NEURAL MODELS OF LANGUAGE PROCESSES

PERSPECTIVES IN
NEUROLINGUISTICS, NEUROPSYCHOLOGY, AND
PSYCHOLINGUISTICS: A Series of Monographs and Treatises

Harry A. Whitaker, Series Editor
DEPARTMENT OF HEARING AND SPEECH SCIENCES
UNIVERSITY OF MARYLAND
COLLEGE PARK, MARYLAND 20742

HAIGANOOSH WHITAKER and HARRY A. WHITAKER (Eds.).
Studies in Neurolinguistics, Volumes 1, 2, 3, and 4
NORMAN J. LASS (Ed.). Contemporary Issues in Experimental Phonetics
JASON W. BROWN. Mind, Brain, and Consciousness: The Neuropsychology
of Cognition
SIDNEY J. SEGALOWITZ and FREDERIC A. GRUBER (Eds.). Language Development and Neurological Theory
SUSAN CURTISS. Genie: A Psycholinguistic Study of a Modern-Day "Wild Child"
JOHN MACNAMARA (Ed.). Language Learning and Thought
I. M. SCHLESINGER and LILA NAMIR (Eds.). Sign Language of the Deaf: Psychological, Linguistic, and Sociological Perspectives
WILLIAM C. RITCHIE (Ed.). Second Language Acquisition Research: Issues and Implications
PATRICIA SIPLE (Ed.). Understanding Language through Sign Language Research
MARTIN L. ALBERT and LORAINE K. OBLER. The Bilingual Brain: Neuropsychological and Neurolinguistic Aspects of Bilingualism
TALMY GIVÓN. On Understanding Grammar
CHARLES J. FILLMORE, DANIEL KEMPLER, and WILLIAM S-Y. WANG (Eds.). Individual Differences in Language Ability and Language Behavior
JEANNINE HERRON (Ed.). Neuropsychology of Left-Handedness
FRANÇOIS BOLLER and MAUREEN DENNIS (Eds.). Auditory Comprehension: Clinical and Experimental Studies with the Token Test
R. W. RIEBER (Ed.). Language Development and Aphasia in Children: New Essays and a Translation of "Kindersprache und Aphasie" by Emil Fröschels
GRACE H. YENI-KOMSHIAN, JAMES F. KAVANAGH, and CHARLES A. FERGUSON (Eds.). Child Phonology, Volume 1: Production and Volume 2: Perception

The list of titles in this series continues on the last page of the volume.

NEURAL MODELS OF LANGUAGE PROCESSES

Edited by

Michael A. Arbib
Computer and Information Science
University of Massachusetts
Amherst, Massachusetts

David Caplan
Division of Neurology
Ottawa Civic Hospital
Ottawa, Ontario, Canada

John C. Marshall
Neuropsychology Unit
The Radcliffe Infirmary
Oxford, England

 1982

ACADEMIC PRESS
A *Subsidiary of Harcourt Brace Jovanovich, Publishers*
NEW YORK   LONDON
PARIS   SAN DIEGO   SAN FRANCISCO   SÃO PAULO   SYDNEY   TOKYO   TORONTO

ACADEMIC PRESS, INC.
111 Fifth Avenue, New York, New York 10003

United Kingdom Edition published by
ACADEMIC PRESS, INC. (LONDON) LTD.
24/28 Oval Road, London NW1 7DX

Library of Congress Cataloging in Publication Data
Main entry under title:

Neural models of language processes.

(Perspectives in neurolinguistics, neuropsychology,
and psycholinguistics)
Includes bibliographies and index.
1. Language and languages--Physiological aspects.
2. Psycholinguistics. 3. Artificial intelligence.
I. Arbib, Michael A. II. Caplan, David. III. Marshall,
John C. (John Crook), Date. IV. Series.
QP399.N46   153.6   81-20520
ISBN 0-12-059780-2   AACR2

Contents

3

Brain and Language: The Rules of the Game   45
Oscar S. M. Marin

II

ARTIFICIAL INTELLIGENCE AND PROCESSING MODELS

4

From Artificial Intelligence to Neurolinguistics   77
Michael A. Arbib

5

HWIM: A Speech Understanding System on a Computer   95
William A. Woods

6

Consequences of Functional Deficits in a Parsing Model: Implications for Broca's Aphasia   115
Mitchell P. Marcus

7

Production Strategies: A Systems Approach to Wernicke's Aphasia   135
Pierre M. Lavorel

III

LINGUISTIC AND PSYCHOLINGUISTIC PERSPECTIVES

8

Three Perspectives for the Analysis of Aphasic Syndromes   173
Mary-Louise Kean

9

The Use of Data from Aphasia in Constructing a Performance Model of Language   203
Edgar B. Zurif

IV
NEUROLOGICAL PERSPECTIVES

22

**Organization of Frontal Association Cortex in Normal
and Experimentally Brain-Injured Primates**   469
Patricia S. Goldman-Rakic

23

**Implications of Simulated Lesion Experiments for
the Interpretation of Lesions in Real Nervous Systems**   485
Charles C. Wood

24

**Confrontation Naming: Computational Model
and Disconnection Simulation**   511
Barry Gordon

25

**Perceptual–Motor Processes and
the Neural Basis of Language**   531
Michael A. Arbib

List of Contributors

Numbers in parentheses indicate the pages on which the authors' contributions begin.

Michael A. Arbib (5, 77, 531), Computer and Information Science, University of Massachusetts, Amherst, Massachusetts 01003

Ursula Bellugi (271), The Salk Institute, San Diego, California 92112

Jason W. Brown (447), Neurology Department, New York University Medical Center, New York, New York 10016

Ron Calvanio (371), Neurology Service, Massachusetts Rehabilitation Hospital, Boston, Massachusetts 02114

David Caplan[1] (5, 411), Division of Neurology, Ottawa Civic Hospital, Ottawa, Ontario K1Y 4E9, Canada

Lyn Frazier (225), Department of Linguistics, University of Massachusetts, Amherst, Massachusetts 01002

Albert M. Galaburda (435), Neurological Unit, Beth Israel Hospital, Boston, Massachusetts 02215

Merrill F. Garrett (209), Department of Psychology, Massachusetts Institute of Technology, Cambridge, Massachusetts 02139

Patricia S. Goldman-Rakic (469), Section of Neuroanatomy, Yale University School of Medicine, New Haven, Connecticut 06510

Barry Gordon (511), Department of Neurology, Johns Hopkins University School of Medicine, and Department of Neurology, Baltimore City Hospitals, Baltimore, Maryland 21224

Mary-Louise Kean (173), School of Social Sciences, University of California, Irvine, Irvine, California 92717

[1]*Present address:* Department of Neurology, Temple University Hospital, Philadelphia, Pennsylvania 19140

Andrew Kertesz (25, 327), Department of Clinical Neurological Sciences, University of Western Ontario, St. Joseph's Hospital, London, Ontario N6A 4V2 Canada

Pierre M. Lavorel (135, 367), Laboratoire de Neuropsychologie Expérimentale, INSERM U94, 16 Avenue Doyen Lépine, 69500 Bron, France

André Roch Lecours (345), Centre du Langage, Hôtel-Dieu de Montréal, Montréal, Québec H2W 1T8, Canada

David N. Levine (299, 371), Department of Neurology, Massachusetts General Hospital, Boston, Massachusetts 02114

Mitchell P. Marcus (115), Linguistics and Speech Analysis Research Department, Bell Laboratories, Murray Hill, New Jersey 07974

Oscar S. M. Marin (45), Neurological Sciences Center, Laboratory of Neuropsychology, Good Samaritan Hospital and Medical Center, Portland, Oregon 97210

John C. Marshall (5, 389), Neuropsychology Unit, The Radcliffe Infirmary, Oxford OX2 6HE, England

Howard Poizner[2] (271), The Salk Institute, San Diego, California 92112

Marc L. Schnitzer (237), Department of English, University of Puerto Rico, Rio Piedras, Puerto Rico 00931

Eric Sweet (299), Department of Neurology, Harvard Medical School, Boston, Massachusetts 02114

Charles C. Wood (485), Neuropsychology Laboratory, VA Medical Center, West Haven, Connecticut 06516 and Departments of Neurology and Psychology, Yale University, New Haven, Connecticut 06520

William A. Woods (95), Bolt Beranek & Newman Inc., Cambridge, Massachusetts 02238

Edgar B. Zurif (203, 271), Aphasia Research Center, Boston University Medical Center, Boston, Massachusetts 02130

[2]*Present address:* Departments of Neurology and Psychology, Yale University, New Haven, Connecticut 06520.

Preface

The contributors to this volume share a fascination with the nature of human language and the means whereby we use it. For many, but by no means all, this fascination takes the form of a concern for neurolinguistics, the study of brain mechanisms subserving language. However, a concern for neurolinguistics in no way guarantees unanimity as to methodology. Thus, Parts II–V of this volume serve to group chapters into four methodological classes: artificial intelligence and processing models; linguistic and psycholinguistic perspectives; neurological perspectives; and neuroscience and brain theory. Although there certainly is overlap between these areas, it is a sad truth that few practitioners of any area are expert in another area, and virtually no one is familiar with the literature of all four. There is a danger that building taller edifices *within* the traditional boundaries will make communication *between* them more difficult. The original object of concern—language—tends to disappear behind the walls of anatomy, psychology, and computation. We have therefore tried to organize a volume in which chapters written from the perspective of one discipline will not merely interest but will actually be relevant to scholars who work in another. The ultimate goal is to understand a natural domain of phenomena; we thus look forward to the day when intermediate representations and bridge laws between the neuro- and the -linguistics can be formulated with sufficient clarity so that results obtained under one approach have direct consequences and significance for all others. Only at that point shall we be able to speak of "a biology of language."

Our task, then, has been to select distinguished contributors to all the fields; work with them to increase the accessibility of each chapter to those who do not specialize in that discipline without diminishing its utility to the specialist; and to preface each section with an introduction that will orient the nonspecialist to the basic background material presupposed by individual contributions. We also provide an opening framework that addresses three tasks: to place neurolinguistics in current perspective, to provide two case studies of aphasia, and to discuss the "rules of the game" of the various disciplines that contribute to this volume. The reader thus may find it helpful to read Part I followed by the introductions to Parts II–V before turning to detailed study of the remaining chapters.

The genesis of the book was itself an interesting process, and it was made possible by a grant from the Sloan Foundation to the University of Massachusetts at Amherst for a Program in Language and Information Processing. David Caplan spent 6 months as a visiting scientist at the University of Massachusetts, during which time he and Michael Arbib articulated many of the themes developed in this volume. The editors then conducted two workshops on "Neural Models of Language Processes." The first, held in Amherst in November 1979, brought together many of the authors and helped them understand better the "models of reality" of workers from other disciplines. The second meeting, held in May 1980, not only filled in gaps in the range of topics from the previous November, but also saw the presentation of new research catalyzed by the November meeting. The succeeding months have seen considerable effort by editors and authors alike to prepare chapters that do not report the proceedings of the workshops but, rather, build upon the insights gained there. The resulting volume is designed to provide a new perspective on neurolinguistics that integrates the insights of neurology and neuroscience, linguistics and psycholinguistics, and artificial intelligence and brain theory. Despite the considerable progress made in these integrative efforts, we have nonetheless structured the book in discipline-oriented parts. We have done this for two reasons: first, so that the specialists may have ready access to the chapters in their own fields; second, so that nonspecialists will know where to turn for our exposition of the necessary background for each chapter. Meanwhile, cross-references among chapters and areas should, we hope, persuade specialists to explore beyond the boundaries of their own discipline and so come to appreciate the vital contributions other disciplines can make to their own.

NEURAL MODELS OF LANGUAGE PROCESSES

I
AN OPENING PERSPECTIVE

In this first section, we appoint ourselves three main tasks: to place current neurolinguistics in historical perspective; to present two case studies of aphasia; and to discuss the variety of "rules of the game" that scientists from different disciplines bring to their study of neurolinguistics.

Whatever the range of disciplines underlying current efforts to model the neural underpinnings of language processes, the fact remains that current neurolinguistics is rooted in the nineteenth century efforts of neurologists to correlate symptoms of a variety of language disturbances with the locus of damage to the brain. This nineteenth century "breakthrough" in cortical localization was in turn based on centuries of observation of the effects of head wounds on language and other behavior.

In the first chapter (Arbib, Caplan, and Marshall), we attempt to provide a fair, though necessarily brief, outline of the historical development of the field. We stress the extent to which recent work draws upon many unarticulated assumptions that derive from the earliest days of systematic inquiry into brain–behavior relationships. Our point is not that these "unconscious" constraints from the history of the discipline are necessarily false, or that they necessarily guide modern research into unproductive paths. Rather, the point is that paradigms and research programs must be made explicit if we are to see the ways in which they lead to genuine results and insights and the manner in which they can sever access to new and deeper theories. There is an understandable tendency to regard certain aspects of current research as inviolate. That is, not open to criticism. The definition of syndromes in terms of performance on a restricted variety of tasks is one example; another might be the notational conventions in which a theory is expressed (e.g., boxes and arrows); another is the notion of discrete processing stages. In all these instances, we believe that consideration of the historical development of neurolinguistics can help us to see that all aspects of a theoretical position should be brought into the open and subjected to critical scrutiny. We also stress

*that current linguistic theory has grown with little regard for problems of perfor-
mance (what are the processes involved in the production and perception of language?), let alone neurolinguistics (how are such processes played across the
brain?). Thus, it can be expected that linguistic theory will itself be dramatically
transformed as the data of psycholinguistics and neurolinguistics become accommodated within broader semiotic models.*

*In the second chapter, Kertesz displays, in as neutral a fashion as possible,
some of the primary data to which neurolinguistic theory must be responsive.
Although many other data sources are relevant to our understanding of the representation of language in the human brain, the structure of impaired and preserved
language skills in the patient with (relatively) focal brain damage has always
constituted the major body of crucial observations. Despite the possibility today of
recording the on-line electrical and chemical activity of the normal brain during
the performance of various language tasks, it seems likely that clinicopathological
(including clinicoradiological) correlations will continue to provide the bulk of our
primary data for some time to come. In accordance with our historical remarks, we
note that such observations as those reported by Kertesz can only be "relatively"
neutral. One has already invoked a prototheory when one chooses "archetypal
examples" of Broca's and Wernicke's aphasia because symptoms and symptom–
complexes are as varied as the patients who exhibit them. Indeed, a prototheory is
also summoned when one chooses these disorders for consideration rather than
others, such as the disorders of language seen in degenerative diseases of the brain.
Similarly, one has already adopted a position by assuming that any particular
task such as repetition or picture description is especially revealing. The reader is
particularly urged to note with Kertesz that the symptom-complexes of even a
single patient may vary drastically over time. This diversity across patients, and
within a patient across time, is rarely addressed by current neurolinguistic theory.
Only in the chapters by Goldman-Rakic and Gordon will we introduce the reader
to developments in cell–circuit–synapse neuroscience, rather than the region-by-
region neurology more familiar to neurolinguists, to provide insight into temporal
patterns of adaptation to lesions.*

*The final chapter in our opening perspective is by a neurologist (Marin) who
explores ways in which the lessons of the clinic may be assimilated to the insights of
artificial intelligence (AI), cognitive psychology, neurobiology, and other disciplines so that our analysis of language may be embedded in the integrated perspective of the nascent field of "cognitive neuroscience." Two particular aspects of this
presentation of the "rules of the game" are noteworthy for their departure from
approaches to neurolinguistics rooted in linguistic theory. The first is the stress on
biological evolution. This aspect suggests that without minimizing that which is
unique about language, we can gain much insight in our search for neural
mechanisms by seeking continuities between language abilities and more general
processes of perception, cognition, and movement control (a theme explored by*

Arbib in Part V). The second is that Marin is more impressed by the richness of the lexicon of a language than he is by the number of its syntactic rules, and so urges far more attention to the lexicon than is accorded it in many contemporary approaches to neurolinguistics.

We hope that an understanding of the diversity of 'rules of the game' of the array of disciplines will help associate this varied expertise to topics of common interest and concern. Some way surely has to be found in which results obtained in one discipline can speak to issues raised in another, if the eventual goal of a unified neurolinguistic theory is to be achieved.

1

Neurolinguistics in Historical Perspective

Michael A. Arbib
David Caplan
John C. Marshall

INTRODUCTION

Our purpose in this introductory chapter is both historical and conceptual. We propose to review (very briefly) some of the approaches to brain and behavior that have guided the construction of models of the language faculty over the last 2000 years (or more!). We assume that theories of language must ultimately be formulated within the context of the biological sciences, and our chief reason for choosing a HISTORICAL framework lies in the belief that we can see our CURRENT problems most clearly by considering the slow accumulation of neurolinguistic data and the sometimes dramatic shifts of paradigm within which such knowledge has been interpreted. It is, of course, worth noting at the outset that belief in some variety or other of materialism constitutes a major conceptual advance, and that the discovery that the brain is the primary material substrate of mental life constitutes a major empirical advance. These background assumptions of such hyphenated disciplines as neurolinguistics have surfaced at many times and places in the history of civilization but did not become firmly entrenched until the nineteenth century.

Nonetheless, that brain and behavior are related is an old observation. Cuneiform tablets from Assyria and Babylon remark upon disorders of consciousness and knowledge that may ensue "when a man's brain holds fire [Thompson, 1908, p. 329]." And in the earliest medical documents that we possess, Egyptian surgeons recorded on papyrus their observations of language loss, believing that "the breath of an outside god or death" had entered their patients who henceforth became "silent in sadness [Breasted, 1930]." The practice of trepanning in which these physicians indulged provides practical confirmation of their belief that outside gods were particularly partial to brains.

The brain did not however reign supreme in the ancient world. Plato, it is true, located the rational part of the immortal soul in the head, but placed the

5

NEURAL MODELS OF
LANGUAGE PROCESSES

"baser" components of the mortal soul rather lower down (Riese, 1959). And Aristotle is on record as postulating that the brain is a cold sponge whose primary function is to cool the blood (Clarke and O'Malley, 1968). More acute observers of the medical scene were, however, prepared to grant the brain a rather more extensive and elevated function than this. The author(s) of the Hippocratic treatise *On the Sacred Disease* (epilepsy) conjectured that the brain is "the messenger to the understanding" and the organ whereby "in an especial manner, we acquire wisdom and knowledge [Riese, 1959, p. 78]." Yet when Gall revived the Hippocratic notion that the brain was the source of ALL cognitive capacities, this claim sufficed to have him expelled from Vienna in 1802 and excommunicated in 1817 (Marshall, 1980a). In the long run, however, as Young (1970, p. 3) writes, Gall "convinced the scientific community once and for all that 'the brain is the organ of the mind' [and that] both its structure and functions could be concomitantly analysed by observation rather than speculation." Even his conjecture that the frontal lobes are the seat of one important aspect of the language faculty has not fared too badly as an inductive generalization over the psychological consequences of localized brain injury. But we are jumping ahead of our story; let us return to the ancient and medieval world.

EARLY OBSERVATION AND THEORY

The most important advances in neurolinguistic knowledge in the ancient world we owe to the Greco-Roman physicians who wrote between circa 400 B.C.E. and 135 C.E. The Hippocratic corpus contains numerous references to disorders of speech as a consequence of cerebral trauma and disease, and certain passages are consistent with the interpretation that Greek doctors distinguished between loss of articulation and loss of language. Yet, even if this distinction was familiar to the School of Hippocrates, no theoretical significance seems to have been assigned to it. However, the corpus contains two further pertinent observations. It was noted that injury to one side of the head was often associated with muscular spasms and/or paralysis of the opposite side of the body; it was also noted that speechlessness was frequently associated with paralysis of the right side of the body. Once more, no conclusion was drawn from these correlations (Benton and Joynt, 1960). Some 2000 years were to pass before scholars interpreted the correlation as evidence that the material substrate of the language faculty was intimately bound up with the left hemisphere of the brain. Similarly, no detailed psychological theory of HOW language deficits could arise from brain injury is to be found in classical writings. Hippocrates did, however, throw off some interesting speculations on the variety of putative causes that could be responsible for disordered linguistic output: "Indistinctness of speech is caused either by disease or by defective hearing, or because before a thought is expressed, other thoughts arise; before words are spoken, other words are formed [Adams, 1939, p. 237]."

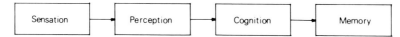

FIGURE 1.1. *A single path serial model of information processing dating back to the time of Aristotle.*

We also note that highly circumscribed behavioral deficits were observed in the classical period. Thus Maximus (circa 30 C.E.) reported on a case of isolated traumatic dyslexia in which an Athenian scholar who suffered a closed head injury lost "the memory of letters" while apparently retaining intact the rest of his knowledge and skills (Kempf, 1888). The historical importance of the case resides in Maximus's explicit commitment to a "memorial" interpretation. From the late classical period until the beginning of the nineteenth century one theory of the overall structure of the mind held almost undisputed sway. The theory derived from Aristotelian analyses of the primary faculties: The Common Sense; Imagination and Phantasy; Conceptual Thought and Reasoning; and Memory. Building upon the original suggestion of Herophilus of Alexandria (circa 300 B.C.E.), the early church fathers located these intellectual functions in the ventricular system of the brain (Clarke and Dewhurst, 1972). All the separate senses were thought to project to the first ventricle (or cell) from whence their internal representations were conveyed to the second ventricle wherein the percept (or image) arose. This in turn was transported to the third ventricle for further conceptual analysis. The elaborated percept then constituted the access code that was used to search among the stored memories (in the fourth ventricle) that had resulted from previous stimulus presentations (Marshall, 1977).

This particular anatomical and physiological hypothesis concerning the material substrate of the mind is no longer held in great esteem. The computational capacities of reservoirs of fluid connected by hollow pipes through which the pneuma flows seem too restricted to do full justice to the complexities of mental life. Nonetheless, it has proved remarkably difficult for later theoreticians to break away from the single path, serial models of information processing (Figure 1.1) that were so extensively debated in the fourth and fifth centuries of the common era.

THE TRANSITION TO MODERNITY

The notion of a storehouse of memory that could be subdivided and sectionalized (like a library) encouraged scholars from Maximus onward to publish reports of cases in which restricted areas of "memory" had been perturbed by brain damage (Marshall and Fryer, 1978). From the fifteenth to the eighteenth century, we witness a steady accumulation of straightforward descriptive reports of the main clinical varieties of language impairment (and associated preservations of function). Severe motor aphasia, in which the patient's speech is restricted to a few isolated words but comprehension is relatively intact, is described, and attributed to central brain damage divorced from paralysis of the tongue (Grafenberg, 1585); nominal aphasia in which the patient cannot produce ("remember") specific nouns (especially proper nouns) is described (Guainerio, 1481); retrieval errors, that is, paraphasias in which the patient produces words that are systematically related (either semantically or phonologically) to the word he is searching for, are described (van Goens, 1789). Preservation of so-called serial or automatic speech is noted (Rommel, 1683). That is, patients are reported whose ordinary conversational skills are almost nonexistent (and who sometimes cannot repeat a word or sentence that the examiner says), but who can adequately recite a list of months of the year, numbers from one to ten, or even a whole nursery rhyme or a prayer from the Bible (Gesner, 1770); it was also reported that patients who were otherwise almost dumb would, if sufficiently annoyed, produce the most glorious (and well-articulated) streams of obscenities and profanities. With respect to disorders of reading and writing, it was noted that the two functions could be dissociated: Patients were described who could write to dictation but then could not read back what they themselves had just written (Schmidt, 1676).

Observations by the medieval and Renaissance physician of restricted loss of particular components of the language faculty were made intelligible by the metaphor of specialized subdivisions within the treasure house of memory. It must, however, be admitted that relatively little effort was made to specify exactly where the relevant pigeonholes were. And toward the end of the eighteenth century, a few farsighted scholars were beginning to wonder what the metaphor brought one beyond essentially ad hoc and nonfalsifiable restatements of the clinical observations.

The work of Johann Gesner is outstanding in this context. Gesner (1770) summarized much previous work and made a number of striking observations of his own. He reported a case of jargonaphasia in which the patient's neographisms showed considerable phonetic correspondence with the neologisms that he uttered. He noted cases of differential impairment in reading between the two languages of bilingual subjects; educated dyslexic patients, including a lawyer and an abbot, appeared to be less impaired in Latin than in German. Gesner also showed that in cases where comprehension is impaired the deficit is disproportionately severe for abstract concepts. In summary, then "just as some verbal powers can become weakened without injury to others, memory also can be specifically impaired to a greater or lesser degree with respect to only certain classes of ideas [p. 125]." Yet the standard theory made no sense to him at all. Gesner writes: "The vessels of the brain are surely not arranged in accordance with categories of ideas and therefore it is incomprehensible that these categories should correspond to areas of destruction [p. 126]." In terms of suggesting a new explanation for the clinical dissociations, however, he can get no further than the proposal that the deficits lie in failures of association between images, ideas, and words. This theme is taken up and made explicit by Crichton (1789). Concerning expressive disorders, Crichton writes: ". . . this very singular defect of memory ought rather to be considered as a defect of that principle, by which ideas, and their proper expressions, are associated, than memory [p. 216]."

Yet the notion that disorders of cognitive functioning could be interpreted as failures of connection between the components of a vast associative machine did not immediately win the day. Rather, the idea of a relatively unstructured and spatially distributed neural substrate for cognition was immediately counteracted by Franz-Joseph Gall's revival and extension of strict, spatially discrete localizationism. Gall (1791, 1810) argued that the talents and propensities that are reflected in behavior can be grouped into underlying faculties and that each faculty has a responsible cortical organ, the activity of which varies according to the organ's size. One method for the in vivo assessment of a cortical organ's size he believed to be the measurement of cranial prominences over the lobes of the brain. Gall's methodology has proved to be somewhat less reliable than modern radiological techniques, and few of his choices of localization are preserved in modern neurology. However, as Young (1970) shows persuasively, Gall's phrenology set the stage for the many developments in cerebral localization in the nineteenth century, which created a doctrine that has survived remarkably well (Galaburda, Sanides, and Geschwind, 1980). (A nice example of the graceful transition from phrenology to modern neuroscience is offered by Brodal's, 1957, monograph—modern neuroanatomy presented as lectures sponsored by the Henderson Trust which was created for the advancement of phrenology.)

When still a schoolboy, Gall had noticed that those of his classmates who were particularly adept at learning verbal material by heart (and at second language learning) tended to have large, protruding eyes. This was to encourage Gall in later life to locate the organ of verbal memory symmetrically in the frontal lobes; "confirmation" of the hypothesis was forthcoming when Gall observed word-finding difficulties in a man with left frontal damage consequent upon a penetrating foil injury. The phrenological journals continued to report cases of aphasia consistent with this localization, but it was not until the publication of a now legendary series of papers by Paul Broca (1861, 1863, 1866) that a modified version of Gall's hypothesis became entrenched. Broca provided evidence (weak evidence it would now appear) that the faculty of articulate language was localized in the posterior part of the third frontal convolution. In both of his most famous cases, the lesion was left sided. Initially this did not strike Broca as worthy of comment; a couple of years later, however, he did remark upon the correlation of left hemisphere injury (and right-sided paralysis) with aphasia, calling it "a strange fact" but making no attempt to explain the coincidence. Eventually, as yet more cases turned up, Broca (and others) formulated the rule that the right-handed person speaks with the left hemisphere. Broca further extrapolated that in the left-handed subject, speech would be mediated by the right hemisphere. He then argued that the left hemisphere was innately preeminent (in the majority of the population) and thus responsible for both the fact that most people are right-handed and the fact that aphasia is most often consequent upon left-sided lesions: Language—man's highest "achievement"—was felt to require an extraordinary neuronal medium. Broca's explication of "innate" was, however, in terms of an inborn predisposition that could be strengthened, modified, or even perhaps changed by experience during certain critical periods. He accordingly guessed, with rather little direct evidence to support him, that if the left hemisphere was injured at birth or shortly thereafter, normal language development, mediated by the right hemisphere, need not be precluded.

Broca himself was not prepared to localize in particular brain areas any subcomponents of the language faculty other than the mechanisms responsible for articulate speech. His patients, he conjectured, had lost "le souvenir du procédé qu'il faut suivre pour articuler les mots." Broca did not, of course, hold that this procedure was an exhaustive description of the language faculty; rather, he believed that the brain as a whole constituted the material substrate for whatever further capacities are involved in the exercise of our linguistic ability.

But Broca's success, seen against the background of Gesner's associationism and Gall's stress upon cortical organs, predisposed other scholars to attempt a thoroughgoing PSYCHOLOGICAL STUDY OF LANGUAGE ON AN ANATOMICAL BASIS. That last phrase is, of course, the subtitle of Carl Wernicke's 1874 monograph in which, for the first time, a unified neurolinguistic theory is outlined.

THE DIAGRAM MAKERS

Carl Wernicke (1874, 1906) and his colleagues attempted to integrate into a single framework the phrenologists' concept of computational centers and the associationists' cortical connections. The theory purported to show how language abilities are organized into functional subsystems whose structure and pattern of interconnection could be interpreted, and in part even motivated, anatomically (Flechsig, 1901; Meynert, 1867). As Arbib and Caplan (1979) point out, the conditions on model construction that Wernicke insisted upon—consistency "with theories in both neuroscience and psychology"—raised the discipline to new heights.

The diagram makers' achievement is basically twofold: They provided a partial formalization of their theories in terms of explicit "box and arrow" notation; they proposed empirical conditions of adequacy that their formalism should meet, namely, that all and only the observed symptom-complexes of aphasia be generated by "lesions" of the diagram. Yet there was an unresolved tension between the requirements of clinical taxonomy and of theoretical understanding that eventually undermined the diagram makers' efforts (Marshall, 1979). We can illustrate this by considering the most famous of the classical diagrams—the Lichtheim "house" (Figure 1.2). The diagram represents Lichtheim's (1885) account of the seven (or eight) major symptom complexes of aphasia: Thus lesion

of pathway 1 = subcortical motor aphasia
of pathway 2 = subcortical sensory aphasia
of pathway 3 = transcortical sensory aphasia
of pathway 4 = transcortical motor aphasia
of pathway 5 = conduction aphasia
of center A = sensory aphasia (or Wernicke's aphasia)
of center M = motor aphasia (or Broca's aphasia)
of center B = anomic aphasia (on other interpretations damage to this center was responsible for "word-meaning deafness")

So far, of course, we have done no more than propose a theoretically unmotivated but (perhaps) observationally adequate taxonomy. On this level, one now simply lists the defining characteristics (positive and negative) of the proposed syndromes. Thus motor aphasia is characterized as a syndrome in which speech comprehension is (basically) intact but speech production (both spontaneous and in repetition) is severely restricted; transcortical sensory aphasia is characterized as a condition in which spontaneous speech is relatively unimpaired, as is the repetition of speech, but comprehension is grossly abnormal. As Arbib and Caplan (1979, p. 449) note, the taxonomy is "centered on the identification of major functional psycholinguistic *tasks*, such as speaking and comprehending speech" and these tasks tend to be treated as "unanalysed wholes." The point of the enterprise is to group these constellations of task-defined functional deficits into symptom complexes or syndromes. As a taxonomy, the Wernicke–

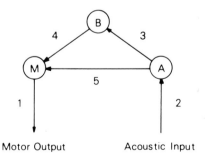

Motor Output   Acoustic Input

FIGURE 1.2. *The Lichtheim "House." Symptom complexes of aphasia are to be explained in terms of lesions to one of three regions (A = Wernicke's area; B = "concept center"; M = Broca's area) or one of five pathways.*

Lichtheim classification is alive and well in the second half of the twentieth century (Benson, 1979; Goodglass and Kaplan, 1972; Kertesz, 1979).

We have not yet, however, used the diagram itself as anything other than a memory aid for the syndromes (Lichtheim, 1885). The diagram makers set their sights considerably higher than this. They gave two further interpretations of the classical drawings. In the first place, they identified the components of the diagram with specific neuronal locales (convolutions and fiber tracts). Thus M was identified as the third frontal gyrus and A as the first temporal gyrus; 5 was identified as the arcuate fasciculus, 1 and 2 as the efferent and afferent "projection tracts" of Meynert (1867). Under the second interpretation, the circles and arrows were identified as FUNCTIONAL devices and codes. Thus, with echoes of the fourth century, Wernicke and Lichtheim labeled A as the center for auditory word memories, M as the center for motor word memories, and B as the center for concepts; similarly, 5 became a pathway that transmitted a phonological code, and 1 a pathway transmitting an articulatory code. This, then, was the way in which Wernicke erected his psychological theory on an anatomical basis. This dual characterization of the diagrams is what Marshall (1979) refers to as "a systematic ambiguity in our interpretation of box-and-arrow notation." The ambiguity in question continues to be exploited by such scholars as Geschwind (1970).

At this point, we can ask, What did the classical diagrams buy in terms of understanding (not merely describing) aphasic symptom complexes? The answer is that SOME MEASURE of theoretical insight was indeed obtained. Consider sensory (or Wernicke's) aphasia, caused ex hypothesi by lesion of A. The disorder of comprehension is interpreted quite straightforwardly as a loss or peturbation of auditory images; the disorder of speech repetition is similarly explained by damage to the auditory forms that provide the input to the direct repetition pathway (5). The two-stage pathway (3–B–4) might, by virtue of running through the concept center (B), be expected to result in semantic paraphasias in repetition. This prediction is borne out in some cases of Wernicke's aphasia. But what of spontaneous speech? At first sight, Lichtheim's model seems to make the wrong prediction about spontaneous speech in the posterior aphasias. The diagram shows a direct innervation of the motor center (M) from the concept center (B). This suggests that spontaneous speech after lesion of A should be normal, yet clinical experience shows that speech in Wernicke's aphasia although fluent is often grossly paraphasic. But Lichtheim turns this possible defect in the model into an advantage. He postulates that center A does play a role in spontaneous speech. Thus NORMAL speech production, according to Wernicke and Lichtheim, involves a double or triple activation of M. Correct output is dependent upon the pathway B–M, but is also controlled by the phonological code that A transmits to M, and perhaps by an indirect path from A to B and thence to M. Lesion of A, and hence perturbation of the route A–5–M, will accordingly result in phonological paraphasias due to incorrect codes being transmitted along 5. Thus the intact pathway from B to M suffices to ensure that speech is produced, but additional (and normal) input from the "sensory" center A is required for well-formed speech.

Wernicke and Lichtheim, then, utilize data from aphasia to support inferences about the identity and neural locations of the basic components of a language processing device. Their inferences include at least a limited notion of interaction between components. Given the level of empirical observation with which they dealt, it is hard to see that any further interaction than that which they postulated could have been justified on the basis of aphasic symptoms. Moreover, the connectionists do go beyond the construction of merely descriptive models. Wernicke attempts to EXPLAIN the reliance of speech production upon memories for the sounds of words by reference to the nature of language learning, a process that he takes to involve repetition and imitation of heard sounds, thus irrevocably tying speech production to sounds stored in a "center" related to speech perception. Lichtheim elevates the distinction between the speech output of aphasics with and without major comprehension disorders to the level of a principle which has PREDICTIVE value: namely, when the performance of a center depends upon two separate inputs, disruption of either will lead to partial performances which are qualitatively different from each other.

Both classical and modern connectionist accounts of the aphasias are replete with detailed arguments of this type. Lichtheim's 1885 paper in particular is a model of clarity, notable both for its close attention to clinical detail, and for the effort to develop a neurolinguistic theory based on as few components and as principled a set of interactions as possible.

PROBLEMS AND ATTACKS

The diagram makers' approach was not (and is not) without its critics. Problems quickly arose in connection with both clinical description and anatomical interpretation. Thus Jackson (1878), for example, drew (or rather redrew) attention to the fact that many patients with severe Broca's aphasia (or even global aphasia) and no usable conversational speech could often produce oaths, "fixed" expressions (e.g., *Good day, How are you?*), and a few single words such as *yes* or *no*. There seemed at the time no obvious way in which such preservation of "automatic" speech could be incorporated into the standard diagrams, and Jackson himself suggested that some minimal capacity for speech could be supported by the right hemisphere. It was also observed that agrammatism (selective unavailability of "closed class" items with relative preservation of uninflected nouns, adjectives, and verbs) was a frequent component of Broca's aphasia (Pick, 1913), and that paragrammatism (incorrect choice, rather than loss, of closed class items) was sometimes seen after posterior lesions (Kleist, 1934). In other varieties of fluent aphasia (Wernicke's aphasia and jargonaphasia), nouns, adjectives, and verbs were peculiarly liable to perseveration, paraphasia, and "replacement" by neologisms (Freud, 1891). Once more, there was no intuitively appealing way in which such observations could be captured within the diagram makers' paradigm. One recourse that they adopted was to invoke rather vague notions about "minimal damage to" or "reduced excitability of" a center, but this stratagem had no predictive power (Marshall, 1974). The diagram makers' only alternative, however, was to multiply their boxes and arrows. Thus Broadbent (1878), for example, postulates a supremodal "ideas centre" that is especially involved in object naming, and a center for "propositionizing." With this latter construct he attempts to bring Jackson's distinction between propositional and automatic speech within the confines of the theory. The marriage was, however, an unhappy one, for Broadbent here broke the strict methodological rule that had guided the diagram makers' attempts to reach beyond mere observational adequacy: As Broadbent (1878, p. 344) himself notes, postulation of a center should "further enable us to represent the causation of *other derangements of speech*" than the one that originally motivated it. It was just such ad hoc proliferation of psycholinguistic components and connections that contributed to the eventual downfall of the system as a productive research program (Head, 1926; Moutier, 1908). As Newcombe and Ratcliff (1975) state in reference to some modern versions of the theory, "this approach—if carried further—would allow one to postulate multiple disconnections of specific pathways to account for the consequences of any cerebral lesion, making the concept of disconnection so flexible as to deprive it of its explanatory power [p. 339]."

An important alternative to the connectionist models was afforded by Jackson's (1874) view of evolutionary levels, with functions represented at all levels, so that the symptom complexes resulting from a lesion at one level could be interpreted as the "release" of the more primitive behaviors mediated by the lower levels. This type of conceptualization has come to play an increasingly important role in the analysis of the visual system, in the understanding of the role of both subcortical systems (Ingle and Schneider, 1970) and the "many visual systems" in cortex (Allman, 1977). With respect to language, the concept of hierarchical organization as developed by Jackson was reflected in theories such as those of Goldstein (1948) which emphasized general psychological factors—such as the capacity to assume the "abstract attitude"—as determinants of a wide variety of quite specific pathological impairments. Debate regarding the extrapolation from symptom to function was thus keen in the period immediately following the first half century of scientific aphasiology, with major disagreements regarding the nature of normative psycholinguistic models and the role that remaining healthy tissue played in the overt behavioral manifestations of disease.

With respect to lesion–symptom correlation there has been relatively little dispute. As Geschwind (1964) points out, the so-called "holists" (Marie and Foix, 1917; Goldstein, 1948; Head, 1926) ended up with taxonomies that were not significantly different from those proposed by the diagram makers, and they agreed also on the locus of the lesion sites. Still, as Von Monakow (1911) pointed out in a particularly lucid discussion, "the diagram-makers employed (at least) three quite distinct concepts of localization: Genuine anatomical localization of nerve tracts and specified cell types; correlations between (grossly) localized pathology and manifest symptoms; localization of basic psychological functions. . . . Nothing has so obscured the problems of cerebral localization or led it so far astray as the confusion between these three different modes."

Jacksonian hierarchies and Goldstein's "abstract attitude" lent themselves to a conceptual approach to language representation in brain that was based upon distributed, or diffusely located, neural mechanisms underlying normal function and, in the explanation of the affects of pathology, to the possibility that lesions could have long-range effects within a neuronally distributed system. This latter possibility was much discussed in the nineteenth century, often by the diagram makers themselves. Thus Bastian (1898) states that a center "may be envisaged as a functionally unified nervous network of variable extension [p. 14]." And indeed the notion that a (theoretical) center need not be (anatomically) punctate is implicit in Lichtheim's (1885) decision to remove Wernicke's diagram from the surface of a brain and present it as an abstract model. This distinction between anatomy and function emerges most clearly in the writings of Gowers (1885, p. 482): ". . . cells may serve a multiplicity of functions, and the same cells may variously participate to different degrees in different centres." For Gowers, a unified functional center "may consist of elements that are anatomically distinct—even situated in different hemispheres."

The ensuing debate, with respect to both the proper psychological characterization of normal and abnormal function and the underlying neural mechanisms, appeared to erode the credibility of Wernicke's program. But it is worth noting with Geschwind (1969, p. 108) that no alternative paradigm "ever matched the successful predictive capacity of the connectionist approach of Wernicke."

WHERE WERE WE IN 1908 AND IN 1958?

Despite criticisms, the connectionist models served to define the essence of the questions asked, methods used, and concepts available for neurolinguistic theory. By 1908, the year in which Pierre Marie and Jules Dejerine confronted each other at the Neurological Society of Paris to debate questions regarding aphasia (Riese, 1947), the following features of the field had emerged:

1. The goal of normative theories of language and brain was to provide a

description—and, if possible, explanation—of the neural mechanisms underlying the primary on-line functions of language: speaking, comprehension of spoken speech, writing, and reading.

2. Such a theory would be constructed on the basis of inferences from the effects of disease upon the brain.

3. The elements of such a theory consisted, on the psychological side, of entire faculties and their interactions, and, on the neurological side, of brain loci specified in terms of gross neuroanatomical structures and their connections.

4. The model of language so-developed was to be related to sensory and motor mechanisms for language perception and production on the one hand and to general intellectual capacities on the other. By and large, the anatomical basis for basic perceptuomotor functions was considered to be subcortical structures and cortical projection areas; that for general cognitive functioning was related to diffuse areas of the brain, in particular the so-called cortical association areas.

5. General psychophysiological factors, such as those which determine Jacksonian functional hierarchies, interacted with the more specific neuropsychological mechanisms whereby language was represented and processed.

6. Conspicuously absent from the descriptions of aphasia and models of language related to brain were detailed considerations of the patterns of language breakdown, and models of language that spoke to the use of specific linguistic forms in the linguistic tasks mentioned in (1).

What progress has been made since the earliest period of neurolinguistic theorizing? Although the basic neurological analysis has not changed in terms of its reliance upon the identification of macroscopic areas of the brain related to psychologically isolable linguistic functions (see Caplan, this volume), the complexity of the models postulated on the basis of observations of aphasics has greatly increased. Arbib and Caplan (1979) drew a distinction between those earlier theories in which components of language located in brain were entire on-line faculties, and those so-called "process models" in which the components that figure in models were responsible for PORTIONS of a psycholinguistic task, the entirety of any task always requiring the interaction of several components. Luria's work (1947) stands as the best example of this development, and also exemplifies another aspect of much of this work: the explicit link between processes related to language function and those which underly sensory-motor function.

In *Traumatic Aphasia* (1947), Luria criticizes the connectionist models for adhering to "the old psychology of faculties." On the other hand, psychological approaches like those of Goldstein (1948) were too general. The answer was to produce "concrete suggestions as to the character of the disorders which are introduced into various functional systems by damage to specific focal areas [p. 18]."

The motor aphasias provide good examples of how Luria sets out to accomplish this research programme. He divides motor aphasias into three groups: afferent motor, efferent motor, and dynamic. The first, in fact, is due to proprioceptive disorders which affect the elaboration of the spatial organization of a "motor analyzer," and follow lesions in the postcentral gyrus. The third, due to lesions in front of the premotor area, affects spontaneous speech to a greater extent than repetition or reading, a language-directed effect of the general "aspontaneity" seen with lesions in this area. We shall now briefly consider his treatment of the second, efferent motor aphasia, which corresponds most closely to the agrammatic aphasia which has been the subject of much recent work.

According to Luria, the prefrontal area is involved in the TEMPORAL organization of movement, as opposed to the postcentral gyrus which is devoted to its SPATIAL organization. Lesions in the former area produce motor disorders characterized by "the patient's inability to master tasks which involve any kind of active motor pattern that must be worked out against a certain dynamic background. . . . the active motor pattern lacks the appropriate dynamic plasticity. The denervation or discontinuation of efforts once they have been initiated ceases to be accomplished automatically and it becomes necessary to generate special voluntary impulses for this purpose [p. 171]."

The effect on speech varies with the site of lesion. Lesions in the more superior aspects of the premotor area, affecting the "marginal" parts of the frontal areas, produce halting speech, difficulty in story narration, simplification of grammatically "expansive sentences, loss of inverted grammatical constructions, and corresponding comprehension difficulties." The disorder involves "a disturbance of what psychologists have referred to as 'inner speech', viz., the abbreviated schema of speech which precedes the speech act itself [p. 177]."

Lesions in the inferior portion of the premotor area, which includes Broca's area, produce more severe forms of this disorder. Disintegration of sentences and words occurs: "Words result from the dynamic organization of the acoustic-articulatory analyzer which makes it possible to carry out the sequential articulations of which words are composed in unitary kinetic patterns. It is this unity which is lost following lesions of the specialized inferior parts of the pre-motor area. With disruption of the dynamic schemata of words, the unit of innervation becomes the individual articulatory act [p. 187]."

More subtle defects "emerge with some clarity when the articulatory difficulties themselves have been overcome [and] are associated with disturbances of inner speech and with the disintegration of the dynamic unity of propositions [p. 188]." Luria stresses that "a proposition always has a predicative aspect . . . behind every proposition there lies a thought. This thought is embodied in a sentence [and] the transition from thought to external speech is invariably mediated by inner speech [p. 188]." And here is the tie-in:

> In its global and purely predicative form, the formulation in inner speech contains the rudiments of the dynamic schema of a sentence. The transition from inner speech to external speech consists in the unfolding of this preliminary schema, i.e. in its transformation into the structure of an externally conveyable proposition [whose grammatical structure is based upon] generalized dynamic schemata to which the linguists refer collectively as the "sense of language." . . . Loss of the dynamic schemata of sentences manifests itself in the fact that even when he has regained the ability to pronounce individual words, the patient is incapable of stringing them together according to proper schemata to form smooth grammatically structured sentences. The defect lies in the fact that the linguistic units innervated are not whole sentences but individual words. Its psychological nature, however, goes even deeper. The most important defect is that the word retains only its static nominative designative function. The dynamic predicative function of the word is completely destroyed . . . such speech is composed of unrelated nouns; verbs are altogether absent (so called telegraph style). . . . The patient has great difficulty in comprehending complex sentences. He must repeat them several times aloud before their meaning becomes clear to him [pp. 188–189, 196].

Luria's solution is, thus, to look to the specific psychophysiological functions of areas of the brain and to apply these functions to the analysis of language. The system is therefore modular, highly interactive, and completely tied in to psychophysiological mechanisms which govern motor and sensory function. Though Luria recognizes that there are areas of the brain that are primarily related to speech, it is not clear that he admits the existence of speech-specific neurophysiological, or even psychological, functions, other than in terms of very general Pavlovian concepts of language as a "second symbol system."

REPRESENTATIONS, PROCESSES, AND INSTANTIATIONS

How then might we eventually reach beyond the understanding achieved by the diagram makers and these first process models? One way is to extend the range of empirical observations regarding aphasic performance to include detailed descriptions of the linguistic structures utilized and the psychological processes whereby they are attained, and to use these enriched descriptions for the development of brain-based models of language. We have already noted that the primary psychological units Wernicke and his colleagues employed were relatively undifferentiated tasks (speaking, understanding, naming, repeating). This emphasis on tasks went hand in hand with rather crude descriptions of the patients' output: Speech was described as fluent or nonfluent, paraphasic or agrammatic, neologistic or anomic. The linguistically ad hoc nature of many of these classifications has long been recognized. Thus Steinthal (1871) summarizes the early literature as follows: "The clinical descriptions are much too incomplete and are inaccurately recorded. Our physicians have as yet no clear concept of what the function of language is [p. 119]." Some nineteenth century scholars, including Delbrück (1886) and Freud (1891), attempted to introduce somewhat finer distinctions, and in the first half of the twentieth century Alajouanine, Ombredane, and Durand (1939) and Jakobson (1941) stressed the necessity of describing language pathologies in terms of categories and relationships that were independently motivated in the study of normal language. But it is only in the last decade or so that such constraints have come to be taken seriously within aphasiology (Goodglass, 1968; Kean, 1978; Whitaker, 1971). Their application to the construction of neurally based models is not, however, without its conceptual (and practical) problems.

Grammatical theory (Chomsky, 1980) explicated linguistic structure by displaying the form of sentences at a variety of representational levels (D-structure, S-structure, Phonological and Phonetic Representation, Logical Form). These levels are regarded by many linguists as the computational targets that the performance machinery is aiming at in the production and comprehension of language. On this view, it becomes possible to characterize aphasic breakdown in terms of failure to compute appropriately a specified representational level, and to study the effect that such failure will have upon other structures that are fed by the (ex hypothesi) impaired level. What is not clear is whether the representations of linguistic theory "cut up the pie" in the right fashion for neurolinguistics.

If we think of formal linguistics as specifying the NATURE of the computations underlying language, a major part of a process model will be a characterization of the algorithms that implement the computation in perception and production (corresponding to the interaction between "top-down" specification of cognitive tasks and their "bottom-up" implementation in neural nets or computer programs [Arbib, 1975; Marr, 1977]). Some success has been achieved, in attempts to construct psychologically plausible parsers (Marcus, 1980; Thorne, 1968) that reflect some of the constraints proposed in linguistic theory, but these models are not "neurologically valid." Proper attention to neurological constraints may lead to the drastic restructuring of our initial top-down analyses. Further analysis of performance models may lead to important modifications of linguistic theory (Bresnan, 1978), and theories of both linguistic structures (Blumstein, 1973) and their processing (Bradley et al., 1980) may have to be modified on the basis of studies of language pathology. Representational models cannot be directly linked to neuronal organization; to glue a transformational grammar to cortical convolutions is to commit an updated version of the diagram makers' fallacy (Caplan and Marshall, 1975).

As several authors have pointed out (Arbib and Caplan, 1979; Kean, 1980), the next step is thus a process model in which the psychophysiological components are directed toward specific linguistic targets in the performance of subparts of particular psycholinguistic tasks. The majority of studies in this volume are directed toward the development of such models.

It is quite reasonable to regard this "linguistic" or "psycholinguistic" approach to the construction of neurally based models of language, as represented by this volume and several other publications (e.g., Coltheart, Patterson, and Marshall, 1980), as a logical continuation of the diagram makers' tradition. The idea is to unpack the contents of Lichtheim's large circles into a set of smaller boxes—with the important proviso that certain boxes may be common to a number of circles. And indeed insofar as most modern work is formalized at all, the notational conventions (boxes and arrows), and their interpretation with respect to lesion data (Newcombe and Marshall, 1980), are identical to those employed in the nineteenth century.

A precise analysis of the data transferred "along the arrows" or of the processes "instantiated in the boxes" is, however, all too often missing. Consequently, these models are, in principle and often in practice, liable to the same disasters that beset their predecessors. It should be stressed that boxes labeled, for example, "phonemic analysis," or "switching control," or "lexical look-up" are not mechanisms. At best, they are hypotheses about the type of mechanisms that may be localized. Moreover, it is likely that smaller symptoms have been squeezed into smaller boxes, and that a proper mechanistic analysis should explain how the residual circuitry functions in the absence of the lesioned circuitry. A detailed analysis of mechanisms of normal function is necessary to provide a framework for the analysis of lesions; lesion–symptom correlation is clinically important, but not the endpoint of explanation. One moral to draw from Arbib and Caplan's "Neurolinguistics must be computational" is the requirement that any mechanism that the theoretician postulates must be able to perform, demonstrably and formally, the role in which it has been cast. Here, the introduction of the neurolinguist to models from artificial intelligence and brain theory may prove particularly helpful. If we demand that mechanisms really be mechanisms, the temptation to invoke a new box or arrow in order to accommodate whatever new data are found when symptom-complexes fractionate might become easier to resist. As the fractionations in questions are usually discovered on the basis of lesion data, one is then further tempted to assume a DIRECT mapping between the theoretical entities of the model (boxes and arrows) and such purported anatomical entities as discrete cell assemblies and fiber tracts, respectively. Although this identification MAY be justified in some cases, it would be a mistake to let the notation prejudge the issue. Again, the requirement that mechanisms be made explicit might serve to reinforce the moral that "There are no free boxes."

CODA

This historical analysis has culminated in the following conceptual observations: Clinicians have developed a vocabulary to describe symptom complexes in the defective behavior of patients with brain damage, and have correlated such symptom complexes with localized lesions. Much neurological observation and theory is in agreement regarding the correlation of "missing function" with "site of lesion"; disagreement arises regarding inferences from these analyses to that of the relationship between normative behavior and brain function. Approaches to the latter question have led to the development of process models in which the production of a variety of behaviors is played across a number of interacting neural systems, with no subsystem constituting a complete "mental faculty," but with each subsystem having a well-defined functional role, the result, presumably, of specific circuitry which transforms and is transformed by that of other neural systems. The development of appropriate theory thus requires both better top-down specification of function and better bottom-up accounts of how the algorithms, posited to affect these functions, may be instantiated in neural circuitry. Modern functional neuroanatomy has revealed subsystems more subtle than simple regions of the brain. Increasingly, linguistic science is providing accounts of the top-down specifications of language, but these "static" accounts need to be supplemented by "dynamic" accounts of language processing which are now appearing in psycholinguistic and artificial intelligence work on language. The application of an interactive, modular approach to language modeling, and the use of data from pathology to justify components of such models, is a natural continuation of the connectionist program of the late nineteenth century, now focused more precisely on the determination of mechanisms underlying the rich and varied structures that constitute human language.

It is worth noting that such mechanisms are the first theoretical entity so far discussed for which it makes sense to raise the question of the nature of the information-bearing neural elements to which they are related. As Vygotsky (1965) emphasized, "the problem of *what* can be localized is not at all irrelevant to the problem of *how* it can be localized in the brain [p. 381]." No one, we trust, would today seek to localize (in either a distributed or a punctate fashion) a grammar (or a component thereof); neither, we hope, would anyone want to localize an algorithm irrespective of the specification of its implementation. But the mechanisms that realize algorithms must have a neuronal instantiation. If we are ever to link "synapse-cell-circuit neuroscience" (Arbib and Caplan, 1979) to neurolinguistics, it must be by way of the mechanisms to which the algorithms that implement a computation are committed (Arbib, 1972; Marr and Poggio, 1977). Neurolinguistics will come of age when we have constructed "functional process models that can mediate between noun phrases and neurones [Marshall, 1980b, p. 106]."

REFERENCES

Adams, F. (Ed.). (1939). *The genuine works of Hippocrates.* Baltimore: Williams and Wilkins.

Alajouanine, T., Ombredane, A., and Durand, M. (1939). *Le syndrome de desintegration phonetique dan l'aphasie.* Paris: Masson.

Allman, J. M. (1977). Evolution of the visual system in the early primates. *Progress in Psychobiology and Physiological Psychology, 7,* 1–53.

Arbib, M. A. (1972). *The metaphorical brain: An introduction to cybernetics as artificial intelligence and brain theory.* New York: Wiley Interscience.

Arbib, M. A. (1975). Artificial intelligence and brain theory: Unities and diversities. *Annals of Biomedical Engineering, 3,* 238–274.

Arbib, M. A., and Caplan, D. (1979). Neurolinguistics must be computational. *Behavioral and Brain Sciences, 2,* 449–483.

Bastian, H. C. (1898). *A treatise on aphasia and other speech defects.* New York: Appleton.

Benson, D. F. (1979). *Aphasia, alexia, and agraphia.* New York: Churchill Livingstone.

Benton, A. L., and Joynt, R. J. (1960). Early descriptions of aphasia. *Archives of Neurology, 3,* 205–221.

Blumstein, S. (1973). *A Phonological Investigation of Aphasic Speech.* The Hague: Mouton.

Bradley, D. C., Garrett, M. F., and Zurif, E. B. (1980). Syntactic Deficits in Broca's Aphasia, in *Biological Studies of Mental Processes.* ed. D. Caplan. Cambridge, Mass.: The MIT Press.

Breasted, J. H. (1930). *The Edwin Smith Surgical Papyrus.* Chicago: University of Chicago Press.

Bresnan, J. (1978). A realistic transformation grammar. In *Linguistic Theory and psychological reality.* ed. M. Halle, J. Bresnan and G. A. Miller, Cambridge, Mass.: The MIT Press, 1–59.

Broadbent, W. B. (1878). A case of peculiar affection of speech, with commentary. *Brain, 1,* 484–503.

Broca, P. (1861). Remarques sur le siège de la faculte du langage articulé, suivies d'une observation d'aphémie. *Bull. Soc. Anatom., 36,* 330–357.

Broca, P. (1863). Localisation des fonctions cérébrales. Siege de la faculté du langage articulé. *Bull. Soc. d'Anth., 4,* 200–208.

Broca, P. (1866). Sur la faculté générale du langage, dans ses rapports avec la faculté du langage articulé. *Bull. Soc. d'Anth.,* Second Series, *1,* 377–382.

Brodal, A. (1957). *The reticular formation of the brain stem. Anatomical aspects and functional correlations. The Henderson Trust Lecture.* Edinburgh: Oliver and Boyd.

Caplan, D., and Marshall, J. C. (1975). Review article: Generative grammar and aphasic disorders. A theory of language representation in the human brain. *Foundations of Language, 12,* 583–596.

Chomsky, N. (1980). *Rules and representations.* New York: Columbia University Press.

Clarke, E., and Dewhurst, K. (1972). *An illustrated history of brain function.* Oxford: Sandford Publications.

Clarke, E., and O'Malley, C. D. (1968). *The human brain and spinal cord. A historical study illustrated by writings from antiquity to the twentieth century.* Berkeley and Los Angeles: University of California Press.

Coltheart, M., Patterson, K., and Marshall, J. C. (Eds.). (1980). *Deep dyslexia.* London: Routledge and Kegan Paul.

Crichton, A. (1798). *An inquiry into the nature and origin of mental derangement.* London: Cadel and Davies.

Delbrück, B. (1886). Amnestische Aphasie. *Jenaische Zeitschrift für Naturwissenschaft, 20,* 91–98.

Flechsig, P. (1901). Developmental (myelogenetic) localization of the cerebral cortex in the human subject. *Lancet, 2,* 1027–1029.

Freud, S. (1891). *Zur Auffassung der Aphasien.* Vienna: Deuticke.

Galaburda, A. M., Sanides, F., and Geschwind, N. (1980). Human brain: Cytoarchitectonic left–right asymmetries in the temporal speech region. *Archives of Neurology, 35*, 812–817.

Gall, F.-J. (1791). *Philosophisch-medicinische Untersuchungen.* Vienna: Gräffer.

Gall, F.-J., with J. C. Spurzheim (1810). *Anatomie et physiologie du system nerveux.* Paris: Schoell.

Geschwind, N. (1964). The paradoxical position of Kurt Goldstein in the history of aphasia. *Cortex, 1*, 214–224.

Geschwind, N. (1969). Problems in the anatomical understanding of the aphasias. In A. L. Benton (Ed.), *Contributions to clinical neuropsychology.* Chicago: Aldine.

Geschwind, N. (1970). The organization of language and the brain. *Science, 170*, 940–944.

Gesner, J. A. P. (1770). *Die Sprachamnesie.* Nördlingen: Beck.

Goens, K. M. van (1789). Einige Beispiele von Geistes—oder Gedachtnissabwesenheit. *Magazin fur Erfahrungsseelenkunde, 7*, 77–80.

Goodglass, H. (1968). Studies on the grammar of aphasics. In S. Rosenberg and J. Kaplan (Eds.), *Developments in applied psycholinguistics research.* New York: Macmillan.

Goodglass, H., and Kaplan, E. (1972). *The assessment of aphasia and related disorders.* Philadelphia: Lea and Febiger.

Goldstein, K. (1948). *Language and language disturbances.* New York: Grune and Stratton.

Gowers, W. R. (1885). *Diagnosis of disease of the brain and of the spinal cord.* New York: Wood.

Grafenberg, J. S. (1585). *Observationes medicae de capite humano.* Lugduni.

Guainerio, A. (1481). *Opera medica.* Pavia: Carcano.

Head, H. (1926). *Aphasia and kindred disorders of speech.* New York: Macmillan.

Ingle, D., and Schneider, G. E., Eds. (1970). *Subcortical visual systems. Brain, Behavior and Evolution, 3,* Nos. 1–4.

Jackson, J. H. (1874). On the nature and duality of the brain. *Medical Press and Circular, 1,* 19–41.

Jackson, J. H. (1878). On affections of speech from disease of the brain. *Brain, 1,* 304–330.

Jakobson, R. (1941). *Kindersprache, Aphasie und Allgemeine Lantgesetze.* Uppsala: Universitets Arsskrift.

Kean, M.-L. (1978). The linguistic interpretation of aphasic syndromes. In E. Walker (Ed.), *Explorations in the biology of language.* Montgomery, Vt.: Bradford Books.

Kean, M.-L. (1980). Grammatical representations and the description of language processing. In D. Caplan (Ed.), *Biological studies of mental processes.* Cambridge, Mass.: MIT Press.

Kempf, K. (1888). *Valerii maximi factorum et dictorum memorabilium libri novem.* Leipzig: Teubner.

Kertesz, A. (1979). *Aphasia and associated disorders.* New York: Grune and Stratton.

Kleist, K. (1934). *Gehirnpathologie.* Leipzig: Barth.

Lichtheim, L. (1885). On aphasia. *Brain, 7,* 433–484.

Luria, A. (1947). *Traumatic aphasia.* English translation (1970). The Hague: Mouton.

Marcus, M. P. (1980). *A theory of syntactic recognition for natural languages.* Cambridge, Mass.: MIT Press.

Marie, P., and Foix, C. (1917). Les aphasies de guerre. *Revue Neurologique, 31,* 53–87.

Marr, D. (1977). Artificial intelligence—a personal view. *Artificial Intelligence, 9,* 37–48.

Marr, D., and Poggio, T. (1977). From understanding computation to understanding neural circuitry. *Neurosciences Research Program Bulletin, 15,* 470–488.

Marshall, J. C. (1974). Freud's psychology of language. In R. Wollheim (Ed.), *Freud: A collection of critical essays.* New York: Doubleday.

Marshall, J. C. (1977). Minds, machines and metaphors. *Social Studies of Science, 7,* 474–488.

Marshall, J. C. (1979). The sense of computation. *Behavioral and Brain Sciences, 2,* 472–473.

Marshall, J. C. (1980a). The new organology. *Behavioral and Brain Sciences, 3,* 23–25.

Marshall, J. C. (1980b). On the biology of language acquisition. In D. Caplan (Ed.), *Biological studies of mental processes.* Cambridge, Mass.: MIT Press.

Marshall, J. C., and Fryer, D. (1978): Speak, Memory! An introduction to some historic studies of remembering and forgetting. In M. Gruneberg and P. Morris (Eds.), *Aspects of memory.* London: Methuen.

Meynert, T. (1867). Der Bau der Grosshirnrinde und Seine örtlichen Verschiedenheiten, nebst einem pathologisch–anatomischen Corollarium. *Vierteljahrschrift für Psychiatrie, 1,* 77–93.

Moutier, F. (1908). *L'aphasie de Broca.* Paris: Steinheil.

Newcombe, F., and Marshall, J. C. (1980). Transcoding and lexical stabilization in deep dyslexia. In M. Coltheart, K. Patterson, and J. C. Marshall (Eds.), *Deep dyslexia.* London: Routledge and Kegan Paul.

Newcombe, F., and Ratcliff, G. (1975). Agnosia: A disorder of object recognition. In F. Michel and B. Schott (Eds.), *Les syndromes de disconnexion calleuse chez l'homme.* Lyon: SPCM.

Pick, A. (1913). *Die agrammatischen Sprachstörungen.* Berlin: Springer.

Riese, W. (1947). The early history of aphasia. *Bulletin of the History of Medicine, 21,* 322–334.

Riese, W. (1959). *A history of neurology.* New York: MD Publications.

Rommel, P. (1683). De aphonia rara. *Miscellanea Curiosa Medico-physica Academiae Naturae Curiosorum, 2,* (second series), 222–227.

Schmidt, J. (1676). De oblivione lectionis ex apoplexia salva scriptione. *Miscellanea Curiosa Medico-physica Academiae Naturae Curiosorum, 4,* 195–197.

Steinthal, C. (1871). *Einleitung in die Psychologie und Sprachwissenschaft.* Berlin: Dümmler.

Thompson, R. C. (1908). Assyrian prescriptions for diseases of the head. *American Journal of Semitic Languages, 24,* 323–353.

Thorne, J. P. (1968). A computer model for the perception of syntactic structure. *Proceedings of the Royal Society Lond B, 171,* 377–386.

Von Monakow, C. (1911). Die Lokalisation im Grosshirn. *Journal für Psychologie und Neurologie, 17,* 185–200.

Vygotsky, L. S. (1965). Psychology and localisation of functions. *Neuropsychologia, 3,* 381–386.

Wernicke, C. (1874): *Der aphasische Symptomenkomplex.* Breslau: Cohn and Weigart.

Wernicke, C. (1906): Der Aphasie Symptomenkomplex. *Deutsche Klinik, 6,* 487–556.

Whitaker, H. A. (1971). *On the representation of language in the human brain.* Edmonton: Linguistics Research Inc.

Young, R. M. (1970): *Mind, brain and adaptation in the nineteenth century.* Oxford: Clarendon Press.

2
Two Case Studies:
Broca's and Wernicke's Aphasia[1]

Andrew Kertesz

INTRODUCTION

The purpose of this volume is to look at a number of issues from neurology, artificial intelligence, psycholinguistics, and neuroscience so as to develop a vocabulary appropriate for discussion of the mechanisms underlying linguistic performance. Our hope is that we may achieve a better understanding of how the brain produces and perceives language. Traditionally we have gained such understanding through the analysis of different types of brain damage. To focus our analysis of these processes more precisely, it seems appropriate to present cases of the two most studied syndromes, Broca's aphasia and Wernicke's aphasia, as background for models from different perspectives which address the issues raised by these syndromes.

One of the most basic issues confronting workers in the field of aphasia is the description and classification of patients with acquired disorders of language. The following two case studies are designed to illustrate common and contrasting forms of language disorders, classified according to a generally accepted nosology. Each of the two cases is, in my opinion, an archetypal example of its category. The first patient is a Wernicke's aphasic who demonstrates neologistic jargon; the second is a Broca's aphasic who recovered from an initial state of being a global aphasic. They represent a contrast in the sensory–motor, expressive–receptive, paragrammatic–agrammatic, syntagmatic–paradigmatic, fluent–nonfluent and asemantic–asyntactic dichotomies that have emerged in the last 120 years of aphasia research.

There is a great deal of variability of patients and it would have been possible to devote this chapter to less frequent forms of language disorders such as isolation aphasia, conduction aphasia, or transcortical motor aphasia. However, not

[1]This work was supported by Ontario Ministry of Health Grant No. PR721.

NEURAL MODELS OF
LANGUAGE PROCESSES

everyone agrees to the existence of all the described categories. In contrast, most investigators in the field subscribe to the basic types presented here, even though their terminology and emphasis on certain features may differ. Moreover, the common occurrence of these two entities in any neurological population makes them available for many studies by a multitude of disciplines. The descriptions that follow differ from numerous previous ones in the literature by the combination of their clinical description with a standardized language examination allowing numerical objective classification, extensive follow-up, and modern methods of lesion localization in vivo.

THE WESTERN APHASIA BATTERY AND CLASSIFICATION

We use a standardized aphasia test, the Western Aphasia Battery (WAB) (Kertesz, 1980, Kertesz and Poole, 1974) developed with a particular view to reliability, practicability, and comprehensive assessment of language following some of the principles and items of the Boston Diagnostic Aphasia Examination (Goodglass and Kaplan, 1972). The WAB scores presented for these patients, therefore, can be compared to those of patients seen in our unit over the past 10 years. The scores for these two patients are highly characteristic of patients seen in the Wernicke's and Broca's groups. Table 2.1 shows our system of synoptic classification based on the scores.

Spontaneous speech is tested by asking standard conversational questions about occupation, illness, etc. and recording the reply, in addition to asking the patient to describe a picture. The amount of information conveyed in the speech is scored as information content and the syntactic and prosodic aspect as fluency. Comprehension is measured by a series of questions with a simple yes–no response, a pointing task (auditory word discrimination), and also a more complex

TABLE 2.1
Classification Criteria Based on WAB Scores

	Fluency	Comprehension	Repetition	Naming
Global	0–4	0–3.9	0–4.9	0–6
Broca's	0–4	4–10	0–7.9	0–8
Isolation	0–4	0–3.9	5–10	0–6
Transcortical motor	0–4	4–10	8–10	0–8
Wernicke's	5–10	0–6.9	0–7.9	0–7
Transcortical sensory	5–10	0–6.9	8–10	0–9
Conduction	5–10	7–10	0–6.9	0–9
Anomic	5–10	7–10	7–10	0–9

sequential comprehension task. The repetition task includes the repetition of words, word and number combinations, and sentences of variable length, complexity, and probability. The scoring is also graded for the complexity, and the number of errors are subtracted. Naming is tested by confronting the patient with objects, by having the patient name as many animals as possible in one minute, and by having the patient complete sentences and respond to simple questions with a single word answer. The scoring of the subtests is already scaled to the same difficulty level. Therefore, the final scoring is a simple addition of the subtest scores, and the total is multiplied by 2 for an aphasic quotient (AQ) which provides a percentage score out of 100 maximum. Because the test has been designed to be relatively simple, free of intelligence or memory factors, a great majority of normal people achieve the ceiling of 100. When reading, writing, praxis, and nonverbal tests are added, the cortical quotient is obtained. The rationale and the standardization which includes test–retest reliability and inter-tester reliability data as well as internal consistency and content validity, has been detailed elsewhere (Kertesz, 1979; Shewan and Kertesz, 1980).

LOCALIZATION OF LESIONS

Substantial progress in our ability to localize lesions in the brain in vivo means that it is no longer necessary to wait for an autopsy or the occasional restricted surgical resection. This compels us to look again at the issue of localization of lesions affecting human behavior. Vascular lesions (strokes) are particularly suited for this because of their large number, their stability, and relative lack of distance effects.

Computerized tomography (CT) is a most important recent advance in neurodiagnosis. Godfrey Hounsfield (1973), its developer, received the Nobel prize in 1979. It combines radiation physics with computer technology to provide an image of the cranial contents. The computer calculates the densities obtained by multiple x-rays focused on a thin section of the skull (*tomography* = imaging with slices), and these densities provide pictures of normal and abnormal structures quite faithfully (Figure 2.1). Less radiation is needed than for an ordinary skull x-ray. The lesions can be seen on the scans long after the initial damage.

Isotope scanning (IS) utilizes the isotope (usually Technecium, TC99) uptake of damaged brain tissue (in addition to the vascular tissues of the face and scalp with normally high uptake) which distinguishes it from normal brain tissue and provides two dimensional pictures of the extent and location of brain damage, if the test is performed at the right time, 1–8 weeks after a stroke. Tumors show growth, and trauma is often negative on these diagnostic procedures used to localize brain damage in our studies.

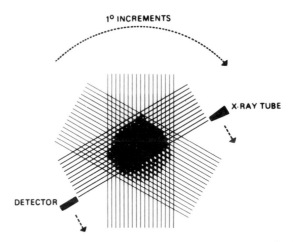

FIGURE 2.1. *This diagram illustrates the principle of computerized tomography. The x-ray source and detectors rapidly circle the head, and density differences from the multitude of intersecting beams are computed to provide an image of the intracranial contents at each successive levels. The images reproduce the anatomy faithfully, and later models produce astonishing details.*

CT cuts are 15° above the orbitomeatal line, and the anatomical relationships of these oblique sections are illustrated on the lateral template of the brain which also summarizes the main gyri concerned with language and associated functions (Figure 2.2). This lateral view of the left hemisphere is a template also used for isotope localization, and the focal planes of the coronal scans (obliquely parallel to the face) are also drawn. For further anatomical detail, the reader is

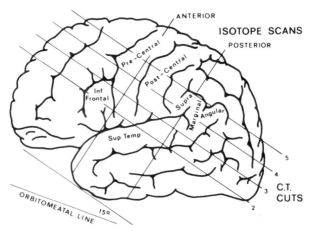

FIGURE 2.2. *A lateral template of the left hemisphere, used for isotope tracing, indicates the location of our CT cuts and the focal planes of the coronal isotope views. The anatomical landmarks of the language areas are illustrated as well.*

advised to consult recent CT atlases (Gonzales, Grossman, and Palacios, 1976; Matsui and Hirano, 1979).

THE SYNDROMES

Broca's Aphasia

In 1861 Broca called this syndrome "aphemia," and subsequently various terms such as "motor," "expressive," "verbal," and "encoding" were used. Broca's aphasia is characterized by a severe disturbance of speech production with relatively well retained comprehension. The speech is effortful, hesitant, and scant (nonfluent), and phonemic distortions and articulatory difficulties are common. Substantive words without connecting grammatical forms lend a telegraphic quality to the output (agrammatism). Writing, reading aloud, and repetition are similarly affected, and there is a great deal of word-finding difficulty, but reading comprehension is relatively preserved.

When the lesion is small or restricted to the posterior portion of the third frontal convolution (Broca's area [Figure 2.2]), the syndrome often recovers within a few months after a stroke and even faster after trauma. Larger lesions which often extend to the central and anterior parietal regions cause a more persistent, severe variety of the syndrome (this is the one Broca himself described, and it is the subject of many linguistic studies and the case report here). Levine argues in this volume (as have others before him) that the inferior portion of the anterior central gyrus is more important in the production of this syndrome, although there is ample evidence in support of Broca's area as well. In the persistent syndrome, both are involved as a rule. At times, entirely subcortical lesions can produce a very similar picture, presumably by undercutting the cortical areas.

The variability of the syndrome is related to the initial severity and the degree of recovery in time. There are two subgroups that share some behavioral features but should be classified separately. One of these is transcortical motor aphasia in which the patient is nonfluent but repeats well; the other is pure motor aphasia or verbal apraxia, which is characterized by pure disturbances of fluency, articulation, and word finding. These can be features of Broca's aphasia as well, but when they occur without comprehension deficit or agrammatism, many authors consider them a separate entity (other names: anarthria, cortical dysarthria, pure word dumbness, apraxia of speech, aphemia).

Wernicke's Aphasia

In 1874 Wernicke called this syndrome "sensory aphasia"; other terms that have been used include "word deafness," "syntactic," "decoding," and "receptive." Wernicke's aphasia is characterized by impaired comprehension but fluent speech. At times, copious unintelligible jargon is produced; such jargon is neologistic if most of the substantive words are unrecognizable, semantic if they are substituted by other words. The prosody and syntactic structure of speech is preserved along with the grammatical modifiers. Comprehension, repetition, naming, and reading are poor. Writing is similarly faulty.

The lesions are located at the posterior regions of the sylvian fissure; the posterior third of the first temporal gyrus (Wernicke's area) and the posterior temporal operculum are commonly affected. In jargonaphasia, the lesions are larger and usually involve the supramarginal gyrus and the underlying white matter.

The variability of the syndrome is related to linguistic and behavioral features, and it is the subject of another contribution by this author in this volume (Chapter 15). In the course of recovery, the features change in the direction of improving comprehension and decreased paraphasias, accounting for some of the variation dependent on the time of examination from onset.

CASE PRESENTATIONS

Persistent Broca's Aphasia

Mrs. D.N., a 59-year-old right-handed female, was found lying on the floor, paralyzed on the right side. She was brought by ambulance to St. Joseph's Hospital, conscious but globally aphasic. Cranial nerve examination disclosed a right hemianopsia, a gaze preference to the left, and a right facial palsy. She had a dense, flaccid, right hemiplegia and an upgoing toe on the right.

She remained in hospital for 6 weeks, during which time she required continuous bladder drainage. On discharge, she was still considered to be a severe global aphasic and was capable only of automatic sentences of up to 3–5 words. The right upper limb showed no movement, the right lower limb had a flicker of movement, and the patient could lift her right knee approximately one inch and move her toes.

The WAB was administered 2 weeks after her stroke. D.N. obtained an AQ of 8.3% and was classified as a global aphasic. The subscores are detailed in Table 2.2. Her nonfluent spontaneous speech was limited to *yes*, *no*, and *well*. Comprehension, repetition, and naming were severely impaired. She showed a severe apraxia to verbal commands on imitation and even when supplied with objects to use. She was unable to read. She did not write, but merely looked at a pencil placed in her hand. Her score on the Raven's Coloured Progressive Matrices (RCPM, a nonverbal visuospatial test of intelligence) (Raven, 1965) was 13 (10th percentile for age).

The WAB was administered 3 months later (see Table 2.2). D.N.'s aphasia

TABLE 2.2
WAB Scores of D.N.—10 Days–6 Years Poststroke

		Patient's Subscores		
	Maximum	10 Days	3 Months	6 Years
Spontaneous Speech				
Information	10	0	2	5
Fluency	10	2	2	4
Total:	20	2	4	9
Comprehension				
Yes–no questions	60	27	45	48
Auditory word recognition	60	2	45	50
Sequential commands	80	2	53	55
Divide Total by 20 for AQ:	10	1.55	7.15	7.65
Repetition	100	6	15	58
Divide by 10 for Total:	10	0.6	1.5	5.8
Naming				
Object naming	60	0	3	33
Word fluency	20	0	0	3
Sentence completing	10	0	6	7
Responsive speech	10	0	0	6
Divide by 10 for Total:	10	0	0.9	4.9
Add Subtotals and Multiply by 2 for AQ:		8.3	27.1	54.7
Taxonomic Diagnosis		*Global*	*Broca's*	*Broca's*

quotient was 27.1%, and her category changed to Broca's aphasia. Her spontaneous speech had improved, but was still nonfluent. Her comprehension for longer commands and complicated material was impaired. Repetition was severely disturbed. Naming was abnormal, but D.N. could now make use of verbal cueing. Reading comprehension was much improved. D.N. was unable to write spontaneously or copy correctly. Tests of apraxia revealed a moderate impairment. She scored 24 on the RCPM (about the mean for her age group). Calculation was markedly abnormal. She was able to recognize 19 of 20 environmental sounds (Vignolo, 1969).

A third assessment on the WAB on September 16, 1974 (1 year poststroke) showed an AQ of 44.2% and a categorization of Broca's aphasia. The patient showed nonfluent spontaneous speech with occasional short sentences and phrases. Comprehension was only mildly impaired on complex material. Repetition was good for single words but poor for phrases and sentences. Naming had improved and continued to show good response to verbal cuing. Reading was good. The patient was able to write her name and part of her address, and she could copy. Her performance on constructional tasks was good. Her score on the RCPM was 30 (90th percentile for age).

Repeat WABs at 2 and 3 years poststroke showed aphasia quotients of 47.6 and 47.9, respectively, indicating a plateau in her level of function.

Mrs. D. N.—transcript of the interview, 4 years poststroke

E   *How are you feeling?*

DN *I–I'm fine.*

E   *Have I ever tested you before?*

DN *No–two, three.*

E   *What is your full name?*

DN *Oh dear.–Henry–oh––––* [correct, but the name for sake of privacy, is omitted].

E   *And your full address?*

DN *Oh dear. Um. Aah. Oh! No–oh. Oh dear.*
     very–there–were–there ave. [veri ðeɚwɚðeɚ] *ave–deversher avenyer* [dɛvɚ ʃɚ
     ævɚnjɚ]. (Correct address. Devonshire)

E   *What kind of work did you do before you became ill?*

DN *Oh. I–I–um. Um–oh dear. I–I–dun know. I don't–want–to.*

E   *Can you tell me what you did for a living? Did you work? Did you have a job?*

DN *Oh yes–I–I–um–um. The–the–say* [se]—*si* [sɪ] *selum* [sɛlʌm] *dum–nogglewife*
     [nɔgɚlwaɪf]. *Oh dear.*

E   *Can you tell me why you're in the hospital, or What happened?*

DN *Oh–y–yes. M–My h–husband is going to–the–the–the–um–um–oh. He was–oh.*

E   *He had an operation?*

DN *Ya–uh–uh. And so*

E   *You went back to St. Mary's?*

DN *Ya. Uh-huh.*

E   *Look at the picture and tell me what you see going on in the picture.*

DN *Oh dear. Um–oh dear. That–oh good–um. Oh, isn't that good i* [ɪ]
     There and there and there and there and there.

E   *Ya, can you tell me what they're called?*

DN *Waving and uh–the–oh dear–and the kite and boy and–and eeth* [ið]. *uh–barking
     and a–a lil boy and a bigs* [bɪgs] *thing in uh–in the–Oh dear he's dreeging*
     [drigɪŋ] *in the uh. Oh dear–I can't say it but he's–ray* [re]. *And a man and–
     woman–do no–no–uh–uh sawst* [sɔst] *all a people–one–two–three and four and–
     and oh–the–oh boy–good and–oh waitingull* [wetŋgʌl] *but no I–oh!*

Six years poststroke her AQ was 54.7% and her categorization still that of a Broca's aphasic (Table 2.2). Her spontaneous speech was still mostly single words. Auditory comprehension was impaired, especially for prepositional commands. She was able to repeat single words but showed difficulty with phrases and sentences. Object naming was impaired, and she continued to benefit from phonemic cues. Reading comprehension of sentences was good. She was agraphic and still manifested difficulty writing her name. She was unable to write words or letters to dictation. She showed facial apraxia. Drawing, calculation, and block design were within normal limits, and her score on the RCPM was 31 (ninety-first percentile for age).

A CT scan was performed 5½ years poststroke. It showed a large fronto-parietal lesion sparing the posterior temporal area and involving posterior frontal and inferior parietal lobe including pars opercularis and the inferior central gyrus, on the left (see Figure 2.3 and 2.4).

Comment

The patient thus shows a persistent severe Broca's aphasia, after an initial short period during which she was globally affected. Her speech is typical for this syndrome, showing agrammatism, hesitation, and mainly single word responses except for automatic sequences: Oh dear—I can't say it." She has good comprehension of spoken and written language, with poor repetition and writing abilities. Visuospatial function and nonverbal intelligence are within normal limits. A limb apraxia has recovered, but a mild facial apraxia persists.

Her syndrome is typical in many respects. Although there are patients who show better comprehension from the beginning and somewhat more recovery, these patients also show agrammatism in speech and, as has been documented in the literature, deficits in comprehension as well (Zurif and Caramazza, 1976). The evolutionary sequence for this severe aphasia is shown to be characterized by considerable initial recovery of comprehension, which changes the category from global to Broca's aphasia. Subsequently there is less recovery; the patient reaches a plateau and remains rather severely incapacitated by the lack of speech output. The diagnosis depends on the stage at which one tests these patients. Up to 1 or 2 months of evolution, they may be called global, but at 3 months they are classified as Broca's aphasics in our system. In Boston, these patients are called "mixed anterior" which is an awkward term with unwarranted anatomical implication and a meaningless adjective. I believe it is much preferable to use the designation severe presistent Broca's aphasia, because it is the severity and persistence of the syndrome which distinguish it from the rest of Broca's aphasia.

Less severely affected cases of Broca's aphasia show less agrammatism and better comprehension. Those patients who have no agrammatism or comprehension deficit but only articulatory disturbance should be classified in the pure motor aphasia category. Marie's term "anarthria" is unfortunate because neurologists use this term for severe dysarthria, related to bilateral subcortical lesions. Some authors have used the term "aphemia" for this condition but this is confusing because Broca and others used the term aphemia originally for the more severe variety of the syndrome. In between the very rare pure motor aphasias and the common severe persistent Broca's aphasia, there are intermediate varieties of Broca's aphasics which are closer to one or the other. Most authors will classify these along with Broca's aphasia which results in some degree of variability within the syndrome.

The localization of the lesion in the patient discussed here indicates that the

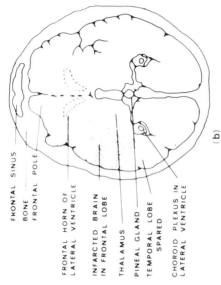

FRONTAL SINUS
BONE
FRONTAL POLE

FRONTAL HORN OF
LATERAL VENTRICLE

INFARCTED BRAIN
IN FRONTAL LOBE

THALAMUS

PINEAL GLAND

TEMPORAL LOBE
SPARED

CHOROID PLEXUS IN
LATERAL VENTRICLE

(b)

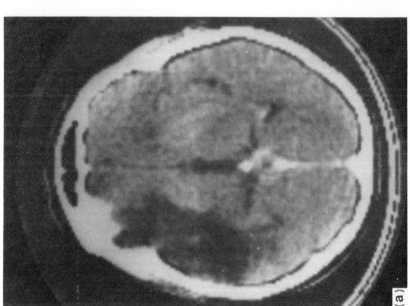

(a)

FIGURE 2.3. This CT cut 2 of D.N. shows a large lesion in the left anterior (frontal) region. The top is the front of the skull with the frontal sinus darkly contrasting the white bone. The lesion is dark representing decreased density from the gray brain tissue. Normally dark areas are the fluid filled ventricles. The white dot in the middle is the calcified pineal gland. Wernicke's area is behind the level of the pineal and is spared, and so are the basal ganglia in the center.

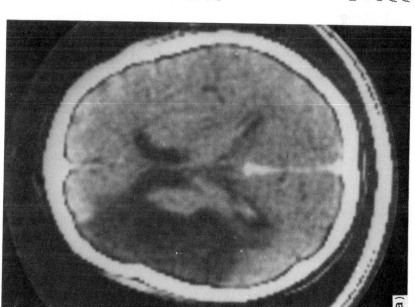

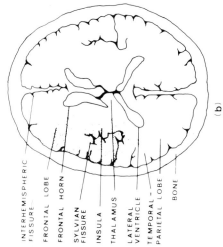

INTERHEMISPHERIC
FISSURE

FRONTAL LOBE

FRONTAL HORN

SYLVIAN
FISSURE

INSULA

THALAMUS

LATERAL
VENTRICLE

TEMPORAL -
PARIETAL LOBE

BONE

(b)

(a)

FIGURE 2.4. This is a CT cut 3 of D.N. The left-sided lesion extends from the frontal to the anterior parietal region. The supramarginal area is spared. Ventricular dilatation on the left side is secondary to loss of tissue and scarring, 3 years before. The white streak posteriorly is the falx cerebri and the dot in the left lateral ventricle is the choroid plexus, useful anatomical landmarks. Newer scanners distinguish even more detail.

persistent variety of this syndrome is caused by a relatively large lesion which indeed occupies Broca's area as well as the more posteriorly lying central inferior rolandic region and the anterior parietal region. Wernicke's area however is spared, correlating with the relatively well preserved comprehension in this case. There are smaller lesions that can cause the persistent syndrome, and I believe that they all involve Broca's area and that a few never go beyond the frontal lobe.

The comprehension of Broca's aphasics is never entirely normal if it is tested with tasks that are difficult enough. However it is so much better than the output of language that this feature has to be emphasized. The preservation of comprehension also distinguishes it from other aphasic syndromes such as isolation or Wernicke's aphasia. Nevertheless, the comprehension scores are often less than they are in milder aphasic syndromes such as anomic aphasia or conduction aphasia. Many authors have correctly pointed out that comprehension is not intact in Broca's aphasia anymore. In the beginning, these patients may have so much difficulty pointing to objects or even shaking their heads in an appropriate yes–no response as a result of apraxia or yes–no confusion, that it is very difficult to determine how much comprehension they have. Other nonverbal behavioral clues and surprising performance on nonverbal tasks provide evidence of preserved cognition and some comprehension. Sometimes a global aphasic who can not respond by pointing or yes–no responses creates an impression, by just being bright and alert and responding emotionally to the stimulation, that he indeed comprehends more than he can let you know. These patients often will show more recovery than those global aphasics who are inattentive and tend to remain severely affected. The difference seems to be related to whether Wernicke's area is involved or not! There is a degree of recovery which is rather substantial in the first few months and then there is plateauing in Broca's aphasia. Often, after 1 year, a patient remains quite stable, like the patient presented here. Change in subsequent years is minor and gradual.

Various comprehension tasks have been designed for aphasics. The Western Aphasia Battery is designed for a wide range of language impairment; it distinguishes between the more severely affected aphasics and yet also provides a good measure of comprehension at a higher level. Elsewhere, comprehension tasks have been used that require more short-term memory and intellectual capacity—some cases are so difficult that a significant percentage of normals have trouble with them. Some of these tasks are complicated enough as to be in fact verbal intelligence tasks. Some of them are long enough that they indeed test the memory of the patient. We tried to avoid both traps in the construction of our test. Therefore, complex, ideational material and excessively long sentences were not used. The more severely affected patients do very well with the yes–no task. We give them the opportunity to respond with the actual words or just with nodding. At times when the nodding is confusing, that is, the patient seems to have a yes–no confusion, we establish a code with eye blinking which may be better preserved than the appropriateness of nodding. An eye blink code such as blinking for no and keeping the eyes open for yes can be used for severely dysarthric or mute patients who comprehend well.

A Case of Wernicke's Aphasia

Mrs. J.A., a 74-year-old right-handed woman was admitted to St. Joseph's Hospital because of sudden onset of jargon speech. The examination in the emergency department showed a right homonymous hemianopia and a mild right arm paresis as well as fluent aphasia. She was admitted with a diagnosis of left cerebral infarction.

She was first tested on the Western Aphasia Battery 2 weeks poststroke. By that time, her arm paresis had disappeared. Her language was characterized by fluent neologistic jargon and severely impaired auditory and reading comprehension. Her writing consisted of neologisms and occasionally correct words. Repetition and naming were severely impaired and stimuli of this sort elicited jargon responses no different from her conversational replies. She showed an apraxia to verbal command, in imitation, and in the use of objects. She could not calculate, draw, or perform the block design of the WAIS or RCPM. Her WAB score showed an AQ of 23.4%; she was classified as a Wernicke's aphasic (Table 2.3).

TABLE 2.3
WAB Scores of J.A. in the Acute and Chronic State

		Patient's Subscores	
	Maximum	2 Weeks	1 Year
Spontaneous Speech			
Information	10	2	0
Fluency	10	7	7
Total:	20	9	7
Comprehension			
Yes–No questions	60	24	21
Auditory word recognition	60	19	15
Sequential commands	80	11	11
Divide Total by 20 for AQ:	10	2.7	2.35
Repetition	100	0	0
Divide by 10 for Total:	10	0	0
Naming			
Object naming	60	0	3
Word fluency	20	0	0
Sentence completing	10	0	0
Responsive speech	10	0	0
Divide by 10 for Total:	10	0	0.3
Add Subtotals and Multiply Total by 2 for AQ:		23.4	19.3
Taxonomic Diagnosis Wernicke's Aphasia			

Mrs. J. A.—transcript of the first interview, 2 weeks poststroke:

E   *How are you today, Mrs. A.?*

JA *Yes.*

E   *Have I ever tested you before?*

JA *No, I mean I haven't.*

E   *Can you tell me what your name is?*

JA *No, I don't I–right I'm right now here.*

E   *What is your address?*

JA *I cud* [kʌd] *if I can help these this like you know–to make it. We are seeing for him. That is my father.*

E   *What kind of work did you do before you came into the hospital?*

JA *Never, now Mista Oyge* [ɔɪdʒ] *I wanna tell you this happened when happened when he rent. His–his kell* [kɛl] *come down here and is–he got ren* [rɛn] *something. It happened. In these* [ðis] *ropiers* [ropiɚz] *were with him for hi–is friend–like was. And it just happened so I don't know, he did not bring around anything. And he did not pay it. And he roden* [rodɛn] *all o these arranjen* [ɚrendʒən] *from the pedis* [pɛdɪs] *on from iss* [ɪs] *pescid* [pɛskɪd]. *In these floors now and so. He hasn't had em round here.*

E   *Can you tell me a little bit about why you are in the hospital?*

JA *No, I don't think I have. . . . No, I haven't.*

E   *Can you tell me what you see going on in the picture?* [A drawing of children flying a kite]

JA *No, I can uh take him.–uh. I haven't read* [rɪd] *'em anybody to right in there. That's the little girl here.*

E   *Anything else? What do you see over here?*

JA *No.* [pause] *I really had pays* [pez] *too. Inste van gup* [ɪnstɛ væn gʌp]. *Here's ee* [i] *little boy being read, too. There he's being there on the ceiling there.*

A Tc99 isotope scan 10 days poststroke showed a wedge-shaped area of uptake in the parietotemporal area on the left (Figure 2.5). The center of the lesion was at the parietotemporal junction. The lesion appeared to involve most of the supramarginal gyrus and the posterior third of the first temporal gyrus and to extend considerably into the underlying white matter (Figure 2.6). A CT scan 3 weeks poststroke showed a decreased density with indistinct edges in the left temporoparietal junction.

She was seen for reassessment 1 year after her stroke. The frequency of neologisms had decreased, but she still had the neologistic jargon. The AQ on the WAB was 19.3%, essentially unchanged from the first test. She was still in the category of Wernicke's aphasia (Table 2.3).

A repeat CT scan at the time of second testing showed a more distinct outline of the previous lesion, and a smaller area of decreased density at a somewhat higher level in the convexity of the right parietal lobe was present, possibly representing a small infarct which had occurred in the intervening year (Figure 2.7).

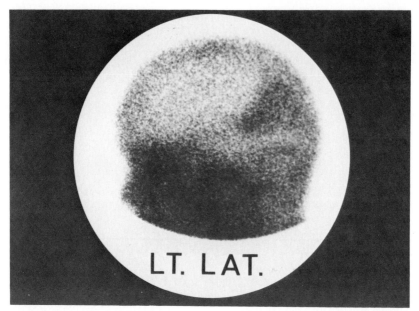

FIGURE 2.5. *The left lateral isotope scan of J.A. in the acute poststroke period. The isotope is taken up by the facial tissues and the scalp but not by the healthy brain. The wedge-shaped uptake posteriorly indicates the extent and location of the infarct.*

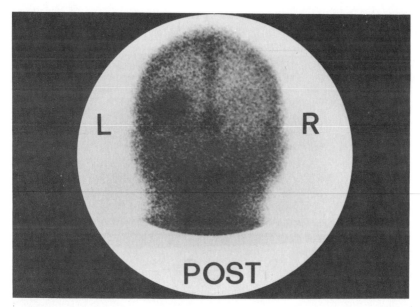

FIGURE 2.6. *The posterior isotope scan of J.A. The abnormal uptake on the left is to be compared with the intact brain on the right. The line of uptake in the midline is the saggital venous sinus.*

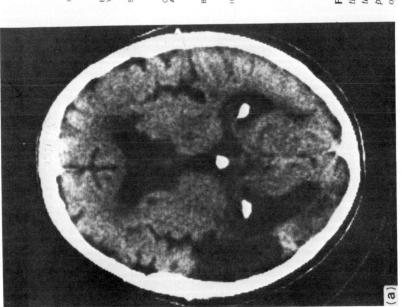

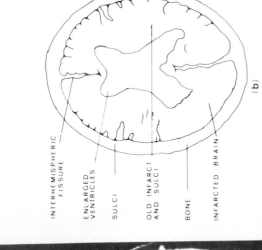

INTERHEMISPHERIC
FISSURE

ENLARGED
VENTRICLES

SULCI

OLD INFARCT
AND SULCI

BONE

INFARCTED BRAIN

(b)

(a)

FIGURE 2.7. The CT scan of J.A. a year after the stroke. The ventricles are larger than normal, especially on the left side. The infarct is well circumscribed in the left temporal region cortically and subcortically. Higher cuts show the lesion to be more posterior. Compare with the lateral wedge in Figure 2.5. Broca's area is in the front (top) of the lesion.

The patient received 6 weeks of speech therapy as an outpatient. Despite the severe language disorder, she manages to live alone with some help from her family. She represents a typical persisting neologistic jargonaphasia subsequent to a left posterior temporoparietal infarction. A small right parietal lesion, probably also an infarction, which occurred between the first and second administration of the WAB, did not alter her symptomatology, and is of doubtful clinical significance.

E   You were in the hospital about a year ago, weren't you?

JA   He was just one und ta dead [ʌnd tʌ dɛd]. You fie, [faɪ] come over, you know. Showed some things over here.

E   What kind of work did you do before you became ill?

JA   No, he was all right. I'd ma deadsnot dog [mɛ dɛdsnɔt dɔg] mine nahthink [nɔθɪnk] or anythink [ɛniθzŋk] No.

E   Is your name Brown?

JA   Oh misstrus prang [mɪstrɚs præŋɔ] went one wissenyer [wɪsɛnjɚ] walking ul [ʌl] thing thing this thing here for thee.

E   OK. Just say yes or no. Is your name Brown?

JA   Well it is here then let me see I just don't know.

E   Is your name A———?

JA   Well my fred [frɛd] mine is my fredmayuv [frɛdmeəv]–of my ed my–my father you know I don't know why what is they doing allike [ɔlaɪk] this thingses [θɪŋzəz] I could not tell you.

E   What's happening here? [Pointing to Schuell's picture of children flying a kite around a pond]

JA   It's just like a–it's a little boy [pointing to girl] fie fie [faɪ faɪ] there you know. An fine.

E   What about here?

JA   The ju si dra da thad 'n theuther. [dʒʌ sɪ dræ dʌ ðæd n̩ ðiʌðɚ] Thuts [ðʌts] all right. Just don't know. Gees I don't know very much of all this suffs [sʌfs]–this all ray [re] I just telling you. I just could not tell you. Because we are air [eɚ] eating–my dadme [dædmi] is a fathermin [fɔðɚmɪn] and he likes to eat and my fader [fɚdɚ] I think everything clean me and I like to clean. Eat my think so I'm all right. I just don't know what is wrong.

Comment

This patient is very fluent, and at times more output is seen than is needed for communication. For some answers, one or two words would suffice and she continues instead with several paragraphs. Thus, there is an excess of speech although she does not display as much pressure of speech as is seen in others.

The syntax and prosody were preserved. She speaks in sentences and uses appropriate pauses and inflectional markers separating lexical items. One can distinguish between words even when they are neologistic. What is even more interesting is that even though there is a string of neologistic words, they are still separated by recognizable grammatical functors. She incorporates prepositions and pronouns in her speech and often there is correspondence between the prepositions and the word endings even though the words are neologistic. English phonology also seems to be preserved. She speaks without articulatory errors or hesitations. However, many of her words are replaced by completely unintelligible paraphasias; at times, these are phonemic, at other times, they seem to be phonemic distortions of verbal paraphasias. When the distortion is complete and one can no longer interpret the word, the paraphasic response is called neologistic. When there are many neologisms in a long string, as in this case, the term neologistic jargon is applied. In contrast with the anomic gaps and hesitations seen in many aphasics, she does not appear to have any word-finding difficulty, but in an extraordinary fashion, neologisms of variable length and phonemic complexity replace substantive words, mostly nouns and verbs. The connecting words, pronouns, modifiers, and other auxiliary elements of the sentence seemed to be preserved.

There is also a curious lack of recognition of errors. She talks as if she spoke without mistakes and she certainly does not have the frustration of Broca's aphasics. There is a rather curious cool and calm manner about her speech as if she did not realize her deficit. This feature is called anosognosia for speech by Alajouanine (1962) and considered by many a very characteristic feature of this disturbance.

There have been several attempts made to decode jargon. This is easier if the jargon responses are elicited on a standard stimulation such as a repetition task or a naming task when the expected answer is obvious to the examiner. In these cases, it is often possible to interpret the jargon words as phonemic distortions of the target word. When the target word is not known, the word is more likely to be interpreted as neologistic. However, even with known targets, the transformation is often completely unintelligible. This led to the theory that some of these substitutions are first verbal paraphasias which then are replaced by phonemic paraphasias in a second-stage transformation.

A severe jargonaphasic illustrates the difficulty of calling these patients "receptive aphasics," a term that reflects only on the severe comprehension difficulty, when such an obvious expressive difficulty is present also. Comprehension difficulty is so severe, however, that even when we employ such techniques as slowing down our rate of speech, repeating instructions, using simple terms—all factors described as important in the literature—we are frequently unsure that the jargonaphasics understand the instructions. The occasional word seems to be comprehended, but never at a sentence level. Comprehension deficits are elicited regardless of the output modality; that is, nonverbal pointing responses to single words cannot be carried out either. Reading comprehension is equally impaired.

In several cases we have played the tape recordings of jargonaphasics back to them, and some seem to show a recognition on hearing their own voice. However, one cannot be sure whether they really understood themselves, although at least one of the patients seemed to point to the tape recorder with a great deal of animation as if to say "Yes, that is it." At times, we responded to the jargon speech with a foreign language but this did not change the output, and patients did not show any more puzzlement. There might be some individual differences in the amount of speech output, but the apparent verbosity of these patients is not correlated very well with premorbid speech patterns. In other words, the usually reticent patients may indeed have a great deal of copious jargon.

Perseveration is another feature that seems to be especially prevalent in the case being presented here. At times, the patient can repeat words although repetition is usually as severely affected as comprehension; this is in clear contrast to transcortical sensory aphasia which shows much better repetition than comprehension.

CONCLUSION

These case presentations serve to illustrate the two most important and common forms of aphasia. The contrast between them exists at clinical, psychological, linguistic, and anatomical levels and is of great interest to linguists, cognitive psychologists, information scientists, and clinicians. The striking difference between the nonfluent patient with an effortful speech who comprehends rather well and the patient with fluent jargon output but without comprehension is powerful evidence against the unitary concept of aphasia. The psychological contrast between the frustrated self-correction of the Broca's aphasic and the calm, matter-of-fact acceptance of jargon of the Wernicke's aphasic who has anosognosia (nonrecognition) of her speech defect is also evident. An obvious neurological difference is the associated persisting hemiplegia in the severe Broca's aphasia and the lack of it in Wernicke's aphasia. On the other hand, the latter is regularly accompanied by hemianopia, as is the case here. There are a host of linguistic distinctions. The agrammatic output in the Broca's versus the preservation of syntax in the Wernicke's aphasia is manifested by the relative preservation of substantive words and the absence of syntactical modifiers in Broca's versus the substitutions of substantives by neologisms but retention of grammatical auxiliaries in the Wernicke's. The lesion location is also different, even though both lesions are large and produce severe persisting deficits. The involvement of the posterior frontal and anterior parietal lobes in Broca's aphasia is contrasted with the posterior temporal and parietal lesions of Wernicke's aphasia.

These cases are examples with typical, replicable anatomical, clinical, and linguistic features. They are commonly available to an interdisciplinary approach to such fundamental questions as the following about how brain and language are related:

1. How can these distinctions be applied to create processing models?
2. Are the clinical, neuroanatomical, and linguistic phenomena related, and, if so, to what extent?
3. Are lesion models and clinical syndromes useful to approach normal function?
4. What is the right combination or modification of holistic or mosaic models applicable to language?
5. Are language processes dependent on neural structures and, if so, which ones?
6. What is the contribution of lesions or normal neural structures to the linguistic, neurological, and psychological distinctions observed?
7. Are lesion models applicable to computational linguistics and vice versa?

REFERENCES

Alajouanine, T., Sabouraud, O., and Ribaucourt, B. (1962). Le jargon des aphasiques: Desintegration anosognosique des valeurs semantiques du langage. *Journal de Psychologie, 45,* 158–180, 293–330.

Goodglass, H., and Kaplan, E. (1972). *Assessment of aphasia and related disorders.* Philadelphia: Lea & Febiger.

Gonzalez, C. F., Grossman, C. B., and Palacios, E. (1976). *Computed brain and orbital tomography—Technique and interpretation.* New York: Wiley.

Hounsfield, G. N. (1973). Computerized transverse axial scanning (tomography): Description of system. *British Journal of Radiology, 46,* 1016–1025.

Kertesz, A. (1979). *Aphasia and associated disorders: Taxonomy, localization and recovery.* New York: Grune and Stratton.

Kertesz, A. (1980). *The Western Aphasia Battery.* Printed by the University of Western Ontario, London, Ontario.

Kertesz, A., and Poole, E. (1974). The aphasia quotient: The taxonomic approach to measurement of aphasic disability. *Canadian Journal of Neurolical Science, 1,* 7–16.

Matsui, T., and Hirano, A. (1978). *An atlas of the human brain for computerized tomography.* Tokyo: Igaku-Shoin.

Raven, J. C. (1965). *Guide to using the Coloured Progressive Matrices.* London: Lewis.

Shewan, C., and Kertesz, A. (1980). Reliability and validity characteristics of the Western Aphasia Battery (WAB). *Journal of Speech and Hearing Disorders, 45,* 308–324.

Vignolo, L. (1969). Auditory agnosia: A review and report of recent evidence. In A. Benton (Ed.), *Contributions to clinical neuropsychology.* Chicago: Aldine.

Zurif, E. B., and Caramazza, A. (1976). Psycholinguistic structures in aphasia: Studies in Neurolinguistics, Vol. 1. New York: Academic Press.

3

Brain and Language:
The Rules of the Game

Oscar S. M. Marin

Pour être effective, la conaissance n'a pas besoin d'être portée à la per-
fection dans aucune direction . . . . Il n'y a pas de connaissance parfaite et
totale: elle est toujours relative aux circonstances, aux limites entre les-
quelles elle doit être valable et aux desseins auxquels elle doit servir.

To be effective, knowledge does not need to achieve perfection in any
direction . . . . There is no perfect and complete knowledge: it is always
relative to circumstances, to the limits of its values and to the end it
must serve.

—FERDINAND GONSETH
Les Mathématiques et la réalité (1936)

Classical clinicopathological studies of language and speech disorders have
been invaluable as diagnostic tools in clinical neurology. They have provided a
first approximation to the study of the relationship between brain and language.
Similar types of correlations have been fruitful in the analysis of perceptual,
sensory, or motor disorders, and in most instances such correlations have confirmed that clinical syndromes are amenable to decomposition into symptomatic
subsets and that the corresponding anatomical lesional substrata may also be
subdivided into fairly independent subterritories. In this way, these studies have
added strength to the notion that the nervous system, and the cerebral cortex in
particular, is organized into distinct areas of relative functional autonomy. This
notion rests, however, on an almost mechanical and surely oversimplified conception of nervous system organization, which views each anatomical locus as
independently capable of processing complex functions and of storing complex
information. The accuracy of this type of clinicopathological correlation has
depended upon whether the function in question is closer to the sensory or the
motor channel, whether the function is entirely related to a specific sensory
modality, whether the information is closely displayed by modality, temporal, or

45

NEURAL MODELS OF
LANGUAGE PROCESSES

spatial characteristics, or whether the information can be represented or conveyed along alternative paths or encoded in nonredundant ways. But, above all, the precision of localized clinicopathological correlations depends on whether one takes into account the complexity and the nature of the function in question.

An understanding of the interrelation of brain and language depends largely on the satisfactory analysis of the various levels and conditions in which the two complex systems—the physical biological entity and the highly symbolic human behavioral and learned manifestation—may correlate. Because there is little scientific interest in the broad approach to this subject, one is initially forced to fragment the problem into partial correlations. This latter approach implies a belief that, at least in broad terms, language as a whole can be understood from the study of its components, and that, similarly, the function of the entire brain can be understood from the study of its subcomponents. More important, the approach implies that in each instance the basic internal structure and interrelation of components is understood. Ultimately, one hopes to associate a significant number of functional fragments or parameters with the distinct biological substrata in which they are processed or stored. In the specific case of language and brain, we must approach this association with some understanding of the cerebral organization of linguistic processes and representations. The fact of the matter is that at the present time, the studies of all three aspects of the equation—knowledge of brain, knowledge of language, and knowledge of their interrelation—are still in preliminary stages of progress and we are forced to rely on assumptions, theoretical concepts, and use of homologies taken from other biological or artificial models.

The problem of understanding the biological foundations of language is complicated by the fact that this function is exhibited only by the human. Thus, the possibilities of its study under experimental conditions or the utilization of inferential knowledge from comparative animal studies are limited. Consequently, one cannot deal with this subject with the aggressiveness and directness that has characterized the study of other functions, or with the application of highly detailed analytical techniques. To a large extent, the study will have to depend on devising experimental techniques that externally manipulate conditions of linguistic information in normal subjects, in cases of language dissociation after brain lesions, or in subjects that are in the process of acquiring this function. This emphasis on the utilization of external intervention in the study of human behavior has coincided with the fortunate emergence of contemporary techniques of cognitive neuroscience, the physioergonomic approach to movement control studies, and the artificial simulation studies of artificial intelligence and computer science. The methodology of behavioral neuroscience has advanced quite dramatically. From the period in which we intended to study directly the modification of performance after stimulation, ablation, or naturally occurring lesions, we have moved to a three-stage methodological approach in

which we (*a*) pretrain and teach a behavioral paradigm, (*b*) introduce the perturbation of the biological substratum, and only then, (*c*) investigate the modification of (*a*) induced by (*b*). Convince yourself of the beauty and elegance of this
approach as utilized by Schneider (1969) in his study of the cortical and tectal
visual system in the hamster. Consider what has followed in research on primate
vision when such approach was extended by T. Pasik and P. Pasik (1973) and
Goldberg and Wurtz (Goldberg and Wurtz, 1972; Wurtz and Goldberg, 1972),
or utilized by Evarts (1974) or Bizzi (1980) in the study of movement controls.
The methodological approach prompted Mountcastle to say, in 1976:

> It has been clear for a long time—at least since the time of Lashley—that the
> quantitative study of behavior, traditionally the domain of the Psychologist,
> and of neural events in the brain, called "Neurophysiology," are conceptually
> different approaches to what are generically the same set of problems, an
> identity long emphasized by Jung (1972). What is new is that it is now possible
> to combine in one experiment the methods and concepts of each to yield a
> deeper insight into the brain mechanisms that govern behavior than is possible
> with either alone [p. 1].

The sudden emergence of language in man and the very central role that it
plays in his behavior can hardly be the de novo result of a fortunate set of genetic
mutations. Its origins and its development must be found beyond the external
manifestations of speech. It is certain that language as an organizing element of
cognition is intimately related to the developmental complexities of other sensory
and motor systems. In this respect, it is difficult to understand how language
could be studied in isolation from other cognitive systems unless one reduces the
entire problem to the study of the most superficial aspects of speech, the medium
by which language is made ostensible. On the other hand, it is equally difficult to
understand how other cognitive systems in man, such as visual, auditory, or
manipulative perceptual skills could be understood by merely comparing them to
homologous systems in other animals. If language and speech interact with other
cognitive systems, the latter must have properties of quantity and quality that
separate them from similar sensory systems in other species. Conversely, linguistic and speech functions must have been influenced by the cognitive functions
they serve.

Language and speech are not unique because of the mode and the way we
display the communication, but because of the kind of things, relations, and
intentions that we are capable of transmitting to others or telling to ourselves.
Recently, there has been a burst of research exploring possible linguistic
capabilities in apes. Initially, that research indicated that language would be
expressed as soon as an adequate means of communication was provided to these
speechless beings. However, over time it became clear that what was already
present in these beings was a rich cognitive apparatus of concepts, images, and
even symbolic representations that enable the experimental subjects to express

direct descriptions of their desires and establish symbolic relations. It became clear that they were able to acquire a respectable repertoire of symbols, a kind of basic lexicon, and to form linkages with referential cognitive contents, but that they were unable to acquire, develop, or expand the linguistic algorithms proper, the combinatory rules of syntax that have enabled man to express all the possible relations and intentions of his language. The use of some linguistic syntactic frames could be taught, but the rules of syntax could not be abstracted to a level that would serve as a model for new combinations or a rich paradigmatic use of models. The further these rules of syntax depart from direct semantic organizational principles, the less evidence has been found that apes can master the structural and algorithmic properties of language itself (Premack, 1976).

These studies, combined with increasing evidence from developmental psycholinguistics and the studies of pathological dissocations, have contributed decisively to confirming the multiple origins of linguistic abilities. One can distinguish the mode: phonological–vocal medium; the content: the semantic organization of cognition and the linguistic interphase proper; the procedural algorithms of syntax and the store of phonological symbols: the lexicon. One must initially recognize the interdependence of speech and language with other functions, but, at the same time, one must acknowledge the relative independence of their functional organization.

Contemporary neurosciences have taken renewed interest in the study of brain activities and structure in relation to higher manifestations of behavior. The almost complete paralysis that followed the impetuous work of the classics was only slightly interrupted by the works and critical studies of Head, Goldstein, Nielsen, or Kleist. In our country, reawakening was prompted by the neoclassical studies of Geschwind (1965), and a new theoretical interest in neurobiological implications was stimulated by the dissociations observed in cases of corpus callosum severance. However, momentous progress has resulted from a refocusing of these studies and of the problem in general: The brain, which classical and neoclassical studies have used as a point of departure, has been recognized as the biological depository of something that must be understood more fully before the physiological interphase can be brought in—behavior itself; in our case, language and speech themselves. No one can expect to make serious progress unless the function is better analyzed and understood. Only then may this knowledge be juxtaposed with physiological or anatomical data or with artificial simulation models. The most basic reason for this different arrangement of priorities is not only methodological, but also conceptual: The contents, the organization, and even the components of behavior are not to be understood simply as the results of brain activity. Biology (the brain) does not fully explain human behavior without the simultaneous consideration of cultural, environmental, and even individual circumstantial factors.

However, in this new approach to the problem, not all traditional disciplines have equal opportunity to affect the current development of our knowledge of the neurobiology of language. Whether traditional disciplines will so affect our knowledge will be dictated by the progress we make in understanding the nature of the problems involved. To this end, for instance, beautiful cytoarchitectonic studies of some areas of the classical speech region, as conducted by Galaburda, Sanides, and Geschwind (1978) and Geschwind and Levitsky (1968) along with many others, are introducing new information regarding cortical asymmetries. These studies, although interesting in themselves, are also suggestive of an as yet undetermined aspect of language. Storage? Speech process? Evolutive trend? Discriminative ability? All the above or nothing at all? It is too early to know; yet, the data are just too powerful and one trick of this game is to be able to match data from different sources within limits of correlative explanatory powers.

ANATOMICAL AND EVOLUTIVE ASPECTS OF BEHAVIOR

The study of aphasia has indicated that language and speech disorders are closely related to the left fronto-parieto-temporal cerebral cortex. This is not the occasion to review the degree of precision of this localization with respect to each of the clinical aphasic syndromes (see, for instance, J. E. Bogen and G. M. Bogen, 1976; Mohr, 1976, Levine and Sweet, Chapter 14, this volume). This cortical lateralization is in some way related to the fact that man, the only primate endowed with extensive acoustic–vocal speech, is also the primate that has the most extensive neocortical development in the phylogenetic scale. We can thus conclude that language is somewhat related to the last stages of man's evolutionary history, a point emphasized repeatedly by many authors (e.g., Geschwind, 1965).

Evolution is the major unifying theme of neurobiology. It is the concept that most radically distinguishes biology from other sciences by providing it with a unique and fundamental sense of direction. For our purposes, evolution can be defined as the description of the functional and structural changes and reorganization occurring in metazoan organisms in relation to the parallel changes that, in time, have taken place between the population and its environment. For our purposes, there is no need to explore the primary forces that have directed this evolutionary process, whether haphazard mutation or the unraveling of a chain of changes that, once initiated, create autonomous circular dynamics toward complexity (Whitehead, 1929). We need only observe that the progressive complexity in the structure and the functions of the nervous system through phylogeny graphically illustrates this biological process. We must recognize that the evolution of interrelations between organism and environment has been dominated by pragmatics and self-centered interests. The organism has (at least to a first approximation) opened and expanded channels of environmental communication and exchange only in those areas and only to the extent required to fulfill its needs. Initially, such channels provided organisms with the information that effected maintenance of homeostasis through biochemical and biophysical exchange with the immediate environment. Later, such channels effected creation of sensory and motor coordinative systems which deal with the immediate surrounding environment through pain reactivity to injuries, mating approaches, or flight by detecting significant signs. The telereceptor systems represent a turning point in evolutive style because (a) they provided the organism with means of gathering and storing information that is spatially and temporally distant, thus enabling a departure from behavior rooted solely in the present, and (b) they radically dislodged the autoreferential polarity of the senses (pain, contact, equilibrium) by providing the organism the opportunity to witness events in which it was not itself involved as actor (vision, audition). However, perhaps the most fundamental change in this evolutionary process occurred when the parameters of sensory information of discontinuous categorization began to replace those based on linear intensity or threshold values. (Such linear activations seem still to prevail in the area of emotion.) It was at this point that perception of the environment began to be fragmented into units of assembled features whose boundaries are dictated by the most salient physical discontinuity of the contents, of the external reality, or even sometimes by arbitrary legal convenience. It is easy to imagine potential consequences of such a cognitive style: The units are recorded as conglomerates; the overwhelming numerosity gives rise to memory overload and to recategorization; the temporal and spatial interrelations of objects with respect to the organism and among themselves give rise to relational concepts of temporal and spatial occurrence of events, a kind of semantically case-oriented frame of reference. The large number of units and the need for categorization and actualization of content and events may have been determinative cognitive forces for the development of a symbolic system that, finally, in man had its biological realization in the auditory modality. It is hardly a surprise that language symbolism, emerging in the midst of telereceptor sensory systems, would not share the same semantic fuzziness and discord that exists amidst its nonverbal contents.

The sensory modalities were not the result of a single master plan, but of the growth of fairly independent subsystems. No set of coordinated environmental physical parameters or units provides coherence to the various receptive channels. Their only points of unitary common reference are the consistency of reality, the unity that results from the singleness of action, and, above all, the relative stability provided by their projection into the symbolic linguistic system. It was impossible to create a unity of cognitive organization out of the diversity and fragmentary information provided by the senses. Thus, the symbolic verbal system was forced to create its own internal linguistic rules as an extension of the pragmatics of the organism as a whole (Marin, Saffran, and Schwartz, 1979).

Trends in cognitive evolution have parallels in the structural development of the nervous system, most particularly in that of the cerebral cortex. The major governing principle of the nervous development was the specialization of neuronal subsets in order to detect important aspects of environmental changes with maximal efficiency. Neurosensory subsets were then guided by physical modes of environmental events (optics, acoustics, chemical). The sensory systems developed complexity in functional and anatomical independence from each other, with the common impetus for growth being pragmatic needs of the organism. No correlations are to be found, for instance, in the degree of discrimination that one sense (i.e., vision) might have developed between color, shape, or texture. Similarly, no correlation is to be found between the ability to discriminate visual features and auditory ones, even when referring to a same object. The efficiency of specialization required the segregation and relative independence of subsystems, but independence created fragmentation and discontinuity.

Single feature detection of significant signs as a stimulus capable of triggering motor behavior would not require elaborate integration between sensory systems. However, the emergence of categorical perception may have been an important determinative factor for more complex subset integrative processes at the vicinity of primary receptive networks, as observed in the early associational stages of visual and somatosensory cortex in mammals. The emergence of object categories, and the alluded intersystem disparities, may have been important factors in the determination of coordinative intersystem representations and processes and the further expansion of the association areas of the cerebral cortex.

The concepts of encephalization and of the hierarchical organization of the nervous system result from these same principles. The cerebral cortex in man, with its specialized sensory and motor subsystems and its significantly expanded intersystem association areas, illustrates the characteristics of a biological substratum organized by these principles.

These principles can be applied to a study of language and speech. Speech has developed into a fairly independent acousticovocal system, with peculiarities that set it apart in perception, production, and cognitive organization. We can demonstrate that there is a parallel tendency for lateralization and localization of the anatomical substratum, just as we demonstrate that speech perception is related to primary auditory cortex and speech vocalization is related to the motor primary cortex. Secondary derivatives of language and speech, such as writing and reading, have been equally lateralized and tend to be in close anatomical proximity with the primary sensory systems from which they develop and on which they are dependent. Isolation of these speech areas from the rest of the cerebral cortex renders the subject spontaneously speechless, without verbal comprehension, and only able to perform occasional verbal repetition: a speech machine with a number of attributes for correct decoding and encoding of speech but without access to meaning or use of language for referential purposes (Marin and Gordon, 1980).

Observation of evolutionary trends in the organization of the cerebral cortex, comparative anatomical studies, evolutionary patterns of change in animal behavior along the phylogenetic scale, and, most significantly, the intense studies of clinicopathological correlations have given us the basis for most of our present knowledge of the brain in relation to language. The reliability of clinical syndrome discriminations, and their preponderant localization, has provided us with a broad picture of the way speech and, to some extent, language are depicted in the brain: Predominant disorders of speech production, articulation, syntactic production, and prosody tend to be disrupted by an anteriorly located lesion in or about the area of Broca; predominant disorders of speech perception and subsequent speech comprehension tend to be the consequence of the more posterior brain in the left paracoustic association area. The certainty of localization for other clinical syndromes is less clear. Authorities disagree as to whether lesions in the left parietal region, with or without involvement of the arcuate fasciculus which associates the temporal and frontal cortical areas, may give rise to the peculiar syndrome of conduction aphasia in which spontaneous speech and comprehension are grossly affected, while repetition is significantly altered or impossible. With respect to naming disorders, the localization of lesions is not specifically determinative, although there is a clear predominance of left posterior localization. Aside from those cases in which the naming disorder seems to be related to a disorder in the input sensory information (modality-specific anomia) or at the output production (production anomia), the large majority of cases involve disorders that compromise the search of the lexical item on the basis of referential knowledge more than the phonological formulation of the lexical item (Goodglass and Baker, 1976). This broader cognitive base for the naming disorder correlates with the inability to assign to the anomias a lesional localization as would be possible in the case of a more instrumental function. The anomia associated with diffuse cortical disorders, as observed in cases of dementia, clearly dissociate the intact lexical phonological level from the disorganized semantic referential one (Schwartz, Marin, and Saffran 1979).

Hence, the problem is not to argue the practical clinical value of classical knowledge of the anatomy of aphasias, but is instead to ask if this level of analysis of the anatomy and the clinical symptomatology is adequate to understand the way the brain operates in reference to speech and language. Despite the claims in its favor (Geschwind, 1970, 1979), I think that the answer to this question is negative. We know too much today about language description, structure, operation, and development to satisfy ourselves with diagrams that depict with fixed arrows or broad anatomical connections the multiple operations that we think are involved therein. Diagrams that overlook the nature, complexities, and dynamics of the functions and oversimplify the way the nervous system operates by reducing the nervous system to a static and passive switchboard, do not give sufficient insight into the understanding of production of oral speech, the reading aloud of a written test, or the repetition or paraphrase of a sentence. It is this better understanding of language as a cognitive system which convicts the classical diagrams of oversimplification. Note that, until recently, a corresponding lack of similar functional analysis seriously hampered the possibility of creative working hypotheses in other fields of cognitive neuroscience, such as movement organization or perception.

It is plausible that, if the problem is viewed from the traditional anatomical approach, we may not be able to improve the degree of detail of localization of language processes beyond that of convolutions or lobes. For some investigators, this may be due solely to lack of good clinical instances which if available would allow us to sample in greater detail the areas of language and perhaps enable us to dissociate the language disorders into finer and finer components. However, for others, the hopelessness of this endeavor is related to the fact that in many cases linguistic functions are of such a nature that they do not permit a static localization; that to try for extreme localization would be like attempting to get a more detailed analysis of a painting using a magnifying glass which would show only the aggregates of color pigments or the direction of brush strokes. Thus, it seems likely that in terms of the anatomical substratum, we have already reached the limits of our effort to isolate macrofunctional operators. Further anatomical discriminations will show a level at which the brain functions are no longer so categorically organized in mental units and, instead, are generically reduced to codes of electrical signals, membrane excitability changes, or columnar aggregates that manifest themselves in cellular biophysical codes (Harmon 1970; Marr and Poggio, 1976).

But there are still more perplexing problems with the concept of anatomical localization of functions: Why is it that a localized function in the left hemisphere may become lateralized with almost unrecognizable difference in the opposite side if an early cortical damage in the left hemisphere should occur? It is obvious that speech, and especially language, is not fully committed to any particular lateralization and that its eventual anatomical localization is primarily determined by a specific need for specialization of some linguistic operation that must be performed by equally specific aspects of an auditory vocal perceptual-motor apparatus. This specialization requires localized subsets; but before such specialization takes place, there are optional alternatives. Thus, localization or lateralization of neuronal subsets is not conditioned by a determined behavioral cognitive faculty (e.g., language or music), but rather (a) by the basic functional operations that one must perform in the realization of such faculties (i.e., in the case of music, perception of temporal sequences of pitch intervals needed to perceive melodies, perception of simultaneous sounds of different pitch in the perception of chords); (b) by the degree of incompatibility that these operations may have with others by virtue of the special computational operations, the special procedural algorithms to be followed, the special sensory code to be employed; and (c) by the special types of content that constitutes the units of such computations (i.e., words of the lexicon). It is only in this way that the concept of cerebral localization may be compatible with the functional plasticity observed during development or during the acquisition of new skills not necessarily shared by all individuals (i.e., reading, music perceptual or performing skills, acrobatics, etc.).

PHYSIOLOGY OF LANGUAGE

Anatomical and clinicopathological studies have provided only a broad frame of reference for analysis of the problem of the relations between brain and language. Would human clinical and experimental physiology carry us any closer? The neurological study of brain function has always been complicated by the enormous conceptual distance that exists between the basic physiological mechanisms or brain structure, and their ostensive behavioral manifestations. When the cardiologist attempts to understand the efficiency of blood tissue perfusion, he can describe the entire function of the circulatory system, from capillaries to the heart, in hydrodynamic and biomechanical terms. From the cardiac hemodynamic forces determined by Starling's law of myocardial contraction, the hydrostatic characteristics of the peripheral resistance, to the permeability of capillaries, there is a perfect continuity of logic and language that permits a direct realization of the relationships between the function of each component and the total performance.

This is not the case in the study of the nervous system. Here, the function is realized only indirectly, through the effect of muscles and sensory organs, which are only transducers in contact with the mechanical and other physical characteristics of the environment. The functional units of behavior are incredible spatiotemporal complexes with no obvious or simple correlation with the activities of the neural substrate. To begin to establish a similar correlation between general function and nervous tissue physiology one must overcome serious problems: (a) the behavioral manifestations of nervous activities must be described and analyzed and their structure and operations understood; (b) these higher levels of structure and operation must be reduced into finer and smaller features capable of being encoded in the language of cells or assemblies of cells; (c) the nervous correlative activities must be recorded, classified, and measured not only at selective loci, but along all their temporal and topographical distribution; and (d) criteria must then be developed for analysis of the units and the codes in which the nervous tissue expresses itself. It is unfortunate that such functional–

physiological correlations are limited because our knowledge in these three areas is insufficient.

When Lettvin, Maturana, Pitts, and McCulloch (1961) and Hubel and Weisel (1962) studied the physiological characteristics of the tectum opticum of the frog and the visual cortex of the cat, they reaffirmed the often neglected principle that the pluricellular organism, complex in its behavior and its structure, is ultimately an assembly of individual cellular units. Cells are biological units that must be addressed in their own cellular terms, regardless of the system to which they may belong, the interactions that may exist within the network to which they are connected, or the specialization or preadaptation that they may have developed for detecting special features.

The neurophysiologist is familiar with this approach of fragmenting subsystem analysis. At the cellular level, he must identify neurons or neuronal aggregates that are specifically and steadily sensitive to special features. Although he may find that a complex object presented as stimulus may excite some calcarine cortical cells, he does not expect that the cell is sensitive to all the physical characteristics of the stimulus, but only to some feature contained by it. He knows that cells in the sensory periphery, in the neural centers, and for that matter anywhere else in the organism, must be addressed in a "language" that is understood by cells: This language is one of the biophysical or biochemical events capable of depolarizing the membrane cells by virtue of their specific receptor membranes and by the temporospatial distribution of the stimuli. He knows that cells are only cells, whether in isolation or in interactive dependence of tissue systems, that their primary interest is the preservation of their homeostatic equilibrium, and that their primary functional characteristic is the reliability of response to low threshold specific elementary stimuli to which they are preadapted. When the visual neurophysiologists were challenged with the problem of vision, they became fully aware that "objects" were composites that cells would never "understand" as wholes. Neurophysiologists understood that objects must be decomposed into effective features. The surprise was to reconfirm both the utilitarian nature of these "significant features" and the fact that any specialization was the result of a biological adaptive pragmatism. In the case of Lettvin and Maturana's frog, the distance between observable visual behavior and cell feature activation was close enough to allow the broad conclusion that the frog saw very much what its cells reacted to. In the case of Hubel and Wiesel, after the analysis of simple, complex, and hypercomplex cell characteristics, the cascade flow of information came to an abrupt end, for in the cat, the distance between visual feature (cellular level) and visual behavior was already immense. Thus, any extrapolation of these results to man indicates that the distance may be even greater because of the complexity of the units that constitute the visual perceptual cognition with which man makes the computations of his conscious mental behavior.

Thus, physiologists have reaffirmed two basic biological tenets: First, throughout evolution, internal or external neural or sensorial cellular codes have remained essentially unmodified in their biophysical or biochemical nature, and specialization has not modified their essential characteristics; second, at cellular levels, organisms are analytical machines whose levels of operation may or may not coincide with the level of conscious cognition at which the whole organism seems to operate in its natural environment. Thus, in most cases, there must exist higher levels of organization that operate as collectors and integrators of simple information into complexes which then correspond to the purposes and the interests of the organism as a whole. When you challenge an insightful neurophysiologist with the question of the interrelation between brain and language, he will respond with the challenge of dissecting behavior into simple enough features to allow analysis of possible neuronal–functional correlations. Currently, one can at most consider the perceptual or articulatory aspects of speech as areas possibly amenable to analytical physiological studies. Other aspects of speech have no such capacity despite the fact that they represent the contents of our cognitive consciousness as visual images, words, thoughts, or musical melodies. However, rudimentary analysis may be possible, if in some instances we force ourselves to reduce mental operations to well-defined sensory codes instead of abstract and poorly defined codes.

The studies of cortical stimulation performed by Penfield and Roberts (1959) were rather disappointing, for they essentially confirmed, instead of advanced, that which was already recognized by lesional studies, namely the existence of a lateralization of speech production and the existence of speech areas broadly limited anteriorly by Broca's area and posteriorly by Wernicke's area. Other regions, such as the motor supplementary areas, were also addressed in these studies. The responses were elementary vocalizations, in rare instances utterances of isolated words, and often arrests of speech phenomena. The more recent studies by Whitaker and Ojemann (1977) have added information regarding naming, repetition, and verbal memory; but on the whole, although quite interesting in their own right, these studies have provided thus far a rather incoherent set of findings that are difficult to integrate into neurolinguistic processing schemas. This type of study does not distinguish those anatomical and physiological substrata which are involved in actual language or speech processing from those which, without such direct involvement, seem to be related to the facilitation or blockage of the verbal flow (i.e., the relation of the supplementary motor areas to mutism). The studies of evoked potentials associated with language or speech activities have not yet advanced to a stage where assessment of their value as physiological analytic tools is possible. The method is crude, and despite the fact that some interesting findings have been observed in lateralization studies or during learning, attentional, or preparatory phases, the method is impeded by the unknown nature of that which is recorded and which serves as a referential marker for the behavior. This method solves one unknown by relating it to another. The trick is not new to scientific study, and one may need to wait before the various components of evoked potentials are related to specific aspects of cognitive processing. Interesting correlations have been found thus far between RT, expectancy, and the P300 and N100 of the cortical evoked response (Hillyard and Picton, 1979; Kutas, McCarthy, and Donchin, 1977; Ritter, Simson, Vaughan, and Friedman, 1979).

It is too early yet to tell whether the Positron Emission Tomography (PET) studies will be able to give some hint as to the topography of cell activations during linguistic tasks.

Other studies are being performed that attempt to relate cerebral blood flow patterns and language operations (Ingvar, 1976). Although these works are interesting, their correlations are vague and far from providing causative linkages between brain and language operations. It is important to remember that in all sciences, coexistence in time or space of various kinds of phenomena may constitute the first link, but that the ultimate goal is to provide conceptual and causative continuations that allow us to transduce codes and understand mechanisms, and not merely to juxtapose isolated events.

In summary, the review of available information concerning physiological events occurring during speech leaves us with isolated data that, in most instances, have not yet reached beyond the classical notion of lateralized areas concerned with speech.

THE VISIBLE AND THE INVISIBLE ASPECTS OF BRAIN ACTIVITIES AND BEHAVIOR

Perhaps the most perplexing problem that arises in studying parallels between function and brain is that in overt behavior one may see more than has actually been actively operated upon by the nervous system. Conversely, behavioral performance levels are usually only part of the nervous system implementation. The other, and often most significant, aspects remain submerged in unconscious processing. Keele (1980) has reminded us that a normal subject is able to write an unfamiliar sentence with his hand in many different positions and in many different planes. He can also perform the task with sets of muscles that, most probably, have never before rehearsed this or any similar tasks. Thus, he can write with his left hand, either of his feet, his nose, or even his forehead. What is remarkable is that, with the exception of size and inaccuracy of details, his performance is remarkably similar and the pecularities of his handwriting can be easily recognized regardless of the particular manner in which he has performed the task.

The immediate conclusion is that the motor program that has served as a template must contain a number of feature specifications, and that it is abstract and largely uncommitted with respect to the muscles that are to be utilized in its performance.

A theory of motor control that presupposes fixed, rigidly wired relations between a program and its elements of implementation may never provide an adequate explanation of these types of phenomena. Such a theory will not even provide an explanation for the fact that the writing of one's signature has notable constancy despite the fact that the exact circumstances of environment (position of paper, friction between pencil and paper, etc.) or the muscles are never the same. Instead, one is forced to accept that the template originates in an internal representation that prefigures the total actions; that for its implementation it can be linked to a number of alternative sets of effectors; and that the template is cast in biomechanical terms that at all times consider the internal and external contextual circumstances. This physioergonomic approach to motor behavior formulated by Bernstein (1967) and his coworkers is a significant conceptual breakthrough in the studies of motor control, for it has provided the necessary external approach alluded to earlier. The approach considers behavior as the tripartite interaction between (a) programs derived from internal representations; (b) implementation of actions based on the instrumentalities available to the organism; and (c) active interactions between the internal and environmental characteristics (see also Shaw and McIntyre, 1974). The characteristics of the body should include biomechanical properties of the effectors, and Houk (1980) has emphasized the importance of peripheral muscular factors such as viscosity, elasticity, or inertial and acceleration forces that are important factors during the realization of even simple movements.

Abbs and Ellenberg (1976) have shown that during vocalization, there is a significant disparity between the actual movements of the jaw and the patterns and timing of the EMG of the corresponding movements. They demonstrated that the organism utilizes inertial and gravitational factors and becomes actively involved in vocalization only during phases in which movement must counteract these forces.

Our understanding of tasks of this type remains incomplete because consideration of the mechanical aspect of the task and the action that executes it ignores the environmental context within which the event takes place. Studies using a broader frame of reference indicate that the traditional single and narrow focus approach to tasks is enriched by the simultaneous study of concomitant environmental and organismic events. Recently Nashner and his coworkers (unpublished observations) have demonstrated that in passive or active hand pulling of a lever, the experimental subject activates a complex set of postural reactions and that the latter, in fact, antecede in time even the fastest phasic motor response. Similar observation has been made by Gurfinkel, Lipshits, and Popov (1979). Also, Massion (1980) demonstrated that cats, during the postural correction of postures of the extremities after mechanical perturbation or electrical cortical motor stimulation of one of the legs areas, make postural adjustments that precede the focal movement. Useful to an understanding of these effects are the findings of Humphrey (1980) which demonstrate through studies of nests of motor cortical neurons that neurons that induce phasic responses are often surrounded by others that induce tonic sustained muscle responses.

Studies of object vision and auditory speech perception, and of motor activity, provide abundant evidence of the importance of considering contextual circumstances and concomitant events. The evidence strongly suggests that studies of isolated processes, or studies focused narrowly on elementary and circumscribed phenomena, may be missing the most important characteristics of the physiological basis of behavior. In many ways, this is what seems to have plagued and virtually paralyzed efforts to understand vocal articulation in speech. The question arises as to why widely accepted phonetic classifications and knowledge of phonetic transitions failed to show any systematic corresponding set of motor articulatory movements. This area, which one would expect to be governed by enviable objectivity, has seen incredible resistance to a one-to-one type of fixed correspondence. In my opinion, this obvious disparity between the motor or receptive surfaces and the external aspects of behavior touches the heart of our conceptual crisis regarding how the nervous system works and constitutes a warning against any expectation that behavior will be implemented by activation of elementary rigid keyboards. The warnings of Hughling Jackson against adopting the concept of the motor cortex as a fixed rigidly wired keyboard of muscles remain unheeded. In neurobiology, the confusion between cellular and organismic levels of organization still requires clarification, long after computer scientists have become fully aware that machine hardware activity has no direct and simple correlation with the units and language of software programs.

INFORMATION PROCESSING ANALYSIS

An attempt to gain insight into the relationship between brain and language through the study of speech perception and production merits special consideration, for (a) it allows us to follow the communication flow from a physical, to a physiological, and then to a psychological level of processing; (b) it permits an experimental methodology in which stimuli can be manipulated along various parameters and response can be quantified; (c) it allows an analysis of the stages and operations that addresses important aspects of the style of brain information processing; and (d) it allows the design and testing of various types of serial, parallel, or interactive models.

There is evidence that might be interpreted as indicating that the nervous system processes complex information through feature-by-feature analysis and amasses information, from simple physical to perceptual complex levels, by a subsequent integration. In cases of sensory modalities, this style of information processing may even be paralleled by the morphological and the physiological display of neural networks that extend concentrically around the primary receptive areas (e.g., Hubel and Wiesel, 1962; Jones and Powell, 1969, 1970). Analogous schematization has been utilized by Marr's (1976) artificial model of early processing of visual information.

At a much higher cognitive level, there is evidence that similar on-line processes occur for auditory and visual presentations of verbal information. Posner (1969, 1978) had demonstrated that reaction times increase when subjects are asked to determine visually the physical characteristics of letters, (e.g., A-a), to determine the name of a particular letter, or to determine if a letter is a vowel or a consonant. Cole, Coltheart, and Allard (1974) have observed similar results for auditory presentations. Studies of verbal perception at even higher levels, as revealed for instance by the analysis of verbal deafness, suggest that information is processed at various stages, at auditory preverbal, and at phonological verbal levels (Saffran, Marin, and Yeni-Komshian, 1976). The cumulative experience gained through the study of various kinds of acquired dyslexias has also suggested that the reading process evolves by gradually integrating pieces of information to word levels and to semantic levels (Shallice and Warrington, 1975). These experimental results indicate the existence of fairly independent stages of cognitive processing and introduce the possibility of ordering them into a chronometric schedule on the basis of RT, or another chronometric procedure. Because of the artificial narrowness implicit in the methodology, these techniques cannot demonstrate whether, under natural conditions, these functional stages in the normal individual, who is already familiarized with the rules of language, are mandatory or merely optional in their sequence. In verbal perception studies, phenomena such as word advantage, pronounceability, familiarity, frequency, or context are known to alter significantly the strict sequential order of operations. It is essential to recognize that language and speech are not processed by cognitively naive individuals and that language and speech are strongly influenced by any prior knowledge of the cognitive system, and by contextual preexisting behavioral biases, all of which decisively interact with the incoming or outgoing information. Marslen-Wilson and Komisarjevsky-Tyler (1980) have recorded important evidence of this interactive style of processing between on-line communication flow and internal representations.

A brief review of the difficulties encountered by one of our patients suffering from a surface dyslexia provides similar evidence. This person was able to read, although with great difficulty, by painfully decoding each letter, assembling these into morphemic clusters, and then translating them into phonemes and then words. She was unable to read words that were orthographically irregular or in which the grapheme–phoneme relation was peculiar (i.e., *night, thought*).

When asked to identify letters in a horizontal display, from center (foveal fixation) to right, her RT increased monotonically in relation to the distance of the target letter from the central initial fraction. Increased separation of letters slightly reduced the curve of RT of this task and the same advantage was noted when a nonverbal symbol was intercalated between letters. However, when the letter search was conducted using a string that alternated letters with numbers that she was instructed to ignore (e.g., the string A3F3R3 . . .), her RT increased three or more times. This dramatic RT increase after introduction of the numbers suggests an inability to avoid the cognitive stage of discriminating letter from number. In tasks of recognizing triads of letters, the same monotonic increase from center to right was observed with no change caused by pronounceability or by the fact that some triads were actually high frequency words (*boy–cat*). Although letter identifications were performed only with great effort, the patient always knew the correct position of the requested item within the total string, and particularly its position with respect to the last items. Such knowledge proved that preverbal visual exploration had been made.

These observations indicate that in higher cortical cognitive disorders and, in particular, in some cases of aphasias or alexias, abnormality may result from the defective interaction between peripheral sensory-perceptual or motor processes and the corresponding internal representations rather than from exclusive functional disconnection, blockage of stage processing, or internal disorganization of internal representation.

ARTIFICIAL MODELS, THEORIES, AND LANGUAGE PROCESSING

Contemporary linguistics, particularly through transformational grammar, has developed a comprehensive description of language. In many ways, this description has served as a structural and functional model. Just as clinicoanatomical studies provided models for the topography of speech function, so linguistic theory can serve as a frame of reference for a psycholinguistic description of the internal representations and the processes involved in language and speech. As has been clearly stated by Chomsky (1965), no claims are made that this performance model must be identical with the psychological processes involved in the language behavior. As indicated by Marr (1977), the linguistic theory may run as a parallel model—what he designates as a Type 2 theory. Thus, an unavoidable prerequisite is the validation of the psychological reality of the various aspects of this description. Broad distinctions between lexicon and syntax have been confirmed in the contrastive studies of aphasias (Saffran, Schwartz, and Marin, 1980; Scholes, 1977). Similarly, phonological and syntactical abilities have been found significantly dissociated from semantic levels in some cases of dementia (Schwartz, Marin, and Saffran, 1979; Warrington, 1975). Studies of naming disorders or of paraphasic errors have begun to shed light on a possible relationship between the lexicon and its referential level, as well as on the possible internal organization of the word representation itself (Buckingham, 1977; Butterworth, 1980; Goodglass and Baker, 1976). It must be remembered, however, that whereas linguistic description is primarily a theoretical and logical description of an almost idealized system of representations, rules of relations, and combinations, the organism and its brain are neither theoretical nor logical, but are overwhelmingly practical, self-centered, compelled by continuous internal urges, and not always parsimonious or precise. In fact, one of the areas of conflict between linguistic descriptive models and available knowledge of neural networks as substratum has arisen as a result of their radically opposite characteristics. Theories tend to embrace the maximal information within minimal sets of generalizations, rules, or storages. Biological evidence of nervous system organization tends to be based on neuronal units or cell assemblies that integrate networks whose properties are too powerful. Whereas, for instance, we have been excessively concerned with the difficulties that might arise during the successful acquisition of syntactic rules, there has been little concern about the much greater demands on memory that are imposed by the learning of an enormous, arbitrary lexicon full of orthographic, phonological, and phonetic exceptions. Of course, this argument does not suggest that cognitive or language acquisition is based only on accumulation of data in an unruly net. The argument does indicate, however, that parsimony and abstract categorical logic may not be the governing, or even primary, style of brain organization. Whereas theory emphasizes the governing rules of syntax and phonology, the organism, healthy or diseased, strives to express primarily its semantic cognitive levels. Thus, to the biologically oriented student of language it is still regrettable that we are unable to develop an extensive semantically based linguistics or a more elaborate case-oriented syntactic theory. It is unfortunate for the biologist that alternative grammars have been too fragmentary and have been more interested in enlarging the descriptive capacity of a theory than in approaching the areas where internal rules and linguistic principles are linked to pragmatic incidences of language. The analysis of governing rules operative in the residual speech production of Broca's aphasics, as studied by Saffran *et al.* (1977), might provide the approach that will permit the analysis of the relations between cognitive and linguistic levels. Advocating the establishment of links among language cognition, and connative behavior in general should not be interpreted as suggesting a commonality of principles of organization and function. Quite to the contrary, what is suggested is that there is as great a need to analyze the interphases of these separated areas as there is to understand the relations between physiological and psychological levels of organization.

The inaccessibility of the internal organization of the physiological or the cognitive representations and processes has required the use of artificial models. In most cases, the models were designed to mimic that which is observed in behavior. In such cases, the computations in the artificial model may or may not be similar to those of the organism, and as Marr (1977) has commented, the model's heuristic value is vastly reduced or nil. However, when different "lesions" of nodes in a homogeneously interconnected network produce quite diverse "focal" or "diffuse" deficits in the output, as in the model created by Wood (1978, 1980), one begins to see the relationship between the kind of information, the kind of "lesions," and the kind of results relevant for biological systems. As Marr (1977) has commented, computational models and theories cannot make any progress by themselves, nor can psychology identify the mechanisms of behavior; both disciplines must evolve in close contact with the other.

.

BRAIN AND LANGUAGE THEORIES: A HISTORY OF DISPARITY

In this chapter, a number of general or specific issues related to the neurobiology of language have been discussed. The skepticism expressed regarding the use of anatomical knowledge as a point of departure for the study of language is based upon the arguments, noted earlier, that justify the conceptual distinction existing between properties of bioelectrical neuronal circuit and behavioral levels that deal with categories, symbols, and complex procedural rules and computational algorithms. Such conceptual distance is not reflected by the naive descriptions of classical clinicopathological cases or syndromes, or by the traditional textbook explanation for how the area of "comprehension of language" is connected to the "speech production area" by the arcuate fasciculus in order to allow verbal repetition. The shallowness of both behavioral and anatomical data make these types of correlations useful merely for broad clinical purposes.

Skepticism about an anatomical approach is strongest among cognitive psychologists who tend to focus attention on psycholinguistic description and processing, and who may even regard the brain as an accidental element. However, this skepticism may not be satisfactory for workers based on the neurobiological side of the problem.

Why is it that this interphase between language behavior and brain has been so hard to conceptualize? In the course of this discussion, I have tried to emphasize the different levels, as opposed to simple specialized subsets, at which the behavior of a total animal, particularly man, must be conceived. I have stressed the heterogeneity of the scope of information and the diverse evolutionary history of the various sensory-perceptual subsystems, and the resulting gaps and disparities that an organism must confront in its relation to the environment. I have stressed the learning and memory load involved in the acquisition and development of cognition and the almost arbitrary nature of some of the symbolic systems. Finally, I have emphasized a utilitarian basis of organismic adaptations as the primal force for subset specialization or for organismic behavior. Looking at the problem from its broadest perspective, I have alluded to the disparities that exist between, on the one hand, the parsimonious internal logic and the economy of any theory conceived by our minds, and, on the other, the heterogeneity, prodigality, and repetitiousness that prevail when the millions of years of evolutionary stress have taught the organism how to survive and deal with its environment. I have observed with surprise the disparity that exists between the parsimony of the linguistic theory and the psycholinguistic processes that is suggested by it, and the almost incommensurable power that emerges from any neuronal model, whether it is based on neurons as units, or columns, or even greater neuronal aggregates. Given the richness of, and the number of, possible units that one can conceive of as operational in any neuronal model, it is easy to explain any of the properties demanded by a psycholinguistic theoretical model. It appears that our knowledge of the biological substratum and our progress and theory in language processing originate in quite different viewpoints. When considering these two views, I must confess that I have always been more impressed with the capacity of the human brain to discriminate, characterize, and store in memory the 30-plus thousand arbitrary words in active use than with the complexity claimed to be involved in learning a few dozen syntactic algorithmic rules. I am impressed by the fact that during his youth, Claudio Arrau won a much sought after musical prize by playing by heart the whole *Well-Tempered Clavier*; or that Saint Saëns, at the age of 12, offered at one of his piano recitals to play by heart any of the 32 Beethoven piano sonatas as an encore. Thus, I am impressed by the fact that numerosity and content are far richer than the combinatory algorithms, or procedural rules. I am similarly impressed that the same disparity in number is characteristic in language by contrasting the extension, richness, and the possible internal structure and cognitive relations of the lexicon with that of the syntax, upon which contemporary linguistics seems to have placed so much emphasis.

Let us consider for a moment another level of biology and consider by analogy the case of biochemistry. One's first impression of biochemistry is that of overwhelming complexity in chemical serial reactions, feedbacks, cycles, and compounds. However, closer observation reveals that the possible biochemical reactions are quite restricted: hydroxylate, dehydroxylate; carboxylate, decarboxylate; aminate, deaminate, transaminate; reduce, oxydize; and a few others. A still closer look limits even further the possible reactions, as only a limited number of operations can be performed on any specific chemical compound (e.g., one can only deaminate an amine or dehydroxylate an alcohol). Thus, the richness and variety of biochemistry result not from the basic reactions, but from the number of compounds that can be submitted to these reactions and, as a consequence of these reactions, the serial chemical algorithms which characterize the biochemical reaction chains and the tissue "context" in which such reactions occur (i.e., whether a specific biochemical reaction occurs in a liver cell, renal cell, or brain cell imposes, in each case, selected barriers to other compounds and creates a special chemical milieu).

Applying this analysis to language, it appears that the basis of linguistic richness and function is the numerosity of the lexicon. Whether the lexical units are words, clauses, or something still higher, they are phonologically symbolic "compounds" whose potential properties are to a large extent predetermined by their semantics and context. For each lexical tag, there is a limited number of possible optional "linguistic reactions." Once the word *school* is introduced, only a restricted linkage can be constructed through the acceptable linguistic operations. Thus, the range of acceptable linkages is drastically curtailed, and the algorithmic syntactic rules must operate within restrictions imposed by semantic reference, contextual pragmatics, and phonological acceptability.

The lexicon may be considered in close functional linkage with the other sensory cognitive contents. Given its respectable size and phonological nature, one would expect to find the lexicon stored and recorded in a sizable neuronal network and in some predictable relation to other cognitive systems. Both aspects are confirmed by the wide—although predominantly posterior—distribution of the lesions producing anomias. In contrast, syntactic algorithms, like basic biochemical reactions, will not occur at any locus. Its apparent anterior localization, as suggested by cases of agrammatism, would be due to the interdependence between syntactic expression and phonological expressive mechanisms.

A change in the center of gravity of language organization, from syntax to lexicon, has obvious consequences for the neurobiology of language. First, it returns to language organization and development the proper semantic and pragmatic foundation that relates language to other cognitive functions and allows language development to be tested as an exercise of the organism's pragmatics.

Second, the impressive growth of the lexicon, its internal organization, and its relationship to other cognitive areas creates a system complex enough to interrelate with the networks already available in the study of nervous system function and structure. Thus, any advance in defining the structure and properties of the lexicon provides a framework for inquiry relevant to the possible correlative properties of the biological substratum. In contrast, like the principles of any theory, and like the basic reactions of biochemistry, the rules of syntax and their algorithms are abstractions of rules and generalizations. Elsewhere (Marin and Gordon, 1979) I have alluded to the abstract nature of syntactic functions and the relative semantic opacity of their means of expression, and, in the special case of syntactic affixes and functions, their strong dependency on phonology. A neurobiological theory of language based on the study of the lexicon should be able to demonstrate that syntax gradually emerges from the properties of that lexical organization, rather than emerging as a totally separate set of rules to be learned as independent cognitive operations. Such a lexically based neurobiology, by virtue of its enormous growth, would interact with the complex neural models at its predominant localization in the midst of the cortical speech association areas. Any such neurobiological theories, however, cannot be based on a progressive utilization of a neuronal network by the developmental growth of a lexical repertoire in the way that seats are gradually occupied by spectators arriving at a concert hall. Instead, such theories will have to consider that such a growth is a history of a process that involves all available neurons in whatever few lexical and syntactical demands. The growth produces an ever-richer, ever-growing network of differentiated units, each more independent, specialized, and narrower in its interconnections and functions. I would like to think that it is in these areas—lexicosemantics, lexicophonology, the study of anomias, the developmental characteristics of the lexicon, and the biological characterizations of the association cortex—that a neurobiology of language and artificial intelligence models will emerge to fill the existing gap between language and the brain.

". . . y entiende con todos tus cinco sentidos que todo cuanto yo he hecho, hago e hiciere va muy puesto enrazón y muy conforme con las reglas de caballería . . . ," exclamó Don Quijote.

"Señor", respondió Sancho, "y es buena regla de caballería que andemos perdidos por estas montañas sin senda ni camino. . . ?"

". . . and understand with all your five senses that all that I do, have done, and shall do is the fruit of sound reasons and wholly in conformity with the rules of Chivalry. . . ," said Don Quijote.

"Sir", said Sancho, "is it a good rule of chivalry for us to be wandering lost in these mountains, without road or paths?"

—*Don Quijote de la Mancha*
First Part, Chapter XXV

REFERENCES

Abbs, J. H., and Eilenberg, G. R. (1976). Peripheral mechanisms of speech motor control. In N. Lass (Ed.), *Contemporary issues in experimental phonetics.* New York: Academic Press.

Bernstein, N. (1967). *The coordination and regulation of movements.* London: Pergamon Press.

Bizzi, E. (1980). Central and peripheral mechanisms in motor control. In G. E. Stelmach and J. Requin (Eds.), *Tutorials in motor behavior.* Amsterdam: North Holland.

Bogen, J. E., and Bogen, G. M. (1958). Wernicke's region—Where is it? In *Origins and evolution of language and speech. Annals of New York Academy of Science, 280,* 834–843.

Buckingham, H. A. (1977). The conduction theory and neologistic jargon. *Language and Speech, 20,* 174–184.

Butterworth, B. (1980). Some constraints on models of language production. In B. Butterworth (Ed.), *Language Production*, Vol. 1. New York: Academic Press.

Chomsky, N. (1965). *Aspects of the theory of syntax*. Cambridge, Mass.: MIT Press.

Cole, R. A., Coltheart, M., and Allard, F. (1974). Memory of a speaker's voice. Reaction time to same or different voiced letter. *Quarterly Journal of Experimental Psychology, 26*, 1–7.

Evarts, E. V. (1974). Sensorimotor cortex activity associated with movements triggered by visual as compared to somesthetic inputs. In F. O. Schmitt and F. G. Worden (Eds.), *The neurosciences. Third study program*. Cambridge, Mass.: MIT Press.

Galaburda, A. M., Sanides, F., and Geschwind, N. (1978). Human brain: Cytoarchitectonic left–right asymmetries in the temporal speech regions. *Archives of Neurology, 35*, 812–817.

Geschwind, N. (1965). Disconnection syndromes in animals and man. Part I and Part II. *Brain, 88*, 237–294, 585–644.

Geschwind, N. (1970). The organization of language and the brain. *Science, 170*, 940–944.

Geschwind, N. (1979). Specialization of the human brain. *Scientific American, 241*, 180–199.

Geschwind, N., and Levitsky, W. (1968). Human brain: Left–right asymmetries in temporal speech regions. *Science, 161*, 186–187.

Goldberg, M. E., and Wurtz, R. H. (1972). Activity of the superior colliculus in behaving monkey, II: Effect of attention on neuronal responses. *Journal of Neurophysiology, 35*, 560–574.

Goodglass, H., and Baker, E. (1976). Semantic field, naming and auditory comprehension in aphasia. *Brain and Language, 3*, 359–374.

Gurfinkel, U. S., Lipshits, M. I., and Popov, K. E. (1979). On the origin of short-latency muscle responses to postural disturbances. *Agressologie, 20*, B, 153–154.

Harmon, L. D. (1970). Neural subsystems: An interpretative summary. In F. O. Schmitt (Ed.), *The neurosciences: Second study program*. New York: Rockefeller University Press.

Hillyard, S. A., and Picton, T. W. (1979). Event-related brain potentials and selective information processing in man. In J. E. Desmedt (Ed.), *Cognitive components in cerebral event-related potentials and selective attention. Progress in Clinical Neurophysiology*, Vol. 6. Basel: S. Krager.

Houk, J. C. (1980). *Neural mechanisms for the control of muscle length and tension*. Paper read at the Symposium on the Organization of Movements, Neurological Sciences Center of Good Samaritan Hospital and Medical Center, Portland, Oregon, April 1980.

Hubel, D. H. and Wiesel, T. N. (1962). Receptive fields, binocular interaction and functional architecture in the cat's visual cortex. *Journal of Physiology, 160*, 106–154.

Humphrey, D. R. (1980). *Motor cortex and segmental mechanisms in the control of hand posture*. Paper read at the Symposium on the Organization of Movements, Neurological Sciences Center of Good Samaritan Hospital and Medical Center, Portland, Oregon, April, 1980.

Ingvar, D. H. (1976). Functional landscapes of the dominant hemisphere. *Brain Research, 107*, 181–197.

Jones, E. G., and Powell, T. P. S. (1969). Connexions of the somatic sensory cortex of the Rhesus monkey, I: Ipsilateral cortical connexions. *Brain, 92*, 477–502.

Jones, E. G., and Powell, T. P. S. (1970). An anatomical study of converging sensory pathways within the cerebral cortex of the monkey. *Brain, 93*, 793–820.

Jung, R. Neurophysiological and psychophysical correlates in vision research, in A. G. Karczmar and J. C. Eccles (Eds.), *Brain and human behavior*. New York: Springer-Verlag.

Keele, S. (1980). *Explorations of the concept of a central clock: Timing of movements*. Paper presented at the Symposium on the Organization of Movements, Neurological Sciences Center of Good Samaritan Hospital and Medical Center, Portland, Oregon, April, 1980.

Kutas, M., McCarthy, G., and Donchin, E. (1977). Augmenting mental chronometry: The P300 as a measure of stimulus evaluation time. *Science, 197*, 792–795.

Lettvin, J. Y., and Maturana, H. R.; Pitts, W. H., and McCulloch, W. S. T. (1961). Two remarks on the visual systems of the frog. In W. Rosenblith (Ed.), *Sensory communication*. Cambridge, Mass.: MIT Press.

Marin, O. S. M., and Gordon, B. (1979). Neuropsychological aspects of aphasia. In R. H. Tyler and D. M. Dawson (Eds.), *Current neurology*, Vol. 2. Boston: Houghton Mifflin.

Marin, O. S. M., and Gordon, B. (1980). Language and speech production from a clinical neuropsychological perspective. The NATO Advanced Study Institute for Motor Learning and Speech. In G. E. Stelmach and J. Requin (Eds.), *Tutorials in motor behavior*. Amsterdam: North-Holland.

Marin, O. S. M., Saffran, E. M., and Schwartz, M. F. (1979). Origins and distribution of language. In M. S. Gazzaniga (Ed.), *Handbook of behavioral neurobiology, 2. Neuropsychology*. New York: Plenum Press.

Marr, D. (1976). Early processing of visual information. *Philosophical Transactions of the Royal Society, Series B, 275*, 483–524.

Marr, D. (1977). Artificial intelligence. A personal view. *Artificial Intelligence, 9*, 37–48.

Marr, D., and Poggio, T. (1976). From understanding computation to understanding neural circuitry. MIT Artificial Intelligence Memorandum 357.

Marslen-Wilson, W., and Komisarjevsky-Tyler, L. (1980). The temporal structure of spoken language understanding. *Cognition, 8*, 1–71.

Massion, J. *Central control of movements*. (1980). Paper read at the Symposium on the Organization of Movements. Neurological Sciences Center of Good Samaritan Hospital and Medical Center, Portland, Oregon, April 1980.

Mohr, J. P. (1976). Broca's area and Broca's aphasia. In H. Whitaker and H. A. Whitaker (Eds.), *Studies in neurolinguistics*, Vol. 1. New York: Academic Press.

Mountcastle, V. (1976). The world around us: Neural command functions for selective attention. *Neurosciences Research Program Bulletin, 16*, Suppl. 2.

Pasik, T., and Pasik, P. (1973). Extrageniculostriate vision in the monkey, IV: Critical structure for light vs. no-light discrimination. *Brain Research, 56*, 165–182.

Penfield, W., and Roberts, L. (1959). *Speech and brain mechanisms*. Princeton: Princeton University Press.

Posner, M. I. (1969). Abstraction and the process of recognition. In G. Bower and J. T. Spence (Eds.), *Psychology of learning and motivation*. New York: Academic Press.

Posner, M. I. (1978). *Chronometric exploration of mind*. Hillsdale, N.J.: Lawrence Erlbaum.

Premack, D. (1976). *Intelligence in ape and man*. Hillsdale, N.J.: Lawrence Erlbaum.

Ritter, W., Simson, R., Vaughan, H. G., and Friedman, D. (1979). A brain event related to the making of a sensory discrimination. *Science, 203*, 1358–1361.

Saffran, E. M., Marin, O. S. M., and Yeni-Komshian, G. H. (1976). An analysis of speech perception in word deafness. *Brain and Language, 3*, 209–228.

Saffran, E. M., Schwartz, M. F., and Marin, O. S. M. (1977). *Semantic factors in agrammatic speech production*. Presented to the International Neuropsychology Society European Conference, Oxford, England.

Saffran, E. M., Schwartz, M. F., and Marin, O. S. M. (1980). The word order problem in agrammatism, II: Production. *Brain and Language, 10*, 263–280.

Schneider, G. E. (1969). Two visual systems. *Science, 163*, 895–902.

Scholes, R. (1977). Syntactic and lexical components of sentence comprehension. In A. Caramazza and E. B. Zurif (Eds.), *The acquisition and breakdown of language: Parallels and divergencies*. Baltimore: Johns Hopkins Press.

Schwartz, M. F., Marin, O. S. M., and Saffran, E. M. (1979). Dissociations of language in dementia: A case study. *Brain and Language, 7*, 277–306.

Shallice, T., and Warrington, E. K. (1975). Word recognition in a phonemic dyslexic patient. *Quarterly Journal of Experimental Psychology, 27*, 187–199.

Shaw, R., and McIntyre, M. (1974). Algoristic foundations to cognitive psychology. In W. B. Weimer and D. S. Palermo (Eds.), *Cognition and the symbolic processes.* Hillsdale, N.J.: Lawrence Erlbaum.

Warrington, E. K. (1975). The selective impairment of semantic memory. *Quarterly Journal of Experimental Psychology, 27,* 635–657.

Whitaker, H. A., and Ojemann, G. A. (1977). Graded localization of naming from electrical stimulation mapping of the left cerebral cortex. *Nature, 270,* 50–51.

Whitehead, A. N. (1929). *The function of reason.* Princeton, N.J.: Princeton University Press. (Reprinted by Beacon Paperbook, 1966.)

Wood, C. C. (1978). Variations on a theme by Lashley: Lesion experiments on the neural model of Anderson, Silverstern, Ritz and Jones. *Psychological Review, 85,* 582–591.

Wood, C. C. (1980). Interpretation of real and simulated lesion experiments. *Psychological Review, 87,* 474–476.

Wurtz, R. H., and Goldberg, M. E. (1972). Activity of the superior colliculus in behaving monkey, III: Cells discharging before eye movements. *Journal of Neurophysiology, 35,* 575–586.

II
ARTIFICIAL INTELLIGENCE AND PROCESSING MODELS

The worker in AI is concerned with writing computer programs that can carry out aspects of such intelligent behaviors as language understanding, picture interpretation, game playing and problem solving. Many workers in this field wish to design systems which will prove technologically useful, without concern for whether or not the systems in any way model mental, let alone neural, processes. Nonetheless, an increasing number of AI workers do see their work as contributing to and being influenced by cognitive psychology. However, virtually none go beyond a behavioral analysis to a concern with how such processes may be realized via interactions within and between structures of the brain. The task of this section, then, is not so much to review as to initiate the contribution of AI to neurolinguistics.

In the following chapters, we meet three AI systems for language perception: the HWIM and HEARSAY systems that proceed from an acoustic input to a semantic interpretation of the utterance it represents, and Marcus' system for parsing sentences presented in text. In studying these, we shall see the virtues of implemented or implementable models: They force us to adopt a rigorous vocabulary, with explicit specification of the different levels of representation of data, and an explicit specification of the processes which act upon them. More importantly, in computational linguistics we are forced to specify the control structures whereby a host of different processes (or knowledge structures) are brought to bear in actual performance. This issue of control has been almost totally ignored in neurolinguistics, except for a few vague words concerning "feedback." The control systems used by HWIM, HEARSAY and Marcus exceed those used by the psycholinguist, and it is our claim that the neurolinguist must assimilate the use of control structures of this complexity if we are to represent adequately the subtle interactions in the brain which underlie language performance.

The phrase "control structures of this complexity" is used without any claim that AI has yet revealed control structures with psychological or neurological validity. As Woods shows in his chapter, the overall architecture of the HWIM system was motivated by a rather informal series of studies of man–machine interaction in understanding spoken sentences. However, HWIM was not meant to model human performance as such, and the evolution of its design was an engineering process focused on "getting the system to work." The HEARSAY system, briefly described in Arbib's chapter, was designed to exemplify the notion that the various knowledge sources were essentially autonomous, and that they interacted only via data (hypotheses at various levels of representation and at various stages of elaboration) displayed on a common "blackboard." Both systems are characterized by the "hypothesize-and-test" paradigm. "Bottom-up" processes (i.e., those which operate on low-level constructs such as phonemes) suggest higher-level hypotheses. "Top-down" processes extend such hypotheses (e.g., by using syntactic or semantic cues to suggest what word category might follow a string of words already hypothesized) and initiate lower-level processes to evaluate such an extension. As a result, "islands of reliability" may be formed anywhere in the sentence, rather than proceeding from a "best possible" analysis of the initial portion of a sentence before subsequent input is processed. Note that these are features of engineering designs; we may also consider them as hypotheses about human language perception. As such, they have been attacked on two grounds: from a psycholinguistic perspective by Marslen-Wilson, and from a theoretical perspective by Marcus.

What evidence do we have that the decompositions in HWIM or HEARSAY are psychologically real, rather than the outcome of decisions made for ease of programming a system? It is a profound question to ask if distinctions of knowledge type made in discussing some performance correspond to distinct processes within a system that embodies that performance. Marslen-Wilson and Tyler (1980) argue that the claim of distinct linearly ordered processing stages is not true of human performance. They argue that speech is recognized by a human as it is heard with words recognized within 200 msec and mapped onto an interpretive structure which affects recognition of later words. This is in contrast to Woods' theory, expressed in the design of HWIM, of working out from "islands of reliability." The problem in current AI systems, as Marslen-Wilson and Tyler see it, is that the low-level representation of the initial portion of an utterance is not reliable enough to provide a basis for processing of this type. However, is it that the signal is underdetermined, or rather that the front ends of present computer systems are inadequate? They agree that the process of understanding involves cooperation between knowledge sources, but suggest that HWIM and HEARSAY do not show how high-level knowledge is used by humans to guide the lower-level processes in the system. They see the perception system as maximizing the speed with which messages are transmitted and received with the main strategy being to move the analysis as rapidly as possible to a domain where all available sources of knowledge are used. The essential link is the word recognition system, and they argue that this provides the basis for invoking the structural and interpretive context that furnishes us with a rather complete analysis of the utterance to date as each new word enters the system. We would caution that while such studies (made with recordings of clearly enunciated speech) show that human input–output behavior can give the appearance of systematic left-to-right processing (which is, presumably, called right-to-left processing in Hebrew and Arabic), it does not rule out the "hypothesize-and-test" paradigm. In fact, with crisp low-level data, word hypotheses can become unequivocal, and a system like HEARSAY or HWIM could proceed in an essentially left-to-right fashion. However, anecdotal data suggest that once the data degrade (the speaker mumbles, speaks too softly, or the radio we are listening to has static), we may indeed have to work back-wards from an "island of reliability" later in the sentence to remove an earlier ambiguity. At the November 1979 workshop, Dr. Marcus uttered the sentence, "The effect's gone after three syllables," but it sounded much more like "the effects go on after three syllables." Note that syntactic and semantic considerations could not clarify this, and that pragmatics were required to reject the acoustically preferred interpretation. With this anecdote we can refer to a brief account of how Marcus' AI parsing model differs from the "hypothesize-and-test" paradigm. Once again, we have a model that does not claim psychological validity, but whose design was nonetheless influenced by a number of observations about human performance.

Marcus is influenced by David Marr's "principle of least commitment": "Never say anything you are not completely sure of." (David Marr made brilliant contributions both to brain theory and to computer vision before his early death of leukemia in 1980. With his death, cognitive science lost one of its most exciting contributors. In Hanson and Riseman (1978), one can find a useful chapter on his approach to vision.) The "principle of least commitment" calls for richer represen-tations to reduce the search space, using a wide enough vocabulary of knowledge types to specify one's understanding without overcommitting oneself.

There is much acoustic information not included in AI systems, and a study by Liberman and Prince (1977) reveals a complex structure of syllables and their interaction "south of the lexicon." This allows for extensive noncommitment below the word level, for example, recognizing stress patterns prior to recognition of individual phonemes. There is also considerable information in the intonational structure of an utterance.

Marcus' parsing model offers a form of "least commitment" for parsing sentences (from text, though, not speech) called "differential diagnosis." Consider the two sentences

Have the boys who you're auditioning sing the song.
Have the boys who you're auditioning sung the song.

The first is a command, the second a question, and have plays a very different syntactic role in the two sentences. Since the first six words are the same in each, this seems a blow to left-to-right parsing since it seems to require nondeterminism with the normal sequence of syntactic decisions. But Marcus shows that if one clumps the structure differently, aware of the various possibilities, and takes the correct notion of context, one can recognize the boys who you're auditioning *as a noun phrase and obtain the "least commitment" analysis*

Have/NP/verb. . . .

A knowledge source with a window just three items wide can then analyze the explicit alternatives to make the decision.

Admittedly, some of these decisions do need semantic interactions. For example, David Marr's work on vision provides examples where bottom-up processing must be supplemented. In an example of a picture of one leaf atop another, it is the knowledge about the shape of leaves that supplies a missing boundary to support the interpretation that the top-left and bottom-right regions belong to the same leaf and are separated by the other leaf which lies atop it. Nonetheless, Marcus argues that, rather than delimit all possible interpretations in advance, we can and should generate an option only when the decision must be made.

To summarize: "Differential diagnosis" and "least commitment" may help reduce the search space and thus simplify the control problem. However, the design of search-limiting representations ultimately may not preclude a "hypothesize-and-test" paradigm. It may well be that all the models discussed here will contribute, albeit in drastically altered form, to psychologically valid models. In any case, it seems clear that the study of these AI models has suggested precise hypotheses amenable to psycholinguistic testing, and that it is therefore appropriate to claim that AI models have become part of the currency of psycholinguistics. With this, in addition to the development of AI language systems for commercial applications ("if it works, it's right"), we may confidently expect to see such systems developed explicitly as psycholinguistic models (e.g., the Moll–Conklin (in preparation) parser being developed at the University of Massachusetts at Amherst reflects both the Revised Extended Standard Theory of transformation grammar, and Frazier's study of human parsing strategies).

Arbib and Caplan (1979) stated "neurolinguistics must be computational," but the confrontation between AI and neurolinguistics has hardly begun. Nonetheless, the chapters in this section do advance the discussion. While Woods gives us a purely AI account of HWIM so that we may see in some detail how a speech understanding system can be implemented on the computer, Arbib confronts the issue of how we may expect the control structures of such a system to change when it is implemented not on a serial computer but rather "in the style of the brain," in terms of the "cooperative computation" of a network of concurrently active systems. He also briefly looks at production as a planning process, but it is Lavorel who most thoroughly addresses the issue of production in offering a sys-

tems approach to Wernicke's aphasia. He presents a (partially implemented) computational model called Jargonaut as a research tool for analyzing language performance. It is worth stressing that there are two levels to the model: The level of the model proper which represents linguistic performance, and a metalevel which enables the human user to conduct "experiments" on the low-level system by changing it in various ways to see whether they adequately represent the effects of various forms of brain damage. The model involves a version of "fuzzy semantics" whereby every item in the lexicon is described by a finite number of features, and where neural calculation may associate different weights to features. The reader will see that this is akin to the priority ratings used for hypotheses in HWIM and HEARSAY.

Both Arbib and Marcus offer what might best be characterized as "contributions toward models," rather than actual models, of Broca's aphasia. Arbib suggests that we explain the comprehension abilities of Broca's aphasics by viewing normal language processing as involving the cooperative computation of syntactic and semantic processes, with the former being impaired in Broca's aphasia. He confesses himself guilty of the crude "faculty in a box" which we have criticized in Chapter 1, stressing that the important points are the notion of cooperative computation and the view of syntax as secondary to semantics. Marcus makes no claim to neurological validity, but offers a pure AI experiment which many neurolinguists have found exciting: He examines the effects on the performance of his parsing model of restricting resources in a variety of ways. Some of the results are surprisingly reminiscent of aphasic data. They offer encouragement to those of us who would develop neurologically valid computational models of language performance.

REFERENCES

Arbib, M. A., and Caplan, D. (1979). Neurolinguistics must be computational. *Behavioral and brain sciences, 2,* 449–483.

Liberman, M., and Prince, A. (1977). On stress and linguistic rhythm. *Linguistic Inquiry, 8,* 249–336.

Marr, D. (1978). Representing visual information: A computation approach. In A. R. Hanson and E. M. Riseman (Eds.), *Computer vision systems.* New York: Academic Press, 61–80.

Marslen-Wilson, W., and Tyler, L. K. (1980). The temporal structure of spoken language understanding. *Cognition, 8,* 1–71.

Moll, R. N., and Conklin, E. J. A *test-bed for parsing strategies in A. I. parsers.* Department of computer and information science, Technical Report, University of Massachusetts, Amherst, Mass. In preparation.

4

From Artificial Intelligence to Neurolinguistics[1]

Michael A. Arbib

INTRODUCTION

Chomsky (1965, p. 5) makes a fundamental distinction between competence (the speaker–hearer's knowledge of the language) and performance (the actual use of language in concrete situations). He argues that in order to study actual linguistic performance, we must understand the interaction of a variety of factors, of which the underlying competence of the speaker–hearer is only one. This has led to the methodological viewpoint that competence is separable from performance, and that linguists can and should study competence prior to the development of models of performance. Chomsky does not concern himself with the articulation of performance models, but he has encouraged the view of a performance system as comprising three "boxes"—a competence box that encodes necessary data about grammar and lexicon, and separate boxes for perception and performance, each of which must refer to the competence box for necessary data. I shall, instead, argue that whereas grammar describes the performance, it is not a subsystem of the system that generates the performance. In the same way, a planet does not use the concept of an ellipse to move in its orbit about the sun. Rather, I would argue that we must separately model the processes of perception and production and chart the manner of their interactions within the brain. We may well find overlapping circuitry in their neural realization, but the hypothesis of a separate "grammar region" is but one among many and has no logical primacy. A competence theory may provide a valuable representation of complex data in a form against which a performance model may be tested, but even here psycholinguistic data that chart the time course of sentence production and comprehension may prove far more valuable than mere judgments of

[1]Preparation of this chapter was supported in part by the Sloan Foundation grant for "A Program in Language and Information Processing" at the University of Massachusetts at Amherst.

NEURAL MODELS OF
LANGUAGE PROCESSES

grammaticality. Finally, note that Chomsky's insistence on competence as the proper focus of linguistics was motivated in part by the desire to penetrate to the heart of language, undistracted by the *ums* and *ahs* of normal discourse. However, there is nothing to preclude—and everything to encourage—the focusing of a theory of language perception and production on just those phenomena which, in our current state of knowledge, appear to be most salient.

In summary, then, although linguistics was revolutionized by Chomsky's insistence that a small body of rules could underlie a vast array of linguistic competence, his emphasis on competence as an abstract representation of grammaticality has been, to my mind, counterproductive to the extent that it has turned attention away from the analysis of process and performance. The neurolinguist must be concerned with process above all and then with how underlying mechanisms can be played across the structures of the brain. To this extent, then, neurolinguistics should build upon recent psycholinguistics, which is providing increasingly refined tools for the characterization of linguistic performance, and upon the increasing ability of workers in artificial intelligence (AI) to write programs that exhibit aspects of language perception and, to a lesser extent, production. One would also want neurolinguists to benefit from the current surge of neuroscience; yet one finds that far more of neurolinguistics is in the style of nineteenth century neurology (a style that can still tell us a great deal) than in the style of synapse–cell–circuit analysis of detailed brain mechanisms. I will attempt in the present chapter to introduce a number of avenues toward a rapprochement between neurolinguistics and AI, and in Chapter 25, a companion chapter, I will attempt to offer bridges from neurolinguistics to neuroscience.

It is important to distinguish the use of the computer as a TOOL for data processing and simulation from the use of the CONCEPTS of computation for the analysis of complex systems. A computationally neurolinguistic model may be analyzed by pencil and paper without computer implementation, but can still provide valuable insights as the subsystem interactions are constrained to yield a model that is linguistically appropriate, that details mechanisms for the linguistic processes, and that goes on to define ways in which disruptions occur such that the distorted performance maps onto the clinical data. Nonetheless, we do expect computer simulation to be a useful part of computational neurolinguistics.

In the following two sections, we shall compare language production to planning processes studied in AI, both to enrich our computational understanding of production and to distinguish a performance view from a competence view by showing how a grammar may be represented for production. In the final section, we shall turn to a quite different AI representation of a grammar suited to perception—the Augmented Transition Network—and use it to develop a pre-theory of certain deficits of syntactic processing and lexical retrieval in Broca's aphasia.

Prior to that, in a separate section, we shall outline a cooperative computation methodology for neurolinguistics. This "C²-methodology" is an example of the use of computational concepts, irrespective of actual computer simulation, to gain insight into neural function. Nonetheless, we shall want to build on AI work to implement computer simulations of brain region interactions, and we should ask what the short-range prospects of success will be. It must immediately be admitted that current AI speech–understanding systems took many man-years to program and do not perform very well. Development of programming methodology will make many aspects of programming such systems relatively routine and efficient—this has certainly been the case with the writing of compilers and operating systems. However, if an AI system achieves less than 90% recognition of sentences based on a 1000-word vocabulary, what is to be gained by implementing a more neurological model to address the data of aphasiology? My answer is to note that our aim is not to predict the exact sentences produced or comprehended by each individual with brain damage, but, rather, to understand the patterns of abilities that survive certain patterns of brain damage—where both kinds of patterns are abstracted from a variety of individual cases. At this level of approximation, we might test whether or not the pattern of performance of a model degrades in a fashion consistent with experiment even if the base of "normal performance" is not the same for model and human.

Another argument for the utility of a general methodology such as that offered by the (still primitive) concepts of cooperative computation comes from Marr and Poggio's (1977) views on the "near independence" of different levels of analysis, or the notion of top-down design in computer programming (Alagić and Arbib, 1978). It seems to be fruitful to describe subsystems in a formalism that is relatively independent of the details of implementation—whether the latter be in terms of neural circuitry in the brain, or the machine language of some computer. Thus a neurolinguistic analysis at the regional level may, to a first approximation, be formalized in terms of cooperative computation. The interactions and internal state transitions posited in this model can then be implemented within some computer programming language. But if the program is properly designed, runs of the program test the high level model, not the details introduced in the implementation. In the same way, a simulation of a dynamic system described by Newton's laws may involve the choice of a Runge-Kutta method for numerical integration of the differential equations, but the resultant trajectories should not depend, save perhaps in fine detail, on the numerical analysis chosen. If distinctions of this kind are rigidly maintained, we can clearly distinguish the use of computation concepts as content in a theory from the concepts used in implementing the theory in a computer program.

SYNTAX AS A SYMPTOM OF TRANSLATION

Many formal accounts of grammar appear to offer a "Give me an S, give me an N, ..." approach to sentence production. A base component "grows" a tree from an S at the root, or describes a path from an initial node in some network, and then further processes elaborate both the semantics and the surface structure of the deep structure (be it tree or labeled path) so obtained. It is, of course, widely understood that this production formalism is not a model of actual human performance, but is rather a rule-based way of characterizing the competence embodied in deciding whether or not a string of words is a well-formed sentence of a given language. Nonetheless, the initial success of transformational grammars as a description of the static structure of languages has encouraged may psycholinguists to look for production models that directly embody the rules of a transformational grammar. However, I would argue that it is more fruitful for psycholinguists and neurolinguists to view sentence production as a process of **translation** from an often ill-defined goal structure to a (relatively) well-formed sentence of the language (embedded with an ongoing action–perception cycle [Chapter 25, this volume]). I shall illustrate this in the present section by the analysis of a simple statement in the programming language Pascal (my analysis should be intelligible to readers unfamiliar with the language). Then, in the next section, I shall relate this posited translation process to **planning** concepts developed in AI.

Pascal syntax contains many rules, including

$\langle$statement$\rangle$ ::= *begin* $\langle$statement$\rangle$; $\langle$statement$\rangle$ *end*
$\langle$statement$\rangle$ ::= *while* $\langle$expression$\rangle$ *do* $\langle$statement$\rangle$
$\langle$statement$\rangle$ ::= $\langle$variable$\rangle$:= $\langle$expression$\rangle$

These are just context-free productions. The items in angle brackets are variables, and the symbol ::= replaces the arrow ($\rightarrow$) more familiar to linguists. Pascal syntax also includes rules for $\langle$variable$\rangle$ and $\langle$expression$\rangle$ that let us "grow" the Pascal program

(1)   *begin* r := x;
         while $r \geq y$ *do* $r := r - y$
      end

according to the syntactic tree shown in Figure 4.1. Pascal syntax does not adequately constrain the production of statements, for example, by proper placement of arithmetic versus Boolean expressions; but the point here is that the program (1) was not obtained as shown in Figure 4.1, but by the following process of "top-down design."

We are given the goal of designing a Pascal statement that will take numbers $x \geq 0$ and $y > 0$ and set a variable r to the remainder $x \bmod y$ when x is divided by y. We decide to do this by subtracting y from x repeatedly so long as $x \geq y$; and we decompose this into

(a) Initialize r to the given value of x; and
(b) So long as r has a value $\geq y$, decrease that value by y.

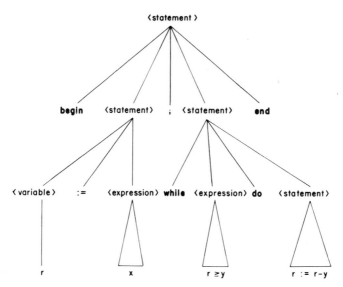

FIGURE 4.1. A *Pascal syntactic tree.*

We then call on our knowledge of Pascal to elaborate (a) and (b), respectively, as

(a') $r := x$
(b') *while* $r \geq y$ *do* $r := r - y$

We know that the Pascal syntax for "do S1 then do S2" is *begin* S1; S2 *end.* Thus, with a certain sense of layout, we combine (a') and (b') to obtain our Pascal program (1).

Here, in short, is the contrast: For the **formal description** of Pascal, we have a syntax whose rules let us "grow" well-formed statements, and a formal semantics that lets us assign, by induction on the height of its syntactic tree, a well-defined input–output function to each well-formed statement.

The "production theory," by contrast, is less well-defined. We start with a **semantic goal** G expressing what input–output function a statement is to achieve. A **planning process** then produces increasingly detailed "program sketches" in some **planning language** by a process of stepwise refinement that may well involve repeated backup (Wirth, 1971; Alagic and Arbib, 1978, Chapter 1, pp. 116, 133–134). Eventually, a level of refinement is reached which allows the **plan** to be translated into a Pascal program that meets the semantic goal. The two points to note here are (*a*) the syntax no longer appears as production rules, but only as translation rules; and (*b*) the planning process invokes a great deal of knowledge (e.g., about arithmetic), only a small amount of which may be well formalized at present. Of course, a major goal of AI is to chart an increasing body of knowledge in terms of well-formalized "knowledge structures" such as scripts, schemas, and frames which are themselves amenable to computational manipulation.

I suspect that relatively little of these "knowledge structures" will be fully formalized in the near future, and that the performance of individuals will depend on idiosyncracies which will be formalizable in principle but not, a priori, in practice. After the fact, we may reconstruct that a particularly novel approach to solving a problem depended on a chance remark overheard in a hotel bar in Copenhagen 7 years before, but the chances of such an item being included beforehand in a workable model of an individual's "long-term memory" are negligible. However, this argument against complete representation does not diminish the importance of seeking an adequate formalism for the representation of knowledge, and of developing computational models of how knowledge is used in planning. Linguists increasingly appreciate the need for an articulated model of the dictionary or lexicon for linguistic theory; the work of AI linguists on knowledge structures may be viewed as the development of an articulated model of the encyclopedia. In neither case is a complete set of entries the criterion for progress.

PLANNING AS AN ONGOING PROCESS

We have suggested that syntax emerges as a symptom of a translation process, and that this translation process is not from a fully elaborated deep structure to a surface structure, but rather involves a planning process that takes us from a (perhaps incompletely specified) semantic goal via a process of refinement until we achieve a plan sufficiently articulated for translation into a well-formed expression of the given language. But this account is still misleading if it suggests that a whole sentence or paragraph is "laid out" in its entirety "internally" prior to the actual production of an utterance. Rather, I would argue that we have a production process in which the next fragment of the utterance depends on the actual utterance generated so far, as well as the semantic goal (which may be redefined as the process continues) and the current state of the plan (much of which will be but partially developed until the utterance nears completion), quite apart from feedback (if any) from the intended audience. In this section, we discuss some notions from AI studies of planning. For a related analysis of the action–perception cycle of visuomotor coordination and its relation to a theory of conversation, see Chapter 25 of this volume.

We start with an approach to planning called the General Problem Solver (GPS) due to Newell, Shaw, and Simon (1959). (For the implications of GPS for cognitive psychology, see Miller, Galanter, and Pribram [1960] and Newell and Simon [1972]. For a brief exposition of GPS in relation to heuristic search and feedback, see Arbib [1972, Section 4.2].) GPS is a general framework for solving problems of the following kind:

1. We are given a set of states and a set of operators. Each operator is applicable to some (but not necessarily all) of the states; when applicable, the result of applying operator f to state s will be to transform it into a new state $f(s)$.

2. We are given an initial state s_0 and a goal state s_g. Our task is to find a (reasonably short) sequence of operators $f_1, \ldots, f_n$ which will transform s_0 into s_g, that is, f_1 is applicable to s_0 and $s_1 = f_1(s_0)$; f_2 is applicable to s_1 and $s_2 = f_2(s_1)$; $\ldots$; f_n is applicable to s_{n-1} and $s_n = f_n(s_{n-1})$.

3. To aid us in our quest for an appropriate sequence of operators, we are given a finite set of differences, and a means whereby, given any ordered pair of states, we can list which differences obtain between them. In addition, we are given an operator-difference table which gives us for each difference a list of those operators that are likely to reduce it.

Unfortunately, the differences give only a rough indication of what needs to be changed, and there is no guarantee that applying a recommended operator will indeed transform the latest state into one that is "closer" to the goal state. Moreover, a recommended operator may not be applicable to a given state—leading us to generate the subgoal of transforming the given state into one to which the operator is applicable. The general control program of GPS is thus designed to develop a "decision tree" which keeps track of the application of various possible operators to various states, "growing" those branches that seem to be leading toward the goal.

To fix our thinking, the states might be the position of a robot in an environment, the initial state its position at the onset of planning, its final state the position to be achieved by the to-be-planned sequence of basic actions. GPS, with its finite set of differences (such as "to the left of" and "ahead of" in this case) is limited in comparison to a system with access to more subtle descriptors of the differences between states (such as actual differences in coordinates modified by information on the presence of obstacles, in this case). This has led to planning techniques based on "heuristic distance" (e.g., using straight-line distance as a "heuristic" approximation to the actual distance to be traversed by the shortest path which traverses all obstacles). Two basic papers in this literature are due to Doran and Michie (1966) and Hart, Nilsson, and Raphael (1968) (see Nilsson, 1971, for a textbook account); and these provided part of the basis for the studies of robot path-planning by Fikes and Nilsson (1971) and Fikes, Hart, and Nilsson (1972). But these studies provided step-by-step planning of the entire path from initial position to the goal, and the attempt to improve upon this with an AI approach to hierarchical planning led Sacerdoti (1977) to elaborate "A structure for plans and behavior" (a title deliberately adapted from the "Plans and the structure of behavior" of Miller, Galanter, and Pribram [1960]). Sacerdoti developed an AI program called NOAH (Nets Of Action Hierarchies) that solves a problem by first creating a one-step solution to the problem (essentially "Solve the given goal") and then progressively expanding the level of detail of the solution, filling in ever more detailed actions. All the individual actions, composed into plans at differing levels of detail, are stored in a data structure called the procedural network. Actions can be initiated before the entire plan is developed to the level of actions which are immediately implementable. If and when more detail is required, or if an unexpected event creates the need for replanning, the system can modify or further develop the plan at any point.

In outlining a theoretical framework for the analysis of skilled motor behavior—such as speaking, typing, writing, drawing, dancing, or playing music—Shaffer (1980) stresses that an extended skilled action starts with a plan that provides a set of goals and the essential structure of the performance. He cites Sacerdoti's (1974) proposal for planning in a hierarchy of abstraction spaces as analogous to his view that the plan is executed in "a continually renewing succession of higher-order units by a motor program, which may construct one or more intermediate representations leading to output, adding the details necessary to specify the movement sequence . . . [Such programs] enable more flexible problem solving and they produce solutions more rapidly than programs that consider all the possible domains of information in a single abstract space. Both these properties, speed and flexibility, are relevant to skilled performance [p. 445]."

TOWARD A C² METHODOLOGY FOR NEUROLINGUISTICS

In Chapter 25 of this volume, I have argued for cooperative computation as a style for brain modeling. Here we extend our concept of computation from the "one instruction at a time" style that used to dominate the programming of electronic computers to a "cooperative" style, which emphasizes the simultaneous activity of many processes in continuous interaction, each modifying the progress of the other, to yield the overall solution to some problem. In this section, we discuss how this style might incorporate lessons learnt from AI systems for language processing such as HWIM (Chapter 5, this volume) and HEARSAY (Erman and Lesser, 1980; for an account in the context of neurolinguistics, see Arbib and Caplan, 1979, Section 4). Such systems have not yet fed into psycholinguistic, let alone neurolinguistic, theory. However, we shall suggest ways in which they let us more explicitly hypothesize how language understanding might be played across interacting subsystems in a human brain. We thus distinguish AI (artificial intelligence) from BT (brain theory), where we go beyond the general notion of a process model that simulates the overall input–output behavior of a system to one in which various processes are mapped onto anatomically characterizable portions of the brain. With Helen Gigley, we have developed a specific neurolinguistic model within the new methodology but we do not yet offer testable hypotheses about anatomical localization of linguistic processes. We predict, however, that future modeling will catalyze the interactive definition of region and function—which will be necessary in neurolinguistic theory no matter what the fate of our current hypotheses may prove to be.

In the next chapter, William Woods describes the HWIM ("Hear What I Mean") speech-understanding system, explaining how the acoustic phonetic recognizer takes speech parameters to construct the segment lattice (assigning various phonemes or features to time intervals with various confidence levels), and how lexical retrieval finds words consistent with high-confidence segment sequences. Sequences of words can then be tested for "acceptance paths" through a grammar in the form of an Augmented Transition Network (ATN). The resultant "theories" (syntactically correct sentence fragments) then suggest possible words or word classes for their extension consistent with the ATN. The control structure that sequences these and other processors is a stack of "theories" obtained so far; the higher the confidence rating of the "theory," the nearer it appears to the top of the stack. In each cycle, the topmost theory is taken off the stack, and whatever theories are obtained by extension (or other processes) are then reinserted in the stack in order of their confidence rating. The process continues until a theory is found that covers the entire utterance—this then provides the highest-confidence hypothesis for the syntactic–semantic structure presented in the speech signal.

The HEARSAY-II system has a similarly explicit representational structure, based on levels of representation. The raw data, whose interpretation is the task of the system, is represented at the "parameter" level as a digitized acoustic signal. The system will, via intermediate levels, generate a representation at the "phrasal" level of a description according to a grammar which contains both syntactic and semantic constraints. The combination of phrasal and lexical information can then be used to generate the appropriate response to the verbal input. Though HEARSAY uses a semantic template grammar rather than an ATN, the difference is perhaps more one of format than of substance since ATN arcs correspond to grammar productions, and since the HWIM ATNs are not purely syntactic, but are "pragmatic grammars" (cf. the "date grammar" in Woods, p. 105, this volume).

HEARSAY uses a dynamic global data structure, called the "blackboard," which is partitioned into the various levels. At any time in the system's operation, there are a number of hypotheses active at the various levels, and there are links between hypotheses at one level and those they support at another level. For example, in Figure 4.2, we see a situation in which there are two surface-phonemic hypotheses 'L' and 'D' consistent with the raw data at the parameter level, with the 'L' supporting the lexical hypothesis "will" that in turn supports the phrasal hypothesis "question," while the 'D' supports "would" that in turn

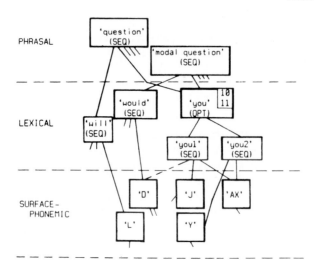

FIGURE 4.2. *Multiple hypotheses at different levels of the HEARSAY blackboard (From Lesser, Fennel, Erman, and Reddy, 1975).*

supports the "modal question" hypothesis at the phrasal level. Each hypothesis is indexed not only by its level but also by the time segment over which it is posited to occur, though this is not explicitly shown in the figure. We also do not show the "credibility rating" that is assigned to each hypothesis.

HEARSAY also embodies a strict notion of constituent processes, and provides scheduling processes whereby the activity of these processes and their interaction through the blackboard data base is controlled. Each process is called a knowledge source (KS), and is viewed as an agent that embodies some area of knowledge, and can take action based on that knowledge. Each KS can make errors and create ambiguities. Other KSs cooperate to limit the ramifications of these mistakes. Some knowledge sources are grouped as computational entities called modules in the final version of the HEARSAY-II system. The knowledge sources within a module share working storage and computational routines that are common to the procedural computations of the grouped KSs.

HEARSAY is based on the "hypothesize-and-test" paradigm which views solution finding as an iterative process, with each iteration involving the creation of a hypothesis about some aspect of the problem and a test of the plausibility of the hypothesis. Each step rests on a priori knowledge of the problem, as well as on previously generated hypotheses. The process terminates when the best consistent hypothesis is generated satisfying the requirements of an overall solution.

The choice of levels and KSs varies from implementation to implementation of HEARSAY, which is thus a class of models or a modeling methodology rather than a single model. In fact, the HEARSAY methodology has been used in computer vision with picture point–line segment–region–object levels replacing the acoustic–phonetic–lexical–phrasal levels of the speech domain (Hanson and Riseman, 1978).

The C2 configuration of HEARSAY-II is shown in Figure 4.3. We see that each KS takes hypotheses at one level and uses them to create or verify a hypothesis at another (possibly the same) level. In this particular configuration, processing is bottom-up from the acoustic signal to the level of word hypotheses, but involves iterative refinement of hypotheses both bottom-up and top-down before a phrasal hypothesis is reached which is given a high enough rating to be accepted as the interpretation of the given raw data.

The HEARSAY model is a well-defined example of a cooperative computation model of language comprehension. We now observe that incorporating it into a regional analysis of neural organization pertinent to language raises several important conceptual questions. We present four of these, along with a brief discussion which sheds light on possible neural mechanisms at this regional level. The result, then, will be to offer a cooperative computation (C²) methodology for neurolinguistic analysis. In what follows, we distinguish the KS as a unit of analysis of some overall functional subsystem from the schema unit of analysis (cf. Chapter 25, this volume), which corresponds more to individual percepts, action strategies, or units of the lexicon.

First, we have seen that the processes in HEARSAY are represented as KSs. It would be tempting, then, to suggest that in computational implementations of

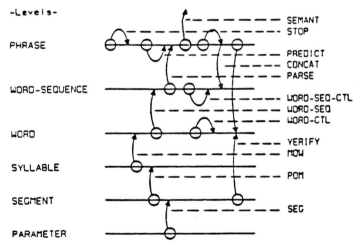

FIGURE 4.3. *The C2 configuration of HEARSAY-II. The levels are represented by the solid lines, labeled at the left. The KSs are represented by the circle-tailed arrows and are linked to their names by the dashed lines. Each KS uses hypotheses at the tail-end level to create or verify hypotheses at the head-end level (Erman and Lesser, 1980).*

neurolinguistic process models such as that of Luria (cf. Arbib and Caplan, 1979, Figure 8), each brain region would correspond to either a KS or a module. Schemas would correspond to much smaller units both functionally and structurally—perhaps at the level of application of a single production in a performance grammar (functionally), or the activation of a few cortical columns (neurally). A major conceptual problem arises because in a computer implementation, a KS is a program, and it may be called many times—the circuitry allocated to working through each "instantiation" being separate from the storage area where the "master copy" is stored. But a brain region cannot be copied ad libitum, and so if we identify a brain region with a KS we must ask, How can the region support multiple simultaneous activations of its function? We may hypothesize that this is handled by parallelism (which presumably limits the number of simultaneous activations). Alternatively, we may actually posit that extra runnable copies of a program may be set up in cortex as needed.

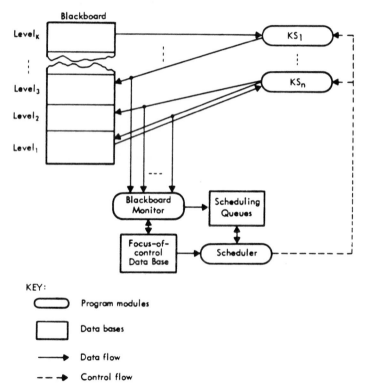

FIGURE 4.4. *HEARSAY-II architecture. The blackboard is divided into levels. Each KS interacts with just a few levels. A KS becomes a candidate for application if its precondition is met. However, to avoid a "combinatorial explosion" of hypotheses on the blackboard, a scheduler is used to restrict the number of KSs that are allowed to modify the blackboard (Lesser and Erman, 1979).*

Both HWIM and HEARSAY are programs implemented on serial computers. Thus, unlike the brain which can support the simultaneous activity of myriad processes, each of these programs must have an explicit **scheduler** that determines which hypothesis (or "theory," to use HWIM terminology) will be processed next, and which process (or "KS," in HEARSAY terminology) will be invoked to process it (Figure 4.4). This is based on assigning validity ratings to each hypothesis, so that resources can be allocated to the most "promising" hypotheses. After processing, a hypothesis will be replaced by new hypotheses which either are highly rated and thus immediately receive further processing, or else have a lower rating which ensures that they are processed later, if at all. In HWIM, the top "theory" is chosen from the stack, and then KSs are invoked which extend that "theory." In HEARSAY, changes in validity ratings reflecting creation and modification of hypotheses are propagated throughout the blackboard by a single processor called the rating policy module, RPOL. As we have seen, these ratings are the basis for the determination, by a single scheduling process, of which hypothesis will next be manipulated, and by which KS. This use of a single scheduler seems "undistributed" and "nonneural." It seems to me that, in analyzing a brain region, one may explore what conditions lead to different patterns of activity, but that it is not in the "style of the brain" to talk of scheduling different circuits. However, the particular scheduling strategy used in any AI "perceptual" system is a reflection of the exigencies of implementing the system on a serial computer. Serial implementation requires us to place a tight upper bound on the number of activations of KSs, as they must all be carried out on the same processor. In a parallel "implementation" of a perceptual system in the style of the brain, we may view each KS as having its own "processor" in a different portion of the structure. I would posit that rather than there being a global process in the brain to set ratings, the neural subsystems representing each schema or KS would have activity levels serving the functions of such ratings in determining the extent to which any process could affect the current dynamics of other processes, and that propagation of changes in these activity levels can be likened to relaxation procedures (cf. Chapter 25, this volume).

The third "nonneural" feature is the use of a centralized blackboard in HEARSAY or the use of a stack of theories in HWIM. This is not, perhaps, such a serious problem. The levels of the HEARSAY blackboard are really quite separate data structures, and they are only linked via KSs. For each level, we may list those KSs that write on that level ("input" KSs) and those that read from that level ("output" KSs). From this standpoint, it is quite reasonable to view the blackboard as a distributed structure, being made up of those pathways which link the different KSs. One conceptual problem remains. If we think of a pathway carrying phonemic information, say, then the signals passing along it will encode just one phoneme at a time. But our experience with HWIM and HEARSAY suggests that a memoryless pathway alone is not enough to fill the computational role of a level on the blackboard; rather the pathway must be supplemented by neural structures which can support a short-term memory of multiple hypotheses over a suitable extended time interval.

An immediate research project for computational neurolinguistics, then, might be to approach the programming of a truly distributed speech understanding system (free of the centralized scheduling in the current implementation of HEARSAY) with the constraint that it include subsystems meeting the constraints such as those in the Arbib–Caplan (1979) reanalysis of Luria's data.

One can expect that psycholinguistic tests will be increasingly integrated into the study of aphasic and other patients so that our neurolinguistic models can fully exploit psycholinguistic cues to "mental structure." But we must expect that our localizations will evolve with our concepts—we may localize a function in a region only to later conclude that there we can only localize some aspect essential to that function.

A virtue of the C^2 methodology is that it provides a framework for future marriage of a parsing system with a cognitive system and an intentional evaluation system. A speech understanding model can thus provide a "growth node" for a comprehensive model incorporating the whole range of human language abilities such as answering questions, producing stories, describing the perceptual world, and carrying on conversations, as well as understanding speech. Whereas the HEARSAY implementation described earlier only addresses speech understanding, the C^2 methodology espoused in this section is meant to accommodate the development of the more general model. As a matter of practicality, the scientist must pick a subtask, whether for modeling or for experimentation, and cannot know a priori whether this subtask is "neurologically valid." One will model it as well as one can, adjusting the subsystems as one seeks to accommodate psychological and neurological data. The real interest comes when we look up from our own subtask to consider a cooperative computation model of another subtask. My expectation is that certain knowledge sources (KSs) in the two models will have major similarities, and that it will take relatively little work to adjust these to have a single definition of each KS compatible with each model. As a result, by identifying the instances of each KS in the two models, we may obtain a single model applicable to both subtasks. (For a hint of this, cf. Figure 7 of Arbib and Caplan [1979], which offers a block diagram of subsystems involved in Luria's analysis of repetitive speech. All the blocks occur in analyses of other language tasks.)

Such AI systems as HWIM and HEARSAY would perform better were the initial acoustic analyses not so crude, sketchy, and error prone as they are in current implementations. In particular, this would reduce the extent to which the hypothesize-and-test style involved in maintaining a "population" of hypotheses is required to analyze a given utterance. Does this mean that the methodology is irrelevant for neurolinguistics? We have not, indeed, proven the neurological validity of the hypothesize-and-test style of cooperative computation—that the brain is modular in a disciplined way, and that it takes hypotheses at one "level" of description and submits them for test against other levels of analysis, with multiple hypotheses active at any time. Perhaps the brain can simply switch in the right process at the right time in a smooth progression from input to output without the "competition and cooperation" of multiple hypotheses. However, such anatomical data as the fact that there are more fibers going "the wrong way" from visual cortex to the lateral geniculate than there are going "the right way" do seem to run counter to straight-through processing (cf. Arbib, 1972, pp. 109–112; Harth, 1976; Singer, 1977). Despite the arguments on both sides, the status of the hypothesize-and-test style is an open question for future research.

ATNS, BROCA'S APHASIA AND THE EVOLUTIONARY SUBSTRATE

A popular approach to parsing (see, e.g., Woods, Chapter 5, this volume) represents the grammar as an augmented transition network or ATN. To tell if a string of words is syntactically correct, we see if they can be mapped into a path on the network. In this process, words fall into two distinctive classes: Words like *the* and *of* occur as labels on arcs. Numbers, nouns, verbs, etc., do not (at least not in principle, though they may do so in certain limited vocabulary implementations); rather, the arc contains an instruction to look in the lexicon for words of the specified category. In this way, ATNs make graphically explicit the familiar syntactic distinction between function words (closed class items) which are in some sense intimately bound into the very syntax of the language itself, and those content words (open class items) which can be lumped into open-ended categories. The fact that the word *sputnik* was added to the category of English nouns in 1957 did not require a change in English syntax—the lexicon contained a new noun, the language remained the English language. The absolute core of our language is bound up in the closed class words like *the* and *of* and prepositions, and also the modifiers like morphemes for past tense and plural, for without these the basic structure of the language cannot be expressed.

The classic description of a Broca's aphasic places much emphasis on the limited ability of the patient to use syntactic cues as an aid to comprehension. This alone is much too crude (see Arbib and Caplan [1979] for a critique of identifying brain regions with overall faculties), but at the rather conceptual level we are pursuing here, it will still be useful to analyze the effect on performance of simply removing all the analogues of ATNs from a neural system. (In Chapter 6 of this volume, Marcus offers an alternative, but similar, view of deficits in Broca's aphasia. It is based on his own deterministic computational approach to parsing.)

However, to analyze the effect of such removal, we must have a theory as to the brain system of which ATNs represent a part. My methodological approach is to view the system in evolutionary terms. This suggests that language did not arrive de novo, but came by differentiation of, and building upon, preexisting systems (such as the perceptual-motor systems examined in Chapter 25). Thus, the removal of finely evolved syntactic structure, as modeled by the ATNs, need not mean that all language has gone. If we hypothesize the ability to perceive objects as laying the basis for the evolution of nouns, then perception of certain patterns of interaction could similarly lay the basis for the evolution of verbs. We can imagine that such a system evolved into a precursor of language with a primitive semantic "presyntax." By this I mean that it contained nouns as well as verbs with associated semantic roles which would ensure that there was seldom ambiguity as to which nouns played which roles; but I do not imply that there were general roles distinct from the particularities of each verb. Nor do I imply any particular significance to word order at this presyntactic stage. Thus *kill/hippopotamus* would not be taken as an imperative to let the hippopotamus kill one, but rather to raise one's spear and attack the hippopotamus. I would suggest that, as this protolanguage evolved, it became possible to go beyond simple relations to generate utterances that were ambiguous. Whereas *boy/apple/eat* offers little ambiguity, *John/Mary/hit* is ambiguous without word order conventions or other syntactic cues. Perception of the roles of the nouns and verb does not unequivocally determine how those nouns are related to that verb.

Relating these evolutionary considerations to aphasia, I would posit that a Broca's aphasic, having "lost ATNs," should still have the more rudimentary ability to use simple nouns and verbs with clearly related semantic roles. Some Broca's aphasics do have enough presyntax to use some word order to choose one reading over the other, to get the active sentences right and passives wrong. Other Broca's aphasics do not seem to make any systematic use of word order, and to the extent that they can hold all the nouns and the verbs together, they will parcel them out in some relatively arbitrary way to come up with an interpretation plausible at the level of the underlying semantic capability. From this evolutionary point of view, it should not surprise us that "knocking out syntax," which one thinks of as a highly evolved system, should leave some residual linguistic capacity.

We now turn to Bradley's psycholinguistic analyses of Broca's aphasics. Subjects shown strings of letters may press one of two keys to indicate their judgment of whether or not the sequence of letters is a word of English. People rarely make mistakes on this task, so the interest is not in whether the subject is right or wrong but rather in reaction time in the cases where the subject is right as an index of how much information processing is required. Bradley, Garrett, and Zurif (1979) observed that for the recognition of the open class words (nouns, verbs, adjectives, etc.) by normals, the more common the word, the more quickly it will be retrieved. However, for the closed class words (the *ofs*, *thes*, etc.) they found a flat curve for normals—no matter how common or uncommon a function word is, it takes roughly the same time for a normal to retrieve it.

This suggests that there are differential routes of access to these two classes. In our crude ATN-based model of language, we had that the open class words are all in the lexicon but that the closed class items occur on arcs of the syntactic graphs. This suggests a model of Bradley's results in which a normal subject can attempt to retrieve a word via two mechanisms, one involving the lexicon, and one involving the syntactic rules. Because there is a relatively small set of rules compared to the number of words in the language, and because of the structure of the grammar, we may posit a uniform retrieval mechanism for the latter case, as distinct from a frequency dependent retrieval from the lexicon.

This model is somewhat wrong, for it predicts that Broca's aphasics should have roughly the same curve of frequency dependence as normals for open class retrieval, but no access to the function words. In fact, the data show that Broca's can still access the function words, but with a frequency dependence akin to that for open class words. Our "Mark II model" thus posits that all words are in the lexicon, but that the function words are also in the syntactic rules. In the normal, both retrieval mechanisms are "turned on" at the same time, with the closed class words retrieved via the uniform rule access to yield a flat reaction-time curve. In Broca's, the grammatical route is no longer available, so access to the function words must be via the lexicon, and thus reaction time exhibits the characteristic frequency dependence.

CONCLUSION

Our discussions of ATNs and Broca's aphasia, and of a neurologized HWIM and HEARSAY, each presented a model-sketch rather than an articulated theory, but I think that they offer a step in the right direction for neurolinguistics to put the account of aphasia within the context of computationally defined processes, while also taking into account an evolutionary substrate that provides basic comprehension without syntactic sophistication. Moreover, as is made clear in Chapter 25, I believe that neurolinguistics will make great progress if it incorporates analysis of the dynamics of neural interaction by looking for rich analogies with visual, auditory, and motor processes that we can study in animals; if it begins to articulate more carefully what is involved in linguistic performance by incorporating the computational methodology of AI models; and finally, if subtle observations in the neurological clinic are reinforced by the development of more refined psycholinguistic analyses of the strategies and timing of linguistic performance.

REFERENCES

Alagić, S., and Arbib, M. A. (1978). *The design of well-structured and correct programs.* New York: Springer-Verlag.

Arbib, M. A. (1972). *The metaphorical brain.* New York: Wiley Interscience.

Arbib, M. A. (1975). Artificial intelligence and brain theory: Unities and diversities. *Annals of Biomedical Engineering, 3,* 238–274.

Arbib, M. A., and Caplan, D. (1979). Neurolinguistics must be computational. *Behavioral and Brain Sciences, 2,* 449–483.

Bradley, D. C., Garrett, M. F., and Zurif, E. B. (1979). Syntactic deficits in Broca's aphasia. In D. Caplan (Ed.), *Biological studies of mental processes.* Cambridge, Mass.: MIT Press.

Chomsky, N. (1965). *Aspects of the theory of syntax,* Cambridge, Mass.: MIT Press.

Doran, J., and Michie, D. (1966). Experiments with the graph transverser program. *Proceedings of the Royal Society A, 294,* 235–259.

Erman, L., and Lesser, V. R. (1980). The HEARSAY-II system: A tutorial. In W. A. Lea (Ed.), *Trends in speech recognition.* Englewood Cliffs, N.J.: Prentice-Hall.

Fikes, R. E., Hart, P. E., and Nilsson, N. J. (1972). Learning and executing generalized robot plans. *Artificial Intelligence, 3,* 251–288.

Fikes, R. E., and Nilsson, N. J. (1971). STRIPS: A new approach to the application of theorem proving to problem solving. *Artificial Intelligence, 2,* 189–208.

Hanson, A. R., and Riseman, E. M. (1978). Segmentation of natural scenes. In A. R. Hanson and E. M. Riseman (Eds.), *Computer vision systems.* New York: Academic Press.

Hart, P., Nilsson, N. J., and Raphael, B. (1968). A formal basis for the heuristic determination of minimum cost paths. *IEEE Transactions on System Sciences and Cybernetics,* SSC-4, 100–107.

Harth, E. (1976). Visual perception: A dynamic theory. *Biological Cybernetics, 25,* 169–180.

Lesser, V. R., and Erman, L. D. (1979). *An experiment in distributed interpretation* (Technical Report CMU-CS-79-120). Computer Science Department, Carnegie-Mellon University.

Lesser, V. R., Fennel, R. D., Erman, L. D., and Reddy, D. R. (1975). Organization of the HEARSAY-II speech understanding system. *IEEE Transactions on Acoustics, Speech and Signal Processing, 23,* 11–23.

Marr, D., and Poggio, T. (1977). From understanding computation to understanding neural circuitry. *Neurosciences Research Program Bulletin, 15,* 470–488.

Miller, G. A., Galanter, E., and Pribram, K. H. (1960). *Plans and the structure of behavior.* New York: Henry Holt and Co.

Newell, A., Shaw, J. C., and Simon, H. A. (1959). Report on a general problem-solving program. *Proceedings of the International Conference on Information Processing,* Unesco House, Paris, pp. 256–264.

Newell, A., and Simon, H. A. (1972). *Human problem solving.* Englewood Cliffs, N.J.: Prentice-Hall.

Nilsson, N. J. (1971). *Problem-solving methods in artificial intelligence.* New York: McGraw-Hill.

Sacerdoti, E. D. (1974). Planning in a hierarchy of abstraction spaces. *Artificial Intelligence. 5,* 115–135.

Sacerdoti, E. D. (1977). *A structure for plans and behavior.* Amsterdam, Elsevier.

Shaffer, L. H. (1980). Analyzing piano performance: A study of concert pianists. In G. Stelmach and J. Requin (Eds.), *Tutorials on motor behavior.* Amsterdam: North-Holland, 443–455.

Singer, W. (1977). Control of thalamic transmission by corticofugal and ascending reticular pathways in the visual system. *Physiological Review, 57,* 386–420.

Winograd, T. (1972). *Understanding natural language.* New York: Academic Press.

Wirth, N. (1971). Program development by stepwise refinement. *Communications of the ACM, 14,* 221–227.

5

HWIM: A Speech Understanding System on a Computer[1]

William A. Woods

INCREMENTAL SIMULATION OF HUMAN SPEECH UNDERSTANDING

This chapter does not itself analyze "neural models of language processes." Rather, it is written in the belief that the space of hypotheses through which the computer searches serially in seeking to provide an interpretation for an utterance is similar to that through which the brain searches, presumably in parallel. In this section, we motivate this claim by looking at a number of experiments on human speech understanding, and the way in which these led to the design of a computerized speech understanding system called HWIM ("Hear What I Mean").

A convenient graphical representation of acoustic information is given by a spectrogram. This is a plot of the spectral energy in a signal over time in which the horizontal axis is time, the vertical axis is frequency, and the gray level at each point of the graph indicates how much energy there is at a given frequency at a given time. In a spectrogram, voiced speech separates into a number of distinct horizontal bands called formants, with the locations of the formants over a short time interval being roughly indicative of vowel quality, and with the shape of the formant transitions into nonvocalic regions providing information about consonants. Denes and Pinson (1963) gives a good general introduction to the acoustic phonetics of speech and the information that is available in spectrograms. An expert can look at short time intervals extracted from a spectrogram, and can come up with a number of alternatives as to the characteristics of the phonemes which are present, rather than unequivocal judgments as to which are indeed present. For example, an expert might judge that an initial segment is an

[1]Work described in this Chapter was done at Bolt Beranek and Newman Inc., in Cambridge, Mass. It was supported in part by the Advanced Research Projects Agency of the Department of Defense and was monitored by ONR under Contract No. N00014-75-C-0533.

95

NEURAL MODELS OF
LANGUAGE PROCESSES

[l] or a [w]; that the next segment is a front vowel, consistent with the hypotheses [iy], [ih], [ey], [eh], or [ae]; that the third segment is an [s] or a [z]; that the fourth is unvoiced and plosive, which could be consistent with [p], [t], [k], or [ch], and so on. In fact, such a judgment was made on a spectrogram of the word *list*, and the reader can see that this is one of the words compatible with the sequence of alternatives given here.

In a classic study of this phenomenon, Klatt and Stevens (1972) looked at samples from a spectrogram through a narrow window, and attempted to transcribe the phonemes based solely on objective acoustic evidence. Stevens, for example, looked at 80 words comprising 299 phonetic segments in all. He was able to correctly (and uniquely) transcribe 24% of the phonetic segments, and gave a correct but incomplete specification of an additional 50%. In 15% of the cases, he made a wrong transcription of the segment, and he actually missed 11% of the segments that were in the utterance. Thus, even when he was allowed to "hedge" on 50% of his judgments, he still had an error rate of 25%. Klatt's performance was comparable. However, if they were allowed to look at more than a single segment, to look at earlier segments and following segments, and to use constraints of syntax, semantics, and vocabulary, they were able to recognize 96% of the words that were presented to them—which is far better than getting 96% of the phonetic segments right. Moreover, most of the remaining 4% of errors were confusions between *a* and *the*, which are hard to disambiguate on local cues, especially if they follow a weak fricative, and which are also hard to separate on the basis of the limited context within a single sentence.

These experiments indicate that people are relatively poor at (visually) recognizing isolated phonetic segments, and must bring syntactic, semantic, and pragmatic knowledge to bear. To this it might be objected that people are far more accurate at *hearing* phonemes than experts are at *reading* spectrograms. For example, people usually speak isolated words sufficiently clearly for them to be correctly heard without supporting syntax and semantics.

Nonetheless, when speaking in a continuous stream of words, people seldom articulate clearly enough for all individual words to be highly intelligible. (Even the comprehension of isolated words depends on a knowledge of the lexicon and phonology of the language, as anyone with an unusual name knows when trying to get it recognized over the telephone!) However, if normal words are embedded in as little as four words of context, the intelligibility rate becomes quite high. In other words, our claim is that when people speak, they rely on the redundancy of the language to economize their articulation, and that when people understand speech they take advantage of their knowledge of the language to make up for this lack of local clarity.

In building upon the Klatt and Stevens work to provide the basis for our design of HWIM, we analyzed a speech understanding system in terms of the components shown in Figure 5.1. **Feature extraction** extracts basic features of

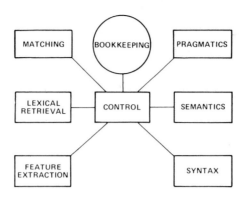

FIGURE 5.1. *Components of a speech understanding system.*

the kind we have discussed. **Lexical retrieval** then searches for words that match these low-level features. Given word hypotheses, **matching** checks the low-level acoustic data to determine the degree to which the hypothesis is supported by the evidence. Once a string of words has been hypothesized, **syntax** checks whether it is well formed; **semantics** checks whether it is meaningful; and **pragmatics** checks whether it is relevant in the present context. As we shall see in more detail in what follows, there is no simple process that can directly yield an unequivocal string of words which through syntactic, semantic, and pragmatic processes yields the unique interpretation. Rather, **control** is required to distribute attention among different subproblems, deciding when to switch from looking at one hypothesis or part of an utterance to another, and when the time has come to go back and reexamine an earlier hypothesis in the light of new data. **Bookkeeping** keeps track of what hypotheses have already been considered.

To get a better handle on how these different components might be implemented as computer programs, we carried out a number of experiments in what we call **incremental simulation** (Woods and Makhoul, 1974).

In each case, we "implement" the system as a combination of human activity and computer programs, and "run" it to discover and test algorithms and to develop an intuition for the problem. In our first experiment of this kind, we had a human carry out all the tasks of Figure 5.1 except that of lexical retrieval, which was handled by a machine. In this way, we could monitor the questions that the human asked, and begin to make hypotheses about his problem-solving strategy. In a second experiment, we had one human carry out the task of feature extraction and another carry out the tasks of control, syntax, semantics, and pragmatics; a machine handled the tasks of lexical retrieval, matching, and bookkeeping, and provided the communication channel between the two humans. In this way, we could get a better idea of the strategies that a human uses in feature extraction when he does not have access to higher level knowledge.

The human carrying out feature extraction looked at the spectrogram through a narrow window—about 1½ phonemes wide—and his error rate suggested that he was indeed not using higher level cues. By having the machine keep track of the communication between the two humans, we were able to form explicit hypotheses about the way in which feature hypotheses are mobilized in forming word level and utterance level hypotheses. In this way, we reached a number of conclusions which formed the basis for the design of the HWIM system to be described in the next section:

1. We learned that small function words are highly unreliable anchors. For example, the sound in *a* is usually the same as that of the vowel in *the*, and it also occurs in many multisyllabic words. Thus, we feel that a speech understanding system cannot utilize the strategy used by several text understanding systems in which the function words provided the framework for determining the syntactic role of other words in the sentence.

2. We found that accidental word matches outnumber the correct ones. Good acoustic matches may in fact be misleading. For example, there is quite a good match for *new* in the middle of *anyway*, and this false local hypothesis must be eliminated on the basis of further processing.

3. Computer scientists distinguish stochastic processes—in which there is a probabilistic element in what will happen next—from nondeterministic processes which are in no way unpredictable, but where at each stage of the process more than one hypothesis may have to be explored. We came to the conclusion that speech understanding is an inherently nondeterministic process in this sense, and that it is necessary to make tentative hypotheses and systematically explore the consequences. For example, once a hypothesis has been made as to several words in the utterance, one should test for syntactically plausible hypotheses that cover the rest of the utterance in a consistent manner, and only maintain the original hypothesis if such an extension proves possible.

4. We found that sequential left-to-right scanning has problems. It is often necessary to provide the ability to recover from a garbled word. The first word of the sentence is often garbled due to high subglottal pressure. But right-to-left scanning is not a viable alternative, as the last word of a sentence can be garbled due to low subglottal pressure that, for example, lengthens phonemes. We thus often find it expedient to work out from those "islands of reliability" provided by the stressed syllables away from the ends of the utterance.

5. When one is dealing with a vocabulary of upward of a 1000 words, there are 10 to the twelfth sequences of length 4. We thus cannot afford to list all possibilities and search them exhaustively, but must rather explore a limited but open-ended space of alternatives based on the data at hand.

6. Even limiting the alternatives in this way, we find that the search space can get too large unless we use merged representations: Many similar hypotheses share common parts, and we can merge these to reduce the search space.

THE HWIM SYSTEM

In this section, we describe the HWIM speech understanding system (Woods, Bates, Brown, Bruce, Cook, Klovstad, Makhoul, Nash-Webber, Schwartz, Wolf, and Zue, 1976). This was designed to handle a vocabulary of 1000 words and had a syntactic/semantic/pragmatic grammar which enabled it to handle sentences such as

> How much is in the speech understanding budget?
> Show me a list of the remaining trips.
> What is the one-way air fare from Boston to London?
> Who went to IFIP?
> Show me Bill's trip to Washington.
> When did Craig go to Utah?
> Enter a trip for Jack Klovstad to San Francisco.
> The registration fee is twenty dollars.

which have to do with contracts, budgets, and conference travel.

The overall system organization of HWIM is shown in Figure 5.2. The speech signal is transduced by a microphone and then processed to yield **parameters** much like those that can be read from the spectrogram. An **acoustic phonetic recognizer** (APR) then processes these parameters to form a **segment lattice** such as that shown in Figure 5.3 corresponding to the spoken input "total budget." Actually, the segment lattice is richer than shown in the figure, since for each segment we list a number of alternatives together with their confidence levels. What is worth noting in Figure 5.3 is that not only do we offer alternative phonemes for a given segment, but we also offer alternative segmentations, as for example in the case of 12–14 and 15–17.

Given a segment lattice and a specified sequence of intervals within that lattice, **lexical retrieval** can return the n best words from any given set of syntactic categories for that region. The **verifier** can proceed through an analysis-by-synthesis process to check the extent to which the parameters support a given lexical hypothesis. Clearly, these processes of lexical retrieval and the verifier must be based on a specified vocabularly stored in the dictionary. In HWIM, this dictionary is produced by expansion from an ordinary pronouncing dictionary and a set of formal phonological rules. Although we will not go into them here, the mechanisms sketched at the top of Figure 5.2 are components that actually determine answers to questions and prepare synthetic spoken utterances for these responses. We shall now turn to the linguistic component, represented by SYNTAX and TRIP in the lower left-hand portion of Figure 5.2. In the current implementation, the SYNTAX component is a general purpose linguistic consultant containing a parser and an ATN grammar that expresses syntactic, semantic, and pragmatic constraints on possible sentences and which interfaces

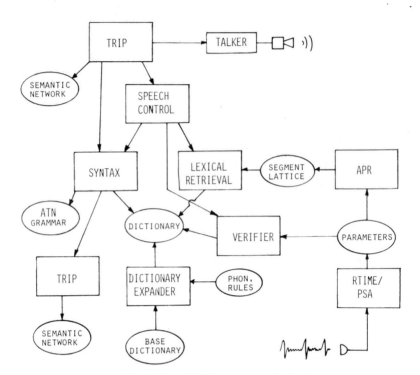

FIGURE 5.2. *HWIM system organization.*

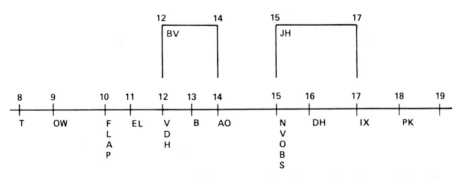

FIGURE 5.3. *A segment lattice obtained from acoustic-phonetic recognition of a speech signal for* total budget.

to a manifestation of the TRIP system for specific factual knowledge such as who has given first and last names, who is taking what trips, etc. The important feature of this linguistic component is that it has to work with sequences of words that have reached a certain confidence level whether or not they form a complete well-formed constituent of a sentence. Thus, the job of the parser is to take an arbitrary sequence of words and judge whether it could be a subsequence of a complete syntactically/semantically/pragmatically appropriate sentence.

While acoustic phonetic recognition is driven bottom-up by the input from the microphone, the verifier, lexical retrieval, and parser are invoked at appropriate times by the speech control system. We shall have more to say of this control after looking at some of these systems in more detail.

Lexical retrieval makes use of a nondeterministic discrimination net. The basic form of such a net is shown in Figure 5.4. Each sequence of phonemes

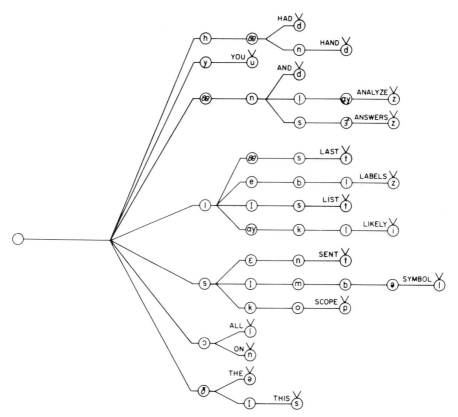

FIGURE 5.4. A discrimination net for word recognition.

determines a path through the net to reach the word, if there is one, formed by that sequence. We see that a branch is taken for each possible initial phoneme, from which there follows a branch for each possible phoneme that can follow it, and so on and so on. In this way, we could—given completely accurate information about the sequence of phenomes that comprise a word—reach the word in a number of steps proportional to the length of the word, irrespective of how many words are contained in the vocabulary. Of course, when we do not have single phoneme hypotheses but instead have likelihoods, we can explore the alternatives, postponing consideration of those initial segments that have a low overall likelihood, while pursuing further through the net those with a high likelihood, until a set of relatively high likelihood words is obtained which covers regions of the segment lattice.

One catch with this is that the pronunciation of a phoneme is highly context dependent. One can certainly handle this for within-word context by designing the tree appropriately. But interword effects seem to pose a different problem, given that one does not know what the adjacent words are when lexical retrieval is being applied. Jack Klovstad, a member of the HWIM project (Woods, Bates, Brown, Bruce, Cook, Klovstad, Makhoul, Nash-Webber, Schwartz, Wolf, and Zue, 1976), discovered an elegant solution to this problem, as indicated in Figure 5.5. Here we see that the net is "wrapped around" so that interword effects can be represented. For example, *hand* usually ends with a [d], but if it is followed by another word, that [d] may be dropped. Thus, the two-word sequence *hand label* may be pronounced as [hanlabel], and we see this indicated in Figure 5.5 by the fact that the final *d* in *hand* is recognized by the "wrap around" network numbered 2 at the left-hand side of the figure, which can alternatively accept an [l] and jump to the place in the main discrimination net corresponding to having matched an initial [l] of a subsequent word. The reader may wish to follow through other wrap-arounds to see how this convention is used in other cases.

The verification component is based on an analysis-by-synthesis approach to word and phrase matching. The pronounciation templates are generated by synthesis-by-rule, which allows a large vocabulary to be generated with relatively low storage, taking into account the contextual dependence in continuous speech and the speaker dependence. The templates thus generated are given via a spectral model which is then compared with the parametric version of the signal to produce a spectral distance measure. More details of the verifier and the other components of the system can be found in Woods *et al.* (1976).

Before going on to see the ways in which hypotheses are formed for various sequences of words within the utterance, and how these hypotheses are grown until one finally has an acceptable hypothesis for the utterance as a whole, let us briefly see what the parser does. Consider the output of the parser given the

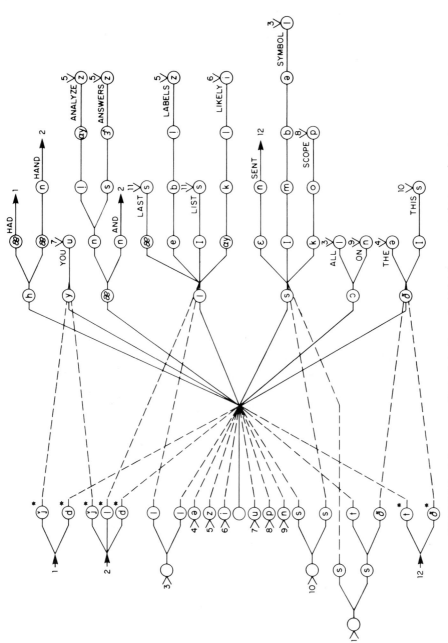

FIGURE 5.5. A "wrap-around" discrimination net which takes account of interword context.

sequence of words *What is the plane fare to San Diego*. The parse tree that will be produced looks as follows:

```
S  Q

    SUBJ NP DET ART THE

           ADJ PLANE

           N FARE

           PP PREP TO

              NP NPR LOCATION (:)1Y SAN@DIEGO

           FEATS NU SG

    AUX TNS PRESENT

        VOICE ACTIVE

    VP V BE

       OBJ NP PRO WHAT

           FEATS NU SG/PL
```

The form of the figure is to be interpreted as a branching tree laid on its side with its root at the top left. The Q of the first line indicates that the overall sentence is taken to be a question. We then see that the subject is a noun phrase which is *the plane fare to San Diego*. Note that the syntax here already contains semantic information, in that it indicates that San Diego is actually a location and a city. The expressions FEATS   NU   SG and FEATS NU SG/PL indicate that their respective noun phrases have syntactic features Number: Singular and Number: Singular/Plural.

The semantic interpretation provided by the parser takes the following form:

```
(FOR:   THE A0007 / (FINDQ: LOCATION ((:)1Y SAN@DIEGO))

      : T ; (FOR: THE A0009 / (FINDQ: DK/FARE (DESTINATION A0007)

                                        (STARTING/POINT BOSTON)

                                        (MODE/OF/TRANSPORT PLANE))

          : T ; (OUTPUT; A0009)))
```

This form has rephrased the question as a program to retrieve the appropriate answer. The first line instructs the question-answering system to set variable A0007 to the location of the city San Diego. The next line tells the system to set variable A0009 to the plane fare for travel to this destination (San Diego) from the starting point of Boston (note the standing assumption based on the fact that the HWIM system was designed in Cambridge, Massachusetts). The last line instructs the system to provide as answer to the question the value so computed for variable A0009.

It would burden this chapter unduly to describe in detail the ATN (Augmented Transition network) grammar and semantic net used by the parser. However, their content can be indicated by a brief look at Figures 5.6 and 5.7. Figure 5.6 indicates the ATN grammer fragment for date expressions in HWIM. (For details on ATN grammars, see Woods, 1970.) The grammar will recognize a sequence of words as being a date expression if it can use these words to move successfully from the initial node marked DATE to the final node marked DATE/DATE at which the final popping out of that level of analysis can take place. For example, 13 May will be accepted by following the path PUSH NUMBER (must be less than 32) from DATE to DATE/DAY; by following the path CAT MONTH (recognizing that May falls in the category of a "month") to then pass to the node DATE/MO, and then taking two jumps that require no further input to get to the final node. On the other hand, 13 May 23 will not be accepted, because the PUSH NUMBER transition from DATE/MO to DATE/NUM can only be done if it was not done during the first transition. To get some idea of the nondetermism of the graph, note that *Wednesday* could be a complete date expression, or could be the first word of a compound expression such as *Wednesday the third of May, 1979.* The reader should check that for each of a wide range of date expressions, there is a valid path through the net, while illegal perturbations of such expressions cannot be accomplished through that net. Thus, indeed, passage through this ATN does provide an appropriate representation of the syntax of date expressions.

Turning now to Figure 5.7, we see that basic **meaning relations** are em-

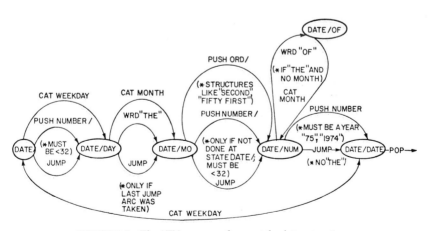

FIGURE 5.6. *The ATN grammar fragment for date expressions.*

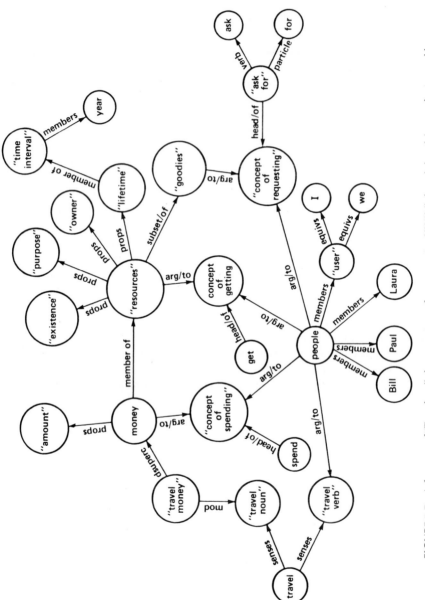

FIGURE 5.7. A fragment of "Travelnet," the semantic net for representing HWIM's knowledge of the travel microworld.

bodied within this net. For example, we may see that Bill is a member of the set of people, that people can provide one of the arguments to "the concept of requesting," for which another argument is "goodies," of which "resources" form a subset, and amongst the properties of "resources" are that they have an "owner." This figure represents the kinds of factual information represented in HWIM and used to answer questions and to perform certain tests invoked by conditions on the arcs of the ATN grammar. For example, the semantic network is consulted by the ATN when it recognizes a person's name to see if it knows anyone by that name. (See Woods, 1975, for a general discussion of semantic networks.)

With this background, we can now briefly sketch the **control strategy** embodied in the HWIM speech understanding system. Briefly, the strategy is one of incremental development of the most likely interpretation of a speech signal as a result of stimulus-suggested word hypotheses, refined by the addition of new words, subject to the constraints of a formalized model (grammar) of possible interpretations. Initially, the segment lattice is generated, and on this basis lexical retrieval will provide an initial set of high-likelihood word hypotheses. A control system can then call upon the linguistic component to use both its pragmatic grammar (as exemplified in Figure 5.6) and its knowledge base (as exemplified in Figure 5.7) to come up with hypotheses which incorporate some of the words previously suggested by the lexical retrieval, but which may also hypothesize further words. On this basis, control can then call the verifier to see whether in fact the newly hypothesized words are supported by the acoustic evidence. And so the process iterates.

The task of the system may be characterized as being high-level perception, in distinction from low-level perception in which one of a small number of stimuli must be recognized. In the present task environment, the system must recognize any member of a potentially immense class constructed from elementary objects via well-formedness rules. Thus, as we have already stressed, analysis must proceed not by enumeration, but by **successive refinement** of partial hypotheses.

We use the term **theory** to refer to a partial hypothesis together with its current evaluation or likelihood level. The control strategy for the growth of such theories, working toward a complete spanning theory to provide the interpretation of the entire utterance, is sketched in Figure 5.8. On the basis of the initial scan, the segment lattice is formed, and lexical retrieval provides "seed theories" which are the initial, stimulus-driven hypotheses based on the purely bottom-up analysis. The resultant seed events are placed on the event queue, ordered by "priority," where they will be joined by other events as processing continues. Events on this queue may be viewed as incipient theories. They consist of either (a) seed events, (b) theories together with adjacent words hypothesized to extend them, or (c) a combination of two "islands" with a word that joins them. The priority of events on the queue can be determined by a number of methods all

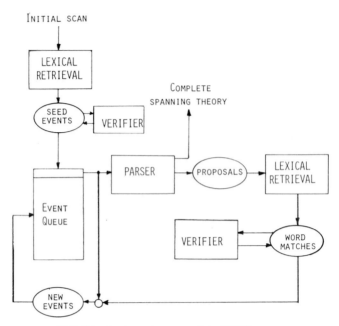

FIGURE 5.8. *Control strategy of the HWIM system.*

based on a semi-Bayesian analysis of the likelihoods of the alternative hypotheses given the evidence considered. One of the most interesting methods, called **shortfall density,** when combined with an appropriate search strategy, can guarantee that the first complete spanning theory found will have the highest likelihood of being correct (Woods, 1977). The events on the queue are maintained in priority order, and the parser at each stage will take the event of highest priority and check whether in fact it could be part of a syntactically/semantically/pragmatically correct sentence. One way of forming a new event is then to hypothesize that a new word be added to one end or the other of an existing theory. Another process, called *island collision,* occurs when some theory1 is posited to be extended to the right by a word which is also posited to extend some theory2 to the left, thus suggesting as a new event the concatenation theory1–word–theory2.

This control, based as it is on an event queue ordered by some priority score, does not work necessarily from left to right, but instead tends to work out from "islands of reliability." The algorithm does not guarantee that those hypotheses which are processed early on will prove to be correct, but some strategies (e.g., **middle-out shortfall-density with island collisions**) do guarantee that the search will eventually find the best complete spanning theory that provides an interpretation of the entire utterance.

Finally, we note that our serial computer strategy uses the priority ordering to tell what to do next; we would speculate that analogs of such rankings may be used within the parallel computations of the brain to determine how resources are to be allocated among the various hypotheses.

A SAMPLE ANALYSIS OF AN UTTERANCE

In this final section, we shall look briefly at the analysis of an utterance to get a better feel for the control strategy indicated in Figure 5.8. The utterance to be analyzed is *Do we have a surplus?* and the analysis that we shall follow is fairly typical, save that it is much shorter and has less branching than what one would encounter on the average. Figure 5.9 appears to be overwhelming, but we hope to convince the reader that it is quite comprehensible. Look, first, at the first panel, in which we see 15 theories. For each theory we list its priority score, and the region of the utterance that supports it. In this example, the search strategy used is called **left-hybrid shortfall-density** and consists of using seed events near the left end of the utterance with a shortfall-density priority score.

You will note that the theories are arranged in descending order of their score, and we have shown the top 15 of the total of 54 seed theories. To make it easier for you to keep track of the processing, we have marked the correct theories with an exclamation mark, and you will note that many incorrect seed theories have higher priority than the correct seed theories before higher level syntactic and semantic processes are brought into play. Now, as we invoke these higher level processes, new theories will be developed, and these theories are to be inserted into the event queue on the basis of their priority ordering. For example, we see that Panel 2 of Figure 5.9 is obtained from Panel 1 by inserting the theory [WHO IS between WERE and WORK on the basis of its score which is intermediate between theirs. Arrows single out the new theories in each panel. Note that WHO has disappeared from the event queue after its use to construct this new theory WHO IS. We shall describe in more detail the process whereby the new theories are created, but for the moment let us just make sure that we understand the way in which these theories, once created, are inserted into the event queue. The transition from Panel 2 to Panel 3 is based on the creation of at least six new hypotheses, together with their scores, and their insertion in the event queue in the appropriate priority ordering. Note that the hypothesis WE has been removed, but that among the new hypotheses that subsume it is [WE, namely the hypothesis of WE not simply as a word somewhere in the sentence, but of WE as the initial word of the sentence. The reader should now be able to follow the way in which the remaining panels are formed from their predecessors. The arrows indicate the items that are added. Items are removed from the queue as they are used to form new hypotheses, and some are pushed down the queue by new higher priority events. The process continues until, in this case in Panel 9, we

①

#	SCORE	REGION	THEORY
1	3.53	1-5	WHO
2	1.92	3-6	WE I
3	0.0	0-1	-PAUSE- !
4	-2.43	2-3	A
5	-3.24	5-10	ELEVEN
6	-4.32	5-9	IRAQ
7	-5.36	1-3	HER
8	-6.00	1-4	WHOLE
9	-6.18	1-5	DO I
10	-6.21	3-6	WERE
11	-6.53	3-7	WORK
12	-6.85	1-4	HIS
13	-7.00	1-5	NOW
14	-7.12	1-6	HAWAII
15	-7.21	3-6	WHERE

+ 39 ADDITIONAL EVENTS

④

#	SCORE	REGION	THEORY	
1	1.12	3-6	[WE I	
2	1.10	1-9>	[DO WE HAVE- !	↓
3	0.0	0-1	-PAUSE- !	
4	-1.13	<2-6	ARE WE	
5	-1.96	<2-6	WILL WE	
6	-1.96	<2-6	WERE WE	
7	-2.43	2-3	A	
8	-2.83	<0-6	WHAT DO WE	↓
9	-3.20	<2-6	CAN WE	
10	-4.03	5-10	ELEVEN	
11	-5.26	5-9	IRAQ	
12	-5.36	1-3	HER	
13	-6.00	1-4	WHOLE	
1?	-6.18	1-5	DO I	
15	-6.21	3-6	WERE	

+ 48 ADDITIONAL EVENTS

②

#	SCORE	REGION	THEORY	
1	1.92	3-6	WE !	
2	0.0	0-1	-PAUSE- !	
3	-2.43	2-3	A	
4	-3.24	5-10	ELEVEN	
5	-4.32	5-9	IRAQ	
6	-5.36	1-3	HER	
7	-6.00	1-4	WHOLE	
8	-6.18	1-5	DO I	
9	-6.21	3-6	WERE	
10	-6.40	1-7>	[WHO IS	↓
11	-6.53	3-7	WORK	
12	-6.85	1-4	HIS	
13	-7.00	1-5	NOW	
14	-7.12	1-6	HAWAII	
15	-7.21	3-6	WHERE	

+ 41 ADDITIONAL EVENTS

⑤

#	SCORE	REGION	THEORY	
1	1.10	1-9>	[DO WE HAVE !	
2	0.0	0-1	-PAUSE- !	
3	-1.13	<2-6	ARE WE	
4	-1.96	<2-6	WILL WE	
5	-1.96	<2-6	WERE WE	
6	-2.43	2-3	A	
7	-2.65	3-9	[WE WENT	↓
8	-2.83	<0-6	WHAT DO WE	
9	-3.20	<2-6	CAN WE	
10	-4.03	5-10	ELEVEN	
11	-5.26	5-9	IRAQ	
12	-5.36	1-3	HER	
13	-6.00	1-4	WHOLE	
14	-6.18	1-5	DO !	
15	-6.21	3-6	WERE	

+ 51 ADDITIONAL EVENTS

③

#	SCORE	REGION	THEORY	
1	1.82	<1-6	DO WE I	↓
2	1.12	3-6	[WE	↓
3	0.0	0-1	-PAUSE- !	
4	-1.13	<2-6	ARE WE	↓
5	-1.96	<2-6	WILL WE	↓
6	-1.96	<2-6	WERE WE	↓
7	-2.43	2-3	A	
8	-3.20	<2-6	CAN WE	↓
9	-4.03	5-10	ELEVEN	
10	-5.26	5-9	IRAQ	
11	-5.36	1-3	HER	
12	-6.00	1-4	WHOLE	
13	-6.18	1-5	DO I	
14	-6.21	3-6	WERE	
15	-6.43	1-7>	[WHO IS	

+ 47 ADDITIONAL EVENTS

⑥

#	SCORE	REGION	THEORY	
1	.99	1-10>	[DO WE HAVE A !	↓
2	0.0	0-1	-PAUSE- !	
3	-1.13	<2-6	ARE WE	
4	-1.55	1-10>	[DO WE HAVE EIGHT	↓
5	-1.96	<2-6	WILL WE	
6	-1.96	<2-6	WERE WE	
7	-2.31	1-11>	[DO WE HAVE LESS	↓
8	-2.43	2-3	A	
9	-2.50	1-13>	[DO WE HAVE OVER	↓
10	-2.65	3-9	[WE WENT	
11	-2.83	<0-6	WHAT DO WE	
12	-2.84	1-13>	[DO WE HAVE UNDER	↓
13	-3.20	<2-6	CAN WE	
14	-3.67	1-10>	[DO WE HAVE MORE	↓
15	-4.27	5-10	ELEVEN	

+ 56 ADDITIONAL EVENTS

⑦

#	SCORE	REGION	THEORY
1	0.0	0-1	-PAUSE-!
2	-1.13	<2-6	ARE WE
3	-1.27	1-17>	[DO WE HAVE A SURPLUS ! ←
4	-1.55	1-10>	[DO WE HAVE EIGHT
5	-1.96	<2-6	WILL WE
6	-1.96	<2-6	WERE WE
7	-2.31	1-11>	[DO WE HAVE LESS
8	-2.43	2-3	A
9	-2.50	1-13>	[DO WE HAVE OVER
10	-2.65	3-9	[WE WENT
11	-2.83	<0-6	WHAT DO WE
12	-2.84	1-13>	[DO WE HAVE UNDER
13	-3.20	<2-6	CAN WE
14	-3.30	1-15>	[DO WE HAVE A THOUSAND ←
15	-3.67	1-10>	[DO WE HAVE MORE

+ 57 ADDITIONAL EVENTS

⑧

#	SCORE	REGION	THEORY
1	-1.13	<2-6	ARE WE
2	-1.27	1-17>	[DO WE HAVE A SURPLUS !
3	-1.55	1-10>	[DO WE HAVE EIGHT
4	-1.96	<2-6	WILL WE
5	-1.96	<2-6	WERE WE
6	-2.31	1-11>	[DO WE HAVE LESS
7	-2.43	2-3	A
8	-2.50	1-13>	[DO WE HAVE OVER
9	-2.65	3-9>	[WE WENT
10	-2.83	<0-6	WHAT DO WE
11	-2.84	1-13>	[DO WE HAVE UNDER
12	-3.20	<2-6	CAN WE
13	-3.30	1-15>	[DO WE HAVE A THOUSAND
14	-3.67	1-10>	[DO WE HAVE MORE
15	-4.21	0-3>	[-PAUSE- HER ←

+ 64 ADDITIONAL EVENTS

⑨

#	SCORE	REGION	THEORY
1	-1.27	1-17>	[DO WE HAVE A SURPLUS ! ←
2	-1.37	2-6	[ARE WE
3	-1.55	1-10>	[DO WE HAVE EIGHT
4	-1.96	<2-6	WILL WE
5	-1.96	<2-6	WERE WE
6	-2.31	1-11>	[DO WE HAVE LESS
7	-2.43	2-3	A
8	-2.50	1-13>	[DO WE HAVE OVER
9	-2.65	3-9>	[WE WENT
10	-2.83	<0-6	WHAT DO WE
11	-2.84	1-13>	[DO WE HAVE UNDER
12	-3.20	<2-6	CAN WE
13	-3.30	1-15>	[DO WE HAVE A THOUSAND
14	-3.67	1-10>	[DO WE HAVE MORE
15	-4.21	0-3>	[-PAUSE- HER

+ 64 ADDITIONAL EVENTS

FIGURE 5.9. *Nine successive views of the top of the event queue in recognizing the utterance Do we have a surplus?*

111

come up with a theory that not only reaches the top of the stack but also covers the entire utterance. When the top event of Panel 9 is evaluated and determined to produce a complete spanning theory, it is produced as the interpretation and no new events are added to the queue. (Clearly, the process could be continued to produce second best interpretations and so on.)

In growing new events from old, the system has the following options:

Doing left-end event forms the hypothesis that the event comes at the beginning of an utterance, and indicates this by placing a [in front of the event; similarly **doing right-end event** places a] after the event.

Noticing on the right adds a new word at the right end of an event; while **noticing on the left** adds a new word at the left end of the event.

In what follows, we shall simply indicate what new events are proposed at each stage.

In getting from Panel 1 to Panel 2, the system starts from the top hypothesis WHO of Panel 1; does a left-end event to create the proposal [WHO, and then performs noticing on the right to create [WHO WILL, [WHO WENT, and [WHO IS. Of these, only [WHO IS has sufficiently high priority rating to enter the top 15 items of the stack as shown in Panel 2.

The system then takes the event WE from the stack as shown in Panel 2 and, by noticing on the left, creates 7 new hypotheses of which 5 enter the top 15 items of the stack as shown in Panel 3 and, by noticing left-end event, forms the new theory [WE which enters second place of the stack at that time. Note that WE has now been subsumed in the other hypotheses and is removed from the stack. The stack contains only a list of hypotheses that have not yet been fully considered.

At the next stage, DO WE is removed from the top of the stack and the system provides 3 new theories: WHAT DO WE by noticing on the left; [DO WE by doing a left-end event; and then [DO WE HAVE by noticing on the right. [DO WE is extended to [DO WE HAVE without creating an intermediate event on the event queue since its score is unchanged by the addition of the left-end hypothesis.

By now, the reader should be able to see the processes that led to the hypotheses which enter the stack in each succeeding panel, and to understand why other hypotheses have been removed from the stack. It is worth noting that the correct but rather unilluminating –PAUSE– comes to the top of the stack at Panel 7, but that an incorrect hypothesis temporarily bubbles to the top of the stack in Panel 8.

The correct hypothesis [DO WE HAVE A SURPLUS enters the stack in almost final form in Panel 7, when [DO WE HAVE A SURPLUS is formed from DO WE HAVE A by noticing on the right. However, it is not until [DO WE HAVE A SURPLUS comes to the top of the stack as shown in Panel 9 that we can finally do a right-end event to form [DO WE HAVE A SURPLUS], which at last provides a complete parse and thus the spanning theory that provides the interpretation of the entire utterance.

ACKNOWLEDGMENT

Grateful thanks to Michael Arbib who produced the first draft of this chapter from tapes, notes, and slides of a talk presented at the conference.

REFERENCES

Denes, P. B., and Pinson, E. N. (1963). *The speech chain.* Murray Hill, New Jersey: Bell Telephone Laboratories.

Klatt, D. H., and Stevens, K. N. (1972). Sentence recognition from visual examination of spectrograms and machine-aided lexical searching. Paper presented at the Conference on Speech Communication and Processing, Newton, Massachusetts, April 1972.

Woods, W. A. (1970). Transition network grammars for natural language analysis. *Communications of the ACM* **13** (10).

Woods, W. A. (1975a). Syntax, semantics and speech. In R. Reddy (Ed.), *Speech recognition.* New York: Academic Press.

Woods, W. A. (1975b). What's in a LINK: Foundations for semantic networks. In D. Bobrow and A. Collins (Eds.), *Representation and understanding.* New York: Academic Press.

Woods, W. A. (1977). Shortfall and density scoring strategies for speech understanding control. Proceedings of the International Joint Conference on Artificial Intelligence, MIT, Cambridge, Massachusetts, June 1977.

Woods, W. A. (1978). Semantics and quantification in natural language question answering. In M. Yovits (Ed.), *Advances in computers,* vol. 17. New York: Academic Press.

Woods, W. A. (1980). Cascaded ATN Grammars. *American Journal of Computational Linguistics,* 6, 1–12.

Woods, W. A. (forthcoming). Optimal search strategies for speech understanding control. *Artificial Intelligence.*

Woods, W. A., Bates, M., Brown, G., Bruce, B., Cook, C., Klovstad, J., Makhoul, J., Nash-Webber, B., Schwartz, R., Wolf, J., and Zue, V. (1976). Speech understanding systems. Final Report. BBN Report No. 3438, Bolt Beranek and Newman Inc., Cambridge, Massachusetts.

Woods, W. A., and Makhoul, J. I. (1974). Mechanical inference problems in continuous speech understanding. *Artificial Intelligence,* 5, 73–91.

6

Consequences of Functional Deficits in a Parsing Model: Implications for Broca's Aphasia

Mitchell P. Marcus

This chapter is an attempt to provide some insight into possible causes of the comprehension deficit that is part of the symptom complex of Broca's aphasia. It examines a previously developed computational model of one aspect of normal language understanding and investigates in detail the kinds of performance degradation caused by "damage" to one particular part of that mechanism. In particular, this chapter will focus on a computational model for *parsing* English sentences; this model consists of a procedure that, given a sentence of English as input, decides what the grammatical structure of that sentence is.

I make two assumptions about the language understanding process: First, deciding what the grammatical structure of a sentence is, that is, deciding what part of the sentence functions as subject and what part as predicate, is normally a prerequisite to assigning a semantic structure to the sentence and thus to deciding what the sentence means. Second, the components of the language processing system that assign meaning are capable of doing so using pragmatic and semantic knowledge alone if syntactic information is missing. This "meaning-based" mode of understanding is presumably similar to the case in which a normal person attempts to understand a passage in an unknown foreign language, given translations of the individual content words, but without full knowledge of word-order restrictions, case-marking, etc. In such a situation, it is often possible to figure out what must have been meant. However, as will be shown, the (perhaps partial) lack of such syntactic information can severely degrade the recovery of the intended meaning of the sentence. It will be demonstrated that "destroying" various specific parts of the parser causes the assignment of grammatical structure to be degraded in particular ways, with each particular "deficit" causing a variety of degradations that may in turn be reflected by a variety of deficits in the assignment of semantic structures.

The structure of the parser to be described was motivated by a set of concerns unrelated to the modeling of cognitive deficits. It was designed to show that

NEURAL MODELS OF
LANGUAGE PROCESSES

English in particular and natural language in general could be parsed in a very efficient manner, contrary to the conventional wisdom accepted by computational linguists. More specifically, it was intended to provide support for what I call the *determinism hypothesis*, which means that a properly designed process can correctly assign syntactic structures to English sentences, working left to right, without ever being forced to either change or discard some structure previously built. For further discussion of these issues, see Marcus (1980).

What I will demonstrate here is that "damage" to specific elements of this machine's structure will cause the resulting system to exhibit deficits that are arguably similar to some of those that make up the symptom complex of Broca's aphasia. Again, it should be stressed that the damage will be to aspects of the machine's structure that are motivated by independent considerations of normal function, although some evidence from aphasics will be used to argue for one aspect of normal structure. More specifically, I will show an example of one kind of structural deficit that causes the parser to construct only fragmentary parses of input word strings and will further suggest that the size of the fragments will vary as a function of the particular kind of damage inflicted upon the machine. It will be argued that the behavior resulting from the production of only fragmentary syntactic analysis, in conjunction with assumptions about semantic processing, is suggestive of the comprehension deficit exhibited by Broca's aphasics.

I must admit at the outset that current knowledge of exactly what comprehension deficits are common to those with Broca's aphasia is not sufficient to fully evaluate the validity of such a model; an admission that may call into question the usefulness of such an enterprise. The point of this inquiry, however, is to show that the specificity of a computational model leads to an ability to predict, for a given functional deficit inflicted on the model, a wide range of specific consequences, many of which are prima facie unrelated to the form of the functional deficit. These consequences, in turn, become specific predictions of the model that can be put to the test of experimental confirmation to determine the truth of the model. Thus, such a computational model, given that its details are well motivated, can provide valuable insight into the indirect manifestation of particular functional deficits within a simple model of one component of cognitive function. [In this respect, this chapter is similar to that of M. L. Kean (Chapter 8, this volume).]

A SKETCH OF THE LANGUAGE UNDERSTANDING SYSTEM

While this chapter focuses on the process of assigning grammatical structure to input word strings, it must be explicitly recognized that this process occurs only as a part of the larger process of determining the meaning of word strings as parts of larger utterances, and that the function of syntactic processing must be viewed within the context of the containing system. For the sake of this chapter, we will assume that the process of understanding a sentence can be schematized as shown in Figure 6.1. (We ignore here the problem of word recognition, which can be argued to occur logically prior to the processes discussed here. See Woods in this volume [Chapter 5] for further discussion of this issue.)

We assume here that the incoming word stream serves as input to a parser, which in turn outputs an analysis of the syntactic structure of the input. For example, given the word string shown in Figure 6.1b as input, the parser might produce a representation equivalent to the tree structure shown in Figure 6.1c. This representation indicates that the word string is a sentence, which is in turn made up of the noun phrase (NP) "all boys" and the verb phrase (VP) "love their mothers." The VP itself contains two constituents, namely the verb "love" and the NP "their mothers" as the object of the verb. This syntactic representation serves as input to the next stage of processing, *semantic analysis.*

As indicated in the schematic, the word stream itself may also serve directly as an input to the semantic processor, where it might be used, for example, just

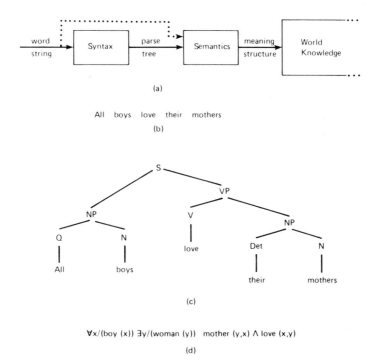

(a)

All   boys   love   their   mothers

(b)

(c)

$\forall x/(boy\ (x))\ \exists y/(woman\ (y))\ \ mother\ (y,x)\ \wedge\ love\ (x,y)$

(d)

FIGURE 6.1. *Postulated information flow and intermediate representations of the understanding process.*

in case the syntactic component can produce only fragmentary output. Another possibility is that the semantic component attempts to do a purely associative analysis of the input while awaiting the outcome of syntactic analysis. In simple cases, however, the parse tree contains all the information conveyed by any given sentence that is needed for semantic analysis.

In any case, the semantic processor produces some meaning representation for the current input that makes explicit the logical structure of the sentence, as exemplified by the predicate calculus representation given in Figure 6.1d). (Figure 6.1d says, more or less, that for each X such that X is a boy there can be found some Y, where Y is a woman, such that Y is the mother of X and X loves Y.) This representation is then assumed to serve as input to a much larger system of cognitive processing that somehow determines the full meaning of the input sentence, given world knowledge and knowledge of the current discourse context.

We further assume that each stage of processing works according to the principal of graceful degradation stated by Norman and Bobrow (1974), that each processing component may give degraded output, given degraded input, but cannot operate in an all or none manner. In the case of syntactic analysis in particular, this means that the parser must be capable of giving as output fragments of what syntactic structure can be derived from noisy or fragmentary input, rather than producing either full parses or no parse at all. [For some speculations on a plausible overall architecture for such a system see Bobrow and Webber (1980).]

To summarize, the crucial aspects of this sketch for our purposes are (a) that the input to semantic processing is the output of a stage of syntactic recognition; (b) that semantic processing therefore assumes that those aspects of syntactic form relevant for the determination of meaning will have been determined by this previous syntactic stage; (c) that semantic processing is nonetheless sufficiently robust that it can make a determination of meaning even in the face of a fragmentary syntactic analysis.

THE PARSER

We now turn to the parsing model itself. The reader should note that the sketch presented here contains only enough detail to enable the discussion of those aspects of the parsing model relevant to this chapter; for a full discussion of the parsing model see Marcus (1980). The parsing model to be discussed here has been embodied in a working computer program called Parsifal, and for ease of reference, I will often refer to this specific parsing model as Parsifal in the following sections.

Parsifal can be viewed as being composed of a *grammar of parsing rules* that act upon the incoming word string to build up syntactic structures contained in internal *data structures*. More specifically, the grammar rules first examine the contents of Parsifal's internal data structures and the incoming word string, and then, contingent upon what structures already exist, add to the contents of those data structures.

All structures built up by Parsifal are contained in two data structures in particular, the push down stack and the buffer, as shown in Figure 6.2. The push down stack contains constituents whose internal structure can not yet be determined to be complete, whereas the buffer contains constituents that are complete (to a first approximation), but that have not yet been assigned a syntactic role in some larger structure.

Thus, for example, in Figure 6.2, the stack contains two nodes, a sentence (S) node and a verb phrase (VP) node, with the VP a daughter of the S. (Note that the stack grows downward so that the root of the emerging parse tree will always be at the top of the stack.) The noun phrase (NP) "you" is also a daughter of the S node; however, it is neither in the stack nor the buffer because both its internal structure and its role in a larger structure have already been determined by the parser. While the verb "plan" of the VP has been found, the VP can not yet be guaranteed to be complete because the verb at least potentially takes an object, and thus it is still kept in the active node stack. The S node above the VP must be kept in the active node stack not only because it has an incomplete daughter, but also because it may take clause-final modifiers.

The buffer in this example contains two constituents, the noun phrase (NP) "the meeting" and the prepositional phrase (PP) "for Friday." We can see that these constituents will ultimately be attached to the VP node, but they are in the buffer in Figure 6.2 exactly because this has yet to be determined.

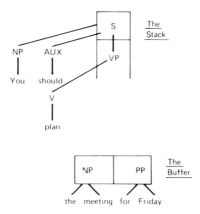

FIGURE 6.2. *Parsifal's two data structures.*

One major utility of the buffer to the Parsifal model is that it allows grammar rules to examine both right and left surrounding contexts before deciding what to do with the constituent in the first (the leftmost) buffer position. As already mentioned, the Parsifal model was motivated by the hypothesis that the syntactic structure of a natural language input can be determined without error in an entirely incremented way by some kind of computational process. The existence of the buffer and the access to righthand context that it allows is crucial to enabling Parsifal to operate in this kind of error-free incremental manner. To allow such context to be utilized wherever necessary while keeping the amount of unincorporated structures to a minimum, it has been determined empirically that a buffer of three constituents seems to be optimal. Thus in what follows it will be assumed that the buffer is three constituents long.

The form of grammar rules is illustrated in Figure 6.3, which shows schematically the operation of one grammar rule that attaches the subject NP of a sentence to its parent S node. Grammar rules are a kind of *pattern-action rule* (Newell and Simon, 1972), with a pattern part that determines when the rule is applicable and an action part that determines what to do when it is. This is indicated in this chapter by two configurations of the parser with an arrow between them; the leftmost is to be viewed as a pattern and the rightmost is to be viewed as the result of applying the action. (For the sake of pedigogical clarity, the result of actions will be shown here with the action itself implicit. In the grammar rules themselves, the action itself must be made explicit.)

In Figure 6.3, the pattern of the rule shown will trigger if the first position in the buffer contains an NP, the second a verb, and the node at the bottom of the active node stack (i.e. the node to which the parser is current attempting to attach daughters) is an S. As a result of the action of this rule, the NP in the first buffer position is attached to the S node, thereby indicating that it is the subject of the sentence under construction. Note that the NP has not only been attached, but it has also been removed from the buffer, and the verb that was previously in the second buffer position has shifted left into the first position of the buffer. This

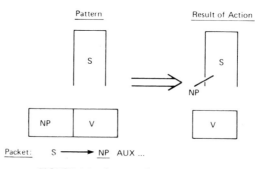

FIGURE 6.3. *An example grammar rule.*

is a general property of the parser; when the parent of a constuent in the buffer has been determined, there is no longer any reason for it to remain in the buffer and it is automatically removed.

Most grammar rules are not always in an active state, however; the parser does not always attempt to determine whether or not the pattern of a rule matches the configuration of the parser. Rather, each grammar rule is contained in a *packet* of rules that is activated only under particular circumstances. Each packet is associated with part of a *phrase structure rule* whose left hand side indicates the type of node that must be at the bottom of the active node stack when the packet is to be activated. A packet itself is associated with one position on the right hand side of a phrase structure rule; the parser will only activate the rules that a given packet contains when the parser is currently attempting to fill that position in the phrase structure template. Thus, for example, the rule shown in Figure 6.3 is part of a packet that is to be activated when the parser is currently constructing an S node; it is associated in particular with the subject position of the sentence; this is indicated in the figure by italicizing the subject NP of the S. The phrase structure rule as a whole indicates that to build a sentence, the parser should first activate the packet of rules that finds the subject NP of the S, then the packet to find the auxiliaries (i.e. the "helping verbs") of the sentence, etc.

It should be noted, however, that some grammar rules are in fact active almost all of the time; for example, the rule that initiates the construction of noun phrases. This rule is only deactivated when the parser is busy building an NP, otherwise it is always active. This means that NPs are initiated only on the basis of incoming information (to a first approximation); current context has little role to play in the activation of such constituents.

The parser operates by creating a top level parse node, normally an S node, and then by attempting to attach the relevant constituents to the emerging parse tree in the order specified by the phrase structure rule for that constituent. If a node of the appropriate type can be found sitting in the buffer already constructed by earlier processes, that node can simply be attached to the current bottom of the active node stack. Sometimes, however, it will be necessary for the parser to create a new node of the appropriate type at the bottom of the stack, "pushing" the node currently under construction into the interior of the stack. Then it is necessary for the parser to find all the constituents of that subconstituent before "popping" the subconstituent from the stack and continuing with the construction of the higher level structure.

Parsing Fragmentary Input

Because the parser is committed to never creating any incorrect grammatical structure, even in passing, there is no provision for the machine to undo any structure if, for some reason, it is unable to complete a given grammatical analysis either because it has in fact made an error or because the input itself is fragmentary or noisy. Given the principal of graceful degradation previously mentioned, the parser must take some other kind of action when confronted with problematic input if it is not to simply bog down and stop.

The most natural recourse for the parser in case it cannot construct a full analysis of any given input is simply to construct a number of partial analyses. When no active rule matches the current configuration, the parser can continue by (1) outputing whatever partial structures it has completed, (2) by clearing the stack, and then (3) by activating a special set of grammar rules designed to initiate fragmentary input in a primarily data driven way. An appropriate set of rules will then produce an analysis of either the remainder of the input or else some portion of the input, in which case the machine will be cleared again and the fragment parsing process repeated

Whatever the form of rules for parsing fragmentary input, the reader should note that they need not be postulated ad hoc for this purpose alone. Such rules are needed independently to handle the kinds of ellision and gapping that occur in such normal sentences as "Sue gave Bob a lollipop and John a Hersey bar" and "George thinks vanilla." (The last is in response to the question "What is Bob's favorite flavor of ice cream?"). To see this most clearly, consider the kinds of continuations that can follow the conjunction "and" in the fragment

> I gave Sue five freshly-picked apples and
>> oranges
>> equally fresh oranges
>> two rotten bananas
>> Herbert the same
>> watched her eat two of them
>> she gave me a bottle of cider in return

The kinds of constituents that the parser must be prepared to build after a conjunction in this situation include a simple noun, an adjective-noun fragment of a noun phrase, a full NP, a verb phrase fragment, a full VP, and an S node.

To parse fragmentary or heavily ellided input without ever initiating any structure that might have to be discarded as incorrect, the parser must be able to initiate phrase fragments essentially without expectations; almost anything can continue such a conjunction. The point here is that if such rules can be found to handle these fully grammatical sentences, they will be adequate to handle fragmentary input as well. A trivial example of such a rule is shown in Figure 6.4; this is the rule that will always initiate an NP upon seeing a determiner (or an adjective or . . .) as long as an S node is at the bottom of the stack. [The actual mechanism implemented to do this is actually quite a bit more complex than is indicated here, but the basic idea is the same. For full details, see Marcus

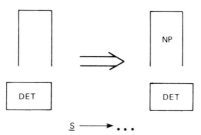

FIGURE 6.4. *A grammar rule triggered without expectations.*

(1980)]. The action of this rule, as indicated in the figure, simply creates an NP node at the bottom of the stack, causing the parser to initiate the building of an NP according to the packets that will be activated while scanning the phrase structure rule for NPs.

HYPOTHETICAL DEFICIT I—LOSS OF CLOSED CLASS LEXICON

With the basic parser model now presented, this section will investigate one possible "lesion" that can be afflicted upon the parser model, explicating the functional loss that results from this posited loss of structure. As discussed in the introduction, the primary point of this exercise is to demonstrate the ways in which fairly straightforward structural deficits in the underlying machine can express themselves in complex functional patterns. In particular, this section will investigate the result of rendering the parser unable to recognize the *closed class words* of the language, that is, the "function words" such as determiners like *the*, and *a*, prepositions like *by* and *to*, quantifiers like *all* and *some*, and assorted other words that serve primarily as the grammatical "glue" that holds the content words of a sentence together.

This line of investigation is suggested by the well known difficulty in the production of function words that Broca's aphasics exhibit, as well as by the seeming inability of Broca's aphasics to detect function words in language recognition tasks (Zurif, Caramazza, and Meyerson, 1972). It is also suggested by the results of recent psychological experiments (Bradley, Garrett, and Zurif, 1979) investigating the organization of the mental lexicon. They suggest that there are two distinct lexical access mechanisms for open and closed class words, and that the closed class access mechanism is somehow nonfunctional in Broca's aphasics. These experiments also suggest that the open class lexicon includes in fact *both* classes of words, but that occurrences of closed class items in this full lexicon are somehow inhibited from interfering with entries in the other as long as the closed class access mechanism is functional.

We begin here by suggesting that a grammar for the parsing mechanism already discussed be modified to include explicit reference to all closed class lexical items rather than to the word class of such items. (Next, we will posit "damage" to exactly this extension and see what follows.) Thus, for example, instead of the rule shown in Figure 6.5a, which says to start a prepositional phrase (PP) whenever a preposition (P) is followed by an NP, the grammar will have a large number of rules each of whose patterns will be triggered by one particular preposition, as exemplified by those shown in Figure 6.5b. This position suggests that closed classes are closed exactly because their items are "hard wired" into the grammar; this provides a possible explanation for the fact that new closed class items are exceedingly hard to coin or acquire.

Such a move is motivated not only by the kinds of psychological results previously discussed, but also by considerations entirely internal to the structure of the parsing process. It turns out that it is already necessary to explicitly include many closed class items within a grammar for a parser of English; thus, the suggestion here merely extends the existing situation to the logical limit. For example, a parsing grammar must include a rule such as that shown in Figure 6.6, which captures the fact that for exactly three quantifiers of English, *all*, *both* and *half*, one can either say "all the boys" or "all *of* the boys"; the word *of* can optionally be deleted. (This rule must be active exactly when parsing the quantifier phrase (QP) of the noun phrase, as the rule shown indicates.) Given that

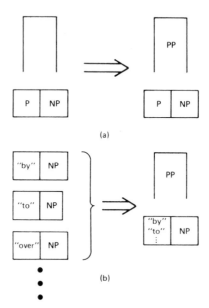

(a)

(b)

FIGURE 6.5. *Rule patterns before and after closed classes are multiplied out.*

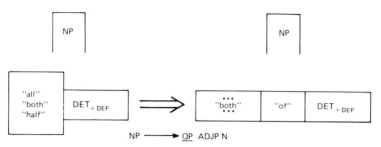

FIGURE 6.6. *A grammar rule that necessarily mentions closed class items.*

these three quantifiers do not seem to define a natural class motivated by considerations independent of this rule, these three lexical items must be explicitly noted in the parsing grammar. Other such rules would include the rule that must note that exactly the word *a* followed by a word like *hundred* is not a determiner, but rather a form of the number "one," and all the rules for auxiliaries that must note that each of the forms of the helping verb *have*, for example, must be followed by the perfective form of the verb.

One possible implementation of this scheme might be as follows: Each element of a rule pattern will be viewed as a *demon*, an independent processing unit that continually attempts to match its target in whatever input representations it examines. Demons that search for any member of some *open* word class will trigger on the output of mediating processes that recognize tokens of specific lexical items in the incoming speech stream, and then somehow report on the word class of these items. Demons that search for individual closed class items, on the other hand, will trigger on occurrences of lexical items in the speech stream, triggering on either some kind of phonological representation, or perhaps even some abstracted representation of the speech waveform itself.

Returning to the main thread, let us assume that somehow all grammar rule patterns containing at least one closed class word detector fail to fire. This could result from the detectors themselves having been damaged or from the destruction of the connections between the detectors and the grammar patterns or from damage to the structures in the buffer encoding the information that the closed class word detectors need to operate. What would follow from such a deficit?

Assume that such a parser, with what I will call "Hypothetical Deficit I" (HD-I) is given as input the word string (1):

(1)   The small child could give a present to the teacher.

Were the parser fully functional, the lexical information it would use to construct the parse, given its grammar, is shown in (2), where each open class word is represented by its word class, and each closed class word is represented by itself.

(2)   The   ADJ   N   could   V   a   N   to   the   N.

Given that the parser can obtain no information about closed class words, *ex hypothesi*, what it sees as input is shown schematically in (3); it can determine the word classes of open class words, but closed class items are unidentified.

(3)   ?   ADJ   N   ?   V   ?   N   ?   ?   N.

Let us trace the parser's analysis of the input.

When the first word *the* enters the parser's buffer, no rule can fire, so the parser will simply stop, with further operation of the parser blocked by the unused input sitting in the first buffer cell. In such a situation, as discussed in an earlier section, the parser will output whatever partial structures it has built and reinitiate parsing. In this case, the only partial structure is the word token itself, which the parser will pass on to semantics.

I will assume here, consistent with the results of Bradley and her coworkers, that the processes responsible for the recognition of open class lexical items will recognize closed class word tokens if (and only if) the special closed class procedure is nonfunctional, and will return to the parser the *word class* of closed class words just as it does for open class words. Note, however, that this information is not useful to the parser, since the parsing grammar is expressed in terms of closed class lexical items themselves and not their word classes. Semantics, I assume, however, will know that the determiner *the* was in the input stream, although it will not know what structure the determiner modifies.

The word *small* will now enter the parser's buffer, labeled by the open class lexicon as an adjective. (For the sake of simplicity, I ignore here the problem of lexical ambiguity, e.g. that *small* can be a noun as well as an adjective. For the description at hand, the complications introduced by the handling of this kind of lexical ambiguity are not crucial.) One of the rules that initiates the parsing of noun phrases will trigger, and *small* will be attached to the new NP node and removed from the buffer. When *child* enters the buffer labelled as a noun, it will similarly be attached.

Now the closed class item *could* enters the buffer. No rule for continuing an NP will fire in this configuration, so a special "default" rule (a rule of very low priority whose pattern matches all configurations) now fires, dropping the completed NP into the buffer. Perhaps the default rule will note that *small child* is not a well-formed NP unless it is a vocative, but because the parser is deterministic, it will assume that the NP, though not well formed, has the best structure that can be assigned to it and will continue regardless. The buffer will now contain the NP *small child* in the first buffer cell and the token *could* in the second, as shown in Figure 6.7.

Note that while the completion of the NP at this point is correct, it is serendipitous. If this parser were fully functional, it would have noted, in effect, that the lexical item *could* cannot continue an NP, and would therefore com-

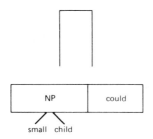

FIGURE 6.7. *The state of the HD-I parser after "could" enters the buffer.*

plete the NP. In the case of this impaired parser, no rule for continuing the NP can fire simply because no rule can be triggered by a closed class word. Had the word following *child* been *who*, a fully functional parser would have begun to construct a relative clause as part of the NP, while this Hypothetical Deficit I parser would terminate the NP incorrectly because *who*, like *could*, is closed class.

What would happen next in the case of a normal parser will depend heavily on exactly how the grammar is written. In the current grammar of English used by the operational Parsifal system, the rule schematized in Figure 6.3 discussed earlier will be triggered, initiating a sentence structure on the basis of an initial NP followed by any type of verb. A rule of this form is useful given a deterministic system because it ensures that an initial NP is followed by a verb before committing itself to the construction of a full sentence, as opposed to some fragment. Given the "multiplying out" of the grammar by the closed class lexicon that I assume here, the grammar will contain not only the rule shown in Figure 6.3, but also one rule for each auxiliary verb, with an action identical to the rule of Figure 6.3 and with an identical pattern for the first buffer position but that triggers on that particular auxiliary in the second buffer position.

Assuming that no other rule than the rule that matches an NP followed by *could* will match the configuration of the parser in the normal case, no rule at all will match in our HD-I parser. While the first pattern element will match the NP in the initial position of the buffer, the second pattern element, which calls for a match against the closed class item *could* is blocked from matching *ex hypothesi*. Once again, therefore, the parser stops, and is forced to flush its buffer before continuing onward. Two fragments are therefore handed to semantic processing: a tree structure corresponding to the defective NP *small child* and the token *could*, labeled as an auxiliary by the full lexicon.

And so the parse will continue. The parser will initiate some larger substructure each time an open class word reaches the beginning of the buffer, but will be blocked from adding any further subconstituents to that structure when some closed class item enters the buffer. Each time a closed class item enters the buffer, therefore, the parser will be forced to close whatever yet incomplete structure it is building, flush it from the buffer, and send that fragment onward to semantic processing. All strings of contiguous open class items that can be incorporated into larger structures will be chunked together into larger grammatical units, but these units will often be incomplete internally and most likely not connected syntactically into some even larger grammatical structure.

After this process has been completed, the input given in (1) will have been assigned the partial structure sketched in (4), where "?" flags a closed class word whose identity the parser could not ascertain. The net result, as far as semantics is concerned, is the string of partial analyses shown in (5).

(4) ? [$_{NP}$ small child]   ?   [$_{VP}$ give]   ?   [$_{NP}$ present]   ?   ?   [$_{NP}$ teacher]

(5) a [$_{NP}$ small child] could [$_{VP}$ give] a [$_{NP}$ present]   to the [$_{NP}$ teacher]

A few general observations about the form of this output are in order. Note that although the structures assigned are partial, they happen to be correct. This is somewhat surprising at first glance, given that any structure with a function word internally will be broken into two pieces, each fragment of which might be assigned some structure by the parser. While one might suspect that this correct assignment of structure is heavily dependent on choice of example, there are some tendencies in the syntax of English that strongly enhance the likelihood of correct NP structures, at least. Chief among these is the tendency of closed class words to group at the beginning of a larger constituent. Thus, the basic noun phrase cluster extending from the determiner and quantifiers of the NP to the head noun consists of a string of function words (determiners, quantifiers, and the like) followed by a string of open class words (adjectives and nouns). The open class tail of the NP, containing, one could argue, the meat of the semantic content of the NP, will thus be correctly structured into one coherent NP fragment.

It is also worthy of mention that this kind of deficit, in some sense, inverts the functional role of closed class words in syntax. Normally, the closed class words serve as the "glue" that holds the content of a sentence together; these words are known as *function words* exactly because they typically serve to indicate the function of the surrounding more contentful grammatical structures in larger syntactic entities. In the case of this hypothetical deficit, however, the function words serve to divide rather than connect the surrounding structures; where they served before as connectors, here they serve as wedges.

A Sketch of Semantic Analysis of Fragmentary Input

We must now ask what semantics will be able to make of this input. For this purpose, let us assume for the sake of definiteness that the semantic representation of an utterance consists of a predicate–argument structure that directly represents the predication encoded in the syntax. The semantic predicate will typically represent the meaning of the verb, while the arguments of that predicate will represent the meaning of the noun phrases and prepositional phrases in the utterance, with the specific argument each NP or PP fills indicating its semantic function in the larger predication. Let us also assume that there are semantic restrictions associated with the prototypic frame for that predicate, indicating the kind of thing that can serve in each given argument position for that predicate. The predicate–argument structure associated with the relevant meaning of the verb *give* used in our example is shown in (6); it derives from the analysis of Fillmore (1968). (I will follow the convention that all upper case indicates a semantic entity; thus GIVE is a semantic predicate while *give* is a verb of English.) This indicates that this meaning of *give* involves an agent, the giver, which must be animate, an object, the thing given, which can be a kind of physical object, animate or not, and a patient, the animate entity to which the object is given.

(6) GIVE
     AGENT +animate-entity
     PATIENT +animate-entity
     OBJECT +physical-object

The account that I will now give is both incomplete and highly tentative; it is intended only to show how the limited amount of partial information supplied by syntax can be used, within a specific framework, to create some reasonable guesses as to the intended message.

Processes responsible for constructing semantic representations of linguistic input could respond in many ways, given only a string of partial structures from syntax. Semantics could simply balk entirely, on the grounds that it expects a single coherent parse tree from syntax and cannot handle this kind of unanalyzed structure. This seems to be simply contrary to fact; people seem to be quite facile at pulling syntactic fragments snatched out of conversation together into a plausible whole. Furthermore, such an approach contradicts the principle of graceful degradation previously cited. Another possibility, and the one that I shall illustrate here, is that semantics could simply try to do what it can with the pieces that it has available. Given the semantic frame for *give* shown in (6), what will semantics do in this latter case with the pieces shown above in (4)? (Yet another possibility: Semantics might make use of the order in which the fragments appear to make sense of the utterance, possibly in conjunction with information in the semantic frame that indicates, for example, that the agent is typically the first NP in the sentence. Note, however, that such information is quite exactly a rudimentary form of syntax. This possibility will not be pursued here; the reader should be able to fill in a sketch of such an approach for him- or herself, given what follows.)

Without order information, semantics has access to the set of pieces (in no particular order) *small child, teacher, present, give, a, the, the, to, could,* analyzed as 3 NPs, a verb, 3 determiners, a preposition, and an auxiliary verb, respectively. (Remember that semantics has access to the word class of closed class words, as already discussed.) A possible sketch of what semantics might do given this information follows.

Semantics will note that the verb *give* is present, and will try to fill the frame of the semantic predicate GIVE as well as it can. (Perhaps it will try to fill predicates corresponding to other senses of give as well; let us assume for simplicity that semantic restrictions will block these other predicates from being successfully filled.) Given the semantic restrictions associated with the frame of give, which calls for its arguments to be two animate entities and one physical object, semantics can see that the predicate/argument structure must be either

GIVE(AGENT: SMALL CHILD; PATIENT: TEACHER
   OBJECT: PRESENT)

or

GIVE(AGENT: TEACHER; PATIENT: SMALL CHILD;
   OBJECT: PRESENT)

I ignore here both the encoding of the modality of *could* and the internal details of the representations of the meanings of the NPs, but the representation will encode, for instance, that the child is small. Thus, it can determine that it is likely that either some small child could give some present to some teacher or else some teacher could give some present to some child, but not which. If the conversation were about the child's birthday, the choice between them could be made easily on pragmatic grounds.

The key point here is simply that given this kind of partial information coupled with semantic knowledge, semantics can construct a reasonable partial account of what is going on. If the verb were not reversible in the sense that the agent and patient of the verb are both animate, and thus the sentence could be put either way, then the meaning reconstructed by this process would be exactly correct. Such a result is consistent with the experiments reported by Caramazza and Zurif (1978), showing that Broca's aphasics correctly comprehend sentences containing center embedded relative clauses if and only if both the matrix clause and the relative clause are not reversible in the sense used here.

A Potential Problem with HD-I as a Model of Broca's Aphasia

I have shown that an HD-I parser fragments much natural language input in a way that, in conjunction with some rather standard suppositions about semantic processing, is at least reminiscent of the comprehension deficit that is part of the symptom complex of Broca's aphasia. However, there are situations in which such a parser performs extremely well; too well, it might seem, to model the comprehension deficit shown by Broca's aphasics. Whether these predictions of the HD-I model are contrary to fact, I believe, must await the outcome of the relevant experiments; experimental evidence relevant to the issue to be raised in this section is, as far as I know, scanty and mixed as to interpretation. (cf. Kolk [1978] for some relevant data.) Indeed, the real point to be made here is that because this model is precise, its implications can be determined with enough detail to facilitate the formulation of potential experiments to either support or falsify these predictions.

One potential problem with the HD-I model is this: Since the parser fragments text only because it cannot analyze closed class words, very long runs of open class words may well be correctly analyzed by the parser. For example, a long string of adjectives and adverbs followed by some noun–noun complex such as

    recent available airline flight guide

or

    big bright red car seat cushion cover

should be correctly analyzed by a HD-I parser.

Perhaps more counterintuitively, an HD-I parser will parse any sentence made up only of open class words absolutely without error. Thus, for instance, any of the following sentences will be fully and correctly analyzed by a HD-I parser:

    Mothers give children birthday presents.
    Big frogs inhabit small ponds.
    Hypothetical deficit I parsers correctly analyze open class word strings.

If this property is inconsistent with the comprehension deficit exhibited by Broca's aphasics, one assumption can be added to the HD-I model that will block this result, although such a move is admittedly somewhat ad hoc: One can stipulate that morphological analysis of verbs inserts into the parser's buffer independent morphemes for tense and aspect. Given that such morphemes should have the same properties as closed class words from the point of view of the parser, and given that any main verb has some such tense and aspect morpheme affixed to it, all main verbs would then cause fragmentation of the input for an HD-I parser. This, of course, would mean that no full sentence could be fully analyzed by an HD-I parser.

CONCLUSION

This chapter has explored just one possible deficit that could be inflicted upon the Parsifal model. Other possible deficits include severely truncating the stack and severely restricting buffer usage, both of which will lead to patterns of syntactic fragmentation that vary somewhat from the pattern exhibited by the HD-I parser discussed here. In each case, the details of the manifestation of the deficit will depend on auxiliary assumptions about adjuncts to the structural aspects of syntactic processing, such as lexical ambiguity resolution and the like; it is because of the complexity of the assumptions that must be made that these other deficits have been avoided in this initial exploration.

Also, I am not unaware that this account, for example, rests on the somewhat problematic assumption that the comprehension deficit of the syndrome of Broca's aphasia is functionally unrelated to the production difficulties that are also included in the syndrome. But it is in some sense irrelevant to the point of this chapter that no strong claim can be made, or is made, about the veracity of this account. It is too early to suggest at this time that this model is correct; the evidence is simply too weak. The crucial suggestion of this chapter, however, is that this may be a theory of the right form; this chapter is intended to illustrate that the manifestations of simple functional deficits upon cognitive mechanisms can lead to manifestations so complex that they can only be explicated by consideration of models worked out in enough specific detail to see what the second- and third-order consequences of the deficit might be. The consequences of simple deficits inflicted upon complex systems are far from simple.

ACKNOWLEDGMENTS

I would like to thank Michael Arbib, David Caplan, Mark Liberman, and Edgar Zurif, variously, for valuable discussion of the ideas contained herein, for comments on earlier drafts of this chapter, and for general encouragement of this enterprise.

REFERENCES

Bobrow, R. J., and Webber, B. L. (1980). Knowledge representation for syntactic/semantic processing. *Proceedings of the first Annual National Conference on Artificial Intelligence*, American Association for Artificial Intelligence.
Bradley, D. C., Garrett, M. F., and Zurif, E. B. (1979). Syntactic deficits in Broca's aphasia. In D. Caplan (Ed.), *Biological studies of mental processes*. Cambridge, Massachusetts: MIT Press.
Caramazza, A., and Zurif, E. (1978) Comprehension of complex sentences in children and aphasics. In A. Caramazza and E. Zurif (Eds.), *Language acquisition and language breakdown*. Baltimore, Maryland: Johns Hopkins Press, 145–162.

Fillmore, C. J. (1968). The case for case. In E. Bach and R. T. Harms (Eds.), *Universals in linguistic theory*. New York: Holt, Rinehart & Winston.

Kolk, H. (1978). Judgment of sentence structure in Broca's aphasia. *Neuropsychologia*, 1978, *16*, 617–625.

Marcus, M. P. (1980). *A theory of syntactic recognition for natural language*. Cambridge, Massachusetts: MIT Press.

Newell, A., and Simon, H. A. (1972). *Human problem solving*. Englewood Cliffs, New Jersey: Prentice-Hall.

Norman, D., and Bobrow, D. (1974). On Data-limited and Resource-limited Processes. Technical Report # CSL74-2, Xerox Palo Alto Research Center, May, 1974.

Zurif, E., Caramazza, A., and Meyerson, B. (1972) Grammatical judgments of agrammatic aphasics. *Neuropsychologia*, *10*, 405–417.

7

Production Strategies: A Systems Approach to Wernicke's Aphasia[1]

Pierre M. Lavorel

This chapter provides a theoretical perspective on linguistic processing and control during lexical retrieval and sentence building.

Most of the ideas that will be put forward here rest on clinical observation and experiments conducted in Lyon, France. But we shall try to abstract ourselves from the intricacy of natural phenomena and relate the conceptual model to previous studies in the linguistics and artificial intelligence literature.

Wernicke's aphasia has been opposed frequently to other types of aphasia as essentially characterized by a large comprehension deficit. It is, therefore, not possible to deal with the patient's production strategies without considering the general problem of the varying efficiency of the human brain as it processes information that constitutes the mental dictionary for production AND for comprehension.

WERNICKE'S APHASIA SEEN AS A PROCESSING DEFICIT, NOT AS A KNOWLEDGE LOSS

Elsewhere (Lavorel, 1980), I have argued that in order to give a satisfactory account of production deficits in posterior aphasias, it is not sufficient to study paraphasias and anomia. Isolated phenomena like paraphasias should in fact be considered as parts of a set of difficulties (this is in fact a familiar statement for neurologists who look for syndromes). Indeed, the visible signs may only be the

[1]The research reported in this chapter was supported in part by a grant from the Alfred P. Sloan Foundation in support of the University of Massachusetts Program in Language and Information Processing while the author was a visiting scientist at Amherst. This chapter has been improved by interaction with Michael Arbib and Helen Gigley of the University of Massachusetts, and I wish to express my thanks to them.

135

NEURAL MODELS OF
LANGUAGE PROCESSES

tip of an iceberg of processing limitations. **Paragrammatism** for instance, which has often been also considered and analyzed as an isolated symptom seems to be closely related with the breakdown of the neuropsychological functions that cause anomia and paraphasias.

I shall start with some remarks about how paragrammatism and paraphasia are often connected in Wernicke's aphasia, thus hoping to establish a performance-oriented outlook upon Wernicke's aphasia which I shall then partly model.

The Fallacy of the Independent Syntactic Deficit in Wernicke's Aphasia

Several studies (e.g., Ducarne and Preneron, 1980) have implied that paragrammatism is a synonym for "dyssyntactic aphasia" and is characterized by a construal deficit affecting the phrase structure of sentences. One should first distinguish between paraphasic and paragrammatic syndromes which are associated with a parietal or parietooccipital lesion and those which are not. Lesions affecting areas 39 and 40 (Brodmann's classification) may be found to DIRECTLY affect phrase structure processing, by making mental representations difficult (and therefore any calculus of word order or preorder will fail when it is complex) (Luria and Tsvetkova, 1967). But posterior lesions of area 22 associated with phonemic and verbal paraphasias do not DIRECTLY affect those cognitive functions that may be necessary to produce or comprehend syntactic structures. The following experiments were conducted in 1978 in my laboratory with the help of an CII, IRIS 80 computer and of an IBM 365-65 computer: Samples of paragrammatic language produced by temporal lobe Wernicke's aphasics were analyzed using successively a parser with an immediate constituent grammar based on a 5000-word subset of normal language (AMEDE, Lavorel, 1979) and another parser with syntactic–semantic rules AND either dependency rules or lexical context filters (PIAF, Courtin, 1973). The immediate constituent parser accepted 96% of Wernicke's aphasics' language as grammatical but often ambiguous (frequently, alternate structures were calculated). However, the same utterances were rejected as "incorrect" by the second system which basically relies upon semantic-government relations (see Tesnière, 1966).

This study having specified more clearly what is to be analyzed in Wernicke's area syntactic aphasia, I was left with a strong lexical hypothesis to investigate. This hypothesis was that paragrammatism is either the consequence of lexicosemantic errors upon the sequence of words and of phrases, or of incoherence secondary to cascading errors and control difficulties. When a patient writes (the following examples are translated from a French corpus in Lavorel,

1980a): *Near the nursing home there is a* **contractor made   bricks** (*of* was erased by the patient who was not too sure about it), *contractor* is paraphasia for *building*. But the ensuing impression (especially if *of* is erased, after *bricks*) is one of sentence or discourse incoherence. In many cases, such errors in long sentences, when they accumulate, lead to changes in the sequence of ideas, and all sorts of digressions or diverging paths make sentences LOOK ungrammatical or nonsensical:

> *I felt it was hot; so I went to see the* **hot produced** *by the thermo-meter*   (paraphasic perseveration).

In some cases, a similar impression may even be given by recorded normal conversation when speakers tend to talk loosely and be somewhat paraphasic themselves.

The Fallacy of the Independent Semantic Memory Deficit

The bulk of this chapter will be devoted to the study of some **processing functions** that could be impaired in Wernicke's temporal aphasia in such a way that the retrieval of words and of their combinatory properties would become difficult or erroneous. It is only by understanding this processing deficit that we shall be able to approach its consequences upon the structure of an utterance. Thus, I shall address the problem of the identification and selection of **lexical morphemes** with cues about what they should mean; more particularly, I will be concerned only with morphemes that constitute "open classes of words," bearing in mind that some, like prepositions and modal verbs, may be memorized as "open class items" and as "closed class items." It is to be understood that phonic, as well as syntactic or logical, information helps in retrieving (or is retrieved together with) a lexical item. Language research tends increasingly to emphasize the fact that the lexicon must contain much information about the syntactic or logical patterns in which a given item may be inserted. Ray Jackendoff's x̄ syntax is one example (Jackendoff, 1977). Maurice Gross's (1975) distributional constraints provide another. Categorial grammars themselves have always defined all linguistic categories except sentence and noun with reference to knowledge about their left or right environment (Lewis, 1972).

These observations lead the neurolinguist to assume that the mechanism often covered up by the "mental dictionary" notion is not only concerned with a calculation of the adequacy of the form and of the content of words. The "mental dictionary" programs must also include some recall of remembered contextual properties of lexical entries. These properties might be represented in an artificial lexicon by an ensemble of patterns like the following for *to roll:*

FORM
  Articulatory and phonic pattern
  Morphological features and associated phonological properties
  Graphic pattern and associated orthographic properties

CONTENT
  Denotational pattern
  Semantic contexts
  Personal and sociocultural connotations

SYNTACTIC PROPERTIES (notation used : $\bar{\mathrm{X}}$ convention, as in Jackendoff, 1977).
  Category: verb predicate of the class (X, Y, Z)
  Thematic or casual schema:
  1. EX: *The snowball is rolling down the slope.*
        N (ERGATIVE) → ROLL → $\begin{cases} \text{COMP CIRCUMSTANCE)} \\ \emptyset \end{cases}$
  2. EX: *John is rolling the snowball down the slope.*
        N (AGENTIVE) → ROLL → N (OBJ) → $\begin{cases} \text{COMP}\dots \\ \emptyset \end{cases}$

Some evidence can easily be found of the rich information patterns associated with the recall of one morpheme. I shall mention two examples. (a.) The **categorial characteristics** of morphemes are necessary to insert words into a syntactic mold. If those characteristics are fuzzied or confounded, the insertion process may be faulty or even impossible:

Starting France, start by car .... **From** *Paris* **for** *20 hours.*

where: [COMP *starting France*] may well be only a verbal paraphasia for [COMP *leaving France*], but [Š *start by* ...] may be much more intricate paraphasia where *start* is used instead of an adverb plus a verb (*we first took by a car*), thus adding a categorical shift to a semantic error. [?Prep **from** *Paris* **for** *20 hours*] may be caused by some degrading of the categorial properties of an Š or an S because Prep and V properties are not clearly felt as distinct. The utterance should have been something like [S *we left Paris and drove for 20 hours*], or [S *the trip from Paris lasted 20 hours*].
  Similarly, in

When I go hiking in the woods, I try to walk **for a long slow.**

we find a transformation (or a distortion) where conceptual images G_i and G_j become merged:

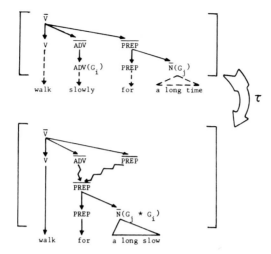

The main paragrammatic impression comes partly from the paraphasic substitution *time* → *slow(ly)* and partly from the ADV → [$_{ADV?}$ categorial slip on *slow* in the lexical retrieval process.

(b.) Another aspect of relational pattern misselection is the poor retrieval and use of **thematic patterns** (or case patterns) associated with verbs and prepositions. In Wernicke patients with this selection deficit, it may all end up with irrelevant case marking (where, in English, prepositions are accessed with improper specifications):

> *He knew the child* **on** *whom he had walked.*
> *A river* **in which** *there is a bridge.*

But even if the lexicon is viewed as including much nonsemantic information, the lexical deficit hypothesis does not itself explain everything in temporal aphasias. Another well-known shortcoming of Wernicke's aphasics is poor transient memory, or what might correspond to limited memory space in processing. Frequently, they cannot repeat sequences of more than two or three words; they cannot process operations where more than two or three actions or two or three objects are involved. This is particularly true of aphasics with large temporal lesions extending far back and up towards the angular gyrus, or affecting the underlying fasciculi—for instance this patient whose short-term memory was found to be very poor:

PSYCHOLOGIST: *What are these dogs doing?*
PATIENT: [speaking quickly] *They follow the interesting the that the the . . . Hm the there is a scent with their noses near for the ground . . .*
PSYCHOLOGIST: *Near the ground.*

PATIENT: *Yes they follow because they want of the catch rabbits . . . Hm, these woods in these woods, to, to, to hide rabbits . . .*

The video-tape shows that the patient is desperately trying to remember the words that he intended to concatenate into a sentence. This effect combines with the lexical deficits in contributing to the impression that syntactic knowledge might be defective.

JARGONAUT, A RESEARCH TOOL IN LANGUAGE PROCESSING

The human language system is so organized that it may fail even when it is not lesioned. Or it may, in the case of a poetic utterance, produce unexpected outputs which have never been encountered before and evoke surprise and admiration.

Starting from these observations, I concluded that it is necessary to conceive a SIMULATION MODEL which will not always yield the same determined output in the same given language situation. Some obvious questions are what dynamics make the system nondeterministic; what could physically degrade this nondeterministic system; how could its knowledge and programs evolve in time?

Block Diagrams Help to Subdivide Problems

Lexical retrieval is a highly complex job. It consists in FINDING IN MEMORY A MORPHOLOGICAL VALUE for some still unexpressed ensemble of **concepts** which together form a **cognitive image**. When I say *horse* (unless I am just reproducing an unknown sequence of phonemes heard before, or generating random sounds and rhythms), I visualize one particular horse, or I have in mind a sort of conceptual definition of that animal, or some learned notions about the English morpheme *horse*, or the French morpheme *cheval*. In other words, there is no initiation of linguistic performance if there is not a purpose on the part of the speaker (to say or write something for some reason), and a more or less sophisticated internal schema or representation of at least the beginning of the message. The matching of these ideas and of phonological (acoustic or articulatory) or graphic (visual or motor) knowledge can be conceived in many ways, as for example in Figure 7.1. In this figure, "memory" remains unknown; it is not exclusively linguistic. "Matching" is downstream of another process called "speech planning," which has access to "memory"; but "matching" also has access to "memory" via a (virtual or real) short-term lexicon which is being activated (or built) during one speech event (which could be thought of as a linguistically oriented disinhibition of long-term memory).

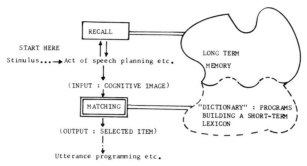

FIGURE 7.1. *Rough building code for lexical selection processor.*

In the case of other discourse stimuli, as in the case of dictation or reading, the initial input is a morphological pattern, but what in Figure 7.1 is labeled as "act of speech planning, etc." will take place. A "cognitive image" will be used jointly with the (heard or seen) stronger morphological definition of the target words which will facilitate the matching or complicate it when the subject has some perceptual or associative deficits which distort the morphological pattern.

But Figure 7.1. has to be improved. First, some control process of the matching may seem to be necessary if matching cognitive images and lexical entries is a little tricky. It may lead to several correction paths like I and II in Figure 7.2., which, respectively, recycle an unsuccessful "cognitive image" or reformulate it inside a new utterance planned to replace the aborted one. Second, Figure 7.1. should specify what the computation called "lexicon-building" could look like. The mental dictionary is more likely to be an active remembrance program than an ordered catalogue as Forster (1978) saw it. This very powerful documentary center certainly deals with the data bank of past experi-

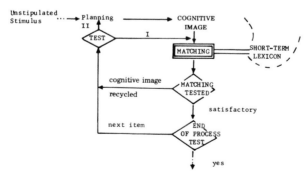

FIGURE 7.2. *An elementary looped system. Rectangular boxes represent more or less complex processes; diamonds represent tests and decisions between alternative pathways.*

ence which has left what might be conceived of as perceptual (acoustic, visual, etc.), as well as linguistic, motor, proprioceptive, traces, themselves often equated and integrated into abstract knowledge about what we might call "physical, psychological, and anthropological worlds." We obviously require a basic model of memory management that will incorporate a lot of physiological constraints on its inputs, and perhaps some open options as to what logical code and reasoning neuropsychological subsystems (of the parietal lobes, of temporo-occipito-temporal juncture areas, of frontal and prefrontal areas?) can develop in order to learn how to organize and remember a few things, how to forget a lot, and eventually how to retrieve what may be useful for a task by activating, disinhibiting, or calculating functional information.

Whatever this model may be (and there are many candidates), it must be understood that both cognitive images used in planning and lexical definition are calculated from a common background of knowledge. (A good overall state-of-the-art assessment is presented in Edelman and Mountcastle, 1978. For updated models, see Lavorel and Arbib, forthcoming. An AI model can be found in Fahlman, 1979.) Only, the purpose of the "act of speech planning" is necessarily urgent, somewhat synthetic and perhaps open to modification, whereas the selection of words, which comes later, is less urgent, certainly more sophisticated, and should converge to only one solution. So, the conceptual input into the "matching" process postulated here will or will not give graphic and acoustic cues about the morphemes that can be associated with the cognitive images being formed. Some of us will for instance expect any kind of pasta to have a long name full of vowels and ending in $-i$.

The lexical retrieval task can now be understood as a matching of conceptual targets and of lexical definitions, and simultaneously as some sort of interactive specification or simplification of initial cognitive images. This is why in Figure 7.2, I and II control pathways together with the tests that determine them, appear to be essential for relevant and pertinent selection (and have to be analyzed thoroughly).

Let us now concentrate on the subsystem around the "matching" box, where some target is going to be equated to a linguistic code (in one or several passes).

JARGONAUT, A Conceptual Model

A system that simulates lexical retrieval will be described here as a complex device comparing conceptual planning and lexical definitions (whatever their nature may be, conceptual or other). As an example, I shall comment on the selection of lexical morphemes by a system using conceptual patterns that only have to do with the denotational value of words. Some parts of the process which will be presented here have been implemented on a CII, IRIS 80 computer, others on a CDC 6600 computer, and others on an IBM 360-65 computer. However, JARGONAUT has not yet been programmed as a whole. I shall thus restrict my comments to the concepts that have been used to design the system.

In this theoretical system, a set of **conceptual formulas** will be generated from a vocabulary of "primitive concepts" with "categorial rules" (a categorial grammar of the type recommended by Bar-Hillel, 1964):

$$\left.\begin{array}{l} \vartheta \text{ concept} \\ \mathscr{G} \text{ category} \end{array}\right\} \rightarrow \text{conceptual formulas}$$

The nature of such a grammar can be shown with an example. Let us suppose that ⟨*horse*⟩ and ⟨*young*⟩ are primitive concepts (angle brackets will be used to differentiate the conceptual level from the word level); then the conceptual formula:

$$\langle\langle \; n \mid (n) \text{ young } \rangle \text{ n horse } \rangle$$

possibly defines *colt*, n being a characterization of the category including ⟨horse⟩ and n | (n) being a characterization of the category including concepts expressing attributes of n's, like ⟨young⟩. Read:

n	|	(n)
form an "n"	if there is an	"n" to the right (Bar-Hillel, 1964).

This categorial metalanguage, using "⟨ ⟩" brackets, categories like n, and relations like "|" and "( )" to represent the structure of conceptual formulas, is as it were the abstract code of JARGONAUT, an imaginary lexical selector. Categorial language appears to be practical because it can be used as a representation of classification trees used by thesauri as well as of dictionary definitions that are sentences. It might be useful to point out here that "primitive concept" is only a tag for actual words of the language which have proved frequent, useful to define others, and unambiguous: They have been raised to the level of metalanguage. A concept may be connected to others in order to form a conceptual formula or a structure of conceptual formulas. But it may also disappear or be decomposed itself if it no longer satisfies the three conditions stated here. So, concepts are either primitive or composite.

Let us now postulate the existence of an automaton that can identify two subsets of conceptual formulas, namely, purely conceptual formulas (**conceptual formulas**, or Cs for short) and conceptual formulas associated with lexical morphemes (**lexical formulas**, or Ls for short). Any C will be considered as an abstract equivalent for a prelinguistic message to be translated in a sort of interactive manner into a given human language. Any L will be considered as the abstract denotation of an entry in the activated lexicon of this given language.

Basically, the procedural plan could be schematized by Figures 7.3, 7.4, and 7.5. In this representation, we find a choice of sequential or of simultaneous

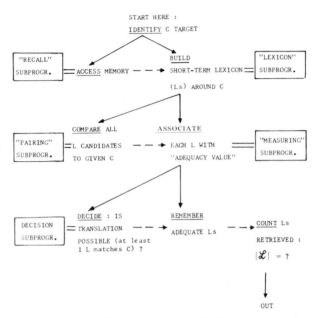

FIGURE 7.3. *The matching process (represented as a network of successive or simultaneous actions for easy reading). The parts of JARGONAUT that have been implemented on a computer system are indicated in the Appendix. But this diagram can be read without any reference to actual computing tricks; it merely states what processing steps are likely to be taken.*

processing. This might be of interest for further research. Furthermore, as was indicated in Figure 7.1, the "lexicon" is a short-term construction which is built and rebuilt as a speech event is being carried on. "Access memory" with one cue which is C (one conceptual formula) means that some kind of parallel search is propagated through the knowledge network (representing memorized data) with one cue which is C. "Build lexicon" means that a small lexicon will be ready (built or modified if it already exists) in order to incorporate many items conceptually related to C. It can be materialized here as anything from a transient stack to a more lasting complex space. Each entry (L) is extracted from long-term memory and has at least a "morphological representation" and a "conceptual image" attached to it. For example, | #koult# |... , and ⟨⟨ ... young⟩ ⟨ ... animal⟩ ⟨ ... in ranch⟩⟩ can be one of the possible definitions of a colt.

Some of the subprograms in Figure 7.3 will be commented upon later because they are specific to computer systems and probably not of interest for current problems in neuropsychology (see Appendix).

As for the decision phase (in Matching), it is a well-known issue, for mathematical psychologists have devoted much time to it (preference–indifference models in Lavorel, 1980c and Luce, 1956).

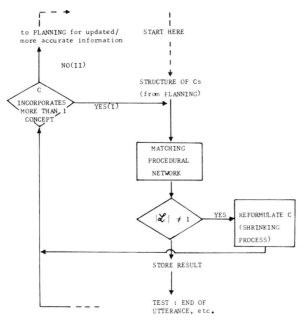

FIGURE 7.4. *Matching control: Rectangular boxes are processes, diamonds are tests for alternate pathways. The first test after "matching . . ." ($|\mathscr{L}| \neq 1$) means "is the total number of lexical morphemes selected not equal to one?" and if so, selection will have to be done again after having reformulated the target, that is, C, the conceptual formula. The second test on the left (just in case C has been shrunk too much) acquires or revises concepts at the planning level.*

What do we know of the actual processing control of lexical selection by the neuropsychological system? Are all these pathways relevant? "Structures of Cs," or "structures of conceptual formulas," are just an input which is a more or less clear purpose to say or write something to someone else. Such an approximation of a cognitive image should in fact be paired with a formulation of

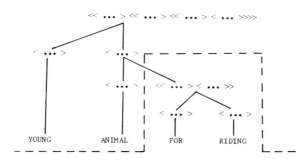

FIGURE 7.5. *How a conceptual formula can be pruned.*

presuppositions and prejudices about the communication context (in order to account for discursive and rhetorical phenomena that affect a choice among equally convenient words). But what is more important to understand at this stage is that "structures of conceptual formulas" are not really upstream of lexical selection and that the "II" control pathway in Figure 7.4 materializes interaction phenomena made obvious when subjects update, replan, or abort their utterances while they are halfway through delivery:

What is interesting is that the first test after "Matching," together with the **shrinking device**, depicts the difficulty arising from the fact that if comparison and decisions are not made in a loose way, words and ideas do not always match one another (words do not always express ideas satisfactorily, ideas may be too vague, etc.). Then, the shrinking device is a processing equivalence to what happens in the mind. Some INACCURACIES ARE PRODUCED AS A RESULT OF A NORMAL PROCESS which takes place when the system is in difficulty for a number of reasons and does not plan to run the RISK OF INADEQUACY. When asked to name or to comment upon an overelaborate impressionistic picture, we often want to form an idea of it as a whole and we do away with some details. The more difficult something is to talk about, the more we want to step backward and wink at it from afar, in order to merge details into a simple pattern. The same happens for all recognition tasks that have to be followed by a verbal characterization (comments on sculpture, music, speeches, books, etc.). When the brain cannot find a word for conceptual representations which are too elaborate, it must shrink them. In the case of intricate prelinguistic conceptual structures we do not know what shrinking really is. All we know is that subjects paradoxically come up with overgeneralization, like hyperonymic metonymies (e.g., *silver* for "very strange fork which looks like a fork but has only two prongs, and is very small, and might be used to eat snails"). Or they may come up with inaccurate or irrelevant words because they do not give enough consideration (or "weight") to specific features (e.g., *The Chinese eat* **swallows' nests** for "a specified kind of seaweed incidentally used by sea-swallows to build their nests"). The shrinking of conceptual formulas can easily be materialized by some pruning operations in a tree structure as in Figure 7.5.

This structure can be pruned at the level of the dashes (and so, instead of *colt*, one could fancy any young animal's name to be a second best solution. Shrunk formulas will, then, be considered as conceptual simplifications and should be distinguished from **freaks** which will be studied later as formulas transformed by a distorting effect like a lesion which interferes with access, calculation, retention, or information transfer at one or several levels of the system.

The processes and controls presented here owe much to systems programming actually implemented in automatic documentation (Salton, 1968) or in artificial intelligence (Bobrow and Winograd, 1977). They are not the actual clockworks of the brain but computing metaphors which help in a Cartesian decomposition of the set of operations or functions that the brain knows or has learned to implement (but in a different way), in order to achieve the lexical selection task. Studying the logics and the possible errors of these artificial processes seems to yield interesting hypotheses about the basic sets of operations that underlie such a wide field of linguistic performance as lexical access. Sentence building, or morphophonological transformations, can also be approached through successive approximative simulation experiments.

NEURAL MACHINES AND FUZZING EFFECTS

As a complement to systemic metaphors to neurolinguistics and neuropsychology, artificial intelligence has also provided some stimulating hypotheses about the neurophysiology of the associative areas of the posterior path of the dominant hemisphere. This research may provide complementary insight into the dynamics of anomia and of paraphasia in normal and aphasic subjects.

The Identification and Comparison of Linguistic Patterns in a Many-Level Calculus Carried Out by a Nondeterministic Machine that Learns as It Processes

In the last two decades, more and more experiments have been attempted (Arbib, 1964; Nilsson, 1965) to define the principles of all the machines (machines being taken as a very general term) that learn how to detect, discriminate, measure, describe, and recognize "patterns" or to segment input into "features" and assemble these again into "schemas" (Arbib, 1977).

From Pattern Classifiers to Layered Machines

I do not want to go into this vast field of research any more than is necessary. Let us only look at two of the figures found in Nilsson's *Learning machines* (1965) which reviews work that has served as a base for useful hypotheses in the study of adaptive networks. Developments of this line of research are exemplified by Anderson, Silverstein, Ritz, and Jones (1977) and Wood (1978). Figures 7.6 and 7.7 give an idea of neural net levels serving as bases for elementary operations in a layered machine. Some physiologists have claimed that there are neuron columns or modules that actually process information in a comparable way (Andersen and Eccles, 1962; Szentágothai, 1975). If only the structure of the arrays of cells working in the cortex was roughly a network or a forest of hierarchical trees, it could be assumed that the processing principles in pattern analysis might not be very different from what Nilsson has suggested.

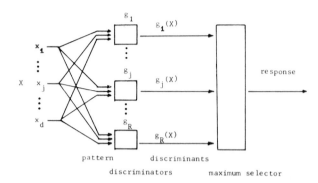

FIGURE 7.6. *Basic model for a pattern classifier. (From Nilsson, 1965, p. 7).*

Further Approaches to Networks

One of the insufficiencies of the learning machines of Figures 7.6 and 7.7 is that they play down the role of reafferent information. In order to really mimic what the cortical cells can do it is necessary to assess the part played by feedback loops (dashed lines in Figure 7.8). These loops would carry downstream information back to upstream neurons and, so to speak, "punish" (inhibit) or "reward" (stimulate) them instantaneously or later, according to whether their spikes match or do not match the final decision of the subnet they belong to.

This major function has been better approximated globally by the Amari–Arbib theory of conflicts between excitation and inhibition in columns and layers of cells of the frog's tectum (Amari and Arbib, 1977), building upon former models of Didday (1975), of Kilmer, McCulloch, and Blum (1969), and of Dev (1975). "Cooperation" and "competition" seem to play an important role. The Amari–Arbib model represents the regulation of hysteresis phenomena measured in vivo by physiologists. Amari and Arbib address equilibrium states and their stability, showing that when "a number of primitive competition models are interconnected" it is possible to establish output functions which represent the behavior of a layered neuron calculator as a threshold-controlling mechanism.

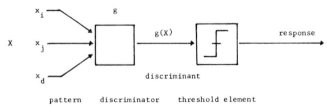

FIGURE 7.7. *Basic model for a pattern dichotomizer (2-category pattern classifier). (From Nilsson, 1965, p. 8.)*

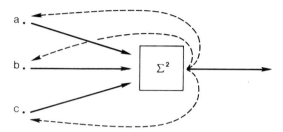

FIGURE 7.8. *Feedback Loops after a Summing Device.*

Arbib's and Manes's Fuzzing Machines

As they tried to tackle the more general question of the dynamics machines, Arbib and Manes (1976) introduced a new notion: an arbitrary "category" of abstract definitions of machines which unifies the theories of sequential machines, linear control systems, tree automata, and stochastic automata.

The fundamental theorem of Arbib and Manes (1976) proves that only very weak conditions are required on a specific input process to determine one class of theoretical machines or another in the Arbib–Manes category: Given a minimal realization theory, that is, a computational model, where all states are possible successors of the initial state, small changes can have striking consequences on the dynamics (on the style of processing) of the machine. Thus, machines like theoretical neuron nets can in some cases be assimilated to stochastic automata, or in other cases to arrays of deterministic machines if some of the conditions stipulated by Arbib and Manes are fulfilled or not. This basic assumption will be taken for granted in the following pages.

Theoretical variations in the classification of abstract representations of machines may correspond to real machine dynamics, for instance when "state-blurring" effects are observed. If the brain is considered as a processing machine, some "input dynamics" may act upon data, to use Arbib and Manes's (1975a,b) notions. We can finally imagine that the networks of the previous section would be characterized as anything from stochastic automata and tolerance automata (Arbib and Manes, 1975a) to nondeterministic fuzzy automata, depending on what inhibitory effects, or what parallel processing effects, or what learning effects may be verified.

The approaches presented on pages 147–148 may be thought of as electronic intelligence or as narrow-minded conjecture about the extremely complex biochemical, electric, and magnetic functions of neuron layers. However, after McCulloch and Pitts's (1943) artificial neurons, after Didday and Arbib's (1975) collicular model, we have had many specific models (eye movement control, spatial representations, and hand control) where ratiocination about intelligent functions has not infrequently later been proved right by research in neuroanatomy and in the physiology of neuron modules (see Mountcastle, 1978 and chapters by Goldman-Rakič and by Gordon, this volume). Theoretical models often help observation.

Moreover, even though I have sketched a complicated processing device allowing for a relative uncertainty of outputs in some cases, we may look for more sophisticated models in a few years' time. Remez (1979) implied that, in order to be efficient, neural nets probably had to take risks in their decisions. Feedforward may then also have to be thought of in order to account for the remarkable processing speed of humans in speech recognition. Specialization of subnetworks may also be a key to efficiency, as indicated by Capranica, Frishkopf, and Nevo (1973) or by Winter and Funkenstein (1973).

Fuzzy Semantics

I would like to integrate the theories discussed here and only consider the general hypothesis of a **fuzzing effect** of a calculation at one level or another of an intelligent machine (brain or computer). Note that the fuzzing concept is a natural concept, and use of the term does not endorse any particular theory of fuzzy sets. This fuzzing effect will be restricted in normal conditions and increased in case of a lesion or in other cases (which have something to do with learning, memorizing, or adaptation).

Although I cannot easily imagine how sets of abstract objects representing language can be defined as fuzzy, I will admit in a general statement about neurolinguistic processing that the (phonemic, graphic, or semantic) discrimination of linguistic units may become approximate or impossible in some performance situations. Everything then works as if a subset F of biological measurements (e.g., a subset of measurements on the sound pattern of words or a subset of measurements on the conceptual image of words) was misclassified, or not classified uniquely, by some fuzzing pattern recognition process δ:

$$F \xrightarrow{\delta} F'$$

Then, if I wish to give an intentional definition of F' (one that uses properties or features of elements in F'), it may be fit to associate to each feature f_i a confidence level or a weight w_{f_i} which will be defined here as a part of the $[0, 1]$ interval (Figure 7.9). This confidence level could vary possibly like the activity level of some pools of associative neurons (Erman, Hayes-Roth, Lesser, and Reddy, 1980) (Figure 7.10).

Now, in a production process related to the one described in Figure 7.3, at any moment of the selection program, one and only one conceptual formula C is being considered. It should now be added that the "planning" input in Figure 7.3 is probably not the only possible one. As soon as the lexical selection process

$$0 \qquad\qquad w_{f_i} \qquad 1$$

FIGURE 7.9. *Measure of the weight of a given feature* f_i.

starts, some lexical items L_i, L_k, etc., are retrieved and those already available Ls are associated with their definitions (conceptual formulas, morphophonological characterization). Such definitions may, just as well as the planned conceptual structure, serve as cues for next step selection. We therefore have to consider the hypothesis of parallel processing and of distributive control of searches in a fuzzing machine (Amari, 1971).

At this level, it is necessary to imagine possible conflicts between results (they might yield speech errors like blending [Frécon and Lavorel, 1980]), or a success of the fastest process (context-determined speech errors being again possible), or a late evaluation device which keeps the lexical morpheme L whose conceptual formula C is the best solution (in terms of probability for instance). But we shall not study this point in the present chapter because it has not been implemented and needs to be tested by some computer work.

After having gone a little further into the definition of either analytical or contextual selection of lexical units, we can study the fuzzing effect of the "neural machine" on the two types of inputs into the matching subprograms ("contextual theme" being opposed to "planned conceptual image" as in Figure 7.11).

Let us remember that every unit L in the short-term lexicon is described by a "conceptual formula" built on primitive concepts, which in fact are equivalent to a finite number of **features** (p. 143). Let us also remember that the "fuzzing effect" of neural calculation may associate different **weights** to features (Figure 7.9). The situation at time t of a given selection stage ("Match") can be represented as a decision to be made with regard to a characterization space where candidate units are more or less **distant** from one another:

With three features, units can be defined in a three dimensional space; for k features, units can be defined in a k-dimensional space. For any three objects in

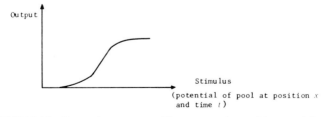

Output

Stimulus
(potential of pool at position x
and time t)

FIGURE 7.10. *Output from a monostable neuron pool at position x and time t.*

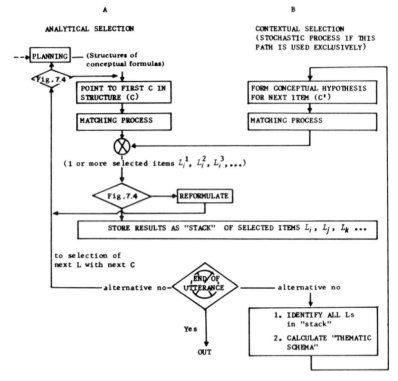

FIGURE 7.11. *Alternate A and B processes (for missing details see Figure 7.3.). "Theme" calculation may be carried out with the "stack" or with information from a pragmatic level not envisaged here. Evaluation of conflicting solutions may be necessary at ⊗. [Perhaps a "committee" evaluation unit as studied by Nilsson (1965) or a blackboard as implemented in HEARSAY. From Erman, Hayes-Roth, Lesser, and Reddy (1980)]*

the space, it is possible to establish an order, and perhaps a metric can be defined to evaluate **conceptual distances.** Many topological spaces can be thought of (Lavorel, 1975) which will suggest different types of metrics.

If, because of the fuzzing effect, morphemes are not clearly characterized (possibly not easily differentiated in the lexical space by their associated conceptual formulas), selection may be perturbed. *Sparrow* and *eagle* will rarely be confounded if they appear together in the lexicon, but *falcon* and *buzzard* may often be.

In the "contextual selection" alternative (Figure 7.11), this will occur when an estimated or conceptual target (thematically defined) is not sufficiently probable, often beccuse context itself is formed of ill-characterized or of ambiguous morphemes. For instance: ⟨ . . . *on the mat there is a black* . . . ⟩ may relate to a discourse whose theme is laying the table and *cat* will become a little less plausible.

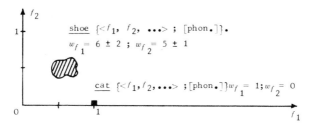

FIGURE 7.12. *Fuzzied cross-characterization of* shoe *and* cat. f_1: *⟨fits into the context on the mat there is a black . . .⟩* f_2: *⟨footwear⟨worn⟨⟨to play⟩⟨basketball⟩⟩⟩⟩*

HOW ERRORS ARE GENERATED

Given a JARGONAUT-type processing system and fuzzy characterization dynamics as they have been defined here, we will now study the errors that are normally expected when a selection decision is made about candidate items in a short-term lexicon.

Selection will be more certain and appropriate either if lexical morphemes are well defined and can be properly matched with conceptual formulas or, alternatively, if contextual thematic cues help to reach a preferable solution. On the other hand, selection will perhaps be uncertain or inappropriate if either lexical morphemes are ill defined (weights, for instance, greater than .3 and less than .7), or the contextual input is vague and fragmentary. In some cases it will be impossible (all solutions being indifferent). Slips of the tongue, verbal paraphasias, and even some types of semantic jargon can thus be produced by modifying the weights of individual features associated with lexical items. This may correspond to "threshold logic unit" decisions in Nilsson's neural machines which vary with the weights attributed to "discriminants" (see Appendix).

If no preference can be reached, three cases will be observed.

(a.) The machine may be blocked IN A CLOSED LOOP which yields no selection. This corresponds to sudden interruptions and long pauses in anomia where subjects just feel that there is a blank in their minds, till they plan another utterance.

(b.) The machine may ENUMERATE ALL EQUI-PREFERABLE UNITS. This corresponds to subjects who hesitate, suggest lists of possible words, and wait for the interlocutor to confirm or condemn.

(c.) A RANDOM CHOICE among the set of units in the short-term lexicon is a third possible behavior.

PREFERENCE can be reached even IF THE CHARACTERIZATION of lexical units or the characterization of conceptual images IS FAR FROM THE NORMS OF LANGUAGE AND OF THOUGHT. Such is the case of glossomania and of some cases of schizophasia where the patient's attention may be concentrated on connotations of words or on some unfathomable personal associations. This case, like the others, is illustrated in nonpathological language by cryptophasia prevailing among poets and initiatic sects who relish practises amounting to a *délire à deux*.

The machine may decide to select one unit. But because of a low threshold level while units are not distinct (features may be fuzzied), or because of some drastic pruning of the conceptual formulas, two types of errors are generated:

(a.) If only the HEAD FEATURES of the structures of conceptual formulas (which often happen to be generic) are taken into account, a slight mistake may crop up (*bus* instead of *subway*, *salt* instead of *pepper*, *spoon* instead of *fork*). These substitutions inside a class of related units are common in normal language and very frequent in all types of Wernicke aphasia. They might be called the **near miss phenomenon.**

(b.) If, on the contrary, GENERIC FEATURES happen to be pruned off or not clearly discriminated, the machine will carry out what Jakobson (1966) called a **metonymic substitution.** These errors can sometimes be difficult to retrace:

lock for *key*
to eat for *spoon*
salt for *salt-cellar*
smoke for *pipe*
for coffee for *cup*

The mechanics of the **Freudian slip** are related to this process; a specific feature of a conceptual image being for some private reason attributed more weight than generic features, an irresistible substitution may then take place (as in Type b errors) while other features are ruled out:

this session will be **cancelled,** instead of **opened**
(said by a French Prime Minister on the day when he was defeated by a vote).

But this process announces the possibility of a composition of elementary errors which will be defined later.

Metonymic processes are frequent in Wernicke's aphasia. They are also current in poetry, and at the origin of the evolution of languages (see *Oxford English Dictionary*: Bluestocking).

One other class of errors is particular to context-sensitive processes. It occurs when context is ill-perceived or pruned and cannot serve as a proper cue for lexical selection. A stochastic automaton implementing this would probably indifferently produce poetic metaphors, blunders, or semantic nonsense, depending on what features of the context are given more weight for selection (Lavorel, 1980c.).

The **blending** of two related solutions can be caused by parallel processing envisaged in Figure 7.9 when no evaluation control is applied to conflicting results.

Other blendings (of related or unrelated solutions) may be caused by sentence processing, as Garrett (1980) rightly implies. But this is obviously another type of speech error not exclusively characteristic of Wernicke's aphasics.

Deloche, Lecours, and Lhermitte (1973) have argued that first order speech errors, some of which have just been defined, can be combined into second order speech errors, etc. But theirs is a descriptive approach to slips of the tongue of all sorts: They basically justify their simulation program on a statistical frequency of errors without addressing the underlying dynamics which may distinguish how and where the mechanics of speech go wrong.

In the following section, I shall suggest a hypothesis about composite speech errors in pathology. In normal verbal behavior, which we are dealing with now, second order lexical paraphasias as well as anticipation probably take place during syntactic or phonological processing, or are related to praxic or motor control. As a matter of fact, Garrett (1980) recently suggested several arguments in favor of a sentence structure sensitive mechanism, and motor and praxic studies (Itoh, and al., 1980; Macneilage, 1980; Butterworth and Whittaker, 1980; Marin and Gordon, 1980) provided a few useful leads to control failures in articulatory dynamics. However two particular instances can be considered to be of interest in lexical selection mechanics and should be mentioned now. First, the frequent composition of a semantic paraphasia and of a phonemic paraphasia (a phenomenon that we chose not to study now because that would require more hypotheses about interaction between phonic cues and semantic cues in retrieval, e.g., *ambolus* for *ambulance*, heard in hospital). Second, the composition of two or more successive substitutions cascading into what looks sometimes like undecipherable riddles:

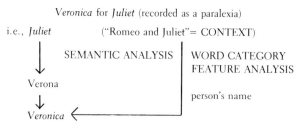

Although this last mechanism is characteristic of schizophrenia as well as of aphasia, it can also (in rare instances) be found as "normal" slips of the tongue.

THE EFFECT OF LESIONS UPON THE FUZZIED SYSTEM: DISTORTING TRANSFORMATIONS

After having designed a performance system for lexical recall as a processing unit that is always LIABLE TO GENERATE ERRORS, the impact of pathology will be studied.

A lesion itself never produces any kind of PATHOLOGICAL LANGUAGE. Pathological language is produced by what remains of the system when it is still functioning, or sometimes when it is running amok (*a*) without the help of a destroyed (or inaccessible) subsystem, (*b*) in the midst of parasitic phenomena due to the lesioned subsystem (noise, false alarm, resonance. . etc.).

Two Types of Pathology

(1) In clinical observation and classification of aphasia, we may find some statistical indications about what could be the role of the rest of the brain when there are temporal, temporooccipital, temporoparietal, or connection lesions. Severe jargonaphasia could for instance occur when the frontal lobe is no longer checked by a posterior left hemisphere or by a lesioned thalamus (when semantic or proprioceptive control which slow down and optimize performance are, as it were, short-circuited). Severe anomia mixed with phonemic and semantic paraphasia, slow delivery or agrammatism, and hypertonic rhythm could be what the right hemisphere is still trying to do when not only the posterior part but also the anterior part of the left hemisphere are damaged. Good parrot-like repetition and poor spontaneous production could be what the system is doing when there is no longer a good connection between areas that have a major part to play in the formation of concepts (lesions of parietooccipital, temporo-parietal, or temporooccipital areas sometimes associated with what has been called "transcortical sensory aphasia").

But the study of pathology would depend less upon clinical generalities if some simulation of isolated cases was possible by using a computer model of performance like JARGONAUT. It is always possible to erase automatically some data, some rules, or to shunt operations which have to do with planning and control. The scientist can then observe how a system is behaving when it is more or less severely reduced.

I shall suggest a way to develop such a research methodology in the following pages.

(2) Just as was the case for the simulation of the systems dynamics when subsystems are dramatically reduced, I claim that successful or catastrophic strategies developed consciously or unconsciously by the individual to overcome degrading effects should be studied for individual pathological cases with the help of a computer.

There are no cybernetic or physiological proofs about the nature of the parasitic effect of lesions affecting more or less layers of the cortex, more or less underlying white matter, and involving millions or hundreds or thousands of neurons. But we can imagine that the transfer of excitatory or of inhibitory information must be disrupted to the point that operations normally carried out by various levels or by various areas (like identification, comparison, preferential decisions) will be either nonexistent (well replaced by internal control or parallel processing), or distorting to language (assuming that the "fuzzing effect" of brain calculation would be increasing the entropy of the system), or relatively compensated (by heuristic strategies depending upon interlocutors' feedback, and by nonlinguistic modalities). In order to mimic all that, the **distorting mechanism** would have to be some huge facility reproducing faithfully the physiology of the whole or of part of the multibillion neuron net in the human brain. I think that in the coming decades the experimental distorting mechanism could more easily be a **programming device compiling transformational operations** at several functional levels (phonemic, morphemic, phrase structure, semantic structure) without paying much attention to what kind of hardware is used. The compilation would consist (*a*) in generating ordered structures of transformational rules and constraints by combining degrading effects like discrimination fuzzing, memory limitation, disrupted timing, inhibition level lowering or raising, decision threshold modification, etc; and (*b*) in applying these distortion programs to an artificial system like JARGONAUT.

Composite distortions suggested in (*a*) could be **metaoperations** like the following (which generates substitution):

ERASE X AND ADD NEIGHBORING VALUE → SUBSTITUTION.

Application rules suggested in (*b*) could also be complex, like the following (which specifies conditions for a SEMANTIC paraphasia):

(SEMANTIC) SUBSTITUTION [CONSTRAINT: TERMINAL NODES IF NOT FUNCTION—WORD] → (SEMANTIC) PARAPHASIA.

Simulation Project for Further Research

No thorough computer work has yet been attempted in this field. The automatic generation of distortion programs has been implemented by the author using an ALGOL compiler and a CDC 6600 computer (the only difficulty being to write rules in Backus Normal Form). But the application of such programs to a production system has not been possible. Consequently, what follows is a project which would enable us to test theoretical hypotheses about composite neurolinguistic pathology before we consider studying distorting effects in neural nets. Luria's interpretation of interaction between subsystems of disturbance could for instance be tested by real distortions applied to JARGONAUT.

Reduction or distortion can actually be implemented on a language production system with the introduction of distorting factors. But before characterizing them, it is necessary to show at what levels distortion experiments are to be carried out.

Here is another block diagram showing how some of the subsystems of

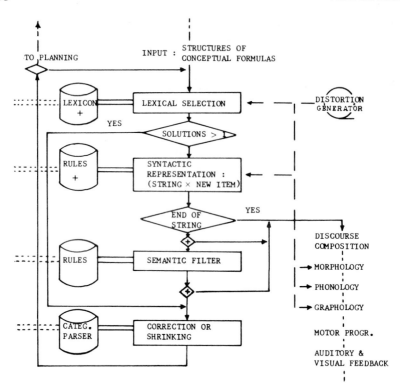

FIGURE 7.13. JARGONAUT.

JARGONAUT are connected (Figure 7.13). Other subsystems are merely mentioned here (e.g., planning, discourse composition, morphology, phonology, graphology). Lexical selection, which has been studied in the previous sections of this chapter, now appears as a single box. What is important about this representation is that it shows that distortions can be programmed to interfere with the system at several levels of processing ("-- →" lines) and that permanent reductions could be introduced by JARGONAUT users on what might be called "competence" or "linguistic knowledge" ("+" in the lexicon and in syntactic rules) or on control paths ("+" supressing shrinking or semantic filtering).

Distortion programs have to be completely determined for each pathological case. In such a system, users first have to choose hypotheses of **degrading effects** from a list of experimentally studied and codified deficits, for example: auditory perception fuzzing, auditory agnosia, visual perception fuzzing, visual agnosia..., spatial recognition fuzzing..., resonance effect (for perseveration) ..., syntactic buffer limitation, phonological buffer limitation.

Then a computing device must be used to compile composite distortion programs as indicated on page 157. The details of the rules and operations of the distortion generator are predetermined. They can reflect the user's linguistic performance theory about the relationships between clinically observed language deficits and anatomical, physiological and psychological measurements. Users only have to decide what comes of what and word the decisions as rewrite rules. But let us look at an example:

SEMANTIC FUZZING is the axiom with which we will start. The compiler first applies a MEGARULE redefining this first notion:

SEMANTIC FUZZING (means) : PARAPHASIA (applied to) A LEXICAL SELECTION PROCESS (or a) BLEND (applied to) PARALLEL SELECTION PROCESSES.

Simultaneously, the compiler stipulates more clearly the processes that have been named, by applying MEGAOPERATIONS:

LEXICAL SELECTION PROCESS (is a) :LEXICAL SELECTION PROGRAM (associated with) CONDITIONS OF REALIZATION; PARALLEL LEXICAL SELECTION PROCESSES (are):... etc.

The results of this first level (called MEGAPRODUCTION) are immediately fed into a second level of compiling where HYPERRULES redefine all the terms:

PARAPHASIA (means) : SUBSTITUTION (*or*) SUBSTITUTION + other things... (*or*)... etc;
CONDITIONS OF REALIZATION (applied to) A LEXICAL SELECTION PROCESS (means): ACCESS LEXICAL SELECTION ('COMPARE' program studied above) WITH CONSTRAINTS, like what kinds of words it applies to (e.g., nouns), whether it is iterative, etc.

Simultaneously, METAOPERATIONS stipulate more clearly what elementary operations are involved:

SUBSTITUTION (is a) : ERASE X (where X represents a conceptual formula),X (being associated with) CONSTRAINTS, like [pick the formula with the lowest confidence values for its features].

As an interesting computational fact, the basic operations used by metaoperations are: ERASE X [constraint]; ADD X [constraint]; PERMUTE X AND Y [constraint]. The following are second order operations: ERASE X AND ADD Y; BLEND W AND Y (which uses syllable arrangements in X and Y). More complex compounding is still to be thought of for interplay between several subsystems, in order to simulate the compensation or amplification of errors. But this would mainly concern phonemic paraphasias.

It seems that distortion programs compiled by many-dimensional compilers, as exemplified by orthogonal grammars also called "W grammars" (Van Wijngaarden, 1965) can serve as artifacts to degrade a language production system. But we have no evidence as to their relevance to brain processing in aphasia, or more generally to distributed compiling of complex transformations (whether distorting or not).

This conceptual outlook has addressed some strategies that may underlie the speech deficits in Wernicke's aphasia. I would like to add that simulating language pathology is not only a promising approach to refine aphasia diagnosis; it should also help us to form prognoses and to study therapy.

Therapy can be simulated by interfering with the lesioned system in different ways:

a. The first of these involves suppressing degrading sources (distortion programs will not be triggered off). This corresponds, for example, to surgery which, when applied to a tumor, will often do away with jargonaphasia.

b. Guided learning (an increase or a suitable modification of some rules of various unlesioned subsystems) may yield interesting improvements, whereas misguided learning or poor adaptation to a deficit will lead to clumsy or minimal performances.

c. The most interesting kind of artificial therapy that could be simulated with JARGONAUT is the development of SEMANTIC CONTROL.

A semantic filter is necessary (even when the system is not lesioned) to IDENTIFY AND THEN ELIMINATE OR SHRINK any illegal linguistic occurrence or any string of occurrences. (See Figure 7.13, page 158, and follow the loops in the lexical retrieval, planning or input, semantic filtering, shrinking subsystem: a loop back to syntactic processing will rebuild an utterance with what is left of it after it has been shrunk).

It is to be hoped that modifying the semantic rules in a computer system or by-passing semantic filtering operations will teach us more about natural LINGUISTIC CONTROL and conscious SELF-CHECKING which have been underestimated in competence models. Some aspects of Wernicke's aphasia called auditory agnosia, verbal deafness, anosognosia, low comprehension, will then appear as elements of bad prognosis because they prevent the elaboration of successful safeguard heuristic strategies in discourse and sentence planning (like uttering short simple sentences, avoiding anaphora, prepositions, and deictic words, using pragmatic cues and logical inference, developing dialogue skills and circumlocution). It is even possible to conjecture that Wernicke's aphasia would not exist or would be greatly reduced if comprehension was not marred at many levels by the very lesions that disrupt production.

APPENDIX

I. The matching of conceptual formulas has been achieved using a documentation retrieval system on a CII, IRIS 80 computer in Grenoble, France, via the Cyclades network. It is interesting to notice how the retrieval of the titles of books and papers from a documentation bank resembles lexical retrieval. Both types of search use a conceptual formulation and matching subprograms.

II. Shrinking processes have been developed in a pattern-recognition system on a CDC 6600 in Paris (Université Descartes). Linguistic patterns as well as pictures or voice formants can be processed in terms of concatenated features. Concatenation corresponds to various types of relations and may be represented by networks. Only, conceptual representations are formed of discrete entities whereas pictures and sounds are first discretized before they can be shrunk.

III. Distortion programs have been compiled (as if they were grammars) but not applied to the above two subprograms. An ALGOL Compiler on an IBM 360-65 was used. Linguistic distortion BNF rules were entered instead of BNF rules of a programming language.

I shall briefly indicate what may be of interest in these programs for the AI readers.

IV. A. The comparison of formulas

Let us assume that a formula defining the conceptual image of colt as ⟨⟨ . . . YOUNG⟩ ⟨ . . . ANIMAL ⟨ . . . IN A RANCH ⟩⟩⟩ has to be matched with a formula defining the lexical entry *colt* as ⟨⟨ . . . YOUNG⟩ ⟨ . . . ANIMAL ⟨ . . . FOR RIDING⟩⟩⟩. It is easy to cmpare the two formulas feature by feature in the lexical space because the two structures are isomorphic at this level of representation:

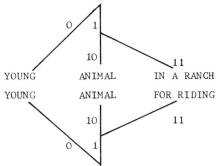

In many cases, only partial morphisms between formulas can be found. And so, only comparable subtrees will be equated. This is how pruning becomes useful even before comparison, until some subformula of the conceptual formula can be matched with at least part of one lexical formula. In other cases, complete conceptual structure reformulation will be necessary (e.g., when no partial morphism is found, or when pruning reduces a C to a mere **skeleton**, i.e., one feature): see second test in Figure 7.4.

IV.B. Reformulation of formulas

As for the shrinking algorithm used, it is sufficient to know that, when applied to a given conceptual formula with brackets, it will at each pass erase the innermost terms. These may be given by a counter calculating the number of newly opened brackets:

$$\langle \quad \langle \quad \rangle \quad \langle \quad \langle\langle \quad \rangle\langle\rangle\rangle \quad \langle \quad \rangle \quad \rangle \quad \rangle;$$
$$1 \quad 2 \quad \quad 2 \quad 2 \quad 34 \quad 4443 \quad 3 \quad \quad 3 \quad 2 \quad 1$$

then an erasing operation is applied to the highest values obtained. Here 4s will be erased first, then 3s, etc.

IV.C. The basic decision principle of analytical selection (Figure 7.11.) works by referring one or several lexical formulas to one conceptual formula and transforming similarities into multimapping probabilities, in the following way:

morphisms or partial morphisms between formulas are associated with a metrics on the reference set of primitive concepts (see page 143).

The choice of this metric has been dictated by an available documentation language which handles hierarchical relational trees. A Hamming summation of ultrametric distances is calculated:

$$\mathcal{H}\,(f_A,\,f_B) = \sum_{i=1}^{n} \frac{s_i^A\,u\,s_i^B}{n}$$

where f_A and f_B are any two formulas, s_i^A and s_i^B are corresponding features respectively of f_A and of f_B; u is the ultrametric distance between any two features s_l and s_m in T given by Metzger's measure

$$s_l\,u\,s_m = \frac{D}{N_{lm.}+1} \times \frac{L_{l.m}}{2.H}$$

where D is a dispersion coefficient of the tree T ($0 < D < 1$) equal to the cardinal value of T, N is the level of the common "ancestor" of s_l and s_m in the hierarchical tree, $L_{l.m}$ is the length of the shortest pathway linking s_l and s_m, H is the height of the hierarchical tree (number of levels).

Resulting Hamming distances are converted into probabilities by

$$P_{A.B} = \exp\,[-\mathcal{H}\,(f_A,\,f_B)].$$

Finally, probabilities for different source formulas to match one target formula are compared, and a selection decision is reached whenever probability is greater or equal to a predefined value (this "level" is taken to be an analogue to Nilsson's thresholds).

IV.D. This process would work rather well if all the features were not affected with a weight reflecting a possible decreased confidence level (or activation level). Since all the features are associated with this weight in the [0, 1] interval, the probability obtained above is regulated by an information coefficient applied to ultrametric distances between features, Entropy would be maximal if

$$\tfrac{1}{2}\,(w_{f_l} + w_{f_m}) = 0,$$

and would be null if

$$\tfrac{1}{2}\,(w_{f_l} + w_{f_m}) = 1.$$

The alternative stochastic process (Figure 7.11) has not been implemented.

REFERENCES

Amari, S. I. (1971). Characteristics of randomly connected threshold element networks and network systems. *Proceedings of the IEEE*, 59, 35–47.

Amari, S. I., and Arbib, M. A. (1977). Competition and cooperation in neural nets. In J. Metzler (Ed.), *Systems neuroscience*. New York: Academic Press.

Anderson, J. A., Silverstein, J. W., Ritz, S. A., and Jones R. S. (1977). Distinctive features, categorical perception and probability learning: Some applications of the neural model. *Psychological Review*, 86, 413–451.

Anderson, P., and Eccles, J. (1962). Inhibitory phasing of neuronal discharges. *Nature*, 196, 645–647.

Arbib, M. A. (1964). *Brains, machines and mathematics.* New York: McGraw-Hill.

Arbib, M. A. (1977). Schemas: Cognition, reality, and mechanism. *Brain Theory Newsletter, 3,* 2, 14–23.

Arbib, M. A., and Manes, E. G. (1975a). A category-theoretic approach to systems in a fuzzy world. *Synthese, 30,* 381–606.

Arbib, M. A., and Manes, E. G. (1975b). *Arrows, structures, and functors: The categorical imperative.* New York: Academic Press.

Arbib, M. A., and Manes, E. G. (1976). Machines in a category: An expository introduction. *SIAM Review, 16,* 163–191.

Bar-Hillel, J. (1964). *Language and information.* Reading, Mass.: Addison-Wesley.

Bobrow, D. G., and Winograd, T. (1977). An overview of KRL: A knowledge representation language. *Cognitive Science, 1,* 3–46.

Butterworth, B., and Whittaker, S. (1980). Peggy Babcock's relatives. In G. E. Stelmach and J. Requin (Eds.), *Tutorials in motor behavior.* Amsterdam: North-Holland.

Capranica, R., Frishkopf, L., and Nevo, E. (1973). Encoding of geographic dialects in the auditory system of the cricket frog. *Science, 183,* 1272–1275.

Courtin, J. (1973). Un analyseur morphologique et syntactique pour les langues naturelles. *Proceedings of the Association for Computational Linguistics,* 1,1 (Pisa Conference).

Deloche, G., Lecours, A. R., and Lhermitte, F. (1973). Paraphasies phonémiques: Description et simulation sur ordinateur. *Colloque IRIA, Information Medicale.* Rocquencourt, France: Institut de Recherche en Informatique et an Automatique.

Dev, P. (1975). Computer simulation of a dynamic visual perception model. *International Journal of Man–Machine Studies, 7,* 511.

Didday, R. G. (1975). A model of visuomotor mechanisms in the frog optic tectum. *Mathematical Biosciences, 30,* 169–180.

Didday, R. G., and Arbib, M. A. (1975). Eye movements and visual perception: A "two visual system" model. *International Journal of Man–Machine Studies, 7,* 547–569.

Ducarne, B., and Préneron, C. (1976). La dyssyntaxie. *La Linguistique, 12,* 2, 33–54.

Edelman, G. M., and Mountcastle, V. B. (1978). *The mindful brain.* Cambridge, Mass.: MIT Press.

Erman, L. D. F., Hayes-Roth, V. R., Lesser, V. R., and Reddy, R. (1980). The HEARSAY-II speech understanding system: Integrating knowledge to resolve uncertainty. *Computing Surveys, 12,* 2, 213–253.

Fahlman, S. E. (1979). *NETL: A system for representing and using real-world knowledge.* Cambridge, Mass.: MIT Press.

Forster, K. I. (1978). Accessing the mental lexicon. In E. Walker (Ed.), *Explorations in the biology of language.* Montgomery: Bradford Books.

Frécon, L., and Lavorel, P. M. (1980). Context-sensitive selection models for speech errors. Paris: Klincksieck *T.A. Informations,* 1, 38–44.

Garrett, M. F. (1980). Levels of processing in sentence production. In B. Butterworth (Ed.), *Language production.* New York: Academic Press.

Gross, M. (1975). *Méthodes en syntaxe.* Paris: Hermann.

Itoh, M., Sasanuma, S., Hirose, H., Yoshioka, H., and Ushijima, T. (1978). Articulatory dynamics in a patient with apraxia of speech. *Brain and Language, 11,* 1, 66–75.

Jackendoff, R. S. (1977). X̄ *syntax: A study of phrase structure.* Cambridge, Mass.: MIT Press.

Jakobson, R. (1966). Linguistic types of aphasia. In E. C. Carterette (Ed.), *Brain function,* Vol. 3. Berkeley: University of California Press.

Kilmer, W. J., McCulloch, W. S., and Blum, J. (1969). A model of the vertebrate central command system. *International Journal of Man–Machine Studies, 1,* 279–309.

Lavorel, P. M. (1975). *Eléments pour un calcul du sens.* Paris: Dunod-Masson.

Lavorel, P. M. (1979). Grammaires pour les analyseurs morphosyntaxiques: Rappels théoriques et recettes pratiques. *T. A. Informations*, Vol. 1. Paris: Klincksieck.

Lavorel, P. M. (1980a). *Aspects de la performance linguistique: Contribution neurolinguistique et psycholinguistique à l'analyse des systèmes langagiers*. Lyon: Université Lyon II.

Lavorel, P. M. (1980b). Interpretation lexicaliste de l'incohérence verbale dans les aphasies postérieures. *Etudes de Linguistique Appliquée*, Vol. 2. Paris: Sorbonne.

Lavorel, P. M. (1980c). Sept formes de jargon. Troubles de la sélection dans le lexique mental. In J. L. Nespoulous (Ed.), **Etudes neurolinguistiques**. Toulouse: Presses de l'Université de Toulouse: *Grammatica*, 1981.

Lavorel, P. M., and Arbib, M. A. (Forthcoming). Towards a theory of language performance, *Theoretical Linguistics*, 1981, 1.

Lewis, D. (1972). General semantics. In D. Davidson and G. Harmon (Eds.), *Semantics of natural language*. Dordrecht: Reidel.

Luce, R. D. (1956). Semi-orders and a theory of utility discrimination. *Econometrica*, 24, 178–191.

Luria, A. R., and Tsvetkova, L. S. *Les troubles de la resolutions des problemes*. Paris: Gauthier-Villard, 1967.

MuCulloch, W. S., and Pitts, W. A. (1943). A logical calculus of the ideas immanent in nervous activity. *Bulletin of Mathematical Biophysics*, 5, 115–133.

Macneilage, P. F. (1980). Distinctive properties of speech motor control. In G. E. Stelmach and J. Requin (Eds.), *Tutorials in motor behavior*. Amsterdam: North-Holland.

Marin, O. S. M., and Gordon, B. (1980). Language and speech production. In G. E. Stelmach and J. Requin (Eds.), *Tutorials in motor behavior*. Amsterdam: North-Holland.

Metzger, J. P. (1978). *Dialogue homme-machine: System d' explication automatique du discours documentaire*. Lyon: Université de Lyon I.

Mountcastle, V. B. (1978). An organizing principle for cerebral function: The Unit Module and the distributed system. In Edelman and Mountcastle (Eds.) *The mindful brain*. Cambridge, Mass.: MIT Press.

Nilsson, N. J. (1965). *Learning machines*. New York: McGraw-Hill.

Remez, R. E. (1979). Feature detectors in speech. *Cognitive Psychology*, 11, 1, 38–57.

Salton, G. (1968). *Automatic information organization and retrieval*. New York: McGraw-Hill.

Scott, D., and Suppes, P. (1958). Foundational aspects of theories of measurement. *Journal of Symbolic Logic*, 23, 113–128.

Szentágothai, J. (1975). The "module concept" in cerebral cortex architecture. *Brain Research*, 95, 475–696.

Tesnière, L. (1966). *Elements de syntaxe structurale*. Paris: Klincksieck.

van Wijngaarden, A. (1965). *Orthogonal design and description of a formal language*. (Technical report MR 76.) Amsterdam: Mathematische Centrum.

Winter, P., and Funkenstein, H. A. (1973). The effect of species-specific vocalization on the discharge of auditory cortical cells in the awake squirrel monkey. *Experimental Brain Research*, 18, 489–504.

Wood, C. C. (1978). Variations on a theme by Lashley: Lesion experiments on the neural model of Anderson et al. *Psychological Review*, 85, 582–591.

III
LINGUISTIC AND PSYCHOLINGUISTIC PERSPECTIVES

Linguistic and psycholinguistic studies of normal and pathological language capacities have somewhat different relationships to the theoretical developments of neurolinguistics. Studies of the structural properties and psychological mechanisms involved in normal language provide hypotheses as to the natural division of elements of language and their organization in use. These hypotheses would be greatly strengthened by the discovery of correlations between items, levels of representation, constraints on processing, etc., and neurological analysis. The situation is analogous to the relationship which exists between theories of genetic inheritance such as Mendelian genetics, which were based on observations about the transmission of phenotypic characteristics, and observations regarding DNA's structure and function. The genetic theory led to the search for a physical structure capable of fulfilling a particular function. Thus, the discovery of DNA confirmed central aspects of genetic theory. Linguistic and psycholinguistic studies of language disorders can, within limits, test the "neural reality" of linguistic and psycholinguistic hypotheses, and, when conjoined with information about the physical nature of the injury to the nervous system, provide hypotheses regarding the specific physical mechanisms involved in language. (The proviso within limits draws attention to the notorious difficulties involved in arguing from observations of pathological symptoms to normal functioning.)

Three of the chapters in this section focus on nonaphasic language behavior. Grammatical descriptions are, for obvious reasons, always considered neutral between perception and production: Successful communication presupposes that one speaks the language one understands. But the extent to which the production and perception of speech draw upon the same algorithms and mechanisms is an open question. To some extent, they must differ. The path from thought to speech cannot simply "run backward" the machinery for the path from the sound wave to comprehension. It is possible, however, that some of the more "central" mechanisms involved may be held in common across the two tasks.

   Garrett's chapter and the chapter by Frazier examine the evidence that the operations of speech production and speech comprehension make use of an independently registered set of linguistic forms and rules with the additional possibility that some of the procedures employed by the processes of speech production and perception are common to both. Bellugi, Zurif, and Poisner explore the nature of linguistic systems which develop in individuals deaf from birth in whom the normally preferred modality of language perception is unavailable. One of the most exciting developments of the last decade has been the extensive, detailed study of sign language, such as American Sign Language (ASL), that constitute the primary means of communication in some deaf communities. For many years such systems had been regarded as little more than crude pantomime or the simple stringing together of "natural" gestures. It is now apparent, however, that ASL has a rich syntax, morphology, and (manual equivalent of) "phonology," and must be regarded as a system that is structurally no less a language than English or Japanese. But the demands of the modality (visual-manual) do shape the language, just as the properties of the ear and vocal tract must, to some extent, shape spoken languages. Bellugi et al. provide a state-of-the-art chapter in which they outline current thinking on the linguistics and psycholinguistics of sign language. Ultimately, we hope that comparisons of sign and speech will help us to factor out the "central" components of the language faculty from the peripheral modality-driven components that provide the interface between abstract systems and physical signals. The Bellugi et al. chapter also raises the prospects of studying aphasic ASL users. The evidence regarding breakdown patterns in sign, as well as the considerations of Garrett and Frazier, suggest that areas of the brain are committed to abstract aspects of the linguistic code and the processes which utilize them, rather than to particular modalities or to motor or sensory functions. Garrett presents evidence that vocabulary classes and the mechanisms of access particular to each, the distinction between phonological form and semantic readings of individual words, and certain aspects of morphology are common to speech production and perception. Frazier considers the possibility that syntactic knowledge and certain processing units are common to the two processes. Bellugi et al. review their evidence that the abstract elements which comprise ASL are similar to those of languages which use auditory-vocal mechanisms, although the visual-manual system utilizes different physical realizations of these elements (such as superposition rather than temporal concatenation).

   The most widespread clinically-based models of language representation and processing in the brain do not clearly dissociate language mechanisms from the motor and sensory mechanisms invoked by speech. The familiar view of language–brain relationships (see the chapters by Arbib, Caplan, and Marshall, and Levine and Sweet), modified little since its statement in the late nineteenth century, is that language comprehension is closely associated to auditory perceptual mechanisms: The role of the temporal association cortex (Wernicke's area) is the representation of the sound patterns of words and the decoding of incoming speech; the function of the anterior "language area" (Broca's area, but see Levine and Sweet's chapter) is the representation of the motor engrams for speech output. It is certainly true that classical theorists allowed for other "centers," such as the "concept center" of Lichtheim, and that modern theorists postulate functions less directly associated to speech perception and production as parts of an overall model of language with a neural basis. (Geschwind's view of the inferior parietal lobe associating auditory and other nonlimbic stimuli to establish meaning and/or reference is one example.) However, functions considered outside of the acts of speech perception and production are limited in number and scope, and many, such as Lichtheim's "concept center," are not unambiguously linguistic. We now argue that there are many central aspects of language representation and of processes which utilize linguistic information in speaking and listening which are unrelated to motor or sensory speech processes per se. This position is incompatible with a strong interpretation of clinically derived theories, which claims that the most important aspects of language representation and processing are closely and necessarily linked to either the sensory or the motor representations of speech. Note, however, that our suggestion (reinforced by the study of ASL) of the importance of "nonperipheral" representations and processes in neurolinguistics in no way vitiates our concern with perceptual-motor mechanisms in Part V. We shall see that perception and motor control are also linked by complex central processes, and suggest that the understanding of such processes will provide a link to animal studies, as well as offering hope of integrating aphasia with agnosia, apraxia, etc., in a unified neuropsychology.

There are two possible consequences for neural mechanisms of this "move from the periphery." The first possibility is that a good deal more language processing occurs outside areas of the brain committed to modality- and task-specific functions than is currently claimed by many clinical theories. The second is that the association cortices now conceived as related to sensory or motor function are not so narrowly committed, but are instead areas responsible for abstract operations and the representation of structural properties of language (and other cognitive abilities). There is some preliminary evidence in favor of the second possibility: Neville has reported that, in deaf-mute signers, late components of visual evoked potentials appear over scalp areas that are not activated by similar stimuli in normals, even though those scalp areas are thought to be related to the auditory association cortex in which auditory potentials appear in normals. This suggests the commitment of these cortical areas to abstract qualities of the signal, rather than to modality-specific features.

Two of the contributions to this section, those of Kean and Zurif, analyze a particular aphasic syndrome, Broca's telegrammatic aphasia, to test the "neural reality" of linguistic and psycholinguistic hypotheses. The same syndrome was addressed in the "steps toward a model" taken by Arbib and Marcus in their contributions to Part II. The syndrome has been the focus of considerable study in the last few years, the results of which are summarized in several places (e.g., Berndt and Caramazza, 1980, Marshall, 1977). Kean and Zurif now extend previous analyses in important ways. Kean proposes that the levels of representation made available in modern generative grammars constitute exactly the targets that process models must compute, and the (psychological) locus at which aphasic syndromes can be defined in a principled, cross-linguistic fashion. She groups together the free standing "function word," "closed class" vocabulary of English with a certain group of affixes, those which do not alter the stress patterns of words to which they are adjoined. Her claim is that these two classes of linguistic items are members of a single group, defined within the phonological component of a transformational grammar. It is a close approximation to empirical fact that these elements of language are most severely affected in telegrammatic aphasic's speech. In other work (Kean, 1980), Kean discusses the interaction of this linguistic characterization of the deficit in these patients with processing mechanisms, an interaction which complicates the observed pattern of speech actually produced. Here she describes a structural level which constitutes an interface between purely syntactic and purely phonological processes. It is at this level that the distinction between P-words and P-clitics (P for phonological) is stated, the distinction which she claims characterizes the pattern of preserved and impaired items in agrammatic Broca's aphasia. She also indicates that work on normal sentence production and lexical retrieval implicates the distinctions describable at this level of structure. The existence of a language disorder, which is explicated in terms applicable to the analysis of normal psycholinguistic operations, supports the validity of the linguistic model which naturally establishes these two classes of items.

Zurif reviews and extends the view of agrammatic aphasia as an inability to construct syntactic structures which incorporate the "closed class" vocabulary of English. He and his colleagues have shown that the speech deficit in this syndrome is parallel to a comprehension disorder that is not always clinically apparent upon informal testing. The disorder affects the comprehension of sentences which require syntactic structures to be established on the basis of this set of words. Here Zurif reports new work which suggests that these patients may know the semantic value of "closed class" elements in a sentence (when given sufficient "processing time"), even though they cannot use these elements for structure building purposes. Such results are consistent with the characterization of the disorder in this syndrome as one of lexical retrieval of "closed class" items that are required in the elaboration of syntactic frames in both sentence production and comprehension.

These two chapters provide evidence for the isolation of certain components of psycholinguistic processing, such as lexical retrieval and the creation of syntactic structure, for the limited and still somewhat hypothetical commonality of aspects of these components to the production and comprehension of sentences, and for a particular division of vocabulary and morphological items in language which interacts with psycholinguistic processing.

These results also suggest a role for particular brain structures: The effect of the lesion that produces this syndrome is expressed as an abstract division of language inventories and particular components of psycholinguistic processes. If the normal function of a lesioned locale is to support the functions disordered when it is damaged (for discussion of the legitimacy of these assumptions, see the chapters by Marshall, Caplan, Schnitzer, and Wood), we can claim that the lesioned area normally represents one part of the vocabulary of English (or another natural language) that underlies certain psychological routines utilizing this vocabulary. This hypothesis is a specific example of the sort of intrinsic linguistic representations and psycholinguistic functions that are to be related to areas of the brain (or to other aspects of neural structure and function) which, to refer to the earlier theme, are unrelated to motor or sensory function per se.

The contributions of Garrett, Frazier, Kean, and Zurif are bound together by the presupposition that the targets are (approximately) as described in the standard (or extended standard) theory of transformational grammar. Schnitzer's chapter, on the other hand, takes its point of departure from stratificational grammar. Schnitzer describes how linguistic structure is characterized by stratificational grammar and shows how the symptomatology of Broca's and Wernicke's aphasia can be elucidated in stratificational terms. His analysis pays special attention to the superficially different symptomatology of anglophones and hispanophones. The resulting theory distinguishes "morpholexical" and "logicosemantic" aspects of language, and postulates that each is related to its own psychological processes in the production and perception of sentences. Broca's and Wernicke's areas are seen as the substrates responsible for the representation of these aspects of language structure and for their activation in processing. The reader may find it instructive to contrast Kean's claims for a "phonological deficit" (in a rather extended sense) in Broca's aphasia with Schnitzer's emphasis on a "morpholexical" deficit. It is also worth noting that Kean sees little place for general considerations of "implementation" (memory, parallelism, etc.) in her analysis of language. By contrast, Schnitzer claims one of the advantages of stratificational grammar is the ease with which it may be used in psycholinguistic processes, because the notation of stratificational theory provides a relatively direct mapping from the linguistic structure of language to the neuronal instantiation of language, though network nodes are not thought to represent individual neurons. Essentially, Schnitzer adopts a structural realism for which the neuronic representation includes the same structural description as the language. It remains to be seen whether or not significant generalizations are overlooked when one draws few distinctions between the theory of a computation, the algorithms and mechanisms that realize the computation, and the neuronal hardware in which they are instantiated. It is debatable whether there is room in the stratificational network for the control structures which played such an important role in the HWIM and HEARSAY systems discussed in Part II. To what extent must neurolinguistics generate models for the neurological analogues of such control structures, and to what extent are they automatically provided for by an account of interaction between levels?

Formal descriptions of language and language processing are the basis for searching for neurophysiological correlates of language. Schnitzer uses evidence from data on regional blood flow. The development of techniques for identifying evoked electrical potentials, as well as limited extracellular recording from the brain, will allow investigators to look for electrophysiological events related to language structures and tasks (a subject to which we return in Part V). The more precise and better established a characterization of a level of linguistic structure or a psycholinguistic process, the easier it will be to isolate the physiological basis of such functions. In addition, if we know from studies of pathology where to look for physiological events correlated with a function, we are one step ahead.

Both logic and experience, however, caution against high expectations in this regard. In his chapter, Wood warns of the danger of inferring that a function is localized on the basis of lesion studies. Clinical studies can serve as a guide to localization, but do not establish that a function is localized. What they do establish, in principle at least, is the best analysis of a functional disturbance.

Despite Marin's warning in his discussion of the "rules of the game," chapters in this section emphasize syntax (where general principles are represented) at the expense of the lexicon (where idiosyncracies are represented). One subpart of the lexicon presumably contains the "names" of objects that are perceptible to the senses. It is obvious that synchronically the relationship between a cat and "cat" is unprincipled. It is equally obvious that the fluent user of a language must have ready access to the cat–"cat" (or "chat") pairing. Confrontation object-naming is the clinician's tool for investigating the "word-finding difficulties" that are so frequently found in aphasia. Ojemann and Whitaker (1978) have investigated the wide variety of forms that such difficulties can take, and attempted to elucidate some of the brain areas that are involved. Unfortunately, they do not attempt to analyze the neural mechanisms, or even the functional principles, underlying these effect. Nonetheless, sophisticated studies of "reversible" deficits provoked by electrical stimulation of the exposed cortex during brain surgery should continue to be a source of valuable clinical information to augment the traditional accounts derived from trauma and disease.

But what linguistic model best coordinates with clinical studies? Among the issues raised by Schnitzer's chapter is one that affects the evaluation of many studies of aphasia, namely, what justification is there for the adoption of one or another framework for the description of language structure and processing as the basis for analysis of aphasic performance? The terms of analysis determine the characterization of disordered functions. Moreover, any inferences about normal function and its relation to brain mechanisms must take into account the justification of the theory of language adopted as a model of normal linguistic functioning. While there is some congruence of several models currently applied to the analysis of aphasic syndromes, as Kean's chapter stresses, convergence is not always the case. When we see how the AI representations of language in terms of interacting knowledge sources (discussed in chapters by Woods and Arbib in Part II) differ from the representations posited by stratificational or transformational-generative grammar, the question of the appropriateness of a framework of analysis is critical.

One response which does not suffice is to exercise ecumenical tolerance. If there are good reasons for rejecting a theory of language on the basis of its inability to account for normal language, the fact that it can be used to account for abnormal performance does not justify its adoption as a theory of normal function. The brain may have reorganized itself significantly as a result of injury and no inferences to the normal state may be justified (see Marshall's and Caplan's chapters). While descriptions of aphasic syndromes are not necessarily linked to justifiable normative theories, inferences from the underlying functions revealed by pathology to descriptions of the normal state are linked.

Adoption of more formal linguistic, psycholinguistic, and AI theories in the analysis of the aphasias should begin to resolve such disputes. As Kean emphasizes, close attention must be paid to the particular claims made in an analysis of an aphasic disorder so that one can distinguish terminological from substantive disagreements. Are Schnitzer's morpholexotactics and Kean's phonological structures the same levels of linguistic structure? If not, and we suspect not, what distinguishes the two? Are the facts of Broca's telegrammatic aphasia best accounted for as a disorder of P-clitics or of morpholexotactics? Though answering such questions will not be easy, the more formal and precise the theories of language characterizing aphasic impairments, the greater the opportunity for sharpening the issues and finding data to resolve opposing claims. In particular, it becomes important to shift the focus from levels of representation per se, and pay far greater attention to the processes which act upon them, and the control structures which coordinate these processes. That is why we view the goal of a "computational" neurolinguistics as so important.

REFERENCES

Berndt, R. S., and Caramazza, A. (1980). A redefinition of the syndrome of Broca's aphasia: Implications for a neurological model of language. *Applied Psycholinguistics, 1*, 225–287.

Kean, M. L. (1980). Linguistic representations and the description of processing. In D. Caplan (Ed.), *Biological studies of mental processes*, Cambridge, Mass.: MIT Press.

Marshall, J. C. (1977). Disorders in the expression of language. In J. Morton and J. C. Marshall (Eds.), *Psycholinguistics Series*. Vol. 1. Ithaca, New York: Cornell Univ. Press.

Ojemann, G. A., and Whitaker, H. A. (1978). Language localization and variability. *Brain and Language, 6*, 239–260.

8

Three Perspectives for the Analysis of Aphasic Syndromes[1]

Mary-Louise Kean

Until quite recently, there has been a striking paucity of attention to theories of the structure of language and "normal" human linguistic capacity in behavioral analyses of aphasic deficits. Analyses have typically relied on naive notions of linguistic structure that would, in many cases, shock elementary school students brought up on Reed and Kellogg sentence diagrams.[2] The level of discussion took a marked turn upward with the work of Harold Goodglass in which, for the first time, there was a serious attempt made to pay attention to systematic taxonomies of linguistic structure in a broad body of aphasia research. With only sporadic and isolated exceptions (e.g., Whitaker, 1971), the contribution of Goodglass was allowed to remain static rather than be seen as suggesting an aphasia research program where theories of linguistic structure would be more and more incorporated into functional analyses of aphasic syndromes. Thus, despite significant advances in the last 20 years in both linguistics and psycholinguistics, little effort was made to bring those research results directly to bear on the analysis of linguistic deficits. However, within the last few years, there has at last been a concentrated effort to follow just such a research program as was suggested by Goodglass's work. This is most notable in research that has recently

[1] Preparation of this chapter was supported in part by NIMH fellowship 1-F32-MH07189-01 and by a research fellowship at the Max Planck Institute for Psycholinguistics.

[2] Reed and Kellog sentence diagrams were the backbone of elementary school grammar lessons until relatively recently. The following is an example of such a diagram.

The class gave Mary presents in gay wrappings.

NEURAL MODELS OF
LANGUAGE PROCESSES

been carried out on agrammatism in Broca's aphasia. At this point we now have relatively detailed analyses of agrammatism in terms of grammatical theory and in terms of processing theories of comprehension and production. The virtue of such analyses should be self-evident. For the first time, we have empirically predictive hypotheses which not only aim toward an understanding of deficits at a considerably deeper level than previously known, but which also serve to open up the field to serious debate about the nature of deficits in the context of models of the structure of the linguistic capacity of normal mature human beings. One does not have to be sliding down the slippery slope of confusing lesion sites with function to recognize that such analyses are a necessary component of any attempt to understand the structure of the organism.

Agrammatism can be characterized for English as the selective loss of "function words" and various bound grammatical elements (e.g., tense markers on verbs). In this chapter, we shall consider the recent work on agrammatism—work that may be grouped into three sets of studies. First, there is the work of Bradley and her colleagues on comprehension. On the basis of a series of lexical access studies, Bradley and Garrett (in preparation) argue that in the normal course of linguistic events there is a differential access for "function words" than for members of the major lexical categories (nouns, adjectives, verbs). These results suggested that it might be profitable to consider whether agrammatic aphasics demonstrated the same sort of differential access systems. The research of Bradley, Garrett, Kean, Kolk, and Zurif (in preparation) addressed just this issue, and it was found that the normal pattern of access was indeed disrupted in the agrammatic subjects. This work served as the basis for developing processing analyses in comprehension studies of agrammatism (Bradley, 1978; Bradley, Garrett, and Zurif, 1980; Kean, 1981).

The second set of studies involves work on sentence production. In an extensive study of normal spontaneous speech errors, Garrett (1975, 1976, 1980) proposed a model of the successive levels of representation which a linguistic string would, minimally, have to pass through in the course of the processes of sentence production. Garrett's model was adopted in Kean (1977) and served as the basis for an attempt to account for aspects of variation in agrammatic production. Extending and revising Garrett's basic model, Kolk (1979) attempted to provide a processing analysis of the production deficit of agrammatism. Garrett and Kean (1980) have also outlined a (partial) production analysis of agrammatism based on Garrett's "normal" model.

The third approach to be considered here is the grammatical analysis of agrammatism. Traditionally, agrammatism has been viewed as a syntactic deficit, in work which attempted to analyze the linguistic structure of agrammatic language use in terms of grammatical theory. More recently, it has been argued that the deficit must be located at the representational interface of what are traditionally thought of as syntactic rules and phonological rules (Kean, 1977,

1979, 1980, 1981). Under this analysis, the apparent grammatical variety of agrammatism—syntactic, morphological, semantic, phonological—is argued to be accountable for in terms of the interaction of various components of the grammatical system.

It will be argued here that the three models of grammar and processing that figure in these accounts of agrammatism each represents a necessary component of any psychological theory of human linguistic capacity. Furthermore, it will be argued that the three models can, as currently constituted, be viewed as components of the same theory of human linguistic capacity. Superficially, the analyses of agrammatism proposed in the context of each of these models appear to be inconsistent: In the case of comprehension the deficit seems to be in lexical access; in the case of production in syntax; and in the case of grammar phonological. Given the fundamental consistency of the models across consideration of normal linguistic function, this apparent inconsistency in the deficit analyses that each leads to seems curious, at best. And as will be seen, appearances to the contrary, when taken together the three analyses provide a framework for a full and consistent analysis of the deficit which has implications for further research not only in the local domain of deficit studies, but also in the broader domain of the structure of (normal) human linguistic capacity.

Three issues will be the central foci of this chapter:

1. A minimal condition for the development of functional analyses of linguistic deficits is that there be a consistent use of technical terminology. Unless systematic definitions are given to theoretical notions such as "phonology" and "syntax," and those definitions rigidly adhered to, what are terminological divergences of no theoretical or analytic content can be too easily confused with those actual theoretical and empirical distinctions which warrant our closest attention. The recent history of aphasia research is fraught with use–mention confusions of terminology which have served to shed no light on the nature of linguistic deficits. In this chapter an effort will be made to enforce an explicit terminology to the end of determining to what extent, if any, the models being considered provide empirically inconsistent analyses of human linguistic capacity in general and of agrammatism in particular.

2. It is an indespensable condition of the analysis of linguistic deficits that they be put forward in the context of models of the structure of normal linguistic capacity. One cannot characterize analytically any linguistic behavior, normal or deviant, without appealing to explicit characterizations both of the structure of human languages and of the way in which knowledge of language is exploited in language use. The usefulness of any analysis as a guide to future research resides in its explicitness and in its predictive capacity. There is no advantage to be taken from an analysis of a deficit which makes no contact with accounts of the structure of normal human linguistic capacity. Thus,

analyses based on grammatical theories that are clearly misguided as models of human linguistic capacity are of no utility—no one would, for example, attempt to put forward an analysis of deficits in terms of the grammatical model of Reed and Kellogg or on the basis of Panini's grammatical theory. Yet when it comes to more recently proposed linguistic and psycholinguistic models, in much of aphasia analysis it seems to be taken as totally irrelevant that the model in question may have been discredited. My point is that the attempt to provide insightful analyses of deficits must be based on the best available models of linguistic capacity.

3. The combined grammatical–production–comprehension model to be discussed here provides a framework for the analysis of deficits. Although the model is skeletal, it has the essential characteristics that one would find in more fully elaborated models. In particular, it allows for the serious and systematic analysis of deficit data, it suggests explicit lines of research, and it allows for the construction of empirically explicit analytic hypotheses. It is, as far as I know, the only model that both has scope over the central components of a linguistic performance theory and is worked out in sufficient detail to allow for precise predictive analyses. A review of the aphasia literature quickly reveals that much of the experimental research has the following two properties: (a) the experimental design is not based on explicit accounts of the structure of language and thus the variables manipulated are arbitrary, and (b) the analyses of the data obtained are either pretheoretic or post hoc appeals to whatever linguistic analysis is most convenient at the time. Neither of these characteristics permits a systematic research program in neurolinguistics. It is my hope that in outlining an analysis of agrammatism here, I will simultaneously illustrate the necessity—and the availability—of a systematic approach to deficit studies.

ON MODELING LINGUISTIC CAPACITY—SOME GENERAL CONSIDERATIONS

It is taken here as an obvious and necessary assumption of the study of human linguistic capacity that a human being with normal mature command of his native language both knows something (his native language) and can use that knowledge to produce and comprehend sentences. A theory of human linguistic capacity that incorporates accounts of not only the knowledge of language but also the processes of the use of that knowledge in comprehension and production will be called a **linguistic performance theory.** Thus, each of the models to be considered here is a component of some performance theory. Beyond that rather weak relation among them, the three can be taken together as constituting an attempt to develop a complete linguistic performance theory, skeletal though that theory may currently be; that is, they are not to be viewed as competing models.

A central assumption of all three models is that linguistic capacity under any conceptualization must be viewed as a partially ordered set of autonomous components. Each component is autonomous in the sense that the substantive vocabulary it operates over is a specific and limited subset of the universally available vocabulary of linguistic elements and that the formal devices available for any one component of the system are a proper subset of those available universally across the whole system. To take a concrete example: In the theory of transformational generative grammar, there are two so-called syntactic components in any grammar, a phrase structure component and a transformational component. Both components operate over a categorial vocabulary of N (noun), V (verb), Adj (adjective), etc., and the phrasal projections of those elements (NP, VP, AdjP, etc.). Viewed as formal rule systems the two components are fully distinct; the phrase structure rules are context-free rewrite rules whereas the rules of the transformational component are transformational rules which move constituent elements of a linguistic string, subject to a set of universal constraints on the application of such rules. As the phrase structure rules are ordered just "before" the transformational rules, the representations of syntactic structure that they generate must be such that a proper syntactic derivation will be obtained in consequence of the application of the transformations. Needless to say, the formal theory of transformations must, by the same token, be so formulated as to function over the structures generated by the phrase structure rules. There is, then, an interaction among the components of the system. The output of any component of the system is a representation of a linguistic string with respect to the component of the system which generated it. Such representations serve as the interface of components. To the extent that any component may "directly" interact with any other component, that interaction is modulo their interface representation. Thus, pursuing our example, if there is a proposed phrase structure system consisting of 10 distinct rules, no transformation can demand reference to the structure of a string at any arbitrary intervening level of representation generated by those rules—for example, no transformation may require particular reference to the output of the phrase structure rules as they applied up through but not beyond the fifth rule in the set. The interaction of components in these models is therefore restricted to those which arise through their ordering relations; two components not linearly ordered with respect to each other or not both feeding (perhaps indirectly) a third component cannot in any way interact. Such interactions as there are are captured in the systematic representations generated by the components. It is assumed that substantively and formally the components of the grammatical and processing models are universally (i.e., language independently) specified, as are their ordering relationships.

The general structural parallelism among the models noted thus far hardly warrants the claim that they are to be viewed as components of the same performance model. However, this general structural parallelism plays a central role in how deficits are to be analyzed in the context of each of the models. Consider the partially ordered set (1).

$$D$$
$$\searrow$$
(1) $A \rightarrow C \rightarrow E$
$$\nearrow$$
$$B$$

Assume that A, B, C, D, and E are autonomous components of some system in the same sense as are the components of the linguistic models. If C is impaired there will be a deviant output from the system. It should be evident that although the contributions of A and B to C will be well-formed, that well-formedness will be obscured through the deviance of C; at the same time, although D and E are unimpaired, the imparied contribution of C to E where it interacts with D may well have the attendant consequence of thoroughly obscuring the fact that both D and E are intact. Thus, the deviant output which arises solely from the impairment to C will not be transparently or trivially labelable as "deviant because C is imparied." To arrive at the conclusion that C is the functional culprit would require an analysis of the data with respect to the particular contributions made by each component to the formal realization of the output function. Under such circumstances, it would then be more than misleading to characterize the output as showing, for example, a deficit in E; surely there would be a "failure" in E, but that failure would be caused entirely by factors extrinsic to E; that is, in no strict sense would we be justified in characterizing the realized deficit directly in terms of or with respect to E.

This rather obvious point has long been noted in the localization literature. Yet, although Jackson's (1882) injunction against confusing a lesion site with the locus of function is frequently cited in the literature, to judge from the analyses themselves little more than lip service has been paid it in behavioral work. The confusion Jackson noted in the context of functional localization work (diagram making) has been chronic in the more restricted domain of functional analyses of deficits. In the analysis of agrammatism, the typical error in this regard is the claim that agrammatism is a syntactic deficit because agrammatic sentences are syntactically ill-formed. All realized linguistic strings, well-formed and ill-formed, are products of the full set of components of the linguistic system—the phonology, morphology, syntax, etc.; all strings are therefore a priori phonological strings, syntactic strings, morphological strings, etc. Pursuing this point for a moment, compare the strings in (2), where (2a) is well formed and (2b) is ill formed.

(2)   a.   *Fred and Ethel are living near the Ricardos.*
      b.   *Fred ... Ethel ... living near ... Ricardos.*

A priori one is as justified in claiming that (2b) is phonologically deviant (due, for example, to the lack of phonetic realization of certain necessary elements) as in claiming that it is syntactically deviant or morphologically deviant. For any ill-formed string it is impossible to have any preanalytic insight into the source of its deviance(s). In this regard, it seems appropriate to recall Goldstein (1948): "The question of the relationship between the symptom complex and a definitely localized lesion becomes a problem, no longer, however, in the form: where is a definite function of symptom localized? but: *how does a definite lesion modify the function of the brain so that a definite symptom comes to the fore?* [p. 45]." The italics are Goldstein's.

The relatively constrained notion of interaction of components that is admitted by the models considered here should not be confounded with interactions that arise as a consequence of the interaction of linguistic capacity (as characterized by these models) and other cognitive systems. The models are all sentence grammar models, their domain that which "goes on" within a sentence. This abstraction away from intersentential phenomena such as discourse anaphora is in no way a denial of the assertion that there is some type of structure associated with discourse; rather it is a denial of a more particular claim, to wit, that the well-formedness of a sentence of a language can only be determined in the context of discourse. That is, the string *The man bit the dog* will always be a well-formed sentence independent of whether or not in any instance of its being uttered it is uttered in a discourse in a pragmatically appropriate fashion; by the same token, the string *Is the man who wearing green shorts is here?* will invariably be ungrammatical independent of whether or not it is uttered in the context of a discussion of whether or not some man who is wearing green shorts is about. Similarly, the knowledge of the real world that is clearly brought to bear on our everyday language use plays no role in these models. To take a long discussed example, the sentence *Colorless green ideas sleep furiously* is certainly semantically anomalous in terms of what we know or expect of the world—sleeping is an activity we typically restrict to animates, and even for those possessed with vivid imaginations we would be unlikely to ascribe animacy to their ideas; however, the apparent anomaly of that string can be made to disappear in poetic contexts. Surely no account of the structure of what it is to know, for example, English can be held responsible to such phenomena.

The appropriate everyday use of a language therefore involves not only our linguistic resources but also a myriad of other resources ranging from etiquette to general conceptual knowledge. It is well to keep in mind the logical dissociation that although it may be true that much of our knowledge of the world was acquired through the vehicle of language use, from that it in no way follows that our language faculty incorporates what we know of the world. To take one last example on this point: I know where my mother lives, and I can use that knowledge together with my knowledge of English to tell people where she lives; however, my knowledge of English would in no way be altered if I did not know where she lived and therefore could not use my knowledge of English to tell people where she lived.

Keeping such distinctions in mind is not only crucial to the development of models of normal cognitive structure (including linguistic capacity); it is also crucial in considering the effects of brain damage on the manifest realizations of cognitive capacity. Deviant use of language surely does not logically entail an impairment of linguistic capacity per se. Just as the components of linguistic models interact with each other, so too must linguistic capacity interact with other components of human cognitive capacity. In attempting to develop precise functional analyses of cognitive deficits that arise concomitantly with brain damage, it is essential that there not be pretheoretical conflation across domains.

In addition to abstractions away from general knowledge and the like, these models also abstract away from mechanisms that are intimately connected with the exploitation of linguistic knowledge in language processing. Thus, all the models involve an abstraction away from human memory capacity. To acknowledge that our ability to process sentences is severely constrained by limitations on working memory. Nonetheless this does not entail that linguistic models of processing incorporate models of memory directly. If there are general constraints on memory load independent of particular cognitive systems (e.g., linguistic, visual imaging), then it would surely be wrong to incorporate those constraints directly into the theory of human linguistic capacity. Instead what would be needed is a theory of memory that could operate over the distinct vocabularies of cognitive domains, and, quite independently, theories of those cognitive domains such that they are capable of appropriately interacting with the memory theory to provide an account for the relevant phenomena. By the same token, were one to show that there are qualitative and quantitative peculiarities to the memory systems invoked on-line in the employment of some particular cognitive system then such peculiarities would have to be modeled into the account of that cognitive system. At this point, there is no reason to believe that there is some peculiarly linguistic memory system for on-line processing; thus, memory factors are not to be directly incorporated in the models.[3]

To take a second relevant case, consider the fact that language processing occurs from "left-to-right"; that is, we do not wait until a complete sentence has been presented and then process it holistically in some fashion. To the extent that this left-to-rightness is a shared property of multiple cognitive systems, it is not a component of the language faculty per se, and the responsibility of linguistic models to the fact resides only in being able to properly interface with left-to-right implementation. Similarly, if parallel processing is the only processing available for our mental exercises, then it is not directly a component of the language faculty. The exploration of these issues is still in its relative infancy, and

[3]Frazier and Fodor (1978) have proposed a parser which explicitly interfaces with memory constraints; their proposal specifies where short-term memory limitations come to bear on syntactic parsing and as well as the vocabulary of linguistic elements over which such constraints operate. See also Frazier (Chapter 11, this volume) for further discussion.

we may yet be led to incorporate more and more of such apparently independent systems into our models of the language faculty, but at this point, for the cases noted here, the evidence does not seem to warrant such a radical step.[4] It might be noted in this regard that in much of the work in artificial intelligence (AI) where modeling does not involve abstraction away from knowledge of the world, memory, etc., the people carrying out that work typically deny that they are trying to characterize the language faculty at all. What is desired of models of cognitive systems is that they be as impoverished as an appropriate analysis of the data will allow. In abstracting away from many independent but interacting cognitive systems, the models to be considered here represent attempts to determine the limits, the impoverishment, of the human capacity to know and use natural human languages in the normal course of experience. It is, of course, a constraint on such models that they (ultimately) be realizable, that is, executable, when implemented in a system which takes into account the structure of on-line memory, temporal resolving power, left-to-rightness, parallel implementation, etc.

It is a regrettable and all too frequent fact of the modeling of some specified behavioral domain under different conceptualizations that there be terminological vagaries and contradictions which obscure any attempt to consider the analyses of more than one model at a time. Each of the models considered here divides the language system up into what are essentially the same sets of component parts, a fact which has in the literature been somewhat obscured by slightly different uses of the same terminology. So, before progressing further in considering these models, it is necessary to fix some systematic terminology so that potential empirical (in)consistency not be clouded.

A theory of human linguistic capacity is responsible for accounting for the mapping between the sound realization of a string and its semantic interpretation. At the most general level of description the linguistic system can be seen as consisting of three parts: a syntax, a phonology, and a logical form component, plus a lexicon (including a derivational morphology). The component(s) of the model that capture those aspects of sentence structure that contribute both to the sound interpretation (above the level of isolated uninflected words) and the logical interpretation of a sentence are components of the syntax; the phonological component provides an account of those aspects of sentence realization

---

[4]For the sake of argument, let us assume that there exists some constraint C which operates across all domains of human cognitive capacity. In such circumstances we would not be motivated in directly incorporating C into our models of those systems. This would remain the case even were we to discover (a) that for the cognitive systems in question each was discretely neuroanatomically localized, and (b) that the neuroanatomical substrate of C was equipotentially realized across each relevant area. In this it is not the case that the functional models are not responsible to a physical interpretation; rather, one could not justifiably propose an equipotential physical substrate for C were it incorporated independently into the models of each cognitive system.

which effect the final phonetic form of a sentence but have no impact on its logical form; the logical form component of the grammar is concerned with the structure of the realization of logical syntax of, for example, quantification, in sentence grammar. Roughly speaking, then, the kinds of systems we are concerned with have the structure given in (3).

(3)

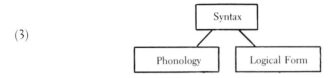

Given this broad framework of analysis, let us consider to which of these components we should assign the analysis of various aspects of sentence structure. The order of constituent elements in a sentence affects its ultimate phonetic shape, so from this it follows that all rules affecting the phonetically realized order of constituents must be incorporated in the syntax or the phonology. Any constituent structure ordering of elements that affects the logical form of a sentence as well as its phonological realization must be accounted for in the syntax, and any rule affecting the structural relations among constituents that has no impact on the logical interpretation of a sentence must be a rule of phonology.

Throughout the rest of this discussion, the terms *syntax*, *phonology*, and *logical form* will be used in the senses outlined here. That the linguistic data as characterized in each of these models can be analyzed with respect to this terminology is certainly in itself not sufficient to justify the claim that the three models are potentially components of the same performance theory. Justification of such a claim must rest on what one takes the relation between the components of such a theory to be—how the components must be related to each other.

First, it should be clear that the same components will not be found in each of the models even when they are fully developed. For example, an essential component of processing language is the mechanism(s) of lexical access—the retrieval of lexical items in the course of production and comprehension. The grammar, being a characterization of what it is to know a language, independent of the mechanisms of use of that knowledge, will contain no access component. Therefore, whatever systematic relations we posit as necessarily obtaining between the grammar and the processing models, we cannot demand full isomorphism of component systems.

As was noted at the outset, each of the models characterizes linguistic capacity as a partially ordered set of components, each component generating a representation, the characteristics of the function of the components and their output representations being universally specified. It is postulated here that it is a constraint on performance theories that the levels of representation generated by the grammar are all systematically realized by the processors. It should require no discussion that this constraint is quite distinct from a constraint that demands isomorphism of the components themselves. The claim here is not only that the representations generated by the grammar are realized in processing, but that they are the only linguistic representations systematically realized in processing.

Agrammatism in Broca's aphasia is typically behaviorally characterized (for English) in terms of a selective inability to exploit "function words" and inflectional elements in spontaneous speech. In a wide variety of studies, this selective failure of the normal capacity to exploit function words and inflections has been shown to be a deficit that pervades virtually every modality of language use, including metalinguistic abilities.

A GRAMMATICAL ANALYSIS OF AGRAMMATISM

As the grammatical analysis of agrammatism has been discussed extensively (Kean, 1977, 1979, 1980, 1981), it will only be reviewed in outline here. A systematic grammatical analysis of agrammatism must, minimally, provide a bifurcation of the elements in a string into two classes—function words and inflections versus other items. It has been argued that in the grammar this distinction is captured at a level of phonological structure; no other level of grammatical analysis would seem to provide anything systematically approximating the distinction.

The claim of the so-called phonological analysis of agrammatism is, then, simply this: At all levels of representation and with respect to all components of the grammar, save for one level of the phonological component, any grammatical analysis of agrammatism will be purely stipulative.

The class of items typically omitted in agrammatism is on the surface quite diverse grammatically. As a case in point, let us consider prepositions. It is typically said that prepositions tend to be omitted. In terms of the surface categorial vocabulary of the items in sentences this is approximately true; however, the class of surface prepositions is in fact itself quite diverse grammatically. There are in English four distinct classes of elements that are superficially designated prepositions:

1. There are lexical prepositions, true independent lexical formatives which can (up to anomaly) be freely inserted in strings. The sentences in (4) are illustrative of this class.

(4) a. *The man is standing* **on** *the table.*
     b. *The man is standing* **near** *the table.*
     c. *The man is standing* **under** *the table.*
     d. *The man is standing* **by** *the table.*
     e. *The man is standing* **in** *the swimming pool.*

2. The second class of interest consists of prepositions that are idiosyncrati-
cally associated with (occur "idiomatically" with) particular verbs. For these
prepositions there is no free substitution, and there is no (obvious) compositional
semantics of a string involving the lexical semantics of these items. This class is,
for adult second language learners, a considerable nuisance. In (5) some examples are given.

(5)   a. *We count on Fred to win.*
      b. *They took advantage of Harry.*
      c. *You should keep tabs on Reuben.*

3. The third class of interest is verb particle constructions. Again there is an
idiosyncratic relation between the verb and the following element, however, verb
particle constructions are syntactically quite distinct from the first two classes
mentioned. As with the second class, there is no free lexical substitution; unlike
both the first and second class, particles may "move" across a following noun
phrase sequence. This contrast is illustrated in (6), where an asterisk is used to
mark an ungrammatical string.

(6)   a. *John looked up Mary's address.*
      b. *John looked Mary's address up.*
      c.* *John is standing the table on.*
      d.* *You should keep tabs Reuben on.*

It should be noted that not all cases of *look up* are particle constructions. The
sentences in (7) show that *look* can also be followed by lexical prepositions,
including *up.*

(7)   a. *John looked up Mary's dress.*
      b.* *John looked Mary's dress up.*

(4). The fourth and final class is the set of items that are simply
grammatical formatives, that simply mark grammatical (and thematic) relations.
Thus, for example, when the subject of a derived nominal occurs after the
nominal it is preceded by *of* (8a–8b); the agent of a passive sentence is marked
invariably by *by* (8c–8d); there are two classes of datives, marked by surface
prepositions *to* and *for* (8e–8f).

(8)   a. *the city's destruction (by the Huns)*
      b. *the destruction of the city (by the Huns)*
      c. *The man bit the dog.*
      d. *The dog was bitten by the man.*
      e. *The boy gave the flowers to the girl.*
      f. *The boy bought the flowers for the girl.*

Given this diversity, were there in fact uniform loss of surface prepositions, there
would be no explanatory force to the claim that the category preposition was

undermined in agrammatism, and such a claim would simply be empirically false at deeper levels of analysis.

The diversity evident in the class of surface prepositions is characteristic of the diversity of classes of items cited in descriptions of agrammatism. To take one further example, consider the -s suffixes in English. The -s suffix is the plural marker of nouns. Number on nouns has interpretive force, delimits the class of specifiers a noun may take, is crucial to verbal agreement, and is not predictable grammatically. The -s suffix is also the verbal inflection that marks third person singular present tense verbs. The suffix of the verb in *Sally eats salami* reflects not only the person and number of the verb, derived by agreement with the subject of the sentence, but also the tense of the sentence, where tense is determined independently of number and person and is not syntactically predictable in any given sentence. Finally, -s is the genitive suffix. When a noun takes another noun as its specifier, the specifier noun is marked with the genitive. Frequently called the possessive in English, the genitive is not restricted to noun phrases with possessive interpretations. Thus, although one does assign a possessive interpretation to *Bill's books* in *Bill's books are on the table*, as the noun phrases in (9) illustrate this is only a use of the genitive and the genitive is not simply "the possessive" in any transparent semantic sense.

(9) a. *Rembrandt's picture of Aristotle which the Met now owns*
     b. *the city's destruction*
     c. *a pinhead's capacity to seat angels*

Thus, if we consider the grammatical "sources" of the items generally characterized as being a set that agrammatic aphasics tend to omit, there is apparently little sense to be made of that set. Furthermore, if it is the surface we consider, the set seems to make equally little sense. Surely a description that appealed to such notions as suffixes that are *s*, surface elements that are prepositions (or homophonous with prepositions), etc., would hardly be satisfying, much less satisfactory. Note also that such an account begs a variety of analytic questions. How, if we really are appealling to the surface, that is, to the phonetic string, do we know that the final syllable of *churches* in *The churches are open on Sunday* is a suffix but that the phonetically similar syllable in *We saw Usric* is not? Or that *up* is a preposition in *John looked up at the sky* but not in *I read the Hitopadsha, Upanishad, . . .*? That is, the most surface analysis available presupposes some degree of constituent structure analysis. Obviously, then, the question is, Is there a level of grammatical analysis where these superficially disparate classes have some uniform analysis?

The grammatical analysis we are concerned with here claims that there is indeed a level of grammatical structure, just one, in which the class in question is unified. That level is a level in the phonology. It should not require argument that the syntax does not treat this class uniformly; the observations that have already been made as to its diversity should suffice. In order to outline the grammatical analysis we must first consider some general, and too often over-looked, properties of the phonological component. The phonological component of the grammar, among other things, assigns the prosodic and segmental structure to sentences. The structures to which the segmental and prosodic rules apply are called phonological representations. It is the character of these representations that is central to the grammatical analysis. The segmental and prosodic phonological rules are sensitive to constituent structure. In English, for example, when two nouns occur adjacently as a compound, as in *kitchen towel*, it is the left one which receives the dominant stress; however, when two nouns occur adjacently in a sentence, not as a compound, as in *Fred gave* **students books,** the noun on the right that receives the dominant stress. Because phonological rules attend to constituent structure, one of the properties of phonological representations must be that they include the constituent structure characterization of a string. The constituent structures that the phonology appeals to are not inevitably identical with those derived through the syntax. Consider, for example, (10) where we have a sentence which syntactically has two embedded relative clauses.

(10)   *This is the princess that didn't sleep on the pea that was under the mattress.*

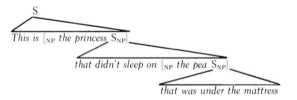

The phrase *that didn't sleep on the pea* is an embedded modifier of *the princess,* and *that was under the mattress* is an embedded modifier of *the pea*. The architectonic structure of the sentence as is (grossly) illustrated in (10) captures these relations, relations that must be taken into account in assigning the appropriate logical relations to the constituent elements of the string. When such a complex sentence is uttered, all the typical phonetic traces of embedding (relatively weaker stress, lowered intonation) are lost; such sentences are realized as if they were coordinate structures, structurally analogous to (11).

(11)   *Bill played baseball, Fred rowed on the crew, and Harry avoided all sports.*

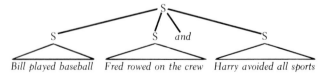

Thus, for these sentences, a rule is needed to readjust a structure of such as that in (10) to a structure such as that in (12).

(12)   *This is the princess—that didn't sleep on the pea—that was under the mattress*

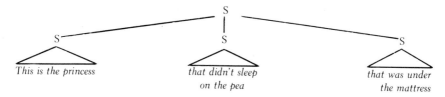

Thus the phonological component of the grammar is sensitive to constituent structure, and the constituent structures that the prosodic phonology operates over are distinct from syntactic constituent structures. The sensitivity of the phonological component to the structure of a string goes beyond gross clausal structure. Consider, for example, the interaction of deletion with the phonology. As the sentences in (13) illustrate, there can be "deletion under identity."

(13)   a.   *John is in the kitchen and Harry is in the kitchen too.*
       b.   *John is in the kitchen and Harry is—ø—too.*

Given that the deleted sequence receives an interpretation in the logical form component, it must be the case that that sequence is retained throughout the syntax. Such deletion should be viewed as the marking of a string of elements as opaque to phonological interpretation.

Deletion interacts with the phonological rule of contraction in English.

(14)   a.   *John's in the kitchen and Harry's in the kitchen too.*
       b. **John's in the kitchen and Harry's too.*
       c.   *John's in the kitchen and Harry is too.*

As is illustrated by the paradigm (13, 14), contraction of *be* is blocked when the element to be contracted (e.g., *is*) immediately precedes a deletion site. Contraction, like the prosodic rules mentioned earlier, is therefore a rule that is sensitive to the structure of a sentence. If we consider another observation about stress in English, yet another property of phonological representations emerges. In nonemphatic declarative sentences in English, not every orthographic word receives a "word stress"; thus, in *The boys played in the sandbox* the words *boys*, *played*, and *sandbox* all carry stress, whereas *the*, *in*, and *the* do not. Nor do these latter three words contribute to the overall sentential stress pattern; *Students read books* and *The boys played in the sandbox* have the same sentential prosody. If we consider the stress patterns of words in English we note that some affixes will cause a change in stress on words, whereas others never do. In English, inflectional morphemes (e.g., the plural, tense markers, the comparative, and the genitive) never affect the stress on a word even when they are realized as full syllables; other affixes, some of the derivational affixes of the lexicon, do affect the stress pattern of a word. Thus, we can contrast the gerundive and progressive suffix -*ing* with the derivational affix -*ation*, as in *divíne*, *divíning*, *divinátion*. What is required is some means for the grammar to distinguish, in the case of English, the stress sensitive elements from the stress insensitive elements. The sequences that participate in stress assignment in English are the major lexical categories and the phrases dominating these categories. In the structure (15) the units that contribute potentially to the stress and intonational pattern are given in uppercase; no other units can participate in neutral nonemphatic stress assignment.

(15)   *The BOYs WALKed to SCHOOL on SUNNY DAYs.*

There is a simple algorithm for distinguishing these sets of units that can be used to make available a principled notation for distinguishing the stress contributing words form everything else. The algorithm proposed by Chomsky and Halle (1968) is: Insert a word boundary (#) to the right and left of very major lexical category and category dominating a major lexical category. [Details are omitted in (16)]

(16)   [$_S$ # [$_{NP}$ # the [$_N$ # [# boy # $_N$]s # $_N$] # $_{NP}$][$_{VP}$ # [$_V$ # [$_V$ # walk # $_V$] ed # $_V$]
       [$_{PP}$ # to [$_{NP}$ # school # $_{NP}$] # $_{PP}$] [$_{PP}$ # on [$_{NP}$ # [$_A$ # sunny # $_A$] [$_N$ # [$_N$ #
       day # $_N$] s # $_N$] # $_{NP}$] # $_{PP}$] # $_{VP}$] # $_S$]

Applying this algorithm, we can now distinguish those items that are properly bracketed strings of the form [#——#], where —— contains no #s, from everything else. [For convenience and ease of reading in what follows rather than using the # notation, just those items that are properly bracketed strings of the form #——#, where —— contains no #s, will be given in uppercase, as in (15); such items will be termed **phonological words** (P-words). Everything else, **phonological clitics** (P-clitics), will be given in lower case.]

      If the division of the elements in a string by this algorithm into two systematic phonological classes is an idiosyncratic property of English, then the distinction would have to be built into the grammar of English per se. However, given that the algorithm is totally structural, we can apply it to the representations of strings in the grammar of any other languages to yield two distinct classes and, having established those two classes within other languages, we could then consider whether the grammars of those languages treat the classes established in any systematically different ways. If we find that the distinction that shows up in English with respect to stress shows up in other languages with respect to either segmental or prosodic parameters, then that would motivate incorporating the distinction (the algorithm, as it were) into the theory of grammar and not just into the grammar of English. In fact, the P-word–P-clitic distinction is extremely phonologically potent cross-linguistically. It figures in liaison phenomena in French, a final consonant devoicing rule in Russian, and a vowel deletion rule in Klamath, to cite a few examples. Because this distinction pervades the segmental and prosodic domains of phonology, it must be representationally captured prior to the application of such rules. It is important to note that there are no segmental or prosodic rules that MUST apply prior to the introduction of this distinction into the representation of a string, and, by the same token, there is no rule operating in any domain prior to the segmental and prosodic phonology that must take this distinction into account. On the basis of such considerations it must be concluded that the distinction between phonological words and everything else must be given in phonological representations.

To summarize: The role of the phonological component is the phonetic interpretation of a sentence. The assignment of a phonetic interpretation involves the application of segmental and prosodic rules. These rules apply to phonological representations. Phonological representations, like, for example, syntactic structures, are hierarchical constituent structure representations. These representations are not isomorphic with the representations that are the output of the syntactic component. In addition to expressing the phonological constituent structure of strings, phonological representations, unlike representations associated with other components of the grammar, must make available the bifurcation of the elements in a string into P-words and P-clitics. The "phonological analysis" of agrammatism consists, then, of the following empirical hypotheses: (a) the distinction between the class of items that tend to be omitted and the class of items that are typically retained involves a single principled grammatical distinction among items, and, furthermore, (b) that distinction is captured in phonological representations.

As should be evident from this cursory overview, the grammatical analysis of any aphasic deficit as simply "a phonological deficit" would be unrevealing; phonological structure and organization are of such richness that any such description would be without explanatory force. A phonological deficit might involve an impairment with respect to the utilization of the segmental distinctive features or with respect to (some aspect of) the realizations of constituent structure in phonological component. There is, of course, work in aphasia in which these very distinct aspects of phonology have played distinct and critical roles. In Blumstein's (1973) analysis of segmental (phonemic) paraphasias, it is the feature system that is central. By contrast, in Kean (1979, 1980, 1981) it is phonological representations, and explicitly not features, which provide the pivotal issue in a phonological analysis of agrammatism. Just as distinctive feature theory is an empirical hypothesis as to the parameters of segmental confusion, so too the distinction between P-words and P-clitics in phonological representation constitutes an empirical hypothesis as to a parameter of potential categorial dissociability.

There are several significant empirical consequences to this analysis. First, consider its predictions with respect to English. Because the analysis is based on a general structural property of the language, it is in fact greatly underdetermined by the data that motivated it. This is, of course, going to be a property of any analysis that attempts to reach a level of descriptive adequacy. By virtue of being so underdetermined it makes a variety of predictions about classes of items previously not considered in analyses of agrammatism, thereby raising new and specific research questions. For example, as the suffix -*ness* is a P-clitic in English, the prediction is that it should pattern with the "function words," whereas the suffix -*ity* which is not a P-clitic should not, ceteris paribus. Several objections have been raised to this sort of claim. Curiously, it has been suggested that because there are no data from agrammatism that directly support that claim, this can be taken as constituting an argument against the phonological analysis (Kolk, 1978). Surely the relative truth or falsity of a prediction cannot be evaluated if the relevant data are not available. Yet another objection has been that Broca's aphasics do not typically use long multimorphemic words, such as words in -*ness* or -*ity*, and therefore the analysis must be wrong because it predicts that they will use such words, in particular, words with -*ity*. As the analysis makes no claims about actual production capacities, and no purely grammatical analysis could, such putative arguments are totally beside the point. To accept any such line of argument would lead one also to accept arguments that there is a grammatical difference between *Dogs don't eat plankton* and *Orangutans don't eat plankton* due to the fact that there are processing distinctions between the two because *orangutan* has more syllables and is of lower frequency than *dog*. Finally, it has even been suggested that the analysis must be wrong because, even if Broca's aphasics did use words of sufficient complexity to make the hypothesis easily testable, it is highly doubtful that -*ness* would pattern exactly with, for example, the plural, and -*ity* would be fully retained. It would be in no way surprising if this conjecture were true; it would also be totally irrelevant to the grammatical hypothesis. It is not the case that the deficit of agrammatism compromises all function words and inflections in equal degree; there is a hierarchy of loss, with -*ing*, an inflection, being relatively well retained, and -*s*, the verbal inflection, being just about completely "lost." Thus, given that there is such a hierarchy one would anticipate that items like -*ness* and -*ity* would fall somewhere within it. Where they would fall is another question. It has been suggested (Kean, 1977) that this hierarchy is found in normal production and that it reflects the diversity of the class of P-clitics; Kean and Garrett (1980) also note the necessity for mechanisms of construal in the lexicon which would give rise to a production hierarchy. Whatever the appropriate analysis of that hierarchy, that is totally independent of the claim that phonological representations provide the proper grammatical domain for analyzing agrammatism.

A second empirical consequence of the analysis is that it makes explicit cross-linguistic predictions. The P-word–P-clitic distinction is a structural distinction to be found in all languages. Thus, *modulo* the role this distinction plays in processing, the analysis gives a principled description of agrammatism for all languages. There are two virtues in this. In describing agrammatism cross-linguistically, there is a chronic confusion of translation. In a language like English, the oblique cases (i.e., dative, locative, ablative, etc.), with the exception of genitive, are basically captured in the language through special uses of prepositions; in other languages (e.g., Latin) these cases are captured by special case affixes on nouns. If in characterizing agrammatism one were restricted to descriptions arising under translation then it would surely be the case that the deficit would be totally unsystematic cross-linguistically. The structural relation of a case marker to a noun is not necessarily the same as that of a preposition to a noun; case inflections need not be P-clitics. Since one knows from consideration of one language, English, that the deficit is systematic, then it must be the case that some systematic nontranslation analysis is available. Whether or not the phonological analysis is correct, it does have the clearly necessary property of any potentially adequate analysis in being language independent. Secondly, as with the consideration of English alone, the analysis goes far beyond the available corpus of data on agrammatism and in doing so suggests new areas of inquiry and at the same time opens itself to rather direct falsification.

Although grammarians have long noted that any analysis of the phonology of a language involves more than just description of how a linear sequence of unit segments (systematic or taxonomic phonemes) interact with one another, this has typically been ignored by people working in domains outside the study of the structure of human languages. Thus some people have rejected the phonological analysis of agrammatism because it involves something other than linear strings of segments. Such rejection amounts to little more than a pun. Clearly an analysis cannot be rejected on the basis of a terminological disparity. If one wanted to maintain that phonology is solely concerned with the way segments interact in linear sequences in various languages, then the phonological analysis could not be properly termed "phonological" (and such phenomena as stress, intonation, and contraction in English would also be nonphonological). As the domain of phonology in grammar has never been so arbitrarily restricted in the past (for good reason it would seem), it would hardly seem warranted to change the definitions of phonology and syntax simply in the service and furtherance of ignorance.

Simply because the phonological level of representation stands at the interface of rules that attend to the order of constituents and rules that attend to prosodic and segmental realization, it does not follow that the phonological analysis of agrammatism makes the prediction that there will be a segmental or prosodic deficit in agrammatism. In fact, the phonological analysis does not make such a claim. First, that claim would only make sense if one took the grammatical model also to be the processing model completely. One might plausibly anticipate that because there is a deviance with respect to the input to the processes of segmental and prosodic realization in production, there would, as a by-product, be some segmental and prosodic disruption in production and identification, but this is all. By the same token, because phonological representations do not in themselves determine the segmental analysis of a string in comprehension but are, rather, product (at least in part) of segmental analysis, lexical access, etc., one might anticipate no significant comprehension deficit at the segmental level. But these are only speculations, of rather limited force in the absence of serious analyses of how phonological representations actually interact with the segmental processes of production and comprehension.

TWO PROCESSING ANALYSES OF AGRAMMATISM

Lexical Access and Sentence Parsing

In a series of experiments, Bradley and Garrett (in preparation) found different lexical access patterns for members of the "closed class" (i.e., function words) as opposed to members of the "open class" (i.e., the major lexical categories). In considering the implications of this finding for modeling comprehension processes, they suggested that there is a rapid exhaustive lexical search of the "closed class" file, and that items so accessed provided the crucial cues to initial "syntactic" hypotheses as to the constituent structure of a sentence.[5] On the basis of lexical access, a preliminary constitutent structure representation is realized.

(17)   a.   ... segmental sequence

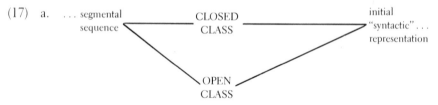

CLOSED CLASS

initial "syntactic" ... representation

OPEN CLASS

The distinction between the "closed class" and the "open class" noted in this work is, for the range of currently available data, aproximately the same as the P-word–P-clitic distinction of phonological representation. It has long been hypothesized by linguists that phonological representation is the preliminary constituent structure representation of a sentence which is realized in processing.[6] Bradley, Garrett, and Zurif (1980) and Kean (1981) suggest that it may

---

[5] Alternatively, on the basis of these data one might posit a single lexical file and attribute the difference between the classes to differential postaccess deployment in parsing. For the present purposes, this analysis is equivalent to that in the text.

[6] Chomsky and Halle (1968), for example, state:

It appears that the syntactic component of the grammar generates a surface structure Σ which is converted, by readjustment rules that mark phonological phrases and delete

be/is in fact phonological representation that is the initial "syntactic" hypothesis, which is the realized output of the lexical access system. Following that interpretation of the results of the lexical access studies, (17a) can be translated as (17b). It should be evident from this example, that many specious arguments can, potentially, arise due solely to nonempirical terminological confusions. In terms of (17a), any analysis made with respect to the representation realized in consequence of lexical access will be called "syntactic," whereas in terms of (3) and (17b) an analysis with respect to phonological representation would be termed "phonological." A failure to use systematic terminology across the models within theories of grammar and processing can only serve to obscure the substantive issues at stake in analyses put forward.

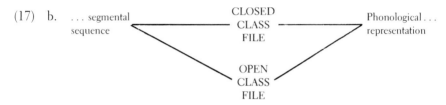

Bradley and Garrett (in preparation) have argued on the basis of experimental data that in sentence comprehension there are distinct lexical access systems for function words (closed class items) versus other words (open class items), a distinction that essentially parallels the P-word–P-clitic distinction over the range of experimental data. They hypothesize that this distinction in access systems plays a crucial role in the construction of initial "syntactic" hypotheses in parsing: Members of the closed class provide crucial cues to the constituent structure of a sentence; items in the open class are with great frequency ambiguous as to syntactic category; their ambiguity can in large measure be resolved by attending to the particular closed class items(s) in their local domain. In virtue of this two-track system an initial constituent structure representation is realized.

Bradley, Garrett, and Zurif (1980) note that it has been hypothesized by linguists that phonological representations are the initial level of constituent structure realized in comprehension (see Note 6). Given the characteristics of phonological representations—that they apparently distinguish open from closed class items and provide a gross constituent structure analysis of a string—such a hypothesis is natural. Following the traditional nongrammatical description of these structures they have termed them "syntactic" rather than "phonological." To reiterate, we have here simply a difference in terminology. To the extent

---

structure, to a still more superficial structure Σ'. . . . We might speculate, then, that the first stage in perceptual processing involves recovery of Σ' from the signal using only the restricted short term memory, and that a second stage provides the analysis into Σ and the deep structure which underlies it [p. 10].

that there are relevant data available, those data rather directly implicate phonological representations.

Given the evidence that there is a comprehension deficit (on-line) which parallels the production deficit (on-line) of agrammatism, in the light of the Bradley and Garrett (in preparation) results the question naturally arises as to whether one would find evidence of the same sort of two-track access system with agrammatic subjects. Bradley, Garrett, and Zurif (1980) carried out a study with Broca's aphasics which directly addressed this question. The results of that study were that the aphasic subjects did not show the capacity to do a rapid search of a segregated file of closed class items, but rather, appeared to treat those items as if they were members of the open class. Under the hypothesis that an independent access system for members of the closed class plays a crucial role in the realization of initial hypotheses as to the constituent structure of a string, the agrammatic access data can only be interpreted as indicating that because they have lost the ability to exploit the closed class file, agrammatic aphasics are therefore unable to make the appropriate initial constituent structure parsings of sentences—that is, they have an impairment to a crucial component of the capacity to realize phonological representations.

The lexical access studies discussed here all involved visual presentation of individual stimulus items. Obviously, such studies must be supplemented by auditory studies if the general comprehension argument analysis is to be maintained. In a recent auditory study using a word monitor technique, Swinney, Zurif, and Cutler (1980) obtained results consistent with those of the visual studies. They too describe the deficit in terms of an inability to realize an initial "syntactic" representation; this again simply reflects the tradition of psycholinguistics to refer to all matters of constituent structure as "syntactic." There is in these data and their analysis no basis for claiming a substantive empirical difference, incompatibility between this analysis of agrammatism and that termed "phonological."

Although the comprehension model of (17) makes claims about stages in processing, it makes little claim as to the nature of the mechanisms available for these stages. To be sure, the model demands that the mechanisms attend to a distinction between open and closed class items, but it makes no claim as to how these two classes of items are integrated in the initial realization of constituent structure. In a recent comprehension experiment, Schwartz, Saffran, and Marin (1980) provide some experimental evidence that agrammatic aphasics have difficulty with the proper realization of word order in comprehension. Those data are both suggestive of the scope of the deficit and deserving of considerable attention in any attempt to develop hypotheses as to the nature of the mechanisms in question. Surely, whatever the mechanisms involved, they must be capable of the maintenance of word order. How that is effected is the issue. If, for instance, the positional constituent structure frames made available through the closed class access and/or parsing system were in some sense crucial keys to maintaining appropriate word order relations in comprehension, then the limitation in the capacity to utilize the closed class access system would provide at least a partial explanation for any failures in agrammatism, in maintaining word order relations in comprehension. This is, to be sure, speculation, but it is suggestive of the avenues of inquiry that must be pursued, if attempts to provide principled analyses of deficits are to be pushed with any degree of seriousness. At this time, the relevant data for making justifiable proposals along these lines are wanting.

Levels in a Sentence Production Model

If we turn now to the production model in question, we find it is also necessary to carry out some "translation" in order to see whether or not it can be incorporated into the linguistic performance theory which includes the grammar and comprehension models already discussed. The model in (18) is taken from Garrett (1976); this model was developed on the basis of an extensive study of the structure of normal spontaneous speech errors. The logic of the approach to speech error analysis in the development of production models is quite straightforward: There must be processing mechanisms for sentence production, speech errors are not random deformations of well-formed sentences, therefore, speech errors must be constrained by the mechanisms of sentence production. Under this line of reasoning, a systematic taxonomy of speech errors can be taken as indicating (some of) the component systems of the production processor (see Garrett, Chapter 10, this volume). The model in (18) characterizes the minimal number of levels of representation that must be incorporated into any model of production that attempts to account not only for well-formed productions but also the range of potential deviances from well-formedness. Under such a model, the notion "impossible speech error" has essentially the same status that the notion "ungrammatical sentence" has for the theory of grammar.

(18)

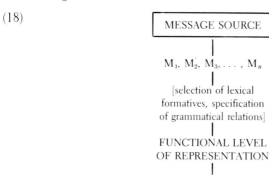

MESSAGE SOURCE

|

$M_1, M_2, M_3, \ldots , M_n$

|

[selection of lexical
formatives, specification
of grammatical relations]

|

FUNCTIONAL LEVEL
OF REPRESENTATION

|

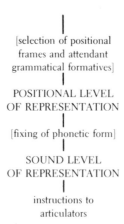

[selection of positional
frames and attendant
grammatical formatives]

POSITIONAL LEVEL
OF REPRESENTATION

[fixing of phonetic form]

SOUND LEVEL
OF REPRESENTATION

instructions to
articulators

At first glance, it would seem that this model has little in common with the grammatical and comprehension models discussed so far. There is no obvious equivalent to the functional level in the grammatical model, or, to be more precise, it is not clear what the appropriate grammatical equivalent might be. We can think of grammatical relations in two ways. First, in terms of the structure of a sentence, we can characterize grammatical relations on purely structural grounds. Thus, for example, the subject of a sentence can be characterized as that NP immediately dominated by S.

(19)

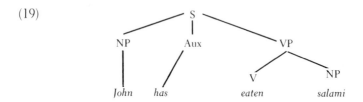

If we appeal to underlying grammatical relations, then *John* is the subject of both the active sentence (19) and its passive counterpart, *Salami was eaten by John*. At the level of the output of the syntax, however, under the structural definition of subject *John* is the subject of the active sentence, and *salami* the subject of the passive. Yet another type of grammatical relation one might think of is the thematic relations of the different elements in a sentence, the relations *agent*, *patient*, etc. Thematic relations are determined in the lexicon and the logical form components of the grammar. At this time, the functional level is not sufficiently specified to allow for a specific hypothesis as to its possible appropriate grammatical analogue(s).

The positional level is more readily localizable in terms of the models we have been considering. The characteristic of the positional level is that there is a systematic distinction between function words and inflections, on the one hand, and everything else on the other. This, then, is apparently once again phonological representation, the one level of grammatical representation where the distinction between these classes—P-words and P-clitics—is made. Further evidence that it is phonological representation that is at issue here comes from the fact that the order of elements as represented in the positional level is the same as the order of elements as they are phonetically realized. Again, phonological representation has just this property. Garrett (1975) described the positional level as the surface "syntactic" level. Thus, here we find another case where there is a potential confusion arising solely out of terminological variation. In terms of the models under consideration, each proposes a level of representation with what would appear to be the P-word–P-clitic bifurcation of items in which the elements of a sentence have their realized order; there is no substantive distinction between the models with respect to postulating such a level.

The claim that the models in question can be taken as components of the same linguistic performance theory may still seem like so much wishful thinking. There surely are differences among the models, the most notable being the considerable disparity in the degree of specificity of each. In the case of comprehension, we only have a small fragment of a model, and, although the production model is more fully outlined, it still lacks the detail of the grammatical model. The production model covers a broader range of stages in processing than does the comprehension fragment, but in its account of the details of those stages it lacks the specificity of the comprehension fragment. Neither of the processing models as currently developed posits as many levels of representation as does the grammatical model; however, nothing can be said to follow from their failure to postulate, for example, a logical form–underlying syntactic distinction. That is, it is not that the proponents of these models deny the logical form–underlying syntactic distinction; rather, it is that at this time they have no data that bear on that distinction with respect to the models of processing. There can be no substantive dispute over a domain that consists of an open question. To the extent that these models are developed they are mutually consistent. Whether they will remain consistent when they are all more fully elaborated is something only a clairvoyant might know. Given the current form of these models it can be claimed that they can be taken as components of the same linguistic performance theory because they are consistent with each other. Obviously, it is a research goal to develop more fully specified and related models.

Although production traditionally has received the greatest attention in describing agrammatism, particularly in clinical descriptions, it has received the least attention in the development of systematic and principled analyses. As the most salient characteristic of agrammatism is the selective failure to exploit function words and inflections in spontaneous speech, in terms of the production model it is the positional level which is implicated. The positional level involves a phonological representation of sentence frames consisting of the superficial constituent structure bracketing of a sentence and its grammatical formatives, that is, function words and inflections, or closed class items, or P-clitics. Into these frames, the lexical formatives, that is major class items, or open class items, or P-words, are inserted under Garrett's (1975, 1976, 1980) model.

What is unclear at this point is how exactly the positional level is implicated. As with the previous two analyses, the production analysis suggests specific avenues for research. Extrapolating from the comprehension analysis, it would be reasonable to attempt to further refine the production analysis in terms of an inability to exploit the closed class lexical file to the end of establishing appropriate positional frames in production. As Garrett (Chapter 10, this volume) points out, this is one area where there is good evidence of an overlap of the production and comprehension systems. If the deficit is ascribed to a failure in establishing positional frames, and if, following Garrett's model, these frames are the vehicle for establishing the appropriate surface word order in normal production, then it would be predicted that agrammatic aphasics would have as a byproduct of the deficit a problem with word order in sentence production. Research by Saffran, Schwartz, and Marin (1980) provides evidence that there is in fact a word order problem in production. It is essential to keep in mind that under the analysis being suggested here there is no deficit with respect to establishing the word order of major lexical formatives per se, but rather there is a deficit that has the consequence of impeding the normal appropriate execution of the insertion of major lexical formatives into appropriate positional frames. At this point there are insufficient production data to allow for the further refinement of this hypothesis. What is required are studies in which the P-clitic–P-word distinction for production can be systematically contrasted for normal and agrammatic subjects as well as studies of both populations that would allow for closer scrutiny of the mechanisms for relating major lexical items to positional frames in production and comprehension.

It has been suggested by Schwartz, Saffran, and Marin (1980) that their word order studies provide evidence against the grammatical phonological analysis. By the logic of the situation, such evidence can only come from showing either (a) that the word order production data are inconsistent with the predictions of the phonological analysis under the appropriate production model, or (b) that a better explanation is available under some other model. As has just been outlined, there is reason under the production analysis coordinate of the grammatical phonological analysis to anticipate some problem with word order, though the precise character of that problem is currently left open. Saffran, Schwartz, and Marin suggest an analysis in terms of case grammar (Fillmore, 1968). It is implausible to think that that analysis will in the end provide a better explanation of the data, given that case grammar has been abandoned by linguists because of its fundamental inadequacies in accounting for the basic structure of human languages. At this point, the production model is not sufficiently specified and the relevant data are wanting to be able to closely consider whether the production analysis with respect to the phonological representation of the positional level will provide an adequate analysis of agrammatism or not. What is currently provided by the production analysis is the outline of a framework for systematic research in the future.

Another study of agrammatic production has been carried out by Kolk (1979). Kolk used a story completion paradigm to elicit contrasting pairs of sentences like *The lion is able to kill* versus *The lion is easy to kill*. Although the surface linear word order of such pairs is identical, they differ significantly in that *the lion* is the subject of *kill* in the former sentence, its object in the latter—a distinction that is grammatically captured by the fact that there is a significant structural syntactic difference between the sentences. Kolk trained subjects on sentences of the *able* type in story completion, and in his training would explicitly tell his subjects what the appropriate target was and encourage them to produce it. Having been trained on the *able* type sentences, the subjects were then given stories that demanded an *easy* type sentence for completion. Kolk found no transference of training to the *easy* sentences. He argued that this provided strong evidence against the phonological analysis and in favor of a syntactic analysis. However, given that the distinction between *able* and *easy* type sentences is syntactic and not phonological, the failure of transference provides evidence that the subjects were tacitly aware of at least that aspect of English syntax. Thus, if the experiment points to anything it points to an intact syntactic capacity.

Kolk notes that the majority of the errors his subjects produced were "syntactic" errors, where "syntactic" errors included all errors that were neither segmental paraphasias nor omissions of function words or inflections from THE APPROPRIATE TARGET SENTENCE. Thus, if a subject produced a sentence that was not of the target structure, but rather some alternative structure, and that production was ill-formed in virtue of the omission of a function word, such an error was called "syntactic," whereas an error involving the omission of a function word from a target sentence was not called a syntactic error. Using this rather curious differentiation, Kolk claims that the phonological analysis is not supported as it fails to predict that the majority of errors will be "syntactic." Such reasoning hardly warrants discussion. To be sure, Kolk's error data deserve close scrutiny. For example, his subjects showed definite preferences for producing some of the possible alternatives to the target constructions; little is known of nature of structural preferences in processing, and as Kolk's corpus is a controlled sample over a restricted set of structures it is a valuable resource for beginning to develop some understanding of preference phenomena.

Kolk has attempted to interpret the production deficit of agrammatism in terms of Garrett's model. Initially, Kolk (1978) argued that the deficit should be associated with the positional level; as Garrett (1975) had characterized the positional level as "syntactic," Kolk argued that if the analysis in terms of the positional level were correct then the phonological grammatical analysis was wrong. This is yet another instance of the confusion of terminological differences with empirical differences (Garrett and Kean, 1980).

CONCLUSION

Looking at agrammatism from the perspectives of grammar, production, and comprehension where the models of the conceptualizations of language are mutually consistent, we begin, I think, to have a framework for the close scrutiny of functional deficits. Without such models, analysis of deficits will remain capricious; an anarchic approach to functional characterization has had no theoretical utility. Although this work is still in its early infancy, it does allow for the liberation of research from pretheoretic conceptions of the structure of language and human linguistic capacity. Agrammatism and at least some of its concomitants are no longer a random collection of symptoms; one begins to see some functional coherence to the symptom-complex. Experimental studies have enriched our conception of agrammatism; no longer can one think of the agrammatic Broca's aphasic as a person with just a production deficit. The systematic analyses of agrammatism which are beginning to emerge direct our attention to new avenues of inquiry where we can, I think quite safely, anticipate experimental research that will enrich our appreciation of the scope of the agrammatic deficit. And it is also quite clear that as such research proceeds our understanding of the structure of normal function will in turn be enhanced.

REFERENCES

Blumstein, S. (1973). A phonological investigation of aphasic speech. The Hague: Mouton.
Bradley, D. C. (1978). Computational distinctions of vocabulary type. Unpublished Ph.D. dissertation, MIT.
Bradley, D. C., and Garrett, M. F. (In preparation). Computational distinctions of vocabulary type.
Bradley, D. C., Garrett, M. F., Kean, M.-L., Kolk, H., and Zurif, E. B. (In preparation). Distinguishing vocabulary type: Normal versus agrammatic speakers.
Bradley, D. C., Garrett, M. F., and Zurif, E. B. (1980). Syntactic deficits in Broca's aphasia. In D. Caplan (Ed.), Biological studies of mental capacities. Cambridge, Mass.: MIT Press.
Chomsky, N., and M. Halle (1968). The sound pattern of English. New York: Harper and Row.
Frazier, L., and Fodor, J. D. (1978): The Sausage Machine: A new two-stage parsing model, Cognition, 6, 291–325.
Fillmore, C. (1968). A case for case. In E. Bach and R. Harms (Eds.), Universals of linguistic theory. New York: Holt, Rinehart, and Winston.

Garrett, M. F. (1975). The analysis of sentence production. In G. Bower (Ed.), *The psychology of learning and motivation.* New York: Academic Press.

Garrett, M. F. (1976). Syntacitic processes of sentence production. In R. Wales and E. Walker (Eds.), *New approaches to language mechanisms.* Amsterdam: North-Holland.

Garrett, M. F. (1980). Levels of processing in sentence production. In B. Butterworth (Ed.), *Language production,* Vol. 1. New York: Academic Press.

Garrett, M. F., and Kean, M.-L. (1980). Levels of representation and the analysis of speech errors. In M. Aronoff and M.-L. Kean (Eds.), *Juncture.* San Francisco: Anma Libri.

Goldstein, K. (1948). *Language and language disturbances.* New York: Grune and Stratton.

Jackson, J. H. (1882). On some implications of dissolution of the nervous system. *Medical Press and Circular 7.* (Reprinted in J. Taylor, Ed., *Selected writings of John Hughlings Jackson,* London: Hodder and Stoughton, 1932.)

Kean, M.-L. (1977). The linguistic interpretation of aphasic syndromes: Agrammatism in Broca's aphasia, and example. *Cognition, 5,* 9–46.

Kean, M.-L. (1979). Agrammatism: A phonological deficit? *Cognition, 7,* 69–84.

Kean, M.-L. (1980). Grammatical representations and the description of processing. In D. Caplan (Ed.), *Biological studies of mental capacities.* Cambridge, Mass.: MIT Press.

Kean, M.-L. (1981). Explanation in neurolinguistics. In N. Hornstein and D. Lightfoot (Eds.), *Explanation in linguistics.* London: Longman.

Kolk, H. (1978). The linguistic interpretation of Broca's aphasia. *Cognition, 6,* 353–361.

Kolk, H. (1979). *Where do agrammatic sentences come from?* Paper presented at the International Neuropsychological Society, June 1979.

Schwartz, M., Saffran, E., and Marin, O. (1980). The word order problem in agrammatism, I: Comprehension. *Brain and Language, 10*(2), 249–262.

Saffran, E., Schwartz, M., and Marin, (1980). The word order problem in agrammatism, II: Production. *Brain and Language, 10,*(2), 263–280.

Swinney, D., Zurif, E., and Cutler, A. (1980). Effects of sentential stress and word class upon comprehension in Broca's aphasics. *Brain and Language, 10,* 132–144.

Whitaker, H. A. (1971). *On the representation of language in the human brain.* Edmonton: Linguistic Research.

9

The Use of Data from Aphasia in Constructing a Performance Model of Language[1]

Edgar B. Zurif

GRAMMATICAL AND PROCESSING ACCOUNTS OF BROCA'S APHASIA

Although very few clinicians have ever claimed the comprehension of Broca's aphasics to be entirely normal, it has only lately been recognized that, in some important respects, the Broca's comprehension deficits, though less "public," actually parallel the production deficits, and more particularly, that, whatever else, the problem in both implicates at least the closed class elements, thereby pointing to a grammatical limitation that is general to the language faculty. (For aspects of the development of this notion see, e.g., Caramazza and Berndt, 1978; Goodglass, 1976; Zurif and Blumstein, 1978; Zurif and Caramazza, 1976.) Kean's analysis (Chapter 8, this volume) builds upon this and other recent experimentally based advances in a detailed and interesting fashion; and in the process, her work offers encouraging evidence for the existence of strong connections between the organization of a seemingly language-specific cognitive system and the organization of an underlying neural system.

An important feature of Kean's work is that although it is initiated from the perspective of grammatical theory, the linguistic distinctions provided, very explicitly accomodate a processing device. This device, though hardly detailed at this point, appears, nonetheless, to be geared specifically to the assignment of structural analyses to utterances. Thus, in alignment with her grammatical—specifically, phonological—distinction between open and closed class vocabulary items, there appear to exist separate routes for the lexical access of these two classes. By hypothesis, the closed class route serves as input to a parser, permitting the on-line construction of a structural representation—or as Kean has stated

[1]The preparation of this chapter and some of the research reported in it were supported by Grants NS 11408, NS 06209, and NS 15972.

NEURAL MODELS OF
LANGUAGE PROCESSES

it, a sound–syntax interface (see also Bradley, Garrett, and Zurif, 1980; Bradley, Garrett, Kean, Kolk, and Zurif, forthcoming).

The fact that patients who do not control this specialized closed class retrieval—who treat open and closed class items alike at the point of lexical access—are also agrammatic strengthens this hypothesis. Further, and to add to Kean's descriptions, it must be emphasized that the failure to distinguish open and closed class elements is not a consequence of brain damage in general; rather, it seems to be tied to the agrammatism of left-anterior brain damage. A number of posteriorly damaged patients presenting primarily with a word-finding difficulty in the context of grammatically well-formed utterances have already been tested and have shown the normal dissociation of the two vocabulary classes (Bradley *et al.*, 1980 and forthcoming).

With this by way of summary and added detail, I want now to enter one cautionary note concerning Kean's analysis (with which she is likely to be in agreement) and then, in several following sections, to use her analysis as a means of raising some issues for future research.

The cautionary note: Even though the distinction between open and closed vocabulary classes is worked out by reference to the phonological level, the PROCESSING ramification—that is, the implementation—of this distinction seems, from the evidence at hand, to appear at the point of lexical access, and not as some have claimed (e.g., Kellar, 1978; Brown, Chapter 21, this volume) at the point of assigning a phonological representation to the acoustic input. To be sure, Kean's grammatical characterization is elaborated for English-speaking aphasics in terms of stress, particularly in terms of the fact that closed class items neither receive stress (except for emphatic purposes) nor contribute to sentential stress patterns. But these are grammatical claims, and they are not to be taken as literally indicating that the brain damage underlying Broca's aphasia forecloses grammatical analysis simply by blocking off the analysis of unstressed (closed class) items on a purely acoustic basis. In fact, as Kean (1979) herself has pointed out, closed class items carry no special physical signal that distinguishes them from open class items: Stressless syllables abound in open class items, yet these are recovered by Broca's aphasics.

There is also experimental evidence to suggest that the Broca's comprehension problem is other than one of dealing with the acoustic structure of closed class items (Blumstein, Cooper, Zurif, and Caramazza, 1977; Caramazza, Gardner, and Zurif, 1978; Swinney, Zurif, and Cutler, 1980). In the Swinney, Zurif, and Cutler (1980) experiment, for example, though both Broca's aphasics and neurologically intact subjects responded faster to stressed than to unstressed words in a monitoring task, only the Broca's patients showed an effect of vocabulary class by responding faster to open than to closed class items, REGARDLESS OF STRESS. Again, the fact that closed class items place an extra burden on the Broca's processing capacities may be presumed to reflect the Broca's inability to preferentially access the special closed class file.

ACCESS TO FEATURES OF STRUCTURE AND
MEANING AND SOME ON-LINE CONSIDERATIONS

Yet, although Broca's aphasic patients seem not to have access to the closed class "bin," the fact remains that they do recognize closed class items as belonging to their language. Accordingly, it seems that the closed class is "doubly" registered"—once in its specifically accessed bin, which by hypothesis supports syntactic analysis, and again in the bin that also includes the open class items.

In the context of this speculation, the question arises as to whether a predominantly semantic function can be assigned to the frequency sensitive system, in complementary fashion to the syntactic function hypothesized for the closed class system. Thus, given that the Broca's aphasic patients appear to have access to the first-mentioned route, do they know the semantic value of closed class elements in a sentence, even though they cannot use these elements for structure-building purposes?

One experiment that has been devised to address this question turns on a situation in which articles are involved—appropriately or inappropriately—in the assignment of reference. Specifically, a patient is instructed to point to a single geometric figure from an array of three, the article employed in the instruction being either appropriately or inappropriately definite or indefinite with respect to the array. Presented with two circles and a square, for example, the patient might be told to indicate "the square one"—an appropriate instruction. Or he might be told to point to "the round one"—an instruction in which the definite article is inappropriate given the presence of two circles.

When the instructions are delivered orally at a normal speaking rate, the patients show no evidence whatsoever of processing the article (Goodenough, Zurif, and Weintraub, 1977). However, we have lately been presenting the instructions in written form, giving the patients unlimited time to read the sentences; and each of the three Broca's aphasics tested to date has clearly recognized when an article has been used inappropriately. One patient, for example, when instructed in the written condition to indicate "the round one" in the presence of two circles, pointed to the word *the*; said "no"; then fingerspelled the letter *a*.

To generalize from these preliminary findings (and to suppose their reliability!), it seems reasonable to suggest that the semantic facts arrayed against closed class items are, in principle, available to Broca's aphasics. In the particular case tested, they can be supposed to know that in relation to the highly constrained stimulus situation, the definite article specifies some such notion as "ready identifiability.") But because the patients no longer have the specific closed class retrieval mechanism, which by hypothesis serves as input to a parser, they cannot make on-line use of such information.

Garrett, Bradley, and I plan to investigate this notion in a more precise fashion by delivering the instructions orally under different conditions distinguished by the rate at which the words in the instruction are presented and by whether or not the article receives contrastive stress. At one extreme, the words in the instructions will follow each other at a very slow rate, with additional intensity on the article to make its significance, and hence the relevance of its semantic value, more readily apparent. At the other extreme, the instructions will be presented at a normal speaking rate.

If the closed class retrieval system functions to accomodate the rapidity of syntactic processing demanded by normal speaking rates, then, given its disruption in Broca's aphasia, it should be the case that at a normal speech rate, the patients will be unable to integrate the article structurally and thereby will be unable to apply the semantic information inherent in the article. And this outcome is projected, even though they will have been alerted to, and indeed will have made use of, its semantic value in the slower conditions. Indirectly, then, this work should allow us to determine the on-line significance of the closed class route and to fix the parameters of its operation.

SOME OTHER ISSUES FOR FUTURE RESEARCH

Kean's analysis and, equally, my comments on this point have focused on the distinction between open and closed class elements as a means of reconstructing the consequences of left-anterior brain injury. But the question arises as to whether this is the only structure-building mechanism to be disturbed. It is possible that the brain damage underlying Broca's aphasia more pervasively compromises the ability to deal with relational meanings expressed in sentences, the disruption to the closed class route being, then, nothing other than a reflection of this "larger" deficit. Clearly the tasks of determining what counts as evidence on this issue and then gaining the relevant data remain before us.

Another—and the final—issue to be entered here has to do with the already much discussed relation between comprehension and production processes. Kean rightly introduces the grammar as a component of the performance model, suggesting that it serves at least to specify the representations implemented or targeted by the processors. But although the information inherent in linguistic description must be represented whether we speak or listen, the question remains concerning the extent to which the processes underlying speech and comprehension share components. The data from Broca's aphasia bear intriguingly on this question: Given the convergence of agrammatic output, agrammatic comprehension, and the results of the lexical decision experiments it seems reasonable to suggest at least some form of sharing—the locus of the connection possibly occurring at that point at which the open–closed distinction is exploited (see Garrett, Chapter 10, and Frazier, Chapter 11, this volume). But the resolution of this issue, too, is before us.

REFERENCES

Blumstein, S., Cooper, W., Zurif, E., and Caramazza, A. (1977). The perception and production of voice-onset time in aphasia. *Neuropsychologia, 15,* 371–383.

Bradley, D., Garrett, M., Kean, M. L., Kolk, H., and Zurif, E. B. (forthcoming). Distinguishing vocabulary type: Normal versus agrammatic speakers.

Bradley, D., Garrett, M., and Zurif, E. B. (1980). Syntactic deficits in Broca's aphasia. In D. Caplan (Ed.), *Biological studies of mental processes.* Cambridge, Mass.: MIT Press.

Caramazza, A., and Berndt, R. S. (1978). Semantic and syntactic processes in aphasia: A review of the literature. *Psychological Bulletin, 85,* 898–918.

Caramazza, A., Gardner, H., and Zurif, E. (1978). Sentence memory in aphasia. *Neuropsychologia, 16,* 661–670.

Goodenough, C., Zurif, E. B., and Weintraub, S. (1977). Aphasics' attention to grammatical morphemes. *Language and Speech, 20,* 11–19.

Goodglass, H. (1976). Agrammatism. In H. A. Whitaker and H. Whitaker (Eds.), *Studies in neurolinguistics,* Vol. 1. New York: Academic Press.

Kean, M.-L. (1979). Explanation in neurolinguistics. (1979). *Social Sciences Research Reports, 40.* University of California, Irvine.

Kellar, L. (1978). *Stress and syntax in aphasia.* Paper presented to Academy of Aphasia, Chicago.

Swinney, D., Zurif, E. B., and Cutler, A. (1980). Effects of sentential stress and word class upon comprehension of Broca's aphasics. *Brain and Language, 10,* 132–144.

Zurif, E. B., Blumstein, S. (1978). Language and the brain. In J. Bresnam, M. Halle, and G. A. Miller (Eds.), *Linguistic theory and psychological reality.* Cambridge, Mass.: MIT Press.

Zurif, E. B., and Caramazza, A. (1976). Psycholinguistic and structures in aphasia: Studies in syntax and semantics. In H. Whitaker and H. A. Whitaker (Eds.), *Studies in neurolinguistics,* Vol. 1. New York: Academic Press.

10

Remarks on the Relation between Language Production and Language Comprehension Systems

Merrill F. Garrett

INTRODUCTION

What relation holds between language comprehension and language production processes? To begin with the obvious, production and comprehension processes differ incontrovertibly—at their "extremities," if nothing more. The question is, how far does the separation extend beyond the distinction between mouth and ears? The extreme possibility is that NO overlap of computational procedures and/or of the neurological structures supporting such exists. I prefer to reject that possibility from the outset; not because it would be unimportant if true, or because it is not conceivably true, but, rather, because it is the less interesting answer, and because there are plausible arguments for significant correspondences between the two performance systems.

What might one mean by "overlap" or commonality in the two systems? Certainly it requires more than an interdependence of production and comprehension systems; there must be an equivalence, perhaps an identity, of the procedures used in carrying out some aspect of sentence processing (e.g., of lexical retrieval or assignment of phase structure). Given strong evidence of such an overlap in procedures, one might then consider the issue of a neurological correspondence. This latter, however, is best considered a further and separately evaluated claim.

We know, of course, that the systems ARE interdependent, most clearly in terms of monitoring functions that the recognition system carries out for the regulation of production, especially at the motor levels. One thinks immediately of the dependencies indicated by delayed auditory feedback effects and perhaps of

NEURAL MODELS OF
LANGUAGE PROCESSES

"tongue twisters" as well. I will not consider such matters here, though I believe that they are of intrinsic interest and that we will need an understanding of these sorts of phenomena in order to properly evaluate the evidence for more abstract levels of interconnection between the two systems. It is the possibility of such higher order convergence that I wish to address.

A final preliminary point to raise is the rhetorical question, Why do we care about the relation between comprehension and production systems? There are several answers. It is obvious that knowing something concrete about the connections between comprehension and production could increase our ability to evaluate theoretical proposals within each domain. More to the current interest is the particular promise that this enquiry has for connecting theories of computation with theories of supporting physical structures and also for illuminating the relation between grammatical theory and processing theory. If, for example, one were to discover that the architecture of production and comprehension systems is substantially the same, one might interpret this as evidence that the organization of processing systems for language is more heavily determined by informational structure (e.g., that indicated by rule systems of grammars) than by modality-specific aspects of the physical representations of language. One might then hope to separate those aspects of neural organization which are responsive to modality-specific features of language from those which are responsive to the general features of language structure and computation.

A different possibility is what I will call "Bever's speculation." It depends on a particular claim about the relation between comprehension and production, namely that they are fundamentally different, at least during their developmental course. The resulting "asymmetry of description" for the utterances which a child experiences calls forth a "rationalizing capacity," which in turn eventuates in the system we identify with a grammar (Bever, 1975). I cannot evaluate this or the preceding possibilities here. I raise them in order to indicate the extent to which positions on the production–comprehension question ramify through the whole of the language investigation enterprise, and thus to indicate the potential of serious inquiry into the relation between the two major language performance systems.

In what follows I will consider some proposals and some evidence from studies of normal language processing which indicate correspondences or differences in production and comprehension tasks. I will note some connections to language disorders. Briefly, the position I will hold is that (a) the exploitation of the lexicon is sufficiently similar in production and comprehension for us to seriously consider common procedures; (b) the effects of phrasal structure, especially clausal organization, show differences and similarities whose import is not presently clear; and (c) the architecture of the two systems shows similar influences in areas where it might not have been expected.

STRUCTURAL TARGETS IN PRODUCTION AND COMPREHENSION

The first focus of interest in assessing relations between production and comprehension ought to be the similarities and differences between their respective structural targets. Clearly the argument for commonality of structures is powerful: If communication is to take place, a correspondence must be established between the mental representation of a sentence for a speaker and that for a listener. The nature of the required correspondence, however, is crucial. If it were demonstrable that the representations to be computed by the two systems had striking differences, we would not be so readily concerned by the possibility that the computational systems for the two tasks might be similar or identical in part. It is, indeed, an initial acceptance of the view that both systems are responsible for comparable structural distinctions that makes the whole matter seem compelling. Though I think this view is correct, there is certainly room to question the extent of its relevance; a brief consideration of possible differences in the way a given structural burden may be accomodated is useful to show why.

Two domains, sound structure and syntax, provide convenient examples: For the first, aspects of the "motor theory of speech perception" are relevant, and for the second, the role of underlying and surface syntax.

Consider the motor theory. The claim is that the descriptive parameters for acoustic objects are based on articulatory regularities; the perceptually relevant sorting of phones is, on such a view, determined by control parameters for the vocal tract. Note, however, that this view might be instantiated in an actual performance system in several ways—for example, as an analysis-by-synthesis system in which the normal production apparatus is used to provide matching signals for input, OR as a straight analysis system in which acoustic parameters (organized in terms of their relation to the structure of the vocal tract) are evaluated directly for the assignment of acoustic inputs to perceptual categories. Thus, the convergence of descriptive regularities might, in the first case, signal a genuine overlap in the two systems, or it might, for the second, reflect some other computational exigency (e.g., the need to evaluate contextually induced variations in the acoustic representations of segment types).

Similarly for the syntactic domain, though the details are different: Again we may hold that each system is responsible for a similar range of structural distinctions—in the strongest case, each is responsible for the structural descriptions associated with a sentence by a formal grammar; but again, perhaps not in the same fashion. For example, detailed surface syntax might play only an "after the fact confirmatory" role in comprehension processes rather than being an immediate computational responsibility as it must be in production if stress and intonation are to be gotten right.

Indeed, here one might even consider denying that the same full range of structures must be constructed. Production systems, as we noted, must get the details of surface form right, for the system is responsible for pronunciation. Not so, one might argue, for the comprehension system, which must get only those features of sentence structure that are needed to unambiguously specify the interpretive burden of the sentence. In short, it is not impossible to argue that the production system may be more "form oriented" than the recognition system. However, I am not at all confident about such a speculation, given that all the major features of sentence form are POTENTIALLY of interpretive significance, even if not functional in given sentence types or contextual circumstances. It seems likely that a system that sought to capitalize on the temporary irrelevance of a particular structural feature would often be in trouble. Evidently, for this case, much depends upon the relation of other structural types (notably prosodic and various semantic) to syntactic analysis. We will return to this issue. For now, the point is simply to acknowledge the possible divergence either in the structural responsibilities of production and comprehension systems, or, minimally, in the time course of their assessment.

Granting the possibilities for divergence in the two systems, perhaps now we should turn to what evidence we have.

USING THE LEXICON FOR RECOGNITION AND RECALL

There are at least three areas of significant overlap in performance for word recognition in comprehension and for word recall during spontaneous speech. They are in the roles (a) of word meaning versus word form, (b) of morphological structure, (c) of a syntactically and phonologically motivated vocabulary distinction ("open" and "closed" classes). I will consider each in turn.

Meaning versus Form in Comprehension and Production

There are two salient points to be made about word retrieval processes for comprehension. The first is that the processes dependent upon word form operate INDEPENDENTLY of their meaning consequences, and the second is that the analysis of word form which determines retrieval places a premium upon the initial portions of words. Precisely the same two points may be made about word retrieval for production: Meaning and form are computationally dissociated, and the most significant determinant of form-based retrieval is the initial portion of a word. The evidence for these claims is various; I will cite examples for each area.

The most compelling evidence for the first point in comprehension processes arises from the study of lexical ambiguity and its effects on sentence processing. This is a topic that has received rather systematic attention from a number of investigators with an eye toward determining HOW the comprehension system deals with ambiguous words—they are frequently encountered but rarely noted as conscious decision points. We are simply not usually misled by the opportunity for misinterpretation that such words present. No one, I would wager, has been momentarily misled by the possible interpretation of the frequently occurring word *sentence* (in this discourse) as meaning "term of imprisonment." The question is, how do we simultaneously avoid such a miscalculation here while at the same time insuring that the same word in another circumstance (e.g., a courtroom description of the outcome of a trial) will, with the same apparent facility, be assigned the (presently) nonpreferred interpretation? The answer, on both logical and experimental grounds, is fairly straightforward, though there is sharp disagreement over the details. It seems clear that both (all) the senses of an ambiguous word are temporarily activated (i.e., are "looked up" in the mental dictionary) and that a selection is made among these on the basis of the current syntactic, semantic, and discourse factors. This view contrasts with one in which such contextual factors preselect the relevant sense of an ambiguous form and no activation of the contextually irrelevant sense occurs. The two-stage view of the process is appealing because it rationalizes the flexibility of our use of vague and ambiguous terms and gives sense to the notion of independence of meaning-based and form-based processes during word recognition. A single example of the relevant experimental findings will make the point concrete.

Swinney (1979) has shown that priming occurs for both the contextually selected and nonselected senses of an ambiguous word. In his task, subjects listen to a sentence and at some point during it a string of letters flashes on a screen before them. They must (while continuing to listen to the sentence) decide whether the string of letters constitutes a word or not. This judgment is refered to as a "lexical decision task." Though the subject is not aware of it, the point of presentation of the target letter array just follows the occurrence of an ambiguous word in the sentence he or she is simultaneously listening to. When the letter array forms a word, the subject responds "yes" by pushing a reaction-time key. If the visual test word has been preceded in the spoken sentence by a word related to its meaning, response is facilitated (i.e., the test word has been "primed") relative to an unrelated control-word baseline. One then may compare cases in which the lexical decision target is related to the contextually selected sense of the ambiguous word with cases in which it is related to the nonselected sense. Swinney finds facilitation for both senses of the ambiguous term; this double facilitation is short-lived, however, for at test points approximately three syllables later in the sentence, presentation of the two types of lexical decision targets shows facilitation only for the contextually selected meaning. Similar sorts of results have been reported for other experimental paradigms (see Swinney, 1980, for a review) and they seem most naturally accomodated by the two-stage retrieval process which permits search processes based on word form to proceed independently of the current "meaning" context.

What would evidence for a comparable separation in word retrieval for production be like? It would require an indication that words are recovered at some point during sentence construction solely in terms of their form. On the face of it, such a circumstance seems unlikely—for after all, we select words to convey intended meaning. Of course, the same observation might have been made vis-à-vis ambiguous words in comprehension—we choose the interpretively relevant sense of such items. But, as the ambiguity research shows, the fact of semantic constraint does not obviate the need for selection processes based on word form in comprehension; nor does it do so for language production. Word substitution errors provide a clear illustration; they indicate the existence of a two-stage selection process in production which corresponds in important ways to that indicated for comprehension.

Word substitution errors occur with fair frequency in the normally fluent speech of intact mature speakers of a language. Several investigators have been interested in the properties of these and related types of speech errors, and substantial corpora of such errors have been accumulated by various of them over the years (for some relevant discussions, see Fay and Cutler, 1977; Fromkin, 1971; Garrett, 1980). These errors come in two principal varieties: those that are meaning related and those that are form related. The main features of the issue are not complex: Where there is a meaning relation, form similarities are not obvious, and where there is a strong resemblance of form, meaning is clearly irrelevant. So, for example, one finds substitutions like *hot* for *cold*, *answer* for *question*, *belt* for *collar*, *racquet* for *club*, etc. And, as frequently, one also finds errors like *colloquium* for *colloquial*, *garlic* for *gargle*, *married* for *measured*, *inches* for *innings*, *envelope* for *elephant*, etc. The irrelevance of meaning constraints for these latter errors could hardly be more clear. When we speak, there is a point at which the determination of a semantically constrained lexical target has been made (i.e., identification of a lexical item whose meaning corresponds to that of the intended message) but precise word form has yet to be determined. The process of selection at this latter point is, on the evidence of these errors, independent of meaning, for it is emphatically not the case that form-related errors occur only—or even frequently—between items that are significantly similar in meaning.

Just here, we should also take note of certain features of language disorders that have been widely remarked. So, for example, certain aphasics show deficits in retrieval of word form (as in amnesic aphasia) or in execution of word form (as in conduction aphasia) though meaning based lexical processes are clearly intact (see Buckingham, 1979: Lecours, 1980). In other aphasias (as certain Wernicke's aphasics), one sees frequent meaning based word substitutions with substantially intact retrieval of word form. (In this connection, it is important to bear in mind that an identifiable semantic verbal paraphasia presupposes a successful mapping from the erroneous meaning to an entry in the inventory of word forms.)

We might grant, at this point, a correspondence between lexical retrieval for comprehension and production in terms of this broad organizational feature without being ready to concede a resemblance strong enough to warrant the postulation of common mechanisms. The case is materially strengthened, however, when one examines the specific form parameters that govern lexical look-up in the two systems: The aspects of word form that guide recognition are also the points of similarity between target and intrusion for word substitution errors in normal, spontaneous speech production. The most striking such common aspect is the salience of word initial phonetic elements in the two processes. An examination of the examples of form-related errors cited here will give some idea of the case for production. With some interesting exceptions (involving affixes, discussed later), the overwhelming generalization is that target and intrusion correspond in initial segments and that the probability of correspondence decreases steadily as one proceeds further into the word. Fay and Cutler (1977) present analysis of this correspondence in detail, with discussion of syllable structure and stress (both of which are implicated) as well.

For word recognition in comprehension, the same prominence of word initial portions holds and it is manifest in both auditory and visual presentation of words. Marslen-Wilson's (1979) discussion of cohort effects incorporates this feature: specification of a set of candidate lexical items on the basis of the initial portion of the word form, followed by selection on the basis of semantic and form parameters. For visual presentation, the work of Taft and Forster (1976) is persuasive. Using a lexical decision procedure, they demonstrated, for example, that nonwords that contained a partial analysis corresponding to a real word (e.g., **post***le*) were rejected (i.e., correctly classified as nonwords) with longer latency than nonwords without such a subanalysis (e.g., *puctle*); note that this held only for subanalyses determined by a left-to-right scan, however—a real word embedded at the end of the nonword form was not interfering. Taft and Forster provide a number of other demonstrations and arguments for this sort of account.

Some Effects of Morphological Structure

Much remains unknown about the details of access procedures in both comprehension and production; there is certainly room for intractible differences to appear. But, given what we have in hand, the correspondences between the two systems are striking. We note one further such correspondence at the lexical level before turning to some effects of lexical category. That correspondence is in the role of prefixes in word substitution errors and in word recognition as revealed by the lexical decision task. For the latter, again the most relevant work is that of Taft and Forster (1975). In this case, two types of nonwords are compared: those derived from prefixed words by deletion of the prefix (e.g., *juvenate* from *rejuvenate* or *vive* from *revive*) and those derived from nonprefixed words by a similar letter deletion (e.g., *pertoire* from *repertoire* or *lish* from *relish*). The former type of items have longer response times because, Taft and Forster argue, prefixed words are stored as [stem + affix]; hence *juvenate* contacts a mental entry and must be checked for acceptibility, whereas no such process is engaged by items like *pertoire* and *lish*. Another example of the same point comes from real word items like *vent* when compared with items like *coin*. Such items are paired in terms of length and frequency of occurrence in the language because these variables affect recognition time. They differ in that the former occurs both as a free form and a bound form (e.g., *invent*, *prevent*) whereas the latter occurs only as a free form. Moreover, the bound form of *vent* is more frequent than its free form. If the interpretation of the *juvenate* versus *pertoire* results is correct, one would expect, given that entries are contacted in order of decreasing frequency, that subjects would retrieve the bound form for *vent* first and would then have to reject it before encountering the free form entry. The interference should elevate reaction times for lexical decision. This was the result: Times for items like *vent* were longer than times for frequency- and length-matched items like *coin*. In order to show that this effect does not arise for all bound forms (i.e., that it is not just a matter of overlap with other existing words) the experiment was repeated using bound forms whose free form version was more frequent than their bound form (e.g., *card* from *discard*). By the same assumptions, the bound form entry should not be encountered before the free form entry and no interference should arise. This was in fact the result. Thus, both a frequency effect for organization of word storage and the storage of stems are indicated by this outcome.

   Given this modification of the left-to-right processing model for word recognition (i.e., the addition of a "prefix-stripping" operation), it is all the more striking that when one examines the corpus of word substitution errors, one finds that many of the exceptions to the very strong generalization noted here—namely, a left-to-right correspondence of target and substitution—are cases in which a prefixed word substitutes for its nonprefixed stem (e.g., *envision* for *vision*) and vice versa (e.g., *call* for *recall*) or in which a prefixed word substitutes for another with a common stem (e.g., *advice* for *device* or *inquired* for *required*). Fay (1979) has argued in detail for an account using a retrieval and storage process of the sort sketched here to describe the word recognition data of Taft and Forster. He also offers some evidence that frequency of occurrence in the language affects the likelihood of an interaction between two words for substitution errors. In short, we find here as before evidence of a convergence of recognition and production regularities in word retrieval.

Effects of Vocabulary Type: Open and Closed Classes

The final correspondence I wish to discuss concerns effects of lexical category on word retrieval processes. Again, our comparison will involve data from speech error analyses and lexical decision tasks. Put most succinctly, that comparison suggests that a vocabulary classification motivated by processes of phrasal construction in recognition of sentences (i.e., a parsing process) is also central to processes of phrasal construction for the production of sentences. We will refer to that vocabulary contrast as that between **open** class vocabulary and **closed** class vocabulary (see Bratley and Dakin, 1967; Thorne, Bratley, and Dewar, 1968).

Consider first the production process. In developmental regularities, in language disorders, and in the patterns of spontaneous speech errors, there is a strong indication of the computational separation between open and closed class vocabulary. That division corresponds roughly to the one we are accustomed to label the distinction between "content" and "function" words. I say roughly because that customary label encompasses just free forms, whereas the relevant computational distinction includes bound forms as well—inflectional affixes (e.g., those for number, tense, and aspect) seem to behave like closed class free forms ("function words"). Let me illustrate these points.

The developmental facts are well known. I have in mind the so-called telegraphic stage of language development which is characterized by the selective omission of elements of the minor grammatical categories. In the case of language disorders, of course, I have in mind the differential loss of open and closed class items for agrammatic and fluent aphasics—very roughly, the latter preserve what the former have lost and vice versa (see Saffran, Schwartz and Marin, 1980). Agrammatic patients seem to better preserve open class vocabulary than closed class, and the reverse is true for certain Wernicke's aphasics. I certainly do not mean to suggest that these deficits are entirely reducible to such a rough and ready characterization, but I do mean to draw attention to what is a quite striking manifestation of the vocabulary contrast of interest. How precisely complementary the patterns of loss and preservation are in these aphasics syndromes is not currently determinate—nor is the relation they may bear to the details of language development. I am, at this point, merely being suggestive. There is an area where I feel more confident of the detailed ground, however, and that is in the patterning of speech errors.

Speech errors occur in a variety of forms other than that of the simple word substitutions we discussed earlier. In particular, there are complex errors involving the mislocation of multiple elements of the intended utterance. Those involving sound elements—as, for example, saying *a disorder of speech*, **spictly streaking, is** . . . (for *strictly speaking*) or *They're at* **Ruvver Frint Stadium** (for *River Front Stadium*)—have long been called "spoonerisms." Such complementary mislocations also occur for words and morphemes, however, and it is the patterning of these and other related error types that gives us evidence for the vocabulary contrast in question. Briefly, the salient facts are these:

1. Errors in which two elements EXCHANGE position are confined to open class vocabulary—nouns, verbs and adjectives; rarely do sound, word, or morpheme exchanges arise from minor category words, nor do they involve inflectional affixes.

2. Errors in which a single element SHIFTS its position are characteristic of the closed class vocabulary; that is, minor category words and inflectional affixes are commonly mislocated, as, for example, when one says *All the home team wons* for the intended *All the home teams won*, or *Who did you say else came?* for *Who else did you say came?*

The different characteristics of errors that involve function words and inflections on the one hand and those that involve content words and derivational affixes on the other are quite detailed (see Garrett, 1975, 1980, for discussion) and seem to arise because of differing roles which the two classes of elements play at differing stages of the production process. Closed class vocabulary seems to be recruited at the point where the detailed surface form of sentences is being integrated, whereas the open class vocabulary is retrieved at an earlier stage when the functional roles of words and phrases are being determined. That is, it seems plausible that there is a separate retrieval stage for these two classes of word forms, and that separation is motivated by the different roles these classes play in the constructive processes for sentence production. The production equivalent of parsing procedures in recognition seems, on grounds of these observations, to accord a special role to the closed class vocabulary. That the same separation of computational vocabularies, and for similar reasons, also holds for recognition processes is suggested by a variety of observations—some recent and some long recognized.

Some years ago, Thorne and his colleagues (Thorne, Bratley, and Dewar, 1968; Bratley and Dakin, 1967) emphasized the essential role played by function words and some inflections in fixing the syntactic analysis of sentences, and incorporated the open-class–closed-class dictionary concept in the design of their parsing system. Quite apart from the computational utility of a limited dictionary (an issue to which we shortly return), there are, of course, many formal and informal behavioral indications of the salience of this vocabulary distinction for recognition processes. Syntactically organized nonsense strings (strings constructed by substituting nonsense forms for OPEN class vocabulary (e.g., *a vapy koobs desaked the citar molently*) are more quickly assimilated and recalled than nonsense strings not so organized (see Epstein, 1961); there are sundry experimental demonstrations of this phenomenon though no really satisfying explanations. Similarly, it is clear that our conscious sensitivity to details of the form of elements of the two classes differs—the closed class is in some sense less readily available for report. For example, repetitions or inversions of closed class items are more likely to be overlooked in proofreading than are repetitions of open class items. Although such observations attest a difference in the processing of these vocabulary classes, they do not specifically indicate an access or retrieval account. Some other results, however, do have such an account as their most natural explanation.

I refer to a series of studies that explore the hypothesis that open and closed classes are recognized by distinct retrieval processes. That work explores the thesis that the organization of lexical retrieval systems is tailored to the demands of parsing processes. In particular, it examines the case for a distinct retrieval routine for closed class vocabulary on grounds that such items occupy a special role in the procedures for assigning phrasal analyses to sentences. I will discuss two of the findings as illustrative.

The first of these concerns the effect of frequency of occurrence on lexical recognition. As we noted earlier (in our discussion of Taft and Forster's work), facility in lexical decision tasks is positively correlated with estimates of the occurrence rate for words. This is a finding that has been incorporated into a variety of word recognition models, and it is often used as a diagnostic for treating a particular performance as lexically dependent. However, according to our results for English (Bradley and Garrett, 1980), this frequency effect is confined to the open class vocabulary. When comparable frequency ranges for sets of open and closed class items are compared, there is a strong frequency organization for the former but no such effect for the latter. If access in order of decreasing frequency is characteristic of open class recognition procedures, it does not seem to be so for closed class retrieval.

A second finding is similar in its import. We earlier noted a strong left-to-right or temporal bias in the effects of the letter and sound elements of words, and cited the interference effects arising when a real word is embedded in a nonword. That characteristic feature of word recognition again appears confined to open class vocabulary. When sets of length-matched pairs of nonword items, one set beginning with open class items (e.g., **word**er*ty*) and the other with closed class items (e.g., **such**er*ty*), only the open class set shows the interference effect reported by Taft and Forster (Bradley and Garrett, 1980). Thus, two of the principal diagnostic features of open class retrieval seem not to apply for closed class elements. If the closed class vocabulary is, as we have suggested, privileged with respect to inferences about phrasal analysis, this apparent holistic, direct access may well reflect that priority. Again, there is a good deal more to be determined on this issue, but for present purposes, the results at hand do indicate a reasonable correspondence between production and recognition vis-à-vis the computational contrast of open and closed class vocabularies. One last observation reinforces that point. When the two recognition tests I have just described, that for frequency sensitivity and left-to-right analysis, were done with a group of agrammatic aphasics (n.b. these are patients with a PRODUCTION deficit in the closed class), there was no indication of the access contrast shown by normal speakers: Both open and closed classes showed a strong frequency organization and both classes produced interference effects (Bradley, Garrett, and Zurif, 1980). If dissociation of these vocabularies is indeed a feature of normal language recognition processes, the aphasics' performance suggests a quite specific retrieval loss which is arguably connected to the ability to appreciate or produce phrasally organized word strings. These results must be regarded as preliminary given that the group of patients tested was not large, but they do provide additional indications of a correspondence of production and comprehension deficits in word retrieval processes.

The claim for a correspondence between production and comprehension deficits in Broca's aphasia is, of course, neither unprecedented nor restricted to word retrieval processes (for discussion, see Zurif and Caramazza, 1976). Perhaps it will turn out that, just as the seeming dissociation of production and comprehension performance in this disorder has long provided a bulwark in arguments for the separate representation of production and comprehension capacity, the growing body of observations about correspondences between the two domains of performance in aphasia will be among the richest sources of data in evaluating claims for their overlap.

I have so far drawn a number of parallels between processes of word recognition and processes of word production. They seem compelling enough to warrant serious consideration of the hypothesis that there is procedural overlap in the two systems for lexical access. There now remain two further points in my discussion of the relation between production and comprehension.

PHRASAL STRUCTURE

The issue of phrasal integration in the two systems has in a sense already been broached by our examination of the open and closed class vocabulary effects in production and comprehension domains. I have offered an interpretation of that vocabulary contrast which is linked to processes of phrasal construction. One would, however, like to have a more direct indication of correspondences or divergences of phrasal analysis systems for the two processes. One promising area is in the investigation of segmentation and grouping phenomena during comprehension and production. This is a topic usually pursued under the rubric of "units" of sentence perception or sentence production. In particular, one seeks experimental and observational indications of the macrosegments for sentence understanding or sentence planning. One wants to discover how decision domains for sentence input or output relate to their phonological, syntactic, and semantic analyses.

We are, somewhat paradoxically, in a position to make more detailed claims for sentence planning units than for sentence understanding units. This is because much of the comprehension study has revolved around the role of clausal structure, surface and deep; the positive claims that have been made are primarily about the salience of clausal boundaries in on-line comprehension processes. Effects of detailed phrasal structure internal to clauses have, of course, been shown in a variety of ways, but these have typically been based on postsentence measures (as, e.g., probe latency studies, see Walker, 1976). By and large, the bone of contention has been whether surface or deep clauses (or neither) are the basic determinant of segmentation processes (see, e.g., Carrol, 1979; Fodor, Bever, and Garrett, 1974, p. 329–344; Marslen-Wilson, Tyler, and Seidenberg, 1979), and it is fair to say that the issue is not settled in any very satisfactory way. Some approximation to surface clausal structure may have the best chance of survival, but the exceptions are manifold and complex. Moreover, I should stress that there can be no real question of the relevance of simple phrasal structure to immediate sentence analysis—the question is how and when it is determined. The available experimental evidence is insufficient, and many a complex issue in the theory of parsing will need experimental evaluation before the matter begins to be resolved.

For production processes, we have somewhat clearer indications of the involvement both of simple phrasal structure and of clausal structure. For example, the evidence from speech error patterns seems strongly to indicate simple phrasal planning units. The basic determinant of interaction between words in exchange errors seems to be distinct phrasal membership (with correspondence of their phrasal roles), whereas for sound exchanges, it is COMMON phrasal membership that is the rule. Taken together, these observations (and others) suggest a multiphrasal planning stage (perhaps clausally constrained) and a subsequent single phrase planning level (see Garrett, 1980, for discussion). There is some reason to characterize this latter planning stage in terms of phonological phrases rather than in strict syntactic terms (see Garrett and Kean, 1980).

On the face of it, the preceding observations suggest differences in the phrasal planning operations for production and comprehension. The latter emphasize surface clausal organization, whereas the former, on evidence of speech errors, show clear reflections of simple, nonclausal constituent structures as well as of clausal structure. There is, in addition, one further set of observations to be weighed. Ford and Holmes (1978) and Ford (1977) report that both hesitation distributions and reaction times (to tones heard while speaking) seem primarily dependent upon underlying rather than surface clausal structure. If one accepts the indications that surface clausal structure is a more profound determinant of comprehension processes than is underlying clausal structure, this argues for a production–comprehension difference.

It must be evident that the case for production and comprehension overlap in this problem domain is not clear. Such evidence as we have seems to indicate differences in their detailed phrasal planning mechanisms. The evidence, however, is limited. It might be argued, for example, that the apparent differences are more a reflection of the focus of experimental interest and of the sensitivity of the measurements that have been used in comprehension studies than they are of the lack of an effect of simple phrasal structure in comprehension processes. I suspect this is correct.

ORGANIZATION OF PRODUCTION AND COMPREHENSION SYSTEMS

In my introductory remarks, I raised the question of how seriously one should take the thesis that production and comprehension systems are required to recover the same structural descriptions for sentences. I expressed doubt that one could design a satisfactory comprehension system that constructed less than a full syntactic analysis—that is, one that recovered only the "situationally relevant" structural features. The rub comes in determining, INDEPENDENT OF SYNTACTIC ANALYSIS, what the relevant features are in any given circumstances. The only way such a system could be remotely plausible would be for it to be dynamically dependent upon semantic and pragmatic features of the message and its context. If people are built to such a specification, we might well expect to see pretty definite evidences of it. Specifically, we should expect to see evidence that lexical and syntactic processing based upon parameters of word and sentence form is strikingly altered by such contextual variation. My observation is that this is not what one finds in either production or comprehension; though contextual contraints are indubitably effective in directing our ultimate interpretation of sentences, they do so in ways that preserve the integrity of the form-based lexical retrieval and parsing processes. This is not an uncontroversial view, of course. (See, for example, Marslen-Wilson and Tyler [1980] for evidence that they regard as incompatible with this view.) In its defense, let me remind you of the evidence I cited earlier for separation of meaning and form in lexical access processes for production and comprehension. I suggest that a two-stage access process—of the sort indicated by Swinney's results, for example—is the kind of solution that can accomodate both ranges of observations. For phrasal integration in production and in comprehension, I believe there is again good evidence for a similar separation of effects of meaning and of form. That evidence arises both from normal processing studies (see, e.g., Forster, 1980) and from observations of language disorder, as for example the preservation of certain lexically based inferential capacities in agrammatic aphasics (Caramazza and Zurif, 1976; Saffran, Schwartz, and Marin, 1980). And, in production processes as indicated by speech errors, there is again rather little indication of semantic and pragmatic influences on word and morpheme exchanges or shifts (see, e.g., Garrett, 1976).

The evidence is, of course, scattered and of mixed character. Perhaps it is enough that it strongly suggests, even if it does not prove, a very similar organizational principle for comprehension and production systems—namely, that the decomposition of the processing system reflects the decomposition of language structure in linguistic rule systems. On this view, the architecture of the processing system for production and that for comprehension provides another instance of motivated convergence in the two systems.

CONCLUSION

It would be foolhardy to claim a clear case for particular overlap in production and comprehension processes on grounds of the evidence we have presently available to us. On the other hand, it is a hypothesis of more than passing interest, and there is, particularly in the area of lexical retrieval, more than a little evidence to support its viability. That evidence implicates not only the organization of processing systems, but also the organization of language involved brain tissue. The hypothesis of computational overlap for significant areas of language processing seems worthy of serious and sustained inquiry.

REFERENCES

Bever, T. G. (1975). Psychologically real grammar emerges because of its role in language acquisition. In *Proceedings of the Georgetown Linguistics Round Table*, Spring, 1975.

Bradley, D. C. and Garrett, M. (1980). Effects of vocabulary type on word recognition. Occasional Paper 12, Center for Cognitive Science. Cambridge, Mass.

Bradley, D. C., Garrett, M., and Zurif, E. (1980). Syntactic deficits in Broca's aphasia. In D. Caplan (Ed.), *Biological studies of mental processes*. Cambridge, Mass. MIT Press.

Bratley, P. and Dakin, D. J. A limited dictionary for syntactic analysis. In E. Dale and D. Michie, (Eds.), *Machine intelligence*. Edinburgh: Oliver and Boyd, pp. 173–181.

Buckingham, H. (1979). Linguistic aspects of lexical retrieval disturbances in the posterior fluent aphasias. In H. A. Whitaker and H. Whitaker (Eds.), *Studies in neurolinguistics*, Vol. 4. New York: Academic Press.

Carroll, J. (1979). Functional completeness as a determinant of processing load during sentence comprehension. *Language and Speech, 22*, 347–369.

Fay, D. (1979) Prefix errors. Paper presented at the fourth Salzburg International Linguistics Meeting. Salzburg, Austria, Aug. 15–27.

Fay, D. and Cutler, A. (1977). Malapropisms and the structure of the mental lexicon. *Linguistic Inquiry, 8*, 505–520.

Fodor, J. A., Bever, T. G., and Garrett, M. (1974). *The psychology of language*. New York: McGraw-Hill.

Forster, K. I. (1980). Levels of processing in sentence comprehension. In W. Cooper and E. Walker (Eds.), *Sentence processing*. Hillsdale, N.J.: Lawrence Erlbaum.

Fromkin, V. (1971). The non-anomalous nature of anomalous utterances. *Language, 47*, 27–52.

Garrett, M. (1975). The analysis of sentence production. In G. Bower (Ed.), *Psychology of learning and motivation*, Vol. 9. New York: Academic Press.

Garrett, M. (1976). Syntactic processes in sentence production. In R. Wales, and E. Walker (Eds.), *New approaches to language mechanisms*. Amsterdam: North-Holland.

Garrett, M. (1980). Levels of processing in sentence production. In B. Butterworth (Ed.), *Language production*, Vol. 1. London: Academic Press.

Ford, M. (1977). *Planning units and syntax in sentence production*. Unpublished Ph. D. dissertation, University of Melbourne.

Ford, M. and Holmes, V. M. (1978). Planning units and syntax in sentence production. *Cognition*, 6, 35–53.

Epstein, W. (1961). The influence of syntactical structure on learning. *American Journal of Psychology*, 74, 80–85.

Lecours, A. R. (1980). On neologisms. Paper presented at C.N.R.S. conference on Cognitive Psychology, Royamount, Paris, June 1980.

Marslen-Wilson, W. (1979). Speech understanding as a psychological process. In J. C. Simon (Ed.), *Spoken language generation and understanding*. Dordrect, Holland; D. Reidel.

Marslen-Wilson, W. and Tyler, L. K. (1980). The temporal structure of spoken language understanding. *Cognition*, 8, 1–71.

Saffran, E., Schwartz, M. and Marin, O. (1980). Evidence from aphasia: Isolating the components of a production model. In B. Butterworth (Ed.), *Language production*, Vol. 1. London: Academic Press.

Marslen-Wilson, W., Tyler, L. K., and Seidenberg, M. 1979. Sentence processing and the clause boundary. In W. J. M. Levelt and G. B. F. d'Arcais (Eds.), *Studies in the perception of language*. New York: Wiley.

Swinney, D. (1979). Lexical access during sentence comprehension: (Re) consideration of context effects. *Journal of Verbal Learning and Verbal Behavior*, 18, 645–659.

Swinney, D. (1980). Lexical processing during sentence comprehension: Effects on higher order constraints and implications for representation. In T. Myers, J. Laver, and J. Anderson (Eds.), *The cognitive representation of speech*. Amsterdam/New York: North Holland.

Taft, M., and Forster, K. I. (1975) Lexical storage and retrieval of prefixed words. *Journal of Verbal Learning and Verbal Behavior*, 14, 638–647.

Taft, M. and Forster, K. I. (1976). Lexical storage and retrieval of polymorphemic and polysyllabic words. *Journal of Verbal Learning and Verbal Behavior*, 15, 607–620.

Thorne, J., Bratley, P., and Dewar, H. (1968). The syntactic analysis of English by machine. In D. Michie (Ed.), *Machine Intelligence, Vol. 3*. New York: American Elsevier.

Walker, E. (1976). Some grammatical relations among words. *New approaches to language mechanisms*. Amsterdam: North Holland.

Zurif, E. and Carramazza, A. (1976). Psycholinguistic structures in aphasia: Studies in syntax and semantics. In H. A. Whitaker and H. Whitaker (Eds.), *Studies in neurolinguistics*, Vol. 1. New York. Academic Press.

11

Shared Components of Production and Perception

Lyn Frazier

In principle, there are a variety of aspects of language processing that might be shared by the language production and comprehension systems. Information about the well-formedness constraints of the language might be mentally represented in some form that is neutral between production and comprehension, and thus a common body of grammatical knowledge might be accessed and utilized in both tasks. Likewise, a common set of procedures might be employed to retrieve grammatical information, to schedule the flow of information and decisions, and/or to guide the processor's decisions at choice points.

Garrett (Chapter 10, this volume) has suggested that the actual routines used in lexical retrieval may be common to the production and comprehension systems. However, as his data only show that the same set of distinctions are evidenced in both tasks, they are consistent with the weaker claim that it is only a common body of lexical information, not a common set of lexical retrieval procedures, which is shared.

Garrett's arguments address only the question of shared lexical information or lexical retrieval processes. This chapter will be addressed to the question of what syntactic information or processes may be shared. First, we will consider the question of shared syntactic information. We will then turn to the question of whether there are shared processing units in production and comprehension. Finally, we will explore the implications of production–comprehension correspondences for the development of linguistic theory.

SHARED SYNTACTIC KNOWLEDGE

I am not aware of any arguments or direct evidence that a common body of syntactic knowledge is—or is not—shared by the production and comprehension systems. In the absence of such evidence, perhaps the only way to proceed is by

NEURAL MODELS OF
LANGUAGE PROCESSES

examining what is known about the representation and use of syntactic information in production and perception to determine whether it is at least consistent with the claim that the production and comprehension systems exploit the same body of syntactic information.

Naturally, there are several logical possibilities with respect to the mental representation of syntactic information. The syntactic information used in comprehension might be stored together with, and inextricably intertwined with, the decision principles and action plans used during sentence comprehension. Thus, the very form of the representation of this information might render it inappropriate or useless for purposes of production. For example, there is considerable psycholinguistic evidence that perceivers make certain systematic errors during the comprehension of sentences (see Bever, 1970; Frazier, 1978). In a sentence fragment like (1), perceivers initially tend to analyze the phrase *the solution to the problem* as a simple direct object of the verb *know*, as in (1a), rather than taking it to be the subject of a complement clause, as is necessary for the correct analysis of (1b).

(1)   *Nobody knew the solution to the problem . . . .*
      a. Nobody knew the solution to the problem by heart.
      b. Nobody knew the solution to the problem was easy.

The principles that guide the parser's decisions in such cases of (temporary) ambiguity have been called "parsing strategies." And it is at least a logical possibility that these strategies are inextricably bound up with, and inseparable from, the representation of the syntactic information that is used during comprehension. For instance, the fact that a verb like *know* may legitimately take a sentential complement might be represented by a rule like (2).

(2)   If a noun phrase that has been assigned as the direct object of a verb like *know* is followed by a finite verb, reassign that noun phrase as the subject of the following verb.

Rules like (2) may be used to specify the set of possible syntactic structures in a language indirectly, by specifying perceivers' first and preferred analysis of a sentence, together with permissible changes in this analysis (see, for example, Lakoff and Thompson [1975], where rules of this form were proposed).

From the perspective of sentence comprehension, rules like (2), which directly encode parsing strategies into the representation of syntactic information, do not seem too implausible. However, if SPEAKERS were to rely on such rules when they were formulating utterances, they would have to construct the same incorrect intermediate structures when they produced sentences that perceivers construct when they comprehend sentences. In producing a sentence like (1b), speakers utilizing a rule like (2) would be obliged to construct an intermediate structure in which the ambiguous noun phrase was assigned as the simple direct object of the verb *know*.

The claim that speakers construct the same intermediate hypotheses when they are planning a sentence that perceivers construct when they are garden-pathed by a sentence is extremely implausible and, to my knowledge, there is absolutely no evidence that supports it. Yet, if perceivers' strategies are directly encoded into the representation of the syntactic information used in comprehension, this is precisely what is predicted by the assumption that there is a common body of syntactic information shared by the production and comprehension systems.

Alternatively, the syntactic information used in comprehension might be stored together with, but not inextricable from, perceivers' parsing strategies. In the ATN framework, for example, syntactic information is represented as a network of "states" and "arcs" and perceivers' strategies may be represented in the network itself by ordering the alternative arcs leaving a state (cf. Kaplan, 1972). If we take this sort of representation seriously (rather than thinking of it as merely a convenient notation for indicating the ordering that is imposed on arcs by a separate body of strategies or scheduling principles), then in one sense syntactic information would be stored together with perceivers' strategies. However, the syntactic information contained in the network would not be inseparable from these strategies (as it was in the previous example). Speakers might use the syntactic information contained in this network when they were producing sentences but simply employ different principles (i.e., some principle other than the ordering of arcs encoded in the network) to govern the order in which they attempted different arcs. Hence, this alternative would permit speakers to utilize the same syntactic information as perceivers but would not entail that they relied on the same decision principles (and thus would not lead to the implausible prediction that speakers are garden-pathed by the same set of sentences that garden-path perceivers).

Finally, syntactic information might be stored by itself, completely independent from the processor's decision principles. In this case, syntactic information would be removed entirely from perceivers' parsing strategies and thus isolated from those aspects of processing where there is reason to expect differences between production and comprehension. Hence, this alternative would be entirely compatible with the claim that production and comprehension share a common body of syntactic information.

Fodor and Frazier (1980) argue at length for this third alternative. One of their arguments is that a particular parsing strategy, Minimal Attachment, can be explained very naturally if it is assumed that syntactic phrase structure information is stored in a separate rule library which must be accessed during sentence comprehension.

MINIMAL ATTACHMENT: Incorporate incoming lexical items into the phrase marker being constructed using the fewest nodes consistent with the well-formedness rules of the language.

Given the assumption of a special rule library, Minimal Attachment will follow as an automatic consequence of minimal rule accessing. Assuming that there is some cost (in terms of time) associated with accessing a rule, then accessing more rules will of course take more time. And, thus, if the parser merely accepts the first analysis available to it, this will automatically result in a preference for minimal attachments. In short, given the assumption of separate rule storage, the parser's preference for minimal attachments may simply be attributed to the general time pressures involved in sentence processing.

This explanation of Minimal Attachment enjoys several advantages over conceivable alternative explanations. Since the parser will accept the first analysis available to it regardless of the particular construction under consideration, this explanation accounts for the generality of the preference for minimal attachment across the wide variety of different constructions in English. And, as minimal rule accessing will be operative regardless of the particular details of the rules being accessed, this explanation permits minimal attachment to be generalized not only within a single language, but across different languages as well. Further, this explanation eliminates the need to postulate a special node-counting device in order to account for the parser's preference for minimal attachments. This latter point is especially important. Surely it is more in line with what is known about the human brain to assume that it simply performs operations in the quickest way it can (this is suggested, for example, by the prevalence of "horse-race" models in contemporary psychology) than to assume that the brain has evolved special counting devices whose only purpose is to evaluate the outcome of other operations solely on the basis of the number of steps taken to perform those operations.

Another argument that Fodor and Frazier present in support of syntactic information being stored separately from perceivers' strategies concerns the interaction of different parsing strategies. Specifically, when the parser's preference for low attachment and its preference for minimal attachment are in conflict, Minimal Attachment will prevail in some circumstances (when the minimal attachment site is visible within the restricted viewing window of the first stage processor) and the preference for low attachment will prevail in other circumstances (namely, when the low attachment is visible to the first stage processor, but the minimal attachment is not). If parsing strategies were stored together with the representation of syntactic information, then the interaction of these strategies is extremely difficult to explain. (In terms of an ATN representation in which arc ordering is encoded in the network, capturing this interaction requires placing completely ad hoc conditions on arcs to insure that in cases of conflict the length and structure of preceding constituents, not the relative order of arcs in the network, will determine which strategy will prevail and thus which arc will be attempted first, see Fodor and Frazier, where this argument is laid out in detail.)

If we accept the conclusion that the syntactic well-formedness constraints used in comprehension are stored separately from perceivers' decision principles, then we have at least established that the production system and the comprehension system could share a common body of syntactic knowledge. In sum, the claim of shared syntactic knowledge is at least coherent and consistent with available evidence concerning the mental representation of syntactic knowledge.

Clearly the claim that the same body of syntactic information is exploited by both the production and comprehension systems is a stronger claim than one that allows the representation of the syntactic information used in production to differ in any way at all from the representation of the syntactic information used in comprehension. Hence, at present, surely the best working assumption is that the production and comprehension systems do access and utilize the same body of syntactic information.

SHARED PROCESSING UNITS

Another place where we might expect to find a correspondence between production and comprehension is in the size and nature of the processing units which are important in each of these tasks. Most of the structural units of linguistic theory have at one time or another been proposed as the important processing unit in terms of which sentences are comprehended (e.g., the entire sentence, the surface clause, the deep clause, every syntactic phrase). More recently, Frazier and Fodor (1978) have argued that the important units in sentence comprehension do not correspond to units of any one particular structural type but rather correspond to "phrasal packages" whose size depends largely on the length of the constituents in a sentence. Because of the restrictions on human short-term memory, these phrasal packages will typically contain roughly six or seven words. Thus, a short clause consisting of five or six words might be structured together into a single phrasal package, whereas a long clause might be divided up into a number of different phrasal packages (which would be integrated only at a later stage in the processing of the sentence).

Though the memory and computational capacity of speakers is not very well understood, it is probably safe to assume that there do exist some restrictions on the immediate memory and computational capacity available to speakers when they are formulating utterances. Hence, we might wonder whether these restrictions lead speakers to plan and execute utterances in "chunks" that are roughly the same size as the phrasal packages that are constructed by perceivers during comprehension. A correspondence of this type would be of considerable interest, especially as it would suggest that listeners do not have to construct phrasal packages from scratch when they process a sentence, but rather they might reconstruct—or recover—phrasal packages which have been encoded into the acoustic signal by speakers during the production of the sentence.

Though this hypothesis has not been directly tested to date, there are a number of highly suggestive findings that support it. First, Fromkin (1971) reports that speech errors rarely involve elements separated by more than five or six words, which indicates that the units of sentence production correspond very nicely in size to the phrasal packages constructed by perceivers. Second, Grosjean, Grosjean, and Lane (1979) measured the pauses produced by speakers during the reading of familiar material. This study indicated that the best predictor of pause location was a metric that took into account not only the syntactic structure of the sentence, but also the distance of each possible pause location from the midpoint of the sentence. As all the example sentences presented in the study were twelve words in length, the midpoint was always between the sixth and seventh word of the sentence. Thus, assuming that speakers are most likely to pause between planning units rather than within a planning unit, this study also suggests that speakers are organizing sentences into chunks that are roughly six or seven words long (though, as expected, the exact length of these chunks also depends on the constituent structure of the sentence).

Suci (1967) demonstrated that subjects find it easier to learn a list of sentences if the presentation of the sentences respects the pausal segmentation of the sentence (i.e., if the words that would be included between two pauses when a speaker produces the sentences are presented together) than if the presentation respects only the syntactic structure (major constituent segmentation) of a sentence. This finding implies that the units of sentence production are also ideal units for purposes of perception and thus lends further support to the hypothesis that phrasal packages are involved in both the production and perception of speech.

In a study of pauses in spontaneous speech, Boomer (1965, p. 151) notes that "in order to exceed six or seven words a clause must usually include one or more extended anacolutha. . . ," or syntactically mixed constructions. Boomer's interest was in the study of pauses per se rather than in the presence or distribution of anacoluthic expressions, and thus he does not present the data on which this observation was based. Nevertheless, the observation is intriguing in that it again supports the notion that speakers must restrict the length of their planning units or else risk exceeding their capacity and thus forgetting or losing access to the syntactic commitments which they have taken on in earlier portions of the sentence.

In short, a variety of psycholinguistic findings suggest that speakers plan sentences in units that consist of a constituent or series of constituents that are roughly six or seven words in length. And thus there is converging evidence from different types of production studies in support of the hypothesis that phrasal packages are the basic processing units in production as well as in comprehension.

SHARED COMPLEXITY RANKINGS

From the perspective of linguistic theory, one of the most interesting correspondences between the production and comprehension systems would be a correspondence in the relative complexity rankings they assigned to different sentence types. That is, we might expect the grammar of a language to be most heavily influenced by performance considerations, not in cases where the exigencies of sentence production and the exigencies of sentence comprehension are at odds, but rather in cases where the two systems coincide and thus both exert a pressure on the language to change in the SAME direction.

If some construction or sentence type is particularly easy both to produce and to comprehend, we might expect that construction to be unmarked and frequently occurring both within a single language and across different languages. Similarly, if a construction places an especially heavy burden on both the production system and the comprehension system, we would expect the language either to develop a simpler alternative construction or to incorporate some constraint that excluded the complex construction from the language. Of course, at present very little is known about the complexity ranking that the sentence production system assigns to different sentence types. However, if we pursue the reasoning of the previous section (where it was argued that the limitations on speakers' immediate memory and computational capacity lead them to plan and produce utterances in terms of phrasal packages), then there are a variety of examples that may reasonably be argued to be cases where the complexity ranking of the production system and the comprehension system coincide.

Assuming that speakers and hearers process sentences in terms of phrasal packages, it seems likely that both speakers and hearers would prefer to have items that form a coherent semantic unit occur adjacent to each other in the lexical string (where they may be structured together into the same phrasal package), rather than having these items separated by some long intervening constituent (in which case these items might very well end up in separate phrasal packages). If this "adjacency preference" is in fact shared by both the production and comprehension systems, then this is a case where the grammar could accommodate itself to the needs of both systems simultaneously, and thus we would expect the "adjacency preference" to have a quite strong impact on the grammars of different languages. In Frazier (1979), it is argued that this preference explains many of the implicational universals proposed by Greenberg (1965). For example, it accounts for the tendency for postpositional languages to place relative clauses before their heads, genitives before their governing noun, etc. (see discussion of the "In-positional Universal" and the "Head Adjacency Principle" in Frazier, 1979). This of course supports the notion that constructions that are particularly easy both to produce and to comprehend are "unmarked" and thus correspond to the expected case across a wide variety of different languages. And, in terms of developing a theory of markedness [such as "Core Grammar," see Chomsky and Lasnik (1977)], it may be important to distinguish unmarked constructions that might be widespread simply because they have been favored by both the production and comprehension systems from constructions that are unmarked but may only be attributed to language learners' initial hypotheses about the structure of the language. In short, the theory of markedness will be more revealing of the basic structure of the language acquisition device if we are able to abstract away from (or separate out) the influence of the adult production and comprehension systems.

Turning to constructions that are particularly difficult to process, we may begin by considering a construction that is relatively difficult to comprehend, but not to produce. As mentioned earlier, a sentence like (3) [=(1b)] is more difficult to comprehend than a sentence like (4), where the presence of the complementizer *that* prevents the parser from incorrectly interpreting the phrase *the solution to the problem* as a simple direct object of the verb *know*. However, from the perspective of sentence production, there is no reason to expect (3) to be any more difficult than (4).

(3) Nobody knew the solution to the problem was easy.
(4) Nobody knew that the solution to the problem was easy.
(5) Nobody knew the air was polluted.
(6)* Nobody knew the air.

Given the perceptual complexity of (3) relative to (4), one might have thought that the grammar of English would simply prohibit complementizer deletion in sentences like (3) where the temporarily ambiguous noun phrase (*the solution . . .*) may coherently be analyzed as a simple direct object of the preceding verb [as opposed to (5), where this analysis is semantically incoherent—unless *air* has the rare interpretation of "tune"]. However, given the devices standardly available within a restrictive theory of syntax, a constraint on complementizer deletion could not be formulated in such a way that it would exclude all and only those instances of complementizer deletion that result in perceptually complex sentences [i.e., the constraint would be unable to discriminate between Sentences (3) and (5)]. In this situation, there are only three choices available to the grammar:

1. It could prohibit complementizer deletion across-the-board, thereby excluding the perceptually complex sentences, together with a large range of sentences like (5) which do not pose any particular problem for the sentence comprehension mechanism.

2. The grammar might incorporate some entirely new type of device which would permit it to exclude all and only the perceptually complex sentences.

3. The grammar might do nothing at all (i.e., the language might simply tolerate the perceptually complex construction).

It appears that in general the grammars of natural languages do not resort to extreme options like (1) or (2) in response to constructions which are only difficult to comprehend, but not to produce (see discussion of the Minimal Exclusion principle in Frazier, 1979).

But suppose (counterfactually) that exactly the same instances of complementizer deletion that cause difficulties for the sentence comprehension mechanism also caused problems for the sentence production system. We might speculate that under these circumstances the grammar of English might develop a constraint excluding all and only the complex constructions even though this would entail incorporating some new device into the grammar or relaxing the usual restrictions on the form of syntactic rules. In other words, when the production and comprehension systems are in collusion, speakers and hearers might be willing to "bend" the rules of the grammar or, perhaps, ignore them altogether as will be seen in what follows).

Though speculative, this line of reasoning leads to the hypothesis that whenever we find a "wrinkle" in the grammar (i.e., exceptional behavior whose grammatical treatment requires either expanding the vocabulary of linguistic theory or incorporating some new and otherwise unwarranted type of mechanism into the grammar) the "offensive" construction may be attributed to the collusion of the production and comprehension systems.[1] (The implications of this "Collusion Hypothesis" will be spelled out in a moment.) To take a specific example, in general syntactic rules are completely insensitive to the length of constituents; typically one does not find rules which, say, specify that a verb phrase may consist of a verb followed by a long noun phrase, but not of a verb followed by a short noun phrase. However, there are a few well-known exceptions to this generalization: the rule of Particle Shift [which is responsible for the atrocity in (7b)] and the rule of Heavy Noun Phrase Shift [which is responsible for the sentence in (8b)].

(7)   a.   *Henry sent out some reports about the numerous accidents that occurred at Three Mile Island last year.*
      b.   *Henry sent some reports about the numerous accidents that occurred at Three Mile Island last year out.*

[1]The Collusion Hypothesis does not entail that a grammar will only incorporate a performance-motivated constraint when the complexity rankings of the comprehension and production systems coincide. Rather, it claims that it is only in cases of collusion between the two systems that the grammar will go outside its normally available devices to incorporate a constraint that can not be stated without violating or relaxing the usual restrictions on the vocabulary and operations available in the grammar.

(8) a. *John gave a copy of his latest article about the role of the media in the militarization of American society to Susan.*
     b. *John gave to Susan a copy of his latest article about the role of the media in the militarization of American society.*

(9)* *John gave to Susan a book.*

In the case of Particle Shift, accounting for the apparent sensitivity of the rule to the length of constituents is not problematic, as there are independent reasons for supposing that sentences like (7b) in which the particle has been moved over a long intervening constituent will be unacceptable (see Frazier and Fodor, 1978). However, the sensitivity of Heavy Noun Phrase Shift to the length of the moved constituent is problematic if we wish to maintain the generalization that syntactic rules can not refer to the length of constituents—regardless of whether we formulate this rule as an extraposition rule [in which case we must explain why a short noun phrase like the phrase *a book* in (9) cannot be extraposed] or as an intraposition rule (in which case we must explain why the rule is obligatory just in case the relevant noun phrase is short) it appears that the rule must make reference to the length of the moved constituent. (Notice that this same argument goes through even if we assume that it is the prepositional phrase, rather than the noun phrase, which is moved.) And, by contrast with the Particle Shift example, we cannot explain these facts by appealing to the notion of an unacceptable but grammatical sentence as there is no reason to believe that the sentence comprehension system would find a sequence of SHORT phrases [such as the prepositional phrase and noun phrase in (9)] particularly difficult to process. In other words, the problem in the case of Heavy Noun Phrase Shift is that we must explain why a construction IS permissible just in case certain constituents are long, rather than why a legitimate construction is NOT permissible just in case certain constituents are long.

In the model of sentence comprehension proposed by Frazier and Fodor (1978), there are clear reasons for expecting that a sentence like (8a), which contains a "heavy noun phrase" that has not been shifted to the end of the sentence, should be difficult to parse. If the first stage processor receives a long noun phrase, such as the direct object in (8a), then by the time it receives subsequent material (e.g., the prepositional phrase *to Susan*) the lexical material preceding the long noun phrase will no longer be available within the restricted viewing window of the first stage processor. Thus, in a sentence like (8a), the first stage processor will not have access to the correct attachment site for the phrase *to Susan* (i.e., to the VP node dominating the verb *give*) at the time when it encounters this prepositional phrase. However, if the heavy noun phrase is shifted to the end of the sentence [as in (8b)], this problem will not arise since the first stage processor may incorporate the phrase *to Susan* into the same phrasal package that contains the verb *give*. (And, of course, there will be no problem parsing the long direct object since all of the items contained in it may correctly be structured together with other nearby items and the resulting phrasal packages may be integrated with preceding material by the second stage processor. See Frazier and Fodor, 1978, for details.)

A similar argument holds in the case of sentence production. In sentences like (8a), where the long noun phrase has not been postposed, speakers must remember the predicted prepositional phrase while they are elaborating the long intervening noun phrase. By contrast, in planning and producing sentences like (8b), speakers may relieve themselves of this commitment before they begin elaborating the longer and more complex noun phrase. Hence, the rule of Heavy Noun Phrase Shift appears to facilitate the task of the sentence production system, as well as the sentence comprehension system. In other words, though the rule of Heavy Noun Phrase Shift must refer to the length of constituents, there are independent reasons for believing that, as predicted by the Collusion Hypothesis, "unshifted" heavy noun phrases create complexities for both the production and comprehension systems—complexities that are not engendered by the alternative (shifted) constructions created by this exceptional rule.

If the Collusion Hypothesis can be maintained, it will provide a PRINCIPLED means for imposing stringent constraints on the form of syntactic rules in general, by permitting those constraints to be relaxed under very restricted circumstances (i.e., in cases of collusion). Alternatively, if a sufficiently detailed theory of acceptable ungrammaticality can be articulated (so that it will not incorrectly predict that *any* intelligible ungrammatical string should be judged to be well formed by speaker-hearers of the language, cf. Langendoen and Bever, 1976), then perhaps the rule of Heavy Noun Phrase Shift could be banished from the grammar entirely. If so, then the Collusion Hypothesis may be viewed as simply an initial step toward developing a more constrained theory of acceptable ungrammaticality.[2] In either case, it appears that identifying production–comprehension correspondences will permit us to construct more restrictive theories of natural languages without having to dismiss certain troublesome data in a relatively unprincipled fashion.

REFERENCES

Bever, T. G. (1970). The cognitive basis for linguistic structure. In J. Hayes (Ed.). *Cognition and the development of language.* New York: Wiley.

[2]This latter approach is especially tantalizing insofar as it might provide some insight into the genesis of "free word order" languages. If in cases of collusion speakers and hearers are willing to simply violate certain rules of the language and then proceed to systematically do so in circumstances that are governed by "performance" factors and thus are not describable in terms of a set of innately specified grammatical categories or in terms of a natural class of structural conditions, language learners might well conclude that there are only (or predominantly) stylistic constraints on the word order of the language they are acquiring.

Boomer, D. S. (1965). Hesitation and grammatical encoding. *Language and Speech*, 8, 145–158.

Chomsky, N., and Lasnik, H. (1977). Filters and control. *Linguistic Inquiry*, 8, 425–504.

Fodor, J. D., and Frazier, L. (1980). Is the human sentence parsing mechanism an ATN? *Cognition*,

Frazier, L. (1978). *On comprehending sentences: Syntactic parsing strategies*. University of Connecticut Ph.D. dissertation. (Reproduced by Indiana University Linguistics Club.)

Frazier, L. (1979). Parsing and constraints on word order. In J. Lowenstamm (Ed.), *University of Massachusetts Occasional Papers in Linguistics*, 5, 177–198.

Frazier, L., and Fodor, J. D. (1978). The sausage machine: A new two-stage parsing model. *Cognition*, 6, 291–326.

Fromkin, V. (1971). The non-anomalous nature of anomalous utterances. *Language*, 47, 27–52.

Greenberg, J. H. (1965). Some universals of grammar with particular reference to the order of meaningful elements. In J. H. Greenberg (Ed.), *Universals of language*. Cambridge, Mass.: MIT Press.

Grosjean, F., Grosjean, L., and Lane, H. (1979). The patterns of silence: Performance structures in sentence production. *Cognitive Psychology*, 11, 58–81.

Kaplan, R. (1972). Augmented transition networks as psychological models of sentence comprehension. *Artificial Intelligence*, 3, 77–100.

Lakoff, G., and Thompson, H. (1975). Dative questions in cognitive grammar. In *Papers from the Parasession on Functionalism*, Chicago Linguistics Society.

Langendoen, D. T., and Bever, T. G. (1976). Can a not unhappy person be called a sad one? In T. G. Bever, J. J. Katz and D. T. Langendoen (Eds.), *An integrated theory of linguistic ability*. New York: Crowell.

Suci, G. (1967). The validity of pause as an index of units in language. *Journal of Verbal Learning and Verbal Behavior*, 6, 26–32.

12

The Translational Hierarchy of Language

Marc L. Schnitzer

INTRODUCTION

In arguing against reductionism, Jerry Fodor (1975) has written:

> If psychology is reducible to neurology, then for every psychological kind predicate there is a coextensive neurological kind predicate, and the generalization which states this coextension is a law [p. 17].

He goes on to say:

> Yet, as has been frequently remarked in recent discussions of materialism, there are good grounds for hedging these bets. There are no firm data for any but the grossest correspondence between types of psychological states and types of neurological states, and it is entirely possible that the nervous system of higher organisms characteristically achieves a given psychological end by a wide variety of neurological means [p. 17].

and further:

> What I have been doubting is that there are neurological kinds coextensive with psychological kinds. What seems increasingly clear is that, even if there are such coextensions, they cannot be lawful. For it seems increasingly likely that there are nomologically possible systems other than organisms (viz., automata) which satisfy the kind predicates of psychology but which satisfy no neurological predicates at all [pp. 17–18].

According to Fodor, what is needed is a medium of representation for the computation required for language processing. But the hardware involved might be employed in any number of ways. The position is evidently quite pervasive. Geschwind (1974), one of the most outspoken localizationists has said:

NEURAL MODELS OF
LANGUAGE PROCESSES

I would have to accept the view that what one might call the realization in hardware of an axiomatic system would not necessarily be, so to speak, isomorphic with that system. One would hardly expect that damage to an ideal computer, capable of deriving theorems of Euclidean geometry, would produce loss of individual axioms [p. 505].

I find two objections to this line of reasoning. The first one is theoretical. If all the hardware provides is a medium in which the (presumably mentalistic) computation takes place, one is left with the problem of who or what is doing the computation. Any theory of language that leaves one with little men doing the job we are trying to account for is no theory at all, as one is left having to explain how these homunculi work.

My second objection is on empirical grounds. If the hardware does nothing more than provide a medium for computation, how is one to explain the large number of data relating site of lesion with behavioral deficit in uniform ways across speakers and across languages? Kean (1978) makes a similar point regarding the characteristics symptomatology of Broca's aphasia across speakers of different languages.

Computers can perform grossly differing logical operations with constant hardware because they have been built in such a way that the flow of logic depends largely on software which is interchangeable. And this point pertains only to general purpose computers. Special purpose computers do not share this property. There seems to be little reason to compare the human nervous system to a general purpose computer.

As people did not build human neurological systems, they do not know how they work a priori. Therefore, it seems advisable to follow the admonition of Brown (1977), when he says:

Symptoms should, in fact, be the mortar of the psychology, not just chosen to illustrate this or that theoretical formulation, since the diversity of clinical symptoms is such as to support by the manner of selection almost any a priori assumption [p. 2].

I am not trying to argue that localization studies are the route to discovering how language is represented in the brain. On the contrary, localization is no substitute for explanation: With more refined localization, the homunculi just get smaller and smaller, doing smaller and smaller jobs. Arbib and Caplan (1979) make a similar point in their critique of "faculty models."

Lamendella (1979) in his review of neurolinguistics for the *Annual Reviews of Anthropology* puts it as follows:

Theoretical linguists could not be content to merely identify a "phonological" level of language structure and not go on to derive a theory of the organization of phonological structures. Theoretical neurolinguistics should not be content to identify a *"motor speech region"* (Broca's area) or a *"sensory speech region"* (Wernicke's area) without having as a high priority the description of the organization of speech functions and subfunctions which accounts for the capacity of these areas to process speech [p. 386].

Thus, the question of where language faculties and speech functions are located seems premature. 'What' and 'how' are what we need to know before the question of 'where' becomes intelligible. So we have the problem of having to know what it is we are seeing linguistically when we "see something" neurologically. There are those who would argue as Klein (1978) does that:

it is the job of linguistic theory to provide us with a description of a person's knowledge of his language; it is the job of psycholinguistics to provide us with a description of the processing mechanisms by which that knowledge is put to use. Although neurological evidence may lead to insights as to the most appropriate functional theory and certainly must be consistent with such theories, in general, research must proceed from psychology to neurology. The reason is simple. We will not be in a position to discover how LRCS [= language responsible cognitive structure] is realized neurologically until we know what is so realized. In other words, evidence of the neurological realization of LRCS cannot be properly evaluated except in the context of linguistic and psycholinguistic models of LRCS [p. 5].

But I think that this misses the crucial point that defining human language is not the same as defining an electric motor, or even a general purpose computer. Language can be defined in many different ways, depending on perspective (e.g., social, psychological, cultural, political, formal, etc.), and even within a single perspective. As Bresnan (1978), speaking from a more or less cognitive perspective, puts it:

The difficulty in linguistics is that we can characterize our knowledge of language in too many ways. What has been called the grammatical characterization problem—the problem of representing the language user's knowledge of language—is not very well defined. Therefore, it does not seem reasonable to argue that the grammatical characterization problem should be solved in advance of what has been called the grammatical realization problem: it is not clear that we will ever come to a solution to the grammatical characterization problem as it has been defined in the past.

But the grammatical realization problem can clarify and delimit the grammatical characterization problem. We can narrow the class of possible theoretical solutions by subjecting them to experimental psychological investigation as well as to linguistic investigation [p. 59].

The point can be applied to neurolinguistics as well. The way language appears to be represented neurologically can give us information as to how language is to be characterized. Thus I see the proper direction for investigation to be the opposite of that proposed by Klein: Symptoms should be the mortar of the theory.

A theory of language must be relatable to, and must conform to, what we know about the nervous system, based on evidence from pathology as well as from other investigatory paradigms. There can be little doubt of the hierarchical nature of the nervous system, in which higher levels exert control over lower levels, and in which lower levels operate more or less autonomously in the absence of control exercised from above, and constantly provide input and feedback to higher levels. It can hardly be disputed that language functions to relate cognitions, thoughts, ideas, and feelings to a form of representation such as sound or writing for transmission to other organisms, and to receive the transmitted form and relate it to cognitions, feelings, etc. of the receiver. As a higher cognitive function, language is part of the larger hierarchy which is the human mind–body, and as such, displays hierarchical structure as well. Thus, one can think of encoding as a process by which thoughts are first put into predicational form (in which arguments are distinguished from predicates, topics from comments, etc.) and, along the line, major lexical items are chosen (but not always). From this point, the message is filtered through linguistic "housekeeping" rules, traditionally called (surface) syntactic, morphological, and morphophonemic rules or constraints, before being passed on to be mesotically encoded.[1] The mesotic (i.e., the form encoded for communication) will usually but not always involve phonology. As each level will have input from the next lower level, lower levels will in fact influence higher ones. Thus, the level of cognition could indeed be influenced by the linguistic structure of the language of the speaker. So one can thus conceive of a linguistic hierarchy in which the highest level is cognitive and is really not linguistic per se. The next level down is semantic, in which thought is "linguisticized" into predications, and in which, usually, major class lexical items are drawn from the lexicon. The next level subjects these predications to individual constraints. Here we find superficial syntax and inflectional morphology, and perhaps some derivational morphology, although I suspect that the larger part of the latter is provided ready-made by the lexicon. At this point, the message can be encoded phonologically, graphemically, or otherwise, and hooked up to the appropriate peripheral motor-command systems.

Note that the foregoing discussion entails that a human language is not a set of sentences, but rather a transducer between thought and mesotic (or means of transmission). In DEcoding, it transforms mesotically encoded messages into thought, but I shall postpone discussion of decoding until I have given evidence for the conception I am presenting.

[1]See Schnitzer (1976) for a discussion of the notion "mesotic."

EVIDENCE FROM LANGUAGE PATHOLOGY

I wish now to present evidence for considering Wernicke's area to be the site of what I have been calling the semantic or linguistic predication function, and for considering Broca's area[2] to be the site of what I have been calling the "housekeeping" function.

Broca's Aphasia

In an ideal Broca's aphasic, Wernicke's area is intact. The speech of a Broca's aphasic is characterized by the presence of content words and by intact basic predicational relationships. Broca's aphasics speak as though they were trying to communicate in a language of which they do not know the grammar. When a normal adult learns a foreign language, what he in fact has to learn is "housekeeping rules" (as well, of course, as vocabulary, phonology, phonetics, and orthography). He does not need to learn basic predicational relationships. This kind of speech uttered by the Broca's aphasic is understandable most of the time. We can usually understand telegrams as well. The language used in telegrams differs from normal language by virtue of its elimination of many of the "housekeeping" elements of ordinary language. Pidgins originate in an attempt to facilitate communication with nonspeakers of a language by reducing the "housekeeping" rules.

The receptive ability of Broca's aphasics is generally good. This makes sense. One usually does not need "housekeeping" rules to understand what someone means. One can understand a foreign language, having only imperfect command of the grammar. But in specific tasks requiring attention to morphology or to superficial syntax, Broca's aphasics fail.

Luria (1975) discusses two kinds of tasks presented to aphasics. One set involved testing patients' assessment of constructions expressing logical relationships (such as "the father's brother" versus "the brother's father," or "a triangle over a circle" versus "a circle over a triangle") by having them explain the difference in meaning or point to a diagram picturing the relationship. This sort of task would involve the semantic or predicational level in the hierarchy, which I attribute to Wernicke's area. The other set of tasks involved asking the patient to

---

[2]In referring to Broca's aphasia and Wernicke's aphasia, I do not mean to imply that these syndromes can always be clearly related to specific cortical areas bearing the respective names. What I wish to imply is that, at some of level of analysis, certain cortical areas can be related on a statistical basis to specific kinds of language disorders, as discussed in the remainder of the chapter, and that, functionally, all brains that handle language normally must have a "Broca-type" area and a "Wernicke-type" area, even if these functional units are not found in the traditional Broca's and Wernicke's areas.

judge the grammaticality of sentences, among which were included sentences containing morphosyntactic errors of a relatively superficial nature [e.g., Parokhod idet povodoj (The steamship sailed through by the water) or Zimoj ludi kataiutsya na saniaMY (In winter people travel about on with sleighs)], and to correct the errors, if possible. This task, on the other hand, would involve what I have called "housekeeping rules." Luria finds that patients with anterior lesions have little trouble in performing the first type of task but have difficulty in evaluating the grammaticality of and correcting the morphosyntactic (i.e., "housekeeping") errors in the sentences in the second set of tasks. This result follows from what I have been saying.

If this interpretation of Broca's aphasia is essentially correct, how does one account for the presence of phonemic paraphasias so frequently found in the speech of Broca's aphasics? I would claim that because the level of phonological realization gets input from Broca's area, an impaired Broca's area would send down an imperfect signal which could not be completely specified phonologically. The paraphasias could then arise from indeterminacy in the signal. If this is correct, Broca's aphasics should be able to recognize phonemic paraphasias in receptive tasks, even though they do not recognize agrammatism, as Luria notes. The reason for this will become clear later.

Keller (1979) has argued rather persuasively for a distinction between planning and execution stages in speech production. In so doing, he argues against a strict separation of phonemic and phonetic processing in speech. If he is correct, then phonemics may belong strictly to the realm of perception. In production, Broca's area sends signals consisting of lexical and grammatical formatives encoded for motor commands. Keller's position is consistent with the fact that some phonemic paraphasias found in Broca's aphasia do not violate the phonotactic constraints of the language whereas others do.

Wernicke's Aphasia

In an ideal Wernicke's aphasic, Broca's area is intact. I have claimed that Wernicke's area handles semantics—basic predicational functions. In the speech of Wernicke's aphasics, we find a lack of intelligibility of message, due to the absence of logical structure. We find superficial syntax, morphology, morphophonemics, etc. preserved. The speech patterns of Wernicke's aphasics arise from a functioning Broca's area taking care of "housekeeping," but receiving a distorted input from Wernicke's area. Naturally, comprehension is significantly impaired in Wernicke's aphasia since comprehension is, basically, the interpreting of the encoded message into its basic predicational functions. The housekeeping rules play only a minor role in this.

This accounts for Luria's (1975) observation that patients with posterior lesions have little difficulty with the grammaticality judgments task, but have a good deal of trouble assessing the logical relationships. The grammaticality judgments are handled by the intact Broca's area.

The approach I have been discussing, would also make it possible to account for other syndromes in a straightforward manner. Dementia could be looked at as a nonlinguistic deficit affecting the cognitive level and providing impaired input to the semantic predicational level (Wernicke's area). Isolation syndrome could be looked at as a disconnection between the linguistic and cognitive levels or, in the case of a severely damaged cognitive level, a linguistic system operating in the absence of cognitive input. At least one type of anomia may be due to disconnection in the lexical access path between the cognitive level and the semantic predicational level. Thus such anomics know what they want to say and do not demonstrate agrammatism, but cannot access the lexical item they wish to use. This could be because the cognitive matter on being put into lexical predicational form in Wernicke's area arrives without lexical encoding, due perhaps to some kind of disconnection between the lexicon and Wernicke's area. I really do not wish to speculate on this any further in view of the sizable number of different anomic-type syndromes for which Benson (1979) has adduced evidence.

It would seem that the agnosias and the dysarthrias are not language deficits per se. I will discuss conduction aphasia in due course.

LINGUISTIC THEORY

In *Aspects of the theory of syntax*, in the context of warning against transformational grammars being misconstrued as models of speech production, Chomsky (1965) said:

> A reasonable model of language use will incorporate, as a basic component, the generative grammar that expresses the speaker-hearer's knowledge of the language; but this generative grammar does not, in itself, prescribe the character of functioning of a perceptual model or a model of speech production [p. 9].

A good deal of research was devoted to trying to discover how a generative grammar might be incorporated in a model of language use. In spite of this, no one was able to construct a model incorporating competence grammars of the Chomskyan type that offered any evidence of psychological validity. The results led Bever (1970) to conclude that "the relation between linguistic grammar based on intuition and that based on the description of other kinds of explicit language performance may not just be 'abstract' (as maintained by Fodor and Garrett) but may be *nonexistent* in some cases [p. 345, Bever's italics]."

The failure to find such a relationship led to a reduced interest in transformational grammar among psycholinguists. Some researchers, however, have decided that it may be the linguistic theory which is at fault, and that a criterion for grammar selection should be psychological plausibility (Bresnan, 1978). Probably the aspect of transformational grammars that has shown the least likelihood of having psychological reality has been the transformations themselves. Recently, however, a number of linguists (for example, Brame, Wasow, Bresnan, Jackendoff) have been arguing that the number of transformations should be drastically reduced and that a large number of tasks previously assigned to the transformational subcomponent should be relegated to the lexicon.

Chomsky himself, on "internal linguistic grounds," has been gradually reducing the number of transformations up to the point of proposing that the transformational subcomponent may be reducible to one rule, "Move Category" (Chomsky, 1977). Furthermore, the development of "trace theory," first introduced by Chomsky in 1973, has allowed for semantic interpretation to be done entirely at the level of surface structure. Given that one of the principal arguments for a level of syntactic deep structure had been that this was the only point at which (certain significant aspects of) semantic interpretation could take place, the introduction of trace theory significantly weakened the case for deep structure. With transformations and deep structure significantly reduced in importance to linguistic description, a number of linguists have been moved to do away with them altogether and to develop alternative theories of grammar.

In the past few years, a number of theories of grammar have been proposed which can be grouped, I think, into three main types.

The first type is what I call **functional**. Here I mean 'functional' in the sense of accounting directly for communicative function by means of the model. In this group I place Dik's "functional grammar" (Dik, 1978), Foley and Van Valin's "role and reference grammar" (in preparation), augmented transition networks, being developed by a number of investigators (e.g., Kaplan, 1972; Wanner and Maratsos, 1978; Woods, 1970), and Lakoff and Thompson's "cognitive grammar," which makes use of augmented transition networks (1975a,b). McCawley's recent work also seems to be "functional" in this sense, although he still retains transformational derivations. Clearly the HEARSAY system proposed by Arbib and Caplan (1979) would belong to this group. Although these approaches differ markedly in their formal properties, they share the conception of language as a communicative tool, and regard the goal of linguistics to be the explication of how the tool works to achieve its end.

A second type of theory may be characterized by its emphasis on an **enriched surface structure**. Such models include only one level of morphosyntactic structure. This is achieved by including a lot more in a representation than merely trees with syntactic category lables: Semantic and syntactic functions and relations are all included at the single level as well. In this group, I would classify Hudson's "daughter-dependency grammar" (Hudson, 1976) and Michael Kac's "corepresentational grammar" (Kac, 1978).

I label the third group **axiomatic definitional** systems, for want of a better label. In these, a variety of techniques are used to formally specify the language. The most obvious example of this is Montague grammar, of which a clear exposition for the nonlogician can be found in Partee 1975. A Montague grammar consists of recursive definitions of sets of sentences. I also classify Gerald Sander's (1972) "equational grammar" in the group. Sander's approach involves statements of which linguistic representations are equivalent or nonequivalent to which other linguistic representations. These statements can theoretically be used to prove equivalence or nonequivalence between semantic representations and phonetic representations. I think that Brame's (1979) "realistic grammar" (which differs somewhat from Bresnan's realistic grammar in that the latter still uses transformations) also belongs to this group. Relying heavily on lexical specifications, the grammar consists essentially of compositional and interpretive rules.

I have not intended this list to be exhaustive but merely illustrative of the various trends in linguistic theory at the present time. And it should be borne in mind that the approaches referred to differ greatly in the extent to which they have been worked out, many of them being only at the stage of offering a promissory note.

Stratificational grammar, although belonging to the functional group in terms of stated aims, belongs to the axiomatic definitional class in terms of its formal properties. I have argued (Schnitzer, 1978) in favor of stratificational grammar as a possible framework for neurolinguistic research, because it seems well equiped to model the relationship between static knowledge and dynamic performance in representing hierarchical linguistic structure. Because stratificational grammar has only relations—no items, no processes—one can conceive of knowledge as the static network as always represented, and of performance as the framework put into use with impulses running through it. But as such, stratificational grammar provides only a framework. As is true of any theory of language, research needs to be done with respect to the analysis of specific aspects of specific languages. Perhaps ideas gleaned from some of the approaches just mentioned could be incorporated directly into a relational network of stratificational grammar.

My arguments in Schnitzer (1978) in favor of the adoption of a stratificational model were made in the context of a structural-realist approach to the mind–body problem. If it turns out that the competence–performance distinction, as I have therein defined it in neuropsychological terms (see p. 251), is viable, then we must concern ourselves not only with processing—not only with computation, as it were—but also with KNOWLEDGE. The appearance in a given aphasic of the same linguistic errors across radically different linguistic tasks in all modalities would indicate a deficit not in computation, but in knowledge. Some evidence that such phenomena occur is reviewed in Schnitzer (1978).

In any case, in doing linguistic analysis I think it important to take the cue from Jason Brown in the passage cited at the beginning of this chapter: "Symptoms should . . . be the mortar of the psychology," that is to say, of the LINGUISTIC theory. Various versions of stratificational grammar have been proposed which consist of various numbers of strata. Typically, a stratificational grammar has the following strata:

1. HYPERSEMEMIC (or COGNITIVE). This is, strictly speaking, an extralinguistic stratum which is intended to represent cognitive structure with which the linguistic system interacts.
2. SEMEMIC. This would include basic predicational and thematic relations, logical form, deep cases, focus, topic, etc.
3. LEXEMIC. This stratum deals with basic word order in different types of clausal structure.
4. MORPHEMIC. This level handles inflectional morphology, productive derivational morphology, and part of morphophonemics.
5. PHONEMIC. This would probably include syllable, cluster, and segment structure, contrast, and certain alternations, as well as phonological feature composition.
6. PHONETIC. This level would handle nondistinctive phonetic specifications. Like the hypersememic, this stratum may possibly be extralinguistic.

Each stratum in a stratificational grammar contains a **realizational system,** connecting it with the stratum above and the stratum below; and a **tactic pattern**—that is to say, a specification of the combinatorial possibilities of the units of that stratum. This is one of the key features of the stratificational framework. On the other hand, the particular list of strata that I have presented is meant only to be illustrative. There is considerable diversity in the number and composition of strata among practitioners of stratificational grammar (see Makkai and Lockwood, 1973, for representative papers).

At this point, it seems appropriate to provide a brief (and oversimplified) introduction to stratificational grammar for those readers unfamiliar with the relational network approach to linguistic description. As already noted, stratificational grammar deals with relations only. Its primitives are conjunction (*and*), disjunction (exclusive *or*), precedence (*before* and *after*), and upward (toward cognition) and downward (toward phonetics or other expressive mode) direction. Figure 12.1 shows the basic symbols ('ordered' and 'unordered' refer to the relevance and irrelevance of precedence, respectively). There seem to be no instances of upward ordered *and*s. Figure 12.2 represents a portion of a relational network of English which handles some of the lexotactics, morphotactics, and morphophonemics of the (fragments of) sentences:

$$(1) \quad Why \begin{Bmatrix} do \\ can \\ will \end{Bmatrix} \begin{Bmatrix} you \\ /yə/ \\ they \end{Bmatrix} not \dots$$

(2)　Why ⎰ *don't* ⎱ ⎰ *you* ⎱ . . .
　　　　⎨ *can't* ⎬ ⎨ /yə/ ⎬
　　　　⎱ *won't* ⎰ ⎱ *they* ⎰

(3)　Why ⎰ /downčə/ ⎱ . . .
　　　　⎨ /kænčə/ ⎬
　　　　⎱ /wownčə/ ⎰

(4)

　　　　/waynčə/ . . .

In addition to the symbols noted in the two columns of Figure 12.1, Figure 12.2 contains several instances of the diamond symbol which is an abbreviation for an upward and a downward unordered *and*, in the relation shown at the bottom center of Figure 12.1. (For purposes of this chapter, it is not necessary to go into the reasons for its use.) All written words and symbols in Figure 12.2 are for the sake of readability: The network itself operates without labels; a relational network has no ITEMS.

Let us trace this diagram from top to bottom (sememic to

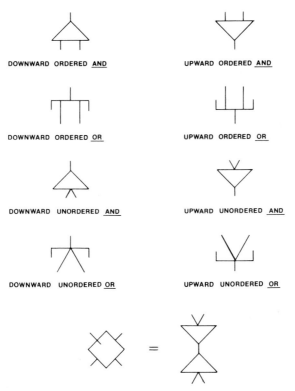

FIGURE 12.1. *Stratificational symbols.*

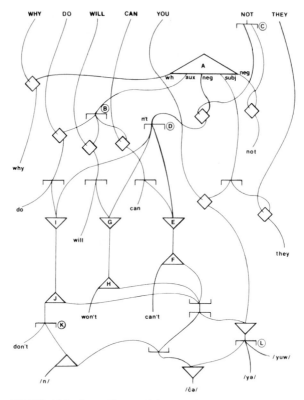

FIGURE 12.2. A stratificational diagram for a sentence fragment.

morphophonemic) to understand what it says. This network can be looked at statically (as representing inherent structure—competence) or dynamically (as representing expression or reception). For convenience of exposition, let us think of this diagram dynamically and expressively, tracing the paths from top to bottom, looking at it as a process through which the ideas carried by sentence fragments (1)–(4) are expressed. In a more complete diagram, many of the phenomena collapsed herein would be dispersed in various strata.

At the top, we find the sememic units WHY, DO, WILL, CAN, NOT, YOU, and THEY. Triangle A represents a portion of English clausal structure, which as a downward ordered *and* node, specifies the possible linear arrangements of wh elements, auxiliaries, subjects, and the negative.

For the sentence fragments (1), the sememic unit WHY is combined with the wh tactic form of A to yield morphemic *why*, the only wh word contained in these fragments. Node A assures its position at the beginning of the clause.

Downward unordered *or* node B combines the tactic auxiliary element with one of the sememic elements DO, WILL, and CAN, to insure second position for the auxiliary element. These elements are not contracted as the right branch of downward ordered *or* node C is chosen, which results in the realization of NOT as *not*, and in its being placed in the rightmost position by node A. Because the rightmost branch of C is chosen, the effect of the third element in A (i.e., neg) is nullified, and the next element chosen (to the right of the auxiliary) is the subject. In the diagram presented, the only two choices are YOU and THEY.

For sentence fragments (2), (3), and (4), many of the relations are the same as for fragments (1). Let us look at the differences.

In sentence fragment (2), the negative element is required BETWEEN the auxiliary and the subject. The necessity of combining the auxiliary with the contraction *n't* at downward unordered node D is handled by the selection of the left branch of node C. In the case of *can*, the impulse which originated at sememic CAN combines with *n't* at node E and is realized as *can't* at node F. As the forms /wɪlənt/ and /duwnt/ do not exist, special network fragments for *won't* (nodes G and H) and *don't* (nodes I and J) are required to derive the forms /wownt/ and /downt/ as realizations of DO and WILL, respectively, when combined with *n't* (node D). For both sets of sentence fragments (1) and (2), the varients /yuw/ and /yə/ are insured by the downward unordered node L.

The major difference between sets of sentence fragments (2) and (3) is that for (2) the rightmost branch or the middle branch of downward unordered *or* node L is chosen to combine with the right branches of downward ordered *and* nodes J, H, and F. In (3), the LEFTmost branch of L is chosen, yielding the /če/ realization of NOT + YOU (in combination with DO, WILL, and CAN).

The sentence fragment (4) allows for a realization of *don't* as /n/ (node K), provided that is is combined with the left branch of L, realized as /če/.

Unfortunately it is not possible to trace a stratificational diagram in complete detail by means of prose description. The reader is urged to follow the diagram according to the principles stated. A good exercise would be to trace the network in the upward direction, starting with sentence fragments (1)–(4). For more technical information regarding stratificational grammar and the construction of relational networks, Lockwood (1972) is highly recommended.

Following Brown's admonition, let us now consider a hypothetical example of two typical Broca's aphasics—one an English speaker and one a Spanish speaker. It might be expected that most of the agrammatism produced by the English speaker would involve SYNTACTIC deviation, whereas most of that produced by the Spanish speaker would involve MORPHOLOGICAL deviation. For example, if the English speaker said "go" or "you go" or "would go" in a context in which a normal speaker would have said "you would go," this would appear to be agrammatism of a syntactic type. But if the Spanish speaker said, for example, "yendo" instead of "irías," this would be considered to be agrammatism of a morphological type. But this is only because in 'you would go' the four morphemes are represented by three lexemes, whereas in 'irías' the three morphemes *ir* ('go'), *ía* ('conditional'), and *s* ('second person') are represented by a single lexeme.

If symptomatology is to be the mortar of our theorizing, then this phenomenon provides motivation for collapsing the lexemic with the morphemic stratum. Not to do so would lead to the absurd conclusion that because lesions in Broca's area affect mainly syntax among English speakers and mainly morphology among Spanish speakers, there must be a physical difference between anglophones and hispanophones.[3] Yet quite clearly, English syntactic relations and corresponding Spanish morphological patterns are performing the same kind of "housekeeping" functions. From a functional perspective, one could say that the loss of "housekeeping" rules would HAVE TO involve principally syntactic problems for English speakers and principally morphological problems for Spanish speakers. This indicates that the lexemic and the morphemic strata should be combined. I shall henceforth refer to this combined stratum as the "morpholexemic level" and to "housekeeping" operations as "morpholexotactics."

In his remarks to the Milwaukee Conference on Current Approaches to Syntax, William Sullivan (1979) mentioned that Henry Gleason had in fact already suggested that lexotactics might be the upper portion of the morphotactics, rather than part of a separate stratum. When I asked for clarification, Sullivan responded in part as follows: "He didn't say that LT [lexotactics] and MT [morphotactics] could be collapsed. He just said that he hadn't seen sufficient convincing evidence for the establishment of two strata. (Personally, I see both tactic and realizational evidence. The former involves idioms like *kick the bucket*, which are lexemic, and *understand*, which are morphemic. The latter involves the time–tense system of English. Other languages I know well also have both kinds of evidence. As I see it, the question is what constitutes necessary and sufficient evidence. That is, there is some, but is it enough? . . .) [personal communication, 1979]." I think that using pathology as the mortar of the linguistics can help deal with questions of this kind.

Kean (1978) has come to a similar conclusion regarding the importance of a multilingual approach to evaluating aphasic symptomatology. However, she claims that what Broca's aphasia affects is not morphosyntax, but rather PHONOLOGY. She says: "A Broca's aphasic tends to reduce the structure of a sentence to the minimal string of elements which can be lexically construed as phonological words in his language [p. 88]." But she does not say why or how. And in the model she implicitly adopts, "phonology" contains much that other approaches

---

[3]Vildomec (1963) noted that one would expect to find different manifestations of agrammatism in analytic and synthetic languages.

have included in morphology, morphophonemics, superficial syntax, and the lexicon.

If, on the other hand, we adopt a hierarchical relational network approach to neurolinguistic modeling, such as I have been arguing for, we can claim that Broca's area contains the morpholexemic stratum and that Broca's aphasia damages the interconnections of the tactic pattern at that level. Thus well-formed semantic units (perhaps coming from Wernicke's area) are passed through Broca's area without being subjected to a properly functioning tactic pattern as they are passed along for speech or other mesotic encoding. This, I am claiming, is the source of agrammatism in Broca's aphasia. I am claiming that Broca's area contains the morpholexemic stratum and that Wernicke's area contains something like what has been called the sememic stratum.

COMPETENCE AND PERFORMANCE

I have been discussing both competence and performance. The Hayekian approach (see p. 256) that I have implicitly adopted in connection with a stratificational network framework allows one to look at input processing, output processing, and linguistic knowledge as all related by a constant structure which can be looked at in both a physical and a mental representation. One can look at POTENTIAL connections in a system, or imagine the system in operation with impulses traveling through it. This applies to the human mind–body in general and to the linguistic system in particular. We can call the static aspect 'competence' and the dynamic one 'performance,' I think, without changing the traditional sense of the words. The main difference is that by adopting structural realism, we can look at a given structure under two representations—one mental and one physical—with the same static–dynamic distinction under both (cf. Hayek, 1952; Schnitzer, 1978; and the section on the mind–body problem in this chapter).

I can now say a word or two about decoding. I have argued that Wernicke's area deals with basic semantic functions: logical form, deep case structure, etc. When speech is heard, impulses, undoubtedly already somewhat analyzed subcortically, arrive at Heschl's gyrus, adjacent to Wernicke's area. Wernicke's area, with direct connections to the lexicon (which is probably diffusely localized) interprets the message in general terms and allows a basic understanding. Usually no more linguistic processing is necessary. If it is necessary, that is, if interpretation depends crucially on morpholexemic analysis, then the partially decoded form can be sent to Broca's area for morpholexotactic analysis.

My proposal thus explains in a straightforward way why Broca's aphasics have relatively good comprehension and why Wernicke's aphasics have relatively poor comprehension. It also explains why, notwithstanding, Broca's aphasics make mistakes on receptive tasks which are analogous to the errors made in their speech.

The fact that Wernicke's aphasics also have problems with reading comprehension may be due to the fact that if what is perceived is linguistic, the impulse winds up in Wernicke's area anyway. This needs to be investigated by various monitoring techniques. (Another explanation is implicit in the discussion of the mind–body problem in what follows.)

I can now also address the question of why the approach I am advocating would entail that although a Broca's aphasic will not recognize agrammatisms when they are presented to him, he should, ceteris paribus, recognize phonemic paraphasias. Because Broca's area handles morpholexemics and not phonology, one would expect someone with a damaged Broca's area to have difficulty evaluating agrammatisms but little difficulty evaluating phonetic deviations, even though he may not be able to correct them. My claim needs to be tested, of course, by presenting Broca's aphasics with phonemic paraphasias and asking them to identify them. Edgar Zurif (personal communication, 1979) said that the fact that these patients keep trying to correct themselves when they produce phonemic paraphasias provides evidence in favor of this claim. I wish now to present some further evidence in the form of phonemically distorted words that were presented to a Broca's aphasic to be judged for correctness and corrected if wrong. Table 12.1 contains the presented distorted word, the correct form, and the patient's response.

In response to Item (1), the patient produced morphologically and semantically related words, but could not produce the correct form. This was true for (6) as well. For Item (5), the patient produced a word phonologically similar to the correct form, but unrelated semantically and morphologically. For (3), the patient produced two phonemically similar words before getting the correct form. The patient succeeded for (7) and (9), and failed entirely for (4) and (8). These data thus tend to support the claim.

TABLE 12.1
Correction of Distorted Words

Item Presented	Correct form	Response
1. telesivor	televisor	TV, televisión
2. ustedas	ustedes	ustedes
3. maripesa	mariposa	mariguana, marimacho, mariposa
4. otupado	ocupado	no
5. sirvilleta	servilleta	cerveza
6. veniendo	viniendo	venir
7. bicicleca	bicicleta	bicicleta
8. /abániko/	/abaniko/	—
9. biccionario	diccionario	diccionario (after 2 minutes)

CONDUCTION APHASIA

Green and Howes (1977), citing various recent summaries, describe the syndrome of conduction aphasia as a disorder of the ability to express oneself in well-formed utterances, but with RELATIVELY GOOD COMPREHENSION: "The spontaneous speech of a conductive aphasic is fluent, yet it is circumlocutory and inadequately structured. . . . Above all, the difficulty in repetition is remarkable. Despite self-criticism and repeated trials, patients characteristically fail to provide a suitable match for the examiner's model [p. 124]."

As noted earlier, each stratum in a stratificational grammar has a tactic pattern, which specifies well-formedness conditions within the stratum, and a realizational pattern, which specifies the connections to higher and lower strata. We can view conduction aphasia as a syndrome in which the semotactics (of Wernicke's area) and the morpholexotactics (of Broca's area) are both operating normally, but in which the realizational network connecting these two strata is disrupted. This is really the classical view of conduction aphasia (a dysconnection between Broca's and Wernicke's areas), but rather than being a box diagram approach it is based on a linguistic theory.

Thus the conduction aphasic has "relatively good" comprehension, as does the Broca's aphasic, since Wernicke's area (and the sememic stratum) is intact. This interpretation would predict that conduction aphasics would show the same kind of receptive deficits as Broca's aphasics show when submitted to those kinds of tasks which require use of morpholexotactics. Similarly, although for the conduction aphasic the sememic stratum is intact, nonetheless, because the realizational connections between the sememic and morpholexemic strata are disrupted, the morpholexemic stratum (of Broca's area) gets a distorted input (as in the case of the Wernicke's aphasic), and thus the speech output resembles that of a Wernicke's aphasic. The characteristically poor performance of conduction aphasics in repetition tasks lends further credence to the view that conduction aphasia represents a disturbance of the realizational pattern connecting sememics with morpholexemics.

NONLESION EVIDENCE

Wood (Chapter 23, this volume), on the basis of some simulated neuronal lesion experiments he conducted, argues cogently against identifying locus of damage with locus of function, in any meaningful sense of the word 'function.'[4]

----

[4]Thus, if complete bilateral excision of the optic nerves leads to blindness, one could conclude that the "function" of the optic nerve is to *inhibit blindness*. But as Wood correctly points out, to use the word 'function' in this way is counterproductive to our attempts to discover how a system operates.

Characteristic deficits of function following removal of a specific brain region cannot suffice to show that that region plays a specific role in the performance of that function in the normal organism, since, as Wood's experiments show, highly selective lesion effects can also be obtained in nervous systems in which each neuronal element participates in a wide range of "functions." (Wood 1980, 24). Thus, as Wood mentioned at the November meeting (following Gregory, 1961), "just because a radio howls when a resistor is removed does not mean the resistor is a howl inhibition center" (cf. Note 4). Thus the step from correlation of characteristically located lesion with loss of characteristic function, to the identification of the lesioned area with the normal performance of that function, is unwarranted: Although it is an interpretation which is consistent with the data, there are many other possible interpretations.

For this reason, I would like at this point to cite some nonlesion evidence which lends support to the position for which I have been arguing. Because these findings involve no lesion-to-function fallacy, their interpretation is not subject to Wood's criticism.

Lassen (1979), using radioisotope xenon-133 injected into the internal carotid artery, found a 30% local increase in blood flow in the following regions under the following conditions:

1. In listening to speech:
   (a) the superior-posterior temporal lobe, and
   (b) INTERMITTENTLY, the inferior frontal region.
2. In automatic speech (i.e., counting from 1 to 20 repeatedly):
   (a) the superior-posterior temporal lobe
   (b) the primary mouth area in the central region
   (c) supplementary motor area in the superior frontal lobe (Penfield's superior speech area)
3. In "fluent normal speech":
   all of the areas in which the increased blood flow was found in automatic speech, PLUS THE LOWER FRONTAL AREA

I have suggested that in decoding, Broca's area would not always be used, as generally the message is understood without recourse to precise morpholexotactic analysis, but that when necessary Broca's area IS used for such analysis. This is consistent with Lassen's observation that in listening, the inferior frontal region[5] shows only "inconstant" hyperactivity, whereas the superior-posterior temporal lobe shows consistent activity.

In speaking, if the contribution of Broca's area is morpholexemic, then it is no surprise that no hyperactivity is found in this region when counting to 20

---

[5]Lassen does point out, however, that since this region overlays the basal ganglia, one cannot decide if the area of increased blood flow is cortical or subcortical.

repeatedly: Morpholexemics would not be needed for such a task. On the other hand, this area was found to demonstrate hyperactivity during "fluent normal speech," as would be predicted by my model.

Also note that the posterior-superior temporal region is an area of hyperactivity in all of these linguistic tasks. This is also consistent with my approach.[6]

THE MIND-BODY PROBLEM

In addition to the nonlesion evidence just cited, there are theoretical as well as biological arguments that vitiate Wood's criticisms. How language is represented in the brain is not merely an engineering problem, and the simulation technique by its very nature ignores some very relevant phylogenetic and ontogenetic aspects of human communication.

1. First, if we could treat the human body as a machine and take it apart and test the various parts and subsystems in any way we wished, and then put them back together, repeatedly, without damaging the organism, this alone would not suffice to answer the question of how language is represented in the

---

[6]There is another interesting datum reported by Lassen, namely that all of these changes in regional blood flow are observed BILATERALLY. Recently Albert and Obler (1978) have claimed that there is a significant right hemisphere linguistic participation among bilinguals. They base their claim primarily on the abnormally high percentage of aphasia cases due to right hemisphere lesions in dextral bilinguals, and on the absence of the predicted right visual field effect in tachistoscopic tests of verbal material in several studies involving bilinguals.

They claim that the right hemisphere is always used in language acquisition at any age, and that as knowledge of a language is perfected, its representation becomes more and more left lateralized. This lateralization occurs with much greater facility prior to puberty. Hence, the only examples of complete left lateralization of more than one language may perhaps be in balanced bilinguals who acquired both languages in childhood.

In a personal communication, Lassen informed me that all of his subjects were Danes who knew another language besides Danish, except for one monolingual. Unfortunately, Lassen did not gather any right hemisphere data for that subject.

Nevertheless, I would like to cite two other studies in support of Albert and Obler's thesis. One is Curtiss's (1977) study of first language acquisition in a postpubescent individual, Genie, in which dichotic listening, tachistoscopic, and cortical evoked potential studies indicate the use of the right hemisphere for language. The question of course remains as to whether Genie's language dominance will ever begin to shift to the left. The other study, Pettit and Noll (1979), involves some dichotic tests that were given to some aphasics over a period of 2 months. The authors found that over this period, the aphasics' performance on general language tests improved, and that their performance on the dichotic tests showed a LEFT ear advantage that increased over the 2-month interval. Right ear scores (inferior to begin with) did not improve during the 2 months. The authors take these data as evidence for a dominance shift hypothesis: Dominance shifts to the right hemisphere in aphasia. But if Albert and Obler are correct, these data may indicate instead that the aphasic is reLEARNING a language, hence the right hemisphere participation. In view of the data from Curtiss and from Lassen, as well as the studies noted by Albert and Obler, this alternative certainly cannot be ruled out.

brain. If the system of human language were a physical system (only), then theoretically, a team of well-trained bioengineers, working under the ideal conditions stated, would eventually be able to solve the problem. But this is even theoretically impossible. Language is inherently a mental phenomenon. Phonemes, morphemes, noun phrases, clauses, linguistic meanings, etc. in themselves could not be found anywhere in the brain. So even if we solved the engineering problem, we would still not understand how LANGUAGE was represented in the brain.

To deal with this problem, we must deal with the mind–body problem in some way. In Schnitzer (1978), I propose the approach of structural realism, suggested implicitly by Hayek (1952), who claims that the gap between the mental and physical orders be bridged by assuming that they have the SAME STRUCTURE. A structure is an abstraction which can be instantiated in various media. The complex of lines, dots, and other markings written on pieces of paper when Beethoven composed the Eroica Symphony has the same structure as the piece when performed by the Cleveland Symphony. Similarly, human languages can be represented in speech, in writing, in manual signs, in Morse code, etc. Grammatical (including phonological and semantic) structure is involved in these representations of language. This structure can be represented in a written grammar of a linguist (perhaps someday). It is represented in the human mind: We KNOW the structure of our language, as is evidenced in the multitude of tasks in which we make use of it. It is also represented in the brain—to deny THIS would be to deny the possibility of doing neurolinguistics at all.[7]

What I have been claiming is that at the appropriate level of analysis, the structure of language as represented in the brain must be the same structure as our (mental) knowledge of the language. The problem remains as to what the appropriate level of analysis is. David Caplan (personal communication, November 1979) said that he thought it dangerous to assume that if the brain is a

[7]I should like to emphasize that the approach I have been advocating is not reductionist. I am not claiming that linguistic structures can be reduced to neurophysiological ones. What I am saying is that the neurophysiological system that represents what we mentalistically and phenomenally call knowledge and behavior, competence and performance, must in some sense have the same structure as the system of language which it represents. For reasons stated in what follows, it seems that this is the only sensible way of dealing with the mind–body problem insofar as language and the brain are concerned.

Nonetheless, the specific linguistic proposal I have made does not require the adoption of structural realism. It is undoubtedly compatible with a dualistic approach to the question of language and the brain, and in view of the growing amount of serious research in the field of parapsychology yielding positive results it no longer seems possible to rule out automatically a two-substance theory (See Randall, 1977, for a cogent review of the literature).

But there is one major problem for dualism: If the mind and the body are of two distinct substances which interact in some way as yet unknown, then why is it that characteristic brain lesions produce characteristic cognitive deficits?

certain way, then language must also be that way (or vice versa). David Levine (personal communication, November 1979) expressed similar reservations, also noting that, at the cortical level, there is no reason to believe the brain to be hierarchical; hence neuroanatomical hierarchy could not be used as evidence for stratificational hierarchy.

These comments miss the point, I think, that the level of analysis at which the mental grammar and the grammar in the brain must have the same structure is certainly not the level of neuroanatomy, nor of box diagram neurophysiology. The hierarchical structure of language may not reflect the evolutionary hierarchy of the development of the brain (although evidence cited in what follows suggests that indeed it may). But at the appropriate level of analysis of brain function, I claim that the two hierarchies are the same.

In a discussion with David Caplan, I mentioned that I could not conceive of a reasonable alternative to my approach. He mentioned that at one time it was believed that pain came about via mediation of special "pain cells." I asked him what supposedly made the cells cause pain. He replied, "Their very nature." But this response does not deal with the problem. To say that we feel pain because of special pain cells ignores the issue of what makes the physical (physiological) happenings represent what we mean when we say we FEEL pain. That is, what about what is going on makes it be the PAINful SENSATION?

Dennett (1978) deals quite elegantly with this problem in a paper entitled "Why You Can't Make a Computer That Feels Pain." The issues are extremely complex, and I refer the reader to that paper. Suffice it to say that the mind–body problem is involved here, and ignoring it will not get us any closer to understanding pain.

Hayek (1952) discusses color perception. He claims that our phenomenal perception of color exactly parallels the physical mechanism of selective sensitivity to different wavelengths of light. His structural-realist solution is to say that the distinctions we make among different hues ('hue' being a phenomenal term) are just those distinctions made among wave lengths by the physical sensory and interpretive apparatus. The difference between the two orders (phenomenal and physical, i.e., neurological) is essentially between two vocabularies. I wish to argue the same point for language: The difference between the linguistic description of language and the neurophysiological one will turn out to be a difference in vocabularly used to describe two orders that have the same structure. This is not a logical point: The relation between the two orders might be otherwise. I cannot think of another plausible solution (but see Note 7). But, to paraphrase George Lakoff, lack of imagination does not constitute evidence.

I do, nonetheless, think that there is evidence for the position I hold. My position depends on there being such a thing as (linguistic) KNOWLEDGE. If what we think of as knowledge is a mere artifact of various tasks that we perform, then there is no reason to assume that the linguistic grammar per se is encoded neurologically. But there is evidence that we do have linguistic knowledge. Those studies which have found error type constancy across widely diverse types of linguistic performance tasks argue for an underlying linguistic competence or knowledge which is brought to bear in performing the various tasks. Several of these studies have been cited here and in Schnitzer 1978. The relational network approach that I have been advocating can be viewed statically as representing the inherent knowledge or dynamically as operating in performing linguistic tasks of various kinds.

Michael Arbib (1979), in reply to my commentary on "Neurolinguistics Must Be Computational" (Schnitzer, 1979) said that he thought I was wrong in viewing knowledge as necessarily task independent. He says "to say that some KSs [knowledge structures] may be involved in a variety of tasks is not to deny that each task may involve a specific set of KSs [p. 478]." Aside from the philosophical point that, as I understand it, what we mean by 'knowledge' (in the sense of knowing THAT, as opposed to knowing HOW) DOES entail task independency, given that Arbib's KSs are computational modules his approach would entail that we have knowledge only when we are computing something, that knowledge exists only when put to use. One of the advantages of relational network representations (as found in stratificational grammar) is that they can be viewed statically as knowledge structures or dynamically as computational mechanisms.

It is possible that knowledge in the sense I am discussing does not exist. But the preliminary evidence from pathology supports my position. Much more evidence is needed since, if my view of knowledge is correct, characteristic errors should appear in patients with linguistic pathology, which affects the knowledge system(s) under ANY linguistic task, not just under certain varieties of tasks.

Before I leave this point, I wish to stress that stratificational relational networks are not intended to represent neuronal relationships directly. The logical relations represented in a network diagram could be realized by any number of possible neuronal level models, including one such as presented by Wood. Stratificational grammar uses as primes only the notions of conjunction, disjunction, precedence, and "upward and downwardness." Certainly these notions are ones used outside of language, and any microlevel neuropsychological theory would have to provide a way of dealing with these notions.

2. Second, there are biological reasons for questioning a line of argumentation that stems from simulation experiments involving isolated neuronal vectors outside of a natural evolutionary context, and from analogies to man-made devices.

Brown (1977), Lamendella (1977), and Givón (1979) have proposed approaches to understanding human (cognition and) communication. These approaches, although differing substantially in focus, emphasis, and detail, are alike in spirit.

In discussing the building up of evolutionary structure in the brain, encephelization, Brown (1977) distinguishes four levels of cognition, of which the first three are phylogenetic and the fourth is ontogenetic: the sensorimotor (subcortical) level, the presentational (limbic) level, the representational (neocortical) level, and the symbolic (assymetric, neocortical) level. He concedes that these may well not be discrete states, but merely landmarks in a continuum. For him, lesions reveal lower levels of function which are normally concealed by the operations of the higher levels. Regarding language, he says:

> Language develops through a formative or microgenetic process as one of several components of cognition. In this development, the content passes from one stage to another, though generally we apprehend only the final products and are not aware of the developmental process itself. These earlier, otherwise concealed (i.e., traversed) levels, however, reveal themselves when they appear as pathological speech forms. . . . With structural brain lesion, however, the earlier stage, the aphasic syndrome, can become a final speech product and may persist indefinitely as a relatively stable form. Pathological language of this type affords an opportunity to study, at a leisurely pace, the psychological determinants of normal utterances [p. 26].

In a similar vein, discussing the role of the limbic system in communication, Lamendella (1977) distinguishes three progressively higher limbic levels: appetitive, affective, and volitional, in which the last (highest) level contains the rudiments of signal communication. Regarding (higher) neopallial systems (which are capable of propositional communication) he says:

> As neopallial systems arose phylogenetically, and as they develop in the human individual, they inhibit certain limbic functions and carry these functions out at a higher level in a novel fashion. Nevertheless, each limbic subsystem continues to exercise control over its sphere of human activity as a subordinate component of the higher neopallial metasystem [p. 196].

Givón's (1979) work is primarily concerned with understanding language and only derivatively concerned with phylogeny and ontogeny. In fact, he scarcely mentions the brain. Nonetheless, in his discussion of communication from the level of one-celled organisms on up, he arrives at a distinction among the **monopropositional** (found in canines, pongids, human babies, and sometimes in adult humans), the **pragmatic** (phylogenetically and ontogenetically—and perhaps diachronically—the earliest stage of language), and the **syntactic** (the highest, most fully developed) modes, as progressively higher stages in language phylogeny and ontogeny.

The monopropositional mode is strictly speaking prelinguistic. Since among animals and babies, distinctions such as topic–comment, past–future, agent–patient, etc. all tend to be contextually determined, communicative acts in this mode are taken to be monoclausal—representing imperatives from the perspective of adult human language. This mode would be limbically mediated for Lamendella and neocortically mediated for Brown.

The pragmatic mode represents the first LINGUISTIC stage in human language development, both phylogenetically and ontogenetically. It is characterized by loose discourse structure rather than tight sentence structure, with minimal presuppositionality in its constructions. Among its transparent properties are the tendencies toward topic–comment word order, concatenation rather than subordination, a low noun-to-verb ratio (roughly one argument per verb), a lack of grammatical morphology, a use of higher intonation contours for new information with the use of low intonation contours for old information, and a lack of anaphora (instead of which we find either repetition or omission of the name of the entity referred to). For Brown, this mode would be symbolically mediated, and Lamendella would agree that this mode is represented at the neopallial level.

Increasing "syntactization" brings about the phylogenetic and ontogenetic shift to the syntactic mode. In this level, we find the syntactization of the pragmatic order of topic–comment into the semantic order of subject–predicate, the introduction of subordination, an increase in noun–verb ratio, and the introduction of grammatical morphology and anaphoric pronouns. We find also the possibility of communication with strangers who do not share much of the background knowledge of the speaker about topics outside the immediate environment. There is an increase in the speed of delivery. This final mode is probably only an ontogenetic (rather than a phylogenetic) development.

Looking at linguistic pathology in these terms, it seems to be relatively clear that Broca's aphasics tend to operate in the pragmatic mode: Their speech tends to lack subordination, anaphoric pronouns, and grammatical morphology. A topic–comment word order predominates, and there is typically a low noun-to-verb ratio. Rate of delivery is slow. In Broca's aphasis, we can see a clear case of what Brown means when he says that pathology reveals function. It seems reasonable to identify, therefore, the syntactic mode with the morpholexemic stratum and with Broca's area.

Wernicke's aphasics are adults who once had a fully developed communicative function hierarchy. If we identify the pragmatic mode with the sememic stratum and Wernicke's area, we can view Wernicke's aphasics as victims of a syntactic mode cut off from the normally subservient pragmatic mode, as their sememic stratum, which can be thought of as working in the pragmatic mode, is disrupted. This same line of reasoning can be applied, mutatis mutandis, to conduction aphasics, people with dissociated pragmatic and syntactic modes.

Implications from the discussion earlier in this chapter of differences between the agrammatism of Spanish and English speakers follow from what Givón calls "morphologicization"—a late stage of syntactization, in which syntactic elements cliticize into prefixes and suffixes, etc. and eventually become fully incorporated morphophonemically in inflectional (and derivational) paradigms. The diachronic tendency is for syntactic elements to evolve into morphological elements, which in turn evolve into morphophonemic elements, which in turn tend to be eliminated. Communicative pressures then require the addition of new syntactic elements. This process can be seen from a comparison of modern French and Spanish. Oral French, which has lost most of its person marking on verbs (still present in Spanish) now requires overt mention of subject pronouns, whereas Spanish does not.

Thus, what is traditionally called (surface) syntax and what is traditionally called morphology are two manifestations of the syntactic mode. Both should be handled by a single stratum, and it seems clear that both are affected in Broca's aphasia.

In view of the foregoing, it is difficult to interpret the place of the cognitive (or hypersememic) stratum. Whence develops this higher nonlinguistic structure? Perhaps this stratum is merely an artifact of a conception of language as an entity that interprets or translates our cognitions but is separate from them. In view of the phylogenetic evidence adduced in the works cited, it is difficult to imagine a place for this stratum.

THE PROBLEM OF CONTROL

Michael Arbib stated (personal communication, November 1979) that he thought that the stratificational network diagram presented here as Figure 12.2 was similar to the system presented by William Woods (Woods, 1980 and this volume) but without CONTROL. I would now like to argue that control is built into the stratificational network.

Woods's system contains independent components of feature extraction, lexical retrieval, matching, bookkeeping, syntax, and semantics, all interrelated only by another independent component called "control." One of the goals of this system is to deal with the indeterminacy of the signal in speech perception. I believe, however, that the relational network approach (stratificational grammar) handles this problem by virtue of the inherent INTERRELATEDNESS (i.e., nonindependence) of the components. In other words, it handles the problem of control in a perfectly natural way. Let us consider some examples from English:

1. If a particular segment of running speech were indeterminate as to voicing, as for example /s/ versus /z/ in the nonsense sequence [ˢ̣zpow], the phonotactics would immediately assign the sequence to /spow/ rather than to /zpow/, since /#zp/ violates English phonotactics.
2. If a similar situation occurred with respect to /k/ and /g/ in the sequence [hiywəzlʊkɪŋæt⁻ðə{ᵏg}ayt⁻], the relational network would assign the

sequence to /kayt/ as no lexeme would be found with a phonological realization /gayt/.

3. If in the course of a conversation, the following sequence occurred (in which the question mark indicates an indeterminate segment):

[ðəsæːndwɪčəzɔnðəbiyčə ? draːy],

the morpholexemic stratum would determine that the segment in question must be either /r/ or /z/, depending on whether the intended message had been "The sandwiches on the beach are dry" or "The sand which is on the beach is dry."

It would be the sememic level, which deals with topics, which would determine whether the segment in question was /r/ or /z/, depending on whether the topic of conversation had been sand or sandwiches.

4. The cognitive stratum (if it exists) would determine between /r/ and /z/, if there indeed existed phonetic indeterminacy between these two, in the sequence

[flaːyɪŋpʰleːynzə ? deːynǰərəs],

since, from a sememic standpoint, presumably in a given conversation either *flying* or *planes* would be a suitable topic. Discourse block considerations would be needed to determine whether the intended sentence was "Flying planes are dangerous" or "Flying planes is dangerous."

Granted these examples are not the most plausible; but I think that they serve to illustrate the way in which the interrelatedness of strata in relational networks can obviate the need for a special "control" component.

RELATIONAL NETWORKS AND APHASIA

In commenting on my paper at the November meeting, Alfonso Caramazza took me to task, correctly, for not dealing explicitly with the details of Broca's aphasia, and accused me, I think unjustly, of providing no more than another "competence" grammar. He suggested that I provide more examples of how specific cases of aphasia would be analyzed in terms of stratificational networks.

Zurif and Caramazza (1976) review some research they did involving relatedness judgments analyzed by hierarchical clustering, among (inter alii) Broca's aphasics and "mixed anterior aphasics." Among their findings are that aphasic patients' control of "functors" shows parallels in their speech and in metalinguistic judgments. This is the kind of result that I take to provide evidence for the existence of a task-independent linguistic "competence," such as discussed here and in Schnitzer (1978).

More importantly, they find that for Broca's aphasics, "such control as is shown, seems determined more by the semantic force of a functor (if it has such force) than by a fully computed syntactic representation [Zurif and Caramazza 1976, p. 272]." This result is in accord with my claim that Broca's area is in charge of "housekeeping," or morpholexotactics. Those functors which are not truly FUNCTIONAL, that is, which are merely required by the morpholexotactics of the language, would be predicted to be more adversely affected than those that have realizational connections to the sememic stratum. Consider the following Spanish sentences:

1. *Aquí tenemos a la señora Sánchez.* ('Here we have Mrs. Sanchez.')
2. *Le dijo Pedro que Juan no iría.* ('Pedro said [to someone] that Juan would not go.')
3. *Le dijo a Pedro que Juan no iría.* ('[Someone] said to Pedro that Juan would not go.')

In the first sentence, the word *a* is required by Spanish morpholexemics because the direct object (*la señora Sánchez*) is human. It has no semantic function and would have no representation in the sememic stratum. On the other hand, the *a* in Sentence 3 serves to mark *Pedro* as the indirect object and to distinguish Sentence 3 from Sentence 2, in which *Pedro* is the subject. My stratificational approach (and the results of Zurif and Caramazza's research) would thus predict that Broca's aphasics would have better control (both in speaking and in metalinguistic tasks) over the *a* in Sentence 3 than over the *a* in sentence 1. The *a* of Sentence 3 would have realizational connections to the sememic stratum (which handles deep cases) and would hence be a FUNCTIONAL functor (from a communicative standpoint—it functions to identify deep cases), whereas the *a* of Sentence 1 would not.

Zurif and Caramazza find that Broca's aphasics have less difficulty with prepositions than with articles. This stands to reason, as in English prepositions frequently mark deep cases but articles have relatively little (and sometimes no) sememic value.[8] The word *to* was found to be under better control when used in

---

[8]Edgar Zurif (personal communication, May 1988; see Chapter 9, this volume) has adduced evidence that Broca's aphasics can in fact deal successfully with articles. In a task in which they were asked, from a display of a black square, a white square, and a black circle, to pick *the* black one, they tended to fail. Nonetheless, if given sufficient time to think about the task, they tended to succeed, that is, they realized that compliance with the instructions was impossible. This experiment is an example of one of the cases in which articles DO have sememic value, as the definite–indefinite distinction is crucial for successful performance of the task. This suggests that articles in English may have two origins—one in the morpholexemic stratum (like the conjugation classes in Figure 12.4, given in what follows) and one in the sememic stratum. Broca's aphasics are evidently able to deal with sememically based articles, but because in English most instances of articles do not have sememic relevance, Broca's aphasics tend to mishandle articles. It is interesting that extra time was a key factor in their success on this task, as this would suggest operation of the pragmatic (slow) mode rather than the syntactic (fast) mode. When one's automatic housekeeping habits are disrupted, successful operation of a vacuum cleaner takes more time.

a prepositional phrase than when used to introduce a complement clause. In the latter case, the *to* is required by English morpholexotactics, but has no sememic representation.

Goodglass (1968) found similar results with Broca's aphasics, noting their tendency to omit "the small words of grammar" and inflectional endings. To deal with these forms he creates the notion of "saliency," about which he says, "The intuitive definition that was suggested is that saliency be considered the psychological resultant of the stress, of the informational significance, of the phonological prominence, and of the affective value of a word [p. 264]." Thus Broca's aphasics perform better (i.e., less agrammatically) when the functors have "salience." As far as informational significance and affective value are concerned, the relational network approach would predict better performance (in all sorts of tasks) with informationally significant functors (since these have sememic realizations) as well as those with affective value (since these would presumably have cognitive realizations, assuming that the cognitive stratum exists).

With respect to Goodglass's other criteria for salience, "stress" and "phonological prominence," it is important to note that when these were the only criteria for salience involved, performance was found to be enhanced on a REPETITION task. It is quite conceivable that the phonological salience allowed the aphasic(s) to repeat correctly by using a strategy for repetition involving processing no higher than the phonemic stratum, bypassing morpholexemic and sememic processing. More research needs to be done to find out whether phonological salience alone is sufficient to improve the performance of Broca's aphasics with respect to nonsememically realized "functors" in tasks other than repetition.

SOME ILLUSTRATIONS

I would now like to illustrate how the stratificational network can be used in the analysis of aphasic errors. First I will briefly review an analysis of some dyslexia data of Whitaker and Keith cited in Schnitzer (1978). Essentially, what was found was that when patients were asked to read aloud sentences of the form $\{^{That}_{This}\}$ is a ADJ N' (e.g., 'This is a general solution'), there was greater average latency between the article and noun-derived or verb-derived adjectives—such as *accidental* (noun-derived) or *reliable* (verb-derived)—than there was between the article and pure adjectives (such as *possible*). Figure 12.3 is a stratificational schematic of this relationship. It illustrates in a highly abbreviated form the relatively greater amount of structure involved in the derived adjectives than in the pure ones. Looking at this structure dynamically (with impulses traveling

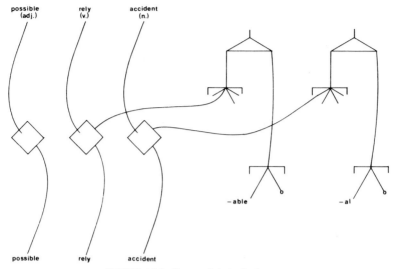

FIGURE 12.3. *Pure and derived adjectives.*

through it in real time by means of whatever neural mechanism turns out to be correct), we would expect a greater latency in processing derived adjectives. This illustrates how a relational network approach can deal with the competence–performance distinction: The relational network represents the always present linguistic knowledge (competence); the ACTIVIATED network represents processing (performance) and allows for relative latency predictions.

I wish to turn now to some data from a moderately agrammatic Spanish-speaking aphasic. Spanish has a highly inflected verb system involving three stem classes and inflecting for person, number, tense, aspect, and mode. It is schematically represented in Figure 12.4. In order to insure legibility, I have included only one complete example, namely, the morpholexemic representation of the sentence 'Ellas hablaron' [They (feminine) spoke (preterite)]. The diagram ignores compound tenses completely. The aphasic had a marked tendency not to inflect verbs, and to substitute gerunds and infinitive forms for inflected verb forms. Table 12.2 is a list of verbal forms which he used in a 5-minute discussion of some photographs. I have been arguing that Broca's aphasia is a disruption of the morpholexemic stratum. Let us now look at the errors to see whether they support this position.

Of the seven incorrect verbal forms in Table 12.2, three are instances of gerunds, and one of an infinitive which replaced an expected inflected form of the verb. In Spanish, gerunds are generally used adjectivally or adverbially and infinitives nominally (as in complement clauses). The gerund and infinitive

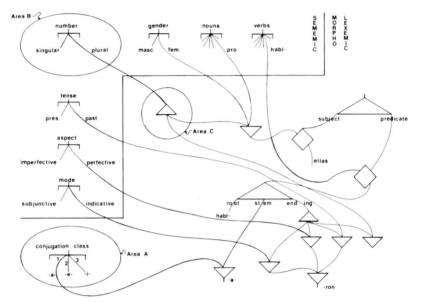

FIGURE 12.4. *Part of the Spanish verbal network.*

TABLE 12.2
Verb Forms Used in an Agrammatic Discourse

Correct forms used	Incorrect forms used	
	Form used	Correct form
está		
empieza	preguntando	pregunta
hablar	/empyese/	empieza
escribir	encontrando	encuentra
está	escribiendo	escribe
será	/komprer/	comprar
fue	encontrar	encuentra
pagar	dice	dicen
es	—	—
parece	—	—
pagarle	—	—
—	—	—

forms do not participate fully in the verbal morpholexotactics, yet they carry the sememic value of the related verbs.

The other three errors can be viewed as errors at the level of morpholexotactics. The form /empyese/ could be looked at either as an error in mode (subjunctive where indicative is expected) or as an error with respect to conjugation class—second (e-stem) where first (a-stem) is expected. If it were an error in mode, it would have ramifications at the sememic level. But conjugation class (Area A of Figure 12.4) has no sememic realizations. This type of error would be purely morpholexotactic. The fact that one of the other remaining errors, *comprer for comprar, can be explained in these same terms, but not in terms of an error in mode, makes the conjugation class analysis more plausible.

This latter example is of a correctly used (but incorrectly formed) infinitive. Infinitives do not inflect for person, number, tense, mode, or aspect. They do each have a characteristic conjugation class, and this example shows this class incorrectly represented. On other occasions, this patient made other errors of this type.

The last error, "dice" for 'dicen,' is an error in number. Number obviously has sememic realizations. But the word was uttered in the context "Dos otros dice" (Two others says). Clearly, the patient had the number of the subject correct and was making an agreement mistake. In a stratificational network, the sememic concept of number would apply to the subject. The number agreement for the verb would be a purely morpholexotactic phenomenon. This distinction can be found represented in Figure 12.4 with Area B representing the sememic singular–plural distinction and Area C representing the morpholexemic agreement phenomenon.

It is important that all of the verbal errors can be accounted for at the morpholexemic level alone. Sememic patterns seem to be preserved. It is also important to note that the four errors that resulted in gerunds are counterevidence to Kean's (1978) theory of Broca's aphasia, since she says that "a Broca's aphasic tends to reduce the structure of a sentence to the minimal string of elements which can be lexically construed as phonological words in his language [p. 88]." These gerund forms certainly do not qualify as minimal strings of elements which can be lexically construed as phonological words in Spanish.

SUMMARY

Language is inherently a mental phenomenon. Thus the representation of language in the brain is not merely an engineering problem. I have proposed a structural-realist approach to the mind–body problem, as exemplified by a relational network approach to linguistic structure.

Language develops in characteristic ways phylogenetically and ontogenetically. Givón's pragmatic and syntactic modes represent the highest level of Brown's and Lamendella's hierarchies. Stratificational networks seem to adequately represent these two human communicative modes in the sememic and morpholexemic strata, respectively. Regional blood flow and lesion evidence support the identification of these modes and these strata with Wernicke's and Broca's areas, respectively.

ACKNOWLEDGMENT

I am grateful to David Caplan, John Marshall, and especially Michael Arbib for their skillful and carefully planned organization of the Conference on Neural Models of Language Processes, as well as to all participants for the expression of their stimulating and provocative ideas and data.

REFERENCES

Albert M. L., and Obler, L. K. (1978). *The bilingual brain*. New York: Academic Press.
Anderson, S., and Kiparsky, P. (Eds.). (1973). *A festschrift for Morris Halle*. New York: Holt Rinehart Winston.
Arbib, M. A. (1979). Cooperative computation as a concept for brain theory. *The Behavioral and Brain Sciences*, 2, 475–480.
Arbib, M. A., and Caplan, D. (1979). Neurolinguistics must be computational. *The Behavioral and Brain Sciences*, 2, 449–460.
Benson, D. F. (1979). Neurologic correlates of anomia. In H. Whitaker and H. A. Whitaker (Eds.), *Studies in neurolinguistics*, Vol. 4. New York: Academic Press.
Bever, T. G. (1970). The cognitive basis for linguistic structures. In J. R. Hayes (Ed.), *Cognition and the development of language*. New York: Wiley.
Brame, M. K. (1979). *Realistic grammar*. Paper presented at the Milwaukee Conference on Current Approaches to Syntax, March 15–17, 1979.
Bresnan, J. (1978). A realistic transformational grammar. In M. Halle, J. Bresnan, and G. A. Miller (Eds.), *Linguistic theory and psychological reality*. Cambridge, Mass.: MIT Press.
Brown, J. (1977). *Mind, brain, and consciousness*. New York: Academic Press.
Chomsky, N. (1965). *Aspects of the theory of syntax*. Cambridge, Mass.: MIT Press.
Chomsky, N. (1973). Conditions on transformations. In S. Anderson and P. Kiparsky (Eds.), *A festschrift for Morris Halle*. New York: Holt Rinehart Winston.
Chomsky, N. (1977). On wh-movement. In P. Culicover, T. Wasow, and A. Akmajian (Eds.), *Formal Syntax*. New York: Academic Press.
Cogen, C., Thompson, H., Thurgood, G., Whistler, K., and Wright, J. (Eds.). *Proceedings of the first annual meeting of the Berkeley Linguistics Society*. Berkeley Linguistics Society. University of California, Berkeley, 1975.
Culicover, P. W., Wasow, T., and Akmajian A. (Eds.). (1977). *Formal syntax*. New York: Academic Press.
Curtiss, S. (1977). *Genie: A psycholinguistic study of a modern day "Wild Child"*. New York: Academic Press.
Dennett, D. C. 1978. Why you can't make a computer that feels pain. In D.C. Dennett (Ed.), *Brainstorms*. Montgomery, Vt.: Bradford Books.

Dik, S. (1978). *Functional grammar*. Amsterdam: North-Holland.

Fodor, J. A. (1975). *The language of thought*. New York: Crowell.

Foley, W. A., and Van Valin, R. D., Jr. (In preparation). *Role and reference grammar: A functional approach to grammar*.

Geschwind, N. (1974). *Selected papers on language and the brain*. Boston Studies in the Philosophy of Science, Vol. 16 (R. S. Cohen and M. W. Wartofsky, Eds.). Dordrecht: D. Reidel.

Givón, T. (1979). *On understanding grammar*. New York: Academic Press.

Goodglass, H. (1968). Studies on the grammar of aphasics. In J. H. Koplin (Ed.), *Developments in applied psycholinguistic research*. New York: Macmillan. (Page references to Goodglass and Blumstein [1973].)

Goodglass, H., and Blumstein S. (Eds.). (1973). *Psycholinguistics and aphasia*. Baltimore: Johns Hopkins.

Green, E., and Howes, D. H. (1977). The nature of conduction aphasia. In H. Whitaker and H. A. Whitaker (Eds.), *Studies in neurolinguistics*, Vol. 3. New York: Academic Press.

Gregory, R. L. (1961). The brain as an engineering problem. In W. H. Thorpe and O. L. Zangwill (Eds.), *Current problems in animal behaviour*. Cambridge: Cambridge University Press.

Grossman, R. E., San, L. J., and Vance, T. J. (Eds.). (1975). *Papers from the parasession on functionalism*. Chicago: Chicago Linguistic Society, Department of Linguistics, University of Chicago.

Halle, M., Bresnan, J., and Miller, G. A. (Eds.). (1978). *Linguistic theory and psychological reality*. Cambridge, Mass.: MIT Press.

Hayek, F. A. (1952). *The sensory order*. Chicago: University of Chicago Press.

Hayes, J. R. (Ed.). (1970). *Cognition and the development of language*. New York: Wiley.

Hudson, R. (1976). *Arguments for a non-transformational grammar*. Chicago: University of Chicago Press.

Kac, M. B. (1978). *Corepresentation of grammatical structure*. Minneapolis: University of Minnesota Press.

Kaplan, R. (1972). Augmented transition networks as psychological models of sentence comprehension. *Artificial Intelligence*, 3, 77–100.

Kean, M.-L. (1978). The linguistic interpretation of aphasic syndromes. In E. Walker (Ed.), *Explorations in the biology of language*. Montgomery, Vt.: Bradford Books.

Keller, E. (1979). Planning and execution in speech production. Paper presented at the Ninth International Congress of Phonetic Sciences, Copenhagen, August 6–11, 1979.

Klein, B. Von Eckardt. (1978). What is the Biology of Language? In E. Walker (Ed.), *Explorations in the biology of language*. Montgomery, Vt.: Bradford Books.

Koplin, J. H. (Ed.) (1968). *Developments in applied psycholinguistic research*. New York: Macmillan.

Lakoff, G., and Thompson, H. (1975a). Dative questions in cognitive grammar. In R. Grossman, L. J. San, and T. J. Vance (Eds.), *Papers from the parasession on functionalism*. Chicago Linguistics Society, Department of Linguistics, University of Chicago.

Lakoff, G. and Thompson, H. (1975b). Introducing cognitive grammar. *Berkeley Linguistic Society*, 1, 295–313.

Lamendella, J. T. (1977). The limbic system in human communication. In H. Whitaker and H. A. Whitaker (Eds.), *Studies in neurolinguistics*, Vol. 3. New York: Academic Press.

Lamendella, J. T. (1979). Neurolinguistics. In B. Siegel (Ed.), *Annual Reviews of Anthropology*. Palo Alto: Annual Reviews, Inc.

Lassen, N. A. (1979). *The physiology and pathophysiology of language function as illustrated by measurements of the regional blood flow in the cortex of the brain*. Paper presented at the Ninth International Congress of Phonetic Sciences, Copenhagen, August 6–11, 1979.

Lockwood, D. G. (1972). *Outline of stratificational grammar*. Washington, D.C.: Georgetown University Press.

Luria, A. R. (1975). Two kinds of disorders in the comprehension of grammatical function. *Linguistics*, 154/155, 47–56.

Makkai, A., and Lockwood, D. G. (Eds.). (1973). *Readings in stratificational linguistics*. University, Al.: University of Alabama Press.

Partee, B. (1975). Montague grammar and transformational grammar. *Linguistic Inquiry*, 6, 203–300.

Pettit, J. M., and Noll, J. D. (1979). Cerebral dominance in aphasia recovery. *Brain and Language*, 7, 191–200.

Randall, J. L. (1977). *Parapsychology and the nature of life*. London: Sphere Books, Ltd.

Sanders, G. A. (1972). *Equational grammar*. The Hague: Mouton.

Schnitzer, M. L. (1976). The role of phonology in linguistic communication: Some neurolinguistic considerations. In H. Whitaker and H. A. Whitaker (Eds.), *Studies in neurolinguistics*, Vol. 1. New York: Academic Press.

Schnitzer, M. L. (1978). Toward a neurolinguistic theory of language. *Brain and Language*, 6, 342–361.

Schnitzer, M. L. (1979). Computational neurolinguistics and the competence–performance distinction. *The Behavioral and Brain Sciences*, 3, 163.

Sullivan, W. J. (1979). Syntax and "Semantics" in Stratificational Theory. Paper presented at the Milwaukee Conference on Current Approaches to Syntax, March 15–17, 1979.

Thorpe, W. H., and Zangwill, O. L. (1961). (Eds.). *Current problems in animal behaviour*. Cambridge: Cambridge University Press.

Vildomec, V. (1963). *Multilingualism*. Leyden: A. W. Sythoff.

Walker, E. (Ed.). (1978). *Explorations in the biology of language*. Montgomery, Vt.: Bradford Books.

Wanner, E., and Maratsos, M. (1979). An ATN approach to comprehension. In M. Halle, J. Bresnan, and G. A. Miller (Eds.), *Linguistic theory and psychological reality*. Cambridge, Mass.: MIT Press.

Whitaker, H., and Whitaker, H. A. (Eds.). (1976). *Studies in neurolinguistics*, Vol. 1. New York: Academic Press.

Whitaker, H., and Whitaker, H. A. (1977). *Studies in neurolinguistics*, Vol. 3. New York: Academic Press.

Whitaker, H., and Whitaker, H. A. (1979). *Studies in neurolinguistics*, Vol. 4. New York: Academic Press.

Wood, C. C. (1980). *Implications of simulated lesion experiments for the interpretation of lesions in real nervous systems*. COINS Technical Report 80–09 (M. Arbib, Ed.).

Woods, W. (1970). Transition network grammars for natural language analysis. *Communications of the ACM*, 13, 591–606.

Woods, W. (1980). HWIM: A speech understanding system on a computer. COINS Technical Report 80–09 (M. Arbib, Ed.).

Zurif, E., and Caramazza, A. (1976). Psycholinguistic structures in aphasia: Studies in syntax and semantics. In H. Whitaker and H. A. Whitaker (Eds.), *Studies in neurolinguistics*, Vol. 1. New York: Academic Press.

13

Prospects for the Study of Aphasia in a Visual–Gestural Language[1]

Ursula Bellugi
Howard Poizner
Edgar B. Zurif

INTRODUCTION

The two cerebral hemispheres function differently in people with normal hearing. In general, the left cerebral hemisphere has been considered dominant for language functions, and the right cerebral hemisphere dominant for processing visual-spatial relations. Patterns of language and nonlanguage disorders following localized brain damage in people deaf from birth who communicate with a visual–gestural language can potentially provide important new input into models of brain–language relationships.

Human languages have been forged in auditory–vocal channels throughout evolution, and, indeed, until recently all that we have learned about human language has come from the study of spoken languages. The very concept of language entails complex organizational principles that have often been thought to be intimately connected with vocally articulated sounds. History records not a single instance of a community of hearing people who have a sign language rather than a spoken language as their primary, native language: Human language in hearing populations has clearly evolved in conjunction with speech and the vocal-auditory modality (Lenneberg, 1967; Lieberman, 1975).

Our research has taken an unusual point of departure for the investigation of language and its formal properties. We study a language that has developed in modalities other than auditory-vocal: American Sign Language (ASL), the system of hand signs developed by deaf people and passed down from one

[1]This work was supported in part by National Science Foundation Grant #BNS79–16423 and National Institutes of Health Grant #NS15175 and HD13249 to The Salk Institute for Biological Studies, and by National Institutes of Health Grants #NS11408 and #NS06209 to Boston University School of Medicine. Illustrations were made by Frank A. Paul; copyright, Ursula Bellugi.

NEURAL MODELS OF
LANGUAGE PROCESSES

generation to the next, has been forged into an autonomous language with its own grammatical mechanisms (Bellugi and Studdert-Kennedy, 1980; Klima and Bellugi, 1979; Lane and Grosjean, 1980; Siple, 1978; Wilbur, 1979). We note that there are different sign languages among deaf communities of the world, not dependent upon the spoken/written languages of the surrounding hearing community. American and British sign languages are mutually unintelligible, for example. If sign languages are independent languages (as the mounting evidence from current research clearly demonstrates), then they constitute an experiment of nature that allows us to address fundamental issues about the human capacity for language, the neural mechanisms for language, the necessary conditions for language, and the forces determining its structural properties—for the first time, quite apart from the speech modality. In order to bring out how the study of brain organization for American Sign Language can help broaden our knowledge of neural mechanisms underlying language in general, we will first describe its linguistic structure.

THE STRUCTURE OF A VISUAL-GESTURAL LANGUAGE

Until recently, the individual signs of sign language were regarded as global wholes without any formal internal structure. Early writers focused on the physical form of the signal only to discuss the images that are generated by that form, and this apparently prevailed over any consideration of the internal structure of the sign. Certainly mimetic representation is the SOURCE of many symbols used in signing (TIME,[2] 'pointing to a wrist watch'; BIRD, 'the opening and closing of the beak of a bird'; VOTE, 'putting a vote in a ballot box'); however, there is another aspect to the form of signs.

The Internal Structure of Lexical Signs

Recent research on the structure of lexical signs has shown that, like the words of spoken languages, signs are fractionated into sublexical elements. The component parameters of signs are different from those of words: signs are constituted by configurations of the hand or hands, places of articulation, and movements (Klima and Bellugi, 1979; Stokoe, Casterline, and Croneberg, 1965). The number of possible configurations the hand can physically assume,

[2]Words in capital letters represent English glosses for ASL signs. The gloss represents the meaning of the unmarked, unmodulated, basic form of a sign. A bracketed superscript following a sign gloss indicates that the sign is made with some regular change in form associated with a systematic change in meaning, and thus indicates grammatical changes on signs. Inflectional forms embedded within other inflections are indicated by nested brackets.

the number of possible places of articulation, the number of possible different kinds of movement is very large indeed. Yet ASL uses only a very limited set of formational components—a set analogous in size to the limited set of phonemes posited for spoken languages. Further, as with spoken languages, there are systematic restrictions on the ways these components can combine.

Structural, historical, observational, and experimental evidence supports this view of signs. Each of the major formational parameters of signs has a limited number of values, which serve to minimally contrast pairs of lexical signs. The signs CANDY, APPLE, and JEALOUS, for example, differ minimally in hand configuration (see Figure 13.1a); the signs SUMMER, UGLY, and DRY differ only in place of articulation (the forehead, nose, and chin, see Figure 13.1b); the signs TAPE, CHAIR, and TRAIN differ only in movement

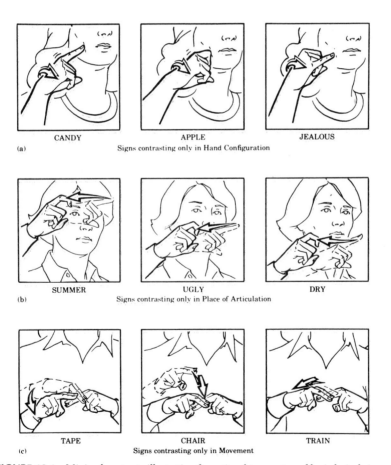

CANDY	APPLE	JEALOUS

(a)   Signs contrasting only in Hand Configuration

SUMMER	UGLY	DRY

(b)   Signs contrasting only in Place of Articulation

TAPE	CHAIR	TRAIN

(c)   Signs contrasting only in Movement

FIGURE 13.1. *Minimal contrasts illustrating formational parameters of basic lexical signs.*

(see Figure 13.1c). Note that sign languages and spoken languages both have sublexical structure, but there is a significant difference in the particular way in which sublexical units combine in forming morphemes. At one level of analysis, the components that distinguish words involve linearly ordered contrasts, whereas the components that distinguish signs are spatially organized and cooccur throughout the sign.

Studies of historical change in signs also provide support for the view that ASL signs utilize a limited number of possible formational specifications for each of the structural parameters. The direction of change in particular signs over the past century has consistently been from the more iconic and representational to the more arbitrary and constrained, conforming to a tighter linguistic system (Klima and Bellugi, 1979, Chapter 3). A classic example of historical change is the current ASL sign HOME, which was found to be an opaque nontransparent sign in a study of the iconicity of signs (Bellugi and Klima, 1976). The current sign HOME is historically a merged compound, deriving from the two highly transparent signs EAT and SLEEP (see Figure 13.2a and 2b). In EAT, an /O/ hand moves as if bringing food to the mouth; SLEEP is made with the cheek laid on the open palm. As a result of historical change the second sign assumed the hand configuration of the first, and the place of articulation of the two contacts are closer together. Today, HOME is a unitary sign with a single handshape

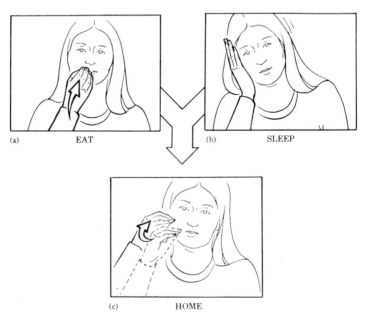

(a)   EAT   (b)   SLEEP

(c)   HOME

FIGURE 13.2. *The suppression of iconicity through historical change in compounds: mimetic signs (a) and (b) modern opaque unitary sign (c).*

touching two places on the cheek (Figure 13.2c). A consequence of these changes is a complete loss of the iconicity of the original two signs: The sign HOME is one of the more opaque signs of ASL. Such historical change in signs suggests that there are systematic pressures in ASL toward constraining its lexical elements in regular, formationally based ways, resulting in more opaque forms.

Evidence for the reality of sublexical structure is revealed in unintended misordering errors which occur in everyday signing—slips of the hands, analogous to slips of the tongue (Klima and Bellugi, 1979, Chapter 5; Newkirk, Klima, Pedersen, and Bellugi, 1980). These slips of the hands, like slips of the tongue for spoken language (Fromkin, 1973), are valuable as spontaneously occurring data from everyday signing behavior that provide clues to the organization of sign language and to the way the signs are coded. As an example, one person intended to sign SICK, BORED (meaning roughly the equivalent of 'I'm sick and tired of it') and inadvertently switched the handshapes of the two signs. The sign SICK was made with the pointing index finger hand intended for BORED, and BORED was made with the bend midfinger hand of SICK. All other parameters remaining as intended (see Figure 13.3).

In slips of the hand, the errors typically produced were not actual signs of ASL; for the most part, these sign forms with single parameters exchanged were POSSIBLE sign forms in ASL—formed from the small set of available handshapes, locations, and movements that comprise other ASL sign forms. In a large number of cases, we found some readjustments of parameter values accompanying some structural substitution to bring the error forms into conformity with

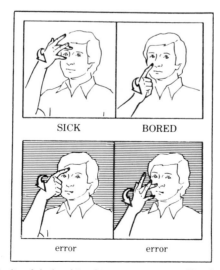

SICK BORED

error error

FIGURE 13.3. A slip of the hand involving transpositions of hand configurations only.

constraints on the combination of parameter values in ASL. Slips of the hand thus provide striking evidence for the psychological reality and independence of individual parameters of ASL; they are behavioral evidence from everyday communication that for deaf signers a sign is organized sublexically and thus that the language of signs exhibits duality of patterning.

Another line of evidence for the view that signs consist of a limited set of combining formational parameters comes from experiments that investigate how deaf signers code ASL signs in short-term memory. These experiments uniformly indicate that the basis of the coding is in terms of the component elements of signs. Thus, intrusion errors in the short-term recall of lists of signs shared formational rather than semantic properties with the presented signs (Bellugi, Klima, and Siple, 1975; Bellugi and Siple, 1974). For example, a common error for TIME was POTATO; for BIRD was NEWSPAPER; for VOTE was TEA. In each of these cases, the common error formed a minimal pair with the sign presented, differing only in one formational parameter. The signs TIME and POTATO are alike except for configuration of the hand; the signs BIRD and NEWSPAPER are alike except for place of articulation; the signs VOTE and TEA are alike except for movement. There was no consistent evidence of any other basis for the intrusion errors: They were neither sound based nor based on the printed word, nor semantically or iconically based. Consistently, the errors were based on the special organizing principles of the signs themselves: configurations of the hand, places of articulation, movements—the arbitrary cooccurring components of signs. Furthermore, just as acoustic similarity of words interferes in the short-term recall of lists of English words, formational (but not semantic) similarity of signs interferes with the short-term recall of lists of ASL signs (Poizner, Bellugi, and Tweney, in press). All of these experiments indicate that the formational parameters of signs have psychological as well as linguistic significance.

Thus, despite the vast differences in the transmission modalities of signed and spoken language systems, both reflect the same underlying principles in the internal organization of their basic lexical units. Clearly these principles do not arise out of the constraints of particular transmission systems; and this suggests more central constraints determining linguistic structure.

Grammatical Processes in American Sign Language

At all levels, there are grammatical devices in ASL that are analogous to those of spoken languages (Klima and Bellugi, 1979; Lane and Grosjean, 1980; Liddell, 1977; Siple, 1978; Wilbur, 1979). American Sign Language is clearly a fully expressive language, with grammatical structuring like that of spoken languages. But many of the formal devices that ASL has developed make use of possibilities either not available or not so used in the vocal-auditory modality of spoken languages. Rather than relying on devices for stringing together lexical stems in linear order in the sign stream, ASL makes elaborate use of grammatical mechanisms that rely on an essentially spatial medium, with simultaneous and multidimensional articulation, and with use of the face and body as well as the hands, all cooccurring as separable layers of structure.

Inflectional and Derivational Processes

Like spoken languages, ASL has developed grammatical markers that function as inflectional and derivational morphemes, resulting in regular changes in form across syntactic classes of lexical items that produce systematic changes in meaning. The elaborate system of formal inflectional devices, their widespread use to vary the form of signs, and the variety of fine distinctions they systematically convey suggest that ASL, like Russian and Navajo, is one of the inflective languages of the world.

Verb signs, for instance, undergo obligatory inflections for indexic reference that identify the arguments of the verb; for reciprocity (e.g., 'to each other'); for several distinctions of grammatical number (e.g., 'to both,' 'to more than two'); for distinctions of distributional aspect (e.g., 'to each,' 'to any,' 'to certain ones at different times'); for distinctions of temporal aspect (e.g., 'for a long time,' 'over and over again,' 'uninterruptedly,' 'regularly'); for distinctions of temporal focus (e.g., 'starting to,' 'increasingly,' 'resulting in'); for distinctions of manner (e.g., 'with ease,' 'approximately'). (See Figure 13.4 for examples of the sign PREACH under a variety of inflections.)

There are also a large number of derivational processes, such as those that form deverbal nouns (a form meaning 'comparison' from the verb COMPARE); derivation of predicates from nouns (a form meaning 'devout' and a different one meaning 'narrow-minded' from the sign CHURCH, see Figure 13.5); nominalizations from verbs (a form meaning 'the actitivy of measuring' from MEASURE); sentence adverbials from basic signs (a form meaning 'unexpectedly' from WRONG); characteristic predicates from verbs (a form meaning 'bossy' from COMMAND); derivations for extended or figurative meaning (a form meaning 'horny' from HUNGRY), and so forth.

Each inflectional process in ASL embeds the sign stem in a superimposed movement pattern, leaving other structural parameters (hand configuration, target locus) intact. One such process, for example, embeds sign stems in iterations along a circle in a horizontal plane; another embeds sign stems in an uneven triplicated, elliptical movement, still another embeds sign stems in a single, fast, tense movement ending in a recoil, and so forth. Interestingly, the global movements that convey the vast array of inflections rarely occur as movement types of uninflected lexical signs. Furthermore, there is evidence that the inflectional level in ASL has psychological as well as linguistic reality (Poizner, Newkirk, Bellugi, and Klima, 1981).

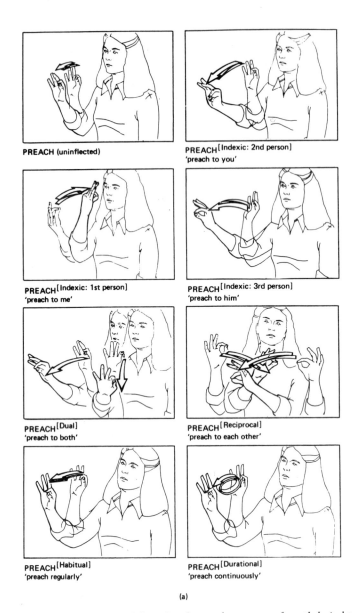

PREACH (uninflected)

PREACH[Indexic: 2nd person]
'preach to you'

PREACH[Indexic: 1st person]
'preach to me'

PREACH[Indexic: 3rd person]
'preach to him'

PREACH[Dual]
'preach to both'

PREACH[Reciprocal]
'preach to each other'

PREACH[Habitual]
'preach regularly'

PREACH[Durational]
'preach continuously'

(a)

FIGURE 13.4. *PREACH (upper left) and its form under an array of morphological processes.*

PREACH[Iterative]
'preach over and over again'

PREACH[Continuative]
'preach for a long time'

PREACH[Multiple]
'preach to them'

PREACH[Exhaustive]
'preach to each of them'

PREACH[Apportionative Internal]
'preach all over'

PREACH[Apportionative External]
'preach among members of a group'

PREACH[Allocative Determinate]
'preach to selected ones at different
times'

PREACH[Allocative Indeterminate]
'preach to any and all at different
times'

(b)

FIGURE 13.4—*Continued*

CHURCH   CHURCH [D:'devout']   CHURCH [D:'narrow minded']

FIGURE 13.5. *CHURCH and its forms under two derivational processes.*

That the inflectional level of structure in ASL is, unlike the lexical level, instantiated entirely in dynamic movement patterns which cooccur with sign stems has been shown by studies in which deaf signers are asked to identify inflectional processes from movement patterns extracted alone. In order to isolate information about movement from information about form (e.g., handshape) in the language, we have utilized a technique developed by Johansson (1975) for studying perception of motion. We place small incandescent lights at selected points on the body of signer corresponding to the major joints of the hands and arms (shoulders, elbows, wrists, index fingertips). Signing is recorded in a darkened room so that on the videotape only the pattern of moving points of light appears against a black background. Even with such greatly reduced information, deaf signers are highly accurate at recognizing and identifying inflections presented in dynamic point-light displays, demonstrating that these patterns of dynamic contours of movement form a distinct isolable (but cooccurring) layer of structure (Poizner, Bellugi, and Lutes-Driscoll, 1981).

Recursive Rules: Nesting of Morphological Forms

In ASL, inflectional processes can apply in combinations to root signs, creating different hierarchies of form and meaning. In these combinations, the output of one inflectional process serves as the input for another, and there are alternative orderings with different hierarchies of semantic structure as well. Figure 13.6 shows the uninflected sign GIVE (a); the sign under the durational inflection ('give continuously') (b); and alternatively under the exhaustive inflection ('give to each') (c). The same sign can also undergo the exhaustive inflection embedded in the durational ('give to each, that action recurring over time') (d), or the durational embedded in the exhaustive ('give continuously to each in turn') (3). Furthermore, such processes are recursive: The output of (e), for instance, can undergo the process in (b) once again (the durational of the exhaustive of a durational of GIVE), resulting in the meaning 'give continuously to each in turn, that action recurring over time.'

Such hierarchical organization and recursive application of rules to create

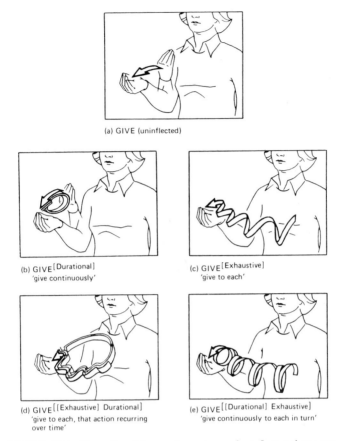

(a) GIVE (uninflected)

(b) GIVE[Durational]
'give continuously'

(c) GIVE[Exhaustive]
'give to each'

(d) GIVE[[Exhaustive] Durational]
'give to each, that action recurring
over time'

(e) GIVE[[Durational] Exhaustive]
'give continuously to each in turn'

FIGURE 13.6. *Hierarchies of form and meaning under inflectional processes.*

complex expressions are also characteristic of spoken language structure at the level of syntax. But the form this takes in a visual-manual language—the sign stem embedded in a morphological process that is spatially and temporally nested in another or in itself—is certainly unique. The proliferation of cooccurring components in spatial patterning brought into play at the morphological level and in the language in general, is consistent with our view of the tendency of the language toward conflation: toward packaging a great deal of information systematically in cooccurring layers of structure.

Other Syntactic Processes

At the level of sentence grammar in ASL, single-unit forms are sequentially presented in phrases, clauses, and sentences. However, even at this level of organization, the language exhibits further cooccurring layers.

In ASL discourse, reference points for noun phrases are established in signing space, either by making the noun sign (or a classifier standing for it) at a particular locus, or by indicating a point in space through pointing, eye gaze, or by body shift. Verb signs can be modulated to incorporate such loci or points in space, in this way specifying grammatical relations. Thus, a grammatical function served in English by linear ordering of words and in other languages by case marking is fulfilled in ASL by an essentially spatial mechanism.

Such spatial mapping also permits anaphoric reference to spatial loci: In discourse, a verb made toward the locus earlier established for a referent noun phrase unambiguously conveys pronominal-like reference. (Aspects of the system of referential indexing and verb agreement have been described in Kegl, 1976; Klima and Bellugi, 1979; Padden, 1979; Wilbur, 1979.) Such use of spatial loci for referential indexing, verb agreement, and grammatical relations is clearly unique to a visual-gestural system.

The functions served by topicalization, conditional clauses, relative clauses, and other types of sentence embedding have become grammaticalized in ASL, but not marked by means of separate lexical manual items or affixes. Rather, these functions are coded in specific facial gestures, and head nods and tilts. The nonmanual gestures constitute a nonredundant part of the grammatical scaffolding of the language; they occur obligatorily and concurrently with the manual signs as a separate and separable layer of form. For example, the equivalent of relative clauses is marked by a nonmanual signal (a head tilt, raising of the eyebrows, tensing of specific muscles that raise the upper lip) cooccurring with the manual signs (Liddell, 1977). In ASL, a variety of specific facial and bodily signals have arisen as a part of the grammaticalized apparatus, cooccurring with manual signals and the structured use of space, thus adding additional "layers" to the grammatical structure of ASL. Thus, American Sign Language, a language developed across several generations of deaf people, exhibits principles of formal organization that are strikingly similar to those found in spoken languages (Bellugi and Studdert-Kennedy, 1980), despite the radical differences in transmission modalities.

BACKGROUND TO THE STUDY OF APHASIA IN DEAF SIGNERS

Aphasia in the Hearing

Given that ASL appears to exhibit a formal system much the same as that underlying spoken languages, it is now timely to ask to what extent the neural representations of the constituent structures of ASL are shaped by the modality of its implementation. We naturally turn to the study of sign language to address this issue, because we cannot solve the problem for language in general within the spoken–auditory modality. By looking at a language with a radically different input–output system, we seek to provide a unique perspective on the relation between linguistic-specific and channel-specific neural mechanisms, and by the same token, to confront fundamental issues concerning brain plasticity.

One way in which we hope to gain the relevant information on these issues is to study the breakdown of ASL under conditions of brain damage. This domain of inquiry has a long history within neurology in relation to spoken languages and is currently being used in interesting ways to constrain and inform linguistic and psycholinguistic theorizing, as many chapters in this book demonstrate. Accordingly, before formulating in more detail the issues involved in constructing a neurology of ASL (and in order to justify the optimism with which we have introduced these issues), it will be necessary to review briefly some of what is known about the effects of brain damage on spoken language.

The central empirical observation to have emerged from the study of "hearing" aphasics is that focal damage to the left cerebral hemisphere (at least for right handers) does not lead to an across-the-board reduction in language proficiency. Rather, lesions within this hemisphere SELECTIVELY undermine language such that the speech and comprehension capacities of aphasic patients often assume one of several distinct patterns, each pattern in turn typically being correlated with a particular lesion site.

Thus, Broca's aphasia, a syndrome produced by damage to the anterior speech region, is marked by relatively good comprehension coexisting with an awkwardly articulated, effortful, and reduced output. Most importantly, although containing words of concrete reference, the output is syntactically impoverished; and it is telegraphic or agrammatic in the sense that grammatical morphemes, both bound and free, are usually omitted with a corresponding reliance on nouns and less often on uninflected or nominalized verbs (Goodglass and Kaplan, 1972; see also Chapters 2 and 14 among others in this volume).

This nonfluent pattern is all the more striking for its contrast with the motorically facile, sometimes even excessively rapid speech observed in Wernicke's aphasics. The output of such patients features syntactically well-formed strings; but this grammatical facility may be illusory, the strings possibly reflecting only a limited number of automatized routines (see, e.g., Gleason, Goodglass, Greene, Hyde, and Weintraub, 1980). Further, the Wernicke's aphasic's speech is typically replete with indefinite noun phrases, errors of word choice, and transpositions of sounds, and is, thereby, remarkably empty of content. Yet another critical feature of this syndrome is that comprehension is notably impaired (Goodglass and Kaplan, 1972).

The speech of anomic aphasics—a second form of "fluent," posterior aphasia—is also relatively empty of substantive words. However, although the output is often circumlocutory and, as in Wernicke's aphasia, marked by indefinite noun phrases, it differs from the Wernicke's output in that neologisms are absent as are errors of word choice and phonemic paraphasias. Further, and again in contrast to Wernicke's aphasia, comprehension in this syndrome is relatively intact. To be sure, some patients initially presenting as Wernicke's aphasics evolve into anomic aphasics in the course of recovery, but the syndromes are nonetheless distinct, and, moreover, the consequence most often of different lesions sites: Wernicke's aphasia results from a lesion in the posterior portion of the first temporal gyrus (Wernicke's area); anomic aphasia, from a lesion in the temporoparietal area which may extend to the angular gyrus (Goodglass and Geschwind, 1976; Goodglass and Kaplan, 1972).

Building upon these descriptions of neuroanatomically specified syndromes, recent experimental analyses have sought to characterize the various forms of language limitation in terms of distinctions among linguistic information types (phonology, syntax, semantics) and in terms of the constituent processing systems that implement each of these types. (For a review, see Caramazza and Berndt, 1978.) By doing so, these analyses have shown that, at least in the case of Broca's aphasia, treating the faculty of comprehension as an unanalyzed whole and emphasizing the distinction between it and production in terms of a simple distinction between a sensory system and a motor system provides a too narrow and somewhat misleading view. Thus, although not readily apparent to clinical observation, it has lately been shown via a number of experimental paradigms that not only do Broca's aphasics have comprehension difficulties, but that these difficulties "parallel" those of the speech disorder (Caramazza and Zurif, 1976; von Stockert and Bader, 1976; Zurif, Caramazza, and Myerson, 1972). Just as these patients omit grammatical morphemes in their speech, so too are they unable to use these items as syntactic placeholders during comprehension. As a consequence, they appear to rely on the meanings of the individual major lexical items in an utterance and attempt to combine their meanings under pragmatic constraints. It seems reasonable, therefore, to propose that, quite apart from its effect on the motor implementation of speech, damage to the anterior speech region produces a grammatical limitation that is general to the language faculty. This limitation, moreover, points to a neurologically natural separation of function between the capacity for semantic inference and the processing of sentence form, sparing the former, disrupting the latter (Bradley, Garrett, and Zurif, 1980; Schwartz, Saffran, and Marin, 1980; see also Chapters by Arbib and Marcus in Part II and by Kean and Zurif in Part III).

Admittedly, reconstructions of the production and comprehension limitations in Wernicke's aphasia in terms of a functional decomposition of the language faculty are less well advanced. The problem is that the distinctions among linguistic information types are less clearly revealed—less palpable—in Wernicke's aphasia than in Broca's. Compared to the latter, the Wernicke's lexical knowledge appears not to be so spared, nor their syntax so disrupted. Yet the disorder has not entirely defied analysis. Even now there exist a number of promising leads that more sharply define the limitations in terms of constituent systems and their interactions—leads such as that provided by Blumstein, Baker, and Goodglass (1977) who have shown that the primary deficit in the Wernicke's aphasic's speech comprehension lies not so much within either of the isolable aspects of phonological and semantic processing as with the interaction between the two. And there are other examples such as Butterworth's (1979) detailed analysis of neologistic output in terms of a lexical search model, and Cooper, Danly, and Hamby's (1979) analysis of fundamental frequency contours in the utterances of Wernicke's aphasics in terms of a model of syntactic–phonetic interactions. In sum, there does not appear to be any principled obstruction to the formation of computational and linguistic characterization of the Wernicke's syndrome (see also Buckingham and Kertesz, 1976; Butterworth, 1979; Delis, Foldi, Hamby, Gardner, and Zurif, 1979; Gleason, Goodglass, Green, Hyde, and Weintraub, 1980).

Language and Motor Skills: Relations between Aphasia and Apraxia in Hearing Subjects

Of particular relevance to our concern to develop a neurology of ASL is Kimura's (1976, 1979) notion that, rather than being specialized for symbolic functions per se, the left hemisphere is specialized for the control of changes in the position of both oral and manual articulators. This control system seems to depend upon the accurate internal representation of moving body parts, not upon sensory feedback, and is fundamental to the production of a series of complex self-generated movements (Kimura, 1979). Although this view of left hemisphere specialization has difficulty accounting for the fact that aphasic output takes different semantic and syntactic forms as a function of lesion site, we must carefully consider the relation between aphasia and the ability to produce a series of self-generated movements. Resolution of the extent to which aphasia can be separated from this control system may perhaps be more directly evaluated in visual-gestural languages than in spoken languages, as manual articulatory movements are themselves directly observable.

Kimura's (1976, 1979) strategy has been to attempt to root speech to the general psychophysiology of motor function. However, attempts to describe common neural organizational principles underlying language and movement in hearing subjects have also taken other forms (c.f., chapter 21 by Brown and chapter 25 by Arbib, this volume; Goldstein, 1948). One of these has sought to link purposive movement disorders (the apraxias) to the aphasias at a more "abstract" level: namely, as two reflections of an underlying asymbolia.

Of the various clinical forms of apraxia—each of which has received detailed, if somewhat conflicting, clinical descriptions (see Heilman, 1979, for a review)—the most relevant for the purpose of exploring a possible link between gesture and language is ideomotor apraxia. This form of apraxia refers to a disruption in the ability to perform familiar purposive movements with either hand in the absence of an associated object—an inability to pretend to use a hammer, for example. Its present relevance turns on a number of factors: Unlike the constructional apraxias which implicate pattern matching and complex non-conventional motor sequences, ideomotor apraxia unequivocally signals symbolic involvement; and is not, as ideational apraxia sometimes is, a part of severe dementia and bilateral damage (Heilman, 1979). Rather, ideomotor apraxia overwhelmingly, results from a left hemisphere lesion, and most importantly, it frequently cooccurs with aphasia. However, we should not infer common neural mechanisms from this cooccurrence. The presence of the ideomotor apraxia does not realiably predict either the severity of the aphasia (Goodglass and Kaplan, 1963) or, more importantly, the clinical form of aphasia. Further, as Bates, Bretherton, Shore, and McNew (in press) point out, to the extent that deficits in gestural symbolic activity do accompany language disturbances, the relationship turns only on that between naming and referential or object-associated gestures. And, clearly, using symbols—whether gestural or linguistic—to refer to objects is hardly the hallmark of natural language (see also Caplan, 1980, for a discussion of this and related issues).

As a general point, then, it appears that the language deficits in the various aphasic syndromes are neither straightforwardly nor simply the consequences of patterns of constraints on the operation of perceptual-motor systems at any level of analysis. Although the neurological capacity for speaking and listening obviously incorporates and is shaped by channel-specific characteristics, the brain seems also to honor linguistic and psycholinguistic processing distinctions—that is, distinctions reflecting "higher-order" linguistic constraints.

Accordingly, it has become an issue for future research to characterize the manner by which channel-specific and language-specific mechanisms interact. And by studying the fate of ASL under conditions of brain damage, we can now hope to approach this issue.

ISSUES IN THE STUDY OF APHASIA IN DEAF SIGNERS

The issue of specifying the relation between aphasia and apraxia has already been raised. And clearly it is of critical interest to the study of ASL. A prior question, however, is whether sign aphasic syndromes will occur that correspond to the fluent–nonfluent syndromes of aphasia for spoken language, quite apart from any lesion-localizing value. If such constellations of symptoms occur in a visual–gestural language, which has a radically different method for packaging linguistic information, then the components of language bear the same relationship to one another whatever the form of the signal. Different constellations of symptoms in sign aphasia, however, might provide insight into how different sensory–motor systems might shape language representation in the brain.

The sign language that is passed down from one generation of deaf signers to the next is an independent linguistic system, not derived from, nor based on, any form of English. There are, however, varieties of signing that are derivative forms of spoken languages. Fingerspelled English, for example, assigns a distinct hand configuration for each letter of the English alphabet, and English words and sentences can be spelled out in the air, letter by letter. Other forms of signing, derivative from English, use ASL signs and invented manual gestures for English morphemes in the order required by English syntax. The few existing clinical reports of sign aphasia do show left hemisphere involvement associated with disruption of signing. But these reports tend not to be especially revealing, in part because the signing systems used by the patients were apparently based on spoken language. Primarily, however, the linguistic impairments of these patients were usually extremely underreported, and testing procedures were insensitive to critical linguistic, psycholinguistic, and sociolinguistic issues of sign languages. (See Poizner and Battison, 1980, for a review of the available reports.)

We have prepared a two-pronged approach to the study of deaf ASL aphasics. In order to provide a careful clinical assessment of any disorder, we have translated the Boston Diagnostic Aphasia Examination (Goodglass and Kaplan, 1963) into ASL. This translation is not a literal one, however, because the change in transmission modality presents special issues. For example, the fact that many aphasics are hemiplegic necessitates that the sign examination be designed so that the patient can respond by using one hand only throughout, both for the language testing and for the testing of apraxia. Apraxia tests are designed to evaluate separately the ability to produce gestures that are with or are without symbolic value, both types of comparable complexity. Second, a battery of experiments that separately evaluate possible ASL disorders for phonetic and phonological processing, for naming and lexical semantics, and for morphological and syntactic processing have been constructed. For each subject, we shall make every effort to ascertain pretrauma level of competence in English and ASL. In the absence of this baseline information, we also plan to provide control data from deaf signers of the same age, with similar language and social background as the brain-injured patient. Furthermore, the same testing constraints such as the use of one hand (indeed possibly the nondominant one) will be applied. Hearing aphasic controls with similar lesions will additionally prove useful for certain nonlanguage testing.[3]

Let us turn to the form of some specific structural aspects of ASL to consider in what ways brain organization for ASL might be determined by characteristics

[3]As we have now prepared a battery of tests, we suggest that aphasiologists contact us for help in testing deaf native signers with localized lesions.

of the transmission system, and in what ways it might be determined by more central processes. It must again be emphasized that the issues we raise are empirical ones. Although we do not have answers to these questions at the present time, we feel that by generating hypotheses we can bring critical issues in this area into focus. It will be very important to determine whether effects of focal brain damage in deaf signers is such that general types of aphasic disorders will be distinguished. If this in fact occurs, will one group of sign aphasics, like Broca's aphasics, strip inflections from stems, even though lexical and inflectional material are simultaneously transmitted in ASL? (We already have evidence that two-year-old deaf children who are learning ASL as a native language do strip off inflections even when they are imitating adult utterances.) Furthermore, will another group of aphasics, like Wernicke's aphasics, properly inflect nonsense signs?

As is typical for ASL morphology, the form of inflections for specifying grammatical relations is heavily tied to the visual modality: The form involves spatial arrangements and movement of signs between points established in the space in front of the signer's body. Consider inflection for person marking: nonpresent third person reference is established with respect to different loci in the signing space, along diagonals which interesect the line of sight between signer and addressee; first and second person reference are specified by a different arrangement of loci. American Sign Language verbs move between such established loci to indicate grammatical roles such as subject and object, as well as to indicate reciprocity and number. A reciprocal inflection, for example, is made by movement of the two hands toward each other between third person loci; see Figure 13.4 for the uninflected sign PREACH (upper left) and for the reciprocal forms of PREACH, meaning 'preach to each other.' Unlike deleting the past tense marker -ed from the English verb played, deleting inflections in ASL requires considerable restructuring of the sign form. To delete the ASL inflection in the example here, only one hand instead of two is used, and the direction of the sign's movement is changed from parallel to the front of the signer's body to perpendicular to it, in a different spatial arrangement. The resulting trajectories of the inflected and uninflected forms would overlap in at most only one point in space; there is no sequentially added suffix-like attachment to be dropped from these inflections.

As grammatical structure and spatial arrangement are interwoven in these signs forms, the very critical issue arises whether lesions to either hemisphere will disrupt the production and comprehension of these forms or whether the linguistic codification involved will primarily implicate the left hemisphere. Important issues also arise as to which areas of the hemispheres mediate specific types of processing. If left anterior damage in a deaf native signer leads to impaired use of grammatical as opposed to lexical morphemes, despite the change in transmission modality, then that area of the frontal cortex would be shown to mediate abstract grammatical functions, independent of the motor and sensory apparatus of the communication channel.

As we have pointed out, a major difference in form between ASL and most spoken languages is that ASL tends to transmit structural information in a simultaneous rather than in a sequential fashion. As the left hemisphere seems better adapted than the right to process sequential rather than simultaneous signals, the simultaneous display of LINGUISTIC structure in ASL allows the study of the interplay of these (opposing) attributes. Will separate linguistic levels in ASL break down independently of one another much as they do in spoken languages, despite the radical differences in the way the linguistic information is packaged in the signed signal? Will the breakdown reflect sublexical structure of the coding process; that is, will there be literal paraphasias? Will the syntax of ASL be disturbed independently of the lexicon? Will syntactic information carried by facial expression (the processing of which is generally right hemisphere controlled) be disrupted by a left hemisphere lesion, and, in particular, by damage to certain anterior portions of the hemisphere?

The spatial as well as temporal packaging of information in ASL also allows given linguistic information to be presented either as a sequence of signs or as a simultaneous modification of a single sign. Thus, certain types of complementizers in ASL can be conveyed either by particular facial expressions or by a sequence of manual signs. Similarly, morphological information can be conveyed either by inflecting ASL signs or by concatenating ASL signs linearly. Thus, one way to sign 'clean all over' is to inflect the sign CLEAN by embedding it in a circular movement in a vertical plane in front of the torso: "CLEAN [Apportionative Internal]." (See Figure 13.4 for an example of the Apportionative Internal inflection on the sign PREACH.) Another way to convey the same concept is through a phrasal sequence which uses uninflected signs: "ALL-OVER CLEAN." Will left- (or right-) sided damage differentially impair the comprehension of the same linguistic information depending upon whether it is realized concatenated in space or sequentially spread out over time? American Sign Language provides an ideal vehicle for exploring the relative importance of physical characteristics versus linguistic characteristics in determining the organization of the brain for language.

Aspects of deafness itself also allow insight into the functional organization of the brain.[4] The two cerebral hemispheres are close, but not exact, neuroanatomical mirror images. One difference between the hemispheres lies in

[4]It is important to note that the hearing loss in hereditary deafness is almost always peripheral in nature, unaccompanied by other neurological involvement (Fraser, 1970). This is not necessarily the case, however, for other causes of deafness. Deaf children of deaf parents not only have a hearing loss that is peripheral in nature, but also are the group of deaf people who learn ASL as a first and native language. For these reasons, familial history of deafness is a critically important variable in research on sign aphasia.

a portion of the auditory association cortex known to mediate language processing. The planum temporale, part of Wernicke's area, is larger in the left hemisphere than in the right, with the difference present at birth. These facts, along with data indicating that even infants show a left hemisphere advantage in processing certain speech sounds have led some investigators to hypothesize that these auditory association areas are important to the specialization of the left hemisphere, and, indeed, that auditory experience is a necessary condition for the development of hemispheric specialization. Clearly this hypothesis could be directly tested by cases of sign aphasia in congenitally profoundly deaf signers who have never had auditory experience. The question remains, however, whether Wernicke's area, that is, auditory association cortex, plays a language mediating role for ASL, a visual-gestural language. If there is a form of aphasia in signers that corresponds in significant linguistic respects to Wernicke's aphasia, will it point to the same lesion site or to a different one? In effect, is it significant that Wernicke's aphasia in hearing patients results from a lesion adjacent to the primary auditory receiving area, or does it reflect, in some indeterminate way, a nonmodality specific type of organization?

Patterns of ASL impairments due to localized lesions in deaf native signers can clearly help illuminate the nature of neural organization for language. However, the brains of deaf people did not evolve independently of those of hearing people, and language mechanisms have certainly evolved to meet the needs of spoken communication. Thus, the neural organization for a visual-gestural language in deaf signers may be determined in part by the evolutionary history of language development in the oral-auditory transmission modality. To the extent that specialized language structures developed for speech govern the representation and processing of ASL, neural mechanisms in deaf ASL signers will be similar to those found for hearing speakers. However, to the extent that the modality in which a language has developed has shaped the structure and processing of the language, modality relevant neural structures may be implicated in its representation. The study of brain organization in deaf ASL signers allows us to address these fundamental questions regarding neural mechanisms for language.

REFERENCES

Bates, E., Bretherton, I., Shore, C., and McNew, S. (In press). Names, gestures, and objects: The role of context in the emergence of symbols. In K. Nelson (Ed.), *Children's language*, Vol. 4. New York: Gardner Press.

Bellugi, U., and Klima, E. S. (1976). Two faces of sign: Iconic and abstract. In S. R. Harnad, H. D. Steklis, and J. Lancaster (Eds.), *The origins and evolution of language and speech*. New York: New York Academy of Sciences, 280.

Bellugi, U., Klima, E. S., and Siple, P. (1975). Remembering in signs. *Cognition*, 3, 93–125.

Bellugi, U. and Siple, P. (1974). Remembering with and without words. In F. Bresson (Ed.), *Current problems in psycholinguistics*. Paris: Centre National de la Recherche Scientifique.

Bellugi, U. and Studdert-Kennedy, M. (Eds.). (1980). *Signed and spoken language: Biological constraints on linguistic form*. Dahlem Konferenzen. Basel: Verlag Chemie.

Blumstein, S. E., Baker, E., and Goodglass, H. (1977). Phonological factors in auditory comprehension in aphasia. *Neuropsychologia, 15*, 19–30.

Bradley, D., Garrett, M., and Zurif, E. B. (1980). Syntactic deficits in Broca's aphasia. In D. Caplan (Ed.), *Biological studies of mental processes*. Cambridge, Mass.: MIT Press.

Buckingham, H. W., and Kertesz, A. (1976). *Neurolinguistic jargon aphasia*. Amsterdam: Swets and Zeitlinger.

Butterworth, B. (1979). Hesitation in jargon aphasia. *Brain and Language, 8*, 133–161.

Caplan, D. (1980). *Cerebral localization and Broca's aphasia*. (1980). Paper presented to Academy of Aphasia, Cape Cod, Mass., 1980.

Caramazza, A., and Berndt, R. S. (1978). Semantic and syntactic processes in aphasia: A review of the literature. *Psychological Bulletin, 85*, 898–918.

Caramazza, A., and Zurif, E. B. (1976). Dissociation of algorithmic and heuristic processes in language comprehension: Evidence from aphasia. *Brain and Language, 3*, 572–582.

Cooper, W. E., Danly, M., and Hamby, S. (1979). Fundamental frequency [F_0] attributes in the speech of Wernicke's aphasics. In J. J. Wolf and D. H. Klatt (Eds.), *Speech communication papers presented to the 97th meeting of the acoustical society of America*. New York: Acoustical Society of America.

Delis, D., Foldi, N., Hamby, S., Gardner, H., and Zurif, E. B. (1979). A note on temporal relations between language and gesture. *Brain and Language, 8*, 350–354.

Fraser, G. R. (1970). The causes of profound deafness in childhood. In G. E. W. Wolstenholme and J. Knight (Eds.), *Sensori-neural hearing loss*. London: Churchill, 1970.

Fromkin, V. (1973). Slips of the tongue. *Scientific American, 229*, 109–117.

Gleason, J. B., Goodglass, H., Green, E., Hyde, M., and Weintraub, S. (1980). Narrative strategies of aphasic and normal subjects. *Journal of Speech and Hearing Research, 23*, 370–382.

Goldstein, K. (1948). *Language and language disturbance*. New York: Grune and Stratton.

Goodglass, H., and Geschwind, N. (1976). Language disorders (aphasia). In E. C. Carterette and M. P. Friedman (Eds.), *Handbook of perception*. New York: Academic Press.

Goodglass, H., and Kaplan, E. (1963). Disturbance of gesture and pantomime in aphasia. *Brain, 86*, 703–720.

Goodglass, H., and Kaplan, E. (1972). *The assessment of aphasia and related disorders*. Philadelphia: Lea & Febiger.

Heilman, K. M. Apraxia. (1979). In K. M. Heilman and E. Valenstein (Eds.), *Clinical neuropsychology*. New York: Oxford University Press.

Johansson, G. (1975). Visual motion perception. *Scientific American*, June 232, 76–88.

Kegl, J. (1976). Relational grammar and American Sign Language. Unpublished manuscript, MIT, 1976.

Kimura, D. (1976). The neural basis of language qua gesture. In H. Whitaker and H. A. Whitaker (Eds.), *Studies in neurolinguistics*, Vol. 2. New York: Academic Press.

Kimura, D. (1979). Neuromotor mechanisms in the evolution of human communication. In H. D. Steklis and M. J. Raleigh (Eds.), *Neurobiology of social communication*. New York: Academic Press.

Klima, E. S. and Bellugi, U. (1979). *The signs of language*. Cambridge, Mass.: Harvard University Press.

Lane, H., and Grosjean, F. (Eds.). (1980). *Recent perspectives on American Sign Language*. Hillsdale, N.J.: Lawrence Erlbaum.

Lenneberg, E. (1967). *Biological foundations of language*. New York: Wiley.

Liddell, S. K. (1977). *An investigation into the syntactic structure of American Sign Language.* Unpublished Ph.D. dissertation, University of California, San Diego.

Lieberman, P. (1975). *On the origins of language.* New York: Macmillan.

Newkirk, D., Klima, E. S., Pedersen, C., and Bellugi, U. (1980). Linguistic evidence from slips of the hand. In V. Fromkin (Ed.), *Errors in linguistic performance: Slips of the tongue, ear, pen, and hands.* New York: Academic Press.

Padden, C. (1979). Verb classes in American Sign Language. Working Paper, University of California, San Diego and The Salk Institute for Biological Studies.

Poizner, H., and Battison, R. (1980). Cerebral asymmetry for sign language: Clinical and experimental evidence. In H. Lane and F. Grosjean (Eds.), *Recent perspectives on American Sign Language.* Hillsdale, N.J.: Lawrence Erlbaum, 1980.

Poizner, H., Bellugi, U., and Lutes-Driscoll, V. (1981). Perception of American Sign Language in dynamic point-light displays. *Journal of Experimental Psychology: Human Perception and Performance, 7,* 430–440.

Poizner, H., Bellugi, U., and Tweney, R. (In press). Processing of formational, semantic, and iconic information in American Sign Language. *Journal of Experimental Psychology: Human Perception and Performance.*

Poizner, H., Newkirk, D., Bellugi, U., and Klima, E. S. (1981). Representation of inflected signs from American Sign Language in short-term memory. *Memory and Cognition, 9,* 121–131.

Schwartz, M., Saffran, E., and Marin, O. S. M. (1980). The word order problem in agrammatism, I: Comprehension. *Brain and Language, 10,* 249–262.

Siple, P. (Ed.). (1978). *Understanding language through sign language research.* New York: Academic Press.

Stokoe, W. C., Casterline, D., and Croneberg, C. G. (1965). *A dictionary of American Sign Language.* Silver Spring, Md.: Linstok Press.

von Stockert, T. R., and Bader, L. (1976). Some relations of grammar and lexicon in aphasia. *Cortex, 12,* 49–60.

Wilbur, R. (1979). *American Sign Language and sign systems: Research and applications.* Baltimore: University Park Press.

Zurif, E. B., Caramazza, A., and Myerson, R. (1972). Grammatical judgments of agrammatic aphasics. *Neuropsychologia, 10,* 405–418.

IV
NEUROLOGICAL PERSPECTIVES

Investigations of the neurological foundation for language function are based almost entirely upon clinical studies. The lack of animal models of language and the restrictions on human experimentation set by ethical considerations have made the great majority of experimental techniques used in other areas of neuroscience unavailable. Thus most of the present dominating theories of language–brain relationships are based upon analysis of the abnormal performances and capacities of patients with disease of the nervous system. (Exceptions include EEG studies, evoked potentials, and measurement of cerebral blood flow.) Theories of neural-linguistic relationships based on clinicopathological correlations extend back in a continuous scientific tradition to Broca, and even, as discussed in Chapter 1, to Gall and his predecessors.

A fundamental dichotomy pervades much clinical work in this field, namely, that between health care and basic research. While they may share our hope that basic research will eventually aid in the rational design of therapy, physicians, speech therapists, nurses, and other health professionals are not primarily concerned with the development of neurolinguistic theory. Rather, they are primarily concerned with the physical health of the patient and secondly with the design of therapy to enable him to reach his ultimate functional potential. Statistically, valid inferences can be made with respect to many disease entities and their prognoses based on patterns of language disturbance by clinicians who do not focus attention on the mechanisms whereby language is represented and processed by the brain.

There are several historical consequences of this prime focus of clinicians upon answering clinical questions about aphasia. It has biased the choice of descriptive terms for the characterization of disordered language, in relative isolation from the development of linguistic theory to describe normal function. As we stressed in the introduction to Part III one of the most obvious ways to combine the study of normal language and aphasia is via a shared set of descriptive terms and operations. If a disorder of language is described as a set of operations affecting phoneme ordering, it is implied that theories of normal language will refer to phonemes and phoneme strings: The disordered language is then seen as some disturbance in the identification or concatenation of these elements. If an analysis of a pathological performance, such as Levine and Calvanio's analysis of dyslexia, claims that a particular ability, in this case, the ability to identify single letters, is not disturbed by the disease, this claim relates to theories of normal function only on the assumption that letter identification is one component of normal reading. Briefly, inferences from the analysis of pathology to that of normal function requires that the two analyses agree on the types of structures and operations which characterize them.

It is at this level, the choice of elements regarding the description of pathological performances, that clinical studies have been most influenced by the concern of health professionals. If correlation between disease entities and prognosis is the chief goal, the choice of descriptive terms is immaterial, as long as it can effectively serve to establish such correlations.

Yet it would be grossly inaccurate to suggest that those who formulated neurolinguistic theories on the basis of clinical analyses were completely unconcerned about the choice of descriptive vocabulary. The founders of scientific neurolinguistics and aphasiology and their contemporary clinical counterparts gave much thought to the description of the abnormal performances they witnessed. The discussion of semiology and pathogenesis of aphasia at the 1908 Society of Neurology Meetings, the insights of Goldstein and Luria, and many other contributions are remarkable not only for their work on pathology and anatomy, but also for the insights gained in language processes and their disorders. Isolated observations notwithstanding, theories of language representation and processing in brain have been largely based on descriptions of pathology which have one noticeable feature: They use descriptive terms that refer to phenomena which are easily observed at the bedside. This feature defines for most neurologists a level of empirical adequacy BOTH *for the description of aphasias* AND *for theories of the brain's language representation.*

The linguistic and psycholinguistic entities that most commonly enter into descriptions of aphasia and thus into neurolinguistic theory are those for whose existence we have the strongest pretheoretical intuitions: words and their component segments; illocutionary force; semantic and psychological associations of words; certain aspects of suprasegmental intonation contours; and the entire congeries of on-line psycholinguistic functions to which the linguistic code is put (speaking, understanding speech, reading, and writing), and several more specialized psycholinguistic functions (naming and repetition). In these descriptions and theories, the greatest effort is made to avoid terminology which refers to abstract levels of linguistic structure or psycholinguistic processes. The descriptions of pathology and the resulting theories are closely associated to observable features of language. In light of the context within which these descriptions and theories have arisen, this is all to the good. It may not be clinically useful to discover that different diseases cause difficulty with empty nodes as opposed to traces (Chomsky and Lasnik, 1977).

Some of the consequences of choosing this descriptive vocabulary are explored in the chapters by Marshall and Caplan. Marshall's concern is with the nature of symptom-complexes: what other than statistical regularity of co-occurrence entitles us to group the various features of the well known aphasic syndromes together? Is there a reason why patients who have dysarthric troubles are those who may have telegrammatic speech? Are the two connected causally or is it simply fortuitous that they co-occur because lesions that affect one usually produce the other due to factors such as the vagaries of vascular anatomy? To answer such questions, more than correlations are needed. Explanatory, mechanistic theories are required to see whether the elements of a syndrome are related by factors which are directly relevant to the way the brain is organized with respect to language. In some cases, the beginning of such causal theories are emerging. The parallel between the production and comprehension deficit in Broca's agrammatic aphasia may have its cause in a single disorder of lexical access for a set of vocabulary items.

Caplan's argument is somewhat different. He examines inferences from an abnormal performance to a deficit analysis of that performance, that is, to a characterization of the performance in terms of a normal system with a missing or misfunctioning component. He states that the argument is valid, only if the normative analysis on which the deficit analysis is based is justified. The link between analyses of pathology and analyses of normal function is required for aphasia to serve as an empirical basis for neurolinguistic theory. Caplan also rehearses Marshall's concerns about the mismatch between the concepts of psycholinguistics and the processes of cell-circuit-synapse neuroscience. Arbib's two chapters discuss strategies for attacking this mismatch by the study of cooperative computation, and by learning from neural models of perception and motor control. We must turn our attention from the question "How did the area that has been lesioned previously provide the missing function?" to "How do the remaining areas cooperate to provide the residual function?"

Lecours' clinical study utilizes a well-defined normative analysis, structural phonetic theory in particular, and the approach to phoneme description developed (for French) by Martinez as the basis for an analysis of an abnormal production, glossolalia. Lecours counts the relative proportions of different phonemic elements and their concatenations in the speech of various glossolalics. He then compares the frequency of occurrence of particular phonemes and phoneme strings in their output with that of aphasic and normal subjects. As opposed to aphasic speech, the distribution of phonemes is different in glossolalia and normal speech, but, as in aphasia, phonotactic constraints are respected. The mechanism by which glossolalia is produced is not clear, more is ignored in its production than simply the semantic aspect of language, and a simulation such as Lecours undertook some years ago with respect to paraphasias may result in a model of how this striking output occurs. If phonemes, features, morpheme structure rules, and similar terms enter into the description and simulation, the abnormal performance will be related to normal language structure by the set of distorting rules. The puzzle in glossolalia is what relation these distorting rules would have to the brain, granted that the brains of (most) glossolalics are normal. The ability of some normal subjects to produce glossolalic output at will provides clues to the mechanisms of speech control. That some elderly aphasics with posterior lesions have output that is related to glossolalia may provide a first hint as to the neural areas responsible for control functions.

As the study of sign language by Bellugi et al. may sharpen our understanding of the neural mechanisms underlying speech by contrasting the visual-gestural with the auditory-oral mode, so may the study of reading illuminate speech mechanisms. The major difference is that the skills of reading and writing are usually acquired subsequent to the mastery of speech, whereas sign language is usually learned by the speechless. Levine and Calvanio investigate both pure alexia (alexia without agraphia) and aphasic alexia. Dejerine explained his classic case of a man who could write but not read in terms of lesions which destroyed the left visual cortex and the splenium (the rear corpus callosum, joining visual areas across the hemispheres), thus isolating the language areas of the left hemisphere from visual input. Levine and Calvanio found that such patients could still name single letters but failed with letter triples on tachistoscopic presentations. Subsequent study of a patient with intact visual cortices but severed splenium suggested that both hemispheres can recognize single letters, but only the left hemisphere develops the complex recognition skills that underlie reading. The right hemisphere is competent for face and object recognition, but not for reading or for color naming (a skill acquired around the age of 3). Turning to aphasic alexia, Levine and Calvanio agree that reading is mediated by multiple regions of the left hemisphere, including angular gyrus, superior temporal region, and precentral gyrus, but they do not see evidence that alexic syndromes vary systematically with the site of the lesion. Nonetheless, there are clear differences between alexic patients, and they argue that the search for the determinants of these differences, without recourse to a 'one task, one box' methodology, poses a major challenge.

The two remaining chapters in Part IV focus on anatomical questions. Levine and Sweet's chapter on Broca's aphasia adopts the classic, clinical definition of the syndrome, and examines the question, What is the minimal area where lesions will produce the syndrome? They argue that the association cortex of the precentral gyrus, that is, the frontal operculum (Brodmann's Area 6), is the region where a lesion may produce the symptoms, not the slightly more anterior area in the pars opercularis and triangularis of F3 as defined by Broca. Because of the locus of the lesion, they suggest that the classic view of Broca's area as sending *motor engrams to the motor cortex for transmission to muscles is incorrect. For Levine and Sweet, Broca's aphasia is an apraxic disorder of speech. Granted their assumptions and observations regarding lesion site, the conclusion is reasonable. But as we noted in the introduction to Part III, it is now unclear whether the telegrammatic type of Broca's aphasia to be considered a disorder of motor planning. If the dysfunction is not analyzed as one of motor systems, arguments from the location of lesions whose effects do not require one to distinguish between apraxia and movement execution in Broca's aphasia are invalid. The description and definition of Broca's aphasia are thus crucial to these arguments. It should also be noted that the analyses of the syndrome in information processing, linguistic, and psycholinguistic terms do not demonstrate that all aspects of the syndrome are nonmotor in nature. Thus, Levine and Sweet's argument is not necessarily incompatible with these accounts.*

Kertesz presents a sophisticated approach to clinicopathological correlation, using the techniques described in some detail in his case studies in Chapter 2, that is, standardized tests of language function, modern radiological techniques of CT scans, and isotope brain scans. The correlation of lesion site with symptom-complex and the evolution of both over time, constitute the link with neural structures which is most frequently made today. Caplan argues against the explanatory adequacy of associating a function with a grossly defined area of the brain, such as a convolution. Regardless of its explanatory adequacy, such associations exist as Kertesz, Levine, and many others have demonstrated. The challenge is to explicate abnormalities in terms of deficits in normal functions (Kertesz briefly sketches such an analysis, but clearly this is an area for considerable speculation and investigation), and at the same time to ask what it is about the neural make-up of an area that causes that area to be responsible for a particular linguistic representation and function. The former statement leads to the information processing and linguistic models of Parts II and III, the latter to the considerations of neuroscience and brain theory of Part V. Thus clinical theories, though focusing on aspects of language that are based on therapeutic concerns, lead in two directions toward contact with more basic science.

REFERENCES

Chomsky, N., and Lasnik, H. (1977). Filters and control. *Linguistic inquiry, 7,* 425–504.

14

The Neuropathological Basis of Broca's Aphasia and Its Implications for the Cerebral Control of Speech[1]

David N. Levine
Eric Sweet

Sudden loss of speech, associated with right hemiplegia, is a very common syndrome, and there are few neurologists who have not seen many such cases. The speech loss, which may be total at first, undergoes a variable degree of improvement over the subsequent days and weeks. Some patients regain no speech, but may moan or cry out to attract attention. Others regain the use of a limited repertoire of neologisms, words, and short phrases that are used in a stereotyped and perseverative manner to respond to questions. Although often slurred and undifferentiated, in some patients these phrases may be enunciated clearly with no significant articulatory difficulty. When speech becomes some-what richer, repetition of single words is often far more successful than uttering these words in naming or in spontaneous speech. But repetition too breaks down beyond the single word or phrase. Still other patients regain even more speech, but it is uttered slowly and effortfully, often in a monotonous measured pace, with frequent stumbling over words and misarticulation. In patients with this degree of recovery, verbal paraphasias are common. Syntax may also be abnor-mal, as words carrying little semantic and/or speech emphasis may be omitted, leaving a bare bones or telegram-like output. Finally, some patients recover normal or nearly normal speech, only occasionally misarticulating slightly or pausing to find a word.

Early workers emphasized that despite lack of speech, use of the orolingual musculature for purposes other than speech was entirely normal. It is now clear, however, that the overwhelming majority of these patients also suffer from in-ability to utilize lips, tongue, and pharynx in a variety of voluntary acts other

[1]This work was supported in part by Grant NS-13102 from the National Institute of Neurologic and Communicative Disorders and Stroke of the National Institutes of Health.

299

than speech. In the first few days of the illness, many such patients have difficulty swallowing their food and saliva, but this dysphagia usually recovers very promptly. Severely affected, speechless patients may be unable to protrude their tongue, either to verbal request or in imitation of the examiner. Less affected patients, such as those uttering some single words or phrases, may protrude the tongue well, but are slow in moving it from side to side. Even when this can be done at reasonable speed, acts such as whistling or clucking are poorly done. In a population of these patients the degree of speech loss is hightly correlated with the degree of such oral apraxia (De Renzi, Pieczuro, and Vignolo, 1966).

Writing with the unparalyzed left hand is almost always impaired. Spontaneous writing or writing to dictation is usually more impaired than copying, but severely affected patients may have trouble with all of these tasks. The correct letters may be poorly formed, incorrect letters appear with frequent perseverations, and letters may be written atop one another or at uneven heights.

Language comprehension is also affected, but to a variable degree. In general, responses to spoken request are poorer than imitation of the examiner's movements, whether these be oral or limb gestures. Thus, the patient may not open his mouth or touch his nose to spoken request but may do so in imitation of the examiner. Not all visual input, however, enjoys such favorable status. Comprehension of written language is usually as impaired as, or more impaired than, comprehension of speech. The same patient who sticks out his tongue to spoken request may be unable to obey the printed command of "STICK OUT YOUR TONGUE." This impairment of comprehension is manifest not only in tests requiring the patient to obey commands, but also in tests requiring matching of spoken or written phrases to appropriate pictures and in tests requiring only binary (yes–no) decisions about spoken or written questions. Such comprehension deficits involve not only ordinary language but also other semantic systems such as that of numbers and arithmetic operations.

The designation of this common aphasic syndrome has had a long history. Broca (1861) called it "aphemia," but Trousseau (1864) argued for "aphasia." When Wernicke (1874) contrasted these aphasics with others who spoke copiously, this aphasia became "cortical motor aphasia" or "Broca's aphasia." "Expressive" (as opposed to receptive) and "nonfluent" (as opposed to fluent) were terms introduced by later authors.

The neuropathological basis of the syndrome has also had a long history, punctuated by polemical attacks and counterattacks. Broca localized aphemia to the third frontal convolution of the left hemisphere (see Figure 14.1). He felt that this region contained the engrams (or programs) for the learned movements that constitute speech. During Broca's era, the prevailing view was that movements could not be elicited by mechanical or electrical stimulation of the cortex, and so the notion of "motor cortex" did not exist. In 1870, Fritsch and Hitzig overturned that view by demonstrating that electrical stimulation of the cortex of the

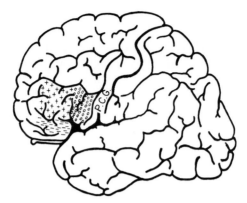

FIGURE 14.1. *Lateral view of a cerebral hemisphere. Markings occupy various portions of the third frontal gyrus, defined by gross anatomical landmarks. Circles occupy the pars opercularis, situated between precentral sulcus posteriorly and ascending limb of sylvian fissure anteriorly. Crosses occupy pars triangularis, situated between the ascending and horizontal limbs of the sylvian fissure. Horizontal lines occupy the pars orbitalis. P.C.G. denotes the precentral gyrus situated immediately posterior to the third frontal gyrus.*

dog could produce various movements. Subsequently, Wernicke (1874) identified Broca's area with that portion of the cortex from which electrical stimulation yielded movements of the speech musculature.

As the anatomy of motor cortex became established, however, it soon became clear that the third frontal gyrus was NOT the motor cortex for the muscles utilized in speech. Instead, the motor cortex straddled the rolandic sulcus, with the lowest thresholds in the precentral gyrus and slightly higher thresholds in the postcentral gyrus. Faced with this situation, Dejerine (1914) and Liepmann (1915) developed a model that has had a tenacious hold on the minds of most students of aphasia ever since. According to this view, the third frontal gyrus (pars opercularis plus varying amounts of pars triangularis depending on whom you read) contains the motor programs for speech. Neurons in this area drive neurons in the precentral gyrus, which is a motor "executor" area, from which axons reach the lower cranial nerve nuclei that innervate the speech musculature. Accordingly, lesions of the motor cortex were thought to produce contralateral facial and lingual weakness and to impair speech output but to leave "inner speech" intact. The patient could thus comprehend speech and print and might write normally if not hemiplegic from extension of the lesion higher or deeper into the precentral gyrus. In contrast, lesion of Broca's area was thought to result in loss of the motor programs for speech, but not necessarily in paralysis of orolingual musculature for nonspeech movements. However, the loss of motor speech programs could have repercussions on other language activities, producing the clinical picture of Broca's aphasia described at the outset of this chapter:

speechlessness with recurrent utterances or agrammatism, agraphia, variable impairment in speech comprehension, and often severe alexia.

The purpose of this chapter is to examine the evidence for this model. The primary source of evidence will be neuropathological studies of patients with Broca's aphasia and of patients with focal lesions of Broca's area. We will also, however, examine some evidence from electrical stimulation of cortex in waking subjects and some evidence from studies of comparative anatomy. We shall conclude that there is little evidence to support the classical model, and shall tentatively propose a different formulation.

EVIDENCE FROM NEUROPATHOLOGICAL STUDIES

Pierre Marie, at the turn of the century, posed the first serious challenge to the classical model. His evidence was assembled and presented in great detail by his student, Moutier (1908), and comprised largely cases of cerebral infarction documented by post-mortem examination. Later, Marie and Foix (1917) studied the aphasias resulting from missile wounds incurred by soldiers during World War I. In this study, post-mortem examination was not usually done, but the large number of cases and the apparent consistency of the wound sites within a given category of aphasia allowed strong conclusions about localization. Later, Niessl von Mayendorf (1926) again summarized the evidence from early cases of cerebral infarction and added cases reported after Moutier's publication. The evidence from traumatic aphasia during war was again vigorously pursued during and after World War II by several investigators (Conrad, 1954; Luria, 1970; Nathan, 1947; Schiller, 1947). Finally, the development of scanning techniques, first radioisotope scanning and later computerized tomography (CT), has allowed the large-scale study of cases with cerebral infarction, even when post-mortem examination cannot be obtained (Benson and Patten, 1967; Kertesz, Lesk, and McCabe, 1977; Mohr, Pessin, Finkelstein, Funkenstein, Duncan, and Davis, 1978).

Evidence against the classical model, derived from these studies, comes from both "negative" and "positive" cases. A negative case is one in which a lesion occurred in Broca's area but either no aphasia developed or the aphasia was unlike Broca's aphasia. A positive case is one in which Broca's aphasia was present but the lesion completely spared Broca's area. Marie appreciated the need for both types of evidence and collected each kind of case.

"Negative" Cases

The literature contains several examples of right-handed patients with infarctions of the left third frontal gyrus who were either never aphasic or who

developed transient mild aphasia. Niessl von Mayendorf (1926) presented summaries of 12 cases, all with infarctions involving the pars opercularis and varying
amounts of pars triangularis and pars orbitalis of the left third frontal gyrus. The
topography of the lesions in four patients who were never aphasic is shown in
Figure 14.2.

Recent evidence from computerized tomography shows that lesions limited
to the third frontal gyrus may show only transient, mild aphasia (Mohr *et al.*,
1978) or no aphasia at all. An example of such a negative case from our own
material will illustrate this clinicopathological relationship.

*A 50-year-old, right-handed, hypertensive man (PM 230-90-86) had a convulsion
with loss of consciousness. He awoke within an hour or two and was confused but not
aphasic. After several further seizures that evening, an endotracheal tube was inserted. A CT scan of the following day is shown in Figure 14.3. On his third hospital
day he was extubated. Examination showed confusion but no aphasia. Asked where he
was, he said, "I am at the airport . . . in a hospital." He subtracted serial 2s from 10
without error. Detailed psychological testing during the following week revealed deficits*

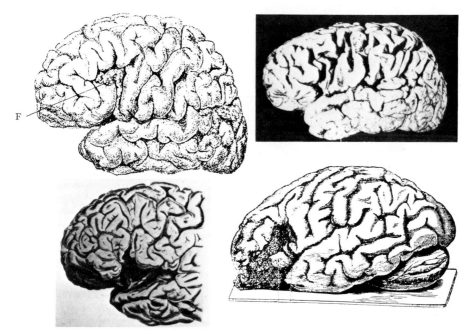

FIGURE 14.2. *Four cases from the literature of lesions of the left third frontal gyrus in right-handed
subjects with no history of aphasia: Top left: Moutier's (1908) case "Proudhomme"; softening of the
pars opercularis. Top right: Archambault's (1913) case; softening of the pars opercularis. Bottom left:
Henschen's (1920) case; softening of the left pars opercularis. Bottom right: Foulis's (1879) case; nearly
complete destruction of the third frontal gyrus; the precentral gyrus intact.*

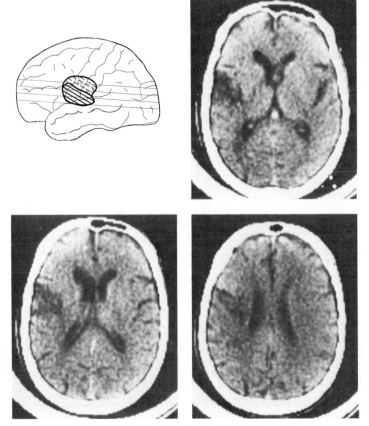

FIGURE 14.3. *Location of lesion in PM. Three levels of CT scan are shown (top right, bottom left, bottom right in ascending order), each showing hemorrhage (densely white area) in left third frontal gyrus. At top left the levels of the section are shown and the projection of the hemorrhage on the surface of the hemisphere is outlined.*

in intellect and memory affecting both verbal and nonverbal tasks. Concreteness of thought, difficulty in shifting mental set with perseverations, and impaired concentration were evident. There was no aphasia.

The occurrence of such negative cases was at least in part realized by advocates of the classical model, who attempted to reconcile this evidence with their view that the third frontal gyrus contained the motor programs for speech. The most common explanation was that in such patients the inferior frontal gyrus of the RIGHT hemisphere took over the programming of speech, resulting in either no aphasia at all, or only transient aphasia.

Recently, we had the opportunity to study a patient who allowed us to test this hypothesis directly (Levine and Mohr, 1979—Case 1). In this patient only mild dysphasia was present even though the third frontal gyrus was destroyed bilaterally.

A 65-year-old man developed sudden mutism and right hemiplegia. The limb weakness improved in 3 days, but speech did not return for several weeks. For a while, he spoke with single words and numerous verbal paraphasias. After several months, his speech was "nearly normal." One year later he again became mute and was unable to swallow, but his speech returned to its previous state within hours. However, severe personality changes ensued. He developed bizarre delusions of persecution and became pathologically compulsive. He displayed little affect except for brief outbursts of anger, and he seemed emotionally distant. Examination revealed moderate dementia with marked concreteness and slowing of thought, poor reasoning and memory, and difficulty with visuospatial tasks. Yet his speech was fairly well preserved. He rarely spoke spontaneously except for an occasional complaint, but he answered readily when addressed, speaking in short phrases. His voice was a husky, breathy monotone, and occasionally sounds were deleted or blurred. But his speech was intelligible and appropriate, as in this conversation:

"What kind of work were you in?"	*"Oil burner work."*
"What did you do?"	*"Install the burners."*
"Anything else?"	*"Made em run."*

His repetition of speech and reading aloud were nearly normal except for mild dysarthria and dysprosody. Naming of visual objects and of objects described verbally was slightly impaired. Speech comprehension was moderately deficient; he could perform two-step commands but not three-step commands. Reading comprehension was impaired only for difficult material. His profile of scores on the Boston Diagnostic Aphasia Examination is shown in Figure 14.4. Thus, language production, although not normal, was only mildly to moderately impaired. There certainly was no evidence of the syndrome of Broca's aphasia. His CT scan (Figure 14.5) showed bilateral low density lesions, consistent with infarction, involving primarily the frontal lobe on the left and frontal and temporal lobes on the right. Broca's area was completely destroyed or undercut bilaterally.

In searching the world's literature for other cases with bilateral lesions of Broca's area, we found six reported cases, all of whom spoke or wrote sufficiently well to exclude them from the category of severe Broca's aphasia (Levine and Mohr, 1979). Recently, we encountered another case reported by Gianulli in 1908 and reviewed by Niessl von Mayendorf (1926).

The patient was a 74-year-old man who had had two strokes. Examination showed dementia. Speech was paraphasic ("pristo" for "tristo") and fluent. Repetition was also paraphasic. Speech and print comprehension were preserved for simple requests

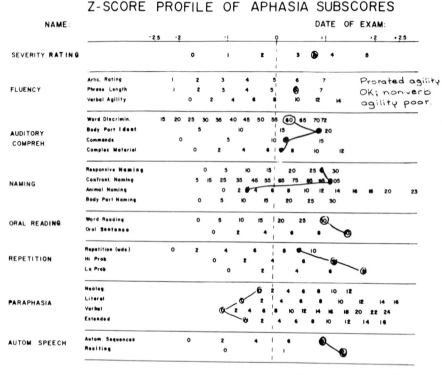

FIGURE 14.4. *Profile of scores for Case 1 of Levine and Mohr (1979) on the Boston Diagnostic Aphasia Examination (Goodglass and Kaplan, 1972). Scores are expressed in number of standard deviations above or below the average score of a standardization group of aphasics. Note the presence of mild to moderate aphasia, very unlike the profile expected for a patient with significant Broca's aphasia.*

but were not normal. Postmortem examination showed atrophic, cavitated lesions in the posterior portions of the third frontal gyri bilaterally (Figure 14.6).

Cases such as these demonstrate that even bilateral lesions of the third frontal gyrus may result in only mild aphasia. Yet the classical model—even the variation that allows for substitution by the right hemisphere—would predict that such patients should be unable to speak at all because the "motor programs" for speech are no longer present.

This evidence poses a serious challenge to any theory that assigns to the third frontal gyrus a dominant role in speech. We must now ask what cerebral structures ARE crucial to speech, if not the third frontal gyri? To answer this question we are required to examine the evidence from positive cases.

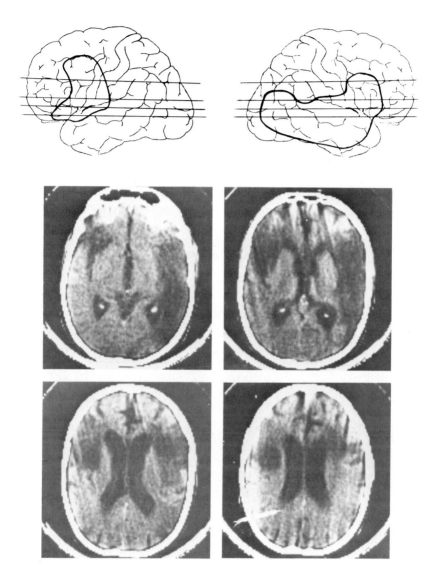

FIGURE 14.5. *Location of lesions in Case 1 of Levine and Mohr by computerized tomographic (CT) scan. The CT scan slices from inferior upward are shown in the middle row left, middle row right, bottom row left, and bottom row right. The top row shows diagrams of the lateral surfaces of the left and right hemispheres. The straight lines depict the centers of the CT sections shown below. The heavy black outline represents the surface projection of the lesion in that hemisphere.*

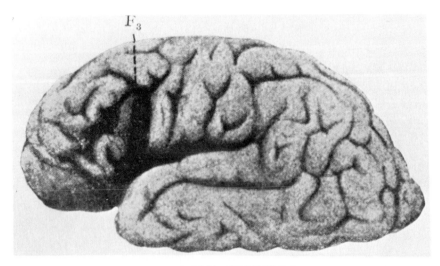

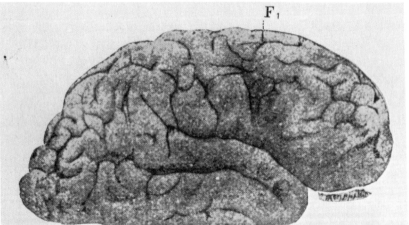

FIGURE 14.6. *Location of the lesions in Gianulli's case. The left hemisphere (top) and the right hemisphere (bottom) both show softenings of the pars opercularis of the third frontal gyrus.*

"Positive" Cases

Marie and Moutier (Moutier, 1908) presented neuropathologic findings in a series of patients with Broca's aphasia. They concluded that patients with Broca's aphasia invariably had lesions in a zone bounded anteriorly by the anterior margin of the insula and posteriorly by the posterior margin of the insula (Marie's "lenticular zone"—Figure 14.7). The superior–inferior borders and medial–lateral borders of this zone were never clearly established. This zone is situated

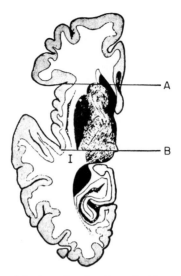

FIGURE 14.7. *Marie's schematic horizontal section of a cerebral hemisphere, illustrating the "lenticular zone" with its anterior (A) and posterior (B) boundaries.*

posterior to the pars orbitalis and pars triangularis of the third frontal gyrus, which were often entirely intact. The "lenticular zone" contained the claustrum, lenticular and caudate nuclei, the thalamus, and the internal, external, and extreme capsules. Cortical components included the insula, frontoparietal operculum, and lower portions of the precentral and postcentral gyri.

The crucial structures within the lenticular zone were never fully elucidated by Marie and Moutier. Many patients had infarction or hemorrhage in the putamen and in the adjacent internal or external capsules. Although Marie often seemed to emphasize the importance of the putamen, this conclusion must be suspect because involvement of white matter lateral, medial, and superior to the putamen must have interrupted projection fibers to and from the inferior and opercular frontoparietal cortex as well as commissural and intrahemispheric association fibers. Indeed, in some cases the putamen was spared, but the lesion involved the inferior portions of the precentral and postcentral gyri and varying portions of the posterior parietal lobe. In his later studies of traumatic aphasia with Foix, Marie concluded that extensive cortical lesions, centered on the inferior pre- and postcentral gyri, produced global or Broca's aphasia. Niessl von Mayendorf (1926), reviewing his own experience and the literature of Broca's aphasia resulting from stroke, concluded that the true Broca's area "coincides with the central projection of those muscles active in speech, an area which can be determined by electrical stimulation of the brain [pp. 141]." Broca's area and motor cortex were not distinct, but identical.

The IDENTITY of motor cortex and Broca's area, first postulated by Wernicke, but later denied by Dejerine and by Liepmann, has been further supported by studies of traumatic aphasia in soldiers of World War II. Nathan (1947) concluded that the most common localization of facial-lingual apraxia, affecting both speech and nonverbal voluntary movement, was the lower precentral gyrus. His patients had deficits of language comprehension as well, although the speech difficulty was most conspicuous. Schiller (1947) found that lesions resulting in articulatory difficulty centered on the lower precentral gyrus. All of his cases showed other aphasic distrubances such as impaired naming. The extensiveness of the aphasia was strongly related to the degree of tissue loss within the perisylvian region. Conrad (1954) showed that wounds resulting in motor aphasia— whether Broca's aphasia or pure word-muteness (subcortical motor aphasia)— centered around the middle and inferior portions of the central sulcus, not the third frontal gyrus. "Practically all foci are situated within the area of the enlarged motor fields of the cortex [pp. 503–504]." The severity of the motor aphasia was related to the size of the lesion.

The results of radioisotope and tomographic x-ray scanning of lesions are consistent with the pathoanatomical evidence supporting the location of Broca's area in the motor cortex itself. Kertesz et al. (1977) found large radioactive uptake over the precentral gyrus in all 14 cases of Broca's aphasia they considered. Using CT scans, Mohr, Pessin, Finkelstein, Funkenstein, Duncan, and Davis (1978) have stressed that only large perisylvian lesions produce severe, permanent speechlessness. Levine and Mohr (1979) have stressed that, within this perisylvian region, the most critical region is the precentral gyrus rather than the third frontal gyrus. These points can be illustrated by two of our most recent cases. The first case (Trojanowski, Green, and Levine, 1980) was a patient with crossed aphasia, that is, he developed a typical severe Broca's aphasia with a left hemiplegia. Over a 9-month period, he recovered no speech except for one or two recurrent utterances. On post-mortem examination, the only major lesion was in the right hemisphere, verifying that this right-handed man had indeed developed speech, for an unknown reason, in the right hemisphere. Of interest to us, however, is that his lesion (Figure 14.8) was almost entirely confined to the cortex and immediately subjacent white matter of the precentral gyrus. It involved nearly the whole extent of this gyrus, but hardly encroached on the frontal gyri anteriorly or the post central gyrus posteriorly. Thus, it appears that (at least in this patient) an extensive lesion of the dominant precentral gyrus is sufficient to result in Broca's aphasia.

The second case was a 70-year-old man who developed sudden speechlessness with right hemiplegia. Six months after his stroke, he had recurrent perseverative utterances but was unable to communicate. He repeated only single words or a short phrase. Moderate deficits in speech comprehension and severe alexia were present. There was some oral dyspraxia. His CT scan (Figure 14.9)

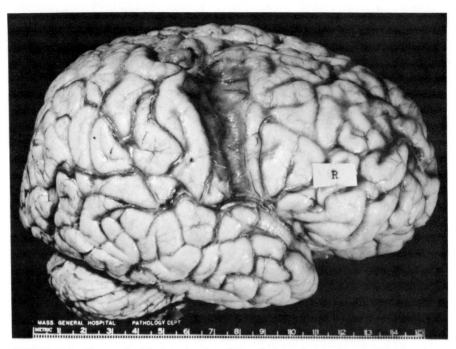

FIGURE 14.8. *Photograph of the lateral surface of the right hemisphere in the case of Trojanowski, Green, and Levine illustrating the large lesion confined to the precentral gyrus.*

showed a focal lesion involving the lower third of the pre- and postcentral gyri. Only slight encroachment on the third frontal gyrus and possibly on the anterior portion of the superior temporal gyrus was present.

In summary, the overwhelming bulk of the neuropathologic evidence seems to indicate that:

1. The third frontal gyrus—including the pars orbitalis, pars triangularis, and even the pars opercularis—can be destroyed in the dominant hemisphere and even bilaterally with only mild dysphasia. Bilateral lesions may result in diminished spontaneity, disorders of affect, and dementia, but do not produce Broca's aphasia.

2. Broca's aphasia is characterized by a deficit in speech output ranging from speechlessness through recurrent, stereotyped utterances, to agrammatic and/or poorly articulated speech; by variable deficits in speech comprehension; and often by severe alexia. It often results from extensive lesions of the inferior frontoparietal cortex, including the third frontal gyrus, precentral and postcentral gyri, and inferior parietal lobule.

3. In this extensive area, it appears that the lower half of the precentral

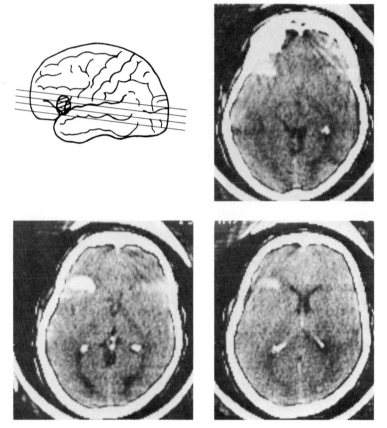

FIGURE 14.9. *CT scan of an unpublished case of Broca's aphasia with a focal lesion of the inferior precentral and postcentral gyrus.*

gyrus is the most critical cortical region. In at least one of our patients, an extensive anatomically verified lesion of the precentral gyrus alone resulted in severe, permanent Broca's aphasia. Destruction of this region or of its callosal and subcortical projections was the one finding invariably encountered in all of our cases and in those reported in the literature.

ANATOMICAL AND PHYSIOLOGICAL STUDIES

The neuropathological evidence that we have reviewed strongly supports a crucial role for lesions of the left precentral gyrus in the production of Broca's aphasia. In this section we shall review some of the neuroanatomical and neurophysiological knowledge bearing on the function of this cortex, particularly its relationship to speech.

The cortex of the precentral gyrus in man and in monkey, consists of two major cytoarchitectural and myeloarchitectural types, both of which are agranular. Area 4, myeloarchitecturally astriate and containing Betz cells in layer V, occupies the anterior bank of the rolandic sulcus and extends forward onto the convexity of the precentral gyrus, less so in man than in monkey. Immediately anteriorly, occupying the remainder of the precentral gyrus, is area 6, which is unistriate and contains no Betz cells.

Pandya and Kuypers (1969) and Jones and Powell (1970) have studied the cortico-cortical connections of these regions in the macaque. Areas 4 and 6 are reciprocally connected. Area 4 is also reciprocally connected to the cortex of the postcentral gyrus; Area 6 is reciprocally connected to Area 5 of the superior parietal lobule, itself a recipient of heavy projections from the postcentral gyrus. Thus, Areas 4 and 6 of the frontal lobe can be considered parts of a more widespread, heavily interconnected system, situated in the frontoparietal region. The system also includes at least Brodmann's areas 3, 1, 2, and 5.

This system appears to function primarily in relation to movement and somatic sensation. The somatotopic motor mapping of the contralateral body-half on the precentral gyrus (MI) is well known. Similar motor maps are present in the postcentral gyrus (SI), in the medial surface of the superior frontal gyrus (MII—supplementary motor area), and in the parietal operculum (SII) (See Figure 14.10). The threshold for movement by electrical stimulation is lowest in the precentral gyrus. It is of interest that the loci for tongue and mouth

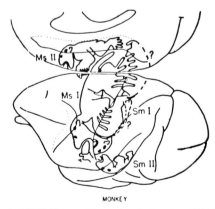

MONKEY

FIGURE 14.10. Woolsey's (1964) diagram illustrating the location of the four major topographically organized areas from which electrical stimulation of the macaque cortex yields movements: MI— (motor) precentral gyrus; MII—(supplementary motor) medial superior frontal gyrus and cingulate sulcus; SI—(somatosensory) postcentral gyrus; SII—(second sensory) parietal operculum.

movements in three of the four motor representations (MI, SI, SII) are nearly contiguous, occupying the inferior portions of the central gyri. It must be emphasized, however, that such maps are potentially misleading. In any given map, there is much overlap of adjacent body parts—that is, movement of a given body part can be elicited by stimulation of an area much wider than its representation on a homunculus or simiusculus (Phillips, 1966). The area depicted on the map is only the most sensitive region in a more widely distributed representation.

Early investigators considered Area 6 and Area 4 to be related hierarchically: Area 6 was a motor association cortex, integrating diverse inputs from all sensory modalities and programming an "executor" Area 4 to carry out complex motor responses. There is, however, little evidence for this view. Woolsey (1952) showed that the somatotopic map MI extended forward, beyond Area 4, into much of Area 6. The map was such that Area 6 mediated movement of the axial musculature and proximal limbs, while Area 4 contained the representations of the distal limbs. Thus Area 4 and the immediately anterior Area 6 appeared to be related not hierarchically but in a complementary manner—that is, as two parts of a single map. Kuypers (1973) and his colleagues, studying the brainstem and spinal cord projections of Areas 4 and 6, have provided evidence consistent with Woolsey's findings. Area 6 projects primarily to the ventromedial portion of the brainstem reticular formation and spinal cord intermediate gray matter. These regions are known to project onto motoneurons controlling the axial muscles and proximal limbs. In contrast, Area 4 projects to the dorsolateral portion of the reticular formation and spinal intermediate zone. These areas project onto motoneurons controlling limb and tongue muscles.

However, the relationship of Area 6 to Area 4 is not completely known. Completion of the motor map MI takes up only some of Area 6. The supplementary motor area is also located in the dorsomedial portion of Area 6 (far from Broca's area), and its functional relationship to MI is unknown. There is still more of Area 6 in the superior frontal gyrus, parts of which yield pupillary dilatation on electrical stimulation (Woolsey, 1952).

Whatever the functional relationship of Areas 6 and 4 actually is, it is clear that the inferior portions of these areas on the precentral gyrus are involved in speech movements. Indeed, Penfield and Roberts (1959) have shown that stimulation of this region (in either hemisphere) in the unanesthetized human can produce rudimentary vocalization. This response cannot be produced from any other cerebral region.

Although the precentral gyrus thus appears to mediate speech, some of the necessary inputs to this area seem to be indirect. One would ordinarily expect that the cerebral region mediating speech should receive strong input from auditory and visual areas of the brain. Yet, if we can extrapolate from the macaque, this does not appear to be the case, at least directly. According to Jones and Powell (1970) and Pandya and Kuypers (1969), the inferior portions of the precentral gyrus (Areas 4 and 6) receive no extensive auditory and visual input. Such input first reaches the frontal lobe via the granular, or prefrontal cortex as well as the cortex of Area 8 that is transitional between agranular cortex (Areas 4 and 6) posteriorly and granular cortex anteriorly. The inferior portion of the transitional and granular cortex, lying in and anterior to the inferior limb of the arcuate sulcus of the macaque, is probably homologous to the third frontal gyrus in man. It has numerous connections to auditory and visual association cortex as well as to polymodal association cortex in the angular gyrus and frontal and temporal poles.

The third frontal gyrus, receiving such a multimodal input, could thus be involved in acts requiring cross-modal integration, including many aspects of language-related behavior. There is little doubt that such is the case. Stimulation of the left third frontal gyrus in man may produce speech arrest or paraphasias, just as does stimulation of the left parietotemporal cortex. But it is also very clear that the third frontal gyrus is not a "motor-memory" store or a motor "association cortex." If it were, stimulation should result in motor phenomena not found with stimulation of other cortical areas. (For example, stimulation of visual and auditory association cortex results in visual and auditory experiences.) But it does not. Penfield and Roberts (1959) could find no difference between the paraphasias produced by stimulating the third frontal gyrus and those obtained from the parietotemporal region. Foerster (1935) was unable to produce any movement by stimulating the third frontal gyrus. It may well be true that activity in the third frontal gyrus indirectly affects Areas 4 and 6. But the connections are unlikely to be powerful and direct.

Thus, although it appears that the third frontal gyrus has a role in language, it is not the specific role of motor learning envisioned by Broca. The lesions producing Broca's aphasia do so by involving the inferior portions of sensorimotor cortex, particularly Areas 6 and 4 of the precentral gyrus. Even these areas may not be related hierarchically: There is no evidence for distinct "memory" and "executor" areas for speech movements.

THE CORTICAL MEDIATION OF SPEECH—AN ALTERNATIVE MODEL

We have outlined the evidence that the true "Broca's area" and motor cortex are not separate cerebral areas but are in fact identical. The classical model, elaborated by Dejerine and by Liepmann, is incorrect. One cannot distinguish a cortex containing "motor engrams" for speech (the third frontal gyrus) from an "executor" cortex (the precentral gyrus), with the former driving the latter. Rather, the sensorimotor cortex for speech musculature, occupying the inferior central gyri, particularly the precentral gyrus, is a single complex whose integrity is necessary for the voluntary movements that we call speech.

We shall now attempt to discuss the pathogenesis of many of the clinical signs of Broca's aphasia in light of this view. This discussion will also serve to refine our understanding of the cerebral control of speech.

Speech and Other Orolaryngeal Movements: Differential Hemispheric Specialization

Broca first observed that although his patient was unable to speak, he had little or no difficulty in utilizing his mouth, tongue, and pharyngeal muscles for other acts, such as swallowing food. This observation led Broca to postulate that the deficit was a loss of motor-speech memories rather than paralysis. The patient no longer could recall "the procedure for articulating words." Later, this distinction between paralysis and loss of "motor-memories" was reflected in models of cerebral localization. A center for motor-speech memories (third frontal gyrus) was distinct from a general, "executor" motor cortex (precentral gyrus) in the left cerebral hemisphere.

We have already pointed out that one rarely, if ever, observes a patient with Broca's aphasia in whom ALL nonspeech movements of mouth, lips, and tongue occur normally (DeRenzi, Pieczuro, and Vignolo, 1966). But SOME acts, such as the ability to move, crush, and ultimately swallow food, are ultimately achieved adequately by nearly all patients with Broca's aphasia. Given that we claim that separate areas for speech and nonspeech movements do not exist, how do we explain why patients who cannot speak can eat? If the lesion in sensorimotor cortex is sufficient to eliminate speech, why do some other orolingual movements still occur?

We suggest that these movements are retained because of preservation of (a) remaining areas of the dominant sensorimotor cortex, and (b) the entire nondominant sensorimotor cortex. We shall discuss the role of the preserved ipsilateral cortex in the next section. Here we shall concentrate on preservation of the entire right hemisphere. In this regard, the orolingual manipulation of food, although admittedly a complex set of movements, can be satisfactorily effected with a single intact hemisphere, which projects bilaterally to bulbar nuclei innervating the oropharyngeal muscles. There is no known difference in the effectiveness of left and right sensorimotor cortex in mediating this behavior (although further study of this matter would be welcome). Speech, however, depends upon the integrity of the left sensorimotor cortex far more than the right. The dominance of left over right hemisphere for speech has been known, of course, since it was postulated by Broca (1861) and by Dax (1865).

It is for this reason, we suggest that a lesion of the left sensorimotor cortex will affect speech more than eating. The following case (Levine and Mohr, 1979—Case 3) illustrates the asymmetry of hemispheric control of speech and the symmetry (and unilateral sufficiency) of the control of eating:

A 20-year-old right-handed woman suddenly became mute with right hemiplegia. After several weeks of speechlessness, she began to use the word here in a stereotyped way and to curse occasionally. Finally, she began to use a variety of single words and an occasional two-word phrase. She retained a good singing voice and was able to sing entire songs with lyrics. She could also recite the Lord's Prayer, the Apostle's Creed, and the preamble to the U.S. Constitution. There was no dysphagia. Nine years later, she suddenly became mute and unable to swallow. One year after this second stroke she swallows with difficulty and remains mute. Her face and tongue are largely immobile, but she often breaks into a broad grin on eye contact with the examiner.

The CT scan of this patient is shown in Figure 14.11. The first stroke was a massive infarction destroying the entire perisylvian region of the left hemisphere. Speech was drastically impaired, and the residual speech was highly similar to that described by Smith (1966) after dominant hemispherectomy for glioma. Nevertheless, swallowing quickly recovered. The second stroke was much smaller and involved the inferior frontoparietal region of the right hemisphere—including motor cortex. This stroke deprived her of her residual speech and significantly impaired swallowing and other oropharyngeal movements.

Hemispheric Specialization is for Tasks—not for "Responses" or for "Comprehension"

It is thus tempting to conclude that some motor acts, such as speech, are left lateralized whereas other acts, such as moving food with the tongue, are not. Although this hypothesis would explain why speechless patients can eat after lesions of the left sensorimotor cortex, it proves to be misleading and oversimplified. It is incorrect to say that "speech" or any other "motor-behavior" is lateralized to the left hemisphere. To specify what is lateralized one must include not only a description of the motor behavior, but also of the CONTEXT in which the behavior occurs—especially the stimulus, if there is one, that provokes the motor act.

Let us take tongue protrusion as an example. A patient with very severe Broca's aphasia (in the early stages following an acute, large left perisylvian lesion) may be unable to protrude his tongue to any form of request, even though he can use the required musculature in swallowing. Somewhat later, he may protrude his tongue in imitation of the examiner but not to spoken or written request. Still later, he may protrude it upon spoken request but not upon written request.

How shall we describe such behavior? We cannot simply say that the deficit is one of output or production. At a certain stage, the patient can deliver the output under some circumstances (e.g., imitation) but not others (e.g., spoken or

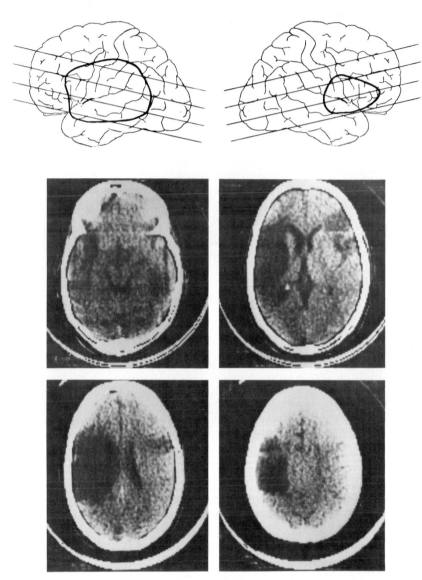

FIGURE 14.11. *Location of lesions in Case 3 of Levine and Mohr (1979) by CT scan.*

written request). We also cannot say that the deficit is one of input or comprehension of speech or print. Some patients, although unable to perform the movement to spoken request, can indicate which of a series of movements performed by the examiner corresponds to the spoken request. Or, although unable to protrude the tongue when asked, the patient may effortfully move the tongue inside his mouth as though "understanding" the spoken request but unable to comply. So either analysis of this behavior as an "output" deficit or as an "input" deficit oversimplifies the picture.

Instead of trying to label the deficit as "output" or "input," it appears better not to subdivide the behavior into such components, but to consider the act as a whole, including the initiating stimulus and the context in which it occurs. In this manner, one can argue that protruding the tongue on imitation, protrusion to spoken request, and protrusion to written request are different acts, each with a distinct neural substrate. These acts became progressively more difficult for the patient with Broca's aphasia because they demand progressively more participation of the left hemisphere.

This hypothesis provides an opportunity to understand the selective deficits of tongue protrusion on an anatomical basis. Ordinarily, activity from the left sensorimotor cortex, projected to the bulbar motor nuclei, is sufficient to mediate tongue protrusion under all of the aforementioned circumstances. This conclusion is warranted because damage to the right sensorimotor cortex, even complete right hemispherectomy, does not usually interfere significantly with such behavior. If the bulbar output of the left sensorimotor cortex is cut off—for example, by infarction in the internal capsule—the various deficits of tongue protrusion occur only transiently or not at all. The explanation for this lack of deficit, we presume, is that output to the brainstem from the right sensorimotor cortex is also sufficient, AS LONG AS THE RIGHT SENSORIMOTOR CORTEX IS CALLOSALLY CONNECTED TO ITS PRESERVED COUNTERPART IN THE LEFT HEMISPHERE. If one adds to the capsular lesion a callosal lesion, disconnecting the left and right sensorimotor cortex, the tongue protrusion deficits will appear. The right sensorimotor cortex will still be able to move the tongue in circumstances such as moving food in the mouth, where activity in the right hemisphere alone is sufficient to mediate the behavior. But where left hemisphere participation is required—as it apparently is to an increasing degree in imitation, response to spoken input, and response to written input—the act becomes increasingly more difficult. The left sensorimotor cortex cannot interact effectively with the right because the main routes for such interaction—the homotopic callosal connections—have been interrupted.

Such double lesions, involving the left internal capsule and the corpus callosum are very rare, although they have been observed (Bonhoeffer, 1914). We have recently seen such a case. The very same effect can be produced by a single lesion, situated deep in the left hemisphere where the projection fibers and the callosal fibers intersect, or it can result from lesion of the left sensorimotor cortex itself. These lesions will interrupt both commissural and subcortical projections, duplicating the effects of the separate lesions described earlier.

The preceding argument is highly similar to that of Liepmann, later reintroduced by Lange (1936) and by Geschwind (1965), to elucidate the neurological substrate of "oral apraxia" associated with Broca's aphasia. We suggest that the same reasoning can be applied to explain the speech deficit as well.

Like the tongue protrusion deficit, the speech difficulty in Broca's aphasia defies description in such simple terms as "output" or "input" disorder. It is not a simple output disorder, akin to the dysarthrias of myasthenia gravis, progressive bulbar palsy, or even pseudobulbar palsy, which involve (bilaterally) the neuromuscular junctions, lower motor neurons, and corticobulbar projections, respectively. In Broca's aphasia, syntactically complex utterances, emitted with little articulatory difficulty, occasionally occur in the form of stereotypes, recitation, or song. Yet, the very same words may fail to occur on request, even in repetition. In those patients whose spontaneous speech amounts to only isolated words, these words may be uttered in some circumstances better than others. For example, such patients usually repeat a noun better than they produce it in naming the corresponding object. This selective failure to utter a word or phrase also cannot be understood simply as a "comprehension" deficit. Some patients may be able to match a spoken or written word or phrase to a picture even when unable to repeat the phrase or read it aloud. Even where this is not the case, the struggling inarticulate output that characterizes Broca's aphasia is hard to reconcile with the notion of a "comprehension" deficit alone.

Accordingly, we propose that, like the "oral apraxia," the speech difficulty in Broca's aphasia can be understood as the effect of (a) depriving the bulbar nuclei of direct output from the left precentral gyrus, and (b) isolating the preserved output of the right precentral gyrus from transcallosal input of the left precentral gyrus. In this way, the bulbar motor nuclei receive input only from an intact right hemisphere that has not learned certain speech acts as well as the left. This effect is most commonly achieved by a single lesion affecting the left precentral gyrus and immediately subjacent white matter.

It might be expected that injury to the sensorimotor cortex itself would have more widespread effects than a combination of interhemispheric disconnection and interruption of the brainstem projections. Lesion of the cortex itself also interrupts intrahemispheric connections between sensorimotor cortex and other areas of the left hemisphere. The combined callosal and capsular lesions may leave these connections intact. We have seen, however, that such intrahemispheric connections are largely within the sensorimotor cortex itself. Noncapsular projections of sensorimotor cortex (such as to the basal ganglia) would also be affected by the cortical lesion but not by the combined capsular–callosal lesions. The significance of these different lesions with regard to the patients' behavior is still unknown.

The Relationship of Speech and Writing

The large majority of patients with Broca's aphasia are agraphic. The right arm is hemiplegic and cannot, of course, write. The left hand usually writes with a coarse, slow, wavering stroke and produces either distorted, unrecognizable letters, or letters that are recognizable but wrong, or an occasional correct word or two. Copying is often better than writing spontaneously or to dictation—but copying, too, may be defective.

To Wernicke and to Dejerine, lesion of the Broca's center of motor-speech memories resulted in BOTH the speechlessness and the agraphia. Writing required "inner speech," and the latter required integrity of Broca's area, Wernicke's area, and their interconnections. Neural activity corresponding to "inner speech" activated the arm area of the left sensorimotor cortex to produce writing.

However, although most nonfluent aphasics are agraphic, not ALL of them are. Conversely, there are rare patients with marked agraphia who have little or no speech deficit. To the classical authors such cases were easily explained. Patients with either pure word mutism or pure agraphia did not have a lesion of Broca's area, but instead had a lesion of "executor" motor cortex. Those who could not speak had a lesion of the portion of executor cortex projecting via brainstem nuclei to the oropharyngeal muscles; those who could not write had unilateral lesions of executor cortex innervating the upper extremity.

But we have done away with separate "motor memory" and "motor executor" areas except insofar as someday sensorimotor cortex itself may become functionally divisible. How, then, do we explain the rare cases of "pure word mutism" or "pure agraphia"?

The answer may lie in lesion size. The sensorimotor cortex runs in a broad strip along the lateral convexity, increasing in width as one ascends dorsomedially from the sylvian fissure toward the interhemispheric fissure. In the homunculus of MI the representation of the upper extremity, although it actually overlaps that of the mouth, has its most sensitive region more dorsally. This anatomical subdivision allows for different effects of lesions depending on their precise location within the sensorimotor cortex.

We propose that "pure word mutism" may result from a discrete lesion of the precentral gyrus, affecting only the inferior portion and sparing the more dorsal representation of arm and hand to a large degree. We also suggest that a more dorsal lesion, affecting the arm and hand area but sparing the inferior face region, may result in right mono- or hemiplegia and agraphia of the left hand without aphasia. A combined lesion of both areas will produce Broca's aphasia.

Existing evidence seems to support this point of view. Three cases of (approximately) "pure word mutism," studied at post-mortem examination, proved to have lesions restricted to the inferior precentral gyrus (Dejerine, 1906; Lecours, 1976). We have seen two such patients, both of whom are still living. Although each clearly had a stroke preceding their aphasia, neither has evidence of an extensive lesion on CT scan. There is only widening of the left sylvian fissure and of the frontal horn of the left lateral ventricle to suggest a small lesion in the appropriate place.

Numerous, but scattered, reports in the literature also suggest that more dorsal circumscribed lesions of sensorimotor cortex may result in agraphia without aphasia. This was probably the stimulus for Exner's (1881) postulating a writing center in the second frontal gyrus. Such cases probably always involve the motor cortex representing the upper extremity in the precentral gyrus.

In contrast to these more circumscribed lesions, patients with Broca's aphasia have larger and/or deeper lesions, compromising BOTH face and upper extremity regions (Mohr, Pessin, Finkelstein, Funkenstein, Duncan and Davis, 1978). We have reported a case of severe, permanent Broca's aphasia, resulting from a superficial lesion of the entire precentral gyrus that did not significantly invade either the frontal gyri anteriorly or the postcentral gyrus posteriorly (Trojanowski, Green, and Levine, 1980). This lesion is shown in Figure 14.8. More frequently, the lesion is smaller but deep, interrupting both callosal and capsular fibers from a wide extent of the precentral gyrus.

We have suggested parallel models for the speech deficit and the writing deficit in Broca's aphasia. Both involve lesions of the sensorimotor cortex— especially the precentral gyrus—of the dominant hemisphere. The mouth and hand areas overlap but are not congruent; so dissociations—occasionally dramatic ones—may occur.

To this point, we have discussed the relationship of deficits of speech and writing with regard to the location of possible lesions within motor cortex of the dominant hemisphere. But is the dominant hemisphere for speech acts and for writing acts necessarily the same? In the neurological literature, surprisingly little attention has been paid to this aspect of the relationship between speech and writing deficits.

The oropharyngeal movements called speech lateralize to the left hemisphere in the majority of people, and most people are also left hemisphere dominant for the performance of many motor acts with the limbs. But speech dominance and limb motor dominance in SOME cases can occur in opposite hemispheres. This is especially the case in left-handed people, presumably right hemisphere dominant for limb motor skills, of whom 60–80% are left hemisphere dominant for speech (Roberts, 1969). In rare instances, right-handed people—presumably left dominant for limb-motor skills—may develop speech in the right hemisphere (Trojanowski, Green, and Levine, 1980).

The lateralization of writing acts is a problem in such cases. Writing is a limb–motor skill, and so might be expected to lateralize with other such skills. However, unlike many other limb movements, writing is learned in intimate association with the hearing, reading, and/or utterance of speech. Acquisition of this skill by the speech dominant hemisphere will be more efficient than by the nonspeech hemisphere, because the latter requires cross-hemispheric integration.[2] In most people who are left hemisphere dominant for both speech and limb praxis, this dual nature of writing creates no conflicts; and this skill happily lateralizes to the left hemisphere. However, what happens to writing in those subjects where speech and limb motor skills lateralize to opposite hemispheres?

The answer is only partially known because the idea of differential lateralization of speech and of imitative limb-motor skills has not been securely established. Left-handed subjects (presumably right-hemisphere dominant for limb-motor skills) who lateralize speech to the left hemisphere may certainly become agraphic with lesions of the speech-dominant hemisphere. It is claimed that such a patient may also become agraphic with lesions of the limb-motor dominant right hemisphere (Heilman, Coyle, Gonyea, and Geschwind, 1973). Can any such patient become agraphic with a suitably placed lesion in either hemisphere? Or do such patients differ from one another, so that some will become agraphic only with lesions of the left hemisphere, and others only with lesions of the right?

Even less is known about the rare right-handers with speech in the right hemisphere. Such patients may become agraphic with lesions of the speaking right hemisphere, as in our case (Trojanowski, Green, and Levine, 1980). We know of no case of a right-handed patient, right dominant for speech, in whom a left hemisphere lesion produced pure agraphia (without aphasia) of the left hand.

Deficits of "Comprehension" in Broca's Aphasia

We have already mentioned that patients with Broca's aphasia usually show some difficulty comprehending speech, marked alexia, and difficulty comprehending numbers and arithmetic operations. Of course, every test of comprehension requires some responses from the patient. When the response is correct, we confidently assert that the patient comprehended. However, when the patient fails we invariably start to wonder whether the failure is one of "comprehension" or of "response generation" (praxis); that is, a "comprehension defect" is not something that most people will allow as directly observable. One approach to this problem is to keep the input constant but to simplify the motor response that is required. If this simplification allows the patient to pass the test, one might argue that "comprehension" is preserved and the deficit is one of "response generation."

---

[2]Myers (1965) has shown that, in the monkey, discriminations that require activity within a single hemisphere only (e.g., input from right visual field, output from right hand) are more efficiently learned than discriminations that require cross-hemispheric integration via the corpus callosum (e.g., input from right visual field, output from left hand). We have suggested that this efficiency difference may be the basis for the normal right ear superiority in dichotic listening and the right visual field superiority in identifying letters (Levine and Calvanio, 1980, and this volume).

In this sense, there is no avoiding the fact that most patients with well-developed Broca's aphasia have deficits of comprehension. Even if one simplifies the motor response to pointing to the correct element in a set of a few choices, there are difficulties. The patient with Broca's aphasia cannot point with normal facility to the printed word that completes an incomplete sentence. He may even show deficits in matching single dictated words or printed words to pictures—whether the words be names of arithmetic operations, numbers, objects, or colors.

It is often suggested that such comprehension deficits result from extension of the lesion into the posterior parietal or posterior temporal lobes. This suggestion, unsupported by evidence, is largely based on difficulty understanding how lesions in "motor" areas of the brain can impair comprehension, especially since "centers" for speech comprehension and for print comprehension supposedly exist in the left posterior temporal and posterior parietal lobes. These posterior centers should be able to activate the right hemisphere transcallosally. Intrahemispheric paths in the right hemisphere should then suffice to activate the right motor cortex, allowing successful performance of the required task. But such is not the case. Severe alexia and considerable speech comprehension difficulty may result from lesions of the left precentral gyrus that leave the posterior temporoparietal language area largely intact. Such was the case in the patients whose lesions we have previously demonstrated (Figures 14.8–14.9). Activation of the right motor cortex from the left posterior region by a combination of posterior transcallosal and right hemispheric activation cannot alone mediate normal comprehension (Levine, Hier, and Calvanio, 1981).

It is thus clear that the cortex of the left precentral gyrus participates actively not only in behavior requiring overt speech or complex limb movement, but in acts of language comprehension as well. Perhaps this results from the fact that the child employs speech and thus activates the left precentral gyrus as he masters comprehension skills during childhood. The cortical substrate of an acquired skill may be no more than the network of cortical neurons activated during its acquisition. If so, it is not surprising that deficits of comprehension as well as speech occur with lesions of the left precentral gyrus.

Regardless of the validity of this speculation, the fact remains that damage confined to the precentral gyrus may impair not only speech but comprehension of language as well. It is incorrect to omit the precentral gyrus in maps of the language area (Dejerine, 1914). More importantly, it becomes clear that identifying abstract psychological functions ("comprehension" or "semantic access"; "production" or "syntactic and/or phonologic encoding") with highly circumscribed areas of cortex is probably quite unwise. Although we might build a brain by interconnecting a set of independent modules, each with a common sense psychological subfunction in the genesis of language acts, nature has evidently chosen another way.

REFERENCES

Benson, D. F., and Patten, D. H. (1967). The use of radioactive isotopes in the localization of aphasia-producing lesions. *Cortex*, 3, 258–271.

Bonhoeffer, K. (1914). Klinischer und anatomischer Befund zur Lehre von der Apraxie und der Motorischen Sprachbahn. *Monatshrift für Psychiatrie und Neurologie*, 35, 113–128.

Broca, P. (1861). Nouvelle observation d'aphemie produite par une lesion de la partie posterieure des deuxieme et troisieme circonvolutions frontales. *Bull Soc Anat Paris*, 6, 398–407.

Conrad, K. (1954). New problems of aphasia. *Brain*, 77, 491–509.

Dax, M. (1865). Lesions de la moitie gauche de l'encephale coincidant avec l'oubli des signes de la pensee. *Gaz. Hebd.* 2 eme serie, 2.

Dejerine, J. (1906). L'aphasie motrice; sa localisation et son anatomie pathologique. *Presse Medicale*, 14, 453–457.

Dejerine, J. (1914). Semiologie des affections du systeme nerveux. Paris: Masson.

DeRenzi, E., Pieczuro, A., and Vignolo, L. A. (1966). Oral apraxia and aphasia. *Cortex*, 2, 50–73.

Exner, S. (1881). Untersuchungen uber die Lokalisation der Funktionen in der Grosshirnrinde des Menschen. Vienna: Braunmuller.

Foerster, O. (1935). Motorische Felder und Bahnen. In O. Bumke and O. Foerster (Eds.), *Handbuch der Neurologie*, Vol. 6. Berlin: Springer.

Foulis, D. (1879). A case in which there was destruction of the third left frontal convolution with aphasia. *British Medical Journal*, 1, 383–384.

Fritsch, G., Hitzig, E. (1870). Über die elektrische Erregbarkeit des Grosshirns. *Archiv für Anatomie, Physiologie, und Wissenschaftliche Medicin*, 37, 300–332.

Geschwind, N. (1965). Disconnexion syndrome in animals and man. *Brain*, 88, 237–294, 585–644.

Goodglass, H., and Kaplan, E. (1972). *The assessment of aphasia and related disorders*. Philadelphia: Lea & Febiger.

Heilman, K. M., Coyle, J. M., Gonyea, E. F., and Geschwind, N. (1973). Apraxia and agraphia in a left-hander. *Brain*, 96, 21–28.

Henschen, S. E. (1920–1922). *Klinische und anatomische Beitrage zur Pathologie des Gehirns*. Stockholm: Nordiske Bokhandeln.

Jones, E. G., and Powell, T. P. S. (1970). An anatomical study of converging sensory pathways within the cerebral cortex of the monkey. *Brain*, 93, 793–820.

Kertesz, A., Lesk, D., McCabe, P. (1977). Isotope localization of infarcts in aphasia. *Archives of Neurolology*, 34, 590–601.

Kuypers, H. G. J. M. (1973). The anatomical organization of the descending pathways and their contributions to motor control especially in primates. In J.E. Desmedt (Ed.), *New developments in electromyography and clinical neurophysiology*, Vol. 3. Basel: Karger.

Lange, J. (1936). Agnosien und Apraxien. In O. Bumke and O. Foerster (Eds.), *Handbuch der Nerologie*, Vol. 6. Berlin: Springer.

LaSalle Archambault (1913). Contribution a l'etude des localisations de l'aphasie. *Nouvelle Iconographie de la Salpettiere*, 26, 20–27.

Lecours, A. R. (1976). The "pure form" of the phonetic disintegration syndrome (pure anarthria): Anatomo-clinical report of a historic case. *Brain*, 3, 88–113.

Levine, D. N., and Calvanio, R. (1980). Visual discrimination after lesion of the posterior corpus callosum. *Neurology*, 30, 21–30.

Levine, D. N., Hier, D. B., and Calvanio, R. (1981). Acquired learning disability for reading after left temporal lobe damage in childhood. *Neurology* 31:257–264.

Levine, D. N., and Mohr, J. P. (1979). Language after bilateral cerebral infarctions: Role of the minor hemisphere in speech. *Neurology*, 29, 917–938.

Liepmann, H. (1908). *Drei Aufsatze aus dem Apraxiegebiet*. Belin: Karger.

Liepmann, H. (1915). Diseases of the brain. In C. W. Burr (Ed.), *Curschmann's textbook on nervous diseases*. Philadelphia: P. Blackiston.

Luria, A. R. (1970). *Traumatic aphasia*. The Hague: Mouton.

Marie, P., and Foix, C. (1917). The aphasias of war. In M. F. Cole and M. Cole (Trans.), *Pierre Marie's papers on speech disorders*. New York: Hafner, 1971. (Originally in *Revue Neurologique*, 1917, 31/32, 53–87.)

Mohr, J. P., Pessin, M. S., Finkelstein, S., Funkenstein, H. H., Duncan, G. W., and Davis, K. R. (1978). Broca aphasia: Pathologic and clinical aspects. *Neurology*, 28, 311–324.

Moutier, F. (1908). *L'Aphasie de Broca*. Paris: Steinheil.

Myers, R. E. (1965). The neocortical commissures and interhemispheric transmission of information. In E. G. Ettlinger (Ed.), *Functions of the corpus callosum*. Boston: Little Brown.

Nathan, P. W. (1947). Facial apraxia and apraxic dysarthria. *Brain*, 70, 449–468.

Niessl von Mayendorf, E. (1926). Über die sog. Brocasche Windung und ihre angebliche Bedeutung für den motorischen Sprachakt. *Monatschrift für Psychiatrie und Neurologie*, 61, 129–146.

Pandya, D., and Kuypers, H. G. J. M. (1969). Cortico-cortical connections in the rhesus monkey. *Brain*, 13, 13–36.

Penfield, W., and Roberts, L. (1959). *Speech and brain mechanisms*. Princeton: Princetown University Press.

Phillips, C. G. (1966). Changing concepts of the precentral motor area. In J. C. Eccles (Ed.), *Brain and conscious experience*. New York: Springer-Verlag.

Roberts, L. (1969). Cerebral dominance. In P. J. Vinken and G. W. Bruyn (Eds.), *Handbook of clinical neurology*, Vol. 4. Amsterdam: North-Holland.

Schiller, F. (1947). Aphasia studies in patients with missile wounds. *Journal of Neurology, Neurosurgery, and Psychiatry* 10, 183–197.

Smith, A. (1966). Speech and other functions after left (dominant) hemispherectomy. *Journal of Neurology, Neurosurgery, and Psychiatry*, 29, 467–471.

Trojanowski, J. W., Green, R. C., and Levine, D. N. (1980). Crossed aphasia in a dextral: A clinicopathological study. *Neurology*, 30, 709–713.

Trousseau, A. (1864). De l'aphasie, maladie decrite recemment sous le nom impropre d'aphemie. *Gazette des Hospitaux* (Paris) 37.

Wernicke, C. (1874). Der aphasische Symptomencomplex. Breslau: Cohn and Weigert.

Woolsey, C. N., Settlage, P. H., Meyer, D. R., Sencer, W., Hamuy, T. P., and Travis, A. M. (1952). Patterns of localization in precentral and "supplementary" motor areas and their relation to the concept of a premotor area. Research Publications. Association for Research in Nervous and Mental Disease 30, 238–264.

Woolsey, C. N. (1958). Organization of somatic sensory and motor areas of the cerebral cortex. In H. F. Harlow and C. N. Woolsey (Eds.), *Biological and biochemical basis of behavior*. Madison: University of Wisconsin Press.

Woolsey, C. N. (1964). In G. Schaltenbrand and C. Woolsey (Eds.), *Principles of Cerebral Localization and Organization*. Madison: University of Wisconsin Press.

15

Localization of Lesions in Fluent Aphasics

Andrew Kertesz

INTRODUCTION

The distinctiveness of fluent aphasics has been recognized since Wernicke. His model was based on a sensory–motor or neural dichotomy rather than the more recently embraced fluent–nonfluent psycholinguistic distinction. It is not entirely accidental that the two overlap to a great extent. This coincidence of neural and linguistic dichotomies provides a framework for interpretation of aphasic data, which may facilitate the formulation of neural models of language processes.

A pragmatic and useful approach is to start with a clinical grouping or taxonomy which has been accepted and refined by generations of neurologists, psychologists, and neurolinguists. An agreement about these clinical entities is to a certain extent essential to the study of localization of lesions producing these impairments. The problems inherent in these taxonomies and in the process of lesion localization have received a great deal of discussion and are detailed elsewhere (Kertesz, 1979).

The many limitations of the autopsy correlations which were relied upon in the past have now been surmounted by a significant advance in our imaging techniques in vivo while the aphasic patient is still under observation (see the case studies in Chapter 2 of this volume). There are numerous problems in methodology but they are partially overcome by administering a quantitative neurolinguistic examination at the time of the anatomical localization. The correlation of the two sets of data is based on the premise that certain combinations of signs and symptoms recur with a predictable frequency. Their clustering may have a neuroanatomical basis, and it is the purpose of this investigation to test that hypothesis.

The taxonomy of fluent aphasics, as given in Table 15.1, is extended beyond the classification based on fluency, comprehension, repetition, and nam-

NEURAL MODELS OF
LANGUAGE PROCESSES

TABLE 15.1
Comprehension, Repetition, Naming, and Speech Output Characteristics of Fluent Aphasia

Aphasia type	Comprehension	Repetition	Naming	Speech Output
1. Conduction aphasia	Good	Poor	Good	Phonemic parapha-sias
2. Transcortical sensory aphasia	Poor	Good	Poor	Semantic jargon
3. Anomic aphasia	Good	Good	Poor	Circumlocutory, empty, few verbal paraphasias
4. Wernicke's aphasia	Poor	Poor	Poor	
Type I				Mainly verbal paraphasias
Type II				Mainly phonemic paraphasias
Type III				Semantic jargon
Type IV				Neologistic jargon
Type V				Undifferentiated jargon
Type VI				Mumbling jargon
Type VII				Pure word deafness

ing emphasized in our case studies (see Chapter 2, Table 2.1) by a consideration of qualitative differences in speech output (for a review of the linguistic features, see Buckingham and Kertesz, 1976; Lecours and Rouillon 1976). The additional categories are the following: neologistic jargon, undifferentiated jargon, semantic jargon, mumbling fluent speech, circumlocutory empty speech, fluent speech with verbal paraphasias, and predominantly phonemic paraphasias. In this classification, comprehension and repetition continue to play an important role in distinguishing various fluent aphasias:

The four main groups of Table 15.1 are accepted by most investigators, although there has been some opposition to conduction and transcortical aphasias, mainly from psychologists who consider these an artefact of emphasizing the role of repetition. Taxonomic studies with objective clustering (Kertesz and Phipps, 1977) indicate that there are probably two distinct groups of conduction aphasias: One group, characterized by a more hesitant speech with many phonemic approximations and excellent comprehension, is labeled "efferent conduction aphasia"; the other, characterized by fluent and paraphasic speech with some comprehension difficulty, is labeled "afferent conduction aphasia." A similar distinction was made on a phonological basis by Blumstein, Cooper, Goodglass, Statlender, and Goltlieb (1980).

The subdivision of Wernicke's aphasia into various groups has been attempted by several investigators (Huber, Stachowiak, Poeck, and Kerschensteiner, 1975). To many clinicians it is clear that what is called Wernicke's aphasia is not a uniform entity and that further subdivisions exist. Just how far one may justifiably subdivide or lump together these patients depends on the purpose and philosophy underlying one's taxonomy.

LOCALIZATION IN WERNICKE'S APHASIA

The history of localization of Wernicke's aphasia began, of course, with Wernicke, who was the first to introduce the motor–sensory dichotomy in the study of language. This motor–sensory dichotomy originated from Meynert who among others recognized that the frontal part of the brain is concerned with motor mechanisms and the posterior part of the brain with sensory physiology. Wernicke applied this insight onto language, publishing two cases with autopsies in his historic article (Wernicke, 1874). One of these involved stroke with generalized atrophy as well, and because of this was considered to be a poor case by later critics. The other case involved a cerebral abscess, which occupied much of the temporal lobe. Wernicke did not distinguish between jargonaphasia or ordinary circumlocutory paraphasic aphasia.

Ever since then, there have been quite a few autopsy cases published with clinical descriptions. One of the first to collect a series of these was an American neurologist, Starr (1889) who analyzed 50 cases of sensory aphasia with autopsy confirmation. He drew the conclusion that there was no difference in the localization between the cases with or without paraphasia.

The most extensive series is Henschen's. Henschen collected all the cases of sensory aphasia with autopsy in the literature up to that time in the sixth volume of his *Pathologie des Gehirns* (1920). His collection is monumental, but it suffers from scanty descriptions and the autopsy material is often mangled or poorly illustrated. Frequently, only one dimension is shown and the extent of the lesion cannot be determined. The majority of the cases do not have illustrations and one has to accept the author's verbal description. In many cases where the photographs available in Henschen's books are quite good the descriptions are telegraphic and inconsistent. Very often there is no description of the patient's spontaneous speech apart from the statement that it is paraphasic. No mention is made of repetition in the majority of cases, and there is a lack of uniformity of the psychological and linguistic examination of the patients. Notwithstanding, Henschen drew several conclusions which were justified to some extent considering the large number of cases. Among his conclusions were the following:

1. Word deafness is in fact part of the paraphasic language disorder, but it may exist separately. In that case, it is justified to call it "pure word deafness."

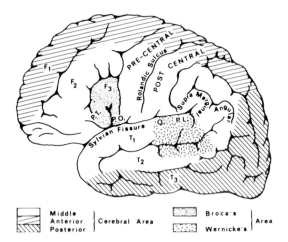

FIGURE 15.1. *The lateral gyri and sulci of the brain after Sobotta and Figge's atlas (1963). The areas of supply by the three major cerebral arteries are indicated. The gyri labeled are: F$_1$, F$_2$, F$_3$ = first (superior) frontal gyrus, etc.; T$_1$, T$_2$, T$_3$ = first (superior) temporal gyrus, etc.; P.T. = pars triangularis; P.O. = pars opercularis; Q. = Heschl's gyrus; and P.L. = planum temporale Q and PL. are inside the sylvian fissure].)*

2. The "Q" (Heschl's) gyrus is always involved, but the lesion does not have to be bilateral.

3. The first and second temporal convolutions (T1 and T2) are also involved, as a rule, in the cases of paraphasic aphasia.

4. For jargon, the lesion involves the Q gyrus plus the temporal operculum behind the Q gyrus plus T1 and T2. This fairly large area thus includes what is generally called Wernicke's area (Figure 15.1).

Subsequent to Henschen, sporadic efforts at localization resulted in some rather speculative and unsubstantiated claims. For instance, Kleist (1962) provided extensive anatomical divisions of the temporal lobe on the basis of myeloarchitectonics but the clinical correlation for the eight cases described was inconsistent. This, then, represents the bulk of the studies in autopsy localization of fluent aphasia, and anybody who claims that we have already as much information about localization as is likely to be useful has to contend with this material.

LESIONS IN NEOLOGISTIC JARGON

The first set presented here concerns the localization of the lesions from neologistic jargonaphasics (Type V). The patients included in this group were selected from a larger group of Wernicke's aphasics because of the unique, voluble, neologistic jargon, with many of the substantives (nouns and verbs) completely transformed so that they represent neologisms which remain, however, within the phonemic and even syntactic constraints of English. The excessive paraphasic speech under pressure (logorrhea), the severe comprehension deficit, and the failure to recognize their disability (anosognosia) characterize these patients to such an extent that most clinicans will agree to the distinctiveness of this syndrome. The most important feature, the abundance of neologisms or unrecognizable paraphasias within the boundaries of normal phonology, is illustrated in the transcripts of J.A. in Chapter 2 of this volume.

One of our cases had autopsy confirmation of the infarct. The difference between our autopsy and Henschen's cases was the opportunity we had had to examine the patient in detail with our standardized aphasia battery. We can establish that this patient does in fact belong to the neologistic jargon group. Figure 15.2 is a photograph of the lateral aspect of the brain. The granular surface and the adherent vascular membrane distinguishes the lesion from the healthy gyri. The lesion is restricted to the posterior end of the sylvian fissure. A cross-section (Figure 15.3) shows that the supramarginal gyrus is greatly involved. The parietal operculum is infarcted, but the posterior aspect of the superior temporal gyrus is not involved to a great extent except the very last

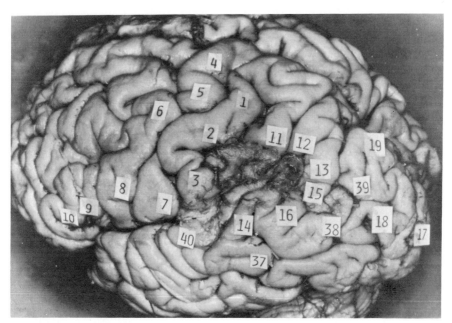

FIGURE 15.2. *The lateral surface of the brain of a case of neologistic jargon 2 months postonset.*

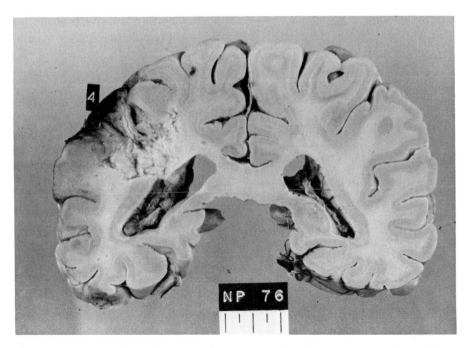

FIGURE 15.3. *Coronal cut of the brain of the same case of neologistic jargon as in Figure 15.2.* (From Kertesz, 1981).

portion (one-fifth) and the inside of the temporal operculum behind Heschl's gyrus. This is a relatively small portion of Wernicke's area. This patient had an isotope scan 4 weeks after his stroke which shows the same size and locus. The isotope scan is positive in the acute state. The clinical examination is also 5 weeks poststroke and the autopsy is 2 months poststroke, so the correlation is close. For a detailed description of the use of isotope and CT scanning, the reader should refer to Chapter 2 of this volume and to my text (Kertesz, 1979).

Lateral views of the isotope scans from our 1970 study of neologistic jargon (Kertesz and Benson, 1970) are overlapped in Figure 15.4. The coronal cut is based on the overlap of five autopsies (Figure 15.5). The reason the autopsies are used for the coronal illustrations is that isotope coronal views are not focused enough to be representative on a single anatomical template. The isotope lateral views are much more useful, but the anteroposterior (coronal) views are very difficult to draw any direct anatomical conclusion from. The overlap is based on the autopsied cases of neologistic jargon in which the crosscuts were available. The supramarginal gyrus and the posterior temporal operculum, that is, the planum temporale, are involved in the overlap. The isotope overlap of our more recent series of cases (Figure 15.6) represents what we collected from 1970 on as

NEOLOGISTIC JARGON-
ISOTOPE & AUTOPSY OVERLAP

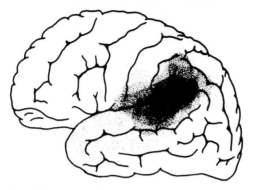

FIGURE 15.4. *Overlap of the tracings of nine lesions from the 1970 study on the lateral template.*

a control study to see if we could confirm the previous results. The overlap areas are identical. Again we found that the lesions involve the temporal lobe and the supramarginal gyrus. The lesions are large, and the isotope overlap indicates that the temporal lobe is usually more involved than in our autopsied case of jargon presented here.

The neologistic jargon overlaps were done on the computerized tomography scans (CT) as well (Figures 15.7–15.9). The lowest cut at the front is across Broca's area (F3) which is intact and the lesions are restricted to the temporal lobe. The next level involves Wernicke's area, and the next goes up to the parietal region, at the level of the supramarginal gyrus. The overlaps indicate that the lesions involve the superior temporal and supramarginal gyrus regions.

AUTOPSIED   NEOLOGISTIC   JARGON

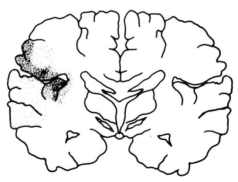

FIGURE 15.5. *Overlap of the tracings of four lesions of the 1970 study where coronal sections were available (all autopsies).*

NEOLOGISTIC JARGON - ISOTOPE OVERLAP

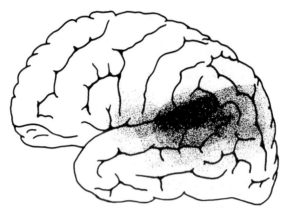

FIGURE 15.6. *Overlap of the lateral isotope scans of neologistic jargon patients since 1970. Note similarity to Figure 15.4. The superior temporal gyrus and supramarginal gyrus are affected in every case. (From Kertesz, 1981.)*

LESIONS IN SEMANTIC JARGON

The second group of patients distinguished have semantic jargon. We separated these patients because they are clinically distinct enough that we feel such separation is justified and useful. These patients are very interesting in that they have a comprehension deficit and when they are asked questions, they respond

NEOLOGISTIC   JARGON CT OVERLAP

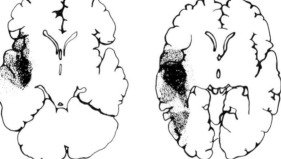

FIGURE 15.7. *Overlap of CT scans of neologistic jargon patients. Cuts 1 and 2 are through the posterior inferior frontal and inferior temporal regions. The overlap is in the temporal lobe. (From Kertesz, 1981.)*

NEOLOGISTIC JARGON CT OVERLAP

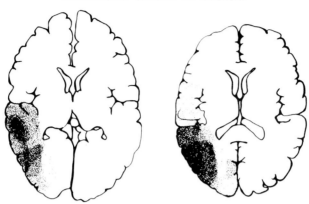

FIGURE 15.8. *Overlap of CT scans of neologistic jargon patients. Cuts 3 and 4 are through the superior frontal, superior temporal, and supramarginal regions. The overlap involves the superior temporal and the supramarginal areas. (From Kertesz, 1981.)*

very fluently but their replies are irrelevant jargon although the paraphasias are not neologistic. When seen for the first time, these patients are often considered to be confused. However, they have a focal lesion and their disturbance is easy to distinguish from confusion by the string of paraphasic words. Their output may be under pressure, but it is without phonemic paraphasia of any significant degree—we exclude patients from the semantic jargon group if they have many phonemic paraphasias. The following transcript serves to illustrate semantic jargon:

NEOLOGISTIC JARGON CT OVERLAP

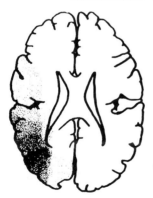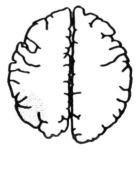

FIGURE 15.9. *Overlap of CT scans of neologistic jargon patients. Cuts 5 and 6 are through the inferior and superior parietal area. The overlap is in the inferior parietal region. (From Kertesz, 1981.)*

E: Can you tell me a little about why you're in Hospital?

P: Well... I had—I cut my thumb off one day.

E: Um-hum.

P: And the boss wanted me change my life. Uh said why don't you make it easy so uh... changed—change a hand out and give a guy a new—Say here, you take the job over and yest you walk around just be the boss.

E: Oh that was good.

P: Al(?) I—fell here and bust this here.

E: Oh, your hip?

P: Yup.

E: Um-hum.

P: Last—two years ago last April.

E: Um-hum.

P: So that was that. Landed in the hospital on a Monday night—laid there Monday, Tuesday, Wednesday... when they let me out.

E: Um-hum.

P: And they... stood me up—and I fell off the tree and umwife—my wife died about six years and I woke up to three and fell out and fell in front of to it. I laid dere fer—at afternoon an' I got out at tree an'—er fell out of the tree I should say—an see [low volume] daughter an'—took me out to St. Joe's and I laid dere and I was there for uh—seven days.

Although there is a definite clinical difference between semantic jargon and neologistic jargon, there apparently is only a minor difference in the localization of lesions producing them: In semantic jargon, lesions do not extend as far posteriorly. There is also a size difference in the lesions: Smaller lesions occur with semantic jargon and larger ones with the neologistic variety. The question then arises, Is semantic jargon only a milder variety of neologistic jargon? This is reasonable in view of the common localization and the common behavioral features such as the fluency, the pressure of speech, and the anosognosia or the nonrecognition of the speech deficit. However, the linguistic difference is substantial, and the appearance of neologisms indicates involvement of the phonemic selector in addition to the impaired semantic selection process. It is possible that further studies in localization will show a significant difference as to the involvement of the supramarginal gyrus region. However the evidence so far is not sufficient to make a distinction on this basis.

TRANSCORTICAL SENSORY APHASIA

Transcortical sensory aphasics have language output similar to that of Wernicke's but can clearly be differentiated by testing repetition (see Chapter 2, case studies). Some authors ignore repetition, arguing that repetition has nothing to do with communication and that it is an artefact of testing. However, if one does not separate these patients on account of their well-preserved repetition, one misses a distinct entity with a different prognosis and localization. We found this localization clearly posterior to anything we had seen so far in Wernicke's aphasia, as shown by Figure 15.10. This figure is an example of a CT scan with

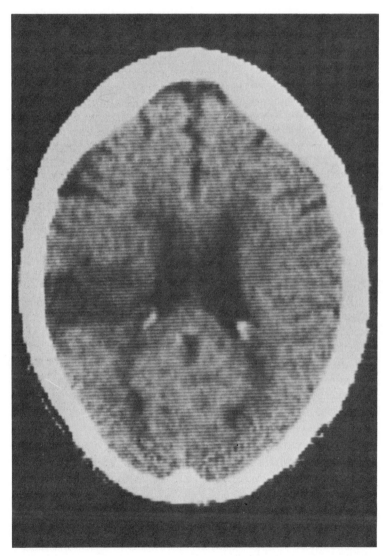

FIGURE 15.10. *CT scan in a case of transcortical sensory aphasia. The darker infarcted area is surrounded by high density contrast indicated excess circulation at the edge of the lesion or "luxury perfusion" outside the ischemic area. The infarct is in the posterior cerebral and its watershed area.*

"luxury perfusion" around the infarct. The patchy whitish appearance is due to the iodine containing contrast injected at the time of the scan. This enhancement is seen in the acute stage and it indicates a functional change around the lesion. The lesion is posterior, in posterior cerebral artery territory and outside the middle cerebral artery territory speech areas (see Figure 15.1). The patient was hemianopic, and had pure alexia without agraphia, seen with occipital infarcts.

Transcortical sensory aphasics recover well. When examined 4–8 weeks later, the whole syndrome may be gone, and therefore it is very important to examine these patients in acute hospitals. In chronic rehabilitation clinics, one will not see transcortical sensory aphasics for the reason that the syndrome is a transient one. Sometimes the lesion is in an area that is not clearly middle cerebral, nor clearly posterior cerebral in distribution, but in between—the so-called watershed area. (See Figure 15.1). According to the disconnection hypothesis, the intact Wernicke's area enables the patient to repeat well, but the lesion cuts the connections to association areas, interfering with comprehension. Spontaneous speech is not monitored by these disconnected areas and therefore the patient's output is semantic jargon, presumably due to a lexical selector running unchecked by an internal monitor, possibly the auditory association (Wernicke's) area.

PURE WORD DEAFNESS

We had a patient who did not seem to hear but whose speech output was reasonably normal, even though at times quite irrelevant to what was asked. He tried to pay attention, asking for the question to be repeated in the manner of the deaf, and often said that he did not hear. He read much better, although he made some mistakes, and he communicated well by asking people to write down what they wanted. His pure tone audiometry was normal and his elementary auditory preception was considered normal by all our methods. Repetition was very poor initially, but his condition persisted only for the first month and then he displayed a transcortical sensory syndrome, when he started to repeat very well. He had a moderate-sized lesion in the superior temporal region. The CT lesion appears less dense and this may account for his substantial recovery.

CONDUCTION APHASIA

The localization of lesions by autopsy in conduction aphasia has been reviewed in several studies (e.g., Benson, Sheremata, Bouchard, Segarra, Price, and Geschwind, 1973; Damasio and Damasio, 1980; Green and Howes, 1977).

Our published CT studies (Kertesz, Harlock, and Coates, 1979) indicate that a relatively small lesion disconnecting posterior temporal and frontal regions is often responsible for the syndrome. Figure 15.11 is an example of the slit-like lesions seen on the CT. Although most of the lesions are anterior to Wernicke's area (posterior third of the superior temporal lobe), some are deep, superior or even posterior to it. All of these locations are compatible with lesions of the arcuate fisciculus, the large path connecting the temporal with the parietal and frontal lobes, first arching back, then curving up to the parietal lobe and forward to the frontal lobe. The involvement of this fasciculus in conduction aphasia was

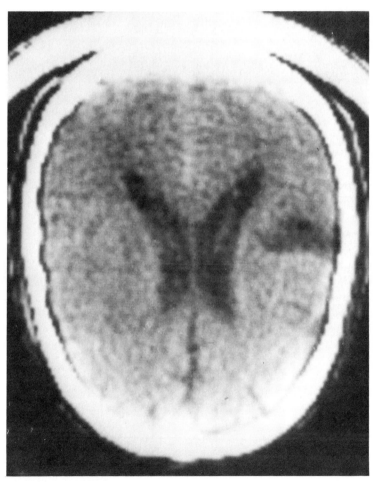

FIGURE 15.11. *A case of conduction aphasia. The lesion disconnects the temporal and frontal speech areas. The insular cortex and the underlying white matter (arcuate fasciculus) are both involved.*

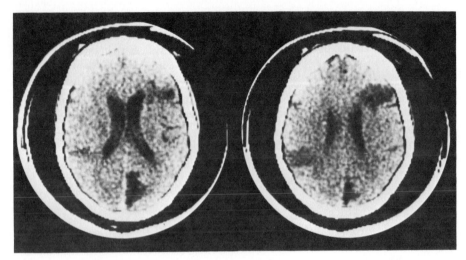

FIGURE 15.12. *Another case of conduction aphasia. The lesion is more posterior probably involving the arcuate fasciculus only. Other lesions in the right hemisphere occurred at different times.*

suggested by Wernicke (1908) and Geschwind (1965). As the arcuate fasciculus curves posteriorly on its way up and forward in the frontal lobes, the posterior involvement indicates that damage to this structure can occur at more than one site in the production of this syndrome. Some of the more anterior lesions have been localized to the insula by Damasio and Damasio (1980). They made the suggestion already postulated by Wernicke 100 years ago, that the sensory-motor speech connections pass through the insula rather than the arcuate fasciculus. The lesion illustrated here also disconnects intact Wernicke's area and intact Broca's area, but is definitely located in the parietal lobe and not in the insula. Whether one considers this an arcuate fasciculus lesion or a supramarginal parietal operculum lesion, it is a matter of putting the emphasis on the cortical or subcortical damage. We had another patient whose lesion did not affect the parietal operculum or the insula but only the arcuate fasciculus (Figure 15.12). It seems that the same clinical syndrome can be produced by lesions at different locations especially when an important connecting system has a long course. The variation in location may contribute to the taxonomic differences referred to in the introduction to this chapter.

MUMBLING JARGON

Mumbling jargon has been observed by us on several occasions, usually in cases in conjunction with large temporal lesions. These are often elderly patients who seem to be globally affected initially, with very poor comprehension and a low volume, barely intelligible mumbling jargon. This is distinct from other forms of jargonaphasia because of the articulatory-phonatory disturbance. Patients are not hemiplegic as a rule, and their behavior disturbance is similar to other cases of Wernicke's aphasia with persisting impairment of comprehension, repetition, and naming, but fluent speech output. By listening carefully, one can discern enough phonemic variability to consider these utterances more than the stereotypics of global aphasics. We do not have enough material for reliably distinct localization, but the lesions appear to be quite extensive although restricted below the sylvian fissure. Just how much cortical or subcortical degeneration on the contralateral hemisphere and in the extrapyramidal system contributes to this rather infrequent phenomenon is as yet unknown. One suspects subcortical or thalamic mechanisms to be involved because of the low volume rapid articulation (palilalia) resembles the voice disorder that is often observed in Parkinson's disease.

UNDIFFERENTIATED JARGON

Alajouanine (1956) coined this term for stereotypic utterances. Since then, it has not been used only for that pattern but also for a string of uninterrupted neologisms without any connecting words or grammatical markers to differentiate them into a syntactic structure (Brown, 1979).

CONCLUSION

The extent of the overlap in lesions of different patients is very good in jargonaphasia. These lesions involve the posterior superior temporal and inferior parietal regions. The point worth making is that only certain parts of the brain are involved for this particular behavior, and yet to produce this syndrome one has to have a certain type of lesion. The only way to create a somewhat similar behavior in normals is by delayed auditory feedback, as in the experiments reported by Lee (1950). These experiments have not been replicated as far as I know, and they produced only certain amounts of paraphasias, not the kind of jargon behavior these patients show. Certainly the whole range of behavior cannot be replicated in any other way than through these particular lesions.

The mechanisms underlying jargon production are obviously complex, but they have to be reconciled with the anatomical evidence. There have been several theories advanced to explain the phenomena. The most durable one, originated by Wernicke himself, is that the lack of auditory monitoring results in a jumble of speech output. This, however, does not fully explain why some patients with conduction aphasia have a great deal of phonemic paraphasias—similar to, although not quite the same as, neologistic jargon—but no comprehension deficit. Another theory is that the phonemic assembly itself is damaged, regardless of the comprehension deficit which may be just a coincidental feature. This may be a suitable explanation for some of the paraphasic phenomena but it is not adequate to explain the anosognosia for the langauge disturbance. A third theory enlarges on the actual production of the neologisms and considers the basic problems of lexical selection to be complicated by a superimposed phonemic selection disturbance. Verbal paraphasias are further distorted by phonemic errors and become unrecognizable in the process. Such a two-stage theory was originally proposed by Pick (1931) and later advanced by Brown (1972) and Buckingham and Kertesz (1976). Some sort of defective inhibition of the selector mechanisms still has to be postulated, otherwise anomic gaps would occur as in other cases of aphasia, such as anomic or Broca's. Indeed, anomic gaps appear as cases of neologistic jargon recover from stroke and their neologisms disappear. Such phenomena suggest the reestablishment of inhibitory mechanisms in phonemic or lexical assembly. That such a process usually parallels the recovery of comprehension argues for the importance of auditory feedback.

As a summary of the possible mechanisms for the various clinical syndromes that are compatible with the anatomical evidence, a simplified block diagram is constructed in Figure 15.13. Four lines across the connections represent distinct syndromes.

    1. The lesion at this site will impair auditory comprehension but the monitoring of lexical and phonemic selection continues. These are the cases of pure word deafness.

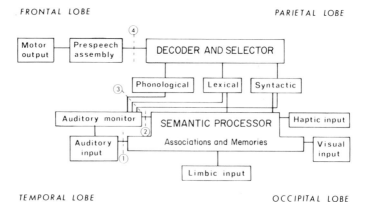

FIGURE 15.13. *A block diagram of basic processes that may be involved in a variety of ways to produce different clinical syndromes. The numbers represent these various clinical entities (see text). (From Kertesz, 1981.)*

2. This lesion produces semantic jargon by disconnecting auditory input from association areas necessary for comprehension and for the appropriate lexical selection.
3. Lesions in cases of neologistic jargon affect both auditory monitoring and phonemic assembly.
4. Lesions in conduction aphasia impair phonemic assembly with preserved auditory mechanisms.

This schema suggests a few of the possible disruptions of the intricate connections between auditory input and auditory monitoring, and between phonemic selection and phonemic assembly. It assumes a simultaneous operation of a lexical selector for both comprehension and preparation of output. Syntactic mechanisms are often intact in fluent aphasias and therefore are not specifically dealt with in the diagram, although they are clearly very important in comprehension and speech production. Their preservation in these posterior lesions has suggested the more anterior neural structures as their substrate.

REFERENCES

Alajouanine, T. (1956). Verbal realization in aphasia. *Brain, 79*, 1–28.

Benson, D. F., Sheremata, W. A., Bouchard, R., Segarra, J. M., Price, D., and Geschwind, N. (1973). Conduction aphasia—A clinicopathological study. *Archives of Neurology, 28*, 339–346.

Blumstein, S. E., Cooper, W. E., Goodglass, H., Statlender, S., and Goltlieb, J. (1980). Production deficits in aphasia: A voice onset time analysis. *Brain and Language, 9*, 153–170.

Brown, J. W. (1972). *Aphasia, apraxia and agnosia—Clinical and theoretical aspects.* Springfield, Ill.: Thomas.

Brown, J. W. (1979). *Neurobiology of social communication in primates.* New York: Academic Press.

Buckingham, H., and Kertesz, A. (1976). *Neologistic jargon aphasia.* Amsterdam: Svets & Zeitlinger.

Damasio, H., and Damasio, A. R. (1980). The anatomical basis of conduction aphasia. *Brain, 103*, 337–350.

Geschwind, N. (1965). Disconnexion syndromes in animals and man. *Brain, 88*, 585–644.

Green, E., and Howes, D. (1977). The nature of conduction aphasia: A study of anatomic and clinical features of underlying mechanisms. In H. Whitaker and H. A. Whitaker (Eds), *Studies in neurolinguistics,* Vol. 3.

Henschen, S. E. (1920–1922). *Klinische und anatomische Beitrage zur Pathologie des Gehirns,* Vols. 5–7. Stockholm: Nordiska Bokhandeln.

Huber, W., Stachowiak, F. J., Poeck, K., and Kerschensteiner, M. (1972). Die Wernicke's Aphasie. *Journal of Neurology, 210*, 77–97.

Kertesz, A. (1979). *Aphasia and associated disorders: Taxonomy, localization and recovery.* New York: Grune and Stratton.

Kertesz, A., and Benson, D. F. (1970). Neologistic jargon: A clinicopathological study. *Cortex, 6*, 362–386.

Kertesz, A., Harlock, W., and Coates, R. (1979). Computer tomographic localization, lesion size and prognosis in aphasia. *Brain and Language, 8*, 34–50.

Kertesz, A., and Phipps, J. B. (1977). Numerical taxonomy of aphasia. *Brain and Language, 4,* 1–10.

Kertesz, A. (1981). The anatomy of jargon. In J. Brown (Ed.), *Jargonaphasia.*

Kleist, K. (1962). *Sensory aphasia and amusia: The myeloarchitectonic basis.* Oxford: Pergamon.

Lecours, A. R., and Rouillon, F. (1976). Neurolinguistic analysis of jargonaphasia and jargonagraphia. In H. Whitaker and H. A. Whitaker (Eds.), *Studies in neurolinguistics,* Vol. 2.

Lee, B. S. (1950). Effect of delayed speech feedback. *Journal of the Acoustical Society of America, 22,* 824–826.

Pick, A. (1931). Aphasie. In O. Bumke and O. Foerster (Eds.), *Handbuch der normalen und pathologischen Physiologie,* Vol. 15. Berlin: Springer.

Sobotta, H., and Figge, F. H. J. (1963). *Atlas of human anatomy.* New York: Halner.

Starr, M. A. (1889). The pathology of sensory aphasia with an analysis of fifty cases in which Broca's center was not diseased. *Brain, 12,* 82–101.

Wernicke, C. (1874). *Der aphasische symptomenkomplex.* Breslau: Cohn & Weigart, Reprinted in *Boston Studies on the Philosophy of Science,* Vol. 4, Dordrecht: Reidel.

Wernicke, C. (1908). *The symptom—complex of aphasia in diseases of the nervous system.* (A. Church, Ed.). New York: Appleton.

16

Simulation of Speech Production without a Computer

André Roch Lecours[1]

In the context of this chapter, the word **glossolalia** designates a fluent, discourselike production that is entirely or nearly entirely neologistic. Glossolalic production can thus be viewed, on the one hand, as essentially a succession of spoken entities that are wordlike although they do not occur in the dictionaries, and that are combined into sentencelike entities bearing no conventional messages that a qualified listener might decode. Glossolalic production can also be viewed and transcribed, on the other hand, as a succession of segments that are assimilable to conventionally pronounced phonemes and syllables.

As a rule, the first impression of one witnessing glossolalic behavior is that one is listening to a bona fide language that one does not know; an "it-sounds-like" reaction is typical. I might add that the contention of many a glossolalic speaker is that he or she is talking, when under the influence of ghosts, gods, devils, the dead, computers, Martians, Russians, and whatnot, one or several bona fide languages that he or she has never learned (and usually does not understand, anyway)—hence, the term **xenoglossia** often used among believers to designate glossolalic behavior (Bobon, 1952; Cénac, 1925). In this respect, my friend Jacques Mehler has told me about a South American believer who managed to be convincing enough, when fluently speaking archaic Babylonian, to have his psychoanalyst indulge in the presentation of an astonished—and astonishing—case report, with a whole set of appropriate Freudian interpretations; likewise, Pierre Marie Lavorel reports, in his comments at the end of this chapter, about an Englishwoman who has become, obviously without apprenticeship, "proficient" in spoken Pharaonic Egyptian.

One might wonder, at this point, if glossolalia has anything to do with the topic of this volume. I would claim that maybe it does, if only because glossolalic

[1]The research reported on in this chapter was subsidized by grant MT-4210 of the Conseil de la Recherche Médicale du Canada.

345

NEURAL MODELS OF
LANGUAGE PROCESSES

behavior shows that the human brain is wired in such a manner that certain components of language production can be turned off while others remain in active function, and also because it shows that the components remaining active can themselves display, in certain circumstances, dissociated functioning. I will later argue that semantics is thus turned off in glossolalia, whereas phonology and prosody are not, and also that prosody remains in line with conventional patterns whereas phonology does so only up to a point. Given that glossolalic behavior has been observed to occur in subjects, both with (Lecours, Travis, and Osborn, 1980; Perecman and Brown, 1981) and without focal brain lesions (Bobon, 1952; Samarin, 1972), one can suggest that suppression of semantic control is voluntary in certain cases and represents the effect of brain damage in others. Given the latter, the glossolalic form of language performance might be considered a potentially relevant one by those who are directly involved in attempts at making neural models of language processes. Moreover, and for the same reason, glossolalia certainly raises an interesting problem for those whose trade is lesion localization, a problem that should be considered together with that raised by the existence of nonglossolalic aphasic jargons in which comprehension of speech is relatively and even sometimes totally spared, which means, as David Levine has suggested (personal communication) that one should distinguish between the "receptive function" and the "speech control function" of the retrorolandic speech areas. It is not my intention here to plead in favor of a "phrenology of convolutions," as Broca did in 1861, yet it seems to me that the study of glossolalia provides further evidence as to the existence of particular neuronal nets specifically attending to particular aspects of language performance.

To date, I have studied 20 samples of taperecorded glossolalic discourse. They were produced by one schizophasic speaker (Lecours, Navet, and Ross-Chouinard, 1981), eight pentecostal charismatic believers, two healthy nurses, one poet and, given my definition of glossolalia, two elderly Wernicke's aphasics. A broad IPA transcription was made in all cases.

Now, provided a set of rules, phonemic and syllabic segmentation of glossolalic discourse is no more a source of difficulty—and sometimes it is appreciably easier—than phonemic and syllabic segmentation of samples of natural tongues one does not know. On the whole, segmentation into sentence-like entities is not a problem either, in view of relatively clear prosodical clues and longer pauses. On the other hand, except for a proportion of strongly wordlike entities, it is more difficult and sometimes impossible to reach common agreement as to wordlike level segmentation, a fact one should keep in mind when examining the transcriptions of glossolalic discourse in what follows. This proportion of strongly wordlike entities varies from one sample to another, depending mostly on pauses and prosodical clues (such as tonic accent), on recurrence of identical or similar strings, on amount of affixlike segments, and so forth.

Given these preliminaries, I will first tell you about 11 of the samples I have studied. They are those of the schizophasic, of 5 of the charismatics, and of the 2 nurses. All of these subjects are exclusive unilingual speakers of Quebecois French. On the other hand, many of them admit to an interest in passive exposure to spoken foreign languages, such as the exposure one gets at night when tuning one's radio along the short-wave bands.

When "speaking in tongues," the schizophasic subject considers himself the reluctant phonatory instrument of malevolent wills from Mars, where he once worked as a crooner. It is thus that he can speak in four different tongues, to which he refers as his "temperaments": One of these, he calls his "English temperament," another his "funny temperament," and the last two his "French temperaments" (the second apparently being an excrescence of the first). Examples of each are given in Insert 1.

The five charismatics, for their part, "speak in tongues" when under the benevolent influence of the Holy Ghost. They are obviously fond of doing it although, like the schizophasic, they consider themselves to be the mere phonatory instruments of a stronger will. Partial transcriptions are provided in Insert 2.

Besides the linguistic aspects I will discuss shortly, the schizophasic and the charismatics have other points in common: (a) all are fully aware of the unconventional nature of their glossolalic utterances; (b) all state that they themselves never decide on the moment of glossolalic behavior, this being the exclusive privilege of the stronger will but, when recorded, all turned out to be capable of

---

INSERT 1

SCHIZO-ENGLISH

[zaRa RakuRu bRubjɛR paRa bRazjɛm nɛRgɛs kaRakuRu bRubjɛR mizœpRiz aRakaska Rœkaœ bRazjɛm nɛRgɛs kɛRakɔRu bRubje Ramisi azumba bɛRgɛs koRo bRubjɛR paRa bRazjɛm nɛRgɛs kɛRakuRu bRubjɛR mizœpRiz aRakaska Rœkaœ bRazjɛm nɛRgɛs kɛRakoRo azumba bɛRgɛs kuʁu bRobjɛR paRa]

SCHIZO-FUNNY

[apalagmala kakili bidi elak kalamala kakisi lipidi kala kakulu ili elak malakala kala kili agumla bala kakisi lipili kala kakulu eli ilak manaka lakala paRa kaza kaRbisi eli biRak kolo malakalk kili paRa kalakolu agumla bala kakisi lipiRi kala kakili ili elak]

SCHIZO-FRENCH 1

[la Rœk3fjɔRanis ʔtRɔbeRɔgad bRakal dœ Rœk3fjɛRjanis ʔtRœbeRɔgad bRakal dœ Rœk3fjɔRjasj3 mãbRal yn bRibɛRgasj3 pineRo peRikal bRabal dœ Rœk3fjɛRjanis ʔtRɔbeRɔgad bRabal la RœkɔmfjɔRasj3 lastRø bœnalfjɛ̃ pineRo peRika bRabal dœ RœkɔmfjœRjanis ʔtRɔbeRɛgal bRakal Rjanik]

SCHIZO-FRENCH 2

[la k3tRavizeRjasj3 la manœRapaRa bRakal dœ Rœk3fjɔRjanis ʔtRøbeRɔgad bRakal dœ Rœk3fjɔRjasj3 bineRomenal bRakal dœ Rœk3fjɔRizi yn bRibɛRgasj3 pineRomenal dœ paRjetegRal epineRopeRika bRabal dœ Rœk3fj3Rjanis ʔtRøbeRɔgal lã lœkoloRjɔl de paRjetegRal epineRopeRikal]

INSERT 2

CHARISMATIC #1

[o kiʀia ʀamatuʀeiʃ silia maʀamakoleiʃ sikolea ʀamataiʃ maʀanataiʃ ʃikolia ʀamataiʃ ʃikolia ʀapataiski o jaʃimdea ʀamatuʀaiʃ ʃekilia soli aʀmakulaiʃ o jaʃimdea ʀakoleiʃ silia
ʀamataʀaiʃ o kulia ʀamataʀaiʃ o kulia ʀapataiski o jaʀa matoiʃ ʃekilia sulia ʀamakolaiʃ]

CHARISMATIC #2

[monoʃkolo kola monoʃkœli kynɔm monokwɔle kwɔmo kɔlekɔmwe aʃkulu kunœkɔmwa alaʃkɔla
kɔʀaja manaʃkolo keʀeʔ manaʃkolo akʀi malaʃkɔlo keʀekɛ monokɛle kɛlokɔlo kɔnœkɛ ʀokœna
mwɛlaʃkolo kyʀija akolo ʀamanaʃ koloka ʀakeja manakolo kuʀane kalakɔ mwanaka akulijam]

CHARISMATIC #3

[o kwena kana maʃe kana maʃina ina kwena ʃanana kanana o kwina kama naʃina naʃena ina
kwena ʃimine nana o kwena kana maʃina ina swina kanama naʃina o kwina kama naja ina
kwina nanaʃa o kwina kana maja ʃana ina kwena ma o kwina mo ina mina ina kwina o na mo]

CHARISMATIC #4

[putʃta jato amadea se atʃtu hoʀa o maʀia ʃtuja talasul e maʀja atunda asuja inʃtigoso
jɛtʃteni o maʀja tuskundea deseu in dios kuna majʃte o njanatʃe maʀjana idonjaʃte kos-
kena ɛ no njɔnɛskena o niʃtɛne maʀja tosɛ no no swoʃtɛnei ɛ no ɛʃeʀo swɔndinu udaʃse]

CHARISMATIC #5

[iljana sepwɛʀe kɛʀeʃte manante kaʀje siljana sapa litekol dɔna hajaʃoʀe dmanin sepeʀja
saiti tuʀjokɔle hedu mɔʃtɔjo poj igmonois hjɔlœ keʀɛs umale nias ajekelena isaʀa janin
tete keʀiʃtea tweʀija kaʀja sijo odnɛnse pwele kahɛntʃe aʀjalijɔns eʀija fajinto kaja]

---

immediate production on demand; and (c), finally, all believe that their glossolalic utterances do belong with real languages, human or not, archaic or
contemporary.

To my surprise (having myself tried without success), I found out that a
certain number of ordinary people—not everybody, by far—are perfectly capable, without rehearsal or even knowledge of the very existence of the glossolalia
phenomenon, of sustained glossolalic discourse in answer to an instruction such
as "try to speak in a language you do not know." The two nurses are among
these. Obviously, they are aware of the unconventional nature of their behavior,
they do not attribute it to possession, and they do not believe it to correspond to
some real language. Examples of their neologistic productions are given in Insert
3.

The 11 samples produced by these subjects all occurred in the form of
monologues, which might be of some importance. As far as I can tell, they
represent imitations of human language production: The attempt at simulation is acknowledged in the cases of the two nurses and is obvious—although
perhaps not fully conscious—in the cases of the schizophasic and the charismatics. My own purpose is to tell you about the outputs in these simulation

---

INSERT 3
<u>   </u>

NURSE #1

[i evistimi tanto elevɛnte bɛste vanto elevɛsti bika anevɛnti mitistan elevɛnti limi
nistaʀe inivindi me dastɔnte elekɛsti kue tikanto eliminimista batɛnto elevanta tɛsta-
mɛnto alavinto e anvekemistan elividimistan elibidimiʃtaj kede vete anto ivaj emindisti]

NURSE #2

[biema kumiku mitʃaou ka bulamiteul tʃibakuʀa bauti mi kaputi dʒabuti kamylabul kwitau
tʃabu ʀinantu mi kabuti amokowti mi kulakutʃi taputu te moʀijɔʀ alamu ʃikolamuki mi
lakulina tuʀi biku miʀɛtu batʃu mitɛltu tijau biʀkma taputa tima tʃiputitau amulaʃ]

---

experiments; it will remain for you to find out about the programs behind these outputs.

I will be brief concerning the semantics of these samples. Indeed, except for being a potential musiclike tool for the communication of moods, glossolalic utterances have no immediately sharable semantic value. Essentially, therefore, it is the formal aspects of language production that glossolalic speakers simulate. This comprises segmental and suprasegmental parameters. Let us deal with the latter first.

It is my impression that prosody is of paramount significance in glossolalic behavior. Nonetheless, I will be brief on this topic also, mainly because I do not know how to tackle the problem. Suggestions are welcome. Meanwhile, I will formulate four comments: The first has to do with general melody, the second with speed of elocution, the third with regional accent, and the last with tonic accent.

Regarding general prosody, one is struck by the obviousness of a major melodical investment in each of the 11 samples. Indeed, one has the very definite impression that a glossolalic speaker's leading choice is that of a prosodical model. In the schizophasic, for instance, the model is apparently Voice of America, or else Radio Tirana; in the charismatics, fervent prayer or imprecation.

A choice in speed of elocution can also be at stake: For instance, a charismatic imprecator can take as little as 7 sec, and an implorer as long as 45 sec, to utter 100 phonemes (as opposed to 13–18 sec in controls). Two years ago, in Urbino, a theologian suggested that this might well be the difference between "bad" and "good" glossolalia.

My third observation concerns regional accent which, as you may know, is nearly as perceptible in Quebec as in, say, south Texas. Regional accent totally disappears in 7 of the 11 samples, and it is very much attenuated in the 4 others (those of the schizophasic). It is a fact of common observation that something of this sort can occur in people singing, acting, reciting, or praying.

The last point is perhaps the most intriguing: But for two samples, those of the schizophasic's "French temperaments," and provided my segmentation in wordlike segments has any validity, there occurs partial or complete replacement of the expected oxytone—with the tonic accent systematically bearing on the last syllable of words, as in French—by a simplified paroxytone, with accentuation of the penultimate or of the ultimate syllable of wordlike entities according to whether they end on a vowel or on a consonant.

I will now turn to segmental parameters of glossolalic simulation, about which I will be somewhat more explicit. For 6 of the samples, those of the schizophasic and of the nurses, who can glossolalize for hours in a row, this aspect of my study is founded on the first 2000 phonemes of each corpus. In contrast, the 5 charismatic samples average only 584 phonemes (442, 1240, 242, 532, and 463 phonemes, respectively). I have compared these 11 samples with various normative data (Léon, 1964; Santerre, 1976), on the one hand, and, on the other, to the first 2000 phonemes of various French control samples. The latter included the productions of two normal persons telling about their work, of one nonglossolalic schizophasic (with occasional neologistic utterances), and of three nonglossolalic fluent aphasics (one with Wernicke's aphasia proper and logorrheic neologistic jargon, one with conduction aphasia and the kind of discursive behavior which I but not Jason Brown would call "phonemic jargon," and the last with transcortical sensory aphasia and verbal jargon).

Let us begin with phonemic choices and frequencies in glossolalic as compared with control discourses. I have several comments on this:

1. The distribution of the 2000 phonemes in each of the control samples, including the nonglossolalic schizophasic and the three nonglossolalic fluent aphasics, is rather close to that in normative data. This is shown in Figure 16.1, Graphs 1–6.

2. From 99 to 100% of the phonemes, in each of the 11 samples, belong with the French phonemic inventory. Occasional foreign-sounding units do appear in a few samples—for instance, English-like [ʀ]s, [l]s, and [h]s, which is hardly an anomaly in Quebec French, anyway.

3. The phonemic distribution in the 11 glossolalic samples is not at all like that in the 6 control samples. As compared with normative data, glossolalic samples are thus characterized by gross overuse of certain phonemes and, complementarily, by gross underuse or even absence of others. Moreover, frequency in mother tongue hardly influences frequency in glossolalic utterances, so that phonemes that are infrequent in French can be overused in glossolalic samples, and phonemes that are frequent in French can be underused or not used at all. A particular profile of phonemic distribution is thus observed in each of the 11 samples: This is exemplified in Figure 16.1, Graphs 7–9.

Several ingenious friends have suggested that another way of comparing the phonemic repartitions in my glossolalic and control samples to that in normative materials was to make some form of entropic measurements. Each provided a formula for this purpose but, for some reason, these turned out to be different from one another. Although I used each of these formulas and thus obtained different sets of data, one striking fact remained whatever the formula: All of the control samples, with their 2000 phonemes each, and even the *Ave Maria* (in French), with its 144 phonemes, yielded measurements that departed little or not at all from those inherent to normative data, whereas all of the glossolalic samples yielded measurements that departed appreciably from the norm, sometimes grossly so. The difference was that the figures related to glossolalic samples were all lower than those related to normative and control samples. My own impression is that this dissociation means something.

I will now turn to modes of interphonemic combination in glossolalia. Just as the phonemic choices in the 11 samples are possible given the French phonemic inventory, so are their modes of combination possible given the French phonological system. Here again, however, mimicry of mother tongue stops at this point in all samples. In other words, combinations that are frequent in French can be utterly neglected, and infrequent ones become predilection linkages. Moreover, only a very small proportion of permitted combinations are actualized in any given sample and, if consonant clusters are (quantitatively and qualitatively) taken as a parameter of phonological "complexity," the 11 glossolalic samples are all "simpler" than control samples. It can therefore be concluded that the 11 samples are phonologically rule governed, which does not really come as a surprise, and that the phonological system subserving their actualization corresponds to a simplified version of the French phonological system, which does not come as a surprise either. I might add that certain phonemic combinations that, in French, are acceptable only at words boundaries, sometimes occur within glossolalic entities that most listeners perceive as wordlike.

I will now turn to glossolalic units of the next level of complexity and will discuss two main points: One of these concerns certain inventories of formally related wordlike units, the other the existence of elements of morphology in glossolalic discourse. Although with various degrees of conspicuousness, both phenomena occur in all of the glossolalic samples I have studied so far.

Thus, each sample comprises inventories of isomorphic wordlike entities, that is, of wordlike entities bearing to one another formal relationships akin to those one observes, in aphasia, between phonemic paraphasias and their corresponding target words (Lecours and Lhermitte, 1969). Take, for instance, the example in Insert 4, excerpted from the discourse of a charismatic imprecator who was admittedly attempting to oust a succuba whom he thought had taken possession of me. Rules of transformation are relatively monotonous in this particular family of isomorphic quadrisyllables: If the most frequent form— [manakala], that is—is arbitrarily considered as a target, these rules allow a few specific permutations on all vowels and on not more than two of the last three consonants, reciprocal metathesis on first and second consonant, and one and

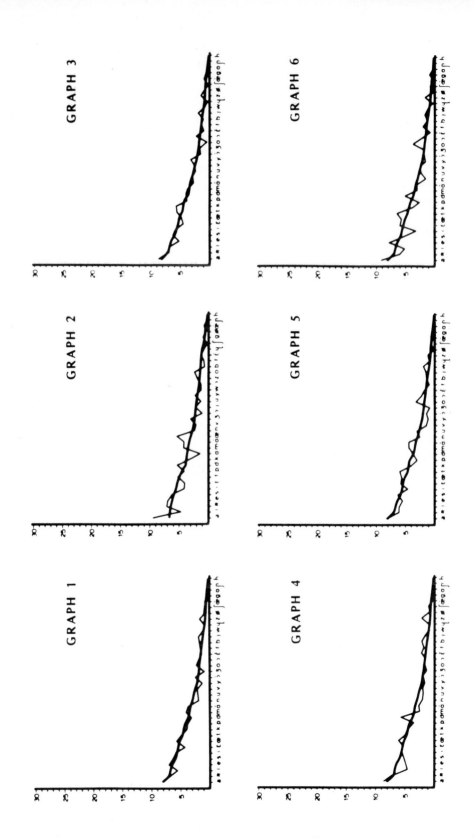

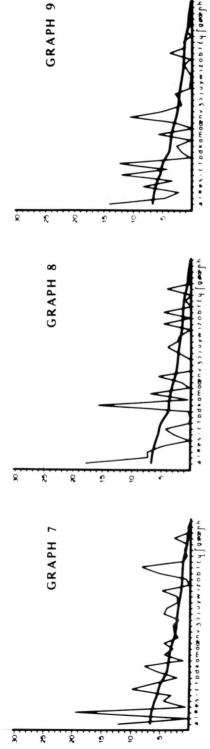

FIGURE 16.1. *Phonemic distributions expressed in percentages. Flat curves: normative data for Standard French in Graphs 1 and 3–6 (Léon and Léon, 1964) and for Quebecois French in Graphs 2 and 7 to 9 (Santerre, 1976). Broken curves: control data in Graphs 1–6 and glossolalic data in Graphs 7–9. Graph 1: normal conversation, Standard French. Graph 2: normal conversation, Quebecois French. Graph 3: neologistic schizophasia without glossolalia. Graph 4: transcortical sensory aphasia. Graph 5: neologistic Wernicke's jargonaphasia without glossolalia. Graph 6: conduction aphasia with an important production of phonemic paraphasias (Lecours and Lhermitte, 1969). Graph 7: schizophasic glossolalia. Graph 8: charismatic glossolalia. Graph 9: unrehearsed glossolalic essay by an unexperimented "ordinary" speaker. The glossolalic sample in Graph 8 comprises 1240 phonemes; all other control and glossolalic samples comprise 2000 phonemes each.*

	INSERT 4	
m a n a k a l a	m a n a ʃk a l a	
m a n a k o l o	m a n a ʃk o l o	mʷ a n a k o l o
m a n a k u ʀ e	m̃ a n a ʃk u l e	
m o n o k o l o	m a n a ʃk u l u	
m o n o k ɛ l e	m o n o ʃk o l o	
m o n o k ɛ ʀ e	m o n o ʃk œ l i	
m o n o k o ʀ a	m o n o kw ɔ l e	
m o n a k ɔ ʀ i	m o n a ʃk u ʀ i	
m o n a k a l e	m ɔ n a ʃk ɔ l e	
m ɔ n a k o l a	m ɔ n a ʃk ɔ l ɛ	
m ɔ n a k u ʀ u	m ɔ n a ʃk u ʀ i	
m ɔ n o k e ʀ i	m ɔ n a ʃk y ʀ i	
m ɔ n e k a ʀ e	m ɔ n a ʃw a l a	
m ɔ n ɔ k u l e	m ɔ n ɔ ʃk o l a	
m u n e k e ʀ e		
m u n u k ʊ ʀ u		
m a l a k a l a	m a l a ʃk ɔ l o	mʷ a l a k a l a
m a l a k o l a	m a l a ʃk u l o	
		mʷ a l o k u ʀ i
m o l̪ a k o l a		
	m a j a ʃk a l a	
	m ɔ j a ʃk o l a	

only one expansion on first and third consonant, as well as on second vowel.

Had one to select a single feature of glossolalic behavior in order to distinguish it from the control standard discourse (poetry excluded), one might confidently select these isomorphic sets.

There also occur, in all samples, sets of wordlike entities in which derivation rules of a sort seem to have been applied. The affixlike units used may be borrowed from the mother tongue or else may be hackneyed foreign prototypes. One of the most complex sets I have observed is from the schizophasic's first "French temperament." Illustrated in Insert 5, it comprises combinatory use of prefixlike entities such as [bi],]ʀœ], [kɔ̃], [kɔ̃tʀa], [epi], and so forth, and of suffixlike entities such as [ezi], [asjɔ̃], [al], [ite], and so forth, all of which belong

INSERT 5

[baʀjɛtɛʀɛzi] ±			baʀ	jɛteʀ	ezi
[ʀɛk3fɔʀjaneʀɛzi] ±	Rɛ	k3	fɔʀ	janeʀ	ezi
[ʀɛk3fjɔʀɛzi] ±	Rɛ	k3	fjɔʀ		ezi
[ʀɛk3fjɔʀani] ±	Rɛ	k3	fjɔʀ		ani
[ʀɛk3fjɔʀanis] ±	Rɛ	k3	fjɔʀ		ɛnis
[ʀɛk3fjɔʀasj3] ±	Rɛ	k3	fjɔʀ		asj3
[k3stʀasj3] ±		k3	stʀ		asj3
[k3tʀavizeʀjasj3] ±		k3tʀa	vizeʀj		asj3
[beʀegasj3] ±			beʀeg		asj3
[bʀibɛʀgasj3] ±			bʀibɛʀg		asj3
[bʀibɛʀgasjɔne] ±			bʀibɛʀg	asjɔ	ne
[bʀibɛʀgasjɔnis] ±			bʀibɛʀg	asjɔ	nis
[bʀibɛʀgal] ±			bʀibɛʀg	al	
[bʀabal] ±			ɒʀab	al	
[bʀakal] ±			bʀak	al	
[ɛ̃tʀabeʀɔgal] ±,	ɛ̃tʀa		beʀɔg	al	
[epinɔʀmenal] ±	epi		nɔʀmén	al	
[binɔʀmenal] ±	bi		nɔʀmɛn	al	
[mɑ̃bʀal] ±			mɑ̃bʀ	al	
[mɑ̃tʀalite] ±			mɑ̃tʀ	al	ite

with French affixial inventories. A simpler example, from one of the paroxytone nurses' samples, is quoted in Insert 6; a few Latin-Italian-Spanish-like affixes occur in this one.

My final point about the 11 samples concerns glossolalic units of a still greater level of complexity, that is, phraselike and sentencelike units. It should be clear, by now, that an outstanding characteristic of glossolalia is the recurrent use of predilection segments of various degrees of complexity. This phenomenon—which one might wish to call perseveration if this were not too pervasive a term to be useful here—can involve phonemes, syllables and other phonemic combinations, morphemelike and wordlike entities, even phraselike and sentence-like entities. When the latter occurs, the listener is often left with the impression of an endless repetition of the same sentencelike entities. This is only partially substantiated by a closer look at the transcriptions. Even in

```
                              INSERT 6

                 [anto] ±
  [e]            anto] ±
  [e]      am    anto] ±        [e]    am    ɔnta] ±

                                [e]    em    antal] ±    [e]    em    asta] ±

                                [a]    am    ɔntala] ±   [a]    am    ɛntɛs] ±

  [e   ʀiv  ist  anto] ±
       [ʀiv        anto] ±
  [e]  ev          anto] ±      [e]   ev    ɛntɔl] ±     [e]   ev    ɛsti] ±
  [in       ist    anto] ±
  [in       im     anto] ±
```

caricatural cases, such as the one illustrated in Insert 7, which is from the schizophasic's "English temperament," wordlike entities behave, within the contexts of predilection sentencelike entities, in the same manner that phonemelike entities behave within the contexts of predilection wordlike entities: One has the superficial impression of a loose although simple Markovian process being applied on two or three different keyboards at the same time.

In Insert 7, I have first listed the 13 basic wordlike constituents of the schizophasic's "English temperament." Nearly all of them can have one or several isomorphic phonological variants, hence the plus-or-minus signs following them in the list. Three preferential phraselike constituents are also listed: They are identified as "a," "A," and "B." The "grammar" of the schizophasic's "English temperament" is thereafter summarized in a formula following the word "SENTENCE."

Keeping in mind this description of the 11 samples, and assuming that ghosts, devils and the like are of only moderate importance (here and nowadays), one can suggest that the programs behind glossolalic simulation are founded primarily on various fragments of learning related to speech production. In unilingual speakers, it is likely that nearly all of these fragments are related to the production of mother tongue, although occasional exposure to foreign languages, however passive and minimal, apparently plays a seasoning role.

Let me now ponder a few questions such as, how successful is glossolalic simulation? How close does it get to a natural language with regard to various formal—segmental and suprasegmental—aspects? How close does it get to sounding "foreign"? To what extent can it be considered to be "semantic"?

As obvious from the reaction of most listeners to glossolalic discourse, the simulation reaches some degree of credibility with regard to segmental aspects: It

```
                                    INSERT 7

1 = [azumba] ±              a = (3 ou 3' + 4)
2 = [bɛRgɛs] ±              A = (5 + 6 + a)
3 = [koRo] ±                B = (8' + 7 + 6 + a)
3'= [keʀœkoRu] ±           ─────────────────
4 = [bRubjɛR] ±                        ┃ 8          ┃
5 = [paRa]                             ┃ or         ┃
6 = [bRazjɛ mnɛRgɛs] ±   "SENTENCE" │       │A│     ┃ (B + 8)    ┃
7 = [aRakaska ʀœkaʀœ] ±            │= +1 ±2 +a +│r│ ±A +┃ or         ┃
8 = [misi] ±                        │       │B│     ┃ (B + B + 8) ┃
8'= [mizœ pRiz] ±                               ┃ or         ┃
                                               ┃ (B - 4)    ┃
```

e.g. [azumba │ bɛRgɛs │ koRo bRubjɛR │ paRa bRazja mnɛRgɛs keR⊃koRo bRubjɛR │
        mizœ pRiz aRakaska ʀœkaʀœ bRazjɛ mnɛRgɛs keRakoRo]

e.g. [azumba │ bɛRgɛs │ koRo bRubjɛR │ paRa bRazjɛ mnɛRgɛs keRakoRo buRbjɛR │
        mizœ pRiz aRakaska ʀœkaʀœ bRazja mnɛRgɛs keRakoRo bRubjɛR │ misi]

e.g. [azaʀœ │ koRo bRobjɛR │ paRa bRasja mnɛRgɛs keʀœkoRo bRobjɛR │ miza pRiz
        aRakaska RakaRœm bRasja mnɛRgɛs kɛRokoRo bRobjɛR │ miza pRiz aRakaska
        RakaRa bRazja mnɛRgɛs keRokoRu bRobjɛR │ mesi]

e.g. [azaRa │ kuRu bRubjɛR │ paRa bRasja minɛRgɛs keʀœkuRu bRubjɛR │ mizœ pRiz
        aRakaska ʀœkaʀœ bRasja minɛRgɛs kaʀœkuRu bRubjɛR mizœ pRiz aRakaska RakaRa
        bRazja minɛRgɛs keRokoRu bRubjɛR │ mesi]

does yield outputs comparable to multiarticulated discourse of a sort, that is, outputs that can be described in terms of simpler units being integrated into progressively more complex ones. On the whole, however, the number of available units, as well as their modes of selection and combination, remains comparatively poor, and this paucity increases with the degree of complexity of the considered units: It is least conspicuous at phonemelike level, intermediate at wordlike level, and maximal at sentencelike level.

Among the 20 samples that I have studied so far, I have found one in which the segmental paucity inherent to glossolalic behavior is appreciably less obvious than in the 19 others. As illustrated in Graph 10, Figure 16.2, this is reflected, at phonemic level, in a repartition that is intermediate between the one in normative and control samples and the one in other glossolalic samples. This difference probably stems from two main factors: On the one hand, this sample comprises a fair number of bona fide French words (indeed, to such an extent that one might wonder if it answers the definition I gave of glossolalia), and, on the other hand, it was produced by a (professional) poet whose "improvisation" was that of one with

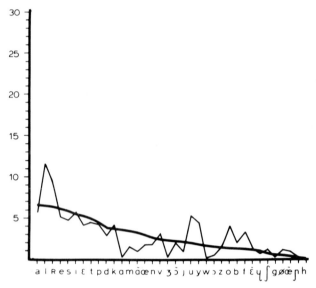

FIGURE 16.2. *(Graph 10) Phonemic distributions expressed in percentages. Flat curves: normative data in Quebecois French (Santerre, 1976). Broken curve: glossolalic data, poetic "improvisation"; 1045 phonemes.*

a long, deliberate experience of utterly calculated, paper-and-pencil glossographic creation.

Suprasegmental aspects now: I am somehow convinced—although I cannot really document my conviction—that prosodic choices are more deliberate than segmental choices in glossolalic behavior. Moreover, there is a basic difference between segmental and prosodic choices in that the former leads to neologistic production whereas the latter does not. Be that as it may, glossolalic mimicry of speech production is quite successful with regard to suprasegmental aspects: Indeed, glossolalic speakers are perfectly capable of sticking to a prosodical model, usually a simple one, with a relatively small number of well-defined melodical features, such as the ones characteristic of recitative prayer, political propaganda, and so forth.

As I have mentioned, there are features in the glossolalic utterances of unilingual speakers that do not represent loans from the mother tongue: After all, the point is to act as if one were not unilingual. This phenomenon can involve segmental as well as suprasegmental aspects: Changes in phonemic repartitions and the use of a few foreign phonemes and affixes are examples of the former, and changes in regional or tonic accent are examples of the latter. But whereas segmental loans remain very sparse, very elementary, and very superficial, suprasegmental ones sometimes evenly dominate the whole of lengthy glossolalic discourse. The striking fact, in this respect, is therefore that minimal passive exposure to foreign languages provides enough information for certain individuals to learn and consistently reproduce suprasegmental components, which is seldom if ever the case for segmental ones.[2] Is not this a rather interesting dissociation? In other words, could not one suggest that certain glossolalists, although they are never segmental xenoglossists, sometimes come very close to being genuine suprasegmental xenoglossists? I wonder if a similar dissociation in reception might explain why listeners to glossolalic discourse usually tend to assimilate what they hear to some language they do not speak but have been exposed to.

Another question that might be repeated and dealt with at this point is the following: Are there semantic components to glossolalic simulation and, if so, how successful are they?

The answer might be yes–there–is–and–quite–successful if one considers only prosodically conveyed messages: For instance, the affect inherent to the discourse of a praying charismatic is very much unlike that inherent to the discourse of an imprecating charismatic.

Things are quite different with regard to segmental aspects of glossolalic mimicry. In this respect, my glossolalic poet teaches that there are indeed messages inherent to phonemic choices; for example, he insists that a production of some length comprising 20% of unvoiced dorsovelar stop consonants will inevitably sound aggressive. This notwithstanding, I think that glossolalic imitation is not semantically targeted as far as segmental values are concerned. More precisely, I do not believe that glossolalic utterances represent systematic transformations of standard utterances, as would be the case, for instance, of several forms of typically aphasic utterances; and I think that glossolalic speakers do not consciously attribute precise meanings to their wordlike and sentencelike productions.[3]

I guess that an argument in this sense might be derived from the study of phonemic repartitions in glossolalic discourse, or again from the omnipresence, in all samples, of families of isomorphic wordlike entities, which is definitely not a characteristic of non-poetic standard speech. Nonetheless, given that most of us are sort of interested in the mutual relationships of brain and language, I will seek my argument in aphasic material.

[2]Unless in circumstances such that segmental values are, as it were, subordinated to suprasegmental ones: Think of how most of us learn songs and of how difficult it can be to recite the corresponding texts isolatedly (on a non-song prosody). This reminds me of the lady who sang in beautiful Italian at La Scala but was unable to order pastas at the restaurant next door, but this is an altogether different matter.

[3]Théodore Flournoy (1900) claims that Hélène Smith was an exception in this respect but, clearly, this girl's game was not glossolalia but cryptophasia: Hers was a CIA-like code—an hermetolect (Lasalle, 1974)—in which each letter or sound of (French) target words was systematically replaced by another sign of her own choice.

INSERT 8

GLOSSOLALIC WERNICKE #1

[sℰ dikte di tʀɔ̃ kɔ̃deʀe dʀikɔ̃dedeʀe digœʀe dis tis tilavɛ klɔʀe œ le dø tʀɔ̃ke ditibɛ
dɛ̃ʀe disœ te kotegoʀe dil kɔ̃deteʀe a wi dœ vilɛbʀiʃ ɔe la lɑ̃bɛtɔʀi de del lɑ̃tetɛʀœme
di kateaɔʀe e œ e ɛlzekute ɛlmœpuʀimakɔ̃te tɑ̃ tutse dœgʀedœgʀe dis gy lateʀe digeloteʀe]

GLOSSOLALIC WERNICKE #2

[vaʀite sœpœ lœbsœ pazezø kœ bœsœmɔse bœdze bosœ bℰ ɔe pje yn bℰ bajesø mɔpɔ mpɔma vjɛ
bɑmbɑ ɔe mapɔzø paɑpuʀ mœʃwø ʃepa bytse bɔvʀe siʀse ɔe va pɑse pɑte gɑ aʃydy mwℰ pise
maɔemɛ mekɔ vjɛse seɔamɛ ɔe peteʀœ samɛ ɔamɛ pɑze pɑ ʀjℰ dzutu ɔamɛ pedœ tepeʀje ɔbℰ]

There have been rare cases of elderly stroke patients with very severe Wernicke's aphasia and a fluent phonatory production that answers the empirical definition I gave of glossolalia. Anna Mazzucchi, from Parma, and Carlo Semenza, from Padova, have each recorded one such patient; as far as I know, these cases have not been reported in the literature. At the last International Neurological Association meeting, Ellen Perecman and Jason Brown (1981) have reported on a third, and I have myself observed two cases (Lecours, Osborn, Travis, and Rouillon, 1981). Exemplary transcripts from these two are presented in Insert 8. The phonemic repartition in the first of these cases is shown in Graph 11 Figure 16.3; compare it with Graph 5, Figure 16.1, which illustrates the phonemic distribution in a control sample from a patient with "regular" logor-

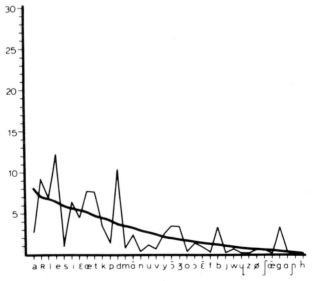

FIGURE 16.3 (Graph 11) Phonemic distributions expressed in percentages. Flat curve: normative data in Standard French (Léon and Léon, 1964). Broken curve: glossolalic data, Wernicke's aphasia; 2000 phonemes.

```
┌─────────────────────────┐
│        INSERT 9         │
├─────────────────────────┤
│    k a t e g ɔ R e      │
├─────────────────────────┤
│    k o t e g ɔ R e      │
├─────────────────────────┤
│    k o t e d œ R e      │
├─────────────────────────┤
│    k o d o l œ R e      │
├─────────────────────────┤
│    k ã t e g o R e      │
├─────────────────────────┤
│    k ã t ɛ g œ R e      │
├─────────────────────────┤
│    k ʒ t ɛ g ɔ R e      │
├─────────────────────────┤
│    k ʒ t e g œ R e      │
├─────────────────────────┤
│    k ʒ t ɛ d œ R e      │
├─────────────────────────┤
│    k ʒ t ɛ b œ R e      │
├─────────────────────────┤
│    k ʒ d e t e R e      │
├─────────────────────────┤
│    k ʒ d y d e R e      │
├─────────────────────────┤
│    k i k ã d œ R e      │
├─────────────────────────┤
│    k i l ʲ d e R e      │
└─────────────────────────┘
```

rheic neologistic jargon. I might add that the two glossolalic samples I obtained from Wernicke's aphasics do show several if not all of the segmental characteristics I have described in the original 11 samples, including—as illustrated in Insert 9 and Insert 10, which I excerpted from the productions of the first of these cases—the families of isomorphic wordlike entities and the elements of morphology. Therefore, their discursive behavior shares more with that of nonaphasic glossolalics than with that of nonglossolalic aphasics.

Now, if you look at the data in Figure 16.3, you will notice an overuse of the three voiced stop consonants, that is, of /b/, /d/, and /g/, in the sample of the first glossolalic Wernicke's; the same holds true for /b/ and /g/ in the sample of the second glossolalic Wernicke's. I come to my argument: Given that Blumstein (1973) has shown that, in phonemically targeted deviations (phonemic paraphasias), replacements of marked phonemes are particularly frequent as compared to replacements of unmarked phonemes, a fact that I have also observed (Lecours, Deloche, and Lhermitte, 1973), one might conceivably expect a decrease—but certainly not an increase—in the frequency of voiced stop consonants if glossolalic utterances represented systematic transformations of conventional ones.

Let me switch now to still another problem raised by the very existence of glossolalia in various categories of speakers: Besides anosognosia, I can identify two basic differences between the discursive behavior of the two glossolalic Wernicke's aphasics and that of the other glossolalics I have considered till now, poet

	INSERT 10			
[mɛtR] ±				mɛtR
[ademɛtR] ±		ade		mɛtR
[digɛtRomɛtR] ±	dig	ɛtRo		mɛtR
[dikelimɛtR] ±	dik	eli		mɛtR
[ɛledœRe] ±		ɛle		dœRe
[dikɑtedœRe] ±	dik	ɑte		dœRe
[gylɑtedœRe] ±	gyl	ɑte		dœRe
[gylɜte] ±	gyl	ɜte		
[gylgydetɜbyl] ±	gylgy	de	tɜb	yl
[detɜbœRe] ±		de	tɜb	œRe
[detɜbɛtRœ] ±		de	tɜb	ɛtRœ
[detɜbɛR] ±		de	tɜb	ɛR
[detɜbe] ±		de	tɜb	e
[vatɜbe] ±		va	tɜb	e

included. The first difference is that glossolalic production represented an exclusive residual behavior in the two aphasics, who had no choice but to shut up if they did not glossolalize, whereas it coexisted with a capacity for standard speech production in the others. I will discuss the second difference later.

The first difference leads one to ask about the brain structures the integrity of which is necessary in order for glossolalic simulation to be possible. If I am not mistaken as to the significance of the formal kinship between the glossolalia in subjects with and that in subjects without brain lesions, whether the latter be schizophrenics, charismatics, or admitted simulators, glossolalic behavior remains possible, at least in right-handed elderlies, in the presence of important left hemisphere destructive lesions: In one of my patients, left posterior temporo-parietal lesions were documented by gamma-encephalography; in the other, CT scan images showed massive left occipital softening, as well as bilateral cortical atrophy, so formidable that it was impossible to tell if unilateral or bilateral temporal and/or parietal lesions had or had not taken place when aphasia had suddenly occurred. The patient reported by Perecman and Brown (1981) had bilateral temporal-parietal infarcts. In other words, when occurring in aphasic subjects, glossolalic behavior—a nondysarthric and phonologically rule-governed fluent speechlike production—does not depend on the integrity of the classical speech area, in particular of its temporal and posterior parietal components. As a matter of fact, having once observed, with Lhermitte, Ducarne, and Escourolle (1973), a case of—nonglossolalic—jargonaphasia resulting from extensive frontoparietotemporal lesions which destroyed the whole of Broca's area and it homologue in the right hemisphere, as well as most of the opercular third of the precentral gyrus in both hemispheres (Figures 16.4 and 16.5), I am bound to claim that there are circumstances, no doubt exceptional, in which even the frontal components of the classical speech area themselves are not necessary to the production of fluent conventionally articulated and phonologically rule-governed meologistic speech.

The second basic difference between the 2 aphasic samples and the 12 others is that all of the latter occurred in the form of monologues, whereas the former could only occur within apparent dialogues, that is, in the form of apparent answers to questions of an interlocutor. Indeed, I thought until recently, that nonaphasic glossolalia always occurred in the form of monologues. I was then given evidence to the contrary: After recording the glossolalic monologues of three British charismatic believers who had never met each other, two friends of mine, Paolo Fabbri and Silvano Fua, from the *Centro Internazionale di Semiotica e di Linguistica* in Urbino, asked them if they thought they were capable of sharing a conversation in tongues. They answered that they were, and they proceeded to do so. Analysis of the phonemic repartitions in the neologistic monologues and in the dialogue of these three native speakers of English yielded results that are comparable, in all respects, entropy included, to those I discussed earlier concerning glossolalia in native speakers of French.

My study of these productions is far from complete, but I think I can say that, on the whole, suprasegmental and segmental characteristics of the monologues, as well as segmental characteristics of the dialogue, are identical to those in other charismatic samples: prayerlike prosody, isomorphic families, and so forth. In contrast, the suprasegmental characteristics of the dialogue are those of a somewhat theatrical animated conversation.[4] Therefore, a striking feature of this particular simulation is again a dissociation between suprasegmental and segmental parameters: Whereas prosody successfully duplicates that of conversation, and apparently leads to holistic semantic exchanges of a sort, a comparison of monologues to dialogue shows that each protagonist keeps using his own unsharable tongues, therefore exerting very little if any influence, for instance as to wordlike entities, on the segmental choices of his interlocutors.

In a way, one might say that general prosody, whether conversational or otherwise, is always appropriate in glossolalic behavior, and consequently need not be considered a part of the simulation; that is, the simulation proper—although supported by regular prosodical apprenticeships and habits—is mostly if

---

[4]Although without the theatrical character, the prosody in the two samples from glossolalic Wernicke's patients is also, appropriately, that of conversation.

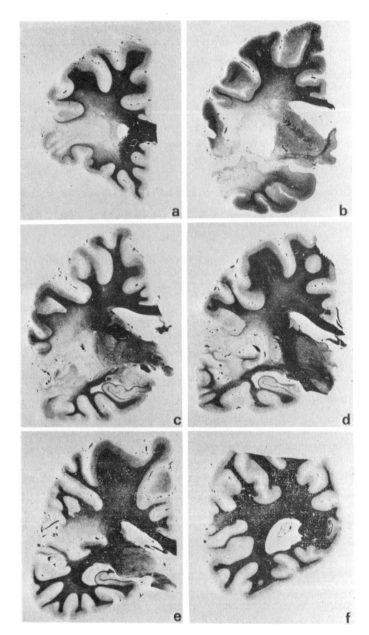

FIGURE 16.4. Nonglossolalic Wernicke's aphasia with logorrhea and neologistic jargon. Coronal sections through the left hemisphere. A gapless ancient cortico-subcortical infarct spreads from the inferior frontal gyrus to the rostralmost part of the inferior parietal lobule. It destroys Broca's area (a, b), the opercular third of the precentral and postcentral convolutions (c, d), the temporal operculum including Heschl's gyrus and Wernicke's area proper (c, d), the anterior (e) but much less the posterior (f) part of the supramarginal gyrus, and most of the insula (b–e). The angular gyrus is spared. Long association fibers are involved, including those of the arcuate bundle, but there exist no important lesions of the subcortical gray. Excerpted from Lhermitte, Lecours, Ducarne, Escourolle (1973).

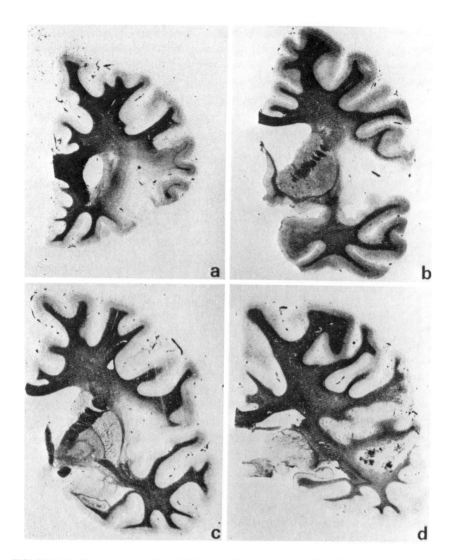

FIGURE 16.5. *Same case as in Figure 16.4. Coronal sections through the right hemisphere. There is an ancient cortico-subcortical infarct destroying most of the homologue of Broca's area (a, b) as well as the rostral part of the insula (b, c), and impinging upon the opercular third of the precentral gyrus (c). Long association fibers are involved rostrally, including those of the arcuate bundle. There are no important lesions of the subcortical gray. Foci of (terminal) hemorragic softening are seen in the caudal halves of the first and second temporal convolutions (d). Excerpted from Lhermitte, Lecours, Ducarne, Escourolle (1973).*

not exclusively directed at segmental aspects of speech production. Well, dissociations of this sort are not unheard of in computer simulation either.

As John Marshall would say, this is all very diverting. But is it of interest? Now, that all depends:

• If you are a theologian (Laurentin, 1974), or else a psychoanalyst, it might be for your own good and interest—however disheartening—to know that, but for

FIGURE 16.6. *Xenoglossia (Pratt, 1973).*

Hugo Pratt's (1973), no recent studies have provided evidence that some people can be proficient in languages they have not learned (Figure 16.6).

- If you are a fan of marginal psycholinguistics, you might be interested in knowing that glossolalia is not a form of cryptophasia (Lasalle, 1974) but rather a learned game—and a rather simple one at that—the foundation of which is a capacity to maintain standard prosodical models and standard phonetics while fluently uttering in line with simplified phonological and greatly impoverished morphosyntactic conventions.
- If you are a buff of stratificational linguistics (see Marc Schnitzer's chapter in this book), you might be interested in knowing that glossolalists also have a few strata, thin ones.
- If you like MIT linguistics, you will have to look for something I have not seen.
- If you dabble in mathematics, maybe you will tell me more about stochastic processes. And maybe not. (See Pierre Marie Lavorel's comment, in what follows.)
- If clinical aphasiology is your trade, it is perhaps not without interest for you to learn—if you did not already know—that certain brain lesions, in certain elderlies, can lead to residual brain functioning such that it yields a jar-gonaphasia behavior sharing more, from a linguistic point of view, with schizophasic and charismatic glossolalia than with other forms of aphasic jargon.
- And finally, if you are an addict of neurolinguistics, whether or not you believe that neurolinguistics must be computational, you might be interested in glossolalia as further evidence of the possibility of dissociated functioning in nerve nets related to speech production. You might even find this evidence comforting if you are yourself involved in simulation experiments in which you have ignored, say, prosody, or maybe semantics.

Process Control and Motivation in Glossolalia: Comments on Lecours' Presentation

By Pierre Lavorel

Is there a syntax of the glossolalic utterance? Are there semantic goals?

It does not seem to be a stochastic process of the simple kind measured by entropy. I drew a state diagram for the first charismatic in Lecours' sample to analyze the basic rhythm and chart the basic elements of recurrence. The coefficient of variation of the rhythmic period seemed too high for a simple Markov model to be convincing. Nonetheless, rhythm is a basic facet of glossolalia.

State diagram for Charismatic #1

If the states correspond to the following equivalence classes:

$$q_1 = \{0\}; \; q_2 = \left\{ \begin{array}{l} \text{kiRia} \\ \text{silia} \\ \text{sikolea} \\ \text{sikolia} \\ \ldots \end{array} \right. \qquad ; \; q_3 = \left\{ \begin{array}{l} \text{RamatuRei}\!\int ; \\ \text{maRamakolei}\!\int \\ \text{Ramatai}\!\int \\ \text{maRanatai}\!\int \\ \ldots \end{array} \right.$$

$$q_4 = \left\{ \begin{array}{l} \text{ja}\!\int\!\text{imdea} \\ \text{jara} \end{array} \right. \qquad ; \; q_5 = \{\text{matoi}\},$$

the state diagram would be:

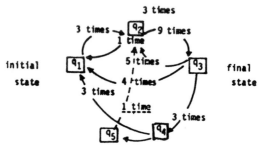

transitions to:

$$q_2 : 12/31; \; q_3 \; ; \; 12/31; \; q_1 : 5/31; \; q_4 \; ; \; 3/31; \; q_5 \; ; \; 1/31.$$

A finite state automaton could be defined to simulate this process.

What is also interesting is the fact that glossolalia is not restricted to simulators. In Lyon, we had a Wernicke's aphasic with glossolalic manifestations. We found the melodic variation in her utterance to be far more regular that that of natural language.

If probabilistic models do not suffice to understand glossolalia, a "systems" approach would perhaps be more helpful. Complex interactive processes involving not only a phonological generator but also symbolic, motor, and proprioceptive functions seem to be at work. We have studied the effect of delayed auditory feedback on people attempting glossolalia. A 500 msec delay is sufficient to hinder the normals, but there is no such impairment with Wernicke's aphasics (or with schizophasics). What, then, are these control processes of euphony and of cacophony which differ in normal and in abnormal speech? Syllable formation and phonic sequence formation seem to be carefully organized in glossolalia and in xenoglossia. I studied an English lady who claimed her glossolalic speech was "Pharaonic Egyptian," but found that she used the English stock phonemes and euphonic principles akin to alliteration, assonance, and complementation which requires a lot of self-control.

Now, what are the semantic goals behind the formal aspects of these elaborate language games? We can always revert to ontogenetic and to phylogenetic arguments. Children, for instance, are known to be good at jabbering repetitive variations. At one lunchtime, I had my children simulate glossolalia by pretending to speak "African" or "Chinese." But they reinvented linguistic strategies. Their intonation became varied to convey the "mood" of an argument; later on they evolved "words" for objects on the table; and by the end of this 35-minute experiment, I had the impression that a "pidginization" of their own syntax (subject, verb, object) began to emerge. Perhaps these mark the basic stages that distinguish true propositional language from glossolalia. Now, in spite of this rather negative experiment, it seems fair to say that incantations have always appealed to children, as well as to poets. Poetry is characterized by alliteration, assonance, and rhyme. *Rhyme* and rhythm are derived from the same Greek root *rhythmos*: Koestler (1956) said that "rhyme is but a glorified pun". Do these various poetic figures, then, all come from forms of rhythm which may themselves be related to the basic characteristics of glossolalia? Perhaps glossolalia, like primitive songs and ancient poetry, exhibits the hidden puns of another world, whether that be the world of devils and gods as claimed by "possessed" glossolalics, or the nether world of the subconscious mind. Sheer articulatory pleasure may indeed be part of the story—Fonagy (1970,1971) claims to have shown that the movements of the vocal tract (tension, relaxation, vibration, constriction) have something to do with deeply rooted oral impulses.

To end my remarks with a neuropsychological hypothesis about glossolalia, we may recall the finding of Luria and Vinogradova (1959) that chloralhydrate makes people associate sounds easily, but disturbs the association of words to convey meaning. What is inhibited? Perhaps mechanisms for planning, possibly located in the frontal lobes or at the tip of the temporal lobes, or in the supramarginal and angular gyri. Besides, one should not disregard subcortical influences. In *The Act of Creation*, Koestler (1956) cites Förster's syndrome. In the 1920s, Förster studied a subject who exhibited manic speech on manipulation of a tumor in the floor of the third ventricle. Each word of the operator would trigger a flood of associations. So we should perhaps consider the role of ventrolateral thalamus.

But there is a lot of fiction in this. The main point is that it is insufficient to look at the surface data if we are to simulate the "simulators," that is, the glossolalics, in their speech.

REFERENCES

Blumstein, S. (1973). A *phonological investigation of aphasic speech*. The Hague: Mouton.
Bobon, J. (1952). *Introduction historique à l'étude des néologismes et des glossolalies en psychopathologie*. Liège: Vaillant-Carmanne.

Broca, P. (1861). Nouvelle observation d'aphémie produite par une lésion de la moitié postérieure des deuxième et troisième circonvolutions frontales. *Bulletin de la Société d'Anatomie, 6,* 398–407.

Cénac, M. (1925). *De certains langages crées par les aliénés—Contribution à l'étude des glossolalies.* Paris: Jouve.

Flournoy, Th. (1900). *Des Ides à la Planète Mars—Etude sur un cas de somnambulisme avec glossolalie.* Paris: Alcan; Geneva: Eggimann.

Fonagy I. (1970, 1971). Les bases pulsionnelles de la phonation. *Revue Française de Psychanalyse* 34, 4; 35, 4.

Koestler A. (1956). *The act of creation.* London: Pan.

Lasalle, J.-P. (1974). Théorie des vicariances dans les hermetolectes. *Grammatica, 10,* 49–61.

Laurentin, P. (1974). *Pentecôtisme chez les Catholiques—Risques et avenir.* Paris: Beauchesne.

Lecours, A. R., Deloche, G., and Lhermitte, F. (1973). Paraphasies phonémiques: Description et simulation sur ordinateur. In *Colloques IRIA—Informatique médicale,* Vol. 1, Rocquencourt: Institut de Recherche d'Informatique et d'Automatique.

Lecours, A. R. and Lhermitte, F. (1969). Phonemic paraphasias: Linguistic structures and tentative hypotheses. *Cortex, 5,* 193–228.

Lecours, A. R., Navet, M., and Ross-Chouinard, A. (1981). Langage et pensée du schizophase. *Confrontations psychiatriques, 19,* 109–144.

Lecours, A. R., Osborn, E., Travis, L., Rouillon, F., and Lavallée-Huynh, G. (1981). Jargons. In J. W. Brown, (Ed.), *Jargonaphasia.* New York: Academic Press.

Lecours, A. R., Travis, L., and Osborn, E. (1980). Glossolalia as a manifestation of Wernicke's aphasia. In M. Taylor-Sarno and O. Höök (Eds.), *Aphasia—assessment and treatment.* Stockholm: Almquist and Wiksell.

Léon, P., and Léon, M. (1964). *Introduction à la phonétique corrective.* Paris: Hachette and Larousse.

Lhermitte, F., Lecours, A. R., Ducarne, B., and Escourolle, R. (1973). Unexpected anatomical findings in a case of fluent jargon aphasia. *Cortex, 9,* 433–446.

Luria A. R., and Vinogradova O. S. (1959). An objective investigation of the dynamics of semantic systems. *British Journal of Psychology, 50,* 2.

Perecman, E., and Brown, J. W. (1981). Phonemic jargon: A case report. In J. W. Brown (Ed.), *Jargonaphasia.* New York: Academic Press.

Pratt, H. (1973). *Rendez-vous à Bahia,* Tournai: Casterman.

Samarin, W. (1972). *Tongues of men and angels.* New York: Macmillan.

Santerre, L. (1976). *Fréquence des phonèmes dans le Français parlé au Québec.* Documents du Laboratoire de Phonétique Expérimentale, Département de Linguistique et Philologie, Université de Montréal.

17

The Neurology of Reading Disorders

David N. Levine
Ron Calvanio

Disorders of reading are extremely common in patients with cerebral lesions and have long interested neurologists and psychologists concerned with aphasia. The nature of these disorders has excited much controversy but surprisingly little controlled experimentation. In this chapter, we wish to summarize our approach to the study of these disorders and to relate our findings to previous work. Before we begin this presentation, we shall briefly discuss the nature of reading and what we mean by a reading disorder.

WHAT IS READING?

Reading is not one thing. It is a name given to a family of activities, and it is difficult to define what these activities have in common without using words (such as "language") more difficult to define than reading itself. Ordinarily, reading involves responding in a conventionally acceptable manner to a set of visual stimuli. However, this statement is both too broad and too narrow. It is too broad because greeting a friend when we see his face is not reading, although a verbal response to a visual stimulus is involved. It is too narrow because, although reading usually involves visual stimuli, most of us would probably accept appropriate responses to tactile stimuli, such as Braille, within the family of reading activities. It is curious that, although we are willing to accept these visual and tactile activities as reading, most of us would not accept as such similar responses to heard speech. The repetition of someone else's speech is not reading aloud, nor is obeying a spoken command evidence of reading comprehension. However, we would be tempted to accept the naming of words spelled aloud as a

[1]This work was supported in part by Grant NS-13102 from The National Institute of Neurologic and Communicative Disorders and Stroke of The National Institutes of Health.

371

NEURAL MODELS OF
LANGUAGE PROCESSES

form of reading. Reciting a message coming across a telegraph in Morse code might also qualify.

Some of this seeming arbitrariness may be resolved by introducing the notion of code or sign. We might consider one set of stimuli (Set A) a code for another (Set B) if the two sets are not identical and if there is a well-defined mapping of Set A onto Set B. The stimuli considered acceptable for "reading" must be signs of speech. The nature of the mapping is highly variable. It may be many-to-one (homonyms) or one-to-many (dialects). It may be phonetic, syllabic, or morphemic. However, there must be a mapping. The rejection of speech repetition but the acceptability of Morse code now becomes more plausible, because in the former, Set A and Set B are identical, that is, there is no code (though there is still the problem of defining "identical").

The term "reading" is many-faceted not only from the perspective of stimulus modality, but also from the point of view of the type of response and the nature of the relationship between stimulus and response. Often, only the crudest distinction is drawn between "reading aloud"—in which the reader recites the coded (Set B) value of the stimulus—and reading "comprehension." But the term *comprehension* encompasses a wide variety of activities that may be no more clearly related to each other than any one of them is to reading aloud. For example, if we consider only speech responses, one test of "comprehension" may involve a propositional response to a written message (*I'll be late* is usually a proper answer to DINNER IS AT SEVEN, but *The pen is red* is usually not), another may involve a yes–no response to whether an array of letters is an English word. The response modality need not be speech but may be writing, pointing, manipulating, ambulating, etc. It is obvious that the variety of acts subsumed under the term *reading comprehension* is limitless.

WHAT IS A READING DISORDER?

A reading disorder exists when a subject cannot read as quickly or as accurately as some arbitrarily agreed upon majority of his age-matched peers. He may never have been taught, or he may have been unable to learn. Alternatively, he may have read competently but then suffered damage to function of eyes, nerves, brain, or muscle. In this latter group, which will primarily concern us, we can avoid the problem of specifying the normative population by defining a reading disorder as a subject's inability to read as he once did.

A reading disorder may be more or less confined to the family of activities we have called reading. The ideal "pure" reading disorder would impair ALL of the acts that we have called "reading" and ONLY those acts. Within a given input modality, such as vision, the impairment should be specific for reading but not extend to other acts, such as face recognition. The impairment should extend across input modalities to involve the retention or acquisition of Braille or Morse code. This lack of input specificity should be matched by a lack of output specificity—affecting all reading acts, whether the response is contractions of skeletal musculature (oral, limb, or body), contractions of smooth muscle, or glandular secretions.

Many reading disorders lack both within modality specificity and across modality nonspecificity. Blindness resulting from bilateral ocular disease will obviously preclude reading, but it will also impair all other visual discriminations as well. Moreover, tactile and auditory reading do not suffer, and if not yet learned, may be readily mastered. A similar situation occurs with some lesions of the brain. Bilateral lesions of optic nerves, lateral geniculate bodies, visual radiations, and striate cortex all produce visual impairments nonspecific with regard to reading but highly specific with regard to modality.

Analogous remarks apply to motor disorders. Bulbar paralysis will preclude oral responses to reading material, but will also impair other uses of these muscles. Mastery of another output channel—such as manual signing—will allow reading "aloud." Again, there is insufficient specificity within the output modality and too much specificity across output modalities.

Other conditions in which reading is impaired are far from "pure" reading disorders for similar reasons. Patients with right hemisphere lesions frequently neglect the contralateral side of space. They may, for example, read the word *islander* as "lander" or "slander." This disorder often, but not invariably, extends across modalities—so that in this sense it may approach a "pure" reading disorder more closely than blindness or bulbar palsy. But there is no specificity within modality. The patient neglects the left side not only in reading words but also in describing pictures, in traversing the environment, etc. Patients with bilateral frontal or diencephalic lesions and the syndrome of akinetic mutism may do poorly on all sorts of reading tests, but also show much more general cognitive and emotional disturbances. The same is true of all the toxic states associated with stupor and coma, as well as of states such as depression, with unknown neuropathological substrates.

In the following discussion, we shall not consider these disorders of reading. Instead, our attention will focus on more specific disorders of reading, which do not yield to such broad explanations as coma, depression, left-neglect, blindness, or paralysis. However, we shall find that these reading disorders are also rarely, if ever, "pure" in the ideal sense described earlier. Instead, they are often associated with (a) varying degrees of impairment of other language activities such as naming, speech comprehension, speaking, and writing, and/or (b) mild to moderate deficits in other visual discriminations besides reading. Nevertheless, unlike the disorders described previously, the reading disorder may stand out as conspicuously severe.

Reading and Hemispheric Specialization

Before discussing the more specific reading disorders in detail, we must note the striking fact that these disorders occur only with damage to the speech dominant hemisphere, usually the left. We know of no instance where a specific reading disorder has occurred with a lesion confined to the nondominant hemisphere. Why is this the case? Why are speech and reading lateralized together?

To answer this question requires a brief look at the ontogeny of reading. The average child does not begin to read until the age of 5 or 6. By this time he has had 4 or 5 years of practice with speech and speech comprehension, at which he has become quite adept. [You will recall that Binet found the average 4-year-old capable of following a three-commission command, something that Marie (1906) found very difficult for most aphasics.] There is considerable evidence that at the age of 6 this proficiency with speech and speech comprehension is more dependent on the left hemisphere than on the right. (Basser, 1962; Lennenberg, 1967). Thus, the child comes to the task of reading with considerable proficiency in speech and in speech comprehension, the integrity and further development of which are more dependent of his left hemisphere than on his right.

Learning to read is learning a code. The child is presented with printed letters or letter arrays, and, by observing the teacher naming, repeating the teacher's speech, and finally practicing on his own, he learns to name them. There are, of course, many different methods, often debated among educators, of teaching the child this code, but almost all methods start with the visual input of print and end with speech.

Let us look at the possible neural pathways utilized by the child in learning to read in Figure 17.1 (A, B, C). The visual input traverses the geniculo-calcarine pathway to reach the striate visual cortex (V) of the occipital lobe contralateral to the visual field in which the stimulus originated [dashed lines of Figure 17.1 (A, B, C)]. We know this is the case because damage to this pathway produces hemianopia—that is, blindness in the contralateral visual field. The speech output originates from the motor cortex (M) of the precentral gyrus, primarily on the left. We know this to be true because lesions of this area severely impair speech. The pathways connecting V and M, although not precisely known, can be divided into three categories, represented by the solid lines in Figure 17.1 (A, B, C). The connections may be entirely within the left hemisphere, if the visual stimulus originates in the right visual field (A). Or the connections may cross from right hemisphere to left if the stimulus originates in the left visual field (B and C). All evidence to date from lower primates suggests that commissural connections are largely homotopic—that is, they are strongest between homologous points of the two cerebral hemispheres. Thus, there are two possible cross-hemispheric pathways: (a) a posterior commissural connection between

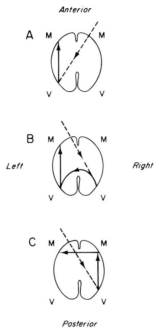

FIGURE 17.I.(A, B, C) *View from above of a schematic horizontal section of the brain. Dashed lines represent input from a lateral visual field to the visual cortex (V) of the opposite occipital lobe. Solid lines represent connections from occipital lobe to that portion of motor cortex (M) mediating speech in the left hemisphere. Such connections may be entirely within the left hemisphere (A) or involve cross-hemispheric integration (B and C).*

visual cortices of right and left hemispheres with subsequent connection, within the left hemisphere, of visual and motor areas (B) and (b) connection of visual motor areas within the right hemisphere with crossing occurring more anteriorly between right and left motor cortices (C).

There is abundant evidence that Pathway (A) is most efficient, Pathway (B) is somewhat less so, and Pathway (C) is extremely inefficient. First, experiments in both animals and man indicate that Pathway (a) is slightly more efficient than the sum of Pathways (B and C). Myers (1965) found that cats and monkeys learn shape discrimination somewhat more efficiently when stimulus and response are on the same side of space than when the stimulus comes from one side and the response emanates from the other. For example, suppose a monkey is to learn to discriminate a circle from a square by pushing a button only when the circle appears. If he is allowed to push the button only with his right hand, he will learn slightly more quickly if the shapes are presented in the right visual field than if they are presented in the left. In the former situation, the stimuli activate the same hemisphere that controls the response [Pathway (A)], whereas in the latter situation cross-hemispheric connections are required [Pathways (B and C)].

If this principle—that learning involving intrahemispheric connections is more efficient than learning involving cross-hemispheric connections—extends to man as well, one would expect that reading print in the right visual field as in (A) would be slightly easier than reading print in the left visual field as in (B or C). Such appears to be the case: Several investigators, beginning with Mishkin and Forgays (1952) have shown that naming words or letter arrays is more accurate and slightly faster in the right visual field than in the left. Again, the pathway of (A) is more efficient than the sum of pathways in (B and C).

Of the two cross-hemispheric routes, there is considerable evidence that (B) is far more important than (C). Literate adults with section of the posterior portion (splenium) of the corpus callosum are unable to read accurately in their left visual fields. (Levine and Calvanio, 1980; Trescher and Ford, 1927). Section of the anterior two-thirds of the corpus callosum, however, results in no reading deficit (Gordon, Bogen, and Sperry, 1971). We have studied a 33-year-old man, (Levine, Hier, and Calvanio, 1981) who at age 6—just as instruction in reading was beginning—developed a hemorrhage in his left temporal lobe and ultimately underwent left temporal lobectomy. An initial fluent aphasia soon improved, but, despite considerable effort, he remains unable to read 27 years later. A Wada test showed that speech output still originated from the left hemisphere. The temporal lobe lesion interrupted the left intrahemispheric pathways needed in (A and B). The connections necessary in (C) remained intact, but they were unable to develop sufficiently to mediate even the rudiments of reading.

Thus, of the three types of connections between visual areas and left motor cortex that are capable of mediating the acquisition of reading, the left intrahemispheric pathway is most efficient, the posterior crossing plus left intrahemispheric pathway is slightly less efficient, and the right intrahemispheric plus anterior crossing pathway does not appear to participate significantly.

ACQUIRED READING DISORDERS (ALEXIAS)

The foregoing remarks lead us directly to a consideration of the relatively specific disorders of reading resulting from brain damage. In following this order, we are doing an injustice to history—for it was the clinical and neuropathological studies of alexia that led to many of the ideas and observations of the previous section, rather than vice versa.

The clinicopathological study of alexia began in earnest with the studies of Dejerine (1891, 1892). He distinguished two syndromes in which alexia was a salient feature: alexia without agraphia (pure alexia, agnosic alexia) and alexia with agraphia (aphasic alexia). He also postulated distinct neuropathologic bases for these two syndromes from the findings on post-mortem examination. His analysis in large part remains valid today.

Pure Alexia

Clinical Features and Pathophysiology

The patient with pure alexia (alexia without agraphia, agnosic alexia) presents a striking clinical picture. Many of his language activities appear intact: He speaks fluently and coherently, although a minor degree of difficulty with word recall—especially proper names—is often present. He understands complex, multistep requests and has no difficulty repeating the examiner's speech. Reasoning capacity, wit, and personality are not obviously changed, although a variable degree of impaired memory for recent events is often present. There is usually no paralysis, but a sensory loss over the contralateral side of the body occasionally occurs. A right homonymous hemianopia is almost invariably present.

Reading difficulty varies from mild to extraordinarily severe. Severely affected patients are unable to name individual printed letters or words, but rarely, if ever, do such patients fail with every letter and every word: Usually, a few are correct but most are not. Perseverative errors are usually very common, but visual confusions (e.g., O for C, N for Z) often occur as well. Auditory confusions (e.g., S for C) are less common but have been reported in some patients. Often, no obvious relationship of target to error is evident.

Less severely affected patients do relatively well in naming single letters but still have major difficulty reading words. They often try to sound out the word letter by letter or guess at the word based on the first few letters. The wrong word may be named as the patient is misled by the seeming context, often created by his previous errors.

Except for a clumsier penmanship, writing both spontaneously and to dictation may be normal (or nearly so). It is common for patients to write a sentence correctly to dictation but then a minute or two later, be unable to read what they wrote. Oral spelling, like written, is intact. The naming of words spelled orally by the examiner is preserved, despite the reading deficit.

The majority of patients with pure alexia including Dejerine's original case, have a lesion in the left temporooccipital region, resulting from infarction in the territory of the left posterior cerebral artery. This finding led Dejerine to a hypothesis regarding the pathological basis of the alexia. Dejerine argued that the lesion isolated an otherwise intact left hemisphere from visual input by interrupting two important fiber tracts. The first is the geniculo–calcarine pathway of the left hemisphere, interruption of which produces right homonymous hemianopia. This lesion eliminates the circuit in Figure 17.1 of (A) and requires that all visual input be projected to the right hemisphere. The second tract is the splenium of the corpus callosum or its extension into the left hemisphere. Interruption of this pathway eliminates the circuit of (B) and deprives the left hemisphere of its remaining access to visual input. Because the language areas of the left hemisphere are largely intact, the patient remains able to perform all language activities not dependent upon visual input. Speech, speech comprehension, oral spelling, and even writing are preserved, but the patient is unable to read.

Experimental Psychological Studies

In the past few years, we have attempted to elucidate the behavioral consequences of this disconnection syndrome. How should one best describe the difficulties of the patient with pure alexia as he attempts to read? Is it fair to say, as have some authors (e.g., Luria, 1966), that he cannot adequately "see" the letters? Or, is it more accurate to say along with other authors (e.g., Geschwind, 1967), the patients "sees" the letters but cannot "name" them? In either case, how are we using the words "see" and "name"?

We began our studies by comparing the performances of patients with those of normal controls on a number of tasks utilizing visual letters and words as stimuli. Our experimental group consisted of three patients with circumscribed left temporooccipital lesions and pure alexia of moderate to fairly severe intensity (Levine and Calvanio, 1978). We subsequently expanded these studies and included two additional patients.

Our patients were able to name nearly all single printed letters accurately, but they had extraordinary difficulty reading words or sentences. We found that if single letters were presented tachistoscopically to their preserved left visual field, our patients had exposure thresholds no longer than those of age-matched controls. We also found that single letters could not be masked by aftercoming random visual patterns any more efficiently in our patients than in normal controls. So, in the sense of exposure thresholds for single letters, a task with which they were successful outside the tachistoscope, our patients' seeing appeared normal.

Quite a different picture emerged when we changed the stimuli from single letters to a horizontal three letter array. Control subjects were able to name three letters with exposure times only a few milliseconds longer than the threshold for single letters. The alexics, however, were able to name only one or perhaps two of the letters with exposures as long as 1500 msec, a hundred or more times the threshold for single letters. So, with multiple letters, a task difficult outside the tachistoscope, "seeing" in the sense of exposure thresholds was abnormal. These findings confirmed earlier reports by Ranschburg and Schill (1932) and by Kinsbourne and Warrington (1962).

But was the elevated threshold with multiple letters truly a difficulty "seeing"? Perhaps the patients, in some sense, "saw" the letters normally but were unable to name them. Several observations and experiments have suggested that this is not the case:

1. In the threshold experiments described here, the average number of letters correctly identified increased steadily as exposure time increased, even though the threshold of three letters correctly identified was never reached.

2. The errors in identifying letter arrays were frequently morphologic in nature (e.g. O for Q, W for V).

3. There was a marked deterioration in performance when morphologically complex letters (e.g., RWK) replaced morphologically simple ones (DVT) or when the letters of a trigram resembled one another morphologically (NXK) instead of being distinct (XOT).

4. If unable to name the three briefly exposed letters, the patient was unable to print them with either hand or to point them out on an answer sheet containing a list of all the letters in the alphabet.

5. If asked to name only one of the three letters, with the spatial position of the target specified by the examiner, the patients were fairly successful if the spatial cue preceded the exposure but not if it followed the exposure.

6. When the patients were required neither to name the letters nor to identify them by copying or matching, but only to enumerate the number of distinct shapes or to state whether all of the shapes were the same, performance was still abnormal.

All of these findings have suggested to us that although "seeing" of single letters may be normal, "seeing" of multiletter arrays is abnormal in patients with pure alexia. The sense in which we are using the word "seeing" must, however, be noted. This abnormality need not be reflected in standard measures of visual acuity. Seeing of stimuli other than written language—even if as complex as faces—may be adequate for accurate identification.

We were able to test these findings in a patient with a lesion confined to the splenium of the corpus callosum (Levine and Calvanio, 1980). Such a patient is not alexic because the left hemisphere is capable of receiving visual input and utilizing the intrahemispheric pathways for reading, as the pathway in Figure 17.1(A) is intact. However, when the visual stimuli are confined to the left visual field, the patient is alexic because this information cannot be transmitted to the left hemisphere as a consequence of the callosal lesion [Pathway 17.1(B) is interrupted]. Cases such as these are extremely valuable because the two hemispheres of a single individual can be compared. The "control" left hemisphere and the "experimental" right hemisphere have the same genetic background and the same environmental history. This case was especially valuable in the latter regard, for there had been no history of childhood damage to either hemisphere, as is the case in most other "split-brain" subjects.

Some of our findings were surprising. We found that the visual fields showed mild concentric constriction and that tachistoscopic thresholds for detecting presence or absence of a black dot or for matching two forms were elevated in each visual field. Thus, the splenium of the corpus callosum was important even in such "elementary" visual discriminations. Even for stimuli projected to a single hemisphere, two interconnected hemispheres are better than one. In these tasks, each visual field showed nearly identical, mild impairment. Such symmetry remained the case when the patient was required to identify, by matching or drawing, briefly exposed nonsensical letterlike shapes or geometric drawings, whether presented singly or in arrays of three. However, as soon as the patient was required to identify arrays of letters, numbers, or colors, performance in the right—but not the left—visual field improved dramatically.

As in our patients with left occipitotemporal lesions, the deficit in letter identification in the left visual fields was present whether the patient had to name the letters, draw them, or match them to an answer card. Errors were more frequently perseverative than in the alexic subjects, but visual errors occurred as well. Sensitivity to increases in the complexity of letter morphology and to the degree of interletter similarity were less marked but present nevertheless. The left visual field remained poorer than the right in a matching task, although the difference was not as dramatic as in the task of identification. In summary, the special sense in which letter arrays were abnormally "seen" in the left visual field of the split-brain patient resembled that in the patients with pure alexia.

It thus appears that the effects of anatomical disconnection of the cerebral hemispheres cannot be simply described as a psychological disconnection between "seeing" and "naming." First, there are effects on elementary visual discrimination in both visual fields. Second, there are special effects on visual identification of letters, numbers, and colors in the left visual fields: Whereas on the right, the number of letters or numerals that can be identified in a single brief visual fixation greatly exceeds the number of geometric or nonsense shapes, the advantage of letters (as well as numbers and colors) over nonsense shapes is absent in the left visual fields.

We believe that this deficit in the span of visual identification of letters can be understood as a consequence of left hemisphere control of speech. The span of visual identification for letters in one's native language expands pari passu with improved skill in reading during middle and late childhood (Hoffman, 1927). Because acquiring reading skill involves the use of speech, the left hemisphere MUST BE ACTIVATED, via the circuit of either (A) or (B). The span of visual letter identification, intimately associated with reading skill, depends, for its integrity, upon the preservation of these pathways. It will be selectively diminished in the left visual field whenever the circuit of (B) is interrupted.

This distinction between this view and that of a psychological disconnection must be emphasized. Our data are not consistent with the view that the act of naming a letter can be neatly subdivided into components of "seeing" and of "naming" that can each remain intact, but be dissociated from one another, following a lesion of the callosum. Rather, we believe that each act must be considered to some degree as a whole—mediated, however, by specific neural circuitry. To the extent that a given act is the manifestation of a skill that is acquired by the use of speech, the left hemisphere must be activated for the act to occur normally. A callosal lesion will severely impair this act when the stimulus is presented in the left visual field, but not when it is presented in the right visual field, because Circuit (A) (or its equivalent in other modalities) is preserved and Circuit (B) is not. Thus, letter identification, whether by naming, drawing, or matching to sample, is severely affected in the left visual field because this group of perceptual skills develops as a direct result of gaining proficiency in reading, a skill that is nearly always learned by the use of speech.

This view allows us to integrate the mild SYMMETRICAL defects of elementary visual discrimination after callosal section with the *asymmetrical* deficits in visual letter, number, and color identification. Fully normal visual perception, even in a single hemifield, requires two callosally interconnected hemispheres. A lesion of the posterior corpus callosum thus produces impairment in each visual field. Some visual acts have no asymmetry in the underlying neural circuitry. For example, under most circumstances, directing one's gaze to a peripheral point of light is probably performed equally well whether the point is in the left visual field (in which case right hemisphere activity predominates) or in the right visual field (in which case left hemisphere activity prodominates). For such acts, callosal disconnection results in SYMMETRICAL deficits, which are only *mild*— because the intact contralateral hemisphere mediates the lion's share of the act. For the deficits to be severe, bilateral lesions are required (Levine, Calvanio, and Wolf, 1980). Other visual acts, however, do have a major asymmetry in their underlying neural circuitry. Such is the case for visual letter identification, which requires a major left hemisphere contribution even for stimuli in the left visual field. For these acts, callosal disconnection results in ASYMMETRICAL deficits. For letter identification, the right visual field defect will be mild, but the left visual field deficit will be severe, because the necessary left hemisphere activation by the visual input cannot take place. Thus perceptual tasks vary in the extent to which they are differentially affected in the right and left fields by callosal section in proportion to the asymmetry of the underlying neural circuits.

The Purity of "Pure Alexia"

We have presented Dejerine's hypotheses that pure alexia represents the isolation of a relatively intact hemisphere from direct and transcallosal visual input. We have hypothesized that the consequences of this isolation are that visual discrimination will in general be mildly impaired, but visual discriminations learned in conjunction with speech will be severely impaired.

This hypothesis would predict that the severe deficits in pure alexia should extend beyond reading to other visual behavior that is learned by the child with the use of speech. Such appears to be the case. Patients with pure alexia usually have difficulty naming colors. Like the alexia, the disorder with colors is not restricted to naming tasks, but usually affects the identification of colors by sorting, delayed matching, crayon selection for coloring a picture, etc. Like alexia, this "color agnosia" is usually sensitive to stimulus variables. For example, the use of pastel shades or of multiple rather than single stimuli may bring out the difficulty in color identification when it is otherwise not immediately apparent. Color identification in children is generally not learned before the third year, and like reading, is taught by means of speech.

The identification of objects and faces is affected to a lesser degree, and varies from one case of pure alexia to another. Dejerine (1892) and Bonvicini and Potzl (1907) reported cases in which the naming of objects was spared. However, at times a large unilateral left temporooccipital lesion results in markedly impaired object naming and identification—that is, "associative visual agnosia" (Caplan and Hedly-White, 1967). The errors are at times visual, and they are often preseverative. We suspect that perseverations, semantic errors, and visual errors may reflect increasing control by the stimulus over the response, so that perseverations may dominate in the more severe cases and visual errors in the milder ones.

The generally milder impairment of object and face identification may reflect the fact that these tasks are mastered earlier than letter and color identifications and the child is capable of many discriminative responses to objects even before he has acquired speech. For example, the preverbal child of 7–8 months discriminates familiar from unfamiliar faces—the basis of "stranger fear." Thus, a unilateral left temporooccipital lesion must be very extensive before face and object identification are impaired, and alexia–color agnosia will always be present.

It is thus clear that the disorder of visual identification in "pure alexia" extends beyond the identification of written language. Nevertheless, there is more within modality specificity in this disorder than, for example, in blindness following bilateral ocular enucleation. Patients with pure alexia are able to reach for objects and traverse an environment without colliding with obstacles. These are examples of activities whose underlying neural circuitry is right–left symmetric.

Pure alexia also to some degree lacks the nonspecificity across modalities that we demanded of our ideal reading disorder. Some investigators of single cases, where alexia was very severe so that single letters were misidentified, have reported that tactile identification of letters was better than visual identification. However, this phenomenon has not been adequately investigated, and there are many patients who do not identify palpated alphabetic characters well. There is, however, one sense in which these alexic patients can "read" (Geschwind, 1965). If an examiner spells aloud the words in a written text, the pure alexic can recognize each word as it is spelled aloud and thus "read" the text much more accurately than he could by eye. Although quite unconventional, it is not completely unfair to consider this activity a form of "reading." It would be of interest to examine a patient with alexia without agraphia who was proficient with Morse code by ear. This form of reading might well be preserved.

Aphasic Alexia

Aphasic alexia differs from pure alexia both pathologically and clinically. The pathological basis of pure alexia is an isolation of a RELATIVELY INTACT left hemisphere from visual input. The intact left hemisphere allows for speech, auditory language comprehension, and even writing. In contrast, the pathological basis of aphasic alexia is destruction of part or all of the language areas in the left hemisphere itself. If we may be permitted the most elementary analogy of brain and computer, pure alexia is the severing of an input channel to an otherwise intact computer, whereas aphasic alexia represents taking a hammer to the computer itself.

The extent and nature of the impairments in language activities other than reading depend upon the location and size of the left hemisphere lesion in aphasic alexia. Dejerine first described aphasic alexia in its purest form as the syndrome of "alexia with agraphia" resulting from lesions of the cortex of the left angular gyrus. The affected patient could not read either visually or by naming words spelled aloud to him. He could not write with correct spelling nor could he spell aloud. Despite these disabilities, speech was intact save for some word-finding trouble; understanding of speech was relatively preserved.

This form of aphasic alexia is closer to our ideal reading disorder than pure alexia in one sense but further away in another. It is closer because the inability to "read" by naming spelled out words confers upon aphasic alexia the nonspecificity across modalities that we required of the ideal reading disorder. However, the presence of impaired writing and minor but definite disorders of naming and of speech comprehension detract from the specificity of the impairment to acts of reading. In other forms of aphasic alexia, where deficits of speech and/or speech comprehension are more marked, this lack of specificity is considerably greater.

The salience of the reading and writing disturbances in "alexia with agraphia" led Dejerine to postulate that the left angular gyrus functioned as a "visual letter and/or word memory store" that had to be activated by visual information for reading to occur. If it were activated instead by impulses from the Wernicke–Broca areas and in turn discharged impulses to the motor cortex related to the arm, writing could occur. Its destruction would preclude both reading and writing.

The concept that the angular gyrus cortex mediates a specific subfunction in the skills of reading and writing has been widely accepted even in modern times. Geschwind (1965) for example, described the function of the left angular gyrus as translation of visual language into its auditory form (as in reading) or vice versa (as in writing).

However, the existence of a precise functional role for the left angular gyrus has never been clearly demonstrated, and later findings have complicated matters considerably. As previously mentioned, alexia and agraphia occur not only with lesions of the left angular gyrus but also with lesions of several other specific areas of the left hemisphere. Lesions of the posterior superior temporal lobe produce alexia and agraphia along with other signs of Wernicke's aphasia. Some authors have suggested that these lesions must extend posteriorly to involve the angular gyrus, but Nielsen (1939b) collected 16 such cases in whom post-mortem examination showed the damage to be confined to the temporal lobe. Alexia and agraphia also occur in Broca's aphasia (Benson, 1977; Nielsen, 1939a; Wernicke, 1874), and the lesion may be confined to the precentral gyrus, leaving the angular gyrus intact (Trojanowski, Green, and Levine 1980).

The mediation of reading by MULTIPLE SPECIFIC regions of the left hemisphere—including the angular gyrus, superior temporal region, and precentral gyrus—is confirmed by studies of changes in cerebral blood flow during reading (Lassen, Ingvar, and Skinj, 1978). Increases of blood flow occurring in these regions presumably reflect the vascular response to increased neuronal energy needs. The energy is needed to maintain the transmembrane ionic gradients which would otherwise break down in proportion to neuronal electrical activity.

The existence of multiple, specific areas to mediate reading—although inconsistent with the notion of a single reading center—is still consistent with the concept of a specific behavioral function for the angular gyrus. Both classical (Dejerine, 1892; Wernicke, 1874) and modern (Luria, 1966) neurologists and psychologists have explicitly or implicitly approached the problem as follows. They assume that a reading act—let us say reading aloud—is a complex that can be broken down into "functional components" which add up to the whole act if performed in some sequential or parallel fashion. The model might be simple, with only two components such as "seeing" and "naming," or exceedingly complex with many components (see, e.g., Gibson and Levin, 1975). These component processes are then transposed to the brain, usually one function per area. Thus, it is assumed that each of the specific brain regions involved in reading mediates a specific functional component of the complex reading act.

This view implies that lesions of the different regions involved in reading should result in distinct alexic syndromes, because each region deals primarily or exclusively with a distinct subcomponent of the reading act. For example, one might expect the alexia associated with Broca's aphasia to have primarily a "motor" character, or to involve syntactic processing, whereas the alexia associated with Wernicke's aphasia might have an "auditory" character with numerous sound-related errors.

These distinct forms of aphasic alexia have failed to materialize, however. Although it is true that Broca's, Wernicke's, and anomic aphasics differ from each other in lesion site and in behavioral parameters such as speech output, the nature of their alexia does not seem to vary systematically with the location of the lesion. The past decade has seen a concerted attempt to establish the existence of distinct forms of aphasic alexia without much success. The analysis of reading has usually been linguistic. Gardner, Zurif, and their colleagues (Gardner and Zurif, 1975, 1976; Gardner, Denes, and Zurif, 1975) have investigated reading performances of Broca's, Wernicke's, and anomic aphasics on a variety of tasks. At the single-word level, they studied such variables as part of speech, word length, abstract versus concrete, and operativity versus figurativity. The type of response—naming, pointing to a picture choice, pointing to the word that does not belong to a group—was also varied. At the phrase and sentence level, factors such as semantic versus syntactic deviations from acceptability, and redundancy of information were examined. No appreciable differences were seen between patients with nonfluent and fluent aphasia. Marshall and Newcombe (1975) have proposed classifying alexia on the basis of error type in reading. Although one patient may differ from another in the relative frequency of type of error, no clear relationship of error type to location of lesion has emerged. For example, semantic paralexias occur in temporoparietal occipital lesions (Shallice and Warrington, 1975), in Wernicke's aphasia, and in Broca's aphasia (Patterson, 1978; Schwartz, Saffran, and Marin, 1977) as well.

These findings must cast doubt on the "functional components" approach to alexia, at least with regard to any of the analyses of the reading act that have yet been proposed. The effects on reading of lesions at these different specific brain sites are too similar to one another for these "functional components" models to be valid. It is possible that different areas involved in a given act within the left hemisphere form a highly integrated unit that does not break down neatly into distinct components except at the very peripheral levels of input and output.

By questioning the "functional components" approach to alexia, we do NOT wish to suggest that the reading disorders of all alexic patients are the same. Indeed, there is ample documentation that for any given measure of reading performance there are clear differences among alexic subjects (Marshall and Newcombe, 1975). However, the determinants of these behavioral differences are still unknown. For example, it may be the case that differences in error profiles reflect varying degrees of severity along a unidimensional continuum with a predominance of visual errors indicating a less severe problem, semantic errors a more serious impairment, and perseverations representing the most severe extreme. This continuum may be reflected pathologically by variations in the "weighted" size of the left hemisphere lesion. By "weighted" size we mean that a lesion counts far more if it involves the perisylvian language area than if it does not. Thus, a large lesion, heavily involving the language area, would result in more semantic or perseverative errors, whereas a lesion posterior to the language zone, of moderate size, would result in a preponderance of visual errors. However, it is also possible that the proper componential analysis of reading acts has not been proposed, or that testing has not been sufficiently fine to bring out differences in reading impairments as a function of the location of the brain lesion that are consistent with current componential analyses. It may still be the case that lesions within the language area affect reading in a fundamentally different way from lesions in the parietooccipital region, and that the two deficits are doubly dissociable rather than variations of severity along a unidimensional contiuum.

The answers to these questions are not all evident. The investigation is complicated by the need to consider variables other than size and location of the cerebral lesion in relationship to the alexia. These include premorbid reading strategy—about which little is usually known—and the degree of hemispheric lateralization in a given patient—about which even less is usually known. It is possible that variations in each of these factors may result in different performances by alexics with lesions of similar size and location.

An adequate investigation of the pathological bases of the different manifestations of aphasic alexia will thus require the investigation of many patients with lesions of different sizes and locations. It will also be necessary to employ a variety of reading and reading-related tasks to insure that we do not overlook significant determinants of alexic behavior. For example, we have found that a patient who made semantic errors on one test (e.g., in a test requiring matching of printed homonyms, MEAT was paired with FLESH rather than MEET) made striking visual errors on another (in speeded crossing out es in a page of text he also crossed out cs). We are currently extending our work on patients with pure alexia to those with aphasic alexia with such goals and precautions in mind.

REFERENCES

Basser, L. S. (1962). Hemiplegia of early onset and the faculty of speech with special reference to the effects of hemispherectomy. Brain, 85, 427–460.
Benson, D. F. (1977). The third alexia. Archives of Neurology, 34, 327–331.
Bonvicini, G., and Potzl, O. (1907). Alexie. Arbeit aus dem Obersteiner Institut Wien 16, 522–560.
Caplan, L. R., and Hedly-White, T. (1974). Cuing and memory dysfunction in alexia without agraphia. Brain, 97, 251–262.
Dejerine, J. (1891). Sur un cas de cecite verbale avec agraphie, suivi d' autopsie. Comptes Rendus des Seances de la Societé de Biologie, 3, 197–201.
Dejerine, J. (1892). Des differentes varietes de cecite verbale. Comptes Rendus des seances de la Societé de Biologie, 4, 1–30.

Gardner H., Denes, G., and Zurif, E. (1975). Critical reading at the sentence level in aphasia. *Cortex, 11,* 60–72.

Gardner, H., and Zurif, E. (1975). Bee but not be: Oral reading of single words in aphasia and alexia. *Neuropsychologia, 13,* 181–190.

Gardner, H., and Zurif, E. (1976). Critical reading of words and phrases in aphasia. *Brain and Language, 3,* 173–190.

Geschwind, N. (1965). Disconnexion syndromes in animals and man, I. *Brain, 88,* 237–294.

Geschwind, N. (1967). The varieties of naming errors. *Cortex, 3,* 97–112.

Gibson, E., and Levin, H. (1975). *The psychology of reading.* Cambridge, Mass.: MIT Press.

Gordon, H. W., Bogen, J. E., and Sperry, R. W. (1971) Absence of deconnexion syndrome in two patients with partial section of the neocommissures. *Brain, 94,* 327–336.

Hoffman, H. (1927). Experimentel-psychologische Untersuchungen uber Leseleistungen von Schulkindern. *Archiv für die Gesomke Psychologie 58,* 325–388.

Kinsbourne, M., and Warrington, E. K. (1962). A disorder of simultaneous form perception. *Brain, 85,* 461–486.

Lassen, N. A., Ingvar, D. H., and Skinhj E. (1978). Brain function and blood flow. *Scientific American, 239,* 62–71.

Lennenberg, E. H. (1967). *Biological foundations of language.* New York: John Wiley and Sons.

Levine, D. N., and Calvanio, R. (1978). A study of the visual defect in verbal alexia-simultanagnosia. *Brain, 101,* 65–81.

Levine, D. N., and Calvanio, R. (1980). Visual discrimination after lesion of the posterior corpus callosum. *Neurology, 30,* 21–30.

Levine, D. N., Calvanio, R., and Wolf, E. (1980). Disorders of visual behavior following posterior cerebral lesions. *Psychological Research, 41,* 217–234.

Levine, D. N., Hier, D. B., and Calvanio, R. (1981). Acquired learning disability for reading after left temporal lobe damage in childhood. *Neurology, 31,* 257–264.

Luria, A. R. *Higher cortical functions in man.* (1966). New York: Basic Books.

Marie, P. (1906). (The third left frontal convolution plays no special role in the function of language.] *Semaine Medicale, 26,* 241–247. (Reprinted in M. F. Cole and M. Cole, trans. *Pierre Marie's papers on speech disorders,* New York: Hafner, 1971.)

Marshall, J., and Newcombe, F. (1975). Traumatic dyslexia: Localization and linguistics. In K. J. Zuelch and *et al.* (Eds.), *Cerebral localization.* New York: Springer-Verlag.

Mishkin, M., and Forgays, D. G. (1952). Word recognition as a function of retinal locus. *Journal of Experimental Psychology, 43,* 43–48.

Myers, R. E. (1965). The neocortical commissures and interhemispheric transmission of information. In E. G. Ettlinger, (Ed.), *Functions of the corpus callosum.* Boston: Little, Brown and Company.

Nielsen, J. M. (1939a). The unsolved problems in aphasia, I: Alexia in "motor" aphasia. *Bulletin of the Los Angeles Neurological Society, 4,* 114–122.

Nielsen, J. M. (1939b). The unsolved problems in aphasia, II: Alexia resulting from a temporal lesion. *Bulletin of the Los Angeles Neurological Society, 4,* 168–183.

Patterson, K. E. (1978). Phonemic dyslexia: Errors of meaning and the meaning of errors. *Quarterly Journal of Experimental Psychology, 30,* 587–601.

Ranschburg, P., and Schill, E. (1932). Uber alexie und agnosie. *Zeitschrift fur die gesamte Neurologie und Psychiatrie, 139,* 192–240.

Schwartz, M. F., Saffran, E. M., and Marin, O. S. M. (1977). *An analysis of agrammatic reading in aphasia.* Paper presented at the meeting of the International Neuropsychological Society, Santa Fe, New Mexico, Feb. 4, 1977.

Shallice, T., and Warrington, E. K. (1975). Word recognition in a phonemic dyslexic patient. *Quarterly Journal of Experimental Psychology, 27,* 187–199.

Trescher, J. H., and Ford, F. R. (1937). Colloid cyst of the third ventricle. *Archives of Neurology and Psychiatry*, 37, 959–973.

Trojanowski, J. Q., Green, R. C., and Levine, D. N. (1980). Crossed aphasia in a dextral: A clinicopathological study. *Neurology*, 30, 709–713.

Wernicke, K. (1874). *Der aphasische. Symptomen complex.* Breslau: Franck and Weigert.

18
What Is a Symptom-Complex?

John C. Marshall

INTRODUCTION

From the inception of the first research program on the aphasias, originally set out by Wernicke (1874) and Lichtheim (1885), the study of acquired disorders of language has been dominated by the notion of symptom-complexes. Confirmation that the notion continues to dominate the field can easily be obtained: One simply notes the effort that has gone into the development of (quasi-) objective tests that are intended to place the Wernicke–Lichtheim taxonomy, or some variant thereof, on a sound, statistically reliable basis (Goodglass and Kaplan, 1972; Kertesz and Phipps, 1977); even more simply, one observes that the vast majority of current "experimental" studies of aphasia subdivide the patient population under investigation into groups that correspond with the traditional syndromes. The validity, and moreover the importance, of the taxonomy is thus frequently presupposed rather than demonstrated, argued over, or otherwise studied.

Given that the idea of a symptom-complex is so central—methodologically, at least—to the entire research enterprise as currently conceived, it is perhaps surprising that there have been so few discussions of the role that the notion plays in aphasia theory. The issue was, of course, keenly and intensively debated in the classical period that culminates in, say, Moutier (1908) but subsequent discussion has been, at best, sporadic (Pick, 1931; Goldstein, 1948; Benson, 1979; Brown, 1979). The remarks that follow are an attempt, then, to open up to discussion a range of topics associated with the notion of symptom-complexes as applied to the aphasias. We might begin by noting that a crude, but useful, response to the question, What is an aphasic syndrome? would be to ask the further question, Do you want a practical or a theoretical answer?

In his superb summary of aphasia theory, Kinnear Wilson (1926) distinguishes anatomical, physiological, and psychological taxonomies. He argues that

NEURAL MODELS OF
LANGUAGE PROCESSES

scientific classification OUGHT to be based upon the pathology of physiological mechanisms, but concludes, "this desirable end not having as yet been attained, the clinician must perforce be content with empirical clinical divisions, the usefulness of which, I repeat, outweighs their patent disadvantages [p. 38]." I believe that there is a real dichotomy here—the two types of classification will overlap only partially. I shall accordingly give a practical answer first, in order to avoid (I hope) some misleading objections to the theoretical issues that are ultimately at stake.

SYNDROMES IN PRACTICE

A standard and, I hope, uncontroversial, definition of a syndrome would be a collection of symptoms (positive and negative) that reliably cooccur. What is the interest of such a definition? Well, it corresponds, one presumes, to the intuitive notion of a clinical entity. And such pathological entities have, at worst, a small number of causes (one hopes), and, at best, a unique cause. Aphasic symptom-complexes fit quite satisfactorally into this framework. Thus Goodglass and Geschwind (1976) define Wernicke's aphasia as a syndrome with the following behavioral aspects:

> Auditory comprehension is impaired, while fluency and ease of articulation are spared. While speech output is rapid, with many long syntactic strings, it is replete with errors of word choice, neologisms, and transpositions of sounds. The patient, unable to find the needed substantive words, products a repetitious, often stereotyped flow, which conveys little information [p. 418].

And the underlying cause, they believe, is damage to "the posterior first temporal gyrus" (of the left hemisphere, in the vast majority of the right-handed population). It is not difficult to see why this framework of behavioral symptom-complexes associated with, more or less, unique lesion sites should assume THE central role in aphasiology (and neuropsychology in general). The nineteenth-century clinician, lacking so many of our current technical devices for the visualization of normal versus pathological brain tissue, needed a reliable in vivo guide to the likely locus of his patient's injury; the pattern of the patient's behavior provided the requisite assay. Differential diagnosis in terms of simple taxonomies of the aphasias, the apraxias, and the agnosias was employed in the explicit service of PREDICTING lesion sites. If the syndrome of Wernicke's aphasia points to pathology of the left posterior first temporal gyrus, then that knowledge may suffice for many clinical purposes. Theoretical speculation as to WHY such a lesion site–syndrome correlation is found can be regarded as a quite distinct issue.

It is sometimes believed that the development of sophisticated twentieth-century technology, leading to such methods of in vivo visualization of brain lesions as angiography, electroencephalography, regional cerebral blood flow measurement, and computerized axial tomography has radically undermined the value of localizaiton by behavioral symptomatology. To some extent, this is no doubt true. But it would seem that no current physical technique (or combination of techniques) provides—at all time post injury—an unambiguous, fail-safe indication of brain damage. For example, Lhermitte, Chain, Chedru, and Penet (1976) have reported on a woman with "an irregular constriction of the visual fields, a left-sided agraphia, and an anomia for objects in the left hand [p. 317]." A brain scan (Ptc 99) performed some 4 months subsequent to the onset of headache and hazy vision showed "two foci of uptake, one in the left temporo-occipital region and one in the right parieto-occipital area [p. 320]." Yet some 2.5 years later, when no marked clinical improvement had occurred, a follow-up brain scan is reported as normal.

To the not inconsiderable extent that there are correlations between symptom type and lateralized, focal injury (as later shown by histology at necropsy), it will continue to be the case that the reliability and validity of in vivo diagnosis will be maximized by employing a combination of "physical" and "psychological" assays. It must, I think, be admitted that the classical taxonomy, and the associated set of lesion sites has stood the test of time extremely well; the only surprises are that such a small number of simple criteria—the pattern of performance with respect to fluency in spontaneous speech, "pragmatic" comprehension, repetition and naming ability, and the information content of speech—should do such a good job (in the majority of cases), and that, broadly speaking, the classical lesion sites, found originally in very small numbers of cases, should generalize quite well to much larger series studied with modern technical aids (Kertesz, Harlock, and Coates, 1979; Kertesz, Lesk, and McCabe, 1977; Naeser and Hayward, 1978; Naeser, Hayward, Laughlin, and Katz, 1981, Soh, Larsen, Skinhøj, and Lassen, 1978). In general, then, the structure erected by the diagram makers and revived by Geschwind (1965) has proved remarkably durable, productive, and ACCURATE.

MODIFICATIONS WITHIN THE CLINICAL PARADIGM

Nothing I have said in the preceding section implies that one cannot attack the clinical paradigm from within and consequently make important advances. On the behavioral side it is obvious that one can deny the STATISTICAL coherence of a syndrome and bring forth evidence to destroy a particular claim about the clustering of symptoms. In modern times, Benton's (1961) demonstration that the "Gerstmann syndrome" is a fiction is perhaps the most striking example of this productively destructive strategy. Although Benton's paper is well known, indeed justly famous, I will quote the summary in its entirety as it is a quite exceptionally elegant and clear account of the problem:

> Systematic, objective analysis of the performances of patients with cerebral disease on seven "parietal" tasks (right–left orientation, finger localization, writing, calculation, constructional praxis, reading, visual memory) indicates that many combinations of deficits, including that known as the "Gerstmann syndrome", may be observed. The syndrome appears to be no different from the other combinations in respect to either the strength of the mutual interrelationships among its elements or the strength of the relationships between its elements and performances not belonging to it. These results hold both for patients with diverse cerebral conditions and for those with focal lesions of the dominant parietal lobe.
>
> The findings are interpreted as indicating that the Gerstmann syndrome is an artifact of defective and biased observation. Further, a review of the pertinent clinical literature offers little support for its alleged focal diagnostic significance. The general conclusion is that the syndrome is a fiction which has perhaps served a useful purpose in the past in certain respects, but which now carries the hazard of retarding advances in the understanding of the organization of abilities and disabilities in patients with cerebral disease [p. 181].

Benton is not, of course, denying either the existence or value of symptoms associated with particular lesion sites; he is simply denying that "Gerstmann's syndrome" is a theoretically meaningful entity. This disavowal does NOT lead one to deny that the greater the number of parietal signs a patient displays the greater one's confidence in diagnosing a parietal lesion.

Within aphasiology, one might quote the case of "conduction aphasia" as an example of a syndrome that may not be one. According to Goodglass and Geschwind (1976), conduction aphasia is

> a syndrome that usually results from lesions of the parietal operculum, manifested by impairment of repetition disproportionate to the fluency of spontaneous speech, and in a setting of near normal auditory comprehension. Speech is marked by a predominance of literal paraphasia (phonemic substitutions and transpositions), especially during efforts to repeat. Word-finding difficulty and severely impaired writing are usually present [p. 418].

Although there is no question that patients who meet this description exist (Benson, Sheremata, Bouchard, Segarra, Prince, and Geschwind, 1973), they are, even on Benson, Sheremata, Bouchard, Segarra, Prince and Geschwind's account, comparatively rare. (They give a figure of 5–10% of all new aphasic admissions.) The clustering algorithm of Kertesz and Phipps (1977) failed to pull out a single class of conduction aphasics; they rather found a bimodal distribution of patients whose repetition ability was severely impaired—one group had high fluency and low comprehension scores, the other low fluency and higher comprehension. There are also a number of well-known problems concerning the lesion site in "conduction aphasia"; although the damage is typically temporoparietal a large number of distinct sites within that rather large area have been implicated in the condition; Table A.1 of Green and Howes (1977) fails to show any particular convergence on the parietal operculum that Goodglass and Geschwind (1976) claim is the primary locus of the damage responsible for the condition. These problems, however, would not in themselves cause anyone to give up the paradigm; one would rather look for plausible ways of subdivding the major syndromes and hope then to obtain a better mapping onto the anatomy. This is precisely what has happened in recent years with the frontal aphasias. Thus it seems that "Broca's aphasia" must be firmly distinguished from "Broca's area infarction." In this latter condition, a lesion of Broca's area (the pars opercularis of the third frontal convolution) and its IMMEDIATE surroundings is associated with mutism which rapidly gives way to speech characterized by effortful and dyspraxic articulation (Mohr, 1973); other language functions are retained in a basically intact form (Mohr, Pessin, Finkelstein, Funkenstein, Duncan, and Davis, 1978). The disorder may thus be related to that seen after infarction of the left supplementary motor area; Masden, Schoene, and Funkenstein (1978) describe a woman with an embolic infarct of the supplementary motor area who was initially mute but rapidly recovered "fluent speech marked by short sentences with normal grammar [p. 1220]." A severe impairment of writing was a persisting symptom. By contrast, it is becoming clear that the full symptom-complex of Broca's aphasia, including stereotyped, fixed expressions and agrammatism, is associated with a far larger lesion of the areas supplied by the upper division of the left middle cerebral artery (Mohr, 1976; Naeser, Hayward, Laughlin and Katz, 1981). Complementing the anatomical picture, behavioral investigations suggest that the clinical impression of relatively intact comprehension in Broca's aphasia may be rather misleading. Caramazza and Zurif (1976) have shown that Broca's aphasics often fail to understand grammatically complex sentences when semantic and pragmatic cues to their interpretation are unavailable; and Goodenough, Zurif, and Weintraub (1977) have found that there is considerable parallelism in expressive loss and comprehension impairment for "non-phonological words" in the sense of Kean (1980). Once more, however, one would not take such findings as a disproof of the clinical claim that Broca's aphasics have relatively good comprehension; instead one would see it as part of a progressive refinement of what "relatively" means in this context.

To summarize the argument so far: It is possible to think of the clinical method as an exercise in actuarial prediction. We have a check list of signs and symptoms; some of these cluster together in regular ways that enable us to predict lesion sites. The research program is progressive to the extent that better check lists, more precise definitions of the terms in those check lists, and more sophisticated statistical measures of central tendencies and family relationships lead to better predictions of lesion sites. It is not NECESSARY that the enterprise include

ANY theoretical content beyond what is required to insure that valid and reliable statistical inferences are drawn. The relevant conceptual apparatus is to be found in conventional test theory. The commentary by Blumstein (1979) on Arbib and Caplan's "Neurolinguistics must be computational" (1979) illustrates exactly the point I am trying to make:

> A & C review in detail various approaches to aphasia research and are especially critical of the so-called connectionist view. In particular, they criticize Geschwind's disconnection theory, primarily because it "fails" to delineate a theory of linguistic processing and brain organization. However, Geschwind's model never attempts to explicate linguistic processing. It merely tries to show the interrelations among a number of behavioral tasks (syndromes) and the areas of the brain implicated in performing such tasks [p. 460].

I think that this quotation is a grossly unfair and misleading characterization of Geschwind's work; but no matter. It expresses perfectly the distinction I want to draw between clinical and theoretical concerns. Yet no connectionist from Wernicke to Geschwind has restricted himself to lesion–symptom correlation.

A LITTLE HISTORY

The history of Lichtheim's diagram (1885) is well known (see Arbib, Caplan, and Marshall, Chapter 1, this volume). I shall accordingly attempt to be brief. By 1866, Paul Broca and many other neurologists were convinced that there was a correlation between (relatively) focal, left frontal damage and severe dysfluency in spontaneous and repetitive speech. Broca (1866) interpreted the association as indicating that one aspect of the language faculty was typically "localized" in the third frontal convolution; the component in question, Broca argued, was "the memory of the procedure that is employed to articulate language [p. 381]." A little later in 1874, Carl Wernicke remarked upon the association between left posterior injuries and a pattern of behavioral impairment that included fluent but paraphasic speech allied to considerable difficulty in speech comprehension. Like Broca, Wernicke (1874) hypothesized that a focally localized component of the language faculty—in this case, the "storehouse" of audiolingual images—could be peturbed by left temporal damage.

But neither Wernicke nor any of the later diagram makers were content to see their work as involving ONLY the discovery of more and more correlations between syndromes and lesion sites. What Wernicke wanted was an anatomical theory that would, in some sense, explain the already observed associations and predict new ones. Wernicke (1874) is quite explicit about his research program:

> My conception differs from earlier ones in its consistently maintained anatomical foundation. Previous theories postulated theoretically different centers (a co-ordination center, a concept center etc.), but paid no attention to anatomy

in doing so, for the reason that the functions of the brain, completely unknown at that time, did not yet justify anatomical conclusions. It is a significantly different approach to undertake a thorough-going study of neuroanatomy and, making use of the now almost universally accepted principles of experimental psychology, to transform the anatomical data into psychological form and to construct a theory out of such material [p. 28].

The aim of Wernicke and of all later diagram makers was to EXPLAIN the varieties of aphasia by invoking localized "centers" of different types linked in specified ways by "association" tracts. The magnitude of their achievement lay in the fact that they formalized their theories by finite state flow charts; a particular diagram would thus generate, without benefit of intuition, a typology of the aphasias through injury to postulated centers and disconnections between them. It was realized that such a notation could, in principle, "explain" any constellation of symptoms by the simple expedient of proliferating centers and connections. In order to protect the theoretical enterprise against trivialization, it was accordingly argued that postulation of a new center or connection was only justified if it enabled one "to represent the causation of other *derangements of speech* [Broadbent, 1878, p. 344]" than the one that initially prompted it; a simplicity criterion was hinted at, so that "the better theory" was the one that generated all the observed symptom-complexes (and no "impossible" ones) by the smaller number of centers and pathways (Bastian, 1897; Moutier, 1908).

It was thus crucial to the entire enterprise that one could NOT simply label a lesioned Wernicke's area with the tag "This produces Wernicke's aphasia," or label a lesion of the arcuate fasciculus with the tag "This produces conduction aphasia" (Marshall, 1979). Rather one had to provide a FUNCTIONAL interpretation of each box and arrow such that the entire system fitted together into a coherent theoretical whole. Unless one accepts that this is what the diagram makers were attempting, none of the traditional criticisms of the diagram makers makes any sense at all. Thus Jackson (1874) did not disagree with Broca's localization evidence; he disagreed with a particular interpretation of it:

> While I believe that the hinder part of the left third frontal convolution is the part most often damaged, I do not localize speech in any such small part of the brain. To locate the damage which destroys speech and to locate speech are two different things [p. 21].

To take another example, Geschwind (1964) has pointed out that Goldstein had rather few reservations about the classical lesion sites. Quite so: But again, the force of the critique in Goldstein (1948) is directed primarily against particular theories of function localization, not against certain facts of symptom localization:

> Particularly after the criticism of von Monakow, based on his enormous knowledge, and my own discussion of this problem with a more detailed

analysis of the clinical pictures, it hardly seemed possible to maintain the classic theory of localization. The question of the relationship between the symptom complex and a definitely localized lesion again became a problem, no longer, however, in the form: where is a definite function or symptom localized? but: how does a definite lesion modify the function of the brain so that a definite symptom comes to the fore? [Goldstein, 1948, p. 45].

It was essential, then, for Wernicke that the system of boxes and arrows in toto had explanatory power; and in order to achieve this it is obvious that—under a particular functional labeling of the components—all the elements of a particular symptom-complex had to "hang together" as a THEORETICAL unity. The long controversy between Wernicke and Kussmaul (1877) provides an excellent example of how deeply Wernicke felt on this issue (Eggert, 1977). To repeat: Wernicke's aphasia includes grossly impaired auditory comprehension and fluent but paraphasic speech. For Wernicke, this association was not merely an accident of anatomy; Wernicke did not conjecture the existence of two boxes (one box per impairment) in close (or overlapping) spatial proximity such that the geometry of the vascular system would ensure that both functions would be impaired after occlusion of the posterior branch of the main left cerebral artery. Rather, he attempted to motivate the dual impairment from a single underlying source. The perturbed component for Wernicke was the storehouse of verbal (acoustic) images, hence the impairment in comprehension; but that same storehouse exerted a guiding, modifying, and monitoring function (via the arcuate fasciculus) over the "primary" route for speech production—a subsystem consisting of the "concept" center and its connection to Broca's area.

And so, finally, to the question I want to ask: Once we leave the pure domain of atheoretical lesion site–syndrome correlations, can we buy the classical taxonomy without also buying the classical theory (or some relatively minor modification thereof)? It is, I think, clear from Geschwind's brilliant discussion of the difficulties encountered by the classical theory—"Problems in the anatomical understanding of the aphasias" (Geschwind, 1969)—that he at least believes that the taxonomy and the theory are inseparable. This raises no difficulties for Geschwind because he obviously believes in the theory (although conceding, of course, that elaborations and modifications are required):

> Let us consider how we name a seen object. A stimulus reaches the visual cortex, goes to the visual association cortex, then to the angular gyrus. This in turn arouses the name in Wernicke's area. From here the impulse is transferred over the arcuate fasciculus to Broca's area where the muscular pattern corresponding to the sound is aroused. From here the impulse reaches the motor cortex and is then conveyed downward [1969, p. 109].

But can an aphasiologist who does NOT believe a story that is at least closely related to such a model justify use of the traditional taxonomic groupings?

The functional issue at stake here is beautifully stated by Brain (1964):

> To put the problem in its simplest form, let us consider two aspects of language which we will merely call a and b to indicate that we habitually distinguish them in our own minds and give them different labels. Let us further suppose that they are both depressed in a particular aphasic patient. There are several possible explanations of this. The primary disturbance may involve a, and the disturbance of b may be secondary to this, or conversely, we may implicate some general function c and say that both a and b are particular examples of disorder c. These are all functional or dynamic interpretations. But there is also the possibility that there is no functional relationship between a and b. They are involved together merely because their pathways, though separate in terms of neurones, run close enough together to be damaged by the same lesion. Examples of all these interpretations can be found in aphasiology [p. 7].

What, then, is the evidence that "Broca's aphasia" or "Wernicke's aphasia" (etc.) are entities that exist at any level beyond that of a random collection of symptoms resulting from the "theoretically accidental" anatomy of the rolandic and the posterior sylvian regions, respectively?

TWO SYNDROMES

Goodglass and Geschwind (1976) describe Broca's aphasia as a syndrome of the anterior speech area

> marked by effortful, distorted articulation, reduced speech output, and ag-grammatic syntax but sparing of auditory comprehension. Writing is usually impaired commensurately with speech, but reading is only mildly disturbed [p. 418].

Under what FUNCTIONAL interpretation would we expect to find this particular grouping of impaired and preserved performance? Well, Broca's original suggestion—a disorder of the procedures for articulating words—combined with the overall structure of the Lichtheim model does quite a good job of unifying the symptoms. If the patient's ability to program the articulatory machinery is impaired, it would not be unreasonable to expect that he would adapt to this condition by reducing his speech output; and, given a desire to communicate effectively despite the output difficulties, one would furthermore find it quite reasonable for such a patient to adopt a "telegram-writing" strategy at an uncon-scious or quasi-conscious level:

> The point of telegram-writing—by normal subjects—is to maximize the "in-formativeness" of a communication whilst keeping "cost" to a minimum. Subjects with agrammatism give the appearance of knowing what they want to say and of trying to say it; in classical cases (e.g. Salomon, 1914), comprehen-

sion of language is relatively well-preserved, and this may be taken as evidence that knowledge of linguistic form is intact (although the data of Zurif, Caramazza and Myerson, 1972, suggests that *some* non-fluent aphasics do suffer receptive loss for the forms they find difficult to express). However, the laborious, distorted and frequently paraphasic quality of the motor aphasic's speech suggests that the cost of expressing this knowledge has risen; communication is effortful. What, then, more reasonable than that verbal elements having a high cost to information ratio should fail to be overtly expressed (although not, of course, by conscious design on the subject's part)? [Marshall, 1977, p. 133].

The intactness of auditory comprehension (and comprehension for reading) then goes through by virtue of the firm distinction drawn in the classical model between the function of Broca's area and of Wernicke's area. The disturbance in writing does not necessitate postulation of an additional lesion (to "Exner's writing center"); rather, one can claim with many of the classical authors that the access code for graphic symbols is the phonological or phonetic representation that ex hypothesi is impaired in Broca's aphasia. In short, then, with the addition of a few minor postulates regarding compensatory adaptations to the primary deficit, the Lichtheim model does excellent service in making Broca's aphasia a FUNCTIONAL unity.

The only difficulty is that, as far as I can see, NO ONE today believes that the preceding description is an adequate characterization of Broca's aphasia, or the syndrome of upper division infarction, as Mohr (1976) terms it. Goodglass and Geschwind (1976) argue convincingly against the "economy of effort" postulate:

> It is true that, for some patients, partial improvement is possible when they are urged to make a complete sentence and when their omissions are pointed out. However, such improvement rarely extends beyond supplying an omitted copula or article. Careful clinical observation shows that the theory of economy of effort is untenable. The patients often struggle with repeated self-corrections, in order to make their output approximate standard English, without succeeding. Obviously their recognition of what sounds correct considerably exceeds their productive ability [p. 408].

And, as previously mentioned, the slow, hesitant speech of patients with disease of the supplementary motor area may result only in short, frequently incomplete, sentences with no trace of the agrammatism that characterizes the Broca's aphasic (Masden, Schoene, and Funkenstein, 1978). Once the "economy of effort" principle goes, we have no explanation WITHIN THE CLASSICAL MODEL of why the patient should have lost the memory for the procedure of articulating *in* but not *inn*, *which* but not *witch*, *all* but not *awl*. Similarly, the classical model provides no account of why comprehension (and metalinguistic judgments) for the elements that are often omitted in spontaneous and repetitive speech should be impaired (Zurif and Caramazza, 1976). Wernicke himself, of course, eventu-

ally noted the comprehension deficit in Broca's aphasia but provided no explanation for it:

> In the main, the power of understanding speech is retained; at least this appears
> to be the case on ordinary tests. . . . There is almost invariably a certain in-
> ability to understand complicated constructions and the finer differentiations of
> speech. . . . I no longer am of the opinion that in pure motor aphasia the
> ability to understand speech always remains unimpaired [1908, p. 798].

The line of argument we have just followed does not in itself show that Broca's
aphasia is NOT a FUNCTIONAL syndrome, but it does I think demonstrate that it
cannot be unified in the fashion originally proposed by Wernicke and
Lichtheim. It is then an open question whether the radically new "syndrome"
conjectured by modern authors can be given an interpretation as elegant and
simple as that appropriate to the older syndrome. The size of lesion responsible
and the fact that Broca's aphasia typically evolves out of a much more global
aphasia (including often a protracted period of more or less total mutism) might
give one cause for doubt.

But let us see. Let us assume that the really critical deficit in Broca's aphasia
lies in the agrammatic quality of spontaneous speech. And let us also accept
Kean's hypothesis (Kean, 1977, 1980) that the appropriate partitioning of the
(relatively) preserved and impaired elements is to be captured within the
phonological component of the grammar:

> The definition of a phonological word is one that is made on the basis of
> phonological representations of sentences. It is a systematic and grammatically
> principled definition. . . . The grammatical analysis, most simply stated, says
> that it is the phonological words of a sentence which tend to be retained in
> agrammatism [1980, p. 256].

As Kean (1980) is careful to point out, nothing follows DIRECTLY from this
analysis. But it does suggest a direction in which to move:

> If . . . agrammatic aphasics have lost the normal ability in exploitation of lexical
> information or accessing routines to make a distinction between phonological
> words and clitics, then to the extent that other processing mechanisms cru-
> cially rely on that distinction those processing mechanisms will be impeded in
> their execution of linguistic computations [p. 262].

This in turn suggests that we should adopt the "two lexica" hypothesis of Thorne
and his colleagues. Bratley, Dewar, and Thorne (1967) have argued that it is
unlikely that the first strategy in processing a word (and then deriving a set of
immediate predictions from it) should consist of looking the word up (under all
potentially available categorial assignments) in a neural representation of a form
class dictionary. In brief, the motivation advanced for this skepticism is as fol-

lows: It is apparent that some arrangements of strings containing nonsense syllables have readily perceived syntactic structure. A famous example of this is Lewis Carroll's "'Twas brillig, and the slithy toves did gyre and gimble in the wabe," in which it is quite obvious that "slithy" is an adjective, "tove" is a noun, and "gyre" and "gimble" are verbs. Dakin and Bratley (1967) continue

> Notice what we are doing—we are not saying 'I know that *tove* is a noun, therefore the syntactic structure is so-and-so'. On the contrary, we are saying, 'The syntactic structure is apparent, and knowing the structure, I can now assert that *tove* is a noun' [p. 174].

Such observations can then be incorporated into an on-line processing model:

> In order to capitalize on these facts and hence to augment the efficiency of their predictive analysis model, Thorne *et al.* reject a dictionary look-up routine that operates (in the first place) upon every word in the sentence. They incorporate a restricted dictionary which includes closed-class items (roughly 'form' words as opposed to 'content' words) such as determiners, conjunctions, pronouns, prepositions, auxiliary verbs, certain adverbs and various inflectional endings. The analyser does not contain any of the normal rules of generative syntax, but rather a simplified generalisation of those rules produced by restating them in terms of open- and closed-class words on the basis of the information elicited from the dictionary look-up of the closed-class items [Marshall, 1970, p. 213].

This line of argument has recently been taken up by Bradley (1978) and Bradley, Garrett, and Zurif (1980). In Kean's summary (1980):

> Bradley has suggested that the reason for the distinction between phonological words and clitics in normal processing is a function of the structure of the syntactic processor. It is her idea that since, as a general class, clitics provide a different sort of cue to syntactic structure than do the items of the major lexical classes, in making the distinction between the two classes relatively early on the syntactic processor is abetted. In particular, she has hypothesized that there are special access routines for clitics (closed class items) and that the parser relies on the clitics to provide the immediate evidential base for determining syntactic structure. If the special access routine for clitics is impaired then the initial basis for making structural hypotheses is lost. Phonological representations provide a partition of strings into a set of phonological words and clitics; the work which Bradley reports here puts forward a hypothesis as to one way that partition is exploited normally in processing and suggests that agrammatism is a consequence of impairment to those routines of exploitation. While the two analyses are independent, each standing on its own, they do fit together and are consistent with each other; there is no ground for suggesting one disproves or undermines the other [p. 262].

It is via such an ancilliary hypothesis that the correspondence between production and comprehension emerges in Broca's aphasia, and it is also via this hypothesis that the appearance of a syntactic deficit is created. Given strings of the following types:

(a) *The man helped the woman.*
(b) *The woman was helped by the man.*
(c) *It was the woman that the man helped.*
(d) *It was the man that helped the woman.*

.
.
.

it can easily be seen that a selective failure to access the "closed class" elements will lead to striking failures in comprehension. As Wales and Marshall (1966) remark, "the greater psychological difficulty of reversible passives may be due not so much to confusions in memory but rather to erroneous (incomplete) analysis of the input [p. 71]." Presented with Example (c), the aphasic subject who only has access to *woman, man,* and *help* may well interpret that string as meaning "The woman and the man help" without requiring us to postulate that a primary deficit in SYNTACTIC processing exists (Newcombe and Marshall, 1967). For understanding longer strings, the gross reduction is short-term memory span that is characteristic of many subjects with Broca's aphasia (Heilman, Scholes, and Watson, 1976) will insure that the patient can only rely on the lexical semantics of those items he can access and the "real world pragmatics" of likely events. Once again, then, one can accept the claim that many Broca's aphasics manifest a "word order" problem (Schwarz, Saffran, and Marin, 1980) without being forced into postulating that a SYNTACTIC deficit is responsible for the surface form of the impairment; and indeed, the failure to cope with word order may not be a LINGUISTIC deficit at all if the patient also manifests serial ordering problems across a range of nonlanguage stimuli. Schwartz, Saffran, and Marin (1980) have demonstrated very clearly that some agrammatic subjects perform poorly on "reversible constructions involving spatial prepositions (e.g., 'The square is above the circle') and verbs (e.g., 'The dancer applauds the clown') [p. 249]." But in the absence of a rigorous analysis of the patients' short-term memory performance it certainly does not follow that their deficit is SYNTACTIC; given the task demands of a forced-choice picture pointing paradigm for assessing comprehension, even the failure of the subjects to map Noun + Verb + Noun sequences onto the canonical Subject + Verb + Object format does not necessarily implicate a syntactic deficit. Perhaps the most dramatic finding of the Schwartz, Saffran, and Marin study is the very wide range of "performance strategies" found when the comprehension of agrammatic subjects is tested with standard forced-choice response mode.

There may, then, be a coherent interpretation of the agrammatism that is shown in both production and comprehension. In order to make the story truly

plausible, however, one would have to show that there are no important dis-
crepancies between the contents of the closed class dictionary that Dakin and
Bratley (1967) motivate on the basis of syntactic parsing criteria and the dictionary that Kean (1980) motivates on the basis of criteria derived (for English) from
cliticization and phonological readjustment phenomena. As far as I know, there
are currently no data available from agrammatic subjects that bear upon this
issue.

Finally, it is worth noting that if the new story does go through there are no
grounds for regarding the "effortful, distorted articulation" and "reduced speech
output" (Goodglass and Geschwind, 1976) as part of the new functional syndrome. Difficulties in accessing a closed class lexicon do not at all imply that the
patient will manifest speech that is in any way dysfluent and dysprosodic over and
above the hesitations that may be caused by (unsuccessful) attempts to access the
closed class lexicon. It may, then, be best to regard the dysfluency as an anatomical accident consequent upon the large lesions that are typically found to extend
to the pars triangularis and Broca's area, adjacent to the primary mouth and hand
areas of motor cortex. For this argument to go through, it should be possible in
principle to find cases of (relatively) FLUENT Broca's aphasia. Cases 3 and 12 from
a paper by Kreindler, Mihailescu, and Fradis (1980) suggest that this may be so
(although, unfortunately, too few clinical details are given for one to be sure of
the conclusion). It should also be the case that the speech prosody of (some)
Broca's aphasics will be far better than the impression that the naked ear obtains
upon listening to them. A paper by Danly, de Villiers, and Cooper (1979) again
suggests that this may be true. Although, as the authors concede, they have only
investigated some "rudimentary aspects" of speech prosody, they did find that 75
two-word utterences from the spontaneous speech of three subjects with Broca's
aphasia exhibited "both terminal falling F_0 contours and declination despite
inter-word pauses of up to 5 seconds [p. 181]." (The timing pattern of the sequences, however, showed no utterence final lengthening.)

In summary, the problem with the classical account of Broca's aphasia is
that the standard interpretation of Lichtheim's diagram fails to unify a fairly
well-grounded set of clinical observations: Impairment to the machinery for the
cortical organization of articulatory plans seems to provide neither a necessary
nor a sufficient explanation for the characteristic behavior of patients who are
CURRENTLY diagnosed as displaying Broca's aphasia. It MAY be the case that the
hypothesis of restricted access to a subpart of the vocabulary (closed class items)
will unify the core symptomatology; it may also be the case that pathology
RESTRICTED to Broca's area, and the white matter underlying it, produces an
impairment, sometimes temporary, that is appropriately described as a "high-
order" articulatory disturbance (Mohr, 1973).

Let us now turn to an example where the classical taxonomy falsely unifies a
variety of disparate conditions. Lichtheim (1885) recognized a further frontal

syndrome in which spontaneous speech is as severely impaired as in Broca's aphasia but other speech functions, including comprehension, confrontation naming, and, most important, repetition of spoken language, are basically intact. In Broca's aphasia, repetition of speech is impaired to approximately the same degree as spontaneous speech; in Lichtheim's "transcortical motor aphasia," repetition ranges between good and excellent. Thus Case 1 of Rubens (1975) could only manage the response *f—f—fine* when asked to make up a sentence about the weather, yet she could repeat *It is a beautiful, warm, sunny day outside* without difficulty; asked to describe the examiner striking a match, the patient managed with much effort to say *fire*, but she successfully repeated the utterence *Doctor, you took out a box of matches from your back pocket and lit one.* At a time when Case 2 of Rubens (1975) was devoid of spontaneous conversation and could only manage one- or two-word answers to questions, the patient correctly albeit haltingly repeated the sentence *The boy who was bitten by John's dog was taken to the hospital in the next town.*

Lichtheim's own account of the condition postulated a disconnection between an ideational "center," the neuronal substrate of which was held to be widely distributed across the left hemisphere, and a higher order articulatory center in the region of Broca's area (Lichtheim, 1885). This conception works in the sense that the classical diagram allows one to trace out pathways for repetition and comprehension that are topologically distinct from the hypothesized locus of impairment in transcortical motor aphasia. But it is difficult to evaluate the cogency of a disconnectionist account of the syndrome in the absence of a formal model of language production that actually specifies the stages of grammatical encoding en route from thought to speech. Lichtheim's model simply conflates impairments that surely must be theoretically distinct.

Thus one interpretation of the condition—the interpretation preferred by Lichtheim himself, by Wernicke (1906), and by Goldstein (1915)—hypothesized derangement of some final "common path" for the expression of language in either speech or writing. Goldstein (1915) cited in support of this subvariety the case of Rothmann (1906) in which transcortical motor aphasia was seen in association with a small white matter lesion immediately beneath Broca's area. This argument was carried to its logical conclusion by Bastian (1898) who located the deficit within the motor speech area itself; Bastian's account, in the summary by Rubens (1976), thus proposes that "mild damage produces a heightened threshold of excitability in which reaction is still possible in response to externally derived auditory stimuli, but not to internally generated volitional stimuli [p. 294]." Other scholars have speculated that the condition is best described as a "lack of speech initiative" (Rubens, 1976); if this is so, transcortical motor aphasia might be regarded as a somewhat specialized form of akinetic mutism, a phenomenon that led Botez (1962) to postulate a "starting mechanism of speech," impairment of which may be seen after lesions (focal or diffuse) at many different levels of the central nervous system. Yet another possibility, suggested by Luria and Tsvetkova (1968) is that transcortical motor aphasia (or "dynamic aphasia" as they rename the condition) is a high-level disorder of syntactic planning and lexical retrieval. Whatever the cogency of any of these suggestions it is clear that postulating a single disconnection between ideation and speech will not take us very far. It may be possible to tease apart subvarieties by concentrating on the pattern of associated impairment in cases that do not match the purest form of the syndrome that can be deduced from Lichtheim's diagram. For example, it can be deduced that confrontation naming should be well preserved in cases of transcortical motor aphasia, and there are indeed reports where this is so (Alexander and Schmitt, 1980). Yet Benson (1979) claims that DEFECTIVE confrontation naming often characterizes the condition. Some such problem is reported in a number of recent studies: Case 1 of Rubens (1975) almost always produced the correct response in object naming but only with long latencies and after some perseveration; Case 2 named objects at the 60% level, with frequent perseveration or total blocking; Cases 2 and 3 of Ross (1980) were severely impaired on naming to tactile or visual confrontation, although they performed well in a multiple choice format. These cases do not seem consistent with Lichtheim's "final common path" hypothesis insofar as that path is distinct from the "naming route" conjectured by Wernicke (1906) and Geschwind (1969).

Benson (1979) also states that in transcortical motor aphasia "conversational verbalization is almost invariably agrammatic [p. 84]." Support for the claim that this is so in some patients may be found in Alexander and Schmitt (1980), whose two cases both show effortful, telegraphic speech. This suggests that one form of the condition is related to Broca's aphasia. But the association is by no means invariable. In both of the cases reported by Rubens (1975), the course of recovery never passed through a stage in which "telegraphic speech" was manifest. Both patients were initially mute, then produced single words, prior to beginning to use short, simple, but grammatically correct sentences. Patient 1 continued to improve, using longer sentences with again no sign of agrammatism.

Some subjects with transcortical motor aphasia show marked echolalia (Rubens, 1975, Case 2); others show "forced completion," that is, they cannot inhibit themselves from completing an overlearned verbal sequence that the examiner starts (Rubens, 1975, Case 1). These frequent but not invariable concommitants are obviously consistent with the good repetition that characterizes the syndrome, but they do not in any sense follow from the structure of Lichtheim's model.

In short, then, Lichtheim's diagram represents transcortical motor aphasia as a single-symptom syndrome, but the model itself provides no real explanation for this symptom of grossly reduced spontaneous speech. Impairment at a wide variety of levels is consistent with the overt manifestation of deficit; and it seems likely that conjectures concerning the actual level that is perturbed in particular patients will need to take into account the associated deficits that do NOT fall within the syndrome as defined by Lichtheim's model. Such an approach to transcortical motor aphasia is consistent with the finding that quite a wide variety of lesion sites anterior or superior to Broca's area have been implicated in the condition.

CONCLUSION

In his exceptionally clear account, Benson (1979) writes that "a syndrome can be considered a group of findings, signs and/or symptoms which occur together in a given disease process with sufficient frequency to suggest the presence of that disease process [p. 57]." He notes that in aphasia, as in many other medical disorders, it is not necessary, or indeed possible, to regard a syndrome as "a fixed group of language findings" in which each and every element must be present before the diagnosis can be made. We can think of Benson's notion of aphasia as a set of family relationships akin to Wittgenstinian analyses of the concept of a game. No individual feature or set of features is strictly criterial, yet the features nonetheless constitute plausible grounds for inference. The features, positive and negative, that are employed in the diagnosis of varieties of aphasia can be thought of as existing in some kind of multidimensional space such that CLUSTERS of features stand out in certain regions. These clusters are the basic forms of aphasia and constitute counterevidence to the claim that aphasia is a unitary phenomenon that varies only in degree of severity. A model of this nature is either implicit (Goodglass and Kaplan, 1972) or explicit (Kertesz, 1979) in the construction and statistical analysis of many recent test batteries for aphasia diagnosis. In support of such an analysis, Benson (1979) employs an analogy due to Geschwind (1977): "Hypotension, scattered dermal pigmentation and low serum sodium do not have specific diagnostic value individually but when they occur together the diagnosis of Addison's disease with pathology in the adrenal glands is probable [p. 58]." So it is with language symptoms: an individual sign may have little significance "but when combined with other findings in a specific grouping they often indicate a specific disorder with specific localization. This is a syndrome [Benson, 1979, p. 58]." To the extent that syndromes so defined predict lesion sites (or other aspects of pathology) one can surely have no quarrel with Benson's stance. We must not, however, forget the disanalogies between aphasia and Addison's disease. Once more, Kinnear Wilson (1926) reaches to the core of the problem:

Aphasia is not a disease, but a symptom. Like all symptoms, it is the expression of departure from a normal state, the external manifestation of disorder of function of a mechanism. When we speak of different types of aphasia, we do not refer to different varieties of a particular morbid entity or disease, but to

certain groups of symptoms, all of which are disturbances of the function of
speech [p. 3].

The primary "morbid entities" that are implicated in the aphasias include
vascular disease, neoplasm, and trauma of the brain. Areas of infarction (or other
damage) consequent upon such processes may or may not correspond with
"entities" that can be justified within some physiological or psychological theory.
As there is no necessary relationship between the spatial areas revealed by histology at necropsy and the units of theoretical analysis, it follows that there will be
some models of brain organization within which the demands of clinical diagnosis and theoretical understanding pull in diametrically opposed directions.
Consider a "mosaic" model of the brain–mind in which functional modules
mapped fairly directly onto discrete, punctate but large anatomical modules. The
behavioral effects of a small lesion within a module would only permit one to
localize the lesion grossly, but the effects of a similarly small lesion at the
confluence of n anatomical modules would permit very fine localization of
pathology. This latter constellation of symptoms would accordingly be of greater
practical utility, but one would be mistaken, ex hypothesi, if one attempted to
unify the deficits theoretically as manifestations of some underlying functional
entity. Given our current knowledge of how the brain instanciates higher cognitive functions, the analogy of aphasic symptom-complexes with manifestations of
adrenal gland pathology may be overoptimistic. In the latter case, we can be
reasonably confident that the adrenal gland is a fusion of two anatomical distinct
organs, cortex and medulla, each of which has a distinct function: The adrenal
cortex, under control of the pituitary hormone adrenocorticotropin, elaborates
steroid hormones; the adrenal medulla elaborates the catecholamines epineph-
rine and norepinephrine. We are, I think, not yet so confident that "Wernicke's
area" elaborates lexical representations and "Broca's area" articulatory representations.

It is implicit in Benson's statistical account of syndromes that even the
best-behaved symptom-complexes should be susceptible to fractionation (Shallice, 1979). Examples where this possibility is realized can be found in Basso,
Taborelli, and Vignolo (1978); Coltheart, Patterson, and Marshall (1980); Heilman, Rothi, Campanella, and Wolfson (1979); Hier and Mohr (1977); Lhermitte and Dérouesné (1974); Low (1931), McKenna and Warrington (1978);
Michel (1979); Spreen, Benton, and van Allen (1966); Warrington (1975). It
would seem to follow that the symptom-complex as defined over the classical
taxonomy is not the best unit of theoretical analysis. We should perhaps pay
more attention to the goal that Wernicke and Lichtheim proposed—to show that
a range of symptoms follows DEDUCTIVELY from impairment to a particular
functional component. And in order to do so it may well be necessary to pay less
attention to the diagram makers' achievements—the discovery of a set of clinically valuable syndromes.

REFERENCES

Alexander, M. P., and Schmitt, M. A. (1980). The aphasia syndrome of stroke in the left anterior cerebral artery territory. *Archives of Neurology*, 37, 97–100.

Arbib, M. A., and Caplan, D. (1979). Neurolinguistics must be computational. *The Behavioral and Brain Sciences*, 2, 449–483.

Basso, A., Taborelli, A., and Vignolo, L. A. (1978). Dissociated disorders of speaking and writing in aphasia. *Journal of Neurology Neurosurgery and Psychiatry*, 41, 556–563.

Bastian, H. C. (1897). Some problems in connection with aphasia and other speech defects. *Lancet*, 1, 1005–1017, 1132–1137, 1187–1194.

Bastian, H. C. (1898). *A treatise on aphasia and other speech defects*. New York: Appleton.

Benson, D. F. (1979). *Aphasia, alexia, and agraphia*. New York: Churchill Livingstone.

Benson, D. F., Sheremata, W. A., Bouchard, R., Segarra, J. M., Price, D., and Geschwind, N. (1973). Conduction aphasia: A clinicopathological study. *Archives of Neurology*, 28, 339–346.

Benton, A. L. (1961). The fiction of the 'Gerstmann Syndrome.' *Journal of Neurology Neurosurgery and Psychiatry*, 24, 176–181.

Blumstein, S. (1979). Phrenology, 'boxology', and neurology. *The Behavioral and Brain Sciences*, 2, 460–461.

Botez, M. I. (1962). The starting mechanism of speech. *Proceedings of the 8th Congress of the Hungarian Neurologists and Psychiatrists*, Budapest: State Publishing House.

Brain, W. R. (1964). Statement of the problem. In A. V. S. de Reuck and M. O'Connor (Eds.), *Disorders of language*. London: Churchill.

Bradley, D. C, (1978). *Computational distinctions of vocabulary type*. Unpublished Ph.D. thesis, MIT.

Bradley, D. C., Garrett, M., and Zurif, E. (1980). Syntactic deficits in Broca's aphasia. In D. Caplan (Ed.), *Biological studies of mental processes*. Cambridge, Mass.: MIT Press.

Bratley, P., Dewar, H., and Thorne, J. P. (1967). Recognition of syntactic structure by computer. *Nature*, 216, 969–973.

Broadbent, W. B. (1878). A case of peculiar affection of speech, with commentary. *Brain*, 1, 484–503.

Broca, P. (1866). Sur la faculté générale du langage, dans ses rapports avec la faculté du langage articulé. *Bulletin de la Société d' Anthropologie*, Second Series, 1, 377–382.

Brown, J. (1979). Language representation in the brain. In H. Steklis and M. Raleigh (Eds.), *Neurobiology of social communication in primates*. New York: Academic Press.

Caramazza, A., and Zurif, E. (1976). Dissociation of algorithmic and heuristic processes in language comprehension: Evidence from aphasia. *Brain and Language*, 3, 572–582.

Coltheart, M., Patterson, K., and Marshall, J. C. (Eds.), (1980). *Deep dyslexia*. London: Routledge and Kegan Paul.

Dakin, J., and Bratley, P. (1967). A limited dictionary for syntactic analysis. In D. Michie (Ed.), *Machine intelligence*. Edinburgh: Oliver and Boyd.

Danley, M. J., de Villiers, J. G., and Cooper, W. E. (1979). Control of speech prosody in Broca's aphasia. In J. J. Wolf and D. H. Klatt (Eds.), *Speech communication papers presented at the 97th meeting of the Acoustical Society of America*. New York: Acoustical Society of America.

Eggert, G. (1977). *Wernicke's works on aphasia: A sourcebook and review*. The Hague: Mouton.

Geschwind, N. (1964). The paradoxical position of Kurt Goldstein in the history of aphasia. *Cortex*, 1, 214–224.

Geschwind, N. (1965). Disconnexion syndromes in animals and man. *Brain*, 88, 237–294, 585–644.

Geschwind, N. (1969). Problems in the anatomical understanding of the aphasias. In A. L. Benton (Ed.), *Contributions to clinical neuropsychology*. Chicago: Aldine.

Geschwind, N. (1977). Psychiatric complications in the epilepsies. *McLean Hospital Journal*, June 1977, 6–8.

Goldstein, K. (1915). *Die transkortikalen Aphasien*. Jena: G. Fischer.

Goldstein, K. (1948). *Language and language disturbances*. New York: Grune and Stratton.

Goodenough, C., Zurif, E., and Weintraub, S. (1977). Aphasics' attention to grammatical morphemes. *Language and Speech*, 20, 11–19.

Goodglass, H., and Geschwind, N. (1976). Language disorders (aphasia). In E. C. Carterette and M. P. Friedman (Eds.), *Handbook of perception*, Vol. 7. New York: Academic Press.

Goodglass, H., and Kaplan, E. (1972). *The assessment of aphasia and related disorders*. Philadelphia: Lea and Febiger.

Green, E., and Howes, D. (1977). The nature of conduction aphasia: A study of anatomic and clinical features and of underlying mechanisms. In H. and H. A. Whitaker (Eds.), *Studies in neurolinguistics*, Vol. 3. New York: Academic Press.

Heilman, K. M., Rothi, L., Campanella, D., and Wolfson, S. (1979). Wernicke's and global aphasia without alexia. *Archives of Neurology*, 36, 129–133.

Heilman, K. M., Scholes, R., and Watson, R. T. (1976). Defects of immediate memory in Broca's and conduction aphasia. *Brain and Language*, 3, 201–208.

Hier, D. B., and Mohr, J. P. (1977). Incongruous oral and written naming: Evidence for a subdivision of the syndrome of Wernicke's aphasia. *Brain and Language*, 4, 115–126.

Jackson, J. H. (1874). On the nature and duality of the brain. *Medical Press and Circular*, 1, 19–41.

Kean, M.-L. (1977). The linguistic interpretation of aphasic syndromes: Agrammatism in Broca's aphasia, an example. *Cognition*, 5, 9–46.

Kean, M.-L. (1980). Grammatical representations and the description of processing. In D. Caplan (Ed.), *Biological studies of mental processes*. Cambridge, Mass.: MIT Press.

Kertesz, A. (1979). *Aphasia and associated disorders*. New York: Grune and Stratton.

Kertesz, A., Harlock, W., and Coates, R. (1979). Computer tomographic localization, lesion size, and prognosis in aphasia and nonverbal impairment. *Brain and Language*, 8, 34–50.

Kertesz, A., Lesk, D., and McCabe, P. (1977). Isotope localization of infarcts in aphasia. *Archives of Neurology*, 34, 590–601.

Kertesz, A., and Phipps, J. B. (1977). Numerical taxonomy of aphasia. *Brain and Language*, 4, 1–10.

Kinnear Wilson, S. A. (1926). *Aphasia*. London: Kegan Paul, Trench, Trubner.

Kreindler, A., Mihailescu, L., and Fradis, A. (1980). Speech fluency in aphasics. *Brain and Language*, 9, 199–205.

Kussmaul, A. (1877). *Die Storungen der Sprache*. Leipzig: Vogel.

Lhermitte, F., Chain, F., Chedru, F., and Penet, C. (1976). A study of visual processes in a case of interhemispheric disconnexion. *Journal of the Neurological Sciences*, 28, 317–330.

Lhermitte, F., and Dérouesné, M. F. (1974). Paraphasies et jargonaphasie dans le langage oral avec conservation du langage écrit. *Revue Neurologique*, 130, 21–38.

Lichtheim, L. (1885). On aphasia. *Brain*, 7, 433–484.

Low, A. A. (1931). A case of agrammatism in the English language. *Archives of Neurology and Psychiatry*, 25, 556–569.

Luria, A. R., and Tsvetkova, L. S. (1968). The mechanism of 'dynamic aphasia.' *Foundations of Language*, 4, 296–307.

McKenna, P., and Warrington, E. K. (1978): Category-specific naming preservation: A single case study. *Journal of Neurology Neurosurgery Psychiatry*, 41, 571–574.

Marshall, J. C. (1970). Mechanisms of linguistic processing. In *Actes du X ͤ Congrès International des Linguistes*. Bucharest: Editions de l'Academie de la Republique Socialiste de Roumanie.

Marshall, J. C. (1977). Disorders in the expression of language. In J. Morton and J. C. Marshall (Eds.), *Psycholinguistics series*, Vol. 1. London: Elek.

Marshall, J. C. (1979). The sense of computation. *The Behavioral and Brain Sciences, 2,* 472–473.

Masden, J. C., Schoene, W. C., and Funkenstein, H. (1978). Aphasia following infarction of the left supplementary motor area. *Neurology, 28,* 1220–1223.

Michel, F. (1979). Préservation du langage écrit malgré un deficit majeur du langage oral (A propos d'un cas clinique). *Lyon Medical, 241,* 141–149.

Mohr, J. P. (1973). Rapid amelioration of motor aphasia. *Archives of Neurology, 28,* 77–82.

Mohr, J. P. (1976). Broca's area and Broca's aphasia. In H. and H. A. Whitaker (Eds.), *Studies in neurolinguistics,* Vol. 1. New York: Academic Press.

Mohr, J. P., Pessin, M. S., Finkelstein, S., Funkenstein, H., Duncan, G. W., and Davis, K. R. (1978). Broca aphasia: Pathological and clinical. *Neurology, 28,* 311–324.

Moutier, F. (1908). *L'aphasie de Broca.* Paris: Steinheil.

Naeser, M. A., and Hayward, R. W. (1978). Lesion localization in aphasia with cranial computed tomography and the Boston Diagnostic Aphasia Exam. *Neurology, 28,* 545–551.

Naeser, M. A., Hayward, R. W., Laughlin, S. A., and Katz, L. M. (1981). Quantitative CT scan studies in aphasia, 1: Infarct size and CT numbers. *Brain and Language, 12,* 140–164.

Newcombe, F., and Marshall, J. C. (1967). Immediate recall of sentences by subjects with unilateral cerebral lesions. *Neuropsychologia, 5,* 329–334.

Pick, A. (1931). *Aphasie.* Berlin: Springer.

Ross, E. D. (1980). Left medial parietal lobe and receptive language functions: Mixed transcortical aphasia after left anterior cerebral artery infarction. *Neurology, 30,* 144–151.

Rothmann, M. (1906). Lichtheimshe motorische Aphasie. *Zeitschrift fur Klinische Medizin, 60,* 87–121.

Rubens, A. B. (1975). Aphasia with infarction in the territory of the anterior cerebral artery. *Cortex, 11,* 239–250.

Rubens, A. B. (1976). Transcortical motor aphasia. In H. and H. A. Whitaker (Eds.), *Studies in neurolinguistics,* Vol. 1. New York: Academic Press.

Salomon, E. (1914). Motorische Aphasie mit Agrammatismus und sensorischagrammatischen Störungen. *Monatsschrift für Psychiatry und Neurologie, 35,* 181–208, 216–275.

Schwartz, M. F., Saffran, E. M., and Marin, O. S. M. (1980). The word order problem in agrammatism, I: Comprehension. *Brain and Language, 10,* 249–262.

Shallice, T. (1979). Case study approach in neuropsychological research. *Journal of Clinical Neuropsychology, 1,* 183–211.

Soh, K., Larsen, B., Skinhøj, E., and Lassen, N. A. (1978). Regional cerebral blood flow in aphasia. *Archives of Neurology, 35,* 625–632.

Spreen, O., Benton, A. L., and van Allen, M. W. (1966). Dissociation of visual and tactile naming in amnesic aphasia. *Neurology, 16,* 807–814.

Wales, R. J., and Marshall, J. C. (1966). The organization of linguistic performance. In J. Lyons and R. J. Wales (Eds.), *Psycholinguistics papers.* Edinburgh: Edinburgh University Press.

Warrington, E. K. (1975). The selective impairment of semantic memory. *Quarterly Journal of Experimental Psychology, 27,* 635–657.

Wernicke, C. (1874). *Der aphasische Symptomenkomplex.* Breslau: Cohn and Weigert.

Wernicke, C. (1906). Der Aphasie Symptomenkomplex. *Deutsche Klinik, 6,* 487–556.

Wernicke, C. (1908). The symptom-complex of aphasia. In A. Church (Ed.), *Diseases of the nervous system.* New York: Appleton.

Zurif, E., and Caramazza, A. (1976). Psycholinguistic structures in aphasia: Studies in syntax and semantics. In H. and H. A. Whitaker (Eds.), *Studies in neurolinguistics,* Vol. 1. New York: Academic Press.

Zurif, E., Caramazza, A., and Myerson, R. (1972). Grammatical judgements of agrammatic aphasias. *Neuropsychologia, 10,* 405–419.

19

Reconciling the Categories: Representation in Neurology and in Linguistics

David Caplan

My purpose in this chapter is to consider the level of empirical observation at which theories of language and theories of brain bave been related, and the descriptive adequacy and explanatory power of theories phrased at that level. To some extent, the analyses and arguments presented here are extensions of those to which I have contributed elsewhere (Arbib and Caplan, 1979; Caplan, in press; Chapter 1 of this volume). Inevitably, given the influence concepts developed in the nineteenth and early twentieth century still exert over contemporary conceptual approaches to language–brain relationships, this chapter will have a somewhat historical flavor.

The elaboration of neurolinguistic theory has, until recently, been undertaken within the context of clinical neurology, by workers who have dual goals. On the one hand, medical men have been concerned with describing and classifying the aphasias and other disturbances of language for clinical purposes of diagnosis and prognosis. Questions such as "Does patient X's mild difficulty with confrontation naming tasks for parts of visually displayed objects represent an early dementia, a mild anomic aphasia, or a depression?" or "Will patient Y's aphasia recover to the point of allowing him to return to work or to return to his family?" are the daily concerns of practicing physicians. For the neurologist, this aspect of the study of aphasia frequently involves the question "Do the signs of language disturbance seen in a particular patient indicate disease of the nervous system and, if so, in what location?"

An important feature to note about such questions is that they can receive answers that represent true empirical generalizations, of a clinically useful sort, without requiring an understanding of the pathogenesis of the symptomatology. Knowing that "if the hemiplegia recovers, the Broca's aphasia usually recovers," is adequate in the majority of clinical situations, and knowing the mechanism that makes this true need not be of further aid to the physician.

The phenomenon of aphasia has, of course, also been studied from the

NEURAL MODELS OF
LANGUAGE PROCESSES

point of view of providing insights into the relationships between language functions, and brain structures and function. In fact, existing theories of language–brain relationships are almost entirely derived from inferences made from the study of aphasic conditions. With few exceptions, the application of such techniques as measuring regional cerebral blood flow (Wood, 1980) and event-related electrical potentials, (Desmedt, 1977; Otto, 1978), which measure physiological events in the central nervous system (CNS) in more direct fashion, has been to verify aspects of a theory of language–brain relationships that has evolved on the basis of inferences from the study of aphasias. Although there are certainly observations regarding language representation in the brain that have come about by the application of methods other than the analysis of aphasia (such as the investigation of the specific comprehension abilities of the surgically isolated right hemisphere [Zaidel, 1978], or the determination of language areas subserving the naming function, which has been discovered by direct stimulation of the cortex [Ojemann and Whitaker, 1978]), it is fair to say that theories of the representation and processing of language by the dominant perisylvian cortex, which is taken to be the principal language-processing area, have achieved their most articulated and interesting form through the analysis of aphasias. No doubt this is, in part, for technical reasons: Although other areas of neuroscience have advanced rapidly because of our ability to record from and stimulate neurological tissue in vivo and our ability to sacrifice animals for morphological studies at specific points of experimentation, there are no appropriate animal models of language, and these techniques are not available in man. The analysis of the so-called "experiments of nature" has largely taken their place.

These two observations—that the study of aphasia has largely been undertaken by physicians whose purposes are partly "medical" in a narrow sense, and that the study of aphasia has formed the basis for the majority of our theories of language–brain relationships—are not unrelated. The requirements of the clinic are for a classification of aphasic syndromes that is reasonably complete and for a technique of assessment of patients that is practicable at the bedside and in the clinic. The work of the so-called "connectionist aphasiologists," as exemplified by Lichtheim's 1885 paper, meets these needs. The clinician must assess the patient's performance in the major on-line functions to which language is put: speech, comprehension, reading, writing; and the special uses of repetition and naming. Lichtheim's article presents a complete classification of aphasic disorders on the basis of observations regarding the relative quantitative impairment of these functions. The partially successful correlation of symptom-complexes defined in this taxonomy with lesion site provided a neurological basis both for the pathogenesis of symptoms and, by a series of inferences, for components of normal language functions, which was conceptually adequate for the clinician. As has been observed many times, the clinical success of this approach led to its reintroduction some 20 years ago after a period of relative abandonment, and, though the details are much debated, this clinical classification and diagnostic examinations associated with it are certainly the most widely used today in North America. The theory of language representation in brain associated with this clinical approach to the aphasias forms the basis for a good deal of our conceptual and investigative approach to the question of language–brain relationships.

It does so in two related ways. First, it provides a level of empirical reality at which descriptions of language function and brain function are to be described in order to be related. Second, it provides a general outline of a theory of language representation and processing in brain based upon descriptions at these levels. I should like to consider both of these aspects of this theory, with respect to their descriptive adequacy and explanatory power, and to explore the impact of more recent approaches upon the notions of description and explanation in neurolinguistics.

Classical studies of aphasia utilized a highly restricted set of linguistic descriptive terms for the characterization of symptom-complexes. Indeed, it seems to be fair to say that the majority of studies undertaken in the first 75 years or so of scientific aphasiology following Broca (1861) focused on individual words as the basic units of language structure. A word was seen as a unit that united two separate levels of description: a level depicting the sound associated with the word, a phonological level; and a level depicting the meaning of a word, a semantic level. Semantic properties of words were primarily referential. Naming and identification tasks figure prominently in the standard methods of assessment. The notion of semantic "associations" to a word also appeared in the writings of Wernicke (1874), Lichtheim (1885), Freud (1891), and many others. The sound structure of words was seen to consist of segmental (roughly phonemic) analyses. Both Wernicke and Lichtheim make reference to an analysis of paraphasias in terms of selection of the sounds of the word. Lichtheim in particular was concerned with the syllable structure of words, and devised a test of a patient's residual inner speech which consisted of his being able to tap the number of syllables in a word that referred to a presented object, even if unable to produce the word orally or in writing.

When areas of language other than these are considered, both "north" and "south" of the lexicon, it becomes clear that classical workers did not have at their disposal a rich and specific set of concepts for the description of linguistic structures. In particular, distinctions among word classes on syntactic grounds, the details of derivational morphological processes, and, most importantly, given current linguistic achievements, the entire areas of syntactic structure and suprasegmental phonology and their relationship to semantics, were not available to classical workers.

I do not mean to imply that aphasiologists were unaware of the existence of levels of linguistic organization other than individual words. For instance, an oft-cited example of their appreciation of these levels is Jackson's (1874) insistence on the notion of a "proposition." It is illuminating to consider his actual definition:

> It is not enough to say that speech consists of words. It consists of words *referring to one another in a particular manner;* and without a proper inter-relation of its parts, a verbal utterance would be a mere succession of names embodying no proposition. A proposition, eg. "gold is yellow" consists of two names, each of which, by conventional contrivances of position, etc. (called grammatical structure in well-developed languages), *modifies the meaning of the other. . . .* A proposition is not. . . a mere sequence. . . . When we apprehend a proposition, a *relation between two things is given* to us—is for the moment, indeed, forced upon us by the conventional tricks which put the two names in their respective relations of subject and predicate. We receive in a *two-fold* manner, not the words only, but the order of words also [p. 130; italics Jackson's].

Jackson's insight regarding the significance of this level of linguistic organization was recaptured independently by numerous investigators (see, for instance, André Thomas's prescient remarks regarding the nature of the "verbal deafness" in Broca's aphasics in the "Great Debate" of 1908).

What is striking about this work, in the light of modern approaches, is that important insights regarding the existence of this supralexical level of linguistic organization were not accompanied by an appreciation of the actual structure of the supralexical organization of language.

Let us consider two more examples of the dichotomy between the rich intuitions that figured in the description of language pathology and the relatively impoverished theoretical vocabulary that was available for the characterization of those descriptions.

The first is the division of vocabulary elements into what is now called "open class" and "closed class" or "P-word" and "P-clitic" vocabularies. Goldstein (1948) clearly recognized the existence of these two classes of words. He described groups of patients who had particular differences in what he called the "finding of the 'small words' such as prepositions, articles, pronouns, grammatical forms, etc. [p. 68]." He was aware of some of the properties of this subclass of vocabulary elements, such as that they are "senseless" when "isolatedly presented," and that there is a "difficulty to pronounce short words [because] words with several syllables are easier to speak because the articulatory units are more precise [p. 70]." What is striking is the discrepancy between Goldstein's remarkably accurate observations regarding the semantic and acoustic-phonetic properties of the closed class vocabulary, and his unsatisfactory general characterization of this class of items. No doubt he was dissatisfied with his own efforts, for he concludes the section by saying "our knowledge of the behaviour of aphasic patients in respect to the small words is limited. Further studies would be of great interest [p. 70]."

As another example, consider Luria's (1973) suggestion that one feature of sentence comprehension is an understanding of the "logical grammatical relations" dependent upon the syntax of sentences. A patient with a difficulty in this sphere is said to have had trouble understanding a sentence such as A *lady came from the factory to the school where Nina was a pupil to give a talk* but not *Father and Mother went to the cinema, but Grandmother and the children stayed home.* It is clear that there are syntactic structural differences between these two types of sentences, but Luria does not say WHICH of these differences are the salient ones in determining the success or failure for the patient group in question. What is lacking, again, seems to be a descriptive framework rich enough to specify the types of distinctions involved. It is not that intuitions about differences between groups of patients are lacking, or that intuitions about differences among types of linguistic and logical structures are lacking. It is rather that a vocabulary sufficiently rich to capture the intuitive differences is not available.

Turning from the characterization of the linguistic concepts that characterize traditional accounts of language–brain relationships and aphasic syndromes to that of psychological functions to which linguistic structures were put, we find, I believe, a historical progression of concepts to which recent work constitutes the logical next step. The traditional observations upon which the description of aphasic syndromes and related neurolinguistic theories were based focused on the description of on-line psycholinguistic tasks of speaking, comprehension, reading, and writing, and the rather special tasks of confrontation naming and repetition, basically forming, as Luria (1947) pointed out, a faculty psychology. Observations that figured in the construction of theories of language representation and processing by brain were directed primarily to the judgment of relative quantitative impairment of each of these faculties. Such observations are suggested by authors as diverse as Lichtheim (1885) and Benson and Geschwind (1976).

Qualitative distinctions in the performance of these various tasks were also noted. It is interesting to see exactly how they figure in the construction of theories of language–brain relationships.

Lichtheim's analysis of the qualitative differences between the abnormalities in speech production in anterior and posterior aphasias constitutes an excellent example (see also Chapter 1, this volume). Lichtheim's model of speech production involved the arousal of the motor images for words in a center, M, from two sources: a "concept centre," B, and the "auditory centre for word sound images," A. Superficially, it might seem that the destruction of center A in posterior aphasia should leave the excitation of M from B intact, with no consequent effect on speech production. This contradicts the observed facts of spontaneous speech in posterior aphasias. Lichtheim therefore concludes that the center A plays a role in spontaneous speech and that normal speech production necessarily involves the double activation of M through two pathways: one from A to M and the second from B to M. Lesions of B or the pathway BM produced one form of speech output disturbance; lesions of A and the pathway AM produced a different type. The underlying principle is that where performance is dependent upon two inputs to one center, disturbance of one input will lead to a partial performance qualitatively distinct from the partial performance seen after the disturbance of the second input. But the details of the actual qualitative nature of disturbance in speech is unexplained.

In our 1979 paper, Arbib and I suggested that there has been a progression of thought in neurolinguistic theories based on observations of aphasias along lines which incorporate more and more of this sort of component interaction. We suggested that the earliest models of language–brain relationships postulated that entire on-line psycholinguistic functions were individual units in a psychological theory of language use. Broca's description of the "faculty of articulate speech" as an isolable psychological function exemplifies this type of theorizing. Progressively more complex interactions, of the type just cited in Lictheim's work, characterized subsequent workers. We suggested that, at the point at which the units of analysis of psycholinguistic function were ALL subcomponents of the major on-line psycholinguistic processes, a state in theorizing had been reached that was qualitatively different from earlier work, and which we termed "process," as opposed to "faculty," modeling.

Given the level of empirical observation of linguistic and psycholinguistic phenomena that characterizes (rather roughly, and with considerable variation among investigators) descriptions of language and language impairments in the faculty and process models, what explanatory power do these models have? To answer this question, it is illuminating to consider specific examples of explanations offered by workers within this tradition. Again, as for the empirical basis of these theories, we may turn to the earliest work for examples of the types of explanations offered.

Wernicke's 1874 paper included two approaches to the explanation of the syndromes he distinguished—the first anatomical, and the second functional. The anatomical explanation of the nature of Broca's and Wernicke's aphasia related both syndromes to the role of the responsible brain areas in motor and sensory processes, respectively. The syndrome described by Broca, in which "the faculty of articulate speech" was disturbed but other language abilities (relatively) spared, followed lesions in the frontal, motor, regions of the brain; Wernicke's aphasia, which he termed "sensory," was due to lesions adjacent to the central terminations of the acoustic pathways and affected comprehension in a marked fashion. These lesion sites were not coincidental, but central to the reasons for the disorders in the language sphere. Wernicke viewed language as a higher order reflex, with a sensory and a motor pole, and he referred to Meynert's discovery of a basic sensory–motor dichotomy between the posterior and anterior portions of the brain as the functional neuroanatomy relevant to the physiology of language and its dissolution.

This appeal to the role of brain loci in sensory–motor function also characterizes the anatomical line of "explanation" of the nature of aphasic symptoms and syndromes in the more complex descriptions and explanations of the process models. Luria's (1947) work provides a good example. In the introductory chapter to this volume, Arbib, Marshall, and I present a synopsis of Luria's description of the pathogenesis of one form of aphasia—efferent motor aphasia—which indicates the explicit link Luria envisaged between the functions of the frontal association areas in motor control and their function in language processing. Just as this area plays a role in the temporal control of movement, it functions in the "dynamic predicative function of the word"; just as lesions here cause motor abnormalities referable to loss of this aspect of motor planning (perserveration, difficulty changing actions, etc.), so too they produce a language disorder in which the patient is "incapable of stringing [words] together. . . to form smooth grammatically structured sentences [Luria, 1947, p. 189]."

Examples of this form of explanation of particular aphasic symptoms are widespread. The claim that the pattern of cerebral connections of the human inferior parietal lobe determines its capacity to act in the formation of "cross-modal, non-limbic associations" which, in turn, underlie the act of naming (Geschwind, 1965), the argument that the speech disorder seen in Broca's aphasia is a high-level articulatory disturbance, a so-called "apraxia of speech" (Levine and Sweet, Chapter 14 this volume), and many other similar analyses come readily to mind.

It is also instructive to examine the PREDICTIVE value of theories of language representation in brain within the perspective of this anatomical form of explanation, since a widely accepted test of the explanatory value of a theory is its ability to make predictions. As Geschwind (1980) has pointed out, the connectionist models have achieved a measure of success in this domain. The work of Liepmann, particularly his analysis of the clinical features of the case of the Regeirungsrat and the subsequently confirmed predictions regarding a lesion in the anterior callosum (Liepman and Maas, 1907), exemplifies this achievement. Without denying the legitimacy or value of this and similar work, we may ask in what domain these predictions have been made. In every case of which I am aware, the predictions deal with one of two general areas: The first is the consequence of the disconnection of a left-hemisphere-based language zone from topographically committed areas of sensory or motor cortex or subcortex such as in the apraxia cases first analyzed by Liepmann. The second is the establishment of "information-flow" between two "centers" of the left hemisphere language zone, WHICH ARE THEMSELVES RELATED TO SENSORY OR MOTOR FUNCTION, as in the prediction that repetition would be abnormal in cases of section of the pathway (be it in the insula or the arcuate fasciculus) between the sensory language center and the motor language center. To my knowledge, these models have never predicted the nature of the language elements affected by disease. That is, the domain in which the models have predictive power is narrowly constrained to the relationship between the language area as a whole and areas of the brain subserving sensory and motor function, and to disconnections of sensory and motor poles within the language zone itself.

The absence of predictions dealing with the detailed linguistic disruption seen with particular lesions reflects the degree to which strictly linguistic characterizations of aphasic symptoms within these models are a sort of epiphenomenon not central to the data the models seek to describe and explain. Though the classical descriptions of aphasic syndromes and symptoms include linguistic characterizations, these qualitative analyses are grafted onto, rather than following from, the nature of the anatomical features of these models.

We have noted one example of this relationship, the case of the qualitative distinction in speech output found in anterior and posterior aphasics noted by Lichtheim, whose attempt to explain these features of aphasic language fell short of an account of the specific nature of the linguistic impairment. Another example is to be found in Luria's explanations of many aphasic impairments, one of which, efferent motor aphasia, we have briefly outlined. Luria's comparison between schemata for temporal organization of movement and the dynamic predicative function of words is allegorical, not mechanistic. One of the reasons for this is that, rich as the descriptions of both motor and language disturbances are in Luria, they are not precise enough for the ultimate purpose of allowing the specifications of detailed correspondences between elements of each. The descriptions of language pathology are still too impressionistic. We cannot tell just what is meant by the term "dynamic predicative function of words," which seems to refer, in Luria, to the role lexical items play in syntactic structures, but might refer to their "sense," as opposed to their "reference." Given the indeterminacy of these terms within the linguistic system, it is impossible to specify the exact way in which they are the formal or substantive equivalent of a term such as "dynamic plasticity of the active motor pattern" used as part of the theory of motor control. In consequence, the explanation of the syndrome of efferent motor aphasia by reference to the motor functions of the area of brain in which lesions produce this syndrome, rests on an imprecise analogy.

Returning to the two modes of neurolinguistic explanation found in Wernicke (1874), let us consider those we may term "functional." Freud (1891) stressed that the occurrence of an abnormality of speech output with posterior lesions does not follow from the "anatomical" analysis; a functional factor needs to be invoked. In Wernicke's view, the reason the sensory center for word sound images is a necessary part of the apparatus for speech production is that language is acquired first by imitation, and the initial reliance of speech upon auditory input establishes the obligatory role of an intact sensory center in this motor activity. Functional factors influencing language performances (and determining the interpretation of the early diagrams) play important roles in all theories, sometimes combined explicitly with notation borrowed from the diagram makers (as in Bastian, 1898) and sometimes without a corresponding formalism (as in Jackson, 1878–1879, and Head, 1926). Perhaps the most heroic attempt to "explain" aphasic symptoms by reference to functional factors is to be found in Goldstein's (1948) recurring appeal to a single disability, the failure to achieve the "abstract attitude," as the cause of a multitude of linguistically deviant performances. Here is his explanation of the failure of certain patients to realize the "small words" (recall his interesting descriptions of this class of items):

> These words are missing apparently because . . . the motor difficulty induces a definite attitude which concentrates on those words which are sufficient for being understood . . . in central motor aphasia, the patient has great difficulty when he must speak or write these words, particularly when they are demanded in isolation, and this is because he is impaired in his abstract attitude [1948, p. 68, 69].

Functional explanations relying on psychological factors not specific to the processes of production and recovery of linguistic representations have been suggested by contemporary authors as well. Goodglass and his colleagues (Goodglass, 1973; Goodglass, Fodor, and Schuelhoff, 1967) have argued that a factor they term "salience," itself a composite of several features of utterances, partially determines Broca's aphasics' production and perception of function words and certain bound morphemes; Wepman and his coworkers (Wepman, Bock, Jones, and Van Pelt, 1956) have reinterpreted the linguistic characterization of anomic aphasia in terms of a disturbance related to infrequent words. There can be little doubt that, just as certain aspects of aphasic performance are the result of (partial or complete) disconnection of language areas from specific sensory or motor "centers," any understanding of language function and breakdown will have to incorporate a variety of nonlinguistic functional factors, some of which may account for the entirety of certain pathological behaviors which, at first, may appear to be the result of a linguistic impairment. On the other hand, as with the anatomical explanations based upon analogies of language and sensory-motor processes and the isolation of language areas from sensory and motor centers, such functional explanations do not account for those aspects of language pathology that are truly the result of the breakdown of linguistic representations and psychological processes specifically related to these representations.

The last dozen or so years have seen progress in the characterization of the linguistic structures affected in individual aphasic patients and in particular aphasic syndromes, in that terms used are both richer and more precise than any previously used. Many of the chapters in this volume are representative of these studies, and it is not my intention to review this growing literature here. Rather, I should like to outline one framework within which these studies can be viewed as contributing to neurolinguistic theory, a perspective that also makes explicit some of the ways in which these studies differ from many previous investigations in terms of their basic assumptions about the nature of neurolinguistic description and explanation.

Chomsky and other contemporary linguists have repeatedly argued that results obtained in modern linguistic studies indicate that language utilizes a set of structures formally and substantively dissimilar to those involved in other aspects of cognitive, motor, and perceptual tasks (see Chomsky, 1980, for discussion). A growing body of work in psycholinguistics implicitly or explicitly assumes the existence of many (unconscious) psychological operations that are unique to the tasks of recovery and production of particular levels of linguistic representations in the production and comprehension of utterances (Fodor, J. A. Bever, and Garrett, 1975; Frazier and J. D. Fodor, 1978). These levels of representation are specifically those that are required by linguistic theory to mediate the sound–meaning relation established by language. Other characteristics of linguistic structures (such as phrase length) are considered to be the reflection of psychological factors, such as constraints on memory, extrinsic to the psychology of language narrowly defined. That linguistic form and the psychological processes devoted to its production and recovery are independent aspects of human cognition is, of course, a hypothesis; one which, at this point, is instantiated in a large body of specific suggestions and arguments regarding the nature of linguistic units, their interaction, and their utilization in psychology in processes of the type described. The justification for this general hypothesis must lie in the ability of particular studies to describe, explain, and predict a significant body of data, a requirement that contemporary linguistic and psycholinguistic studies have begun to meet. Indeed, this approach, which has been described as the attempt to characterize a "language-specific cognitive structure" (Klein, 1977) or a "mental organ" for language (Chomsky, 1977) has been termed "the cornerstone of the most fruitful research in the area of human cognition [Kean and Smith, 1979, p. 469]."

Efforts such as those represented in this volume and in other recent publications to characterize the linguistic and psycholinguistic nature of aphasic and other disorders of language in terms related to this approach to language and language processing naturally add a considerable degree of depth and richness to the descriptions of language pathology. However, they do more than simply provide an additional set of descriptive terms related to language, which can now be applied to language breakdown. They have consequences for the delineation of the biological basis for the human language capacity, and they raise important issues regarding the notion of explanation in neurolinguistics.

The strongest claim of the "independence" hypothesis regarding language structures and their processing would be that, in addition to their independence on the psychological level, cognitive domains are also neurologically independent; that is, each depends upon particular elements or organizational aspects of the nervous system, of which some, such as those putatively related to language, are presumably unique to particular species. The "independence hypothesis" is obviously extended along these organic lines by results that indicate that a set of consequences of acquired disease of the nervous system is characterizable in terms of structures and processing components specific to the language system. For this to be the case would require not only that the independence hypothesis be true, but also that the effects of disease be selective enough to enable us to recognize the contribution to the final behavioral repertoire of a patient of disturbance of independent linguistic and nonlinguistic psychological structures and functions. Though we are certainly a long way from a rich theory of language disturbances phrased in these terms, some of the results of recent years do suggest that what are variably called "knowledge sources," "knowledge types," or "levels of representation," and the processing mechanisms that are associated with them in human cognition, include a number whose role is specific for the representation and processing of human language, and in which the effects of CNS disease can be identified.

The first and central goal of neurolinguistic theory, then, can be conceived as the delineation of the nature of representations that are narrowly linguistic (parallel to the view expressed by Chomsky [1977] when he points out that the study of a phenomenon called "language" has been scientifically supplanted by that of a phenomenon called "grammar"), the psychological processes devoted to their recovery and production, and the nature of the neural elements and operations that are related to both. As has been repeatedly debated in the psychological literature and has been recently pointed out in the neurolinguistic literature (see Kean, Chapter 8, this volume), the identification of appropriate aspects of a linguistic and psycholinguistic ontology and their interaction is a complex theoretical and empirical matter, compounded in the case of language disorders by the variety of possible effects of disease upon these symptoms (see Caplan, in press, for discussion). Our prospects of accomplishing the goal of developing a description of the neural basis of the structures and operations discovered by linguistic and psycholinguistic science, however, is closely tied to our ability to develop such an ontology in detail and, at present, to analyze disorders of language in terms related to it. Analysis of aphasic syndromes of the type outlined by Kean (Chapter 8, this volume) provide the first steps toward functional explanations of aphasic syndromes within this perspective.

If it is at least conceputally clear what some of the requirements are for a functional explanation of an aphasic symptom or syndrome (see Kean, Chapter 8, this volume), the notion of anatomical explanation is less clear within a neurolinguistic framework which emphasizes the identification of neural elements related to language structures and their processing. It appears to me that this conceptual difficulty arises primarily because we are accustomed to thinking of the neural "side" of "neurolinguistics" in terms of a certain type of analysis of the nervous system, one which is inappropriate as the theoretical basis for the type of psychology of language processing contemporary psychology and linguistics is moving toward and for the kind of characterization of language breakdown modern aphasiology is beginning to provide.

The origins of our current neural analysis go back to the first scientific paper on aphasia, that of Broca (1861). Broca's hypothesis that cerebral convolutions were relatively constant landmarks of gross human neuroantomy and that they were functionally significant units, within which psychological faculties could be located, constituted an enormous step forward in the investigation of the neurological basis for language and cognition. However, from 1861 on, the most widespread characterization of neurological structure in theories relating language and brain has been as anatomical units defined by gross neuroanatomical features of the brain. The correlation of aphasic syndromes, and by inference, aspects of the faculty for language, with gyri, parts of gyri defined by gross anatomical inspection, and structures larger than gyri, was a major concern of the nineteenth century and the early twentieth-century aphasiologists, and has carried over into contemporary work. Analyses of neurological structure phrased in terms of neurological elements smaller than gyri are so rare in the field of neurolinguistics that Arbib and Caplan (1979) characterized the neurological aspects of neurolinguistics as fundamentally pre-Sherringtonian, and as almost totally devoid of reference to the most basic units of neurological analysis—cell–synapse–circuit considerations. Recent work (Galaburda, LeMay, Kemper, and Geschwind, 1978; Galaburda, Chapter 20, this volume) has begun to fill the gap in our knowledge of the cellular structure of the language areas.

The effort to establish localization of symptoms and of functions has resulted in what Marshall (1980) has noted to be a neurolinguistic correlational analysis that is in certain ways misleading (see also Chapter 1 of this volume). He points out that

> when connectionist psychological models are "glued" onto the surface of the brain . . . they seem, erroneously, to provide their own physiological interpretation. Students of philosophy or psychology were quick to spot such sleight of hand . . . our flow charts can reasonably be regarded as "specifying abstract conditions that unknown mechanisms must meet" (Chomsky, 1976), but they are surely not physiological theories. And Freud (1891) put it succinctly when he asked rhetorically: "Is it justified to immerse a nerve fibre, which over the whole length of its course has been only a physiological structure, subject to physiological modifications, with its end in the psyche . . ." [p. 126, 127].

Though some components of psychological functions such as those related to particular language functions may in fact correlate with gross neuroanatomical regions, they would do so, as best we now know, because of correlations between elements of these functions and elements of these structures, which both happen to be grouped in particular ways. To suggest, as does Kean (1977), that "there

might be essentially functional equipotentiality for phonological language production across Broca's area [p. 130]" is entirely analagous to saying that stereopsis
is a function of the occipital lobes. In the latter case, we are developing theories
of how elements of the occipital lobes accomplish this function (see Arbib,
Chapters 4 and 25, this volume); we need to do the same for theories of
language–brain relationships.

The most lucid outline of the general form an adequate theory of this sort
might take, in light of our current understanding of the relationship between
neurological events and structures and psychological theories dealing with "information processing," is to be found in the work of Marshall (1980). Based on
suggestions of Poggio's and Marr's, he distinguishes four separate, conceptually
independent, levels of description, which together constitute as complete a description of the neurological mechanisms underlying certain types of psychological function as we currently can envisage. Marr and Poggio term these steps
"from understanding computation to understanding neural circuitry." They are:

1. The level at which the nature of a computation is expressed. With
respect to human language, Marshall suggests that generative transformational
theories of grammer provide a characterization of the structures relevant to
language, that is, a characterization of the features of the mental object attained.

2. The level at which algorithms that implement a computation are characterized. Marshall suggests that work on parsing strategies, both implemented,
and based on the results of psychological experimentation, provides an example
of the beginnings of a characterization of the psychological steps which are
operative in the attainment of the linguistic structures of Level 1. Suggestions as
to the steps of processing involved in language production, based on analyses of
patterns in spontaneous errors in speech, constitute another example.

3. The level at which an algorithm is committed to particular mechanisms,
which has been "the traditional preserve within psycholinguistics of the
aphasiologist."

4. The level at which mechanisms are realized in hardware. Marshall
indicates that it is this level, "the basic component and circuit analysis, which
has been most lacking in neurolinguistics. We just don't know whether the
neurons, synapses, transmitter substances, patterns of conductivity, and so forth,
in the language areas of the brain differ in important respects from those characteristic of other parts [p. 130]."

Marshall's view of the relationship between neural theory and linguistic
theory, namely that we are involved in the search for the "mechanisms to which
the algorithms that carry out a computation are committed [Chapter 1, this
volume]," is an answer to the question of the conceptual framework for describing the neural concomitants of language USE. It does not preclude the search
for neural elements and operations responsible for the "long-term storage" of

linguistic elements—which may be termed "competence" in the sense of modern linguistic theory. Indeed, if, as is implicitly the case in several psychologically justified theories of language processing (Frazier and Fodor, 1978), the basic nature of language processing involves the identification of linguistic structures as tokens of types available by virtue of "knowledge" an individual has of his language, such mechanisms and algorithms will require the identification of neural elements and operations responsible for the representation of such knowledge. Nor need all these linguistic representations or the psychological processes related to their use be of a single type. The distinction between universal and language-specific aspects of linguistic structure, for instance, which overlaps with the distinction between innate and acquired aspects of linguistic competence, must, if valid, be reflected in intrinsic-versus-acquired aspects of neural structure. Everything that DISTINGUISHES Chinese from English, as well as everything that UNITES these two languages as instances of the linguistic competence which can be acquired by a normal human given appropriate exposure at the appropriate developmental stage, must be represented in the brains of Chinese and English speakers. It is possible that the neural mechanisms related to the universal and language-specific aspects of particular languages have different properties. Our psycholinguistic and linguistic ontology will guide our search for neural structures and processes.

Explanatory notions of an anatomical sort will, in this approach, have to await the description and justification of models of neural processes stated at this level of function, which we may call "information bearing." Though we now have only the remotest notions of what the actual substantive form of such an integrated neurolinguistic science will take, we have at least begun the characterization of the phenomena such explanations would be directed to. Anatomical explanation will, ultimately, be related to the computational capacities of neural tissue. Considering the remarkable computational capacity of nonhuman species (Ewert, 1976; see also Arbib, Chapter 25, this volume), it is clearly a nontrivial problem to discover what physical and/or organizational properties of the human nervous system distinguish it from that of other species and permit the representation and use of language.

How might we advance the empirical study of neural mechanisms that underlie language, described at this neurobiological level? I should like to conclude with a brief and very general description of three areas in which further work may be productive.

First, additional studies of the specific linguistic and psycholinguistic capacities of individual aphasic patients and groups of aphasics would serve to increase the range of data relevant to the investigation of such neural elements. As understanding of the structure of language and the psychological processing associated with language increases, we need to know whether patients retain normal structures and processes. An important associated question is the identification of any systematic but aberrant linguistic and psychological principles underlying pathological functions and structures. We know, for instance, that children go through developmental stages in which they construct consistent but erroneous models of language which are, however, related to normal adult grammars (Tavakolian, 1977) and are, apparently, in some well-studied cases, constrained by deep regularities (? universals) of language (Roeper, 1978). Do aphasics do the same?

Second, we need correlation between site of lesion and type of symptoms, in instances where a plausible case has been made that a particular symptomatology reflects the dysfunction of a specific component of a psychological theory of language structure and/or processing. The best work to date concerning the site of lesions that produce aphasic syndromes, such as that of Mohr (1976) and Kertesz (1979), is based on tests and concepts related to the classical clinical analysis. To utilize aphasic data to provide an understanding of the neurological basis of specifically LINGUISTIC capacities and the psychological processes specific to language, we will require further research that is of the traditional clinico-pathological correlational sort but incorporates taxonomies of patients based on available detailed linguistic and psycholinguistic analyses.

Third, the investigation of linguistic and psycholinguistic symptomatology occasioned by different pathological entities would allow aphasiology to approach neural models of a cellular type. It may be that increasing sophistication and availability of more direct physiological observational techniques will make this a secondary approach to the problem. Nonetheless, with more detailed linguistic and psycholinguistic studies of aphasia, it becomes feasible to consider whether particular symptoms occur as a result of particular pathological events. Particularly interesting in this regard would be studies of different types of lesions that occupy the same grossly defined areas of the nervous system (to the extent that different pathological lesions ever do). For instance, Hecaen and his colleagues (Hecaen and Consoli, 1973) have reported that Broca's aphasia follows large and deep lesions that affect the third frontal convolution of the dominant hemisphere. Mohr (1976) has stressed the temporal determinants of this syndrome. If we knew more about how the linguistic and psychological profiles of tumor cases and stroke cases in various stages of evolution compare with those that are seen with stable vascular lesions in the anterior language zone, we would be able to correlate the linguistic–psycholinguistic descriptions with cellular pathological descriptions and begin to construct theories of the neurocellular structures that correlate with language, by a logic identical to that which now relates grossly defined areas of the brain to language functions.

The "revolution" in linguistics has exerted significant, sometimes radical, influences upon the nature of investigation of language in psychology and philosophy. It is beginning to have the same effect in aphasiology and neurolinguistic studies. One of the most exciting and challenging aspects of this process is the dimly perceived notion that we may be on the road to identification of substantive and formal aspects of human cognition which, as Chomsky has said, if not themselves correct, are of the right kind. If so, we may be at the early stages of a significant interdisciplinary scientific enterprise, in which linguistic and neurological theories can be related to each other in rich explanatory ways.

REFERENCES

Arbib, M. A., and Caplan, D. (1979). Neurolinguistics must be computational. *Behavioural & Brain Sciences, 2,* 449–783.

Bastian, C. F. (1897). Aphasia and other speech defects. *Lancet,* 933–942, 1005–1017, 1131–1137, 1187–1194.

Benson, D. F., and Geschwind, N. (1976). The aphasias and related disturbances. In A. B. Baker and L. H. Baker (Eds.), *Clinical neurology,* New York: Harper & Row.

Broca, P. (1861). Remarques sur le siege de la faculte du langage articule. *Bulletin de la Société de Anatome, 6,* 330–357.

Caplan, D. (In press). On the cerebral localization of linguistic functions. *Brain and Language.*

Chomsky, N. (1977). *Essays on form and interpretation.* Amsterdam: North-Holland.

Chomsky, N. (1980). *Rules and representations.* New York: Columbia University Press.

Desmedt, J. E. (1977). *Language and hemispheric specialization in man: Cerebral event-related potentials.* Basel: Karga.

Ewert, J.-P. (1976). The visual system of the toad: Behavioral and physiological studies of a pattern recognition system. In K. V. Fite (Ed.), *The amphibian visual system: A multi-disciplinary approach.* New York: Academic Press.

Fodor, J. A., Bever, T. G., and Garrett, M. F. (1975). *The psychology of language.* New York: McGraw-Hill.

Frazier, L., and Fodor, J. D. (1978). The sausage machine: A new two-stage parsing model. *Cognition, 6,* 291–325.

Freud, S. (1891). *On aphasia.* Reprinted in translation, New Southgate, U.K.: Image.

Galaburda, A. M., LeMay, M., Kemper, T. L., and Geschwind, N. (1978). Right–left asymmetries in the brain. *Science, 199,* 852–856.

Geschwind, N. (1965). Disconnexion syndromes in animals and man. *Brain, 88,* 237–294.

Geschwind, N. (1980). Some comments on the neurology of language. In D. Caplan (Ed.), *Biological studies of mental processes.* Cambridge, Massachusetts: MIT Press.

Goldstein, K. (1948). *Language and language disturbances.* New York: Grune & Stratton.

Goodglass, H. (1973). Studies on the grammar of aphasics. In H. Goodglass and S. Blumstein (Eds.), *Psycholinguistics and aphasia.* Baltimore: Johns Hopkins.

Goodglass, H., Fodor, I. G., and Schuelhoff, C. (1967). Prosodic factors in grammar—Evidence from aphasia. *Journal of Speech and Hearing Research, 10,* 5–20.

Head, H. (1926). *On aphasia and kindred disorders of language.* London: Hafner.

Hecaen, H., and Consoli, S. (1973). Analyse des troubles du langage au cours des lesions de l'aire de Broca. *Neuropsychologia, 11,* 377–388.

Jackson, J. H. (1874). On the nature of the duality of the brain. *Medical Press and Circular, 1,* 19ff, 41ff, 63ff. Reprinted in J. Taylor (Ed.), *Selected writings of J. H. Jackson.* New York: Basic Books, 1958.

Jackson, J. H. (1878–1879). On affections of speech from disease of the brain. *Brain, 1,* 304–330; 2, 203–222, 323–356. Reprinted in J. Taylor (Ed.), *Selected workings* of J. H. Jackson. New York: Basic Books, 1958.

Kean, M.-L. (1977). On the linguistic interpretation of aphasic syndromes. In E. Walker (Ed.), *Explorations in the biology of language*. Montgomery, Vt.: Bradford Books.

Kean M.-L., and Smith, G. F. (1979). Issues in core linguistic processing. *Behaviour and Brain Science*, 2, 469–70.

Klein, V. E. (1977). What is the biology of language? In E. Walker (Ed.), *Explorations in the biology of language*. Montgomery, Vt.: Bradford Books.

Kertesz, A. (1979). *Aphasia and associated disorders*. New York: Grune & Stratton.

Lichtheim, K. (1885). On aphasia. *Brain*, 7, 433–484.

Liepman, H., and Maas, O. (1907). Fall von Linksseitiger Agraphie und Apraxie bie rechtsseitger lahmung. *Journal fur Psychiatrie and Neurologie*, 10, 214–227.

Luria, A. R. (1947). *Traumatic aphasia* (English translation, The Hague: Mouton, 1970).

Luria, A. R. (1973). *The working brain*. New York: Basic Books.

Marshall, J. C. (1980). On the biology of language acquisition. In D. Caplan (ed.), *Biological studies of mental processes*. Cambridge, Mass.: MIT Press.

Mohr, J. P. (1976). Broca's area and Broca's aphasia. In H. Whitaker and H. A. Whitaker (Eds.), *Studies in Neurolinguistics*, Vol. 1. New York: Academic Press.

Ojemann, G. A., and Whitaker, H. A. (1978). Language vocalization and variability. *Brain and Language*, 6, 239–260.

Otto, D. A. (1978). *Multidisciplinary perspectives in event-related brain potential research*. U.S.E.P.A. - 600/9-77-043.

Roeper, T. (1978). Linguistic universals and the acquisition of gerunds. In H. Goodluck and L. Solon) (Eds.), *Papers in the structure and development of clinical language* (University of Massachusetts Occasional Papers in Linguistics, Vol. 4).

Tavakolian, S. L. (1977). *Structural principles in the acquisition of complex sentences*. Unpublished Ph.D. dissertation, University of Massachusetts.

Wepman, J. M., Bock, R. D., Jones, L. V., and Van Pelt, D. (1956). A revision of the concept of aphasia. *Journal of Speech and Hearing Disorders*, 21, 468–477.

Wernicke, C. (1874). *Die Aphasische Symptomencomplex*. Breslau.

Wood, F. (1980). Noninvasive blood flow studies. *Brain and Language*, 9, 1–148.

Zaidel, E. (1978). Auditory language comprehension in the right hemisphere following cerebral commissurotomy and hemispherectomy. In A. Carramazza and E. Zurif (Eds.), *Language acquisition and language breakdown*, Baltimore: Johns Hopkins.

V
NEUROSCIENCE AND BRAIN THEORY

As we begin this final part, it is worth recalling what we have and have not encountered throughout this work. We have met a variety of case studies of aphasic symptom-complexes, and have seen the debates based on neuropathologic studies made at autopsy on aphasic patients and the newer techniques, such as CT scanning, which can be applied to the living human being concerning the cerebral localization of defects that underlie such symptoms. We have seen how psycholinguistic studies can direct analyses of aphasia that make contact with (and perhaps lead to the constructive modification of) current linguistic theory. And we have seen that the processing models of Artificial Intelligence (AI) begin to be confronted by psycholinguistic studies. A promissory note was offered (in the chapters of Arbib, Lavorel, and Marcus in Part II) for the applicability of AI techniques to explain neurolinguistic data via detailed analysis of processing mechanisms. Unfortunately, virtually all work in neurolinguistics has lacked this precise attention to mechanism. Yet there is an even greater fault in neurolinguistics to date: its almost total lack of contact with the insights and techniques of modern neuroscience.

Neuroscience refines region-by-region analysis to probe the cellular structure of different regions and the detailed patterns of cellular connectivity that link them. Comparative anatomy show how these patterns vary and yet retain certain commonalities, from species to species. Neurophysiology records the activity of neurons during certain behaviors, correlating their activity with sensory stimulation, internal states, and motor performance. Brain theory uses computer simulation and mathematical analysis to test the adequacy of postulates about cellular connectivity, coupled with estimates of synaptic weights and time constants, to explain behavioral data, subject to hypotheses about the encoding of behaviorally meaningful information in patterns of cellular activity. It is the task of this final part to initiate a rapprochement between neurolinguistics, on the other hand, and neuroscience and brain theory on the other.

The major stumbling block to rapprochement is that most of the experimental techniques of neuroscience cannot be applied to human subjects and yet it is only human beings who exhibit the full richness of language behavior. Evolutionary and comparative studies may provide the way out of this impasse. Both Galaburda and Brown cite the growing insights these studies afford into the highly differentiated structure of the cerebral cortex. We see the evolution in primates of more specialized structures having connectional relationships with older fields (cf. our growing understanding of the pyramidal pathway as one that can modulate older pathways so that, for example, the pyramidal control of distal musculature can 'ride atop' the extrapyramidal control of the proximal musculature).

The full appreciation of the benefits of comparative anatomy, the present day cross section of the diverse fruits of evolution, will need a major development in conceptual analysis that relates some aspects of human language to the perceptual, cognitive, motor, and communicative abilities of other animals. As Galaburda notes, the application of results on the neocortical organization of rhesus monkeys to the study of the temporal lobe in man is encouraged by the discovery of ear lateralization for vocal communication in macaques. Brown offers a neurological analysis of some relationships between the aphasias, apraxias, and agnosias, whereas Arbib suggests how we might use evolutionary comparisons to raise theoretical brain models from the study of animal (or robot) perceptual–motor systems into neurological analyses that extend from Jackson's notion of levels to Luria's analysis of naming.

A major issue faced by modern neuroscience is that of the proper structural level of analysis. For many purposes of functional correlation, the traditional region is too large a unit, whereas the neuron is too small (though for neurochemists, even the single synapse may become a universe in itself). We now view the visual system of vertebrates as composed of a wide variety of different 'maps,' with several subdividising a single region between them, and each providing a different representation of the visual input (appropriate to a 'control surface' for some subprocess of visuomotor coordination). In the same way, Galaburda's evolutionary perspective on comparative anatomy emphasizes the division of cortical areas into discrete patches with distinct input and output pathways and attendant, distinctive, staining properties. In applying neuroanatomical techniques to human autopsy material, Galaburda finds an unusually high accumulation when staining with lipofucsin granules in a number of areas that are linked (through lesion analysis and neurophysiological testing) to language function. The staining selects Area 44 from the classical Broca's area, and Tpt from the Wernicke region. We thus have what appears to be the first cellular marker for the language areas. Moreover, in the opercular region, Area 44 alone receives direct projections from posterior auditory fields, and Area 44 and Tpt are neatly connected by fibers coursing the arcuate fasciculus. We are reminded of Geschwind's hypothesis that such a connection is an important part of the substrate for language organization in the brain. But there is one catch: The projections dis-cussed in the last sentence but one were shown in anatomical studies of the rhesus monkey. We are forced once again to place neurolinguistics in a broader neuropsychological perspective in which we can come to understand the role of these not-quite-language areas in rhesus, and thus better understand the evolu-tionary pedigree of our own language abilities.

In her chapter on comparative anatomy, Goldman-Rakic makes no attempt to study language-related areas, but rather provides the data on two factors that must enter into any theoretical brain analysis, including one focused on neuro-linguistics. The first is the modular organization of the brain into relatively small functional units (Mountcastle, 1978), far smaller than the "discrete patches" of Galaburda's evolutionary account. Perhaps the best known examples are the "columns" seen by Mountcastle in somatosensory cortex and the "ocular domi-nance stripes" seen by Hubel, Wiesel, and LeVay in visual cortex. It is worth remarking that the layers of cortex (or, as Arbib notes, of cerebellum and other structures) provide an anatomical division "orthogonal" to the patches and modules. Galaburda notes the differential projection of layers within a patch to various targets, while Goldman-Rakic points out that ocular dominance columns are present in Layer 4 of striate cortex in Old World monkeys, but are confined to more superficial layers in New World monkeys.

The second focus of Goldman-Rakic's chapter is of immediate concern to neurologists. It is well known that, unlike an adult who undergoes left hemi-spherectomy, a young child who loses the left hemisphere can still attain remark-ably good language performance. However, Dennis (1980) has shown important linguistic and visuospatial differences between the child with left hemispherectomy and the child with right hemispherectomy. What might the underlying mechanism be? Goldman-Rakic cannot at present provide a mechanism, but does offer a dramatic anatomical correlate. If lesions are made in the frontal association cortex of the pre- or perinatal monkey, there is a dramatic reordering of the modular organization of the residual cortex to accommodate fibers that would have otherwise been projected to the excised cortex. Such rearrangement does not follow lesions in the older monkey. Monkeys who exhibit the anomalous re-arranged connections are precisely the ones who exhibit behavioral sparing after the lesions. While this is a correlation and not a causal relationship, it is an exciting challenge to the development of models of the neural mechanisms underlying recovery. However, it should be stressed that most adult aphasics exhibit a dramatic evolution in their symptomatology, even though they may never recover normal function, as noted both by Kertesz in his case studies (Chapter 2) and by Brown (Chapter 21). Thus, there is also a need for intermediate models between the "large-scale reorganization" so dramatically revealed by Goldman-Rakic's anatomy, and the static view, which sees lesions as producing fixed effects.

Brain theory has developed several challenging models of the reorganization of topographic projections from one region to another. These models suggest that the very mechanisms responsible for orderly projection from one layer to another may also be responsible for the formation of ocular dominance stripes. Constantine-Paton and Law (1978) have shown that if a third eye is grafted to the forehead of a frog, it innervates the tectum and forms alternating bands comparable to the ocular dominance columns of mammalian visual cortex, bands that were not genetically preprogrammed in anticipation of so bizarre a surgical intervention. Von der Malsburg (1979) has shown that a specific model of axonal growth behavior that he and Willshaw had proposed to account for a wide variety of experiments on the reorganization of retinotectal connections following surgical intervention was sufficient to account also for ocularity stripes, including the eye-specific termination bands in tecta of three-eyed frogs.

We do not further consider models of the organization and reorganization of neural projections in this volume. Instead, Wood and Gordon study the effects of lesions on model neural networks that have fixed connectivity, but in which the weights of the various synapses may be adjusted. They use a learning rule attributed to Anderson but fairly well known amongst many neural modellers influenced by Hebb's (1949) suggestion that a synapse is strengthened to the extent that there is a correlation between presynaptic and postsynaptic firing. Wood uses a lesion analysis of a simple associational network (a layer of eight "input neurons" projecting to a layer of eight "output neurons" via modifiable synapses) to demonstrate that, even in this simple preparation, the pattern of lesion deficits and underlying functional organization are not always related in a simple fashion. While such a net may exhibit aspects of Lashley's "equipotentiality" and "mass action" with some types of input patterns, there are marked departures from equal lesion effects when certain input patterns are distinguished by small subsets of the output neuron population.

Where Wood uses a single homogeneous network to develop a critique of lesion analysis, Gordon uses an interconnection of such networks to provide a neural model of confrontation naming (a task discussed briefly in our introduction to Part III). He has subnetworks for visual, tactile, semantic, and motor subsystems. No attempt is made to analyze the details of any of these processes (by contrast see the analysis of visual processing in Arbib, Chapter 25). Rather, his point is to show that a feedback path from the semantic system to the visual system could replace a direct tactilevisual path in enabling tactile experience to supplement defective visual input. Where Wood holds synaptic weights fixed while studying the effects of "lesions" on his computer simulation, Gordon allows rapid synaptic readjustment. More detailed computer studies, perhaps including reorganization mechanisms as well as synaptic readjustment, will be required to better understand the distinction between acute and chronic effects of lesions and the time course of recovery. It must also be noted that Wood and

Gordon only study association networks that are adjusted to pair an input pattern with an appropriate output pattern. In Chapter 25, Arbib gives a small sample of neural models of visual and motor processes that conveys the complexity of the detailed neural mechanisms to be discovered that are required for language performance. These models (see also Szentágothai and Arbib, 1975) assign particular representations to the output of particular cells or to the activity of particular cell groups. When such models make contact with Goldman-Rakic's work, we shall not only understand how neural tissue adapts to insult, but will see how the dynamics of such adaptation relates, via the functional role of neural models in behavior, to the dynamic symptomatology that follows brain lesions.

REFERENCES

Constantine-Paton, M., and Law, M. I. (1978). Eye specific termination bonds in tecta of three-eyed frogs. *Science, 202,* 639–641.

Dennis, M. (1980). Capacity and strategy for syntactic comprehension after left or right hemidecortication. *Brain and Language, 10,* 287–317.

Hebb, D. O. (1949). *The organization of behavior.* New York: Wiley.

Mountcastle, V. B. (1978). An organizing principle for cerebral function: The unit module and the distributed system. In G. M. Edelman and V. B. Mountcastle, *The mindful brain.* Cambridge: Mass.: MIT Press.

Szentágothai, J., and Arbib, M. A. (1975). *Conceptual models of neural organization.* Cambridge, Mass.: MIT Press, 1975.

Von der Malsburg, C. (1979). Development of ocularity domains and growth behaviour of axon terminals. *Biological cubernetics, 32,* 49–62.

20

Histology, Architectonics, and Asymmetry of Language Areas[1]

Albert M. Galaburda

The best anatomical evidence that a given area of cerebral cortex is of particular relevance for language function has been gathered from neuropathological studies of autopsy material obtained from aphasic patients. Additional information on localization has been obtained from intraoperative stimulation experiments on patients undergoing brain surgery, usually for intractable epilepsy. However, recent advances in the understanding of language processes in normal and aphasic subjects based on neuropsychological, neurolinguistic, and psycholinguistic approaches have disclosed some limitations of the classical neuropathological and neurophysiological models. For instance, what is currently known about lesions in Broca's area cannot adequately explain the varieties of Broca's aphasias identifiable in language laboratories. Although it would in all certainty be objectionable to discard the classical anatomical models altogether, as has been suggested by some of their critics, it appears reasonable to make attempts to improve upon these models with the help of modern diagnostic and research approaches.

A major limitation of anatomical studies is that human language is only associated with human brains. Studies sufficiently sophisticated to reveal the detailed organization of the human brain are simply not yet available. However, significant improvements over the classical models might be achieved through the use of modern diagnostic tools such as the computed brain tomogram (New and Scott, 1975), the measurement of regional cerebral blood flow (Ingvar, 1978), of regional cerebral glucose metabolism (Sokoloff, 1976), and of modality-specific evoked cerebral potentials (Molfese, Papanicolau, Hess, and Molfese, 1979). One promising research tool is the venerable study of comparative anatomy. It has been known since the early comparative studies of Gratiolet

[1]Some of the work reported here was supported by NIH grant NS14018 and a biomedical support grant to the Beth Israel Hospital.

NEURAL MODELS OF
LANGUAGE PROCESSES

that the brains of non human primates share many common features of gross and microscopic structural organization with the human brain (insofar as the latter can be determined by the use of classical neuropathological techniques). For instance, findings on neocortical organization in rhesus monkey have been applied to the study of the temporal lobe in man (Galaburda and Sanides, 1980; Pandya and Sanides, 1973). Although there are clearcut interspecies differences in function, especially where it applies to language, the discovery of vocal communication systems showing ear lateralization in some macaques (Beecher, Petersen, Zoloth, Moody, and Stebbins, 1979) makes it more tempting to exploit comparative neuroanatomical data from these primates. The similarities between the two species recommend additional comparative anatomical studies and provide an impetus for the search for common neurolinguistic principles among primate species.

There have also been improvements in the ability to make more accurate lesion–function correlations. Classical neuropathological studies depended on lesions large enough to result in the death of the patient, the only way by which the brain would become available for study. As smaller and more interpretable lesions would not be apt to cause death, most such brains would be lost to study. The few brains with small, well-documented lesions that came to autopsy often showed the ravages of a second illness that had caused the death of the patient and confused the neuropathological evaluation. Computed brain tomography today provides an opportunity to test living subjects with small lesions, an advantage that will undoubtedly lead to better lesion–function correlations. Furthermore, the identification by the computed scan of large numbers of patients with small lesions will increase the chances that some of these patients will be studied neuropathologically. Finally, the identification of small lesions makes it necessary for modern neuropathological analysis to include a description of the exact architectonic extent of the lesion, of degenerated fiber systems, and of atrophy in distant, connectionally related structures, if a better anatomical model is to emerge.

In the remainder of this chapter, I will review some anatomical aspects of the traditional language areas in the light of current information from comparative neuroanatomy, cortical architectonics, and from studies of cerebral asymmetry. The principal goal of such a review is to stimulate ideas for further study of brain–language relationships.

GENERAL PRINCIPLES OF ARCHITECTONIC ORGANIZATION

The most widely accepted theory of cortical organization is based on the findings of the German and Austrian schools in the second half of the nineteenth century, as represented by Flechsig and Meynert respectively. Improvements in microscopy allowed the clear identification by Meynert of areal differentiation in the cortex, and the increased recognition of the value of developmental studies led to the findings by Flechsig of a timetable of cortical maturation. This provided a model of early myelinating "primary" cortical fields which contain discrete projections from thalamic relay nuclei (therefore from the environment), surrounded by "association" areas capable of processing the peripheral information, and maturing later in ontogeny. Interposed amongst association areas were found fields capable of associating or "integrating" different sensory modalities, the highest form of association, best developed and expanded in the human brain, and latest to myelinate.

However, findings of architectonic organization and fiber connections have disclosed a system whereby both pirmary and association fields appear to contain discrete representations of the environment, and these appear to differ in style of representation (see Diamond, 1979; Sanides, 1972). Thus, the cortex appears to have evolved from primitive moieties, the allocortex, and to have proceeded in waves of differentiation away from these roots. In a parallel fashion, subcortical structures such as the thalamus have evolved from primitive cell groups (Yakovlev, 1948), and thalamocortical relationships have been established during each step of cerebral evolution. In this fashion, the primary and association fields do not simply constitute islands and belts of cortex, but rather are representatives of stages of cortical specialization with more or less discrete subcortical connections and maintaining specific relationships to older and newer stages of cortex. In the auditory region, in particular, the primary and association fields, by virtue of their rather more specialized structure, would appear later in evolution than the auditory fields present anteriorly on the temporal lobe. However, they would maintain a connectional relationship to the older fields. Localization of language based on this type of structural model might be expected to be slightly different from the classical models of language areas whereby certain aspects of language (perhaps of clinical relevance) would be localized in posterior fields, whereas other aspects would be localized to more anterior and more primitive auditory fields. Issues of discreteness of connections and bilateral versus unilateral representation might then play a role in lesion–function relationships. The equation of evolution with structural differentiation suggests that specialized fields such as primary motor, somatosensory, auditory, and visual areas and their immediately adjacent neocortical areas are late arrivers in philogeny and largest and most complex in man. In addition, by virtue of their size and time of arrival, they are probably least redundant and, in the more restricted sense of redundancy, likely to be least bilaterally represented. A new model of brain structure, therefore, is apt to be more relevant to modern functional models if it takes into consideration factors of relative architectonic differentiation, topographic relationships among areas on the surface of the brain, as well as their specific patterns of cortical interconnections and connections with subcortical and contralateral regions. Of additional value would be the outline of not only region-to-region connectivity, but also the specific cellular group giving rise to the fibers. One cortical area, for instance, may give rise to discrete projections to another area from its third layer and to diffuse projections to still another or several other areas from its fifth layer (Diamond, 1979). Modern techniques, developed within the past 10 years, are now capable of disclosing such laminar organization of the cortex. Again, lesions leading to, or failing to produce, aphasic disturbances might be explained relative to the discreteness, diffuseness, or even redundancy of the fiber connection pathways affected by a given lesion.

BROCA'S REGION

The exact localization of the lesion causing Broca's aphasia has long been under debate, and it still is not clear what actually is the smallest lesion that can cause this disorder. Although Broca's aphasia can be seen with relatively small lesions involving the opercular portions of the left frontal lobe, more often a much larger area must be lost in order for a permanent deficit to occur (Mohr, 1973). There is no doubt, however, that the lesion must involve at least a major part of the suprasylvian premotor region (Kertesz, Lesk, and McCabe, 1977). The suprasylvian premotor region belongs to a wave of cortical differentiation which begins with the most primitive moiety on the posterior undersurface of the frontal lobe and antero medial temporal lobe and differentiates in a stepwise manner passing through the prefrontal and premotor regions culminating in the most specialized frontal cortex, that of the Brodmann gigantopyramidalis Area 4 (Sanides, 1972) (see Figure 20.1). That Area 4 achieves the highest degree of architectonic differentiation is illustrated by the presence of extraordinarily large pyramidal neurons in Layer V, and the virtual absence of granule cells in Layer IV, features that suggest a specialized function. This area is surrounded on all sides by anatomically less specialized cortex—the intersensorymotor strip Area 3a posteriorly, the premotor Area 6 and the prefrontal Area 8 anteriorly, and a sensory–motor cortex which corresponds to the frontoparietal operculum inferiorly (the subcentral region). The cortex on the frontal operculum represents a

---

FIGURE 20.1. *Semischematic representation of the lateral (top of Figure) and medial (bottom of figure) surfaces of the human brain. The opercular portions of the hemisphere have been spread apart to allow visualization of the insula. There are two proisocortical moieties: One is the insulofrontal pro seen on the anteroventral insula (top) and on the mesioventral frontal lobe (bottom); the other is the perihippocampal pro seen on the medial surface of the temporal lobe and the anterior cingulate gyrus (bottom). The temporal auditory cortex evolves from the temporal pro as stages of differentiation directed in the laterodorsal direction, passing through language area Tpt and ending with the homotypical cortex of the inferior parietal lobule (40 and 39) and the temporooccipital junction (37). The somatosensory representations develop in a similar manner, from the temporal pro, through the*

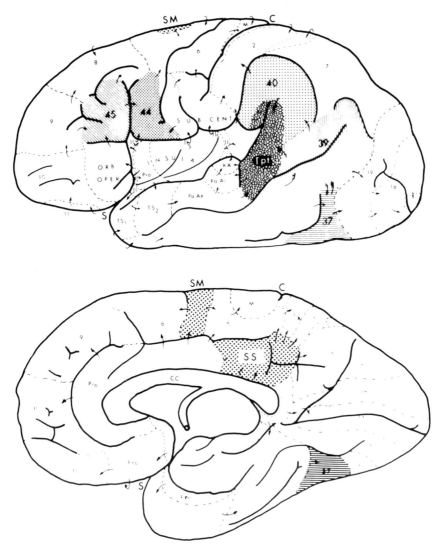

parietal operculum, the postcentral gyrus (3, 1, and 2), then the posterior parietal regions (5 and 7), to Areas 40 and 39. The visual representation also has one of its origins in the temporal pro, and occupies the second and third temporal gyri and the occipital lobe (Areas 17, 18, and 19). The frontal cortex has a root in the insulofrontal pro, evolves in stages in a dorsolateral direction passing through the frontal operculum (orbitofrontal operculum, Areas 45 and 44, and the subcentral region, ending in the homotypical Areas 8 and 9). Cores of superdifferentiated cortex are found in motor area (M), somatosensory area (3) in the depth of the central sulcus, auditory area (KA), and visual area (17). Areas II $_M$, II $_S$, and II $_A$ represent primitive motor, somatosensory, and auditory areas in peri-insular location; a II $_V$ is also found in retrosplenial cortex. Additional primitive motor and sensory areas are found in perihippocampal (pericingulate) location: SM (supplementary motor) containing supplementary motor speech area; and SS (supplementary sensory) containing supplementary sensory speech area. Arrows show general trends of differentiation. Area nomenclature of Brodmann (1909) and Galaburda and Sanides (1980). C = central sulcus; S = sylvian fissure; CC = corpus callosum.

stage that is more specialized than Area 8, but less so than Area 6. Within the operculum, the cortex on pars opercularis has the greatest number of specialized features, that of pars triangularis being intermediate, and that of pars orbitalis being the least specialized, most primitive on the opercular region. The cortex of pars opercularis Area 44 contains large pyramids in Layer IIIc, a feature of specialization not present to the same high degree on pars triangularis Area 45 or on the subcentral sensory-motor cortex lying posterior to Area 44. Area 44, on the other hand, is less specialized in appearance than Area 6 by virtue of its broader granular layer IV and less well developed pyramids in Layer V. Thus the opercular region, upon which Broca's area is engrafted, represents but stages of an apparently uniform sequence of architectonic differentiation in which Area 44 is the most specialized stage, with Areas 45 and subcentral areas being less specialized.

Some preliminary evidence concerning the connectional organization and architectonics of this region points to Area 44 as being the one that might play a special role in aphasia. For instance, when staining for lipofuscin granules in neurons, a substance that results from oxydative cellular metabolism, Area 44 accumulates lipofuscin in an unusual manner not present to the same degree in surrounding opercular areas (Braak, 1979) (see Figure 20.2). Curiously, however, other areas on the cortical mantle accumulate pigment in a similar manner, and they are found on the posterior superior temporal gyrus, on the inferior parietal lobule, on the medial surface of the hemisphere surrounding the cingulate gyrus, and on the preoccipital temporal region of the second and third temporal gyri (Braak, 1980) all areas that have been linked, through lesion analysis and neurophysiological testing, to language function. Another characteristic of Area 44 is that it alone in the opercular region receives direct projections from posterior auditory fields, as disclosed by the study of homologous areas in the rhesus monkey (Pandya and Galaburda, 1980). This auditory–premotor connectional relationship has been suggested as an important part of the substrate of language organization in the brain (Geschwind, 1970). Moreover, Area 44, or more exactly the part of it that shows the unusual accumulation of lipofuscin on pars opercularis (magnopyramidal zone), corresponds in location to a small region that has been found to be particularly vulnerable to aphasic responses after stimulation (Whitaker and Ojemann, 1977). Finally, although consistent asymmetries have failed to be shown for other parts of the frontal operculum, asymmetries in favor of the left side have been recently demonstrated in the frontal operculum's magnopyramidal zone (Galaburda, 1980).

WERNICKE'S REGION

The disagreement concerning the exact location of the lesion producing Wernicke's aphasia is not as heated as with Broca's aphasia. Although aphasic

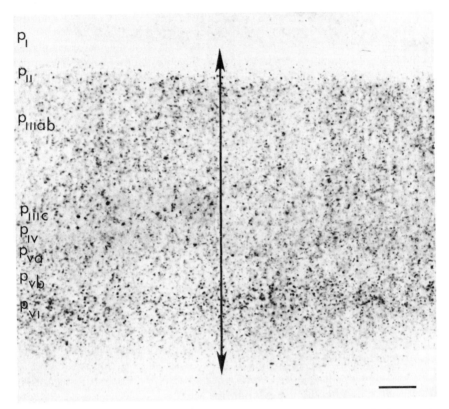

FIGURE 20.2. *Photomicrograph of the frontal opercular region showing the border between the central inferior magnopyramidal zone (left) and a surrounding opercular area (right). Note the lipofuscin accumulation in large pyramidal neurons in layers p_{iiic} and p_{IV} on the left side. At higher magnification this lipofuscin is found in dense aggregates underneath the cell nucleus. Layer nomenclature after Braak (1979). Bar = 250 um.*

disorders with fluent paraphasic speech and poor comprehension can be seen with lesions over a wide area of the posterior half of the left hemisphere (Bogen and Bogen, 1976), there is little doubt that in most cases a significant part of the caudal aspects of the superior temporal gyrus and/or their fiber connections are affected (Kertesz, Lesk, and McCabe, 1977). The superior temporal gyrus and the upper surface of the temporal lobe (the superior temporal plane) house the cortical representation of the auditory system (see Figure 20.1).

Certain parallels may be drawn between the organization of the frontal areas containing Broca's region and the temporal areas containing Wernicke's region. In the superior temporal gyrus, it is the auditory koniocortex (Area 41 of Brodmann) which achieves the greatest degree of architectonic specialization, and it represents the culmination of a series of steps of differentiation beginning in the temporopolar and parinsular primitive proisocortical areas and proceeding in a posterolateral direction (Galaburda and Sanides, 1980). In this cortex, specialization is equivalent to granularization (the acquisition of stellate cells) as opposed to the pyramidalization of the frontal fields, and the auditory koniocortex is the most granular of the auditory fields. Less specialized fields containing primitive features are found rostral and medial to the koniocortex, whereas less specialized, more advanced areas are located caudolateral from the koniocortex. The least specialized yet advanced cortex in this series is found on the inferior parietal lobule (Areas 39 and 40) and the temporo-occipital junction (Area 37), and no longer reflects a predominantly auditory role. The posterior third of the superior temporal gyrus, where left-sided lesions tend to produce Wernicke's aphasia, contains a field labeled Tpt (Galaburda and Sanides, 1980). This field exhibits a degree of specialization like that of Area 44 in Broca's region. It contains prominent pyramids in layer IIIc and a broad lamina IV, but these two features are not as well developed as in the association areas surrounding the koniocortex. Yet the degree of specialization of Tpt is greater than that found more posteriorly in 39, 49, and 37. Thus, 44 and Tpt are equivalent transitional areas between the paramotor and the generalized cortices of the prefrontal area, and between parakoniocortex and the temporoparietal occipital junction areas respectively. Furthermore, these two areas are neatly and separately connected in rhesus monkey by fibers most likely coursing in the arcuate fasciculus (Pandya and Galaburda, 1980). Of additional interest still is the finding of left–right asymmetry in Tpt. The planum temporale, a gross anatomical landmark which contains portions of the posterior auditory parakoniocortical areas and Tpt, is usually larger on the left hemisphere (Geschwind and Levitsky, 1968), and in cases where the planum is larger Tpt tends to be larger as well (Galaburda, Sanides, and Geschwind, 1978). Whether or not other subdivisions of the auditory region have relevance to language is uncelar at this time. Bilateral lesions in the region anterior to auditory koniocortex, which correspond in location to the rostral parakoniocortex, have been associated with word deafness (Barrett, 1910; Schuster and Taterka, 1926), as have lesions more medial in the dominant auditory region, involving more primitive auditory fields (ProA of Galaburda and Sanides, 1980). Again, as with Area 44 rostrally, lesions resulting in clinically recognizable language disturbances may depend not only on the particular architectonic area involved, but also on the topographic relationship of the involved area with respect to architectonic differentiation, and its pattern of connections. If, with progressive architectonic specialization, there is also progressive lateralization, it is conceivable that only a restricted number of auditory fields of relevance to language will be specific enough and lateralized enough to allow for unilateral, highly localized lesions to result in aphasic disturbances. Another point of interest is the fact that in view of the apparent parallel organization of frontal and temporal language areas sharing discrete projections, a certain overlap of symptoms seen in aphasic patients with lesions in either location might be expected.

Consider, for instance, the findings by Blumstein (1973) showing similar phonemic substitutions in patients with Broca's, conduction, and Wernicke's aphasias. The exact mechanism of how this might occur cannot be extracted from an anatomical model alone, but the intimate relationship and similar evolutionary status of Ares 44 and Tpt allows for a certain functional overlap. In fact, architectonic similarities between anterior or posterior language areas, and the overlap in their connectional organization makes it a somewhat surprising finding that lesions in either region produce such different aphasic syndromes.

OTHER LANGUAGE AREAS

Aphasia may occur with lesions involving the supplementary motor region (Masden, Schoene, and Funkelstein, 1978; Rubens, 1975) and the supplementary sensory region (Ross, 1980) on the medial aspect of the left hemisphere (Figure 20.1). The supplementary motor cortex can be distinguished cytoarchitectonically (Brodmann, 1909; Economo and Koskinas, 1925; Sanides, 1962) and by the lipofuscin method (Braak, 1979). The supplementary sensory region is less obvious in its outline, but appears to correspond to the granular perilimbic field LC_1 Economo and Koskinas (1925). The supplementary speech areas can be shown by both anatomical and neurophysiological techniques (Braak, 1979; Penfield and Roberts, 1959). They make up a portion of the supplementary motor and sensory areas, and they are related to the latter in a similar fashion as the perisylvian speech areas are to the motor and auditory cortex, that is, as transitional zones with lesser specialization. The supplementary speech areas are structurally more primitive than the perisylvian ones, and maintain a close topographical and connectional relationship to the primitive cortex of the cingulate region (Sanides, 1962; Vogt and Pandya, 1978). Furthermore, the supplementary regions send fiber connections to the perisylvian speech areas (Pandya, Hallett, and Mukherjee, 1969). Thus, the supplementary areas, with their relation to cingulate cortex and connections to standard speech areas, provide the possibility for an anatomical substrate for the motivational aspects of language functions. For instance, lesions in the supplementary regions produce syndromes whereby speech initiation or attention to language are impaired (Ross, 1980). Similar effects appear to arise from lesions in the deep vascular borderzone territory, presumably because of the likely interruption of supplementary-sylvian connections (personal observations; Damasio, personal communication).

In summary, the neocortex appears to contain the standard speech areas in perisylvian location and two sets of primitive regions with architectonic and connectional association to cingulate proisocortex on the one hand and to temporopolar-orbitofrontal proisocortex on the other. The sylvian language areas are interposed between these two primitive regions, and connected to both.

Perhaps because of the degree of architectonic and connectional specialization (and lateralization), some of the areas discussed appear to be particularly vulnerable to the aphasic effects of lesions. Other regions forming part of a hierarchy of cortical areas extending from the primitive moieties of the orbitofrontal-temporopolar and cingulate roots to the highly evolved generalized cortices of the prefrontal and inferior parietal–temporo-occipital regions may be more resistant to unilateral lesions, or lesions may result in disorders in which alterations of language function are part of a more generalized defect. Thus, lesions in the more primitive areas may lead to disorders of attention and emotional behavior with secondary language deficits (e.g., disorders of writing in confusional states), whereas lesions in generalized-advanced cortex may produce disturbances of intellectual function affecting, amongst other faculties, language function (e.g., the anomia of Alzheimer's disease). Therefore, one can conclude that different aspects of language are localized to a greater or lesser extent in the left hemisphere and that amongst these certain parts of the brain appear to be located and organized in such a manner that they are ideally suited to carry out specialized auditory functions and motor activities necessary for language decoding and encoding processes.

ACKNOWLEDGMENTS

The author gratefully acknowledges Margaret Galaburda for her critical comments and review and Patricia Lamy-Gilbreath for typing the manuscript.

REFERENCES

Barrett, A. M. (1910). A case of pure word-deafness with autopsy. *Journal of Nervous and Mental Disease, 37*, 73–92.

Beecher, M. D., Petersen, M. R., Zoloth, S. R., Moody, D. B., and Stebbins, W. C. (1979). Perception of conspecific vocalizations by Japanese macaques. Evidence for selective attention and neural lateralization. *Brain, Behavior, and Evolution, 16*, 443–460.

Blumstein, S. E. (1973). *A phonological investigation of aphasic speech.* The Hague: Mouton.

Bogen, J. E., and Bogen, G. M. (1976). Wernicke's region—where is it? *Annals of the New York Academy of Sciences, 280*, 834–843.

Braak, H. (1979). The pigment architecture of the human frontal lobe, 1: Precentral, subcentral and frontal region. *Anatomy and Embryology, 157*, 35–68.

Braak, H. (1980). *Architectonics of the human telencephalic cortex.* Berlin–Heidelberg–New York: Springer-Verlag.

Brodmann, K. (1909). *Vergleichende Lokalisationslehre der Grosshirnrinde.* Leipzig: Barth.

Diamond, I. T. (1979). The subdivisions of the neocortex: A proposal to revise the traditional view of sensory, motor, and association areas. Epstein, A. N. and Sprague, J. M. (Eds.), In *Progress in psychobiology and physiological psychology,* Vol. 8, New York: Academic Press.

Economo, C. Von, and Koskinas, G. N. (1925). *Die Cytoarchitectonik der Hirnrinde des erwachsenen Menschen.* Vienna and Berlin: Springer.

Galaburda, A. M. (1980). La région de Broca: Observations anatomiques faites un siècle après la mort de son déconvreur. *Rev Neurol. 136*, 609–616.

Galaburda, A. M., and Sanides, F. (1980). Cytoarchitectonic organization of the human auditory cortex. *Journal of Comparative Neurology, 190*, 597–610.

Galaburda, A. M., Sanides, F., and Geschwind, N. (1978). Human brain: Cytoarchitectonic left–right asymmetries in the temporal speech region. *Archives of Neurology, 35*, 812–817.

Geschwind, N. (1970). The organization of language and the brain. *Science, 170*, 940–944.

Geschwind, N., and Levitsky, W. (1968). Human brain: Left–right asymmetries in temporal speech region. *Science, 161*, 186–189.

Ingvar, D. H. (1978). Localization of cortical functions by multiregional measurements of cerebral blood flow. In M. A. B. Brazier and H. Petsche (Eds.), *Architectonics of the cerebral cortex.* New York: Raven Press.

Kertesz, A., Lesk, D., and McCabe, P. (1977). Isotope localization of infarcts in aphasia. *Archives of Neurology, 34*, 590–601.

Masden, J. C., Schoene, W. C., Funkelstein, H. (1978). Aphasia following infarction of the left supplementary motor area. *Neurology, 28*, 1220–1223.

Mohr, J. P. (1973). Rapid amelioration of motor aphasia. *Archives of Neurology, 28*, 77–82.

Molfese, D. L., Papanicolau, A., Hess, T. M., and Molfese, V. J. (1979). Neuroelectrical correlates of semantic processes. In Begleiter, H. (Ed.), *Evoked brain potentials and behavior.* New York: Plenum Press.

New, P. F. J., and Scott, W. R. (1975). *Computed tomography of the brain and orbit,* Baltimore: Williams and Wilkins.

Pandya, D. N., and Galaburda, A. M. (1980). Role of architectonics and connections in the study of primate brain evolution. *American Journal of Physical Anthropology, 52*, 197.

Pandya, D. N., Hallett, M., and Mukherjee, S. K. (1969). Intra- and interhemispheric connections of the neocortical auditory system in rhesus monkey. *Brain Research, 14*, 49–65.

Pandya, D. N., and Sanides, F. (1973). Architectonic parcellation of the temporal operculum in rhesus monkey and its projection pattern. *Zeitschrift für Anatomie und Entwicklungsgeschichte, 139*, 127–161.

Penfield, W., and Roberts, L. (1959). *Speech and brain mechanisms.* Princeton: Princeton University Press.

Ross, E. (1980). Left medial parietal lobe and receptive language functions: Mixed transcortical aphasia after left anterior cerebral artery infarction. *Neurology, 30*, 144–151.

Rubens, A. B. (1975). Aphasia with infarction in the territory of the anterior cerebral artery. *Cortex, 11*, 239–250.

Sanides, F. (1962). *Die Architektonik des Menschlichen Stirnhirns.* Berlin: Springer.

Sanides, F. (1972). Representation in the cerebral cortex and its areal lamination patterns. In G. H. Bourne (Ed.), *The structure and function of nervous tissue,* Vol. 5. New York: Academic Press.

Schuster, P., and Taterka, H. (1926). Beitrag zur Anatomie und Klinik der reinen Worttaubheit. *Zeitschrift für die gesamte Neurologie und Psychiatrie, 105*, 494–538.

Sokoloff, L. (1976). Circulation and energy metabolism of the brain. In R. W. Albers, G. J. Siegel, R. Katzman, and B. W. Agranoff (Eds.), *Basic neurochemistry* (2nd ed.). Boston: Little, Brown and Co.

Vogt, B. A., and Pandya, D. N. (1978). Cortico-cortical connections of somatic sensory cortex (areas 3, 1, and 2) in the rhesus monkey. *Journal of Comparative Neurology, 172*, 179–192.

Whitaker, H. A., and Ojemann, G. A. (1977). Graded localization of naming from electrical stimulation of left cerebral cortex. *Nature, 270*, 50–51.

Yakovlev, P. I. (1948). Motility, behavior and the brain. *Journal of Nervous and Mental Disease., 107*, 313–335.

21

Hierarchy and Evolution in Neurolinguistics[1]

Jason W. Brown

Many of us would agree that linguistics will not be assimilated to neuroscience without passing through aphasia. But how is the aphasia material to be interpreted? Those in outside disciplines tend to approach the brain-damaged as a neutral battleground on which competing formulations can be tested. When pathological behavior "fits" a given theoretical outcome it is hailed as a proof of the theory; when it does not, it is dismissed as pathological. The problem is that pathological study is not as it should be the starting point of neuropsychological theory, but a test case for theoretical models derived from normal psychology. Studies of abnormal behavior from the standpoint of experimental cognition have the added difficulty that performances tend to be artificially isolated by the experimental design, and deficits tend to be interpreted from the point of view of insufficiency, not as productive qualitative phenomena. As a result, the pathological appears as a kind of degraded normal, and the inner nature of pathological change and its meaning for psychological theory is missed entirely.

One view of pathological language implies that damage to an area of the brain eliminates whatever process, strategy, or representation the area supports. This interpretation is predicted by componential or modular theories of language organization. However, in a patient with a lesion in the left Wernicke area, what is lost in an utterance that is semantically or phonologically deviant? Certainly not the semantics or the phonology. What is the meaning of "loss" when intact performances occur alongside those which are deficient? In what sense is a function lost when it is regained a moment later? For the clinician who deals with symptoms and symptom change, the effects of pathology are more subtle than componential models suppose.

My own view is that a symptom is really a NORMAL event that anticipates

[1]This research was supported by the Institute for Research in Behavioral Neuroscience and NIH Research Grant No. 13740.

447

something, it is a state that is ordinarily traversed in a processing sequence. The effect of the lesion is to display that preliminary state, in language, in perception, or in motility. I might add that this concept of the symptom gives meaning to clinical work. It is the basis of a real clinical methodology. The idea that SYMP-TOMS REFLECT STRUCTURE DIRECTLY allows the clinician to go beyond the usual descriptive approach, classifying behaviors and isolating syndromes without any theoretical underpinnings.

This view of pathological behavior has developed from studies in aphasia, and has led to a new—microgenetic—model of cognitive processing. This chapter will focus on some issues pertinent to the microgenetic account of aphasia, its relation to componential models, and its contribution to theories of mind.

MICROGENESIS AND MODULARITY

Physiological studies of posterior neocortex in monkey have revealed a highly developed functional organization with a considerable degree of topographical specificity. The parcellation of "association" cortex into discrete functional areas, and evidence for a modular arrangement in some of those areas, has seemed to confirm the value of componential approaches to the physiological bases of cognitive processes.

According to such approaches, a behavior is fractionated into subroutines which correspond with areal patterns of functional specification. The fine connectivity within these areas establishes networks of modules underlying common subfunctions. In addition, such networks may be associated into "distributed systems" across regions of brain irrespective of their phylogenetic relationships. The distributed system is really a constellation of intra-areal networks at different levels in brain linked together in a common behavior. This concept of the distributed system derives from the "functional system" approach of Anokhin and Luria in neuropsychology. It takes the mosaicist version of modularity one step further in claiming that the pertinent "component" is a dynamic pattern distributed over intra-areal specifications.

The implication is that these physiological components correspond in some abstract way to cognitive or linguistic components in a process model. However, the human lesion data do not particularly support this approach, at least in its strongest form. Brain damage does not remove functional components from behavior, but gives rise to local symptoms. The symptom is not a deficiency; it does not lack what the damaged area had to contribute but is like a window into the component the damaged area supports.

There is also the problem of neocortical generality, the possibility that regional variation in cytoarchitectonics is not linked to functional specificity but is an accidental feature of fiber density (Creutzfeldt, 1977). The response selectivity of cortical neurons, which is the best evidence for a modular organization, may have to be reinterpreted as a wider range of stimuli are tested. Units that respond to specific features in a visual array may well respond to other nonvisual stimuli which have not yet been tested, especially in the context of an active and more natural perception. This has been demonstrated in the case of reticular units (Siegal, 1979) where individual cells have been shown to enter into many different behavioral routines. A cognitive state presumably arises as an EMERGENT out of a network of cells or columns of cells.

The alternative to a modular theory, however, is not a holistic one, any more than a refutation of cerebral localization is a confirmation of equipotentiality. In fact, to say that language is IN the left hemisphere is already the first step in functional localization (Kuhlenbeck, 1957), a step that ends with functional columns and command cells. The appropriate question is rather along what lines psychological processes and brain states decompose so as to conform to or map onto each other. It is here that the pathological material is important in revealing which chunks of brain are linked to which psychological states, and in what way psychological states degrade. In my view, pathological case study confirms that cognition breaks down along natural lines, and that the products of this breakdown can be viewed as mental states or cognitive levels which are distributed over an evolutionary stratification in the brain. The idea that processing develops sequentially as a series of such states linked to evolutionary structure is termed MICROGENESIS. The theory assumes that a set of psychological and brain levels forms a substructure within a behavior as it unfolds over evolutionary and maturational stages (Brown, 1977).

This approach is entirely consistent with the idea of dynamic patterns underlying behavior, which are distributed over widespread regions. In fact, microgenesis entails that processing stages in behavior are dynamic patterns which structure the behavior over a sequence of such patterns. The issue, however, has to do with which regions of brain are entrained in a particular behavior, and more importantly, with the nature of the relationships between areas in the distributed system. Specifically, the microgenetic concept is that processing is unidirectional, and that the same processing stages are traversed in every behavior that develops to the same endpoint.

Attempts to develop componential models in the framework of evolutionary theory (Arbib, Chapter 4, this volume) have the problem that interaction in a distributed system does not rest well with the idea of constraints imposed on that system by the direction of its evolutionary development. Interactionist models are indifferent to the evolutionary concept that processing reflects the pattern of growth trends in phylo-ontogeny. In contrast, the microgenetic model binds structure, viewed dynamically as a series of emergent strata, to moments in a processing sequence. The sequence unfolds in the direction of evolutionary growth.

Finally, patterns of language breakdown in pathological states seem to correspond to patterns of destructuration in perception and motility. The anterior and posterior language zones develop and degrade in close relation to motor and perceptual systems. These systems are not on the periphery of language as some might suppose; they too have an infrastructure and undergo a microgenetic development. Language exploits or extends perception and motility; it is elaborated through them and emerges on a continuum of evolutionary change. The clinical material argues for common mechanisms underlying all aspects of behavior.

MATURATION AND APHASIA

The modular approach assumes that language components are derived from the genotype and that the distribution of "modules" in the brain is genetically specified. One observation that modularity, or the localization of language components, needs to explain is that of age-specific trends in the effects of focal brain lesions. Age specificity of aphasia type was first proposed by Brown and Jaffe (1975) as evidence for continous lateralization over the life span, and later incorporated into a structural model of the aphasias (Brown, 1977, 1979). The occurrence of age specificity in aphasia was documented by Obler, Albert, Goodglass, and Bensen (1978), and again confirmed in a personal study involving 389 aphasics with vascular lesion seen at the Rheinische Landesklinik für Sprachgestörte in Bonn.

In this population the average age was 48.7, close to that for total and mixed aphasics. In contrast, the mean age of motor aphasics was 45.3, and fluent aphasics 56.5. The percentage of fluent and nonfluent aphasias at 10-year intervals is shown in Figure 21.1. In this curve, mixed and total aphasics were combined as their distribution over the life span was nearly identical. It is unlikely that age specificity reflects a difference in lesion localization between young and old subjects, as the same age-specific trends were present in a separate analysis of 165 trauma cases where a random lesion distribution might be expected. Moreover, it is inconceivable that a bias toward anterior lesions could explain the overwhelming incidence (95%) of nonfluent aphasia in subjects under 30.

These observations have been interpreted as evidence for the view that the Broca and Wernicke zones undergo progressive differentiation throughout life. This process has been characterized as a core differentiation or regional specification within the generalized or homotypical isocortex of the anterior and posterior zones (Brown, 1979). This ontogenetic process is an extension of a comparable growth trend in the evolution of the forebrain (Braak, 1978; Diamond, 1979; Sanides, 1970). Moreover, the idea that regional specification of brain involves a

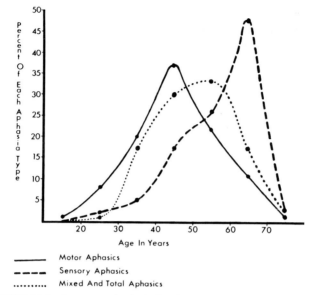

FIGURE 21.1. *Percentage of aphasic disorders at 10-year intervals* (N = 389).

process of cerebral growth that continues into late life is consistent with evidence for dendritic growth in the brain of the normal aged (Buell and Coleman, 1979). The implication is that the Wernicke and Broca zones are not "wired up" at birth or by adolescence, but are functionally specified gradually, over the life span, in the course of maturation (Figure 21.2).

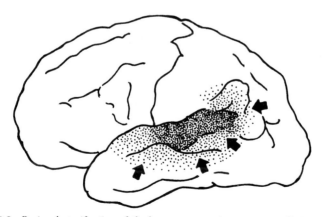

FIGURE 21.2. *Regional specification of the language area. A core zone mediating phonological representation differentiates out of a background zone of semantic representation. A similar process occurs in the anterior region.*

In my view, the Wernicke and Broca zones mediate the phonological component of language (Brown, 1979). This component consists of a phonetic-articulatory stage realized through the Broca area, and a stage of phonemic representation through the Wernicke area. Both the surface phonological components and their submerged antecedents show increasing asymmetry into late life.

THE NATURE OF AGRAMMATISM

Syntax is the soul of modularity in language, and presumed disorders of syntax in Broca's aphasia (agrammatism) are often taken as evidence for modular organization. Yet the pathological data are open to a different interpretation. Several studies from our lab go to this issue.

In one study, Lucia Kellar tested aphasics with the triadic method, and found that anterior and posterior cases had comparable deficits in their grammatical judgments. This indicates that deficient grammatical knowledge, as assayed by these tests, is not necessarily the basis of the agrammatism. In another study, Claudia Leslie found, after Zurif and Caramazza (1976), that aphasics, not surprisingly, have difficulty with reversible sentences. However, when both interpretations are equally improbable, as in *The fish chased the cow,* performance improved dramatically. This indicates that anteriors can decode the syntax of the sentence when they are not required to attend also to the plausibility of the events described. In still another study, Phyllis Ross gave aphasics a letter cancellation task with "silent" and "pronounced" letters. She found that both anteriors and posteriors, like normals, made more errors on functors than content words and that the content–function word difference was the same in the two groups. This suggests that anteriors do NOT treat functors like content words.

This is not to say that anteriors are not deficient in syntax, but rather that this is not the explanation of their agrammatism. Moreover, there are good clinical arguments against the syntax account. For example, the fact that agrammatics tend to read aloud and repeat agrammatically suggests that the problem is bound up with motor planning and production rather than syntactic judgments. Conversely, the relative preservation of grammatical words in posteriors does not indicate that function words are stored in an anterior module, but rather reflects the fact that errors in posteriors are determined by word–meaning relationships. The reduced meaning content of the functors allows them to escape derailment in the posterior system.

What, then, is the problem in agrammatism? Earlier studies by Goodglass and colleagues (Goodglass, 1968; also Kellar, 1978) established the primacy of word stress in agrammatic speech. With a disturbance of the intonational pattern, stress began to play a determining role in speech production. The "loss" of the function words could be explained on the basis of their relatively unstressed nature rather than on purely linguistic grounds. Unfortunately, this line of research was not pursued to its likely conclusion—that agrammatism is bound up with a disturbance of motor timing and the rhythmic structure of the utterance—but instead, under the influence of an aphasiological "syntax clique," drifted off into the vapid domain of closed class words and mental grammars. It is no exaggeration to say that exponents of this view reified a surface description of the agrammatic utterance to a mental component localized in Broca's area.

However, agrammatism is not the same as Broca's aphasia where phonetic-articulatory deficits are distributed over the utterance regardless of word class, and agrammatism is probably correlated not with lesions of F3, but rather of adjacent neocortex. The position of agrammatism in the typology of anterior aphasias and its pathological localization suggest a different interpretation of the agrammatic deficit.

THE DEFECT IN MOTOR APHASIA

The anterior aphasias correspond to stages in a microgenetic series. The framework of this series can be viewed as a rhythmic structure of dynamic waves (see Figure 21.3) developing from upper brainstem and limbic layers through "generalized" to focal neocortex (left F3). This structure elaborates the motor complement of the utterance.

The most primitive level in this structure is that of a "motor envelope" linking vocalization and body motility in the same matrix of rhythmic movement. The act is organized about the axial and proximal musculature. There is a

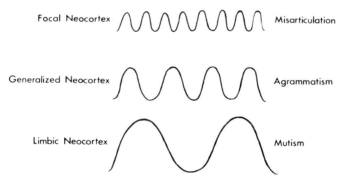

FIGURE 21.3. *Rhythmic levels in motility correspond with the anterior aphasias, and with (disruptions of) evolutionary levels in the brain.*

relationship to respiratory rhythms. With damage to upper brainstem or anteromedial limbic structures (mesocortex), there is inability to initiate or formulate an utterance (mutism) in the context of a generalized motor inertia, of which the mutism is only one element. The subsequent level represents the derivation of this motor rhythm—or base frequency—to the next microgenetic stage. This derivation (?harmonic) is to an oscillator which controls the speech rhythm or intonational pattern. There is greater definition of limb and speech motility, but both are still grounded in a common rhythmic frame. A disruption here gives agrammatism. The final derivation is to the fine articulatory rhythm supporting the terminal program of sound sequences. This level is disrupted in true Broca's aphasia. In a complete series of derivations, discharge would occur into motor keyboards obtaining at a given evolutionary level. The final utterance would blend this process of rhythmic layering into a complex melodic structure.

Deep structural layers in this system are bilaterally organized, requiring bilateral lesions for pathological effects. Intermediate levels are moderately left lateralized. Symptoms occur primarily with left but also with right hemisphere damage (e.g., agrammatism). The final surface level is strongly asymmetric and develops in the course of maturation. This concept of a series of rhythmic levels in motility, unfolding over evolutionary strata in brain organization, and linked to aphasic syndromes arising with lesions of these strata, is illustrated in Figure 21.3.

The idea of a phylogenetic progression from a lower level automatic rhythmic organization to higher level mechanisms directed to the environment has been discussed by several authors (Bernstein, 1967; Jung, 1941; Walter, 1959). The lower organization is probably linked to mechanisms in the rostral brainstem which synergistically relate motor, respiratory, and other autonomic rhythms in a common system. Barcroft and Barron (1937) in a study of the sheep embryo found rhythmic trunk movements timed with respiratory rhythms at an early stage of in utero development. Gradually, these rhythms became independent, but the original relationship could be brought out by anoxic brain damage. Lesion studies indicated that the rhythms were organized at the level of upper midbrain. Schepelmann (1979) reviewed evidence that respiratory rhythms exert an effect on motor activity. He described human cases of brain pathology with synchronous motor and respiratory rhythms, and proposed a primary brainstem rhythm of about 3/min. regulating respiration and motility, and perhaps autonomic functions as well. There is additional pathological evidence for this idea—for example, in the rhythmic palatal and orofacial tremors that occur with brainstem lesions in humans (Brown, 1967). Studies of rhythmic myoclonus in cats injected with Newcastle disease virus have demonstrated spinal and brainstem systems underlying rhythmic motor and respiratory contractions. This system of synergistic motor and respiratory rhythms provides a basis for the generation of an utterance. We know, for example, that an utterance at its inception is organized about respiratory patterns, for example, the "breath group" (Lieberman, 1967) and impairments in respiratory timing occur in motor aphasias (Schoenle, 1979).

There have also been speculations on the relation of speech production to rhythmic activity (Lashley, 1951; Martin, 1972), and the importance of rhythmic factors, tonality, and stress at the earliest stage in speech production. Others have shown similarities between language and motor systems, suggesting common organization principles in terms of oscillatory systems (e.g., Kelso, Holt, Kogler, and Turvey, 1980; Turvey, 1977).

THE DEFECT IN POSTERIOR APHASIA

Naming is the key to an understanding of the posterior aphasias. Arbib (Chapter 25, this volume) has given an apt description of naming as capturing a target in an object field. There are more than incidental similarities between the process of word selection and the visual grasp of an object. Consider the work on monkeys with inferotemporal (IT) lesions. The visual deficit is not solely one of memory or visual discrimination, but is in the selection of an object from an array. Now it is interesting that IT lesions in humans do not give rise to comparable deficits in visual recognition. Visual agnosias in which object meaning plays a part appear to be associated with medial temporo-occipital lesions. Of course, some fragments of the deficit may appear with right temporal lesions, as in the McGill studies, and mild impairments in visual recognition occur with left temporal lesions (see, e.g., De Renzi, 1971). However, the more striking deficit in left temporal cases is an aphasia characterized by lexical-semantic errors. Moreover, these errors are accentuated with a bilateral lesion (Brown, 1981). The possibility that a neural substrate that in monkeys supports visual recognition is in humans involved in lexical selection underscores the relationship between visual search and word search—or naming—and emphasizes the need in aphasia study to go beyond the descriptive material to the underlying perceptual and motor events.

Naming is more than an association of nouns to perceived objects; it is more than labeling an object. There is a common basis for the process of word and object selection. In many ways, language develops in the mind of a speaker like an object in perception. The words of an utterance are represented in the same way as objects in the world. An argument can be made (Brown, 1977) that the subject of a perception does not look up the meaning of an object as a secondary process but has the meaning before the object is fully perceived. This is also true in language perception. Words develop out of a stage of meaning relations and strive toward referential adequacy. Symbolic transformations and mechanisms of the dreamwork come into play at an early stage in object formation. These mechanisms correspond with systems of word meaning relationships in the preliminary stages of lexical selection. The representation of an object in perception and the representation of a word in language are ordered by a common process. In perception, this leads from a stage of symbolic relations to one of form representation; in language, from a semantic operation to a phonological one.

Nouns occupy a special place in this development. They are the figural elements in the perception. The function words, in contrast, supply the matrix within which the content words are positioned. Like the space between the objects of perception, the functors provide the relational context for the abstract space of the content words. The contrast between a noun as an object and a function word as a relational element is comparable to the distinction between object and object relations.

The microstructure of word selection, or the retrieval of a word from memory, is revealed in the posterior aphasias. The different types of word-finding errors display transitions in this microstructure (Brown, 1979). The series leads from a deep bilaterally organized limbic stage, through a stage of generalized neocortex, to focal neocortex (left T1). Semantic representation precedes phonological representation. Deep levels are bilaterally organized and require bilateral lesions for symptoms (e.g., limbic disorders of memory and associated impairments in semantic encoding). Lesions of an intermediate stage of generalized neocortex are moderately left lateralized. Symptoms referable to this level also occur with right hemisphere lesions as will be discussed below. The final surface level of phonemic representation is more strongly left-lateralized. Symptoms occur primarily with focal left hemisphere pathology.

Thus levels in the posterior (perceptual) system correspond to levels in the anterior (motor) system. Moreover, there is a functional relationship between a given level in left and right hemisphere. Evidence for this claim is discussed in the following section.

THE ROLE OF THE RIGHT HEMISPHERE

Lesions of the right hemisphere lead to difficulty in the comprehension of semantic material. Eisenson (1962) first noted an impairment on complex tasks, more pronounced when listening to others. Critchley (1962) mentioned cases with circumlocution and the use of odd synonyms. Language deficits in right hemisphere cases were reported by Marcie, Hecaen, Dubois, and Angelergues (1965) and Archibald and Wepman (1968). Lesser (1974) found difficulty in pointing to objects on a choice card with semantic foils, but not on comparable tests of phonology and syntax; these findings were largely confirmed by Tägert, Chock, Niklas, Sandvoss, and Sipos (1975) and Gainotti, Caltagirone, and Miceli (1979).

The conclusion that can be drawn from these studies is that lesions of the right hemisphere, in perhaps 20–40% of cases, give rise to SEMANTIC IMPAIR-MENTS IN COMPREHENSION. Moreover, if comprehension is sufficiently impaired, production errors may occur, with confabulation or circumlocutory speech, which is an early sign, by the way, of semantic jargon.

In contrast, motor aphasia occurs in 1–2% of dextral adults with right hemisphere lesions (Zangwill, 1967), and in about 7% of adult right-handers after right-sided amytal injection (Milner, 1974). Some years ago, I reported a case of crossed aphasia in a dextral (Brown and Wilson, 1973) and collected seven additional cases in the literature meeting certain minimal criteria: adequate description of the aphasia; right-handedness without family history of left-handedness; a unilateral lesion; and no prior history of a neurological disorder. Since then, many other cases have been described (e.g., April and Han, 1980; April and Tse, 1977, Assal, Perentes, and Diruaz, 1981; Haaland and Miranda, 1980; Trojanowski, Green, and Levine 1980; Wechsler, 1976), confirming the impression that AGRAMMATISM is the chief form of a right hemisphere "expressive" aphasia.

In these patients, there is evidence for BILATERAL LANGUAGE REPRESENTATION. The absence of limb apraxia and the failure to observe a "hooked" writing posture in the right hand argue for a left hemisphere role in writing and skilled movement. The finding in half the cases of marked constructional impairments suggests that spatial ability is not simply shifted to the opposite side in the presence of atypical right hemisphere language. There is also a case (Angelergues, Hecaen, Djindjian and Jarrie–Hazan, 1962) with aphasic deterioration after LEFT carotid amytalization. Finally, as pointed out before (Brown, 1977), the pattern of crossed aphasia in dextrals—initial mutism and agrammatism—resembles that of early childhood aphasia where bilateral language representation might be anticipated.

There is in the literature a case of crossed aphasia with agrammatism who was shown to have a left ear preference on dichotic listening (Denes and Caviezel, 1981). This result was interpreted to indicate right hemisphere language dominance in spite of the well-known problem inferring lateral asymmetries with this method. More important, perhaps, was the dramatic recovery which occurred in this case with a right Sylvian lesion, so large as to probably obviate compensation through the damaged hemisphere. This was also true in the case of Assal, Perentes, and Diruaz (1981).

More problematic are cases with fluent aphasia or jargon. Yarnell (1981) described three crossed aphasics with fluent phonemic paraphasia (phonemic or conduction aphasia). However, in two of the patients there was a history of previous neurological disease, and in none of the cases was family handedness background ascertained. This is important, as left-handedness in a parent or sib would have been grounds for exclusion of the case as a probable "crypto"-sinistral. Pillon, Desi, and Lhermitte (1979) reported two patients with crossed aphasia which resolved leaving a jargon AGRAPHIA. They argued that jargon writing associated with a right-sided lesion implies right language dominance. However, I doubt that Lhermitte would employ the same argument to maintain that cases of left jargonaphasia with GOOD writing, such as he has previously reported, do not have language dominance in the left hemisphere! The significance of preferential involvement or sparing of writing with brain damage is not yet clear. In fact, I am aware of a case of crossed aphasia with AGRAMMATISM and JARGON AGRAPHIA, certainly a peculiar combination in a typical left-damaged patient. Indeed, I have even seen a markedly nonfluent (presumably dextral) crossed aphasic with a type of neologistic jargon. Speech consisted of single-word nonsense utterances. Such cases suggest that fluency and aphasia type may dissociate.

These cases show that fluent aphasia, most often phonemic (conduction) aphasia, possibly even jargon, can occur in crossed aphasic dextrals, though it is probably infrequent. Jargonaphasia occurs in left-handers with right hemisphere lesion, but it is also infrequent (Brown and Hecaen, 1976). With regard to language laterality, there is probably a similarity between the left-hander with a right hemisphere lesion and fluent aphasia, and the right-hander with a right hemisphere lesion and a fluent aphasia. What we are probably seeing is one of a continuum of laterality states irrespective of handedness. Still, in spite of sporadic cases of fluent crossed aphasia, there does appear to be a bias toward nonfluency and, in particular, agrammatism. I do not believe this to be an accident of lesion localization in this patient group, as suggested by some writers. Indeed, the same argument has been used to explain the frequency of nonfluency in younger patients, where it has finally been laid to rest by the data from traumatic cases (see p. 450).

How can the pattern in right hemisphere cases of SEMANTIC errors in comprehension, and AGRAMMATISM in production, be explained? Consider first the situation with lesions of the left hemisphere. As discussed, the LEFT Broca (F3) and Wernicke (T1) zones can probably be viewed as phonological processors. Damage to left F3 gives phonetic-articulatory errors in nonfluent speech; damage to left T1 gives phonemic paraphasias in fluent speech (see Figure 21.4). On the other hand, the anatomical correlation of agrammatism and semantic impairments is less precise. Agrammatism is probably associated with lesions surrounding or partly involving left F3; semantic errors in comprehension (and production) are probably associated with lesions surrounding or partly involving left T1. These are regions of "generalized" neocortex.

Now consider the situation in the right hemisphere, which to a variable extent is deprived of a Wernicke and Broca zone specified for phonological processing. These zones in right hemisphere are comparable, functionally, to the "generalized" neocortex of left hemisphere. This is the neocortical ground out of which the Wernicke and Broca areas differentiate. A lesion of "generalized"

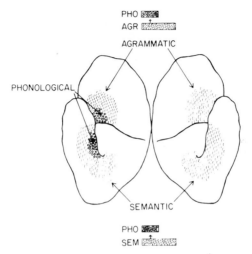

PHO
AGR

AGRAMMATIC

PHONOLOGICAL

SEMANTIC

PHO
SEM

FIGURE 21.4. *Regional specification of the left hemisphere leads to anterior and posterior zones mediating phonological processing. The background zone in left and right hemisphere mediates a prephonological stage. In the anterior system, this concerns a rhythmic oscillator which is linked to the intonational pattern. In the posterior system, this is a stage of lexical selection.*

neocortex in right hemisphere, which therefore includes both the homologous right Wernicke and Broca zones PLUS adjacent areas, gives that form of aphasia associated with left hemisphere lesions of generalized neocortex only.

Specifically, the generalized neocortex adjacent to the Broca and Wernicke areas in the LEFT hemisphere, and the "generalized" neocortex of RIGHT hemisphere (Broca and Wernicke zones plus adjacent neocortex) form a common level mediating a prephonological processing stage. In the anterior sector, the level mediates a rhythmic function elaborating the intonational pattern. A lesion of this level gives agrammatism. In the posterior sector, the level incorporates a multitiered system of word–meaning relationships. A lesion of this level gives semantic errors. The resultant form of aphasia is LEVEL SPECIFIC regardless of hemisphere involved, though more pronounced with left-sided pathology.

Evidence that the isolated right hemisphere is deficient in syntax makes it difficult to understand on this basis the occurrence of agrammatism with right hemisphere pathology. In fact, this is more consistent with a right hemisphere bias for intonation and other rhythmic functions, and possible links to agrammatism. On the other hand, evidence of good lexical-semantic capacity in the isolated right hemisphere explains the finding of semantic impairments in right hemisphere cases as well as clinical observations that bilateral lesions are generally required for semantically anomalous jargon (Brown, 1981). Incidentally, the occurrence of agrammatism and semantic impairments with right hemisphere lesions is a good illustration of the notion that pathology does not just lead to deficient performances but displays processing.

The concept of a bihemispheric semantic level, or one mediating rhythmic functions, and a left-lateralized phonological level helps to explain some observations in commissurotomy patients. Evidence for shared access to axial and/or proximal motor systems—so-called ipsilateral control—points to the unitary organization of primitive levels in motor behavior. It is not simply a matter of ipsilateral nerve fibers; rather, early levels in the temporal structure of a movement develop as part of a unitary bihemispheric system. There is also evidence that each hemisphere in the split has access to a unitary visual field (Holtzman, Sidtis, Volpe, and Gazzaniga, 1980; Trevarthen, 1974). Lesion studies (Denny-Brown and Fischer, 1976) indicate that midbrain tegmental mechanisms construct a unified percept of the two half-fields. Even semantic content may be represented in a unitary field. There are commissurotomy cases who demonstrate semantic sharing between the "disconnected" hemispheres. Verbalizations occur to right hemisphere stimuli, for example, the subject saying "jump" when the word *sit* is flashed in the left visual field (Nebes, 1978). Cross-field semantic priming has been demonstrated in splits (Gazzaniga, 1980).

Such observations indicate that right hemisphere contents are to some extent also in the left hemisphere but "buried" at earlier processing stages. Certainly, there is sufficient evidence from lexical decision tasks and the pathological material to identify semantic processing with preliminary cognition. The degree of semantic sharing in splits reflects the degree to which a content has "come up" in a unitary system of lexical selection. The supposed transfer of affective or experiential relations would instead represent only the most preliminary selection in this unitary system, while the achievement of an adequate conceptual field ("jump" for *sit*) reflects the capacity for a further narrowing down toward the target.

PERCEPTUOMOTOR SYSTEMS AND LANGUAGE REPRESENTATION

The anterior aphasias give evidence for a motor plan underlying the utterance, one that develops as a rhythmic series over evolutionary levels. Similarly, the posterior aphasias suggest a microgenetic development from semantic to phonological levels in retrieval. The utterance involves a simultaneous unfolding over both anterior and posterior systems. This section takes up in a more speculative vein the relationship of this model to several outstanding problems in perceptual neuropsychology.

I would like to begin with the claim that the knowledge of one's own utterance is built up on the same basis as the perception of the speech of others;

that is, that an utterance is represented AS A PERCEPTION. Moreover, the perceptual development of the utterance also elaborates the awareness for that utterance. Posterior aphasia affects the speaker's representation—and thus his awareness—of his own speech. In contrast, the (anterior) motor component, the motor plan or the rhythmic structure of the utterance, does not give rise to mental content directly, but rather contributes an "intentional" quality, a "feeling of innervation" (Innervationsgefühl of Wundt) which enables us to distinguish our own speech from the speech of others. This feeling allows the speaker to determine whether the utterance has come "from within" or "from outside"; that is, whether it is an active or passive movement. The apathy and lack of spontaneity in anterior aphasia point to a disturbance in this function.

In psychotics, the distinction between speech and speech perception may break down. The subject's own voice seems foreign. The utterance takes on the quality of an alien voice, a voice speaking through the speaker. The subject may feel as if he is a vehicle for the speech of others. Speech seems like a passive movement. In such cases, an utterance has a perceptual character. The subject is repeating what another speaker has said. The utterance may also seem like exteriorized inner speech. Thoughts take on the quality of speech and speech becomes more thoughtlike. There may be a confusion of "external" or "heard" speech with inner speech. This is the basis of auditory hallucination. The subject's inner speech appears as a perception of the speech of another speaker. Inner speech seems exteriorized as a perception. Thoughts become perceptions, perceptions become thoughts.

Similar phenomena occur in normal subjects, commonly before sleep or in transitional states. A voice in a darkened room may seem like an exteriorized thought, inner speech may assume a perceptual clarity. There is a collusion of the senses which aids the speaker in making these distinctions. The confusion which may occur between inner speech and perception, or between inner speech and an utterance, points to the common basis of these seemingly disparate performances. In fact, the difficulty we experience in everyday life in trying to speak and to listen at the same time, or in listening to one's own speech while speaking, the necessity for speaker–listener conventions in conversation, the inability to comprehend a speaker when we are distracted by a private thought (inner speech), and the evidence from pathological cases, points to THE COMMON BASIS OF SPEECH, SPEECH PERCEPTION, AND INNER SPEECH.

One may begin by asking, What is the relation between inner speech and auditory hallucination? How is inner speech distinguished from hallucination? One difference is the active quality of inner speech, the feeling that one is the agent or instigator of the behavior, in contrast to the more passive or receptive attitude to auditory hallucination. This difference is like that between active and passive movements. It points to the presence of a motor plan accompanying the inner speech development. This motor plan is the difference between inner speech as an active event, on the way to vocalization, and inner speech as a passive event, on the way to speech perception.

In psychosis, there is a reduced feeling of activity. The patient is no longer the agent of his own inner speech, and so inner speech takes on perceptual characteristics. This link between inner speech and hallucination is supported by numerous observations in schizophrenic patients. It is known that verbal hallucination preserves the intonation and accent of the subject, and is in the language and style of the speaker even though the "voice" seems alien. The so-called "echo of thought" points to a connection with inner speech. During reading, verbal hallucination occurs as an echo or shadow of the material which is read, PRECEDING the actual reading by a second or so or a few words (Morel, 1936). Increasing the reading rate will increase the echo. Verbal hallucination is clearly associated with temporal lobe pathology. It is common in word deafness. Hoff and Silberman (1933) induced verbal hallucination and "echo" phenomena by application of ethyl chloride to an exposed auditory zone in the right superior temporal convolution.

Such observations suggest a continuum between inner speech and verbal hallucination. This continuum may depend on the degree to which the motor plan is activated. If a perceptual content is accompanied by a motor development, the active feeling generated by this development identifies the content as inner speech. If the content is biased toward perception, it is identified as a verbal hallucination. Thus, EMG studies during inner speech show subvocal articulatory movements. This is also true during hallucination (Lagache, 1934). Auditory hallucinations are suspended during respiratory pauses. DeMorsier (1938) noted that auditory hallucination and speech do not occur at the same time. Speaking also tends to interrupt ongoing verbal hallucination. This is because it biases inner speech toward a motor elaboration.

Inner speech and verbal hallucination are at a pivotal stage in thought development. Only the incipient motor development of inner speech allows the subject to separate them as distinct events. The more attenuated the motor plan, the more inner speech is like a perception. The lack of a motor development deprives the subject of an active relation to the mental content. The subject becomes a passive receiver of his own inner speech. This feeling can be recaptured in states of relaxation prior to sleep. As inner speech takes on hallucinatory features, it is not the change in vocal quality that is striking but the seeming detachment of the content, its greater liveliness, the more automatic play of ideas, and their independence from the subject. Such experiences reinforce the impression that inner speech is like a verbal hallucination oriented toward motility. Put differently, inner speech has a PERCEPTUAL basis.

Thus, inner speech and hallucination are preliminary stages leading, respectively, to speech and to perception. Inner speech may vary from a vague, image-laden state, rich in content words or in their precursors, to a more or less well-formed mental sentence, the preverbitum or "unspoken speech." These forms of inner speech reflect a progression leading from a state that is more thoughtlike to the final articulation. Actually, these states are also successive levels of PERCEPTUAL realization. INNER SPEECH DEVELOPS AS A PERCEPTUAL SERIES LINKED TO LEVELS IN THE MOTOR PLAN.

Now consider the relation between verbal hallucination and speech perception. There is considerable evidence from pathological studies (Brown, 1982) that hallucination is a stage leading to perception, it is a preliminary object. One can say that the cognition that fills the hallucination gives itself up in the formation of a veridical perception. The perception develops out of the same ground—or over the same substrate—as the hallucination. This is why hallucination and perception do not occupy the same space. HALLUCINATION IS A PHASE IN A PERCEPTUAL SERIES WHICH TERMINATES IN A VERIDICAL OBJECT. Accordingly, verbal hallucination is a stage on the way to speech perception.

Thus, the deep level in perception that gives rise either to inner speech or verbal hallucination can develop in two directions. One direction, accompanied by an unfolding motor plan, leads through the series of inner speech forms and is the microgenetic path of speech production. Here the perceptual content is represented—perceptually—as an utterance in the mind of the speaker. That is, an utterance consists of a perceptual development, which elaborates the mental representation of the utterance, and a parallel or complementary motor development, which elaborates a feeling of "intentionality." Each level in the perceptual representation corresponds with a level of rhythmic organization in motility. An attenuated development of the parallel motor and perceptual hierarchies gives rise to inner speech. This development is completed in the spoken utterance.

The other direction is to speech perception, and this is also a complex story (Brown, 1982). Briefly, I would suggest that the autonomous content which in the absence of acoustic stimuli gives rise to hallucination is constrained at successive levels by sensory input. The product of the development would then be an object representation oriented to perception and the external world rather than a subjective image formation. That is, the perception is not built up from sensory material, which rather acts to constrain an endogenous system so as to model the external world. In object perception the accompanying motor development would be attenuated. The result would be that the passive or receptive attitude which was so prominent in hallucination, and which reflected the lack of "intentionality" which the motor development provided, is now even more pronounced as the image (object) exteriorizes and seems to detach as an independent thing in the world. The central point is that, from the point of view of mental content, BOTH SPEECH AND SPEECH PERCEPTION DEVELOP OVER THE SAME SET OF PERCEPTUAL LEVELS.

The view of inner speech as a perceptual content linked to verbal hallucination has implications for aphasia study. Goldstein (1948) thought that inner speech developed in relation to perceptual mechanisms, and maintained that phonemic (conduction, central) aphasia involved a disruption at the stage of inner speech. In contrast, Luria assigned inner speech to the anterior region and the motor component of language. This was based on the failure of the motor aphasic to regulate other nonverbal motor activities and the presumed role of inner speech in such regulative functions. However, one might as well argue that nonverbal motor functions are disturbed because motor aphasia represents a disturbance in a motor system rather than a disturbance of language apart from motility. Of course, Luria was also thinking of Vygotsky's characterization of inner speech as predicative and the disruption of predication in agrammatism. Actually, both Goldstein and Luria may be correct. Inner speech should be disrupted by both posterior and anterior lesions but in a different way. Because inner speech is a perceptual content linked to a motor development, anterior lesions should disrupt the motor development and alter the active quality of inner speech. Inner speech might be passive, imaginal, even hallucinatory (see Critchley, 1955). In contrast, a posterior lesion would disrupt the representational content of inner speech, while its intentional quality should be preserved. Certainly, the posterior aphasic gives the impression of a retained active, if not fully critical, attitude to his defective language and toward the world.

MIND AND MICROGENESIS

In this chapter, I have attempted to extend in some new directions the microgenetic account of language. But the concept of microgenesis itself remains elusive. How is microgenesis to be conceived, and what is its relation to theories of mind? In the evolution of a physical structure, a lamination is deposited as a visible trace of what has gone before. The contour of a hill is not what we call the hill; the hill is the subterranean mass within that contour, the contour is only its surface appearance. In living things we can dissect beneath the surface and find no evidence of this evolutionary history. The evolutionary history of an organism constitutes for that organism a kind of abstract structure. The organism presents itself in the here and now as a moment in its span of life. The organism is active in the present. The ontogenesis of the organism is a record in the experience of other living things; its phylogenesis, a theory about a period before the living record. We accept that an ontogenetically active form is captured at a particular stage, and that this form also has an evolutionary background. But to comprehend the structural role of maturational antecedents is not quite so difficult as to understand the comparable role of antecedents in evolution. We infer immediately the derivation of the organism through an ontogenetic process, but we have to understand ABSTRACTLY the continuing activity of evolutionary form.

The evolutionary approach shifts our attention away from mental contents to the process that lies behind them. We are also directed away from the static architecture of the brain to the dynamic activity underlying its structure. The dimensions of, say, the language areas and their interconnections have as little to do with the process of language production as the size, shape, and concatenations of objects in perception have to do with the process of percept formation. There are any number of ways to describe a table or a brain. These descriptions constrain a theory of language or of object formation but are not themselves components of the formative process. We can say that the brain is a microgenetic process through which objects unfold.

Mind is generated over a series of levels. A microstructural development goes on each moment as mind is reconstructed. Mind does not appear at the surface of this structure but obtains at each in a series of emergent states. Mind and world are stratified. Each stratum or mind-state is part of the whole hierarchic series which precedes it. Mind does not consist in the objects, acts, and inner states which fill our conscious awareness, but rather in the antecedents of these states. The real story of mind is in the prehistory of its contents.

REFERENCES

Angelergues, R., Hecaen, H., Djindjian, R., and Jarriè-Hazan, N. (1962). Un cas d'aphasie croisee. *Revue neurologique, 107,* 543–545.

April, R., and Han, M. (1980). Crossed aphasia in a right-handed bilingual Chinese man. *Archives of Neurology, 30,* 342–346.

April, R., and Tse, P. (1977). Crossed aphasia in a Chinese bilingual dextral. *Archives of Neurology, 34,* 766–770.

Archibald, Y., and Wepman, J. (1968). Language disturbance and non-verbal cognitive performance in eight patients following injury to the right hemisphere. *Brain, 91,* 117–130.

Barcroft, J., and Barron, D. (1937). The genesis of respiratory movements in the foetus of the sheep. *Journal of Physiology, 88,* 56–61; *91,* 329–361.

Bernstein, N. (1967). *The coordination and regulation of movements.* London: Pergamon.

Braak, H. (1978). The pigment architecture of the human temporal lobe. *Anatomy and Embryology, 154,* 213–240.

Brown, J. W. (1967). Physiology and phylogenesis of emotional expression. *Brain Research, 5,* 1–14.

Brown, J. W. (1977). *Mind, brain and consciousness.* New York: Academic Press.

Brown, J. W. (1979). Language representation in the brain. In H. Steklis and M. Raleigh (Eds.), *Neurobiology of social communication in primates.* New York: Academic Press.

Brown, J. W. (Ed.). (1981). *Jargonaphasia.* New York: Academic Press.

Brown, J. W. (To appear). *Image and object.* In preparation, 1982.

Brown, J. W., and Hecaen, H. (1976). Lateralization and language representation. *Neurology, 26,* 183–189.

Brown, J. W., and Jaffe, J. (1975). Hypothesis on cerebral dominance. *Neuropsychologia, 13,* 107–110.

Brown, J. W., and Wilson, F. (1973). Crossed aphasia in a dextral. *Neurology, 23,* 907–911.

Buell, S., and Coleman, P. (1979). Dendritic growth in the aged brain and failure of growth in senile dementia. *Science, 206,* 854–856.

Creutzfeldt, O. (1977). Generality of the functional structure of the neocortex. *Naturwissenschaften,* *64,* 507–517.

Critchley, M. (1955). Verbal symbols in thought. *Transactions of the Royal Medical Society, 71,* 179–194.

Critchley, M. (1962). Speech and speech-loss in relation to the duality of the brain. In V. Mountcastle (Ed.), *Interhemispheric relations and cerebral dominance.* Baltimore: Johns Hopkins Press.

DeMorsier, G. (1938). Les hallucinations. *Revue d'Oto-Neuro-Ophtalmologie, 16,* 244–352.

Denes, G., and Caviezel, F. (1981). Dichotic listening in crossed aphasia. *Archives of Neurology,* 38, 182–185.

Denny-Brown, D., and Fischer, E. (1976). Physiological aspects of visual perception. *Archives of Neurology 33,* 228–242.

De Renzi, E. (1971). Visual agnosia and hemispheric locus of lesion. *Fortbildungskurse Schweize Gesamte Psychiatrie, 4,* 57–65.

Diamond, I. (1979). The subdivisions of neocortex: A proposal to revise the traditional view of sensory, motor and association areas. *Progress in Psychobiology and Physiological Psychology,* 8, 1–43.

Eisenson, J. (1962). Language and intellectual modifications associated with right cerebral damage. *Language and Speech, 5,* 49–53.

Gainotti, G., Caltagirone, C., and Miceli, G. (1979). Semantic disorders of auditory language comprehension in right brain-damaged patients. *J. Psycholing Res. 8,* 13–20.

Gazzaniga, M. (1980). *Right hemisphere language: A 20 year perspective.* Paper presented at the Conference on Cognitive Processing in the Right Hemisphere, Institute for Research in Behavioral Neuroscience, New York, 1980.

Goldstein, K. (1948). *Language and language disturbances.* New York: Grune and Stratton.

Goodglass, H. (1968). Studies on the grammar of aphasics. In S. Rosenberg and J. Kaplan (Eds.), *Developments in applied psycholinguistic research.* New York: Macmillan.

Haaland, K., and Miranda, F. (1980). *Case of crossed aphasia in a dextral.* Paper presented at the meeting of the Academy of Aphasia, Cape Cod, 1980.

Hoff, H., and Silberman, (1933) cited in Morel (1936).

Holtzman, J., Sidtis, J., Volpe, B., and Gazzaniga, M. (1980). Attentional unity following brain bisection in man. *Neuroscience Abstracts, 6,* 195.

Jung, R. (1941). Physiologische Untersuchungen uber den Parkinsontremor und andere Zitterformen beim Menschen. *Zeitschrifft Neurologie, 173,* 263–332.

Kellar, L. (1978). *Stress and syntax in aphasia.* Paper presented at the meeting of the Academy of Aphasia, Chicago, 1978.

Kelso, J., Holt, K., Kugler, P., and Turvey, M. (1980). On the concept of coordinative structures. In G. Stelmach and J. Requen (Eds.), *Tutorials in motor behavior.* Amsterdam: North-Holland.

Kuhlenbeck, H. (1957). *Brain and consciousness.* Basel: Karger.

Lagache, D. (1934). *Les Hallucinations verbales et la parole.* Paris: Felix Alcan.

Lashley, K. (1951). The problem of serial order in behavior. In L. Jeffress (Ed.), *Cerebral mechanisms in behavior.* New York: Wiley.

Leslie, C. (1980). *The interactive effects of syntax, pragmatics and task difficulty in aphasic language comprehension.* Unpublished Ph.D. dissertation, Columbia University.

Lesser, R. (1974). Verbal comprehension in aphasia. *Cortex, 10,* 247–263.

Lieberman, P. (1967). *Intonation, perception and language.* Cambridge, Mass.: MIT Press.

Marcie, P., Hécaen, H., Dubois, J., and Angelergues, R. (1965). Les réalisations du langage chez les malades atteints de lésions de l'hémisphère droit. *Neuropsychologia, 3,* 217–245.

Martin, J. (1972). Rhythmic (hierarchical) versus serial structure in speech and other behavior. *Psychological Review, 79,* 487–509.

Milner, B. (1974). Hemispheric specialization. In F. Schmitt and F. Worden (Eds.), *The neurosciences*. Cambridge, Mass.: MIT Press.

Morel, F. (1936). Des bruits d'oreille, des bourdonnements, des hallucinations auditives élémentaires, communes et verbales. *Encephale, 2*, 81–95.

Nebes, R. (1978). Direct examination of cognitive function in the right and left hemispheres. In M. Kinsbourne (Ed.), *Asymmetrical function of the brain*. Cambridge: Cambridge University Press.

Obler, L., Albert, M., Goodglass, H., and Bensen, D. (1978). Aphasia type and aging. *Brain and Language, 6*, 318–322.

Pillon, B., Desi, M., and Lhermitte, F. (1979). Deux cas d'aphasie croisée avec jargonagraphie chez des droitièrs. *Revue Neurol, 1*, 15–30.

Sanides, F. (1970). Functional architecture of motor and sensory cortices in primates in the light of a new concept of neocortex evolution. In C. Noback and W. Montagna (Eds.), *Advances in primatology*. New York: Appleton-Century-Crofts.

Schepelmann, F. (1979). Rhythmic patterns of motor activity after lesions of the central nervous system in man. *Acta Neurochirurgica, 49*, 153–189.

Schoenle, P. (1979). *Speech and respiration in normals and aphasic patients*. Paper presented at the meeting of the Academy of Aphasia, San Diego, 1979.

Siegel, J. (1979). Behavioral functions of the reticular formation. *Brain Research Reviews, 1*, 69–105.

Tägert, J., Chock, D., Niklas, J., Sandvoss, G., and Sipos, J. (1975). Linguistische Funktionsstörungen bei Patienten mit rechtshirnigen Läsionen. *Nervenarzt, 46*, 249–255.

Trevarthen, C. (1974). Functional relations of disconnected hemispheres with the brain stem and with each other. In M. Kinsbourne and W. Smith (Eds.), *Hemispheric disconnection and cerebral function*. Springfield, Ill.: Thomas.

Trojanowski, J., Green, R., and Levine, D. (1980). Crossed aphasia in a dextral: A clinicopathological study. *Neurology, 30*, 709–713.

Turvey, M. (1977). Preliminaries to a theory of action with reference to vision. In R. Shaw and J. Bransford (Eds.), *Perceiving, acting and knowing*. Englewood Cliffs, New Jersey: Erlbaum.

Walter, W. G. (1959). Intrinsic rhythms of the brain. In H. Magoun (Ed.) *Handbook of Physiology* Section 1: Neurophysiology *1*, 279–298.

Wechsler, A. (1976). Crossed aphasia in an illiterate dextral. *Brain and Language, 3*, 164–172.

Yarnell, P. (1981). Crossed dextral aphasia: A clinical radiological correlation. *Brain and Language, 12*, 128–139.

Zangwill, O. (1967). Speech and the minor hemisphere. *Acta neurologica et psychiatrica, 67*, 1013–1020.

Zurif, E., and Caramazza, A. (1976). Psycholinguistic structures in aphasia. In H. Whitaker and H. A. Whitaker (Eds.), *Studies in neurolinguistics*, Vol. 1, New York: Academic Press.

22

Organization of Frontal Association Cortex in Normal and Experimentally Brain-Injured Primates

Patricia S. Goldman-Rakic

Progress in understanding the cerebral cortex has been hindered by its great complexity and by the lack of methods applicable to its study. This is particularly true of areas of association cortex which mediate higher cortical functions. However, recent advances in the physiological, biochemical, and anatomical methods for studying central nervous system organization have allowed us to begin a genuine neurobiological analysis of the association cortex in animals. The studies that I will discuss have been conducted in rhesus monkeys, a nonhuman primate with a brain that is very similar to the human brain in major features of organization, development, and functional topography. Although this animal does not possess a cortical area for propositional speech, we can nevertheless study that portion of the monkey cerebral mantle that comes closest to the association areas of the human cerebral cortex which do mediate language.

In this chapter, I will discuss two recent findings obtained in my laboratory that may have particular significance for human behavior. The first is the discovery of modular organization in the connections of the frontal association cortex in normal monkeys. It is my conviction that neuronal explanations of higher order cognitive processes—including language—need to take account of the brain's predisposition to split its afferent and efferent connections into units. I will also discuss the plasticity of brain connections and how their terminal fields may be altered following injury to circumscribed cortical areas during development. Our findings in this area are relevant to the resilience of linguistic capacity in children that have suffered injuries to their language dominant hemisphere early in life.

469

NEURAL MODELS OF
LANGUAGE PROCESSES

MODULAR ORGANIZATION OF CORTICAL CONNECTIONS

Cortical and Subcortical Connections of Frontal Association Cortex

A well-known feature of brain organization in the sensory systems is the columnar organization of its afferent and efferent fiber systems (Mountcastle, 1978). This type of organization is exemplified by the primary visual cortex in the rhesus monkey. If, for example, radioactive isotopes are injected into one eye, the radioactivity passes through thalamic relays and reaches layers 4a and 4c in the visual cortex (Wiesel, Hubel, and Lam, 1974). A reconstruction of the layer 4 afferents from one eye on a surface view of the occipital lobe demonstrates a spatially periodic pattern, referred to as an ocular dominance stripe, which alternates with stripes representing input from the other eye (Wiesel, Hubel, and Lam, 1974). Thus, the cortical territories subserving the left and right eyes in the cerebral cortex are organized in a pattern of adjacent bands.

We have grown accustomed to viewing the spatially periodic distribution of afferent fibers in the central nervous system as a special adaptation of sensory systems, reflecting primarily the segregation of sensory receptors in the periphery. However, we now know that modular organization characterizes the fiber systems of association cortex as well, and therefore cannot depend wholly upon the structure of sensory receptor surfaces (Goldman and Nauta, 1977a). It is possible that the segregated organization of connections is important for information processing, in general, and language processing, in particular.

The technique involved in demonstrating columnar organization of fiber systems within the primate frontal cortex involves the placing of circumscribed injections of radioactive isotopes in the middle of the dorsal bank of the principal sulcus (Figure 22.1). These substances are taken up by the cell bodies, synthesized into proteins, and transported along the axons which issue from the parent cells. By cutting the brain into serial sections and appropriately processing the sections for autoradiography, it is possible to unambiguously determine the efferent projections of the injected region. The end product of these procedures is a complete series of autoradiograms in which, under dark field illumination, radioactively labeled fibers appear as white grains on a dark surface. For example, a dense accumulation of labeled fibers can be traced from the frontal regions in which the injection is made to the cingulum bundle which is a major efferent pathway of prefrontal cortex. Along their course, axons peel off from the main trunk line and enter the overlying cingulate and retrosplenial cortex where they are distributed in a pattern of bands or columns that alternate with equivalent spaces devoid of prefrontal input (Figure 22.2A). In addition to intrahemispheric projections, the principal sulcus projects significant numbers of axons across the

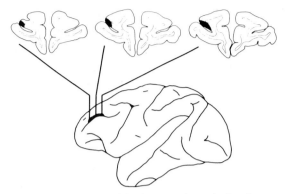

FIGURE 22.1. *Diagram of a lateral view of the rhesus monkey and selected cross-sections through the frontal lobe illustrating circumscribed location of isotope injections into the dorsal bank of the principal sulcus. The black area indicates the site of the injection which labels neurons the axons of which are distributed in a columnar fashion as shown in Figure 22.2. (From Goldman and Nauta, 1976.)*

corpus callosum to the opposite hemisphere where they terminate primarily, though not exclusively, in homotopic cortex. In all of these target regions, the projection fibers originating in the principal sulcus are not uniformly distributed, but rather terminate in areas of high density, separated by areas with lower density or no radioactivity at all (see Figure 22.2). The territories free of prefrontal fibers receive projections from other areas. Recent findings in my laboratory indicate that in the banks of the principal sulcus, callosal (interhemispheric) fiber columns may interdigitate with associational (intrahemispheric) fiber columns to provide a unique set of ipsilateral—contralateral hypercolumns that could provide a modular unit of interhemispheric integration (Goldman-Rakic and Schwartz, 1981).

The use of the autoradiographic technique has also revealed a type of modular organization in cortico-subcortical connections—for example, cortico-striatal (Goldman and Nauta, 1977b), cortico-thalamic (Goldman, 1979), and cortico-tectal (Goldman and Nauta, 1976) fibers. In each of these subcortical structures, fibers originating in the prefrontal cortex surround territories devoid of prefrontal input, which may receive afferents from other sources. Although much remains to be learned about the precise pattern of innervation in these structures, it is already clear that the principal of segregation of afferent information applies as much to subcortical as it does to cortical targets.

Functional Implications of Modular Organization

The demonstration by axonal transport techniques that the distribution of cortico-cortical and cortico-subcortical fiber pathways obeys a modular principle

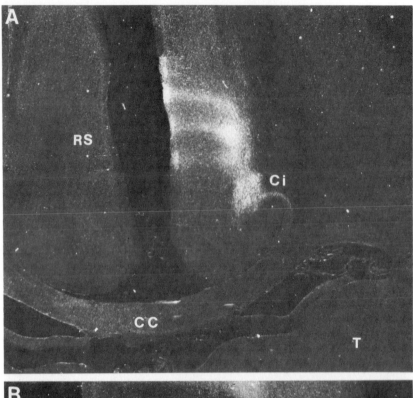

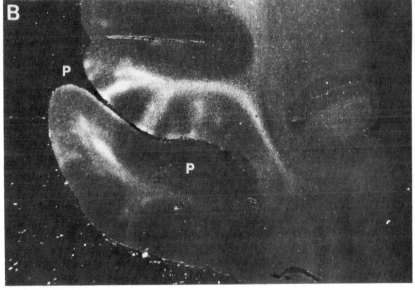

of organization raises the issue of the functional significance of such patterning. This issue can be approached in a variety of ways. Here I will discuss two: deoxyglucose metabolic mapping and comparative neuroanatomy.

Perhaps the most promising evidence that modules may constitute a "functional" unit for brain activity has come from the application of the 2-deoxyglucose method to the study of brain activity (Kennedy, des Rosiers, Sakurada, Shinohara, Reivich, Jehle, and Sokoloff, 1976). Using this method, it has been possible to demonstrate modular organization in the metabolic activity of the cerebral cortex in the behaving rhesus monkey. For example, orientation columns in visual cortex defined originally by electrophysiological techniques (Hubel and Wiesel, 1968) can be visualized when 2-deoxyglucose is given to a monkey that views a particular set of stripes in its visual fields (Hubel, Wiesel, and Stryker, 1978). Likewise, stimulation of certain joint or skin receptors activates a "column" of activity within the somatosensory cortex of the rhesus monkey (Juliano, Hand, Whitsel, Goochee, Karp, and Bajcsy, 1979).

It is important to determine whether association regions of the cerebral cortex also exhibit a modular pattern of metabolic activity which can be correlated with a functional program or psychological demand. Although as of yet it has not been possible to make this type of correlation for associative functions, nevertheless it should be emphasized that the cerebral cortex is not uniformly activated in the alert behaving monkey (Figure 22.3). Rather, cortical activity is prominently discontinuous and takes the form of a spatially periodic distribution of bands of high and low glucose activity (Bugbee and Goldman-Rakic, unpublished observations). The size of these metabolic modules is similar to that of anatomical modules described in the prefrontal association cortex and elsewhere—suggesting that activity may be reflecting impulse flow along a particular set of afferent fiber systems. Indeed, in recent so-called "double labeling" experiments that utilize cortical injections of tritiated amino acids and intravenous ^{14}C-2-deoxyglucose in the same animal, we have succeeded in demonstrating an equivalence between cortico-cortical columns and metabolic columns (Goldman-Rakic and Bugbee, unpublished observations).

Another approach to the functional significance of the modular organiza-

FIGURE 22.2. *Low power autoradiograms illustrating columnar mode of distribution of two classes of cortico-cortical projections emanating from the dorsal bank of the principal sulcus in one hemisphere. A: Associational (ipsilateral) connections terminating in the retrosplenial cortex (RS). B: Callosal (contralateral) projections terminating in the homotopic dorsal bank of the principal sulcus (P) in the opposite hemisphere. In both types of cortico-cortical efferents, fibers are distributed through all layers of the cortex and interdigitate with comparably wide territories that receive terminations of other fiber systems not labeled in these experiments. Determination of the origin of these other sources of input is an important next step in unraveling the connectivity of prefrontal cortex.*

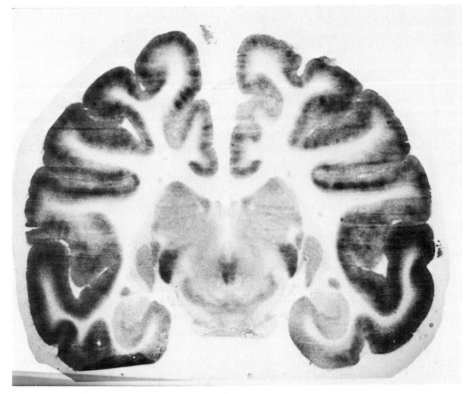

FIGURE 22.3. A 2-deoxyglucose autoradiogram taken through the parietal lobe of a 12-month-old rhesus monkey. Metabolic columns, that is, vertical strips of high glucose utilization bounded on either side by regions of lower activity, are seen in many neocortical regions, but in this section are particularly prominent in parietal cortex. At the time of 2DG labeling, this subject was performing a behavioral task. However, the relationship between an animal's ongoing behavior and the location and number of metabolic columns is not yet understood.

tion of cortico-cortical pathways is to examine phylogenetic differences or similarities in their properties. According to several recent reports, the ocular dominance column, which as mentioned is the central representation of one or the other eye in the visual cortex, appears to be organized differently in Old and New World monkeys. Electrophysiological (Hubel and Wiesel, 1968), 2-deoxyglucose (Kennedy, des Rosiers, Sakurada, Shinohara, Reivich, Jehle, and Sokoloff, 1977) and anterograde transport (Wiesel Hubel, and Lam, 1974) methods have all shown that in Old World monkeys, ocular dominance columns are present in Layer 4 of striate cortex, whereas in the New World species, they are confined to more superficial layers and appear to be totally absent in Layer 4.

Studies in my laboratory have compared the nature and distribution of cortico-cortical modules in the association and limbic cortices of Old World rhesus monkey with those in the New World squirrel monkey (Bugbee and Goldman-Rakic, 1980). Our results revealed a striking similarity in the size, shape, and distribution of cortico-cortical modules in the two species. In both the rhesus and squirrel monkeys, fibers labeled by injections of microquantities of tritiated amino acids into dorsolateral prefrontal cortex formed columns of fibers that extended across all layers in the target territories and alternated in regular sequence with columns of comparable width devoid of prefrontal input.

These findings indicate that module size of the primate cortex is relatively constant from species to species—in spite of large differences in overall brain size and surface area of given cytoarchitectonic fields. Thus, gains in evolutionary capacity may reflect increases in the number, rather than the kind, of afferent fiber module. If these are the functional processing units of brain, then a critical number of them may give rise to qualitative differences in behavioral capacity. It would be of great interest to determine if the distinctively human capacities of consciousness, purpose, and linguistic communication were associated in some way with a quantitative increase in the number of modules.

RECOVERY OF ASSOCIATIVE FUNCTIONS AFTER BRAIN DAMAGE

Perinatal Cortical Injury

There are claims in the literature that if a child has damage to one hemisphere early in life, language can be spared to an extent not seen when a similar lesion occurs in adulthood (e.g., Alajouanine and Lhermitte, 1965; Basser, 1962; Hecaen, 1976). As more sophisticated tests and analyses are performed, it is likely that this simple statement will need to be qualified (Dennis and Whitaker, 1976; Schneider, 1979; Woods and Teuber, 1978). Nonetheless, the resilience of the developing brain in relation to recovery of function is solidly established. Recent studies that we have conducted on fetal and newborn monkeys provide evidence that biological mechanisms exist for aiding recovery after early brain injury in primates.

If frontal lesions are performed in adult rhesus monkeys, and these animals are tested on a delayed response task, they show a permanent impairment in performance which does not recover even when extensive training is given for months or years after surgery. Remarkably, however, if the same lesion is induced earlier in the life of the monkey, the capacity to perform the task is as good as that of nonoperated controls (Goldman, 1971; Goldman and Galkin, 1978; Harlow, Blomquist, Thompson, Schiltz, and Harlow, 1968).

We investigated the question of whether alteration in function could be brought about or explained by modification of neural connections that remain undamaged by cortical injury. In order to do this, we decided to examine the modifiability of frontal lobe connections at the earliest possible stages of development—prenatally (Goldman, 1978; Goldman and Galkin, 1978; Goldman-Rakic, 1981).

The experiments involved the removal of the dorsolateral prefrontal cortex unilaterally both in fetuses at midgestation as well as in neonates aged 1–8 weeks (Figure 22.4). The fetuses either were delivered spontaneously or were taken by caesarean section as they approached full term and allowed to survive for several months. Next, we injected microquantities of ³H-leucine and ³H-proline into the dorsal bank of the principal sulcus in the unoperated hemisphere corresponding to the area resected in the opposite hemisphere (Figure 22.4). One to three weeks later, the animals were sacrificed and their brains were processed for autoradiography. Our studies thus provide unique information about the plasticity or vulnerability of the brain during the perinatal period when most human brain injuries occur.

The main purpose of this experiment was to examine the mode of development of major classes of efferent connections of the dorsolateral cortex in one hemisphere following cortical damage in the other. Here I will describe results obtained so far on two of these classes: the callosal fibers that would normally

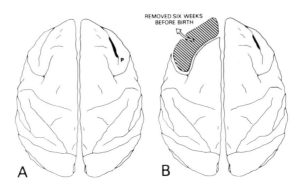

FIGURE 22.4. *Diagrammatic illustration of experimental design used to study modifiability of prefrontal connections consequent to perinatal cortical injury. A: Dorsal view showing site and extent of isotope label in normal brain in which efferent projections of the labeled cortex were studied and compared to those of operated monkeys. B: Same view of an animal in whom the dursolateral prefrontal cortex in one hemisphere was removed at least 2 months before injections of isotope were made in the dorsal bank of the principal sulcus (P) in the remaining hemisphere. In the diagram shown, the unilateral lesion was made 6 weeks before birth, but similar experiments have been conducted on animals operated at various ages after birth. (From Goldman, 1978.)*

connect homotopic areas of prefrontal cortex in the two hemispheres; and the cortico-striatal fibers which represent the main descending projections by which prefrontal cortex ultimately influences voluntary motor behavior.

Plasticity of Callosal Connections

Analysis of prefrontal callosal connections was particularly interesting because, in this instance, the callosal connections of the intact hemisphere had to develop in the absence of their normal target. Our main finding was unexpected: The callosal fibers that would normally innervate the homotopic cortex in the principal sulcus were displaced to the heterotopic dorsomedial frontal cortex adjacent to the resected area (Figure 22.5). As this adjacent prefrontal territory normally receives projections from the ipsilateral principal sulcus, it is partially deafferented by a prefrontal resection within the same hemisphere. Thus, the aberrant callosal fibers could have occupied synaptic space made available in the new location by degeneration or absence of development of the normal ipsilateral principal sulcus—dorsomedial cortical relay. At present, this must remain a working hypothesis, as many details of both the normal and aberrant projection systems remain to be worked out.

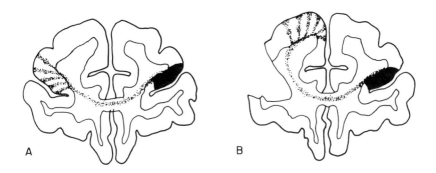

FIGURE 22.5. *Drawing of prefrontal cortex in the left and right hemispheres of rhesus monkeys. A: A normal rhesus monkey whose principal sulcal cortex in the right hemisphere was injected with a mixture of* ³H-leucine *and* ³H-proline *3 weeks before being sacrificed. The drawing illustrates the pattern of alternating callosal fiber bundles in the homotopic cortex of the left hemisphere. B: A monkey in which the dorsolateral prefrontal cortex was resected in the left hemisphere at 8 weeks of age. Two months later intracortical injections were placed in the principal sulcus of the right hemisphere; 3 weeks later the monkey was sacrificed. Callosal fibers deprived of their normal target in the contralateral hemisphere pass by the resected area and become redistributed in the cortex dorsal and medial to the resected area. The anomalous pathway retains its pattern of spatial periodicity. (From Goldman-Rakic, 1981.)*

One intriguing feature of the rearranged callosal pathway that deserves particular notice is that the displaced fibers are distributed in a discontinuous pattern, much as they are organized in their normal field of termination. The finding that a "columnar" mode of termination is preserved by anomalous afferent fibers innervating a foreign territory serves to emphasize not only the modifiability of the nervous system but the importance of columnar organization. This finding also provides evidence that cytochemical specificities between target cells and ingrowing axons need not be overriding factors in determining the ultimate connections that are formed or reformed during development.

Plasticity of Prefronto-Caudate Projections

The second example of modifiability of connections of the primate brain involves the projections from prefrontal cortex to the neostriatum, particularly to the caudate nucleus. We had previously described (Goldman, 1978) the existence of anomalous crossed prefronto-caudate projections in monkeys in which the prospective dorsolateral prefrontal cortex was removed 6 weeks before birth. These results have now been confirmed and extended to monkeys in which the dorsolateral cortex was resected as late as 2 months after birth (Goldman-Rakic, 1981).

In both the monkeys operated prenatally and postnatally the projection to the ipsilateral caudate nucleus is, as might be expected, similar in topography and configuration to that observed in normal monkeys of the same age. The projection to the contralateral caudate nucleus, however, differs markedly from that of controls (Figure 22.6). Whereas in normal animals the contralateral caudate nucleus contains silver grains that only barely exceed background, in the previously operated monkeys dense concentrations of label can be traced in consecutive serial sections throughout the entire extent of the contralateral nucleus over a distance of several centimeters (Goldman, 1978). Significantly, the crossed projection is expanded predominantly in those areas that were deafferented by the unilateral dorsolateral lesions. Furthermore, the anomalous con-

FIGURE 22.6. *Dark-field illumination photomicrographs of the head of the caudate nuclei in the left and right hemispheres of operated and normal monkeys. A: Monkey whose prospective dorsolateral prefrontal cortex in the left hemisphere was resected 6 weeks before birth. The fetus was returned to the uterus and subsequently delivered near term. On the fifth postnatal day, the right prefrontal cortex was injected with tritiated amino acids; the monkey was sacrificed 1 week later. Note intricate pattern of grains in the right (ipsilateral) caudate nucleus, as well as a distinct projection to the left (contralateral) candate. B and C: Normal monkeys that received an injection of mixed ³H-proline and ³H-leucine in the right hemisphere at 5 days of age. The monkeys were sacrificed 1 week later, and their brains were processed for autoradiography. The photographs show the intricate and dense pattern of labeling in the right (ipsilateral) caudate nucleus.*

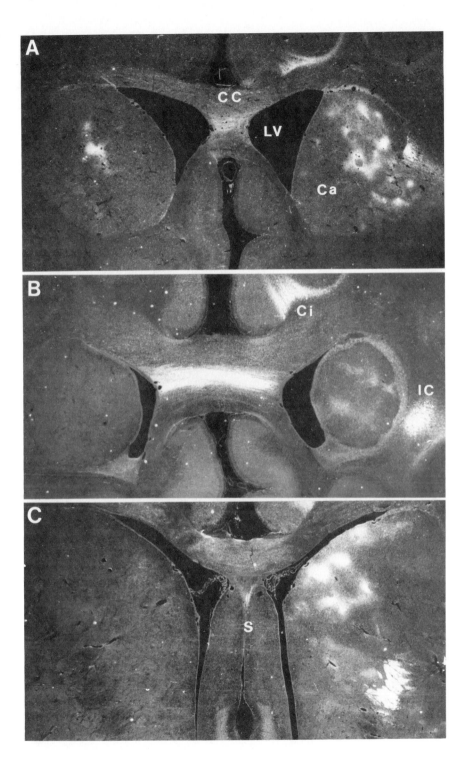

tralateral projections exhibit the same modular pattern of termination that characterize the normal projections.

The several mechanisms, that may be involved in the reorganization of cortico-caudate projections consequent to unilateral prefrontal resection have been discussed elsewhere (Goldman, 1978; Goldman-Rakic, 1981) and need not be elaborated upon here. In essence, we believe that the axons forming anomalous connections belong to the class of efferent fibers that normally innervate the contralateral caudate nucleus only in small numbers. These cortico-striatal fibers, which are not easy to detect even by the sensitive autoradiographic technique, may expand their terminal fields and occupy a number of synaptic spaces on caudate neurons vacated by degeneration of their ipsilateral prefrontal input.

It is of interest and also important to determine whether the anomalous connections described here are functionally useful to the monkey, and in particular, whether they support delayed response performance that is normally mediated by intact prefrontal cortical areas. Although we do not yet know the answer to this question, several lines of argument and ongoing experimentation can be mentioned. Monkeys with unilateral prefrontal resections performed both prenatally and within 2 months of birth are currently being studied in behavioral experiments in my laboratory. As described previously for bilateral prefrontal lesions (Goldman, 1971, Goldman and Galkin, 1978), delayed-response function is spared to a greater degree in monkeys with unilateral lesions operated perinatally as compared with monkeys operated as juveniles or adults. Furthermore, in one of the prenatally operated animals that exhibited functional sparing we subsequently injected tritiated amino acids into the intact prefrontal cortex. In this animal we found rearranged cortico-striatal projections similar to those described earlier. In contrast, expanded cortico-striatal pathways have not been observed so far in the study of animals operated as adults, who were severely impaired on the task. Thus, our preliminary evidence indicates a positive correlation between behavioral sparing and anomalous rearranged connections following unilateral prefrontal removals performed early in life.

It should be emphasized that these considerations do not and cannot establish proof that the alteration of connections in any way accounts for, explains, or provides for recovery of function. We only know that the connections can be modified, and we have evidence that delayed response behavior can be spared following lesions induced within the same critical period. There is much more to do to establish a causal relationship between those two events. Indeed, it is possible that alteration in connections may be responsible for deficits as much as for functional sparing. However, the data from our anatomical studies provides the first evidence that the distribution of cortical connections of the primate brain can be modified and thus indicates that the possibility of a causal relationship between rearranged neuronal connections and sparing of function is worth exploring further.

Theoretical and Biomedical Significance

I have proposed that during the course of normal development, the prefrontal cortex gradually assumes a preeminent role in delayed-response functions (Goldman, 1971). I have argued that prior to full functional maturation of the cortical machinery, certain functions are dependent on subcortical neostriatal components of a frontal lobe integrative circuit (Goldman, 1971, 1974; Goldman and Alexander, 1977; Alexander and Goldman, 1978). In particular, I suggested that sparing of function after prefrontal cortical injury necessarily involved a reliance upon the caudate nucleus as the principal output pathway commanding voluntary motor performance. There is now considerable behavioral (Goldman, 1971; Goldman and Rosvold, 1972) biochemical (Brown and Goldman, 1977) and electrophysiological (Alexander and Goldman, 1976; Alexander, Witt, and Goldman-Rakic, 1980) evidence to support these ideas. The finding that the caudate nucleus figures prominently in the restructured pathways that form after prefrontal resections in the perinatal period lends further credence to the idea that subcortical structures play an important role in cognitive performance not only during normal development but also after cortical injury.

It is my belief that similar kinds of neuroanatomical and neuropsychological mechanisms may be involved in the sparing or recovery of cerebral cortical function that follows injury to the human neocortex at early stages. In particular, if similar kinds of alterations occur in the cortical connections of children that suffer relatively circumscribed cortical injuries in their early life, we may speculate that resilience of certain functions, including language, may in part depend upon rearranged connectivity. Furthermore, if we add the consideration of the human brain's natural asymmetry, we might expect different patterns of connections to form and different functions to be spared depending on the hemisphere injured. Finally, neurobiological techniques have given us evidence to suppose that a lesion of Broca's area or Wernicke's area affects not only that area, but also its projection targets, and perhaps in some cases in which gross lesions and behavioral outcome do not quite correspond, more subtle parameters of central nervous system connectivity. Because we now know that the brain's afferent and efferent fiber systems are organized in a segregated fashion, it could be that the number, configuration, and activity of modular input and output channels could also be altered in cerebral dysfunction.

REFERENCES

Alajouanine, T., and Lhermitte, F. (1965). Acquired aphasia in children. *Brain*, 88, 653–662.

Alexander, G. E., and Goldman, P. S. (1976). Developing prefrontal cortex: Effects of cooling on behavior and on subcortical neuronal activity in rhesus monkeys. *Neuroscience Abstracts*, 2, 189.

Alexander, G. E., and Goldman, P. S. (1978). Functional development of the dorsolateral prefrontal cortex: An analysis utilizing reversible cryogenic depression. *Brain Research, 143,* 233–250.

Alexander, G. E., Witt, E., and Goldman-Rakic, P. S. (1980). Neuronal activity in the prefrontal cortex, caudate nucleus and mediodorsal thalamic nucleus during delayed response performance of immature and adult rhesus monkeys. *Neuroscience Abstracts, 6,* 86.

Basser, L. S. (1962). Hemiplegia of early onset and the faculty of speech with special reference to the effects of hemispherectomy. *Brain, 85,* 427–460.

Brown, R. M., and Goldman, P. S. (1977). Catecholamines in neocortex of rhesus monkeys: Regional distribution and ontogenetic development. *Brain Research, 124,* 576–580.

Bugbee, N. M., and Goldman-Rakic, P. S. (1980). Compartmentalization of prefrontal projections: Comparisons of cortical columns and striatal islands in Old and New World monkeys. *Neuroscience Abstracts, 6,* 822.

Dennis, M., and Whitaker, H. A. (1976). Language acquisition following hemidecortication: Linguistic superiority of the left over the right hemisphere. *Brain and Language, 3,* 404–433.

Goldman, P. S. (1971). Functional development of the prefrontal cortex in early life and the problem of neuronal plasticity. *Experimental Neurology, 32,* 366–387.

Goldman, P. S. (1974). An alternative to developmental plasticity: Heterology of CNS structures in infants and adults. In D. G. Stein, J. J. Rosen, and N. Butters (Eds.), *Plasticity and recovery of function in the central nervous system.* New York: Academic Press.

Goldman, P. S. (1978). Neuronal plasticity in primate telencephalon: Anomalous crossed cortico-caudate projections induced by prenatal removal of frontal association cortex. *Science, 202,* 768–770.

Goldman, P. S. (1979). Contralateral projections to the dorsal thalamus from frontal association cortex in the rhesus monkey. *Brain Research, 166,* 166–171.

Goldman, P. S., and Alexander, G. E. (1977). Maturation of prefrontal cortex in the monkey revealed by local reversible cryogenic depression. *Nature, 267,* 613–615.

Goldman, P. S. and Galkin, T. W. (1978). Prenatal removal of frontal association cortex in the rhesus monkey: Anatomical and functional consequences in postnatal life. *Brain Research, 52,* 451–485.

Goldman, P. S., and Nauta, W. J. H. (1976). Autoradiographic demonstration of a projection from prefrontal association cortex to the superior colliculus in the rhesus monkey. *Brain Research, 116,* 145–149.

Goldman, P. S., and Nauta, W. J. H. (1977a). Columnar distribtuion of cortico-cortical fibers in the frontal association, limbic and motor cortex of the developing rhesus monkey. *Brain Research, 122,* 393–413.

Goldman, P. S., and Nauta, W. J. H. (1977b). An intricately patterned prefronto-caudate projection in the rhesus monkey. *Journal of Comparative Neurology, 171,* 369–386.

Goldman, P. S., and Rosvold, H. E. (1972). The effects of selective caudate lesions in infant and juvenile rhesus monkeys. *Brain Research, 43,* 53–66.

Goldman-Rakic, P. S. (1981). Development and plasticity of primate frontal association cortex. In F. O. Schmitt, F. G. Worden, and S. G. Dennis (Eds.), *The organization of the cerebral cortex.* Cambridge, Mass.: MIT Press. Pp. 69–97.

Goldman-Rakic, P. S. and Schwartz, M. E. (1981). Columnar organization of primate prefrontal cortex: Arrangement of callosal and associational terminal fields. *Neuroscience Abstracts, 7,* 257.

Harlow, H. F., Blomquist, A. J., Thompson, C. I., Schiltz, K. A., and Harlow, M. K. (1968). Effects of induction age and size of prefrontal lobe lesions on learning in rhesus monkeys. In R. Isaacson (Ed.), *Neuropsychology of development.* New York: Wiley.

Hecaen, H. (1976). Acquired aphasia in children and the ontogenesis of hemispheric functional specialization. *Brain and Language, 3,* 114–134.

Hubel, D. H., and Wiesel, T. N. (1968). Receptive fields and functional architecture of monkey striate cortex. *Journal of Phsyiology (London)*, 195, 215–243.

Hubel, D. H., Wiesel, T. N., and Stryker, M. P. (1978). Orientation columns in macaque monkey visual cortex demonstrated by the 2-deoxyglucose autoradiographic technique. *Nature, 269*, 328–330.

Juliano, S., Hand, P., Whitsel, B., Goochee, C., Karp, P., and Bajcsy, R. (1979). A (^{14}C) DG study of somatosensory and associated cortical areas in the monkey. *Neuroscience Abstracts*, 5, 117.

Kennedy, C., des Rosiers, M., Sakurada, O., Shinohara, M., Reivich, M., Jehle, J., and Sokoloff, L. (1976). Metabolic mapping of the primary visual system of the monkey by means of the autoradiographic (^{14}C) deoxyglucose technique. *Proceedings of the National Academy of Sciences of the United States of America*, 73, 4230–4234.

Mountcastle, V. B. (1978). An organizing principle for cerebral function: The unit module and the distributed system. In G. M. Edelman and V. B. Mountcastle (Eds.), *The mindful brain*. Cambridge, Mass.: MIT Press.

Schneider, G. E. (1979). Is it really better to have your brain lesion early? A revision of the 'Kennard Principle." *Neuropsychologia, 17,* 557–583.

Wiesel, T. M., Hubel, D. H., and Lam, D. M. K. (1974). Autoradiographic demonstration of ocular-dominance columns in the monkey striate cortex by means of transneuronal transport. *Brain Research, 79,* 273–279.

Woods, B. T., and Teuber, H.-L. (1978). Changing patterns of childhood aphasia. *Annals of Neurology, 3,* 273–280.

23

Implications of Simulated Lesion Experiments for the Interpretation of Lesions in Real Nervous Systems

Charles C. Wood

INTRODUCTION

Behavioral deficits following brain damage have long been used to make inferences about the functional organization of the nervous system in general and about the neural organization of human language in particular. The work of Flourens (1824, 1825) is generally cited as the first attempt to explore the functional organization of the brain by studying the behavioral consequences of systematic brain lesions in animals (e.g., Boring, 1950, pp. 61–67). Subsequent arguments for and against localization of function in the brain were based almost exclusively upon the results of lesion experiments (e.g., Ferrier, 1876; Franz, 1902; Goltz, 1881; Lashley, 1929, 1950; Munk, 1881). Nowhere has the influence of lesion data been more strongly felt than in the continuing debate between localizationist and antilocalizationist theories of brain organization for language (e.g., Gescbwind, 1974; Head, 1963; Jackson, 1874; Luria, 1973).

In view of the inferential importance of lesion experiments, it is surprising that their interpretation has been discussed (in public, at least) so infrequently. With some exceptions (e.g., Glassman, 1978; Gregory, 1961), the problem of interpreting lesion data has most often been discussed in the context of related questions, rather than as an important issue in its own right. For example, most discussions of of lesion interpretation have appeared in the context of localization of function (e.g., Von Ekardt Klein, 1978; Laurence and Stein, 1978; Uttal, 1978) or recovery of function (e.g., Eidelberg and Stein, 1974; LeVere, 1975; Rosner, 1970, 1974). The question What inferences about the functional organization of the nervous system can be justifiably made from lesion experiments? has received surprisingly little direct attention.

In this chapter, I describe a novel way of investigating what can be learned from lesion experiments, based on simulated lesions in a simple neural model

485

NEURAL MODELS OF
LANGUAGE PROCESSES

of associative memory. There are both advantages and disadvantages to using a neural model for this purpose. On the positive side, three advantages may be noted:

1. Unlike lesion experiments in real nervous systems, simulated lesions in a neural model permit lesion size and location to be precisely controlled and systematically manipulated.
2. Arbitrarily large numbers of lesions, subjects, and behavioral tasks can be studied in simulations, all of which are limited resources in real lesion experiments.
3. Perhaps most important, the mechanisms of information representation and processing in a neural model can be completely and quantitatively specified. Therefore, the problem of inferring functional organization from lesion data can be addressed directly using a neural model in a manner that is impossible for real nervous systems.

On the negative side, simulated lesions are subject to the following limitations:

1. The specific model used to study simulated lesion effects may be inadequate or incorrect in a number of ways; to the extent that its assumptions are invalid, certain conclusions drawn from the simulated lesion experiments may not be generalizable.
2. The range of "behavioral tasks" that can be studied in simulated lesion experiments is constrained by the particular model employed. For example, the capabilities of the model used in this chapter are limited to association of a given pattern of input activity with a given pattern of output activity, with the result that tasks other than those usually termed "association," "recognition," or "discrimination" cannot be investigated using this model.
3. As will be discussed in greater detail in what follows, the specific ways in which simulated lesions are implemented and their effects assessed have important consequences for the conclusions drawn. For example, Gordon (Chapter 24, this volume) discusses the effects of simulated lesions on the "confrontation naming" performance of an association model closely related to that described in this chapter. However, both the model itself and the implementation of the simulated lesions differ in subtle but important ways from those in this chapter.

Thus, the principal aim of this exercise may be stated as follows: Given that we know the mechanisms of information representation and processing that are built into the model by definition, to what extent can those same mechanisms be identified by analyzing behavioral deficits following damage to the model? The model I shall use for this purpose is formulated at a lower level than most that are discussed in this volume, in the sense that it is formulated in terms of the connections and activities of individual neurons instead of abstract processes having no neural realization. Nevertheless, the model has been shown to be capable of approximating a number of interesting "cognitive" phenomena. Regardless of the validity or generality of the specific model employed, the approach outlined here can be applied to any model in which aspects of neural structure are directly represented.

A secondary objective of this chapter is to consider the interpretation of lesion effects in the context of a model in which information processing and storage are DISTRIBUTED across large populations of neurons. It has become increasingly clear on both empirical and theoretical grounds that progress in understanding nervous system function requires consideration of the cooperative activity of relatively large groups of neurons (e.g., Arbib, 1972, 1981; Erikson, 1974; Freeman, 1975; Mountcastle, 1978, Szentagothai, 1978; Szentagothai and Arbib, 1974). Therefore, neural models that involve one or another form of distributed processing have received increasing attention (e.g., Anderson, Silverstein, Ritz, and Jones, 1977; Grossberg, 1976a,b; Kohonen, 1977; Little and Shaw, 1975; Marr and Poggio, 1977; Nuwer, and Baron, 1974; Willshaw, Buneman, and Longuet-Higgins, 1969).[1]

The remainder of the chapter is organized in the following way: The next section reviews the assumptions and mathematical representation of the model, presents a simple numerical example to illustrate the model's properties, and discusses measures for assessing the model's performance. It is followed by a section that describes the implementation of the simulated lesions, the effects of systematic variations in lesion size and location on the model's association performance, and the effects of specific lesions on specific associations. The final section considers the implications of the simulated lesion results for the interpretation of real lesion experiments.

ANDERSON'S MODEL OF ASSOCIATIVE MEMORY

The mathematical model used for the simulated lesion experiments is the one that has been applied to the problems of feature detection, categorical perception, and probability learning by James Anderson and his colleauges at Brown University (Anderson, 1972, 1977; Anderson et al., 1977). Closely related models have been applied to the development of "feature detector" cells in visual cortex (Cooper, Liberman, and Oja, 1979; Nass and Cooper, 1975), item recognition (Anderson, 1973, 1977), vowel perception (Anderson, Silverstein, and Ritz, in press), and to general associative memories (Kohonen, 1972, 1977;

[1]It is worth noting that models in psychology and artificial intelligence have also begun to incorporate distributed processing assumptions (e.g., Arbib and Caplan, 1979; McClelland, 1979).

Kohonen, Lehtio, Rovamo, Hyvarinen, Bry, and Vainio, 1977; also see Little and Shaw, 1975; Roney and Shaw, 1978; Shaw, 1978). All of these models share two fundamental assumptions: (*a*) that associative memory is distributed over a large population of neurons (cf. Palm, 1980); and (*b*) that memory storage involves synaptic modification that depends upon activity in pre- and postsynaptic neurons (Hebb, 1949; Levy and Steward, 1979).

Assumptions and Mathematical Representation[2]

Anderson *et al.* (1977) based their model on the following general assumptions: (*a*) "nervous system activity can be most usefully represented as the set of simultaneous individual neuron activities in a group of neurons [p. 415]"; and (*b*) "different memory traces (sometimes called 'engrams'), corresponding to these large patterns of individual neuron activity, interact strongly at the synaptic level so that different traces are not separate in storage [p. 415]."

The model assumes the existence of two sets of N neurons, α and β, in which every neuron in α is synaptically connected to every neuron in β (Figure 23.1). Set α is assumed to receive its input from some unspecified source (other neurons if α consists of interneurons, sensory receptors if α consists of first-order sensory afferents, or the environment if α consists of sensory receptors). Set β is assumed to send its output to some other unspecified location (other neurons if β consists of interneurons, muscle cells if β consists of motorneurons, or the environment if β consists of muscle cells). For convenience, I shall refer to sets α and β as "input neurons" and "output neurons," respectively.

The activity of each neuron in the model is represented as a continuous variable, assumed to correspond to the neuron's firing frequency relative to some baseline level; thus, activity consists of both positive and negative values relative to baseline. Each input neuron is assumed to be connected to every output neuron with a given synaptic strength, and all neurons are assumed to be simple linear integrators of their inputs. Thus,

$$g(i) = \sum_{j=1}^{N} x_{ij} f(j) \tag{1}$$

where $g(i)$ is the activity of neuron i in β, $f(j)$ is the activity of neuron j in α, and x_{ij} is the synaptic strength connecting neuron j to neuron i. Given these assumptions, the patterns of activity in α and β can be represented as the N-element vectors **f** and **g**, which reflect the activity at a given time over all N neurons in each set. For convenience, the input vectors are assumed to be normalized:

---

[2]The description of the model to be presented here and much of the data presented in following section were originally reported by Wood (1978).

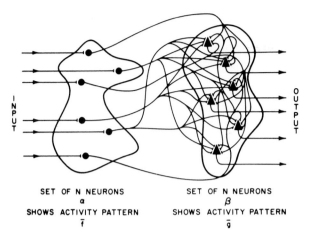

SET OF N NEURONS   SET OF N NEURONS
        α   β
SHOWS ACTIVITY PATTERN   SHOWS ACTIVITY PATTERN
        f̄   ḡ

FIGURE 23.1. *Schematic representation of the structural assumptions of the Anderson, Silverstein, Ritz, and Jones model. Each neuron in input population* α *is synaptically connected to each neuron in output population* β. *(From J. A. Anderson, J. W. Silverstein, S. A. Ritz, and R. S. Jones, 1977.) Distinctive features, categorical perception, and probability learning: Some applications of a neural model.* Psychological Review, *84(5), 413–451. Copyright 1977 by the American Psychological Association. Reprinted by permission of the publisher and authors.*

$$\left[\sum_{i=1}^{N} f(i)^2 \right]^{\frac{1}{2}} = 1. \qquad (2)$$

If a given pattern of input activity, say input vector $\mathbf{f}_k$, is associated with a given pattern of output activity, $\mathbf{g}_k$, perhaps over many trials interleaved with occurrences of other input and output patterns, then the synaptic strengths x_{ij} will be incremented by an amount $g_k(i)f_k(j)$. In other words, the change in synaptic strength can be represented by the $N \times N$ matrix

$$\mathbf{A}_k = \mathbf{g}_k\mathbf{f}_k' \qquad (3)$$

where $\mathbf{g}_k$ and $\mathbf{f}_k$ are N-element column vectors, and $\mathbf{f}_k'$ is the transpose of $\mathbf{f}_k$. Since $\mathbf{f}_k'\mathbf{f}_k = 1$, this ensures that

$$\mathbf{A}_k\mathbf{f}_k = \mathbf{g}_k\mathbf{f}_k'\mathbf{f}_k = \mathbf{g}_k. \qquad (3a)$$

Anderson, Silverstein, Ritz, and Jones (1977) make no explicit assumptions about the learning process by which the synaptic strengths become altered according to Eq. (3); they simply assume that the result of the learning process can be represented as the product of the input and output vectors. For more detailed discussion of this and related synaptic modifiability assumptions, see Anderson (1977), Kohonen, Lentio, Rovamo, Hyvarinen, Bry, and Vainio (1977), Kohonen (1977), and Stent (1973).

Any number of input and output patterns may be associated by first computing the incremental association matrix according to Eq. (3) for each pair and then summing the individual association matrices:

$$A = \sum_{k=1}^{M} A_k \qquad (4)$$

Thus, if pattern f_k is presented to the system with association matrix A, the output of the system will be

$$Af_k = A_k f_k + \sum_{l \neq k} A_l f_k \qquad (5)$$

$$= g_k + \sum_{l \neq k} g_l f_l' f_k.$$

Note that the "error term" vanishes if $f_l' = 0$ for $l \neq k$. In other words, if the input vectors are orthogonal the occurrence of any input vector previously associated with an output vector will produce the appropriate output vector in response.

Anderson, Silverstein, Ritz, and Jones (1977) actually presented two distinct models. The first is the association model just described (Figure 23.1), in which every neuron in one population is connected to every neuron in the other. Their second model makes additional assumptions regarding feedback from each neuron onto itself and adds saturation of the activity of individual elements. The latter model was applied to the specific empirical problems addressed in the Anderson, Silverstein, Ritz, and Jones (1977) paper. For simplicity, the association model without feedback was used for the simulated lesion experiments discussed here. However, simulated lesions could be easily generalized to the feedback model or to any of the other correlation matrix models mentioned earlier (see, e.g., Gordon, Chapter 24, this volume).

A Numerical Example

Anderson *et al.* (1977) presented a numerical example of the model's performance based on eight input and eight output neurons and the four sets of arbitrary input and output vectors shown in Table 23.1. This example will be used here to illustrate some basic properties of the model. The model is first "taught" to associate each input vector with the corresponding output vector in Table 23.1 (i.e., $f_1 \rightarrow g_1$, $f_2 \rightarrow g_2$, etc.) according to Eqs. (3) and (4). The resulting association matrix for this example, A in Eq. (4), is also shown in Table 23.1.

In order to test the model's ability to associate, each of the four input vectors is presented as a stimulus to the model, and the resulting output vectors are calculated according to Eq. (5). These computed output vectors are presented in Table 23.2. As indicated by comparing the computed output vectors with the

TABLE 23.1
Input Vectors, Output Vectors, and Association Matrix for a Numerical Example[a]

Input vectors				Output vectors			
f_1	f_2	f_3	f_4	g_1	g_2	g_3	g_4
.354	−.354	.354	−.354	1.000	−1.000	3.000	4.000
.354	−.354	−.354	−.354	.000	2.000	.000	.000
.354	.354	.354	.354	−1.000	.000	−1.000	−1.000
.354	.354	−.354	.354	.000	−1.000	−1.000	−1.000
−.354	−.354	.354	.354	1.000	−1.000	−2.000	−1.000
−.354	−.354	−.354	.354	−1.000	−1.000	.000	.000
−.354	.354	.354	−.354	−1.000	−1.000	−1.000	.000
−.354	.354	−.354	−.354	.000	2.000	2.000	1.000

Association matrix							
.354	−1.768	2.475	.354	2.475	.354	−1.061	−3.182
−.707	−.707	.707	.707	−.707	−.707	.707	.707
−.354	.354	−1.061	−.354	−.354	.354	.354	1.061
.354	1.061	−1.061	−.354	−.354	.354	−.354	.354
.354	1.768	−1.061	.354	−1.061	.354	−1.061	.354
.000	.000	−.707	−.707	.707	.707	.000	.000
−.354	.354	−1.061	−.354	.354	1.061	−.354	.354
−.354	−1.768	1.768	.354	.354	−1.061	1.061	−.354

[a] From C. C. Wood (1978). Variations on a theme by Loshley: Lesion experiments on the neural model of Anderson, Silverstein, Ritz, and Jones. *Psychological Review*, 85(6), pp. 582–591. Copyright 1978 by The American Psychological Association. Reprinted by permission of the publisher and author.

original output vectors in Table 23.1, association is perfect for the orthogonal input vectors used in this example. That is, the computed output vectors are identical to the output vectors the model was originally taught to associate.

Measures of the Model's Performance

In order to assess the model's ability to associate different types of inputs and outputs, and to assess its performance after simulated lesions, we need a quantitative measure of association performance. What we wish to know is how closely the output vectors computed by the model correspond to the original output vectors the model was taught to associate. Such an index of correspondence could be based on any of the many available parametric or nonparametric measures of similarity (e.g., Mosteller and Rourke, 1973). The most natural measure in the context of the matrix algebra representation of the Anderson, Silverstein, Ritz, and Jones model is the cosine of the angle between two vectors in N-dimensional space. When the activity of each neuron is expressed as a devia-

Charles C. Wood

TABLE 23.2
Computed Output Vectors and Confusion Matrix for the Numerical Example[a]

	Computed output vectors			
	g_1	g_2	g_3	g_4
	1.000	−1.000	3.000	4.000
	.000	2.000	.000	.000
	−1.000	.000	−1.000	−1.000
	.000	−1.000	−1.000	−1.000
	1.000	−1.000	−2.000	−1.000
	−1.000	−1.000	.000	.000
	−1.000	−1.000	−1.000	.000
	.000	2.000	2.000	1.000

Original output vectors	Confusion matrix Computed output vectors			
	g_1	g_2	g_3	g_4
g_1	1.000	−.016	.304	.436
g_2	−.016	1.000	.312	.016
g_3	.304	.312	1.000	.911
g_4	.436	.016	.911	1.000

[a] From C. C. Wood (1978). Variations on a theme by Lashley: Lesion experiments on the neural model of Anderson, Silverstein, Ritz, and Jones. *Psychological Review*, 85(6), pp. 582–591. Copyright 1978 by The American Psychological Association. Reprinted by permission of the publisher and author.

tion score around the mean of the vector, this measure is identical to the product-moment correlation coefficient used by Wood (1978) to assess the model's performance.[3]

It should be understood that the choice of a performance measure implies certain committments about the model's interpretation. For example, the correlation coefficient is sensitive to the pattern of activity across the output neurons, not to the absolute amount of activity. This property reflects the fact that the correlation coefficient is, in effect, normalized over the variances of the two vectors. Thus, a computed output vector with greatly attenuated overall activity can still yield a good correlation to the original output vector, as long as the pattern of activity across the neurons in question is similar. If one wished to include absolute amount of activity as well as its pattern in the measure of similarity, covariances or cross-products could be used instead. However, be-

[3] The randomly generated input vectors used by Wood (1978) to test the model had zero mean and unit variance. Therefore, there was little difference between the product-moment correlation coefficient and the cosine of the angle between vectors for these data. However, with input vectors having means that differ systematically from zero the two measures would differ significantly.

cause the same covariance value could arise from a variety of different input vectors, the correlation coefficient was used as the primary performance measure for assessing lesion effects.

The preceding discussion has emphasized measuring the similarity between the output vector generated by the model in response to a stimulus and the corresponding output vector the model was originally taught to associate. However, we also need to be concerned with the relationship between each computed output vector and other output vectors whose associations the model has learned. A combined measure of association, involving both "recognition" and "discrimination" performance, can be obtained by forming the confusion matrix shown at the bottom of Table 23.2. This matrix consists of pairwise correlations among the computed and original output vectors. The diagonal elements in the confusion matrix may be thought of as an index of the model's "recognition" perofrmance; that is, the degree to which the model responds to each input vector with the appropriate output vector. Thus, larger diagonal elements in the confusion matrix indicate better performance. As noted earlier, recognition performance is perfect ($r = 1.0$) with orthogonal input vectors; with nonorthogonal inputs, however, the diagonal elements would be smaller, as will be illustrated in what follows. The off-diagonal elements in the confusion matrix may be thought of as an index of the model's "discrimination" performance, the degree to which the model responds to each input vector with an output vector appropriate for some other input vector. In this case, lower correlations indicate better performance. A combined index of recognition and discrimination performance is given by the difference between the mean diagonal and mean off-diagonal elements of the confusion matrix. For the confusion matrix shown in Table 23.2, this value is $1.00 - .33 = .67$.

SIMULATED LESION EXPERIMENTS

Simulated lesions were made on elements of the model by assuming that the activity of each neuron included in the lesion would not contribute to the association process represented in Eq. (5). This assumption was implemented by setting the appropriate element of the input or output vector in Eq. (5) to zero.

This mathematical representation of a lesion is a gross oversimplification in a number of respects. First, lesions in real nervous systems not only eliminate the functional contribution of the specific neurons removed by the lesion, but also may produce a variety of indirect effects upon remaining neurons. For example, Sprague (1966) showed that the effects of unilateral removal of superior colliculus in the cat could be offset by removal of the remaining colliculus. Similarly, Sherman (1974) reported that removal of visual cortex led to an improvement of visual deficits produced by visual deprivation. Indirect or "distant" effects of brain lesions were first emphasized in von Monakow's (1974) concept of "diaschisis" and have received increasing empirical attention in more recent investigations of functional recovery following brain damage (e.g. Dail, Feeney, Murrey, Linn, and Boyeson, 1981; Eidelberg and Stein, 1974; Schoenfeld and Hamilton, 1977). Second, the effects of a lesion are not constant but change over time; some effects may disappear (i.e., "functional recovery") whereas others may not (Eidelberg and Stein, 1974; Finger, 1978). Third, in addition to recovery at the behavioral level, anatomical studies have demonstrated structural changes following brain damage, particularly when the lesions are sustained neonatally and to a lesser extent in adulthood (Sidman and LaVail, 1974; Goldman-Rakic, Chapter 22, this volume, Laurence and Stein, 1978). For these reasons, the simulated lesions described here should be viewed as a static approximation to the complex, dynamic set of consequences induced by brain damage. Whether or not it will be profitable to attempt to model these dynamic effects of brain damage is an open question.[4]

Lesions of Neural Elements in the Model

Following a given lesion, the residual performance of the model was tested in the manner already described for the intact model: The four input vectors originally taught to the model were presented as stimuli, and the four corresponding output vectors were recorded in response. The similarity between the computed and original output vectors was calculated from confusion matrices like that shown at the bottom of Table 23.2. Correlations were always based on $N = 8$, regardless of the number of neurons removed by the lesion.

To illustrate this process, Table 23.3 presents computed output vectors and confusion matrices for lesions of Input Neuron 1 and Output Neuron 8 in the numerical example presented earlier. Input Neuron 1 corresponds to the first element in the input vectors and the first column of the matrix shown in Table 23.1, whereas Output Neuron 8 corresponds to the eighth element in the output vectors and the eighth row of the matrix. Three qualitative aspects of the lesion effects shown in Table 23.3 should be noted:

1. Although both lesions produced a decrease in recognition performance, the model was nevertheless able to produce output vectors that closely approximated those produced by the intact model in Table 23.2. Whereas the mean of

---

[4]It would not be difficult to incorporate assumptions about lesion-induced structural changes into the model. At present, however, the available anatomical data are insufficient to constrain the many possible ways in which such an assumption could be implemented. For example, which neurons undergo changes after a lesion? What are the rules by which new connections are established? Are they synaptically functional? In absence of relatively precise answers to these questions, it is not clear how valuable such an exercise would be.

TABLE 23.3
Computed Output Vectors and Confusion Matrices for Lesions of Input Neuron 1 and Output Neuron 8 in the Numerical Example[a]

Computed output vectors for lesion of Input Neuron 1				Computed output vectors for lesion of Output Neuron 8			
$\hat{g}_1$	$\hat{g}_2$	$\hat{g}_3$	$\hat{g}_4$	$\hat{g}_1$	$\hat{g}_2$	$\hat{g}_3$	$\hat{g}_4$
.875	−.875	2.875	4.125	1.000	−1.000	3.000	4.000
.250	1.750	.250	−.250	.000	2.000	.000	.000
−.875	−.125	−.875	−1.125	−1.000	.000	−1.000	−1.000
−.125	−.875	−1.125	−.875	.000	−1.000	−1.000	−1.000
.875	−.875	−2.125	−.875	1.000	−1.000	−2.000	−1.000
−1.000	−1.000	.000	.000	−1.000	−1.000	.000	.000
−.875	−1.125	−.875	−.125	−1.000	−1.000	−1.000	.000
.125	1.875	2.125	.875	.000	.000	.000	.000

Confusion matrices

Original output vectors	Computed output vectors				Computed output vectors			
	$\hat{g}_1$	$\hat{g}_2$	$\hat{g}_3$	$\hat{g}_4$	$\hat{g}_1$	$\hat{g}_2$	$\hat{g}_3$	$\hat{g}_4$
g_1	.987	.047	.225	.475	1.000	−.061	.316	.430
g_2	.125	.997	.374	−.048	−.016	.875	.053	−.120
g_3	.332	.338	.996	.894	.304	.080	.909	.823
g_4	.441	.038	.892	.996	.436	−.101	.949	.977

[a] From C. C. Wood (1978). Variations on a theme by Lashley: Lesion experiments on the neural model of Anderson, Silverstein, Ritz, and Jones. *Psychological Review*, 85(6), pp. 582–591. Copyright 1978 by The American Psychological Association. Reprinted by permission of the publisher and author.

the diagonal elements for the intact model was 1.0, the means for the two lesioned models were .994 and .936, respectively.

2. As indicated by the off-diagonal elements in the confusion matrices, lesion effects on discrimination performance are more difficult to characterize in simple terms; they depend upon similarities of the specific input and output vectors employed. In general, a lesion that removes a neuron whose activity contributes heavily to the difference between two input vectors will have a greater effect on performance. This effect is discussed in greater detail in what follows.

3. Lesions of input and output vectors produce their effects on the model's performance in different ways. Setting the activity of an output neuron to zero directly eliminates the contribution of that neuron to the output vectors but leaves the other elements of the output vectors unaltered (compare Tables 23.3 and 23.2). This is a relatively trivial effect. In contrast, lesions of an input neuron have a more widespread but subtle effect on the pattern of output activity. In this

case, all output neurons are still capable of generating activity, but the pattern of activity across the set of output neurons will generally differ somewhat from that of the intact model (again compare Tables 23.3 and 23.2). Lesions involving both input and output neurons combined these two types of effect.

Effects of Systematic Variations in Lesion Size and Location on Performance of the Model

As noted earlier, an important advantage provided by simulated lesion experiments is the ability to vary both lesion size and location precisely and systematically over a wide range. Equivalent anatomical precision is impossible to achieve in real lesion experiments. In terms of the Anderson, Silverstein, Ritz, and Jones model, lesion size corresponds to the total number of neurons removed, whereas lesion location corresponds to the particular individual neurons removed. The simulated lesions reported by Wood (1978) and reviewed here were based on 8-element input and output vectors like those used in the numerical example described earlier.[5]

Lesion size and location were varied systematically by removing all possible combinations of 1–7 input neurons, all possible combinations of 1–7 output neurons, and all possible combinations of 1–7 input neurons and 1–7 output neurons combined. Thus, there were

$$\left[\sum_{i=0}^{7} \left(\begin{array}{c} 8 \\ i \end{array} \right) \right]^2 - 1,$$

or 65,024 total lesions for a given set of input and output vectors. Because the deficit produced by a given lesion may be influenced by idiosyncratic features of the input and output vectors, the set of 65,024 lesions was repeated for each of 100 randomly selected sets of four input and four output vectors. Each vector in a given set was selected independently from a Gaussian distribution with zero mean and unit variance, and input vectors were normalized according to Eq. 2.

Figure 23.2 illustrates the effects of lesion size, averaged over the 100 randomly selected input and output vectors and averaged over the specific neurons involved. Lesions of input neurons alone, output neurons alone, and combined lesions are shown. The upper left point indicates average performance

---

[5]It is important to ask in this context whether the results of simulations using models of low dimensionality (i.e., with relatively small numbers of input and output neurons) can be generalized to those of higher dimensionality. As will be shown in greater detail in what follows, the answer to this question is in general yes. More important than dimensionality per se in determining lesion effects is the relationship among the input and output vectors. Anderson, Silverstein, Ritz, and Jones (1977) also used 8-element input and output vectors on the grounds that they were "large enough to be indicative of the behavior of a real system, yet small enough to be manageable and of reasonable cost [p. 430]."

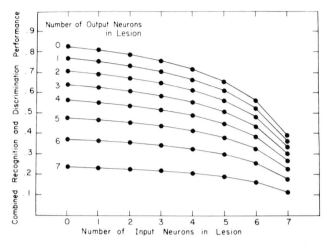

FIGURE 23.2. *Effects of variations in lesion size on performance of the model using a correlation-based measure of performance. From C. C. Wood (1978). Variations on a theme by Lashley: Lesion experiments on the neural model of Anderson, Silverstein, Ritz, and Jones.* Psychological Review, *85(6), pp. 582–591. Copyright 1978 by The American Psychological Association. Reprinted by permission of the publisher and author.*

of the intact model; the mean on-diagonal and off-diagonal values were .85 and .02, respectively. This result illustrates the point made earlier regarding orthogonality of the input vectors; when they are not orthogonal, recognition performance is less than perfect. Nevertheless, the .85 value shown here is a reasonable performance level for a model with small dimensionality.

Figure 23.2 also demonstrates that lesions of increasing size produced a corresponding increase in the size of the performance deficit for lesions of both input and output neurons. However, even with relatively large lesions performance remained well above chance on the correlation measure. Figure 23.3 illustrates the effects of the same lesions using cross-products instead of correlations as the similarity measure. The same general relationships are preserved, except that the decrement in performance with increasing lesion size appears somewhat larger in relative terms than that shown in Figure 23.2. This difference is simply a consequence of including the mean value of activity in the cross-product measure as well as the pattern of activity across neurons. Any lesion will tend to reduce overall activity, leading to larger deficits when cross-products are used instead of correlations as the performance measure.

Figure 23.4 summarizes the effect of lesion location averaged overall lesion sizes. The deficit produced by removal of any given neuron was, on average, equivalent to that of any other neuron. This relationship corresponds closely to Lashley's classic concept of "equipotentiality" (Lashley, 1928, 1933; Lashley and Wiley, 1933). Similar results were seen with the cross-products measure.

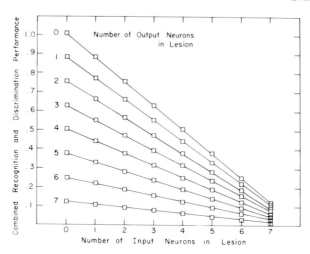

FIGURE 23.3. *Effects of variations in lesion size on performance of the model using a performance measure based on cross-products instead of correlations.*

Effects of Specific Lesions on Specific Associations

The lesion effects just described were based on average results over a large number of individual lesions and many different input and output vectors. Can we expect the same pattern of results from a single set of input and output vectors? The answer is yes and no. It is yes when the input and output vectors are mutually orthogonal. In this case the deficit produced by any given input (or output) neuron closely approximates that produced by any other input (or output) neuron.[6] However, if the input or output vectors are highly correlated, marked departures from equal lesion effects can be obtained. Table 23.4 presents an example constructed by Wood (1978) to illustrate just how marked certain departures from equal effects can be.

In this example, input vectors f_1 and f_2 are distinguished from each other and from f_3 and f_4 by the activity of each of the eight input neurons. In comtrast, input vectors f_3 and f_4 are distinguished from each other only by Input Neurons 1 and 2 and are identical for Input Neurons 2–8. Therefore, as the confusion matrices at the bottom of Table 23.4 illustrate, lesions of Input Neurons 1 and 2 produce a disproportionately large and selective effect on performance relative to lesions of the other input neurons. This effect is selective in that it is limited to as-

---

[6]For the case of mutually orthogonal inputs, Wood (1978) stated that the deficit produced by a lesion of any neuron was "precisely equal" to that of any other neuron. This is incorrect, because it is possible to choose of set of input vectors that meet the global orthogonality criterion but in which the activity of one or more neurons is identical in different input vectors. Lesions including such neurons produce somewhat smaller deficits on average than lesions including neurons that are not redundant across input vectors.

TABLE 23.4
Input Vectors, Output Vectors, and Confusion Matrices Illustrating Localization of Function[a]

Input vectors				Output vectors			
f_1	f_2	f_3	f_4	f_1	f_2	f_3	f_4
−.196	−.229	.114	.912	1.000	−1.000	1.000	−1.000
.000	−.459	.912	.114	1.000	−1.000	−1.000	−1.000
−.196	.459	−.114	−.114	1.000	1.000	1.000	1.000
.392	.229	.228	.228	1.000	1.000	−1.000	1.000
.558	−.459	.114	.114	−1.000	−1.000	1.000	1.000
.558	.000	−.114	−.114	−1.000	−1.000	−1.000	1.000
−.196	−.229	−.114	−.114	−1.000	1.000	1.000	−1.000
−.196	.459	.228	.228	−1.000	1.000	−1.000	−1.000

Confusion matrices

Original output vectors	Computed output vectors for lesion of Input Neuron 1				Computed output vectors for lesion of Input Neuron 2			
	$\hat{g}_1$	$\hat{g}_2$	$\hat{g}_3$	$\hat{g}_4$	$\hat{g}_1$	$\hat{g}_2$	$\hat{g}_3$	$\hat{g}_4$
g_1	.943	−.299	.083	.276	.960	−.319	.209	−.087
g_2	−.309	.898	−.315	.081	−.259	.933	.163	−.127
g_3	.088	−.322	.914	.803	.064	.062	.526	.251
g_4	.088	.025	.241	.522	−.086	−.154	.809	.956

[a] From C. C. Wood (1978). Variations on a theme by Lashley: Lesion experiments on the neural model of Anderson, Silverstein, Ritz, and Jones. *Psychological Review*, 85(6), pp. 582–591. Copyright 1978 by The American Psychological Association. Reprinted by permission of the publisher and author.

sociations between $f_3 \rightarrow g_3$ and $f_4 \rightarrow g_4$; lesions of Input Neurons 1 and 2 produce minimal deficits for vectors $f_1 \rightarrow g_1$ and $f_2 \rightarrow g_2$. For the intact model, recognition performance for input vectors f_3 and f_4 was .89 and .92, respectively, whereas the corresponding values following a lesion of Input Neuron 1 were .91 and .52. In contrast, recognition performance for the same two input vectors was .53 and .96 following a lesion of Input Neuron 2. Table 23.4 also shows that confusion errors between input vectors f_3 and f_4 were significantly and selectively influenced by lesions of Input Neurons 1 and 2.

Examples such as the one in Table 23.4 can be generated ad infinitum and can be extended to include any number of neurons. For example, it is easy to see that a set of input vectors could be constructed so that lesions of, say, Input Neurons 3 and 4 would produce one highly selective effect, lesions of Input Neurons 5 and 6 would produce a different highly selective effect, and lesions of Input Neurons 1, 2, 7, and 8 would have roughly equivalent effects on performance. The important point, by way of summary, is that the pattern of performance deficit depends upon the mutual relationships between the input and output vectors. When the input vectors are orthogonal or nearly so, lesions of specific neurons have minimal selective effect on performance. However, when the input or output vectors can be distinguished by the activity of only a subset of the total population of neurons then highly selective deficits can be obtained. It should be emphasized that this conclusion applies regardless of the dimensionality of the model (i.e., the size of the input and output populations). Selective effects are less probable with models of larger dimensionality simply by virtue of the decreased likelihood of redundant sets of vectors of larger dimensions. However, highly selective effects can occur with a model of any dimensionality.

IMPLICATIONS FOR THE INTERPRETATION OF REAL LESION EXPERIMENTS

A Continuum of Lesion Effects from a Single Model

The lesion effects described in the preceding sections cover the entire continuum of those reported in real lesion experiments. At one end of the continuum are highly diffuse effects like those shown in Figures 23.2 and 23.4, in which removal of any individual neuron produces a roughly equivalent deficit to that of any other neuron and the magnitude of the deficit is roughly proportional to the total amount of tissue removed. As has already been noted, these results are similar to those from which Lashley derived the principles of "mass action" and "equipotentiality":

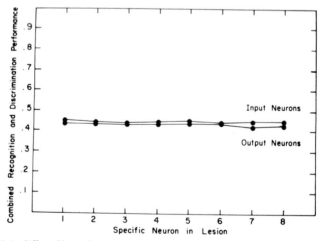

FIGURE 23.4. *Effect of lesion location on performance of the model, averaged over lesion size. From C. C. Wood (1978). Variations on a theme by Lashley: Lesion experiments on the neural model of Anderson, Silverstein, Ritz, and Jones. Psychological Review, 85(6), pp. 582–591. Copyright 1978 by The American Psychological Association. Reprinted by permission of the publisher and author.*

Equipotentiality of parts [is] the capacity to carry out, with or without reduction in efficiency, the functions which are lost by destruction of the whole. This capacity varies from one area to another and with the character of the functions involved. . . . Equipotentiality is not absolute but is subject to a law of mass action whereby the efficiency of performance of an entire complex function may be reduced in proportion to the extent of the brain injury within an area whose parts are not more specialized for one component of the function than for another [Lashley, 1929, p. 25].

At the other end of the continuum are highly selective effects in which removal of one neuron produced large deficits on one association and minimal effects on other associations. In fact, the results shown in Table 23.4 go beyond selective lesion effects to provide a clear example of the "double dissociation" result often interpreted as strong support for localization of function: "Genuine proof of specificity ('localization of function') always requires minimally some evidence of what Teuber has called 'double dissociation of symptoms' so that one lesion produces one set of symptoms and the other lesion another set [Eidelberg and Stein, 1974, p. 208]." Such selective effects should be compared to those obtained by Gordon (Chapter 24, this volume) using the feedback version of the Anderson, Silverstein, Ritz, and Jones model.

In light of this continuum of lesion effects produced by a single neural model, let us return now to the question with which we began: To what extent can the mechanisms of information processing and storage that are built into the model be unambiguously inferred from behavioral deficits following brain damage? The mechanisms of information processing and storage of the Anderson, Silverstein, Ritz, and Jones association model are stated clearly and concisely in Eqs. (1), (3), and (4), together with the assumption that every input neuron is synaptically connected to every output neuron. From these equations and the synaptic connectivity assumption, it is clear that the model's capacity to associate inputs with outputs is DISTRIBUTED throughout the entire structure of the model and is not limited to specific subregions. That is, each input and output neuron performs exactly the same elementary operations [Eq. (1)] on every input, and all neurons in the input and output populations perform those operations in every association. Moreover, each neuron operates on its inputs without regard to the operations of other neurons; and no individual neuron has global information about the activity of the output population as a whole. Rather, the output is determined by "a population of neurons, none of which has more than local information as to which way the system should behave [Arbib, 1981, p. 15]" (see also Pitts and McCulloch, 1947).

Given such a system in which association mechanisms are distributed, one might predict that systematic variations in lesion size and location should produce effects similar to "mass action" and "equipotentiality" in Lashley's terms. Increasingly large lesions should produce increasingly large deficits in performance, and lesions of any given neuron should produce roughly equivalent deficits to lesions of any other neuron. This is exactly the pattern of results shown in Figures 23.2–23.4. Thus, in this case the straightforward inference from lesion effect to conclusions about functional organization would be in reasonable accord with the mechanisms of information processing and storage built into the model.

Now consider the interpretation of the results in Table 23.4, which constitute a "double dissociation of symptoms" by Teuber's definition. If such a double dissociation were interpreted in the traditional manner, one would infer that association mechanisms of the model are highly localized. In the extreme, one might be tempted to conclude that the association of f_3 with g_3 is mediated solely by Input Neuron 2 and association of f_4 with g_4 is mediated solely by Input Neuron 1. Yet the mechanisms of association embodied in Eqs. (1), (3), (4), and the connectivity assumption have not changed. The difference between the results in Table 23.4 suggesting localization of function and those in Figures 23.2–23.4 suggesting "mass action" and "equipotentiality" is not the mechanisms of association in the model, but the specific patterns of activity being associated.[7]

An instructive exercise in this context is to think of the input and output neurons in the present model as receptors and effectors in a simple nervous system having no interneurons. Whether the effects of a given lesion appear to indicate that association mechanisms are distributed or localized depends upon the specific stimuli (i.e., input vectors) and specific responses (i.e., output vectors) being associated. For example, consider a lesion experiment using the numerical example in Table 23.4 in which the only task investigated is discrimination between input vectors f_4 and f_3. As noted earlier, a lesion of either Input Neuron 1 or 2 produces a large deficit in discrimination between these two input vectors, whereas lesions of Input Neurons 3–8 produce little or no decrement in performance. From these results, one might be tempted to conclude that association mechanisms are highly localized. However, if the experiment had tested discrimination between f_4 and f_1, a very different conclusion might have been reached. In this case, discrimination performance is only slightly decreased following lesions of any of the input neurons and one might conclude that association mechanisms are more distributed. In both cases, however, the model's response to input vector f_4 and the mechanisms of association of f_4 with g_4 are precisely identical. What differs in the two cases is the experimental context (in this case the alternative input and output vectors) in which the model's association of g_4 with g_4 is evaluated.

In summary, the fact that the entire continuum of empirical lesion effects can be obtained from this or any other model with no changes in structure of

[7]See Dean (1980) and Wood (1980) for additional discussion.

information processing mechanisms demonstrates a clear dissociation between the pattern of lesion deficits and underlying functional organization of the model. This dissociation poses an important difficulty for attempts to infer principles of functional organization from lesion data alone. A persistent and specific behavioral deficit following removal of a given brain region is often regarded as demonstrating that the region in question plays a specific functional role in the behavioral capacities that appear to be damaged following the lesion. Although such a conclusion may be correct, it does not necessarily follow from the data. As the simulated lesion results demonstrate, highly selective lesion effects can also be obtained in nervous systems in which each neural element participates in a wide range of functions, depending upon task requirements (and probably a host of other variables in more realistic models).

Distinguishing between Deficit and "Function" in the Interpretation of Lesion Data

The conclusion that principles of functional organization cannot be directly inferred from lesion data is certainly not new, although the simulated lesion results do provide a particularly clear illustration of certain aspects of the problem. Writing from the perspective of "The Brain as an Engineering Problem," Gregory (1961) posed the problem of lesion interpretation in the following way: "Suppose we ablated or stimulated various parts of a complex man-made device, say a television receiving set. And suppose we had no prior knowledge of the manner of function of the type of device or machine involved. Could we by these means discover its manner of working? [p. 320]." Gregory's analysis of this question led him to the following conclusion: "Stimulation and ablation experiments may give direct information about pathways and projection areas, but their interpretation would seem to be extremely difficult, on logical grounds, where a mechanism is one of many inter-related systems, for then changes in the output will not in general be simply the loss of the contribution normally made by the extirpated area. The system may now show quite different properties [p. 325]."

The fundamental distinction between the pattern of behavioral deficits produced by removal of a given region and the function(s) of that region in the normal operation of the brain as a whole has long been recognized yet is often ignored. In the context of human language function, Jackson (1874) wrote that "to locate the damage which destroys speech and to locate speech are two different things [p. 130]." Gregory puts the distinction this way:

> Although the effect of particular type of ablation may be specific and repeatable, it does not follow that the causal connection is simple, or even that the region of the brain affected would, if we knew more, be regarded as functionally important for the output . . . which is observed to be upset. It could be the case that some important part of the mechanisms subserving the

behavior is upset by the damage although it is most indirectly related, and it is just this which makes the discovery of a fault in a complex machine so difficult [1961, p. 323].

Von Ekardt Klein (1978) suggests that behavioral deficits produced by lesions should be interpreted in terms of a functional analysis of the *normal* behavioral capacity. Other discussions of the distinction appear in Glassman (1978) and Laurence and Stein (1978).

We have little difficulty making the distinction between deficit and functional role for peripheral parts of the nervous system whose functional roles are, relatively speaking, reasonably well understood. In this case failure to distinguish between deficit and function leads to obvious absurdities. For example, complete bilateral section of the optic nerves produces total loss of vision, yet few would conclude that the function of the optic nerves is "vision." The optic nerves obviously play an important role in vision, but that role is not identical to "vision" as a whole nor can the details of their functional role be deduced from the deficits caused by optic nerve section.

For regions of the nervous system not located near the periphery, we seem much more willing to make direct inferences from the pattern of deficit to hypothesized functional organization. At least three reasons can be cited for such willingness: (*a*) we know less from other data about the functions performed by central regions of the nervous system: (*b*) for central regions there are fewer obvious anatomical constraints of the type available for peripheral regions (e.g., all information from the retina to the brain travels via the optic nerves); and (*c*) the pattern of deficit following central lesions is usually more subtle and complex than for lesions near the periphery. In the content of this volume, Broca's area provides a particularly clear example of our willingness to equate functional role with pattern of behavioral deficit. Based on language production deficits following damage to the posterolateral portion of the left frontal lobe, Broca (1861) and subsequent workers proposed a model "that has had a tenacious hold on the minds of most students of aphasia ever since. According to this view, the third frontal gyrus... *contains the motor programs for speech* [Levine and Sweet, Chapter 14, this volume; my italics]." It is not difficult to find contemporary examples of such a model. For example, Geschwind (1979) writes: "Much new information has been added in the past 100 years, but the general principles Wernicke elaborated still seem valid. In this model the underlying structure of an utterance arises in Wernicke's area. It is then transferred through the arcuate fasciculus to Broca's area, where it evokes *a detailed and coordinated program for vocalization* [p. 187, my italics]." Similarly, Schnitzer (Chapter 12, this volume) discusses "evidence for considering Wernicke's area to be the site of... the semantic or linguistic predication function, and for considering Broca's area to be the *site of what I have been calling the 'housekeeping' function*" (my italics) (where 'housekeeping function' covers what are "traditionally called (surface) syntactic, morphological, and morphophonemic rules of constraints." These interpretations may very well be correct, but it should be understood that they are based upon the same relatively direct inference from deficit to function that seems so inappropriate in the optic nerve example just given.

Eidelberg and Stein (1974) and Gregory (1961) provide extreme examples of the failure to distinguish between deficit and function:

> A serious semantic stumbling block may lie in the lack of agreement between neurophysiologists and behavioral scientists on what is meant by "the function" of a particular neural system. The danger of circularity in operational definitions is nowhere more obvious, for if "the function" of a set of neurons is defined by the permanent deficit in performance that remains after its removal, the conclusion that true functional recovery may not occur is inescapable, because that was the hidden premise of the argument [Eidelberg and Stein, 1974, pp. 234–235].

"The removal of any of several widely spaced resistors may cause a radio set to emit howls, but it does not follow that howls are immediately associated with these resistors, or indeed that the causal relation is anything but the most indirect. In particular, we should not say that the function of the resistors in the normal circuit is to inhibit howling [Gregory, 1961, p. 323]."

Thus, the term "function" as used in the context of lesion data appears to have two distinct meanings which are often confused. The first is the function of a given brain region as it would be specified if we knew how the entire system worked. This type of specification is consistent with an engineering level description of how a system operates (cf. Gregory, 1961) and appears to be what many investigators have in mind by the term "functional organization" (cf., Cummins, 1975; Simon, 1969; Von Ekardt Klein, 1978; Wimsatt, 1974). The second meaning is the function of a given region defined in terms of behavioral deficits produced by its removal. To define "function" from the first perspective we need to know the global capacities and input–output relations of the system as a whole, the elementary functions or operations performed by individual components of the system, and the structural and functional relationships among individual components of the system that are the basis of the functions of the whole. Yet what we learn from lesion experiments is limited to whether or not removal or a given brain region produces reliable deficits in the behavior or behaviors tested.

Let us consider the two general outcomes of a lesion experiment in which the effects of one lesion on one behavior are assessed. If the lesion produces a reliable behavioral deficit, then we are justified in concluding only that the region is in some unspecified way INVOLVED in or related to the production of that behavior. This involvement could be direct, in the sense that if we knew how the brain worked as a whole we would attribute to that region an important causal role in the production of the behavior in question. However, as in Gregory's "howl inhibitor" example, the involvement could be very indirect and the observed deficits could be produced by a very circuitous route indeed. Finally, a lesion that produces a reliable behavioral deficit is sometimes said to demonstrate that the damaged tissue is NECESSARY for normal production of the behavior. This conclusion is correct as far as it goes, but it should be viewed as tentative because a very different conclusion would be drawn if additional lesions are found to alter or eliminate the deficit (e.g., Sherman, 1974; Sprague, 1966).

Alternatively, if a lesion produces no detectable deficit in the behaviors assessed, we cannot conclude that the region plays no functional role in those behaviors. The issue here is more than concluding in favor of the null hypothesis, although that problem is involved as well. The fact that a given lesion produces no detectable behavior effect is evidence only that the region is NOT NECESSARY for production of that behavior and that remaining intact regions are SUFFICENT; it does not demonstrate that the region is uninvolved. The simulated lesion results described earlier provide a clear example of this situation. Some lesions produced little effect on the association between a given input vector and a given output vector (see Table 23.4), even though at the level of "how the system works" [i.e., Eqs. (1), (3), (4), and the connectivity assumption] every neuron participates in every memory.

In summary, I have attempted to distinguish between two different ways in which the term function is used in the context of lesion data—the first defined in terms of complete knowledge of how a complex system works, and the second defined in terms of performance deficits of the system following damage to its parts. If function is defined in the second of these two senses we run the risk of making two types of interpretive errors: (a) attributing direct involvement of a given brain region in a particular behavioral capacity when its involvement is in fact indirect; and (b) failing to detect the involvement of a region whose contribution is clear if the functional organization of the system is known but which shows little or no detectable lesion effect. The latter error is powerfully illustrated by the simulated lesion results in which removal of one or more neurons produces little or no disruption in association performance.

Systematic lesion experiments are important, in my opinion, but not because they provide a direct or unambiguous means of inferring the functional role of the brain structures damaged. Rather, the results of lesion experiments should be viewed as: (a) providing one of many types of available evidence from which theories about the functional organization of the brain may be formulated (no one of which is conclusive); and (b) providing a particularly stringent criterion by which any such theory may be judged.

REFERENCES

Anderson, J. A. (1972). A simple neural network generating an interactive memory. *Mathematical Biosciences, 14,* 197–220.

Anderson, J. A. (1973). A theory for the recognition of items from short memorized lists. *Psychological Review, 80,* 417–438.

Anderson, J. A. (1977). Neural models with cognitive implications. In D. LaBerge and S. J. Samuels (Eds.), *Basic processes in reading: Perception and comprehension.* Hillsdale, N.J.: Lawrence Erlbaum, 1977.

Anderson, J. A., Silverstein, J. W., and Ritz, S. A. (In press). Vowel pre-processing with a neurally based model. In *Conference Record: 1977 I.E.E.E. International Conference on Acoustics, Speech, and Signal Processing.*

Anderson, J. A., Silverstein, J. W., Ritz, S. A., and Jones, R. S. (1977). Distinctive features, categorical perception, and probability learning: Some applications of a neural model. *Psychological Review, 84,* 413–451.

Arbib, M. A. (1972). *The metaphorical brain: An introduction to cybernetics as artificial intelligence and brain theory.* New York: Interscience.

Arbib, M. A. (1981). Perceptual structures and distributed motor control. In V. B. Brooks (Ed.), *Handbook of physiology, Vol. 3: Motor control.* Bethesda, Md.: American Physiological Society.

Arbib, M. A., and Caplan, D. (1979) Neurolinguistics must be computational. *The Behavioral and Brain Sciences, 2,* 449–483.

Boring, E. G. (1950). *A history of experimental psychology.* New York: Appleton-Century-Crofts.

Broca, P. (1861). Remarques sur le siège de la faculté du language articulé, suives d'une observations d'aphémie (perte de la parole). *Bulletins de la Societe Anatomique de Paris,* Vol. 6., 36, 330–357.

Cooper, L. N., Liberman, F., and Oja, E. (1979). A theory for the acquisition and loss of neuron specificity in visual cortex. *Biological Cybernetics, 33,* 9–28.

Cummins, R. (1975) Functional analysis. *Journal of Philosophy, 72,* reprinted in N. Block (Ed.), *Readings in the Philosophy of Psychology Vol. I,* Cambridge, Harvard University Press.

Dean, P. (1980). Recapitulation of a theme by Lashley? Comment on Wood's simulated-lesion experiment. *Psychological Review, 87,* 470–473.

Dial, W. G., Feeney, D. M., Murray, H. M., Linn, R. T., and Boyeson, M. G. (1981) Responses of cortical injury: II. Widespread depression of the activity of an ensyme in cortex remote from a focal injury. *Brain Research, 211,* 79–89.

Eidelberg, E., and Stein, D. G. (1974). Functional recovery after lesions of the nervous system. *Neurosciences Research Program Bulletin, 12,* 191–303.

Erikson, R. P. (1974). Parallel "population" neural coding in feature extraction. In F. O. Schmitt and F. G. Worden (Eds.), *The neurosciences: Third study program.* Cambridge, Mass.: MIT Press.

Ferrier, D. (1876). *The functions of the brain.* London: Smith Elder.

Finger, S. (1978) *Recovery from brain damage: research and theory.* New York, Plenum.

Flourens, P. (1824). *Recherches expérimentales sur les propriétés et les fonctions du système nerveux dans les animaux vertébrés.* Paris.

Flourens, P. (1825). *Expériences sur le système nerveux.* Paris.

Franz, S. I. (1902). On the functions of the cerebrum, I: The frontal lobes in relation to the production and retention of simple sensory-motor habits. *American Journal of Physiology, 8,* 1–22.

Freeman, W. J. (1975). *Mass action in the nervous system.* New York: Academic Press.

Geschwind, N. (1974). *Selected papers on language and the brain.* New York: Reidel.

Geschwind, N. (1979). Specializations of the human brain. *Scientific American, 241,* 180–199.

Glassman, R. B. (1978) The logic of the lesion experiment and its role in the neural sciences. In S. Finger (Ed.) *Recovery from brain damage: Research and Theory.* New York, Plenum.

Goltz, F. (1881). *Ueber die Verrichtungen des Grosshirns.* Bonn: Strauss.

Gregory, R. L. (1961). The brain as an enginerring problem. In W. H. Thorpe and O. L. Zangwill (Eds.), *Current problems in animal behavior.* Cambridge: Cambridge University Press.

Grossberg, S. (1976a). Adaptive pattern classification and universal recoding, I: Parallel development and coding of neural feature detectors. *Biological Cybernetics, 23,* 121–134.

Grossberg, S. (1976b). Adaptive pattern classification and universal recoding, II: Feedback, expectation, olfaction, illusions. *Biological Cybernetics, 23,* 187–202.

Head, H. (1963). *Aphasia and kindred disorders of speech.* New York: Hafner.

Hebb, D. O. (1949). *The organization of behavior.* New York: Wiley.

Jackson, J. H. (1874). On the nature of the duality of the brain. *Medical Press and Circular, 1,* 19–63, reprinted in J. Taylor (Ed.), *Selected Writings of John Hughling Jackson, Vol. 2,* London, Staples Press, 1973, pp. 129–145.

Kohonen, T. (1972). Correlation matrix memories. *I.E.E.E. Transactions on Computers,* C-21, 353–359.

Kohonen, T. (1977). *Associative memory: A system-theoretic approach.* Berlin: Springer-Verlag.

Kohonen, T., Lehtio, P., Rovamo, J., Hyvarinen, J., Bry, K., and Vainio, L. (1977). A principle of neural associative memory. *Neuroscience, 2,* 1065–1076.

Lashley, K. S. (1929). *Brain mechanisms in intelligence.* Chicago: University of Chicago Press.

Lashley, K. S. (1933). Integrative functions of the cerebral cortex. *Physiological Review, 13,* 1–42.

Lashley, K. S. (1950). In search of the engram. In *Symposia of the society for experimental biology* (No. IV). Cambridge: Cambridge University Press.

Lashley, K. S., and Wiley, L. E. (1933). Studies of cerebral function in learing, IX: Mass action in relation to the number of elements in the problem to be learned. *Journal of Comparative Neurology, 57,* 3–56.

Laurence, S., and Stein, D. G. (1978) Recovery after brain damage and the concept of localization of function. In S. Finger (Ed.) *Recover from brain damage: Research and Theory.* New York, Plenum.

LeVere, T. E. (1975). Neural stability, sparing, and behavioral recovery following brain damage. *Psychological Review, 82,* 344–358.

Levy, W. B., and Steward, O. (1979) Synapses as associative memory elements in the hippocampal formation. *Brain Research, 175,* 233–245.

Little, W. A., and Shaw, G. (1975). A statistical theory of short and long term memory. *Behavioral Biology, 14,* 115–133.

Luria, A. R. (1973). *The working brain.* Hammondsworth, England: Penguin.

Marr, D., and Poggio, T. (1977). Cooperative computation of stereo disparity. *Science, 194,* 283–287.

McClelland, J. L. (1979). On the time relations of mental processes: An examination of systems of processes in cascade. *Psychological Review, 86,* 287–330.

Mosteller, F. R., and Rourke, R. E. (1973). *Sturdy statistics: Nonparametric and order statistics.* Reading, Mass.: Addison-Wesley.

Mountcastle, V. B. (1978). An organizing principle for cerebral function: The unit module and the distributed system. In G. M. Edelman and V. B. Mountcastle (Eds.), *The mindful brain.* Cambridge, Mass.: MIT Press.

Munk, H. (1881). *Uber die Funktionen der Grosshirnrinde.* Berlin: Hirschwald.

Nass, M. M., and Cooper, L. N. (1975). A theory for the development of feature detecting cells in visual cortex. *Biological Cybernetics, 19,* 1–18.

Palm, G. (1980) On associative memory. *Biological Cybernetics, 36,* 19–31.

Pitts, W. H., and McCulloch, W. S. (1977). How we know universals, the perception of auditory and visual forms. *Bulletin of Mathematical Biophysics, 9,* 127–147.

Pribram, K. H., Nuwer, M., and Baron, R. J. (1974). The holographic hypothesis of memory structure in brain function and perception. In D. H. Krantz, R. D. Luce, R. C. Atkinson, and

P. Suppes (Eds.), *Contemporary developments in mathematical psychology, Vol. 2: Measurement, psychophysics, and neural information processing*. San Francisco: W. H. Freeman.

Roney, K. J., and Shaw, G. L. (1978). Assemblies of neurons in brain function and memory—theory and experiment. *Neuroscience Abstracts, 4*, 262.

Rosner, B. S. (1970). Brain functions. In D. Mussen and M. Rosenzweig (Eds.), *Annual Review of Psychology*. Palo Alto, Ca.: Annual Reviews.

Rosner, B. S. (1974). Recovery of function and localization of function in historical perspective. In D. G. Stein, J. J. Rosen, and N. Butters (Eds.), *Plasticity and recovery of function in the nervous system*. New York: Academic Press.

Schoenfeld, T. A., and Hamilton, L. W. (1977) Secondary brain changes following lesions: a new paradigm for lesion experimentation. *Physiology and Behavior, 18*, 951–967.

Shaw, G. L. (1978). Space–time correlations of neuronal firing related to memory storage capacity. *Brain Research Bulletin, 3*, 107–113.

Sherman, S. M. (1974). Monocularly deprived cats: Improvement of the deprived eye's vision by visual decortication. *Science, 186*, 267–269.

Sidman, R. L., and LaVail, J. (1974). Biology of the regenerating neuron. *Neuroscience Research Program Bulletin, 12*, 191–303.

Simon, H. (1969) The architecture of complexity. In *The Sciences of the Artificial*, Cambridge, MIT Press.

Sprague, J. M. (1966). Interaction of cortex and superior colliculus in mediation of visually guided behavior in the cat. *Science, 153*, 1544–1547.

Stent, G. S. (1973). A physiological mechanism for Hebb's postulate of learning. *Proceedings of the National Academy of Sciences, 70*, 997–1001.

Szentagothai, J. (1978). The neuron network of the cerebral cortex: A functional interpretation. *Proceedings of the Royal Society London B, 201*, 219–248.

Szentagothai, J., and Arbib, M. A. (1974). Conceptual models of neural organization. *Neuroscience Research Program Bulletin, 12*, 307–510.

Uttal, W. R. (1978). *The psychobiology of mind*. Hillsdale, N.J.: Lawrence Erlbaum.

Von Ekardt Kelin, B. (1978). Inferring functional localization from neurological evidence. In E. Walker (Ed.), *The biology of language*. Montgomery, Bradford Books.

von Monakow, C. (1914). *Die Lokalisation im Grosshirn und der Abbau der Funktion durch kortikale Herde*. Wiesbaden, Germany: Bergmann.

Willshaw, D. J., Buneman, O. P., and Longuet-Higgins, H. C. (1969). Non-holographic associative memory. *Nature, 22*, 960–962.

Wimsatt, W. C. (1974) Complexity and organization. In K. F. Schaffner and R. S. Cohen (Eds.) *PSA 1972*. Dordrecht, Holland, Reidel.

Wood, C. C. (1978). Variations on a theme by Lashley: Lesion experiments on the neural model of Anderson, Silverstein, Ritz, and Jones. *Psychological Review, 85*, 582–591.

Wood, C. C. (1980). Interpretation of real and simulated lesion experiments. *Psychological Review, 87*, 474–476.

24

Confrontation Naming: Computational Model and Disconnection Simulation

Barry Gordon

This chapter will present a qualitative model of confrontation naming cast in a neural modeling framework, along with a quantitative simulation of the model's performance after pure disconnection lesions. Confrontation naming is a reasonable target for such modeling and simulation, partly because it is widely used as a neurolinguistic task, and partly because at least some of its constituent processes probably have a role in other psycholinguistic functions, such as lexical retrieval. Additionally, its mechanisms are probably simple enough so that cognitive psychology and neurophysiology can be used as guides to the modeling effort.

One of this chapter's specific goals is to address some of the provocative criticisms Marshall (1980) and others have raised against many neurolinguistic models. As it is therefore important to make both model and modeling motivations as lucid as possible, I will briefly present the stepwise construction and justification of the qualitative model and of its simulation.

QUALITATIVE MODEL OUTLINE

A guiding principle has been to construct the qualitative model from evidence and hypotheses that are as well established as possible, even if the immediate results at first seem to be too general to be useful. On this basis, we can differentiate the naming task into several functional stages [see, for example, Ross (cited by James, 1890, pg. 57), Kussmaul (1877), Lichtheim (1885), Heilman, Tucker, and Valenstein (1976), Geschwind (1967), and Benson (1979)], as represented in Figure 24.1:

(1) Input processing is done by independent, modality-specific recognition stages. These potentially can function in isolation, but normally they convey information to (2) an intermediate, modality-nonspecific common stage. So long

511

NEURAL MODELS OF
LANGUAGE PROCESSES

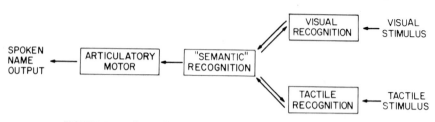

FIGURE 24.1. *Stages for confrontation naming assumed by the model.*

as this stage remains both common and nonspecific, most of our simulation results will be unaffected by whatever label we choose to give it. However, I have called it "semantic" because this metaphoric label is both heuristically useful and reasonably accurate (cf. Coughlan and Warrington, 1978; Goodglass, Barton and Kaplan, 1968). This intermediate stage in turn drives (3) a final articulatory motor output stage.

I have deliberately left out direct input-stage to motor-output connections on grounds of parsimony, even though they have appeared in a number of classical schemes (e.g., Lichtheim, 1885), and even though they can be readily justified in other contexts; they simply proved unnecessary here.

In additional to the forwards connections between the stages, there are reasons for assuming that information can be communicated from the common stage to the modality-specific ones. The best of these reasons are psychological: Intuition (Benson, 1979, p. 323), theory (Finke, 1980; Kosslyn, 1978, p. 252), and some experimental evidence (e.g., Posner, 1978, p. 51) all suggest that a "perceptual" representation can be generated internally. And although there is no direct anatomical evidence to verify this assumption, it seems reasonable to suppose that the extreme connectivity of the brain permits such information flow.

Beyond just functional independence, the classical neuropsychological data also support a low-resolution anatomical separability of the perceptual and motor stages, which is probably true of some crucial aspect of "semantic" processing as well (see Coughlan and Warrington, 1978). In keeping with the principle stated earlier, our model will have these separate functions subserved by separate neural networks. This is a first approximation; both stronger and weaker claims for anatomic isolatability can be argued.

PROCESSING DYNAMICS

Although we now have a model outline, the clinical and other evidence on which this outline is based says very little about the dynamics of representation and processing within and between these stages (see Arbib and Caplin, 1979). It becomes both necessary and appropriate, then, to sketch in these details by analogy with simple recognition and response tasks which have been extensively studied in experimental psychology. For such tasks, there is abundant evidence that within-stage item recognition is not fully achieved all at once. Rather, representation strength begins at some quasi-zero value, and grows over a period of many tens to several hundreds of milliseconds to ultimately reach an asymptote (McClelland, 1979; Wickelgren, 1977).

The stages involved in confrontation naming are probably in **cascade** (McClelland, 1979): Between-stage information transfer is probably rapid compared to the slow tempo of information growth within a stage. This assumption can be justified on a number of grounds. First, the potential pathways between the areas that might participate in naming are oligosynaptic, so the "functional cerebral distance" (Kinsbourne, 1979) between them is probably small. More convincing—albeit still indirect—support for this possibility comes from psychological tasks of equivalent (or greater) complexity, which Wickelgren (1976), Ericksen and Schultz (1979), McClelland (1979), and McClelland and Rumelhart (1980) have reviewed in the context of their own concerns. We will not depend upon cascading in much of what follows, or will only require a weak form of this hypothesis in predicting the temporal course of system behavior and feedback effects. However, cascading is a natural consequence of the assumptions made here, and it will have to be given more consideration in the future.

NEURAL BASIS

To translate this outline into a neural language, I shall draw upon neurophysiology and neural modeling.

What neurophysiologic evidence relates to this point generally implies that the internal representation of items is distributed over many cells and synapses; item recognition corresponds to the development of relatively distinct spatiotemporal patterns of activity (e.g., Mountcastle, 1978). With this formulation, it is possible to characterize within-stage item recognition as the development of a pattern of activity within that stage which has been associated with that external stimulus in the past (cf. Anderson, Silverstein, Ritz, and Jones, 1977; Cavanagh, 1976; Liepa, 1977; Murdock, 1979). This is advantageous because measures of neural pattern match fitness, and of choice alternatives, can be readily equated with psychologic indices of strength describing more macroscopic behavior (cf. discussions by Lappin, 1978, pp. 157ff.; Townsend and Ashby, 1978, pp. 201ff.). Moreover, these kinds of neural models can have the dynamics that the psychologic evidence requires: a growth of patterns of desired activity (macrostates) out of initially less organized neuronal microactivity (cf. Amari, 1977a,b; Anderson, Silverstein, Ritz, and Jones, 1977; Freeman, 1979; Grossberg, 1977; Little, 1974; Sejnowski, 1976a,b).

Together, these considerations constitute a reasonably well-specified outline of a neural model of confrontation naming: individual neuronal recognition networks in immediate and continuous communication with each other, whose lingua franca takes the form of distributed patterns of activity. As a system that is both locally and globally cooperative (Arbib, 1975; Marr and Poggio, 1976), it is potentially capable of a rich repertoire of behaviors. I will focus now on showing how the model can account for some existing confrontation-naming data as strict "disconnection" effects. In doing so, I hope to demonstrate that much of the otherwise puzzling behavior of patients with partial disconnections—puzzling enough so that some interpretations have assumed additional damage must be responsible—can be explained by mechanisms derived from our general principles: the interaction of partial disruptions of between-stage information flow with the nature of intrastage processing. Actually, the explanations given will only touch the surface of a few of the powerful mechanisms generated by these deceptively simple postulates. This reserve power represents one of the strengths of the present approach.

I do not intend to give the impression that these mechanisms are the only ones that can explain such data; rather, I simply wish to show how relatively general principles can lead to such specific explanations. In fact, one conclusion I would like to draw from this work is that even generally accepted principles can allow a plurality of explanatory possibilities.

I will present a fairly detailed quantitative simulation of the qualitative model in order to illustrate its principles and to demonstrate its application to some of the confrontation naming data. The simulation should not be misconstrued as the general model itself or as the basis for a full-scale working model. It is only intended to capture some of the general principles I have developed and show how they might work together to give a post hoc explanation of some aspects of the data. In what follows, I will discuss this data in detail, together with its qualitative and simulated explanation.

ASSUMPTIONS FOR SIMULATION

Simulating the model necessitated a number of specific assumptions, often with unpredictable and sometimes undesirable consequences. I will present the bulk of these assumptions, again in an effort to make the modeling explicit; moreover, some of these choices have additional importance as they highlight the kinds of options that may be available to the brain as well.

A number of computational models can have the properties required for single-stage processing (cf. the literature cited earlier), but at our level of specificity none is more likely to be correct than another. I have therefore adapted the neural network models developed by Anderson and his colleagues (Anderson, 1977; Anderson and Silverstein, 1978; Anderson, Silverstein, Ritz, and Jones,

1977) as the basis for implementation, as they are comparatively transparent and have been exhaustively studied.

The Anderson, Silverstein, Ritz, and Jones' models represent a neuron as a simple linear integrator, summing weighted synaptic inputs into a number which corresponds to neuronal firing frequency. This axonal activity can then serve as the input to other neurons. Anderson, Silverstein, Ritz, and Jones constructed two types of networks from this neuronal representation. In their **associational** network, each input axon is connected to every neuron of the network (see Figure 24.2). With adjustments of the synaptic weights, this network can be taught to generate specific output patterns when presented with specific input ones. Wood (Chapter 23, this volume) elaborates on the mechanisms and properties of this associational model.

The Anderson, Silverstein, Ritz, and Jones' **feedback** network more explicitly allows for the temporal dimension of neuronal processing. In the feedback model, each input axon terminates on only a single neuron, but output from each neuron is fed back onto all the neurons in the network, including itself (see Figure 24.2). Processing through the feedback network proceeds in discrete

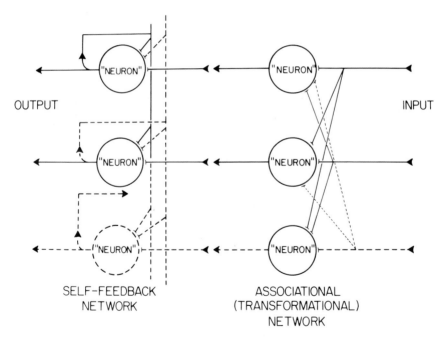

FIGURE 24.2. *"Neuronal" mechanisms of a single simulation stage. Three neurons of the associational and self-feedback substages are represented; each substage in the simulation acutally used sixteen. In the simulation, disconnections, if present, affect only the "external" input or output of these stages; the internal connections and "neurons" shown in this figure are never affected.*

steps: The input pattern of activity is transiently imposed on the network and immediately added to the pattern it engenders via the feedback synaptic weights to produce a new pattern. In both the Anderson, Silverstein, Ritz, and Jones' (p. 426) simulation and our own, this whole process is defined to take one quantum of "neural time." In the next time quantum, the new pattern is summated with a version of itself as modulated by the synaptic weights to produce yet another pattern, and so on. To prevent an explosive growth of neural activity because of the strong positive feedback this model uses, Anderson, Silverstein, Ritz, and Jones (p. 427) impose a saturation limit on individual neural activity. The overall result is a network that "recognizes" patterns it has been taught through modification of its synaptic weights (patterns which we will call "prototypical" for reasons to be explained), by reproducing these input patterns in its own pattern of activity after one iteration.

Other input patterns may evoke one of the learned patterns after a variable number of iterations. These more or less easily recognized patterns are classified as similar (in the network's view) to the patterns it was initially taught (Anderson, Silverstein, Ritz, and Jones, 1977, pp. 403ff.; Anderson and Silverstein, 1978). Correspondingly, if a presented pattern does not induce any identifiable pattern despite many feedback cycles, the network is indicating that the pattern is unlike any it was taught; the pattern is not recognized.

In our simulation, "items" and their internal codes are 16-component column vectors representing neural activity patterns. In order to achieve the behavior we desire from a single stage, each of the simulation stages is formed from an Anderson, Silverstein, Ritz, and Jones 16-neuron associational network coupled with a 16-neuron feedback network (see Figure 24.2). The associational substage is necessary to interconvert the codes of the different stages, as there is no reason to presume that they are the same. The feedback substage is employed (along with degraded input; see p. 517) to give an approximation of the slow temporal evolution of intrinsic activity into the desired pattern (recognition; cf. Anderson and Silverstein, 1978) earlier argued for. (This hybridization would not have been necessary with some of the other neural models cited. Also, there are other ways the temporal evolution of activity could have been achieved, as Wood [1980, personal communication] has suggested, which would have probably resulted in a simpler intrastage structure. But, given that subsequent lesioning would not affect the stages themselves, for present purposes modeling overall stage dynamics was more important than the specifics of intrastage structure.)

Figure 24.3 is presented as an overview of how these stages are interconnected for the simulation, following the specifications of the qualitative stages model of confrontation naming. The reader should beware of a terminological problem: The feedback networks (with the self-loop structure shown on the left of Figure 24.2) are NOT on the feedback paths. The "backwards networks" on these paths are all associational networks (of the kind shown on the right of Figure 24.2).

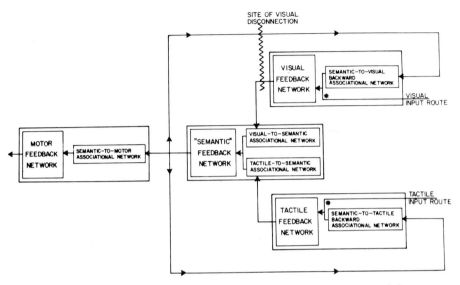

FIGURE 24.3. *Simulated system for confrontation naming: stage interconnections and disconnection sites. For convenience, "external" inputs to the modality-specific stages are presented directly to the feedback substage, instead of going through an associational substage; they are assumed to already be in the desired code. The location of a simulated "visual" disconnection (partial or complete) is indicated; "tactile" disconnections are in a homologous position. At points marked by a "*" the relative weights of the summating inputs were modified for different situations (see text).*

To learn a single "item," each of the four different feedback substages (which are NOT on feedback paths) was taught a different orthogonal vector "prototype" (drawn from a total of 16), and the five associational substages (which are all on intermodality pathways, two of which are feedback paths) were taught to link appropriate patterns with each other. In this manner, for example, a prototypical pattern of activity in the "visual" network would induce a (different) prototypical pattern in the "semantic" network. Associated patterns were considered different aspects of the same "object" (its visual representation, articulatory motor code, and so forth). The system was taught in this fashion how to name four such objects, prior to each simulation run. The steady-state representations of the intact network after presentation of a typical "visual" item are shown in Figure 24.4.

To make each simulated stage's activity grow over time, as we postulate it does in an actual stage, the stimulus items are nonprototypical vectors, specifically selected to be "recognizable" (in the manner discussed earlier) by the modality-specific stage as equivalent to the learned prototypical vectors (cf. Anderson and Silverstein, 1978). They can be thought of as degraded representatives of the original prototypical forms. When these inputs are presented to a

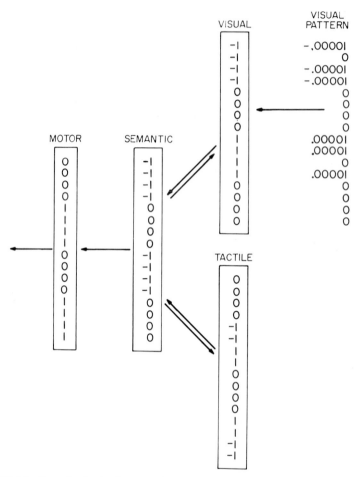

FIGURE 24.4. *Example of a simulation result (compare Row 1 of Table 24.1). A visual pattern has been presented to the undamaged system, and the asymptotic activity patterns of the self-feedback substages are shown. The visual pattern has been successfully recognized and named. Following the conventions of Table 24.1, these activity patterns might be metaphorically identified as the retinal, central visual, central tactile, semantic, and articulatory motor neural representations of a "chair."*

stage, the output of the associational substage is likewise imperfect, and the feedback substage must iteratively find the prestored pattern with the closest match possible (cf. Anderson and Silverstein, 1978). Subsequent stages will show similar temporal behavior, as they receive the activity of the preceeding stage's feedback substage, no matter how unfinalized. The criterion for pattern recognition success within a stage is simply that it achieve a prototypical pattern it was taught.

The general model permits different stages to have different intrinsic processing times; within a stage, items may differ in their "strengths" (eigenvalues; see Anderson, Silverstein, Ritz, and Jones, 1977, pp. 436ff.) and processing dynamics. In the absence of experimental guidelines for estimating these parameters, I have allowed for flexibility within certain limits in the simulation: Stages have a uniform amount of self-feedback, but this is adjustable as necessary; item "strengths" can be set globally or individually. Item processing times (machine iterations) are dependent upon these two parameters and upon interstage feedback.

The interconnections between the stages are made in accord with the qualitative model's principles. Thus I assume, in keeping with our earlier speculations, that appropriate feedback from the common "semantic" stage to the "tactile" and "visual" input ones induces the same representation as would have been produced by the appropriate stimulus to the input stage itself. This is what the associational networks on the feedback paths are taught. This implies, for example, that in the quantitative model, the "visual" representation produced by feedback from the "semantic" stage is (ideally) identical to the one generated by "visually" presenting the item itself.

The qualitative model does not necessarily specify how tightly interconnected the different stages must be; the feedforward contributions (such as the joint "tactile" and "visual" input to the "semantic" stage) have been made equal in strength, but the balance of "perceptual" and feedback activity to an input stage remains adjustable.

The qualitative model allows small interstage transmission and conversion times. In the computer simulation, there is no delay between stages; interstage communication occurs within one iteration.

In the qualitative cascade model, there is a smooth, continuous interplay of (developing) stage activity with information being received from the other stages. In our simulation, however, because the feedback substage might be discontinuously "reset" by new input activity, single-stage transitions might be abrupt, and the interplay is then less a function of a single stage than of the system as a whole.

LESIONING

The lesioning methodology utilized is derived from Wood's (1978 and Chapter 23, this volume) work. His demonstration of the consequences of lesions in an Anderson *et al.* associative network can be easily generalized to intrastage lesions within the present model. I therefore studied pure disconnection lesions which disrupt only interstage communication, and which leave the stages themselves (as well as their self-feedback pathways) intact. To do this, each neuron's interstage efferents were mathematically gathered up into a single "axon," and these axons were lesioned prior to branching (see Figure 24.5a). A disconnection lesion was simulated by "cutting" a variable number of these interstage efferents [note that Wood (1978; Chapter 23, this volume) lesioned the neurons themselves]. "Complete" disconnections disrupt interstage transmission from every neuron; for "partial" disconnections, a variable number (usually 25–75%) of the 16 forward axons (and 16 backward axons; see p. 525) were semirandomly disabled mathematically (Figure 24.5a).

To simulate the desired disconnection behavior, various lesions were tried until one was found to be sufficient; this often required concomitant manipulation of item "strengths" and network feedback coefficients, as has been mentioned. No attempt was made to explore fully any single set of such parameters; it is possible that one set might have been sufficient to give the full range of performance needed. But even if it were not overly optimistic to expect a static collection of 144 simple elements to duplicate all human naming behavior, it

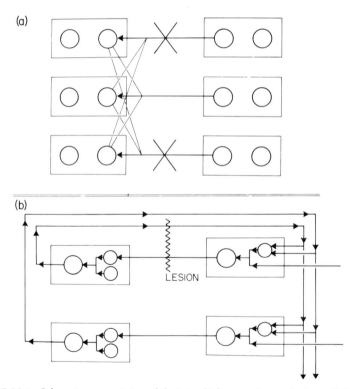

FIGURE 24.5. *Schematic representation of the "visual" disconnection at the "neural" level in the simulation: (a) Partial disconnection (only forwards connections illustrated for clarity); (b) In the simulation, interruption of any single forwards connection also implied lesioning of that neuron's "most direct" interstage feedback connection, as illustrated (see text).*

seemed pointless to try, because of the lack of experimental justification for any particular parameters. It should be apparent, however, that these same parameters will be important experimental constraints when their equivalents in the qualitative model are evaluated in the future. What is impressive is that the model's principles are sufficient enough so that these parametric adjustments ARE capable of making such a simple model yield such realistic behavior.

MODEL RESULTS

Some of the predicted implications of the qualitative model, and the results with the quantitative one, are presented in Table 24.1, along with suggestions as to how they may correspond to actual syndromes. Table 24.1 also presents the activity in intermediate stages, as well as an illustration of the time (network iterations) it took each stage to achieve that asymptotic activity. For clarity, the different orthogonal activity patterns associated together in teaching the networks an "object" have been given the same label.

The completely intact network (Row 1 in 24.1) responds with the correct name to a visually presented item after a finite time interval, as is appropriate.

Complete or nearly complete disruption of the connections between an input stage and the central stage obviously reproduces many of the features of the classical modality-specific naming disorders with modality-intact recognition (e.g., "optic aphasia"—Lhermitte and Beauvois, 1973; "tactile aphasia"—Beauvois, Saillant, Meininger, and Lhermitte, 1978; and "auditory modality specific anomia"—Denes and Semenza, 1975). When the visual stage has been completely disconnected from the rest of the network (Row 2), it still shows recognition of the presented item (but, of course, no recognition is shown by other stages). But visual recognition does take longer than normal, even without direct damage to the stage itself, because it cannot access information about the item which is stored in the other stages.

For partial disconnections, the qualitative model predicts that recognition and naming from subsequent stages may well be slower than normal, even though still correct, as information is being degraded in transmission; this is frequently observed in actual pathology (e.g., Beauvois, Saillant, Meininger, and Lhermitte, 1978), and was sometimes true in the simulation as well (although not illustrated in Table 24.1). With more extreme disconnection and interference, it is conceivable that such networks could require many seconds and a combination of internal and external (auditory) feedback to converge upon the correct answer; compare the behavior of Lhermitte and Beauvois's (1973) patient. In the same manner, multimodal input to a damaged system might add a critically necessary amount of redundancy, even though its contribution may not be apparent when the system is intact; this is a common clinical observation.

TABLE 24.1
Computer Simulation Results[a]

Input route and vector name	Disconnection location and type	Asymptotic recognition				Suggested analogous behavior
		Peripheral tactile	Peripheral visual	Semantic	Motor output	
1. Visual–chair	None		chair $T=4$	chair $T=6$	"chair" $T=6$	Normal
2. Visual–chair	Complete visual		chair $T=5$	$\emptyset$	(no name)	"Optic aphasia"
3a. Tactile–sandpaper ("poor visual" representation)	Partial tactile	sandpaper $T=8$		$\emptyset$	(no name)	"Tactile aphasia"— patient of Beauvois et al. (1978)
3b. Tactile–broom ("good visual" representation)	Partial tactile	broom $T=3$	broom $T=5$	broom $T=5$	"broom" $T=5$	
4. Visual–tree	Partial visual		tree $T=4$	house $T=5$	"house" $T=5$	Compare patient of Marin and Saffran (1975) with "pathologic verbal dominance"
5a. Visual–comb	Partial visual	(???)	comb $T=6$	(???)	(no name)	Undirectional dis- connection (Mohr, 1976)
5b. Tactile–comb	Partial visual	comb $T=3$	comb $T=5$	comb $T=5$	"comb" $T=5$	
5c. Visual–brush	Partial visual	brush $T=5$	brush $T=3$	brush $T=5$	"brush" $T=5$	

5d. Tactile–brush	Partial visual	brush $T = 3$	(???)	brush $T = 5$	"brush" $T = 5$	Semantic representation and name response available before item fully recognized
6. Degraded stimulus: visual–spoon	None		(???)	spoon $T = 20$	"spoon" $T = 20$	visual recognition and motor naming accomplished before semantic recognition achieved (cf. Heilman et al., 1976)
7. Degraded stimulus: visual–butter	None		butter $T = 20$	(???)	"butter" $T = 20$	
8a. Visual–pen	None		glass $T = 3$	glass $T = 3$	"glass" $T = 3$	
8b. Visual–pen	Complete		pen $T = 4$			misperceptions

[a] Stages have been given their labels for the reasons mentioned in the text. The activity patterns within these stages have been identified with "names" for convenience. Input vectors are named according to the prototypical activity pattern they induced in the isolated peripheral stage; vector patterns in other stages are given the same name if they have been associated together in teaching the networks. As explained in the text, different runs generally were done with different model parameters, with the exception of runs 1, 2, and 5, which were done with the same coefficients. $T =$ an illustrative value of the number of machine iterations required to reach a stage's asymptotic response, a measure of "recognition time." For clarity, these are not actual run times (which varied widely), but adjusted relative values; (???) = no clear representation was in evidence at this stage, even though others had reached their asymptotic limits; $\emptyset$ = no activity present at all; a blank space indicates the stage was not included in the computer run. The implied resemblance between the behavior of these stages and item activity vectors, and that of actual processes and item representations is, of course, intentional.

With partial disconnections, in fact, even just the information latent in other stages might become essential if the system is to surmount one pathway's poor information quality. Such a mechanism could explain the behavior of a patient tested by Beauvois, Saillant, Meininger, and Lhermitte (1978). Within what was otherwise a classical syndrome of partial tactile disconnection, their patient showed a puzzling preservation of his ability to tactually name items that have good visual representations (e.g., "chair," "broom"), despite difficulty in tactually naming items that do not have such strong and distinctive visual characteristics (e.g., "wool," "rice"). (This is an interpretation of their terminology and their examples.) Beauvois, Saillant, Meininger, and Lhermitte did not explain this discrepancy directly, but their anatomical discussions might imply that they felt it necessary to invoke direct tactile–visual connections that had been spared by the disconnection. Yet with a model such as ours, this extra pathway is not necessary (even though it may exist on other evidence); the qualitative model allows prestored modality-specific information to make a contribution to naming through the common stage. With the appropriate partial disconnection, our simulation is also unable to name tactually items lacking a "visual" representation (Row 3a), while correctly naming those that have such a representation (Row 3b). (In the actual simulation, differences in visual representation were mimicked by either including a visual stage or leaving the entire stage out of the simulation.)

Partial disconnections and degraded information can account for other behavior. I recently examined a patient who was able to visually match a pencil with another pencil, when given a choice of objects which included a spoon. Yet this patient misnamed the pencil a "spoon" and tried to use it as such. When I gently asked why the "spoon" was not doing a very good job, the patient explained that it was not a very good spoon! Overtly similar perversities of naming and/or behavior have often been described (compare patients of Lhermitte and Beauvois, 1973; Marin and Saffran, 1975). These problems undoubtedly have a number of plausible explanations, including simple perseveration. But one other explanation in our context might be that a partial disconnection has degraded information in such a way that a subsequent stage (such as the semantic one) is misled. The simulation can mimic this (Row 4 of Table 24.1): With a partial visual disconnection it can recognize a visually presented item within the visual network correctly, but its semantic network believes it is seeing a different item, and evokes that (erroneous) name from the motor network. Our model cannot, of course, mime its semantic understanding as the patient could, nor give a circumlocutory description of the contents of its semantic network. But one can imagine that this is how the corresponding human situation would be expressed. As the semantic stage is otherwise intact, we would also expect a patient with this kind of disconnection to name correctly from dictionary definitions (cf. Lhermitte and Beauvois, 1973).

I do not claim that these parallels prove that our present model can easily account for the critical differences between these reported patients: Saffran and Marin's (1975) patient had a multimodal deficit; Lhermitte and Beauvois's (1973) seemed to have relatively intact semantic registration of visually presented objects, often miming their use correctly even while misnaming them. They are simply a suggestion that one type of dysfunction may underlie a considerable variety of abnormal behaviors.

The model also allows a different perspective on other observations. Classical disconnectionism predicts BIDIRECTIONAL disruptions of information flow, as the forwards and backwards pathways are not grossly distinguishable anatomically (cf. discussion by Heilman, Tucker, and Valenstein, 1976). Yet some patients seem to have only unidirectional disorders (Heilman, Tucker, and Valenstein, 1976; Mohr, 1976), an embarrassment that has been accommodated by postulating additional functional or anatomical subdivisions or different informational requirements for the tasks.

The neurally based model could potentially also incorporate these explanations. But if we consider even the strict connectionist hypothesis, then it is apparent that the qualitative model can still predict apparently unidirectional disconnections. This is because under some circumstances the forwards and backwards microcoding could be distinct enough to be differentially affected by the same lesion. In the quantitative model, this has been simulated by lesioning forwards and backwards "axons" in pairs; when one is lesioned, the other suffers obligatory sectioning as well (see Figure 24.5b). It is then almost trivially easy to show that the simulation can overtly behave like a unidirectional disconnection, even though a bidirectional one is present at the neural level. For example, seeing the item does not evoke the name (Table 24.1, Row 5a), whereas tactile presentation of the item not only produces the name but also allows a visual representation of the item to be formed (Row 5b), similar to the performance of Beauvois, Saillant, Meininger, and Lhermitte's (1978) patient. Our model cannot perfectly parallel their clinical situation as it does not incorporate any matching process, but it is easy to see how the intact visual representation in this situation could be used as a basis for matching. The reverse situation is also easy to simulate (Rows 5c and d). (The illustrated results in this and previous runs had the first, second, etc., neurons of each network paired with each other, but many different assignments could have given the same results.)

The intact system can demonstrate interesting "pathological " behaviors, which are predictable from the qualitative assumptions, and which surfaced during trial runs. With the appropriate model parameters or with a very degraded input stimulus, some stages reach asymptote before others have even begun to develop recognizable patterns. Under these conditions, the semantic representation and naming response could be available before the item had been fully recognized visually (Table 24.1, Row 6), or visual recognition and naming might be accomplished in the absence of full semantic knowledge (Row 7). This latter case, although occurring in an intact system, is phenomenologically similar to that of a patient described by Heilman, Tucker, and Valenstein (1976), who could name without understanding. This suggests another mechanism that could potentially account for such behavior, in addition to the existence of direct visual–articulatory connections. (As I noted earlier, I do accept the existence of such direct associations. I further feel that Heilman, Tucker, and Valenstein's explanation is the preferable one for their patient. My point is merely that it is not the ONLY explanation of any similar behavior.)

With some parameters, the simulation initially gives the "wrong" result but after further iterations corrects itself (not illustrated in Table 24.1). With other parameters, the model has "misperceptions" or "hallucinations": The intact system misperceives and misnames an item, but the visual stage is capable of correct recognition by itself when it is cut off from the rest of the "deranged" system (Row 8). Both of these behaviors can be understood from the qualitative model.

DEFICIENCIES

As presently developed and explored, the model cannot account for all the varieties of naming performance of even the patients cited here. Yet, whatever the intrinsic deficiencies of the model, at least some of its present limitations may be artifactual. I have not tried to make full use of available options: The locus and effect of lesioning is narrowly circumscribed, and there has been no serious attempt to incorporate all of the ramifications of the model's feedback complexity and temporal behavior.

Most importantly, neither the qualitative model nor the simulated system has been given certain readily justifiable intrastage capabilities. For example, the model and simulation do not explicitly account for the semantic paraphasias that are a prominent feature of many of the patients cited. But it is easy to see how these could be produced by allowing for a true semantic substructure within the "semantic" stage—for instance, if items were represented componentially by lists of features. Likewise, the model does not account for other aspects of naming or related language abilities that probably depend upon intrastage processes, such as semantic facilitation by "spreading activation" (Collins and Loftus, 1975), and word-category specific problems (e.g., McKenna and Warrington, 1978; Yamadori and Albert, 1973). Again, however, there are already suggestions available as to how the model's neural representation assumptions might be enhanced to give it analogous capabilities, as well as more realistic memory performance (e.g., Liepa, 1977; Murdock, 1979; Ratcliff, 1978).

ACCOMPLISHMENTS

I have primarily intended to suggest explanatory OPTIONS for the pathological behaviors discussed, rather than to rigorously identify single mechanisms (which may be beyond the reach of present evidence anyway). I have chosen to focus on the consequences of between-stage lesions for explicitness; even without enhancements of the model, its present capabilities are interesting. It should be emphasized that most of the features incorporated into the model are fairly well accepted within their original disciplines; here they have simply been linked together with a common purpose and a common underlying mechanism, in what has hopefully been a useful example of a more general methodology (cf. Arbib and Caplan, 1979, and following discussions).

Perhaps I have also answered some of the methodological objections Marshall (1980) and others have had to neurolinguistic theorizing: Marshall (1980) attacked its abuse of metaphor; although I could not avoid metaphor, the metaphorical points of correspondence between the model's function and that of an actual brain are hopefully clearer. Marshall (1980) objected to diagrammatization because it was too tempting to "add another box or another arrow [p. 8]" as a substitute for real understanding. I have tried to keep box proliferation to a minimum, and have even been able to eliminate one of Lichtheim's (1885) arrows as unnecessary for most of our model's results. Marshall questioned whether traditional neurolinguistic diagrams would be interpretable now that we know their substrate consists of an interwoven, variegated web of neurons and neuronal connections (to paraphrase Beneke, 1833, as cited in Marshall, 1980). As we have seen, such macroscopic diagramming still embodies a considerable amount of information, and can be eminently interpretable, so long as we encourage our understanding of what the clinical descriptions actually imply to similarly evolve. For example, the model I have presented is, in a sense, a "connectionist" model: Every stage (or substage) has a specific processing function, and these stages are serially (and deterministically) interconnected. Nevertheless, this model directly contradicts other assumptions of classical connectionism: Neural stage function is not readily predictable from behavior; there is no simple sequential processing of overt "functions"; the QUANTITATIVE extent of a lesion can QUALITATIVELY affect its resultant symptomatology; a simple additivity or substractability of degrees of function or dysfunction does NOT hold. The rules that do apply require a reassessment of what the neural stages actually do and how they communicate with each other.

A final problem Marshall (1980, p. 8) posed was "how can we constrain diagrams so that they become theories [and] not just summaries of the data?" I have shown, in one specific case, that even a very broad characterization of classical data can be synthesized with hypotheses which are almost simple data summaries from other, newer, fields, to produce a very powerful, yet potentially verifiable/falsifiable model. This model might in turn serve as a reasonably secure base for further elaboration.

At the very least, I have provided more support for Wood's (1978; Chapter 23, this volume) conclusions from simulated lesion studies: Wood lesioned neurons within stages, whereas our lesions spared the neurons and disrupted only their interconnections. But in both cases, our results imply that the relationship between overt symptomatology and underlying dysfunction (and function) in the real brain is going to be extraordinarily complex. If so, these results may indicate what kinds of observations or experiments will be necessary to help distinguish among competing models of this and other tasks.

ACKNOWLEDGMENTS

I thank Renee Taub Gordon for her unflagging support during every stage of this effort. Alfonso Caramazza, Oscar S. M. Marin, and Charles Wood offered many helpful comments on the manuscript.

REFERENCES

Amari, S.-I. (1977). Neural theory of association and concept formation. *Biological Cybernetics, 26*, 175–185. (a)
Amari, S.-I. (1977). Dynamics of pattern formation in lateral-inhibition type neural fields. *Biological Cybernetics, 27*, 77–87. (b)
Anderson, J. A. (1977). Neural models with cognitive implications. In D. LaBerge and S. J. Samuels (Eds.), *Basic processes in reading: Perception and comprehension.* Hillsdale, N.J.: Lawrence Erlbaum.
Anderson, J. A., and Silverstein, J. W. (1978). Reply to Grossberg. *Psychological Review, 85,* 597–603.
Anderson, J. A., Silverstein, J. W., Ritz, S. A., and Jones, R. S. (1977). Distinctive features, categorical perception, and probability learning: Some applications of a neural model. *Psychological Review, 84,* 413–451.
Arbib, M. A. (1975). Artificial intelligence and brain theory: Unities and diversities. *Annals of Biomedical Engineering, 3,* 238–274.
Arbib, M. A., and Caplan, D. (1979). Neurolinguistics must be computational. *The Behavioral and Brain Sciences, 2,* 449–460.
Beauvois, M. F., Saillant, B., Meininger, V., and Lhermitte, F. (1978). Bilateral tactile aphasia: A tacto-verbal dysfunction. *Brain, 101,* 381–401.
Benson, D. F. (1979). Neurologic correlates of anomia. In H. Whitaker and H. A. Whitaker (Eds.), *Studies in neurolinguistics,* Vol. 4 New York: Academic Press.
Cavanagh, P. (1976). Holographic and trace strength models of rehearsal effects in the item recognition task. *Memory and Cognition, 4,* 186–199.
Collins, A. M., and Loftus, E. F. (1975). A spreading activation theory of semantic processing. *Psychological Review. 82,* 407–428.

Coughlan, A. K., and Warrington, E. (1978). Word-comprehension and word-retrieval in patients with localized cerebral lesions. *Brain*, 101, 163–185.

Denes, G., and Semenza, C. (1975). Auditory modality-specific anomia: Evidence from a case of pure word deafness. *Cortex*, 11, 401–411.

Eriksen, C. W., and Schultz, D. W. (1979). Information processing in visual search: A continuous flow conception and experimental results. *Perception and Psychophysics*, 24, 249–263.

Finke, R. A. (1980). Levels of equivalence in imagery and perception. *Psychological Review*, 87, 113–132.

Freeman, W. J. (1979). EEG analysis gives model of neuronal template-matching mechanism for sensory search with olfactory bulb. *Biological Cybernetics*, 35, 221–234.

Geschwind, N. (1967). The varieties of naming errors. *Cortex*, 3, 97–112.

Goodglass, H., Barton, M. I., and Kaplan, E. F. (1968). Sensory modality and object-naming in aphasia. *Journal of Speech and Hearing Research*, 3, 488–496.

Grossberg, S. (1977). Pattern formation by the global limits of a nonlinear competitive interaction in *n* dimensions. *Journal of Mathematical Biology*, 4, 237–256.

Heilman, K. M., Tucker, D. M., and Valenstein, E. (1976). A case of mixed transcortical aphasia with intact naming. *Brain*, 99, 415–426.

James, W. (1890). *The principles of psychology*, Vol. 1. New York: Henry Holt.

Kinsbourne, M. (1979). Mapping a behavioral cerebral space. *The INS Bulletin*, Sept. 1979 (Text of Presidential Address at Sixth Annual Meeting, Feb. 1978).

Kosslyn, S. M. (1978). Imagery and internal representation. In E. Rosch and B. B. Lloyd (Eds.), *Cognition and categorization*. Hillsdale, N. J.: Lawrence Erlbaum.

Kussmaul, A. (1877). *Die Storungen der Sprache*. Leipzig: Vogel.

Lappin, J. S. (1978). The relativity of choice behavior and the effect of prior knowledge on the speed and accuracy of recognition. In N.J. Castellan and F. Restle (Eds.), *Cognitive theory*, Vol. 3. Hillsdale, N.J.: Lawrence Erlbaum.

Lhermitte, F., and Beauvois, M. F. (1973). A visual–speech disconnexion syndrome: Report of a case with optic aphasia, agnostic alexia, and colour agnosia. *Brain*, 96, 695–714.

Lichtheim, L. (1885). On aphasia. *Brain*, 7, 433–484.

Liepa, P. (1977). *Models for content addressable distributed associative memory* (CADAM). Unpublished manuscript, University of Toronto.

Little, W. A. (1974). The existence of persistent states in the brain. *Mathematical Biosciences*, 19, 101–120.

McClelland, J. L. (1979). On the time relations of mental processes: An examination of systems of processes in cascade. *Psychological Review*, 86, 287–330.

McClelland, J. L., and Rumelhart, D. E. (1980). An interactive activation model of the effect of context in perception (Part I). University of California at San Diego CHIP Report No. 91.

McKenna, P., and Warrington, E. K. (1978). Category-specific naming preservation: A single case study. *Journal of Neurology, Neurosurgery, and Psychiatry*, 41, 571–574.

Marin, O. S. M., and Saffran, E. M. (1975). Agnosic behavior in anomia: A case of pathologic verbal dominance. *Cortex*, 11, 83–89.

Marr, D., and Poggio, T. (1976). Cooperative computation of stereo disparity. *Science*, 194, 283–287.

Marshall, J. C. (1980). Neurolinguistics, "coding," and the interpretation of models. In M. A. Arbib (Ed.), *Neural models of language processes* (COINS Technical Report 80–09). University of Massachusetts at Amherst.

Mohr, J. P. (1976). An unusual case of dyslexia with dysgraphia. *Brain and Language*, 3, 324–334.

Mountcastle, V. B. (1978). An organizing principle for cerebral function: The unit module and the distributed system. In G. M. Edelman and V. B. Mountcastle, *The mindful brain*. Cambridge, Mass.: MIT Press.

Murdock, B. B. (1979). Convolution and correlation in perception and memory. In L.-G. Nilsson (Ed.), *Perspectives on memory research*. Hillsdale, N.J.: Lawrence Erlbaum.

Posner, M. I. (1978). *Chronometric explorations of mind*. Hillsdale, N.J.: Lawrence Erlbaum.

Ratcliff, R. A theory of memory retrieval. (1978). *Psychological Review, 85*, 59–108.

Sejnowski, T. J. (1976a). On global properties of neuronal interaction. *Biological Cybernetics, 22*, 85–95.

Sejnowski, T. J. (1976b). On the stochastic dynamics of neuronal interaction. *Biological Cybernetics, 22*, 203–211.

Townsend, J. T., and Ashby, F. G. (1978). Methods of modeling capacity in simple processing systems. In N.J. Castellan and F. Restle (Eds.), *Cognitive Theory* Vol. 3. Hillsdale, N.J.: Lawrence Erlbaum.

Wickelgren, W. A. (1976). Network strength theory of storage and retrieval dynamics. *Psychological Review, 83*, 466–478.

Wickelgren, W. A. (1977). Speed–accuracy tradeoff and information processing dynamics. *Acta Psychologica, 41*, 67–85.

Wood, C. C. (1978). Variations on a theme by Lashley: Lesion experiments on the neural model of Anderson, Silverstein, Ritz, and Jones. *Psychological Review, 85*, 582–591.

Yamadori, A., and Albert, M. A. (1973). Word catagory aphasia. *Cortex, 9*, 112–125.

25

Perceptual-Motor Processes and the Neural Basis of Language[1]

Michael A. Arbib

INTRODUCTION

Neurolinguistics developed in the context of clinical medicine with the goal of predicting lesion sites from symptom-complexes and vice versa. But, in the words of Hughlings Jackson (1874), "to locate damage which destroys speech and to locate speech are two different things" Luria (1973)—developing the idea of "functional system" from the work of Anokhin (1935), Bernstein (1935, 1968), and Vygotsky (1934)—asserts that our fundamental task is to ascertain "which groups of concertedly working zones are responsible for the performance of complex mental activity [and] what contribution is made by each of these zones to the complex functional system." This transfers the emphasis from the brain-damaged patient to the normal subject. We seek a theory of how brain regions interact in some normal performance. Because data on abnormal behavior provide some of our best clues about the neurological validity of processes postulated in a model of the normal, it makes sense to develop neural models for normal function with reference to the neurological data.

The performance of the patient with damage to some brain region (though lesions and tumors show scant respect for the boundaries of such regions) is to be explained in terms of the interaction between the remaining brain regions, rather than in terms of the properties of the region removed. The system must still be able to perform despite deletion of some portion—quite unlike the breakdown that would follow removal of a subroutine from a serial computer program (cf. Arbib, 1975, Section 5). One should append additional mechanisms to the model to account for the effects of damage only if it has been shown that the

[1]Preparation of this chapter was supported in part by the Sloan Foundation grant for "A Program in Language and Information Processing" at the University of Massachusetts at Amherst.

531

properties of the remaining regions will not automatically account for these effects—though it may require a rather subtle theory to determine just what does follow "automatically." For this reason, we should be cautious about Lecours's explicit postulation of "error generators" as underlying phonemic paraphasias (Lecours and Lhermitte, 1969; Lecours, Deloche, and Lhermitte, 1973).

One's perspective on neurolinguistics would seem to depend a great deal on one's starting point. We have seen that the classical starting point is the neurological clinic. My own starting point is the study of neural mechanisms of visuomotor coordination and an evolutionary perspective which leads me to serach for common mechanisms for "action-oriented perception" (Arbib, 1972) and "language use" to provide a base from which to explore their differences. Thus, rather than assert the existence of a separable grammar that interacts with processes for understanding or production, I would rather see a variety of processes (e.g., in production and perception) whereby "internal models" of meaning are related to utterances of the language via a "translation" process. This hypothesis (developed in Arbib, Chapter 4, this volume) is based on a view of language as evolving in a context of well-developed cognitive abilities (which are then modified in turn, just as visuomotor processes in superior colliculus are modified by descending pathways from visual cortex). In total contrast are those linguists and philosophers who look for an "autonomous" theory of language processing. They reject the thesis that diverse information is used in language processing and see the core of the linguistic processor to be the generation of phonological, morphological, syntactic, and logical representations, with the diverse nonlinguistic information exploited in everyday language use inaccessible to this core. This thesis seems to have evolved from Chomsky's original claim (1965, Section 1.3) for autonomy of syntax, a claim based on a divorce of linguistics from processing, let alone neurological, issues. Without wishing to discourage intensive efforts in neurolinguistics which are primarily linguistic, I would suggest that these can only be part of the overall emphasis when the goal is to understand the interaction of multiple brain regions. Here I believe that the neurologist, neuroanatomist, and brain theorist have much to offer that the linguist does not.

The integrated theory that I envisage will incorporate a great deal of neuroanatomy as we try to better characterize regions within the brain and the detailed projections that link them. But what manner of "region" will enter meaningfully into neurolinguistics? Such gross anatomical regions as the parietal lobe or the cerebellum are too large, whereas individual "columns," let alone individual neurons, are too fine to make contact with conceptualizations at the level we diagram in what follows. (Does a word in the lexicon have its own set of columns in the cortex? Would such a set contain one column or many thousands? It is perhaps premature to speculate, but we find some clues in a study of changing visuomotor representations in the cortex of the cat [Spinelli and Jensen, 1979].) Classic cytoarchitectonics and modern biochemistry provide different answers for differentiating the brain into a multiplicity of separable populations. Szentágothai and Arbib (1975, Figure 19) schematize the neuron network of the cerebellar cortex into five two-dimensional matrices, reminding us of the insight to be gained by subdividing a region into interacting layers. Boylls's synergy controller model (presented in Szentágothai and Arbib, 1975, Chapter 5) suggests that the cerebellar cortex in isolation cannot be viewed as a meaningful unit in motor control, and that it is only in relation to a number of adjacent nuclei that its posited role in the adjustment of motor synergies can be defined. What is interesting for our discussion of methodology is that Boylls's choice of units resulted from the confluence of a theoretical analysis refining the Bernsteinian theory of synergies which influenced Luria, and a detailed review of the constraints and mechanisms documented in the anatomical and physiological literature.

The paper by Arbib and Caplan (1979), and the attendant commentaries, suggested the following conclusions about neurolinguistics:

1. There is a body of moderately reliable information relating symptom-complexes to localized lesions, but much needs to be done to relate symptom-complexes to the interaction of remaining brain regions rather than to properties of the site of the lesion. It is an article of faith shared by most neurolinguists that such an analysis is in principle possible.

2. There is a body of psycholinguistic research that seeks to refine linguistic categories to provide clues to the "neural code" of language processing. The neural validity of many of the posited codes is still controversial.

3. A new framework is needed to develop, modify, and integrate the approaches outlined in (1) and (2). Arbib and Caplan suggested that precise models using the language of cooperative computation (based on studies in both brain theory and artificial intelligence) may provide such a framework. This proposal needs full experimental testing on the basis of detailed modeling.

4. Computational models are abstract models and must not be confused with crude comparisons of brain and computer. Much can be learned from computational models by pencil-and-paper theorizing, but computer simulation should allow more detailed study of their properties.

5. Neurolinguistics has been too isolated from general issues of neural modeling, and from an appreciation of the relevance of issues in visual perception and motor control. We argue that the cooperative computation style of modeling can integrate neurolinguistics with studies of visuomotor coordination, and that the "modules" posited in a cooperative computation model can provide a bridge to synapse–cell–circuit neuroscience.

JACKSONIAN LEVELS AND COOPERATIVE COMPUTATION

Many neurologists have been concerned with the relationship of aspects of language to perceptual, motor, and other cognitive systems. Examples include Jackson's (1878–1879) view of propositions, Geschwind's (1975) approach to the agnosias and apraxias, and Luria's (1973) concern with start–stop mechanisms shared between linguistic and nonlinguistic motor activities. We have already mentioned the influence on Luria of Bernstein (1968), whose work laid the basis for the Moscow school which combines neurophysiological and mathematical analyses of motor control with the construction of actual robots (Fel'dman and Orlovsky, 1972; Gelfand and Tsetlin, 1962; Okhotimskii, Gurfinkel, Devyanin, and Platonov, 1979).

Pursuit of these connections will, I have argued (Arbib, 1975, this volume, Chapter 4; Arbib and Caplan, 1979), require a framework of cooperative computation in which, in addition to interaction among components of a language processor, there are important interactions among components of linguistic and nonlinguistic systems. Careful analysis of the components of perceptual, motor, and linguistic tasks and of their patterns of breakdown will, it is predicted, lead to the identification of a (presumably limited) number of components that share and/or compare linguistic and nonlinguistic representations. One should then be able to infer something of the neural mechanisms underlying language from an appreciation of those underlying related nonlinguistic processes. As stressed by Arbib and Caplan (1979), we are confronted with the need for explicit representational systems, in this case for nonlinguistic as well as linguistic entities, coupled with a cooperative computational analysis of processing which determines which representations are "translatable" and "shared" between linguistic and nonlinguistic systems. In this section, we shall give an explicit example of a cooperative computation model of a low-level perceptual function to indicate the style in which future computational neuropsychology might be conducted.

Jackson (1878–1879) argued that observations of the "propositionalizing" of patients with "affections of speech from disease of the brain" would lead to a theory of language function which was not task-specific, and to a theory of brain function which did not consist of centers and connections. However, he offered no theory of the representation of propositions, nor did he distinguish between the ideational and linguistic form of propositions. In a highly similar vein, Goldstein [1948] argued that general functional principles were lost in aphasia. A modern development of this approach is found in Locke, Caplan, and Kellar (1973) in which Jacksonian functional capacities are related to a hierarchical model of the neuraxis based on Yakovlev's (1948) work.

The Jacksonian approach incorporates the claim that the functional capacities lost with respect to language functioning are also lost in other realms of behavior in the aphasic patient (cf. Brown, 1972, 1977; Pick, 1913). It emphasizes the overlap of linguistic and nonlinguistic functions, but uses only a rudimentary characterization of language itself. Although this approach avoids the central issue in neurolinguistic theory, which consists first of the study of the representation and utilization of the LINGUISTIC code in and by neural tissue, it does help us understand how this code is subject to functional factors which also regulate other cognitive and perceptual-motor capacities.

I want to show that the Jacksonian view of the brain in terms of evolutionary levels is entirely compatible with computational modeling of the brain; and I shall even claim that such modeling can deepen and enrich the Jacksonian viewpoint. An example is provided by a model (Prager, 1979; Prager and Arbib, in press) of the computation of optic flow. The model is "in the style of the brain" in that the computation is spread over interacting layers of processing units akin to such systems in the vertebrate brain, but no claim is made as to the detailed veridicality of the present model. Nonetheless, the "evolutionary style" of this model should provide insight for neuropsychology and neurolinguistics.

Consider the problem of matching corresponding features in two visual images. We may think of this as either the stereopsis problem or the optic flow problem. In the former, we match patterns falling on two eyes as a basis for depth perception. In the latter, we take a sequence of images from one moving "eye," and seek to match features from two snapshots separated by some small period in time to estimate velocities of corresponding features in the environment. Optic flow is the term for the pattern of vectors indicating the velocity (interframe displacement) of features. For concreteness, consider oriented edges—Hubel–Wiesel feature—as our features in each frame. Imagine an oriented edge in one frame, and several edges of similar orientation and position in the next frame. A feature from a rotating object may change its orientation between frames, but as long as the interframe interval is not too great the orientation will be similar. Thus, rather than look for an exact match of features between frames, we should look for a match that is "nearby" in some metric that increases both with image distance and feature variation. Nonetheless, a convincing nearest neighbor match as judged in some local window might differ quite drastically from the global flow pattern, as is suggested in Figure 25.1.

An algorithm is required to resolve various local estimates to come up with a plausible, globally coherent pattern. As in a number of stereopsis algorithms (e.g., Dev, 1975; Marr and Poggio, 1977), the present approach is based on the observation that the world is made up of objects which present surfaces to our gaze. Nearby features of the visual world are more likely than not to lie on the same object, and so are more likely than not to move similar amounts, that is, to have similar optic fow. These considerations suggest two ways to adjust the current estimate of optic flow.

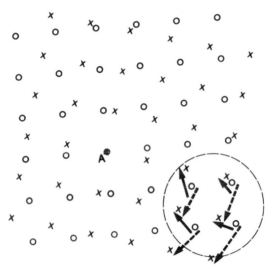

FIGURE 25.1. *Frame 1 comprises the dots indicated by circles; Frame 2 is obtained by rotating the array about the pivot at A to place the dots in the positions indicated by crosses. The dashed circle at lower right is the receptive field of a local processor. The solid arrows indicate the best local estimate of the optic flow; the dashed arrows show the actual pairing of features under rotation about A.*

1. **Feature matching** simply adjusts the optic flow from a Frame 1 feature toward a match with the Frame 2 feature that is nearest in the combined metric.

2. **Local smoothness** adjusts the optic flow at a point toward the average optic flow of features in some neighborhood.

The algorithm is then as follows: Start with all the distinctive features in Frame 1, and establish initial hypotheses for the optic flow vectors (e.g., by the nearest neighbor rule). Then the hypotheses are updated through a number of iterations. As shown in Figure 25.2, each iteration requires updating the optic flow hypothesis for each feature by a linear combination of feature matching and local smoothness. Our computer simulations (Prager, 1979) show that some 10–20 iterations suffice to yield a fairly reliable estimate of the actual optic flow. This algorithm is an example of what is called a **relaxation procedure** because it is similar to the procedure introduced in the 1930s for looking at stress analysis in beams, which starts with an initial estimate of a displacement of each point in a beam and then uses local stress relations to adjust nearby points to minimize the stress, eventually converging to the actual beam placement (Southwell, 1940).

We know from the work of J. J. Gibson (1966) that the optic flow has enough information to support the inference of where a collision might occur,

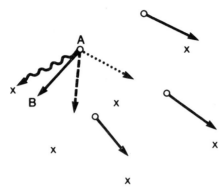

FIGURE 25.2. *The circles indicate features in Frame 1, the crosses features in Frame 2, and the solid arrows the current estimate of the optic flow—the head of the arrow shows the posited position in Frame 2 of the feature corresponding to the Frame 1 feature at the tail of the arrow. "Feature matching" alone would adjust A's optic flow to the wavy arrow pointing to the Frame 2 feature nearest to B (the current estimate of A's Frame 2 position); "local smoothness" would yield the dotted arrow, the average of the optic flow of the neighbors; while our relaxation algorithm yields the dashed arrow as a weighted combination of these two estimates.*

and how long it would be until contact if a collision would occur (cf. Arbib, 1981). This inference does not require recognition of distinct objects moving through the world, and may well correspond to how the brain uses information from the peripheral visual field to enable jumping aside to avoid a collision well before recognition of a distinct object as such. Of course, an overall analysis of adaptive visual behavior will include the recognition of objects as well. One way to recognize objects is based on first separating them from their background. A hypothesis as to what region of an image is the surface of an object yields information about the object's texture, depth, and shape which can greatly speed the recognition process. We now indicate how an estimate of optic flow can also be used in this process of **segmentation.**

When one object moves in front of another, there is occlusion, as the object in front covers up more of the object behind so that features visible in Frame 1 are no longer visible in Frame 2. Thus, one way of finding edges between surfaces is to try to find curves joining points in Frame 1 that do not have good feature matches in Frame 2 specified by the converged optic flow. Similarly for disocclusion—if the object in front is moving to reveal more and more of the object behind, then features in Frame 2 will not be matched by the optic flow with similar features in Frame 1.

There is another way to get edge information. If two surfaces move past each other, then the velocity of their projections upon the retina will be different. Thus another indicator of an edge between surfaces is a curve following a sharp gradient of the optic flow. As shown in Figure 25.3, we thus have two different systems that can build upon the basic optic flow algorithm to find edges, cooperating to find edge hypotheses with the highest confidence level.

Although this is not meant to be a neurologically valid model of the brain, I do claim that it is in "the style of brain." We started with a basic optic flow algorithm with parallel interactions distributed over several surfaces. Once this system has "evolved" (to use biological terminology) there are patterns of information available that were not directly available from the retina. Then two systems can evolve for edge detection: one can exploit difficulty of feature match, the other can exploit high gradient of the optic flow. These can cooperate to come up with adaptive information about where objects begin and end in the environment, and so may be referred to as "cooperative segmentation algorithms." Even more interestingly, once these algorithms have evolved, the original optic flow algorithm—(1) in Figure 25.3—has in its environment estimates as to where edges are; and now it can evolve so that instead of the neighborhood of each feature in the matching process being a fixed locality, it can instead be adjusted to those cells in the locality that are on the same side of a posited edge. Because the edge hypothesis is itself tentative, this adjustment must be a bias rather than being all-or-none.

We have thus seen an explicit computational analysis of a system which may be described in the following biological terms: An evolutionarily more primitive system allows the evolution of higher level systems; but then return pathways evolve which enable the lower level system to evolve into a more

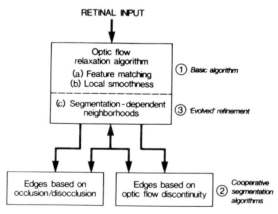

FIGURE 25.3. *Our basic optic flow relaxation algorithm uses the consistency conditions of feature matching and local smoothness. (2) The resultant optic flow estimate permits the hypothesization of edges on cues based on both occlusion/disocclusion cues and on optic flow discontinuity. (3) The resultant edge hypotheses can be used to refine the computation of optic flow by dynamically adjusting the neighborhoods used in employing the consistency conditions.*

effective form. To a first approximation we might want to call the system of Figure 25.3 hierarchical; yet in some sense the lowest level system is the highest because it exploits the middle level!

If we "ablate" the high-level system (the segmentation algorithms of Figure 25.3), we do not see the extended optic flow algorithm per se, but rather the debased version deprived of data from the higher level return pathways. In some sense, the lesion does not reveal the performance of the lower level system in the absence of higher level edge extraction so much as it exhibits an evolutionarily more primitive form of the function of this system. It is instructive to see all these aspects of a Jacksonian analysis—hierarchical level, return pathways, evolutionary interaction, evolutionary degradation under certain lesions—exemplified in so computationally explicit a model, based on cumulative refinement of parallel interaction between arrays. Although the computation of optic flow is a far cry from language processing, I believe that the style of analysis exemplified here is of great potential for neuropsychology in general, and for neurolinguistics in particular.

FROM THE ACTION-PERCEPTION CYCLE TO CONVERSATION

Having placed a computational analysis of an aspect of visual perception within a Jacksonian framework, we now turn to a brief description (following Arbib, 1981) of the relation between visual perception and the control of movement. We then turn to analogies between this process and the analysis of conversation. We shall then see how such analogies may offer a bridge from neurolinguistics to cell–circuit–synapse neuroscience.

We propose that the following internal structures and processes are necessitated by the visual control of locomotion: the representation of the environment, the updating of that representation on the basis of visual input, the use of that representation by programs which control the locomotion, and the cycle of integrated perception and action. We seek functional units whose cooperation in achieving visuomotor coordination can be analyzed and understood irrespective of whether they themselves are further decomposed in terms of neural nets or computer programs. Our style of analysis will seek to decompose functions into the interaction of a family of simultaneously active processes called schemas, which will serve as building blocks for both representations and programs.

The control of locomotion may be specified at varying levels of refinement: the goal of the motion; the path to be traversed in reaching the goal; the actual pattern of footfalls in the case of a legged animal; and the detailed pattern of motor or muscle activation required for each footfall. It is well known that the fine details of activation will be modified on the basis of sensory feedback, but we stress that even the path-plan will be continually modified as locomotion proceeds. For example, locomotion will afford new viewpoints which will reveal shortcuts or unexpected obstacles which must be taken into account in modifying the projected path. We thus speak of the action–perception cycle—the system perceives as the basis of action; each action affords new data for perception.

In terms of "units independent of embodiment," we may seek to postulate basic motor processes for, for example, locomoting which, given a path-plan as input, will yield the first step along that path as output. Another such unit would direct a hand to grasp an object, given its position as input. We refer to such units of behavior as "motor schemas." Our analysis will descend no further than the level of motor schemas, and will leave aside details of mechanical or neuromuscular implementation. Our claim will be that crucial aspects of visuomotor coordination can be revealed at this level of aggregation.

The raw pattern of retinal stimulation cannot guide locomotion directly. Rather, it must be interpreted in terms of objects and other "domains of interaction" in the environment. We also use the term "schema" for the process whereby the system determines whether a given "domain of interaction" is present in the environment. The state of activation of the schema will then determine the credibility of the hypothesis that that which the schema represents is indeed present; other schema parameters will represent further properties such as size, location, and motion relative to the locomoting system.

Consider a schema that represents, say, a chair; and consider an environment that has two chairs in plain view. It is clear that two copies of the chair-schema—or, at least, two separate sets of chair-schema-parameters—will be required to represent the two chairs. We refer to these two copies as "instantiations" of the same schema, each with its own set of parameter values. We may thus view the internal representation of the environment as an assemblage of spatially tagged, parametrized, schema instantiations.

Object-representing schemas will not be driven directly by retinal activity, but rather by the output of segmentation processes that provide an intermediate representation in terms of regions or segments (usually corresponding to the surfaces of objects) separated from one another by edges, and characterized internally by continuities in hue, texture, depth, and velocity. As locomotion proceeds, and as objects move in the environment, most of these regions will change gradually, and the segmentation processes must be equipped with a dynamic memory which allows the intermediate representation to be continually updated to provide current input for the object-schemas, so that the schema-assemblage representing the environment will be kept up to date.

Note that a schema is both a process and a representation. The formation and updating of the internal representation is viewed as a distributed process, involving the parallel activity of all those schemas which receive appropriately patterned input. The resultant environmental representation interacts with those processes that represent the system's goal structures to generate the plan of action—exemplified by the projected path in the case of locomotion—which can provide the input to the various motor schemas that directly control behavior.

We may view the schema-assemblage—the structure of perceptual schemas that relates the animal to its environment—as a spatial structure that has temporal characteristics (e.g., representing the motion of objects relative to the animal). We shall shortly discuss the possible nature of "coordinated control programs" which can coordinate the activation of motor schemas. Such a program serves to control the temporal unfolding of movement but has spatial characteristics since interaction with objects will usually depend on their position in the environment.

There is no simple stimulus–response relationship here. Perception of an object (activating perceptual schemas) involves gaining access to motor schemas for interaction with it, but does not necessarily involve their execution. Although an animal may perceive many aspects of its environment, only a few of these can at any time become the primary locus of interaction. A process of planning is required to determine the plan of action (the appropriate program of motor schema activation) on the basis of current goals and the environmental model. Perception activates, whereas planning concentrates. Coming upon unexpected obstacles can alter the elaboration of higher level structures—the animal continually makes, executes, and updates its plans as it moves.

The language of "coordinated control programs" addresses the description of the coordinated phasing in and out of the brain's manifold control systems. Although certain basic programs are "hard wired," most programs are generated as the result of an explicit planning process. We exemplify this notion by the hypothetical program of Figure 25.4 for a human's grasping an object.

The spoken instructions given to the subject drive the planning process that leads to the creation of the appropriate plan of action—which we here hypothesize to take the form of the distributed control program shown in the lower half of the figure, involving the interwoven activation of motor schemas for reaching and grasping. Broken arrows convey "activation signals," solid arrows indicate transfer of data. Activation of the program is posited to simultaneously initiate a ballistic movement toward the target and a preshaping of the hand during which the fingers are adjusted to the size of the object and the hand is rotated to the appropriate orientation. When the hand is near the object, feedback adjusts the position of the hand, and completion of this adjustment activates the actual grasping of the hand about the object.

The perceptual schemas hypothesized in the upper half of the figure need not be regarded as a separate part of the program. Rather, they provide the algorithms required to identify parameters of the object to be grasped, and to pass these parameter values to the motor schemas. This analysis of visual input locates the target object within the subject's "reaching space," and extracts the size and

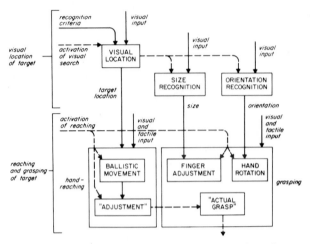

FIGURE 25.4. *A hypothetical coordinated control program for visually directed grasping. The perceptual schemas atop the figure serve as identification procedures for the motor schemas in the control program of the lower half of the figure (---→ control path, ⟶ data path).*

orientation of the target object and feeds them to the control surface of the grasping schema. When the actual grasping movement is triggered, it shapes the hand on the basis of a subtle spatial pattern of tactile feedback. (For data on visuomotor mechanisms in reaching within extrapersonal space and a careful review of the relevant literature, see Jeannerod and Biguer, 1981.)

With this background on the action–perception cycle, we can now see that there are important parallels between visual perception and speech understanding on the one hand, and speech production and motor control on the other. The basic notion is that speech perception, like vision, requires the segmentation of the input. Certain segments may then be aggregated as portions of a single structure of known type, with the whole being understood in terms of the relationship between these parts (see Arbib, Chapter 4, this volume, and Woods, Chapter 5, this volume, for a more detailed analysis). We have suggested that the animal's internal model of its visually defined environment is an appropriate assemblage of schemas, and we offer the same for the human's internal model of the state of a discourse. Because the generation of movement requires the development of a plan on the basis of the internal model of goals and environment to yield a temporally ordered, feedback-modulated pattern of overlapping activation of a variety of effectors, we would argue that the word-by-word generation of speech may be seen as a natural specialization of the general problem of motor control.

If an utterance is a command, the listener must recognize it as such and translate it into a "program" for carrying out the command—which may well involve first translating the command into an internal representation, and then calling upon planning processes to translate this into a detailed program of action tailored to the current situation. If the input is a question, the system must recognize it as such and translate it into a plan for recalling relevant information. A second translation is then required to express this information as a spoken answer. We thus suggest that the task of speech perception is to organize a string of words into pieces which map naturally into internal processes that update the listener's "internal model"—whether or not there is an overt response to the utterance. Production serves to express some fragment of a "brain representation" as a syntactically correct string of words. We stress translation between "internal" and linguistic representation of meaning.

We may then view the action–perception cycle as corresponding to the role of one speaker in ongoing discourse. One can view the deployment and decoding of the linguistic signal as responsive to a series of constraints. The first are those inherent in the structure of the linguistic code itself, and their characterization is the goal of the theory of linguistic competence. We presently have far more information about these constraints than about the remaining levels. The second type of constraint arises from psychological limitations of the human language-processing systems. Frazier and Fodor (1978) have advanced hypotheses regarding the intrinsic nature of these psycholinguistic devices, and suggested interactions between the nature of human processing routines and the nature of language structures. A third type of constraint results from the social and pragmatic facts of conversational situations. Other levels can be suggested. We can view the utilization of language, at each of these levels, as consisting of the interaction of a stored long-term representation of the items and processes at some level and the analysis of the incoming and outgoing signal at the same level to yield a fluid and continually updated current model of the total language act. Seen this way, there are overall similarities between sensory-motor and language computations which should allow us to investigate aspects of the neural mechanisms of language by examining the neural mechanisms relevant to perceptual–motor activity. We close this section, then, by briefly reviewing the extent to which such perceptual–motor mechanisms have yielded to detailed neural analysis.

Neuroscience has taught us how to trace the coding of information in the visual periphery (Hubel and Wiesel, 1977; Lettvin, Maturana, McCulloch, and Pitts, 1959); how to view the cerebral cortex as composed of columns or modules intermediate in complexity between single cells and entire brain regions (Hubel and Wiesel, 1974; Mountcastle, 1978; Szentágothai and Arbib, 1974); how to analyze spinal circuitry involved in motor outflow, and the later stages of its cerebral and cerebellar control (Eccles, Ito, and Szentágothai, 1967; Granit, 1970; Phillips and Porter, 1977). To some extent these analyses may be integrated into models of perceptual and motor precesses (Figure 25.5).

We have good neuroscientific data on retinal response to neuronal stimula-

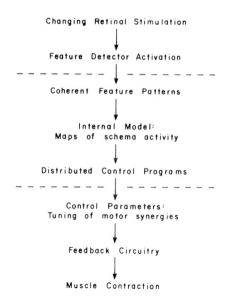

FIGURE 25.5. *Stages in visual perception and control of movement. Many aspects are omitted, as are all of the important "return" pathways.*

tion, and of various "feature extractors" in a number of different animals. At the motor periphery, we have good neuroscientific data on basic motor patterns, their tuning by supraspinal mechanisms (the Russian school has been particularly productive here), and the spinal cord rhythm generators and feedback circuitry which control the musculature. This partial list could be extended and could be complemented by a list of major open problems at these levels: The important point here is that near the visual and motor peripheries there is a satisfying correspondence between single-cell analysis and our processing concepts.

In between, the results are fewer and tend to be somewhat more speculative. By what process are the often disparate activities of feature detectors wedded into a coherent "low-level" representation of the world? How is the representation integrated into the ongoing internal model (the "schema-assemblage" as we have posited it to be)? How are the internal model and goals of the organism combined in a planning process which yields the distributed control programs which orchestrate the motor synergies? There are models for these processes (reviewed in Arbib, 1981), but many are couched in a language closer to artificial intelligence than to neurophysiology, and the body of available neuroscientific data with which they can make contact is still relatively small. Nonetheless, it does seem to us that progress is well under way in the neural analysis of "perceptual structures and distributed motor control."

FROM PREY SELECTION TO OBJECT NAMING

Figure 25.6 shows a model of prey selection by frogs which is of the same general class of brain models as the optic flow algorithm of Figure 25.3: interacting arrays of neurons, with an evolutionarily basic array, together with "more evolved" arrays which modulate the lower system and thus increase the subtlety of the animal's repertoire. This model represents the tectum as controlling basic approach movements to moving objects, with the pretectum being able to modulate such approach for selectivity of targets and for avoidance of larger objects. Ingle (1976, for a review) studied frogs confronted with one or more fly-like stimuli. When confronted with two "flies," either of which was vigorous enough to elicit a snapping response when presented alone, the frog could snap at one of them, not snap at all, or snap at "the average fly." Didday (1970, 1976) designed a plausible network (consistent with data on frog tectum available in 1970) that can take a position-tagged array of "foodness" intensity and ensure that only one region of activity, usually, will persist to influence the motor control systems (Figure 25.6). In the model, the cells of the "foodness" layer feed a "relative foodness" layer whose output is to affect motor control systems. Didday also posits a population of what we shall call S-cells in topographic correspondence with the other layers. Each S-cell inhibits the activity that cells in its region of the "relative foodness layer" receive from the corresponding cells in the "foodness" layer by an amount that increases with increasing activity outside its

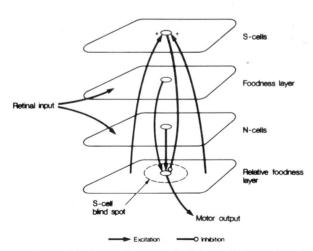

FIGURE 25.6. *Didday model of prey selection. Refined input yields a retinotopic map of prey location in the "foodness layer." This map is projected on the relative foodness layer, where different peaks "compete" via S-cell mediated inhibition. Build-up of inhibition yields diminished responsiveness to changes in the retinal input; N-cells signal such changes to break through this hysteresis.*

region of the relative foodness layer. This ensures that high activity in a region of the foodness layer only "gets through" if the surrounding areas do not contain sufficiently high activity to block it.

One trouble with the circuitry described so far is hysteresis: The build-up of inhibition by the S-cells precludes the system's quick response to new stimuli. Didday thus introduced what we shall call an N-cell for each S-cell. The job of an N-cell is to monitor temporal changes in the activity in its region. Should it detect a sufficiently dramatic increase in the region's activity, it then overrides the S-cell inhibition to enter the new level of activity into the relative foodness layer. With this scheme, the inertia of the old model is overcome and the system can respond rapidly to significant new stimuli.

I claim that the model of Figure 25.6 provides a style of brain theory directly applicable to neurolinguistics. To see this, consider Figure 25.7, taken from Arbib and Caplan (1979), which encapsulates Luria's analysis, in his book *The working brain*, of lesions related to naming. The arrows have no particular significance, for, despite Luria's emphasis on functional systems, he paid little explicit attention to patterns of functional interaction between subsystems. Before suggesting how parallels with Figure 25.6 may lead us toward such a functional analysis, we briefly review Luria's analysis of the individual "boxes" of Figure 25.7. The roles ascribed to the boxes labeled "articulatory system" and "phonemic analysis" seem to correspond to Wernicke's analysis suggesting that speech production will be defective without a phonemic base on which to match the shape of the words. This dispels the naive view that phonemic analysis is irrelevant to the naming task of going from a visual input to a speech output.

The box labeled "visual perception" takes an array of retinal stimulation and

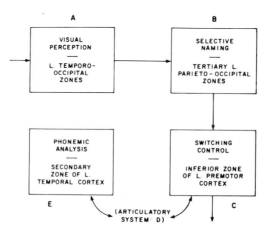

FIGURE 25.7. *Block diagram of subsystems involved in Luria's (1973) analysis of naming of objects* (Arbib and Caplan, 1979).

integrates it into a percept (or percepts), whether or not a name can be given to that percept. A person with a lesion here still has vision in the sense of being able, shown a drawing, to copy it by copying the lines, but is not able to name the object, and—crucial to showing that this can be called a visual perception deficit rather than a naming deficit—is unable, shown a drawing, to recreate it in the way that having seen a drawing of a cat one can draw another cat thereafter even if the second cat is graphically quite different from the first. Luria says that a person who has a lesion of the region called "selective naming" will come up with a name, but that name is as likely as not to be the wrong name, and can be wrong while being semantically similar or phonemically similar. Finally, a patient with a lesion of "switching control" will have no particular problem with a single test; but, if shown object after object, will be very likely to perseverate with a particular name, and will use it repeatedly. The two main areas for building upon Luria's work afforded by Figure 25.7 are as follows: First, as mentioned earlier, the arrows are arbitrary and do not reflect any analysis of functional interactions. Second, boxes are labeled not in terms of what role they might play as a subsystem of the whole functional system, but rather in terms of the deficit associated with a lesion of the subsystem. For example, Luria does not speak of a subsystem whose removal blocks the proper implementation of switching, but rather calls it the subsystem for switching control.

I will now offer a tentative account of functional interaction that is logically akin to the prey selection model we developed for the frog. In Figure 25.6, the foodness layer develops preliminary input-based estimates of what might be appropriate actions before any processing to choose among those alternatives. The ultimate motor output is produced in concert with other areas of the frog's brain to bring about an action which will in general correspond to picking out one target among many. The S-cell monitors activity of other "candidates" elsewhere in the system to suppress a less likely candidate, so that by this process of interaction one candidate will finally emerge victorious and control the motor output. The N-cells stop the system from becoming locked into one response, detecting novel input to interrupt S-cell inhibition and give the new "candidate" a chance to enter the competition.

Figure 25.8 is a re-presentation of Luria's analysis of naming using these concepts. Box A, "visual perception," is given the crudest possible reanalysis on the analogy with foodness and relative foodness. Basic processing activates an array of possible schemas, the internal representations of objects. The system is to choose for utterance a name associated with just one of these schemas, and so we posit an array in which various processes are carried out in interaction with other arrays to bring one schema up to peak activity and suppress others. Of course, the linguistic analogue of the S-cell array cannot be as simple as the somatotopic array of the frog model. Nonetheless, it again seems appropriate to posit S-cells to monitor activity and on that basis provide local inhibition and insure that only

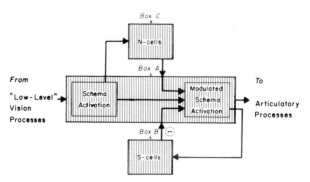

FIGURE 25.8. *A reanalysis of Boxes A, B, and C of Luria's (1973) analysis of naming.*

one of a range of alternatives would be emitted. A lesion to these S-cells would remove control over which schema-name would first reach the motor output, and so an S-cell lesion is precisely analogous to what Luria calls a lesion of selective naming. Note that, in distinction from Luria, we no longer view "selective naming" as the function of a separate "box," but rather as the outcome of intimate dynamic interaction between several "boxes." We do not hypothesize here how the "linguistic S-cells" might take semantic, contextual, and syntactic cues into account.

To complete this exposition, note that the N-cells of our posited model correspond to the function of "switching control" called for in Luria's analysis. Unlike Luria's "box-at-a-time" analysis, however, our analogy with Figure 25.6 offers precise hypotheses on the neural interactions whereby switching control is achieved, and reveals hysteresis in the selective naming circuitry as responsible for lack of switching when the N-cells are lesioned. In this way, we have initiated a more sophisticated neurolinguistic analysis which stresses how a pattern of dynamic interaction could achieve the effects of selective naming and switching control.

CONCLUSION

Among the few contributions to neurolinguistics in the style of modern neuroanatomy is Galaburda's discovery (cf. Chapter 20, this volume) of lipofuscin-staining magnopyramidal cells as a cellular marker of the language areas of the brain. That anatomically homologous areas occur in the monkey brain is encouraging to the anatomist who wishes to have material for detailed studies; but it is discouraging to anyone who believes in the study of linguistics as an autonomous discipline, for monkeys do not have language in anything approaching the human sense.

To make contact with modern neuroscience, neurolinguistics must be embedded within a broader framework in which to analyze the evolutionary continuity between man, monkey, and frog in anatomy and behavior. Such a framework would relate speech perception to other forms of perception, and speech production to other forms of motor control. Since my own work in brain theory has emphasized the study of visuomotor coordination, I have stressed analogies with visual perception and the guidance of the animal's motion in its environment. Even more direct links can be drawn between neurolinguistics and the animal experiments of neuroscience in the study of auditory mechanisms, birdsong, vocal mimicry, the vocal repertoire of the bullfrog, etc.

The connectionist style of analysis of brain mechanisms of language, initiated by Wernicke in extending the observations of Broca, received a simple yet surprisingly full expression in the diagrams of Lichtheim. Here, consideration of lesions localized at one of a few centers or as disconnexions localized on one of a few pathways allowed a gross but insightful account—noting the different roles of multiple pathways connecting two centers—of a wide variety of aphasias. The different centers were characterized psychologically rather than anatomically. Moreover, the model was a "faculty model" in that each "box" was characterized in terms of some high-level "faculty of the mind." We have tried to augment this by using "cooperative computation" to give rich content to Luria's concept of the "functional system" in which such "faculties" are seen as embodied in the concerted working of many zones of the brain, with each zone contributing to a variety of complex functional systems. Despite this philosophy, Luria still talked of the functions of a region in terms of the deficits resulting from lesions which were localized there, and we have indicated how a functional analysis may yield a reinterpretation of Luria's data which leads to a characterization of a region as part of a network of dynamic interactions, quite different from the role-in-isolation of Luria's original analysis. The pursuit of this program needs a better conceptual analysis of the "cooperative computation" of multiple brain regions; a more flexible understanding of just what constitutes a region (column, module, layer, net of interacting layers, etc.); and an increasing subtlety of psycholinguistic description of the performance that is to be modeled.

REFERENCES

Anokhin, P. K. (1935). *Problems of center and periphery in the physiology of nervous activity.* Gorki: Gosizdat. (In Russian.)

Arbib, M. A. (1972). *The metaphorical brain.* New York: Wiley Interscience.

Arbib, M. A. (1975). Artificial intelligence and brain theory: Unities and diversities. *Annals of Biomedical Engineering,* 3, 238–274.

Arbib, M. A. (1981). Perceptual structures and distributed motor control. In V. B. Brooks (Ed.), *Motor control,* Vol. III, Section on Neurophysiology, *Handbook of Physiology.* Bethesda, Md.: American Physiological Society.

Arbib, M. A. and Caplan, D. (1979). Neurolinguistics must be computational. *Behavioral and Brain Sciences*, 2, 449–483.

Bernstein, N. A. (1935). The relationship between coordination and localization. *Arkhiv Biologicheskii Nauk*, 38 (In Russian).

Bernstein, N. A. (1968). *The coordination and regulation of movements*. Oxford: Pergamon Press.

Brown, J. (1972). *Aphasia, apraxia and agnosia: Clinical and theoretical aspects*. Springfield, Ill.: Charles C. Thomas.

Brown, J. (1977). *Mind, brain and consciousness: The neuropsychology of cognition*. New York: Academic Press.

Chomsky, N. (1965). *Aspects of the theory of suntax*. Cambridge, Mass.: MIT Press.

Dev, P. (1975). Computer simulation of a dynamic visual perception model. *International Journal of Man–Machine Studies*, 7, 511–528.

Didday, R. L. (1970). *The simulation and modelling of distributed information processing in the frog visual system*. Unpublished Ph.D. dissertation, Stanford University.

Didday, R. L. (1976). A model of visuomotor mechanisms in the frog optic tectum. *Mathematical Biosciences*, 30, 169–180.

Eccles, J. C., Ito, M., and Szentágothai, J. (1967). *The cerebellum as a neuronal machine*. New York: Springer-Verlag.

Fel'dman, A. G., and Orlovsky, G. N. (1972). The influence of different descending systems on the tonic stretch reflex in the cat. *Experimental Neurology*, 37, 481–494.

Frazier, L., and Fodor, J. D. (1978). The suasage machine: A new two-stage parsing model. *Cognition*, 6, 291–325.

Gelfand, I. M., and Tsetlin, M. L. (1962). Some methods of control for complex systems. *Russian Mathematical Surveys*, 17, 95–117.

Geschwind, N. (1975). The apraxias: Neural mechanisms of disorders of learned movement. *American Scientist*, 63, 188–195.

Gibson, J. J. (1966). *The Senses considered as perceptual systems*. London: Allen and Unwin.

Granit, R. (1970). *The basis of motor control*. New York: Academic Press.

Hubel, D. H., and Wiesel, T. N. (1974). Sequence regularity and geometry of orientation columns in the monkey striate cortex. *Journal of Comparative Neurology*, 158, 267–294.

Hubel, D. H., and Wiesel, T. N. (1977). Functional architecture of macaque monkey cortex. *Proceedings of the Royal Society of London B* 198, 1–59.

Ingle, D. (1976). Spatial vision in anurans. In K. V. Fite (Ed.), *The amphibian visual system*. New York: Academic Press.

Jackson, J. H. (1874). On the nature of the duality of the brain. *Medical Press and Circular*, 1, 19–63.

Jackson, J. H. (1878–1879). On affections of speech from disease of the brain. *Brain*, 1, 304–330; 2, 203–222, 323–356.

Jeannerod, M., and Biguer, B. (In press). Visuomotor mechanisms in reaching within extra-personal space. In D. J. Ingle, R. J. W. Mansfield, and M. A. Goodale (Eds.), *Advances in the analysis of visual behavior*. Cambridge, Mass.: MIT press.

Lecours, A. R., Deloche, C., and Lhermitte, F. (1973). Paraphasies phonemiques: Description et simulation sur ordinateur. *Colloques IRIA–Informatique Medicale*, 311–350.

Lecours, A. R., and Lhermitte, F. (1969). Phonemic paraphasias: Linguistic structures and tentative hypotheses. *Cortex*, 5, 193–228.

Lettvin, J. Y., Maturana, H., McCulloch, W. S., and Pitts, W. H. (1959). What the frog's eye tells the frog's brain. *Proceedings of the Institute of Radio Engineers*, 47, 1940–1951.

Locke, S., Caplan, D., and Kellar, L. (1973). *A study in neurolinguistics*. Springfield, Ill.: Charles C. Thomas.

Luria, A. R. (1973). *The working brain*. Harmondsworth, England: Penguin.

Marr, D. M., and Poggio, T. (1977). Cooperative computation of stereo disparity. *Science, 194,* 283–287.

Mountcastle, V. B. (1978). An organizing principle for cerebral function: The unit module and the distributed system. In G. M. Edelman and V. B. Mountcastle, *The mindful brain.* Cambridge, Mass.: MIT Press.

Okhotimskii, D. E., Gurfinkel, V. S., Devyanin, E. A., and Platonov, A. K. (1979). Integrated walking robot development. In D. Michie (Ed.), *Machine intelligence 9.* Edinburgh: Edinburgh University Press.

Phillips, C. G., and Porter, R. (1977). *Corticospinal neurones: Their role in movement.* New York: Academic Press.

Pick, A. (1913). *Die agrammatischen Sprachstorungen.* Berlin: Springer.

Prager, J. M. (1979). *Segmentation of static and dynamic scenes.* Unpublished Ph.D. dissertation, University of Massachusetts at Amherst.

Prager, J. M., and Arbib, M. A. (In press). Computing the optic flow: The MATCH algorithm and prediction.

Southwell, R. V. (1940). *Relaxation methods in engineering science.* Oxford: Oxford University Press.

Spinelli, D. N., and Jensen, F. E. (1979). Plasticity: The mirror of experience. *Science, 203,* 75–78.

Szentágothai, J., and Arbib, M. A. (1974). *Conceptual models of neural organization. Neurosciences Research Program Bulletin, 12,* 307–510. (Also published in hardcover by MIT Press, 1975).

Vygotsky, L. S. (1962). *Thought and language* (translated from the Russian original of 1934). Cambridge, Mass.: MIT Press.

Yakovlev, P. I. (1948). Motility, behavior and the brain. *Journal of Nervous and Mental Disease,* 107, 313–335.

Index

PERSPECTIVES IN
NEUROLINGUISTICS, NEUROPSYCHOLOGY, AND PSYCHO-LINGUISTICS

A Series of Monographs and Treatises

FRANCIS J. PIROZZOLO and MERLIN C. WITTROCK (Eds.). Neuropsychological and Cognitive Processes in Reading

JASON W. BROWN (Ed.). Jargonaphasia

DONALD G. DOEHRING, RONALD L. TRITES, P. G. PATEL, and CHRISTINA A. M. FIEDOROWICZ. Reading Disabilities: The Interaction of Reading, Language, and Neuropsychological Deficits

MICHAEL A. ARBIB, DAVID CAPLAN, and JOHN C. MARSHALL (Eds.). Neural Models of Language Processes

In Preparation:

R. N. MALATESHA and P. G. AARON (Eds.). Reading Disorders: Varieties and Treatments